BASIC HUMAN ANATOMY

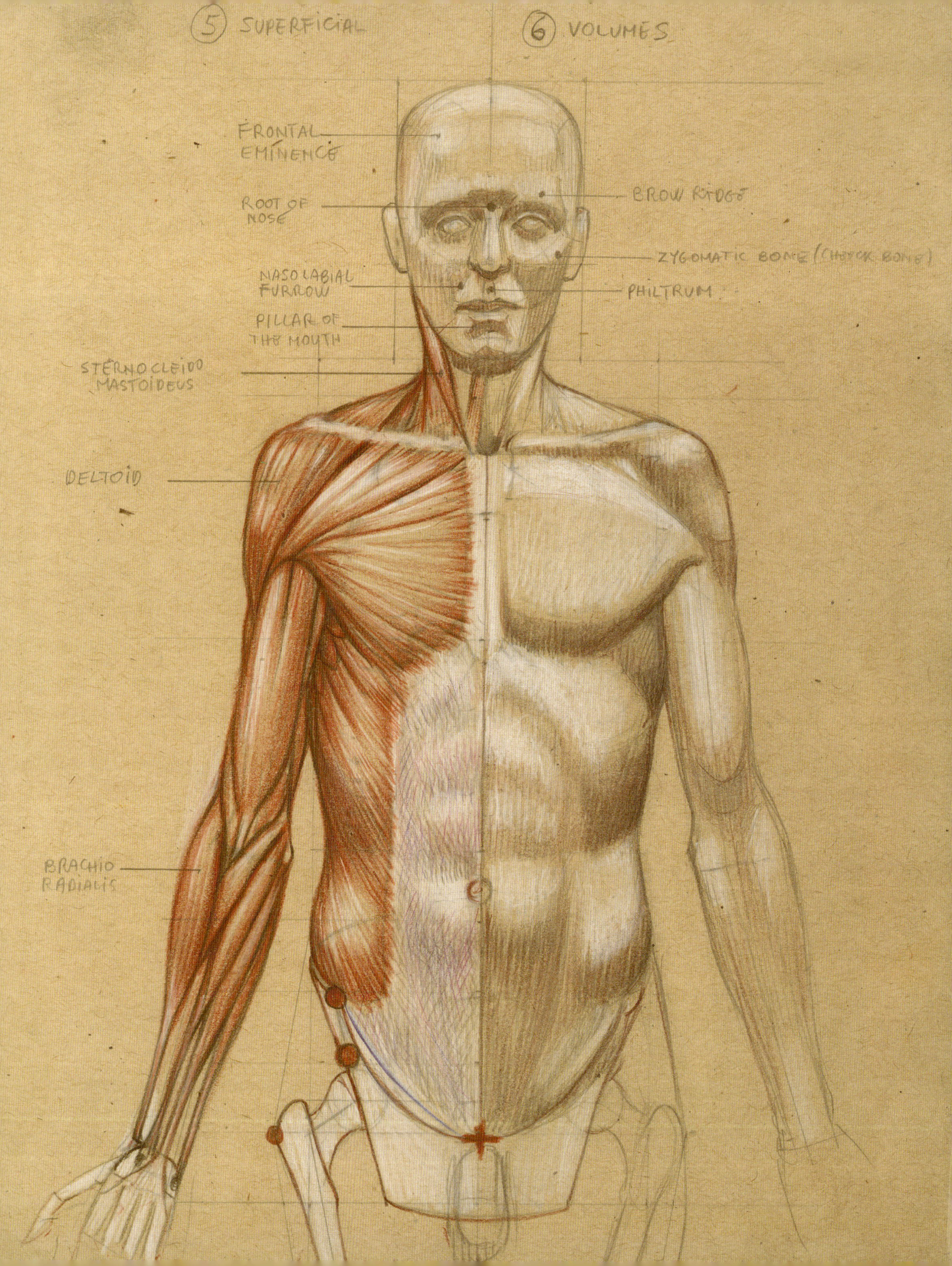

5 SUPERFICIAL
6 VOLUMES
FRONTAL EMINENCE
ROOT OF NOSE
BROW RIDGE
ZYGOMATIC BONE (CHEEK BONE)
NASO LABIAL FURROW
PHILTRUM
PILLAR OF THE MOUTH
STERNO CLEIDO MASTOIDEUS
DELTOID
BRACHIO RADIALIS

BASIC HUMAN ANATOMY

AN ESSENTIAL VISUAL GUIDE FOR ARTISTS

ROBERTO OSTI

FOREWORD BY PETER DRAKE

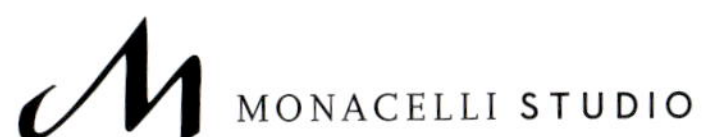

Copyright © 2016 Roberto Osti and The Monacelli Press

Illustrations copyright © 2016 Roberto Osti
Text copyright © 2016 Roberto Osti

Published in the United States by Monacelli Studio,
an imprint of The Monacelli Press

All rights reserved.

Library of Congress Cataloging-in-Publication Data
Names: Osti, Roberto, author.
Title: Basic human anatomy : an essential visual guide for
artists / Roberto Osti.
Description: New York : Monacelli Studio, 2016.
Identifiers: LCCN 2016002506 | ISBN 9781580934381
(hardback)
Subjects: LCSH: Anatomy, Artistic. | Human figure in art. |
BISAC: ART / Subjects & Themes / Human Figure. | ART /
Study & Teaching. | ART / Reference.
Classification: LCC NC760 .O88 2016 |
DDC 700/.4561--dc23
LC record available at http://lccn.loc.gov/2016002506

ISBN: 978-1-58093-438-1

Printed in China

Design by Jennifer K. Beal Davis
Cover design by Jennifer K. Beal Davis
Cover illustrations by Roberto Osti

10 9 8 7 6 5 4

Monacelli, a Phaidon Company
111 Broadway
New York, NY 10006

Phaidon SARL
55, rue Traversière
75012 Paris

www.phaidon.com/monacelli

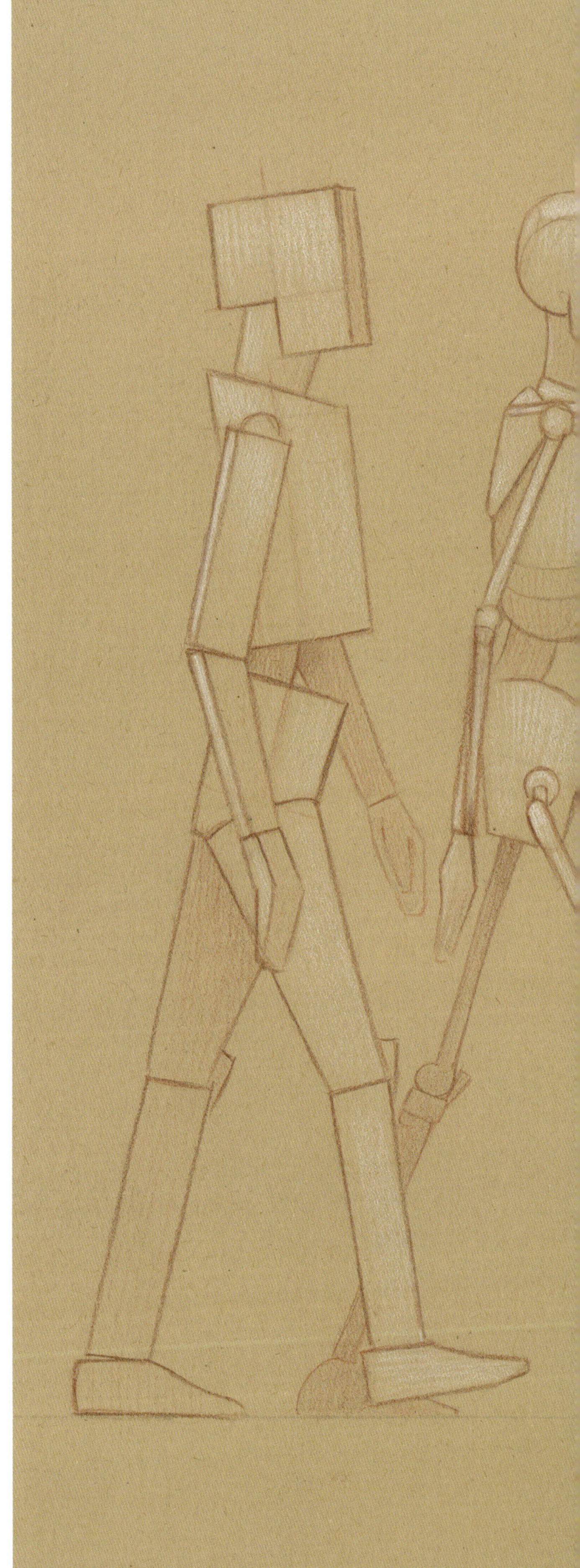

right
PROGRESSION FROM CONCEPTUAL
TO ORGANIC FORM

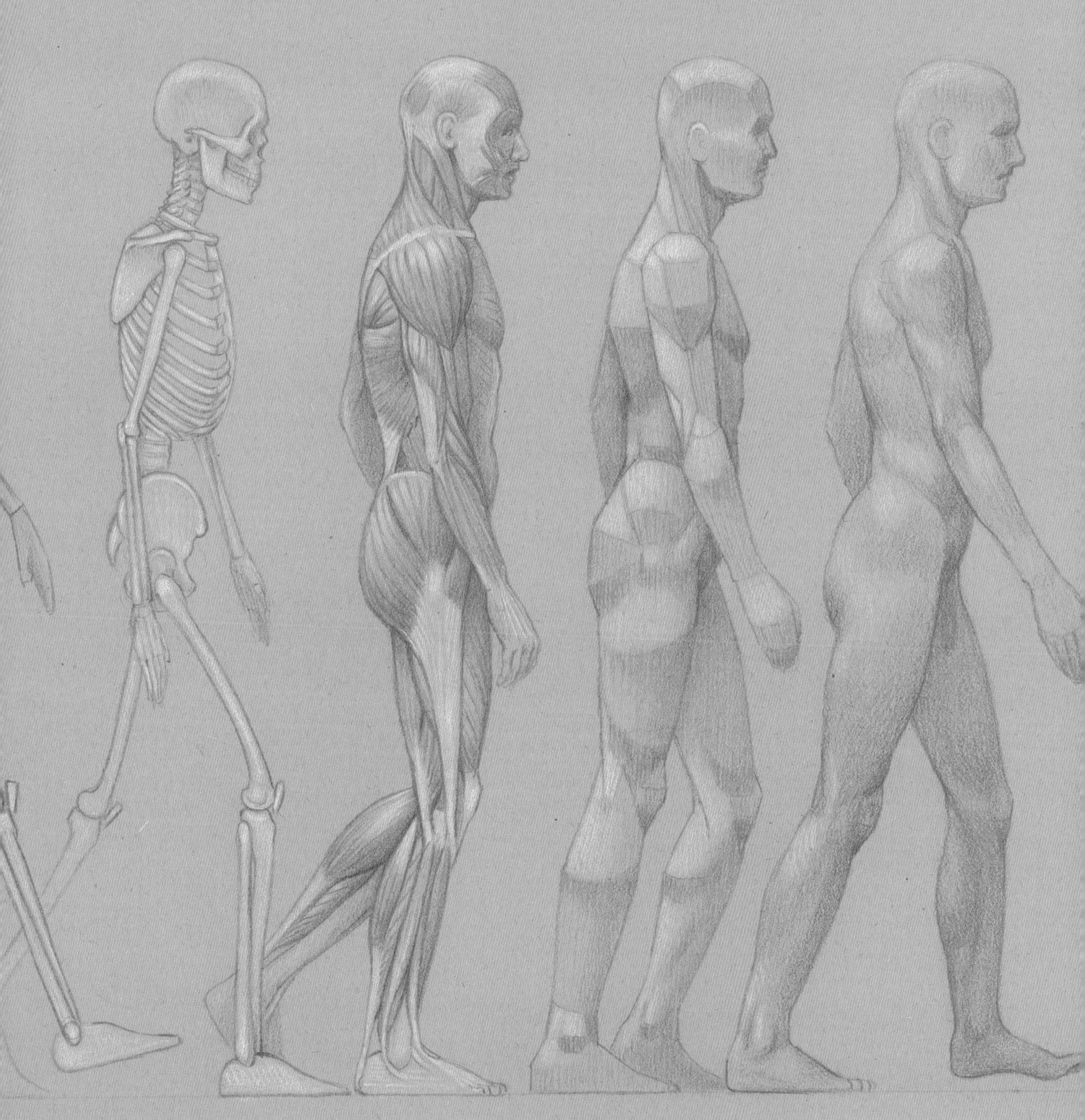

To my father and mother, Nerino and Mirella
To my wife, Angela, and my daughter and son, Emilia and Massimo

CONTENTS

ACKNOWLEDGMENTS

I first want to express my gratitude to those who guided me through my study of human anatomy and the human figure. I first studied anatomy at the Scuola Superiore di Disegno Anatomo-Chirurgico at the University of Bologna, in Italy. There, I underwent a thorough course of studies in anatomy oriented toward scientific-surgical purposes under the guidance of great teachers and artists: I especially want to thank the late Professor Gigliola Gamberini, who taught anatomical and pathological drawing and painting. My gratitude also goes to Professor Maria Acquaviva, my professor of anatomical and surgical drawing and painting.

During my years of professional practice as a scientific illustrator, I had the good fortune of working with Edward Bell, senior art director at *Scientific American* magazine. Under his guidance, I was able to create a great number of artworks concerning various scientific topics.

The pivotal moment when I transitioned from scientific to artistic anatomy came when I studied at the New York Academy of Art, where I obtained my master's in fine arts. My two years there permitted me to expand my study of human anatomy and the human form, this time with an aesthetic approach. At the academy, I had the good fortune of studying with great teachers with deep knowledge of the human figure: the late Martha Mayer Erlebacher, teacher, mentor and friend; Professor John Horn; Professor Harvey Citron; Professor Frank Porcu; and Professor Edward Schmidt.

I also want to acknowledge the work of authors of anatomy and figure-drawing books whom I am indebted to and who must be thanked for keeping the tradition of figure anatomy alive: the superb Gottfried Bammes, author of various books on the topic; Eliot Goldfinger, author of *Human Anatomy for Artists* and *Animal Anatomy for Artists*; and Alberto Lolli, Mauro Zocchetta, and Renzo Peretti, authors of *Struttura Uomo*. Fundamental texts on human anatomy that I often consult are by Sobotta, Netter, Testut-Latarjet, Spalteholz, and Richer, among others.

I must also acknowledge the universities and colleges I collaborate with: the New York Academy of Art, the University of the Arts, and the Pennsylvania Academy of the Fine Arts. I must give credit to these schools for the *lungimiranza* (commitment) it takes to keep alive the invaluable tradition of the study of the human figure for artistic purposes and for giving students a skill that not many artists today possess. I want to thank the many students I have had the pleasure to work with during my years of teaching at these institutions. Working with them has permitted me to continually explore and develop my study of human anatomy and, just as important, to get to know and help fantastic young artists who share the same passion for the human figure.

A grateful acknowledgment also goes to the many talented models I have worked with. Their contribution is very important for my class demonstrations and essential to the artist for the creation of inspired and beautiful artworks.

I also want to thank my editor, James Waller, for the fantastic job he did in streamlining the text and improving the book's structure and flow.

Finally, I want to thank my wife, Angela, from the bottom of my heart for the support and encouragement she has always given me.

FOREWORD
BY PETER DRAKE

There is an assumption in contemporary art instruction that the authentic can only be found in the work of the outsider or the "deskilled." This is a holdover from early Modernism, which defined itself in opposition to what had become a formulaic French academic tradition. Now the pendulum has swung so far in the opposite direction that the embrace of the deskilled has become all but academic itself. In this move from the deeply rigorous and analytic training that had been the centerpiece of historical art education to our present pluralist state, there lies an equally dubious assumption that rigorous training is beyond the capacity of today's artists. This represents an infantilization of the artist that Roberto Osti's volume on anatomy seeks to redress.

Osti has become one of the leading voices in the application of rigorous anatomical study to progressive figurative art. In his teaching, Osti displays all the passion, determination, and enthusiasm for anatomy that you would associate with a Renaissance master. His classes are laboratories for those artists driven to understand the human form from the inside out. For Osti, painting or sculpting the figure without this depth of knowledge would be like copying a Chinese character without knowing its meaning; yes, it can be done, but why bother? To truly understand the human form and, consequently, the human condition, one has to build the figure like an écorché, from its deepest attachments to the most superficial forms. This kind of training allows artists to work from their imagination without references, freeing them to embrace invention, anatomical anomalies, and, ultimately, their own creative vision. To put it more clearly, training isn't a hindrance in Osti's world; it represents creative freedom.

One of the hallmarks of Osti's teaching is his extraordinary devotion to preparatory drawing for each class. This is something that I have had to adjust myself to every year. It is one thing to prepare exceptional drawings; it is another thing entirely to retrain yourself for teaching by redrawing your own lessons every year. This is the kind of preparation that Osti demands of himself. It is the kind of preparation that makes his classes so dynamic and in demand.

In his own work Osti applies what he teaches. Perhaps more than any living artist, Osti represents that ideal commingling of an immersion in an analysis of the human form with a level of invention that releases him from the mimetic role of painting's history. In pieces like *Shaman in Spring* (2008), Osti re-enlivens representation by applying an almost scientific analysis of an imaginary being. The plausibility of the anatomical structure of the image allows the viewer to imagine a world where werewolves and humans gather and the need to understand werewolf anatomy is as essential to life as human anatomy.

Peter Drake is Dean of Academic Affairs at the New York Academy of Art.

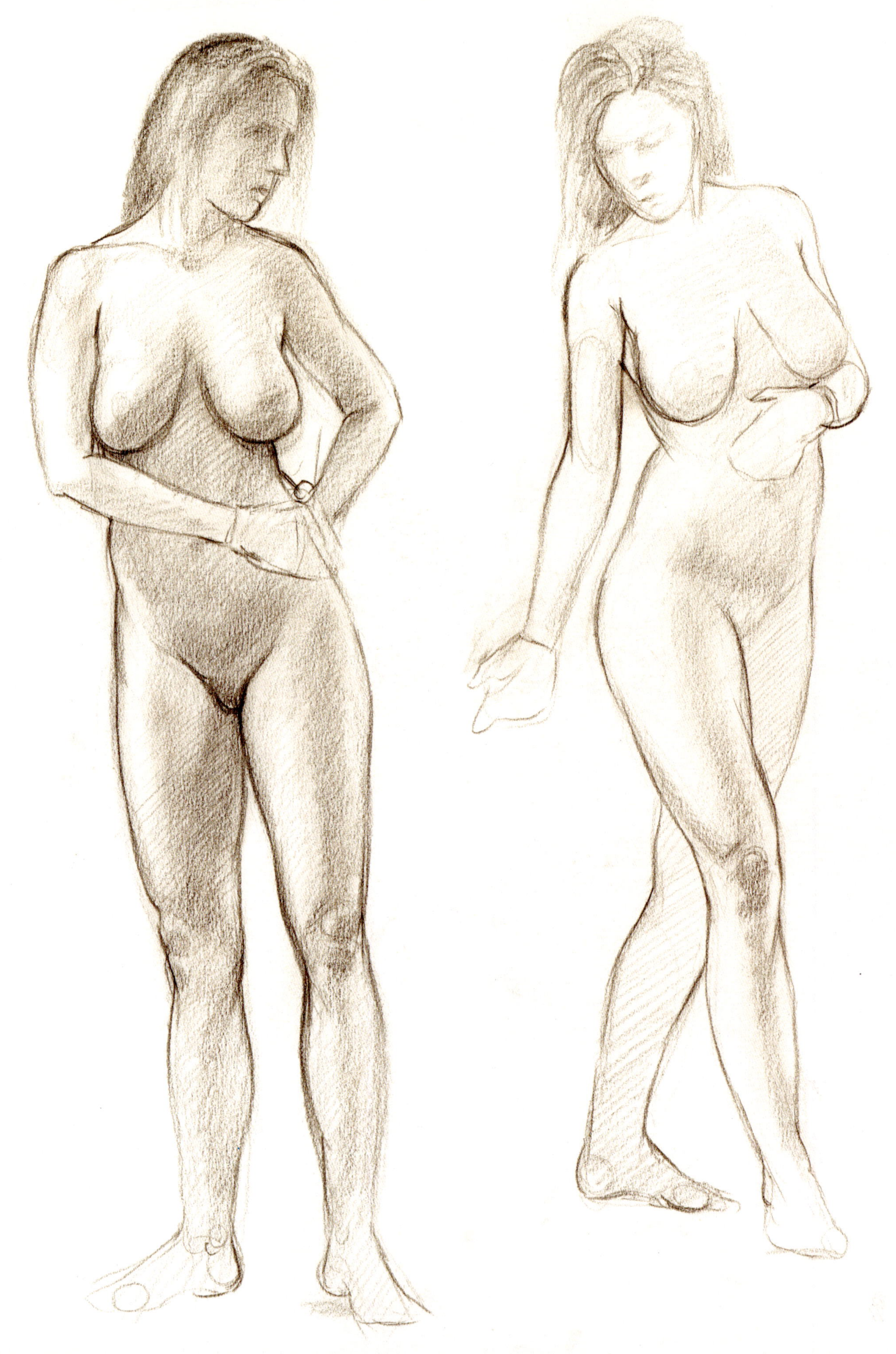

INTRODUCTION

This book is about learning to see; it is about acquiring skills conducive to the active interpretation of the human form, an approach that can be extended and applied to the physical world that surrounds us.

Drawing or painting the figure using a mimetic approach—that is to say, drawing without understanding but just by imitation—is comparable to copying the words of a book without understanding their meaning.

The artist with a good knowledge of anatomy will be able to create more beautiful and accurate artwork because he or she will have the means to better understand the forms of the body.

We draw what we know; the more accurate and extended is our knowledge of the subject, the more accurately we can visually represent it. The artist with theoretical and technical training in anatomy, when examining the human figure, will not just see nameless and localized bumps but specific forms interacting with adjacent forms creating flows, rhythms, and harmonies. The artist will understand specific characteristics of each anatomical structure by its function, leading to solid, harmonious, three-dimensional representations of the human figure.

The protean quality of the human figure makes it a very intimidating yet stimulating subject to depict; the body is standardized and idealized in its anatomical representations, but it presents itself in an incredible number of variations in real life. It changes with age, gender, weight; with the light; at rest or in movement; in health or illness, making it an arduous task to capture it graphically.

The conceptual approach to the human body will permit us to focus on only a limited number of specific aspects of the body at a given time, making it possible for us to understand its language. This book is therefore organized into a series of progressive and interconnected conceptualizations of the human body. Each one will deal with limited aspects of the figure: the volumes, the structure, the anatomy, and so on. The chapters are organized according to an analytical progression that goes from very synthetic forms (the basic volumes) to realistic rendering.

Each chapter will explore specific aspects connected with the human form, limiting the amount of information discussed and making it easier to assimilate it. Specific exercises at the end of each chapter will guide the student to the practical application of the notions discussed.

By the end of this book, readers will be able to understand the human figure from a variety of points of view—volumetric, structural, anatomical—and will be able to analyze its planes and patterns. They will also learn the basics of various drawing techniques, enabling them to transition from "looking" to "seeing."

Drawing the Figure

KEEP AN ANATOMY SKETCHBOOK

In between the chapters of this book, you'll find a series of tips on drawing the figure, each illustrated with drawings of my own. To begin this series, let's discuss what I think is an essential practice for any artist studying anatomy: keeping a sketchbook.

Keeping a sketchbook devoted exclusively to your anatomy studies is a great way to organize your notes and observations. In fact, I'd even call it essential. Every time I teach an anatomy class, I create a new sketchbook filled with visual and written notes, which I find is a very good way of discovering better, clearer ways of presenting the material. For your sketchbook, make sure to buy one of good quality, with paper that can withstand erasing, reworking, and watercolor or ink washes. Use the sketchbook only for your notes on anatomy and for the exercises given at the end of each chapter of this book. Once you start using a sketchbook, you'll feel compelled to add more and more drawings, and you'll have fun seeing your book develop and grow along with your knowledge of anatomy and figure drawing. The images here are taken from some of my own sketchbooks.

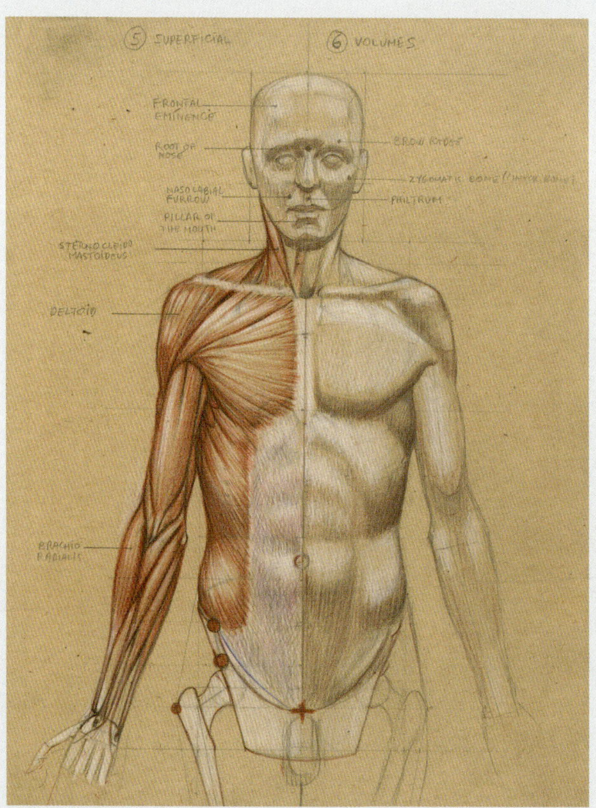

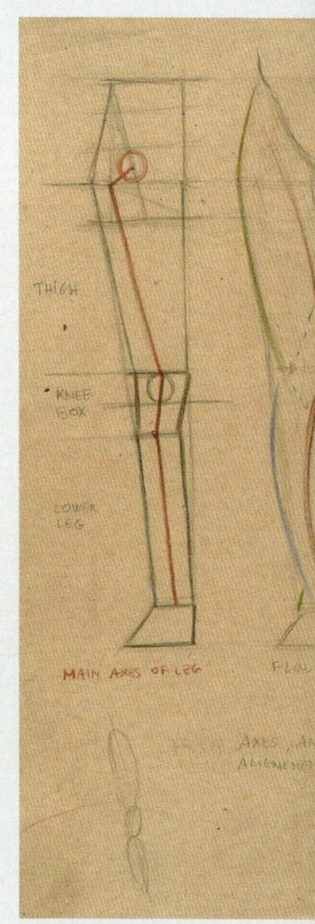

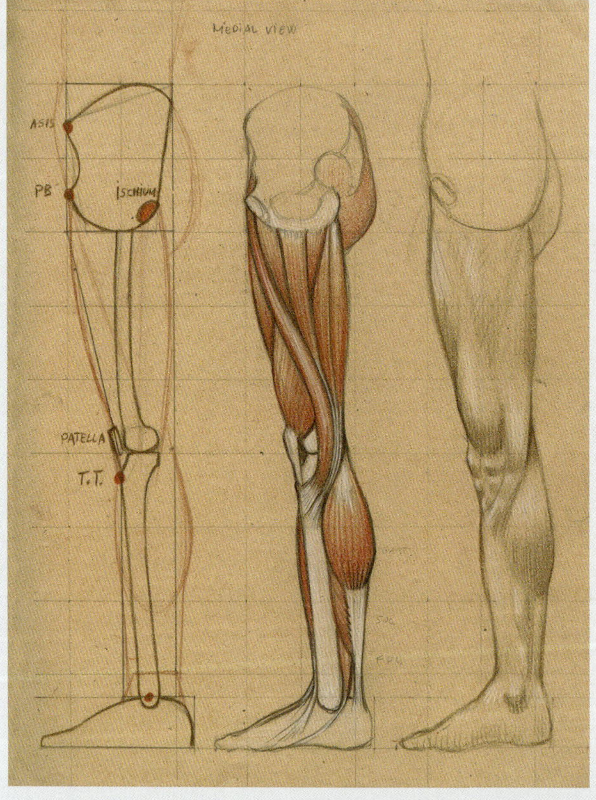

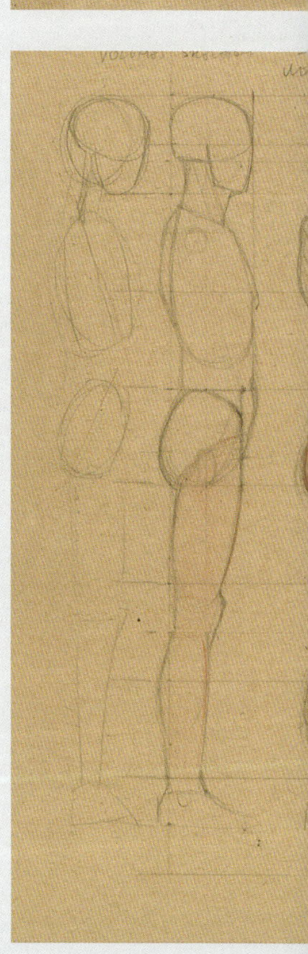

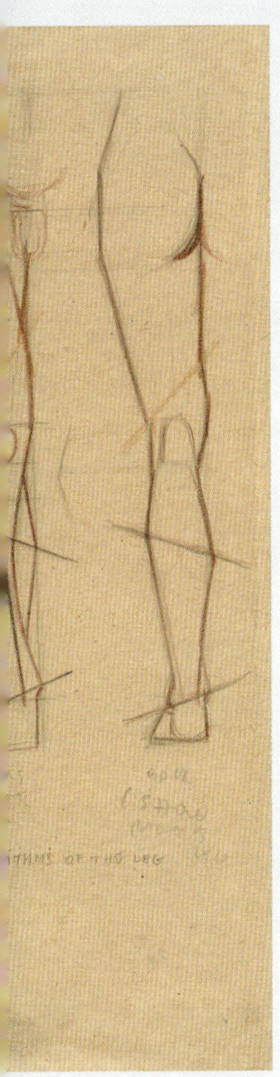

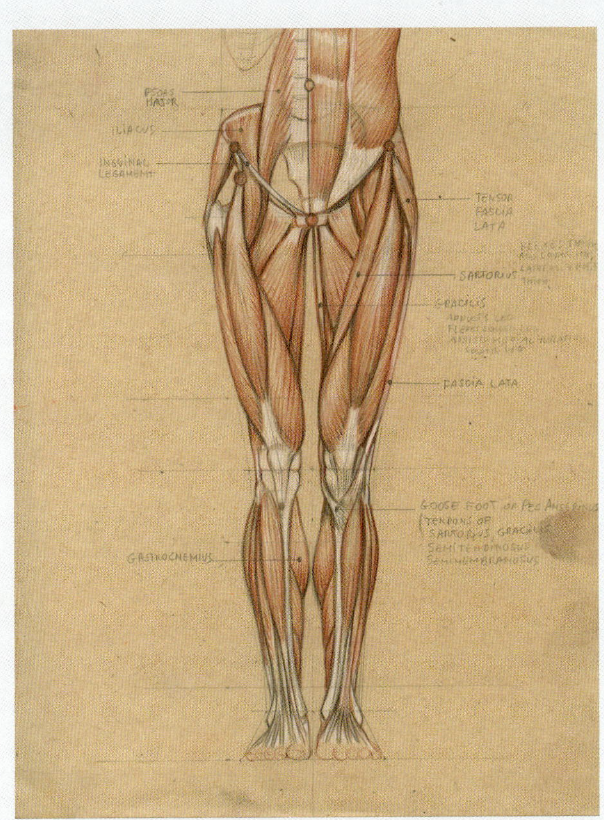

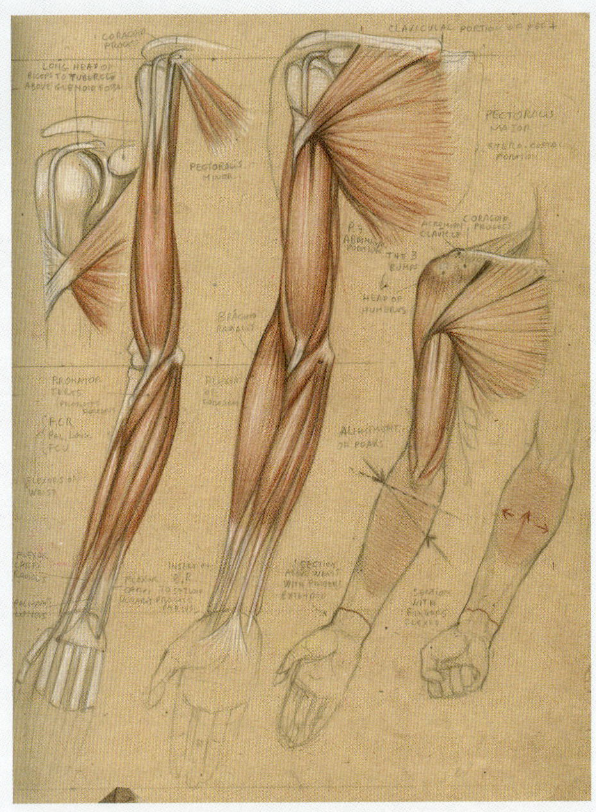

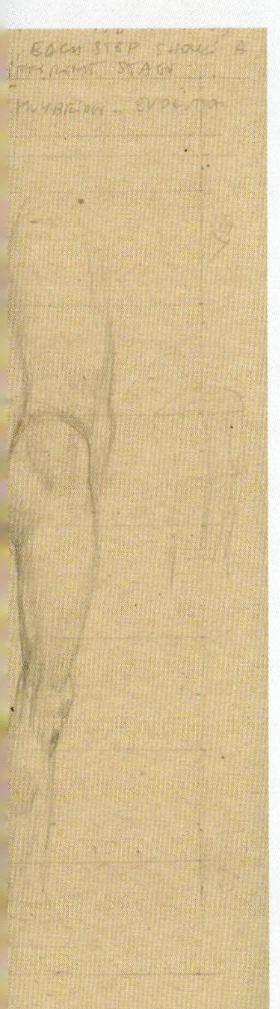

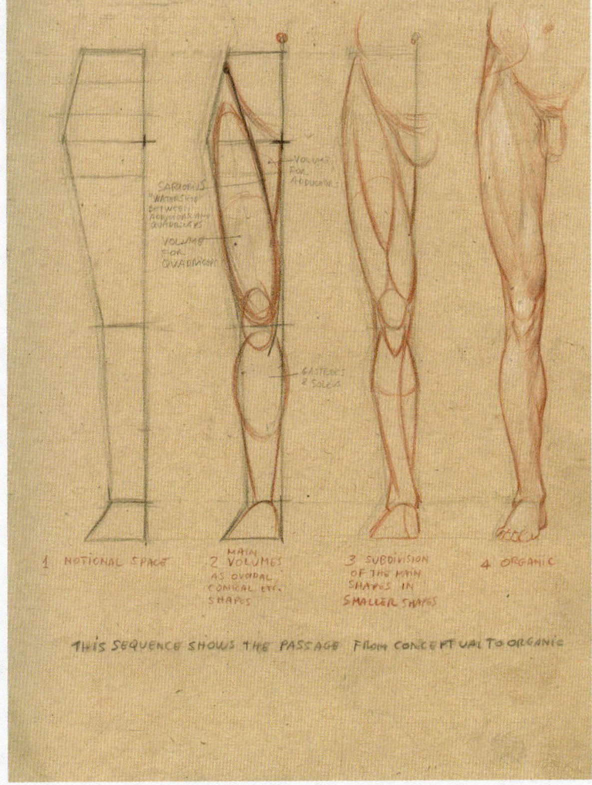

THIS SEQUENCE SHOWS THE PASSAGE FROM CONCEPTUAL TO ORGANIC

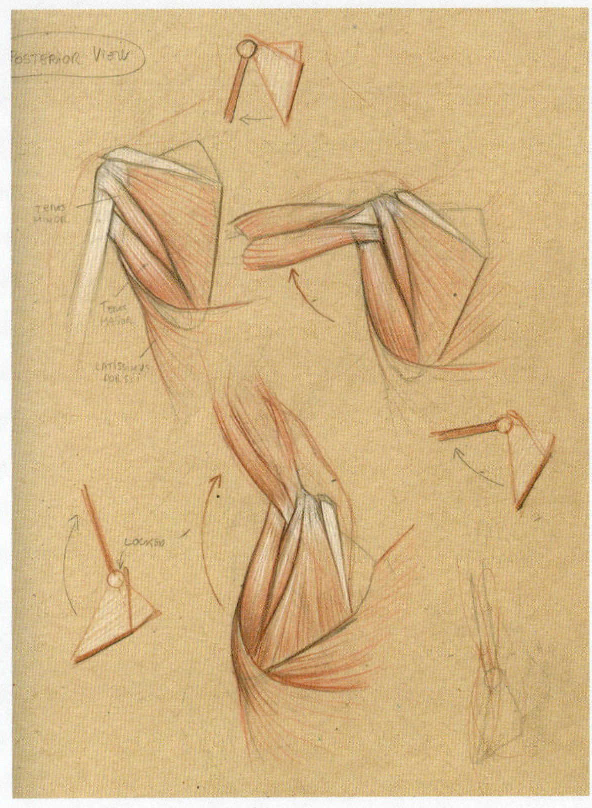

HEAD:
UPSIDE DOWN EGG

CUT AND SQUARE
THE EGG

* 1/2 - 1/3   THIS LINE IS BETWEEN
THE 7TH AND 8TH RIB = WIDEST
POINT IN RIBCAGE

CLAVICLE
PEAK

1/6

3/4 ±

OR
(2/3)

3/4

RIBCAGE:
UPRIGHT EGG

1/3

1 1/4

1 3/8

STERNUM
3/4

TORSO
ANT

1 5/8
TORSO
POST

1 3/8

1/3
1/2

1 1/8

1/8

7/8

1/2

1/2

STERNUM
3/4
WITHOUT
XYPHOID

WIDEST
POINT

1/2

1/3

1 1/2
THIGH

1/4

7/8

-126°
ANGLE
BETWEEN
NECK AND
SHAFT OF
FEMUR

BOX OF
KNEES
ABOUT
1/2 HEAD

2

LOWER LEG
AND FOOT

2/3

1

THE STEREOMETRIC APPROACH TO ANATOMY

Stereometry is one of the fundamental approaches to the study of structural anatomy. In the stereometric approach, the figure is conceived as a collection of geometric solids, such as cubes, spheres, cylinders, tetrahedrons, and so on. The approach has its roots in the early Renaissance, when artists started using mathematics, geometry, and perspective to create more realistic artworks. For example, the Italian painter Piero della Francesca, who was an accomplished mathematician, structured his works according to mathematical ratios, as did his countrymen Paolo Uccello and Leonardo da Vinci. The German artist Albrecht Dürer, who developed stereometry to a very high level, applied geometry and mathematics to the study and depiction of the human figure.

Stereometry reduces the various sections of the body to basic volumes that are easy to measure and to relate to each other. At first, we will use stereometry only to establish proportional

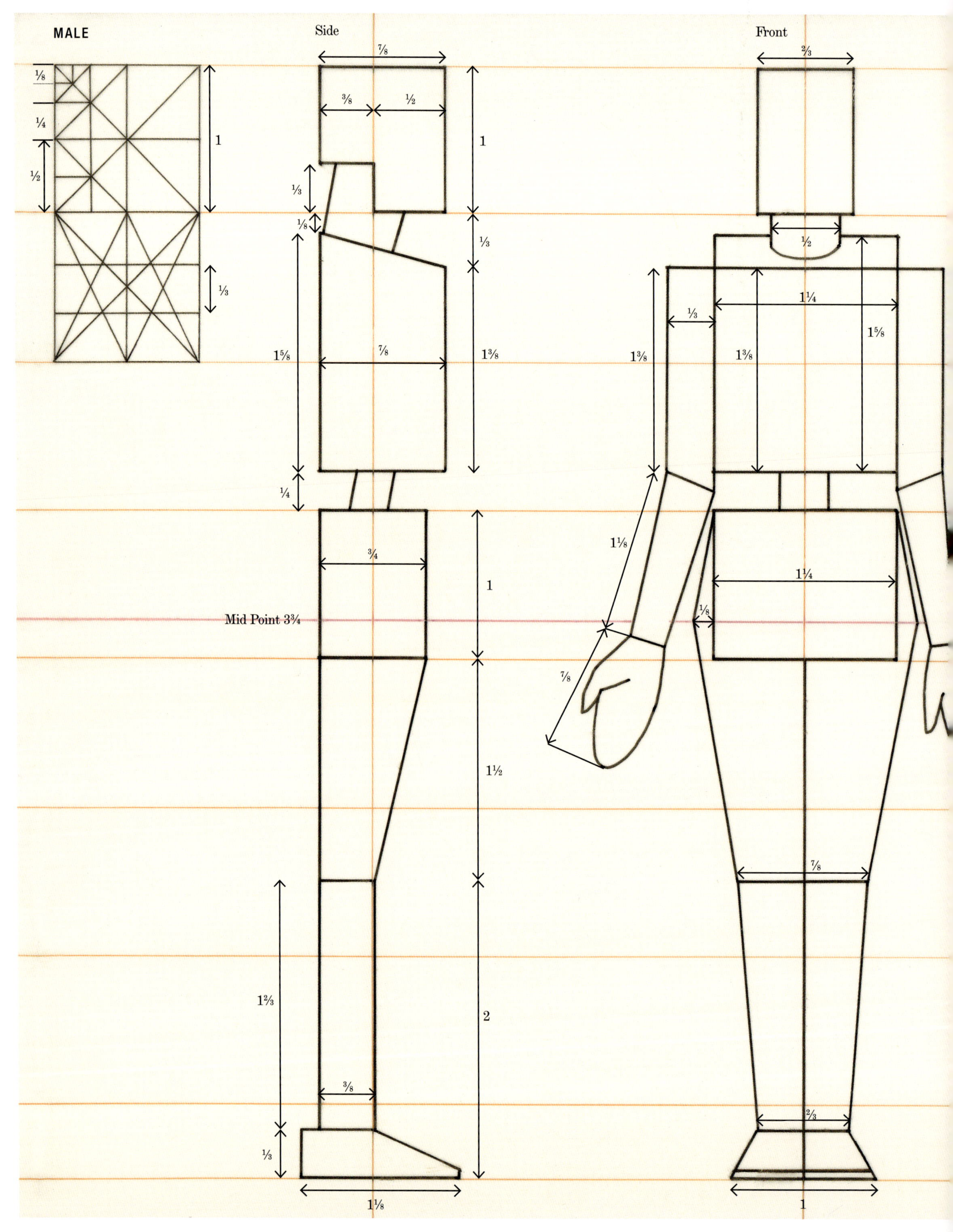

MALE
Side
Front
1/8
1/4
1/2
1
1/3
7/8
3/8
1/2
2/3
1
1/3
1/3
1/8
1/8
1/2
1/3
1 1/4
1 5/8
1 5/8
7/8
1 3/8
1 3/8
1 3/8
1 3/8
1/4
3/4
1 1/8
1 1/4
1/8
Mid Point 3 3/4
1
7/8
1 1/2
1 2/3
2
3/8
7/8
1/3
1 1/8
2/3
1

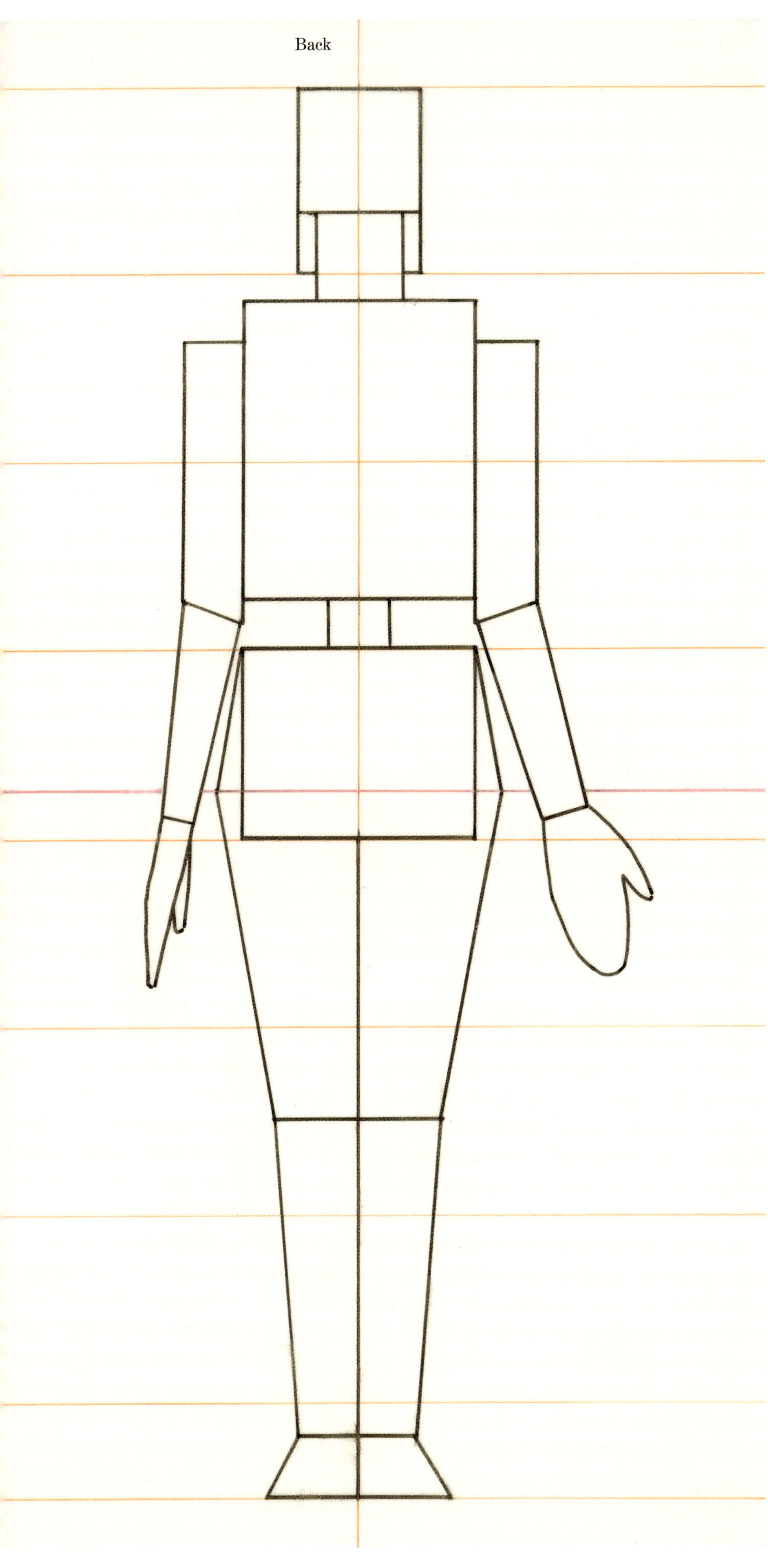

relationships between various segments of the body. Later, we will practice drawing the figure from life using the specific proportions of the actual model, which can vary significantly from person to person. But the basic concept of analyzing the proportional relationship between the various segments of the body will be the same.

The figures here and on pages 18 and 19 show stereometry applied to the male and female figures, as seen from the side (also called the lateral view), front (the anterior view), and back (the posterior view). Here and elsewhere in the book, I use the classic head-to-body ratio of 1:7 ½—that is, a ratio in which the height of the entire body, from the crown of the head to the soles of the feet, is 7 ½ times the height of the head. (Another commonly used head-to-body ratio, 1:8, is discussed in the sidebar on page 22.)

As you look at these figures, note the differences in proportions between the male and female bodies. In the upper left corner of each figure, you see a scale of two gridded squares that will help you easily determine the specific measures of

STEREOMETRY OF THE MALE FIGURE

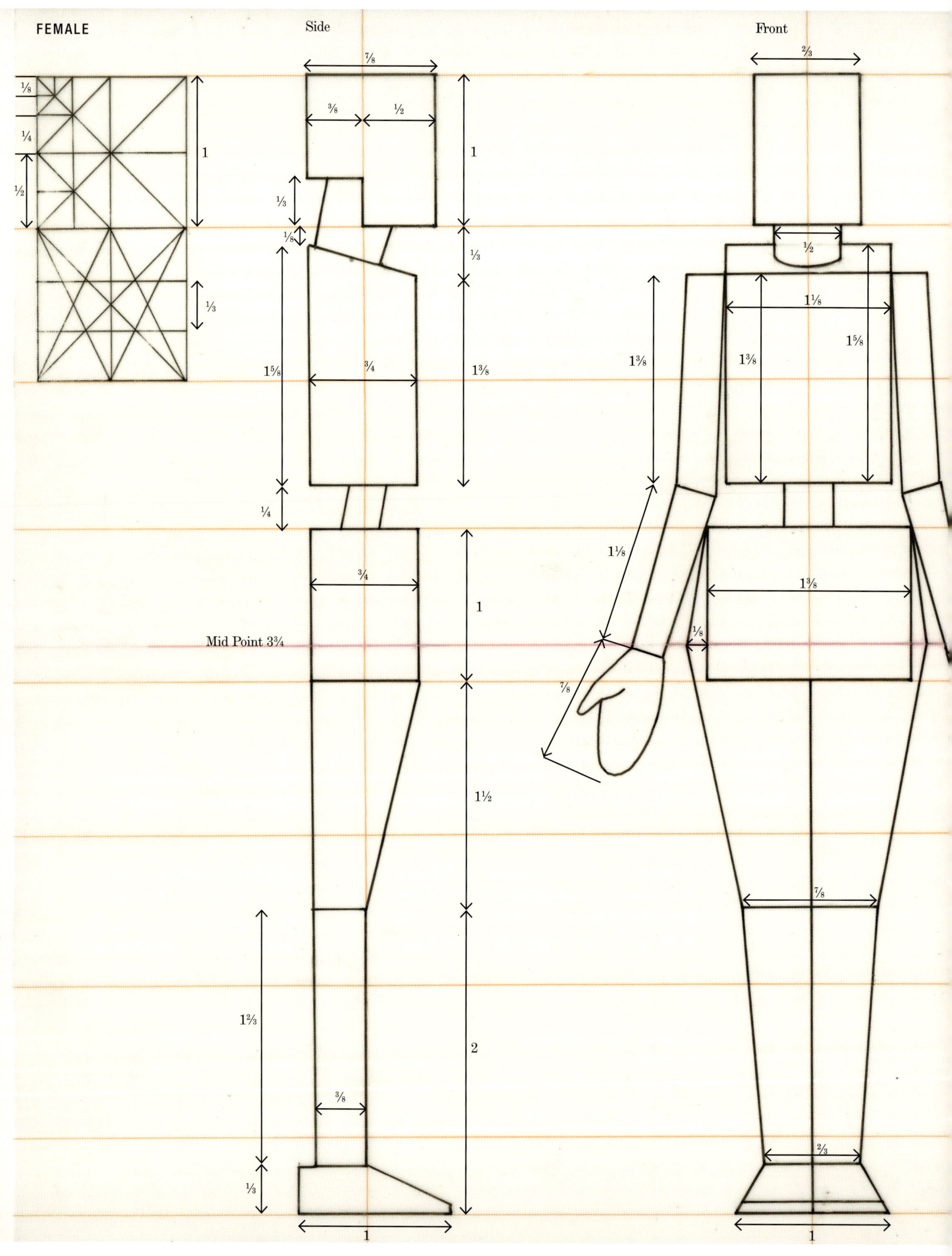

FEMALE
Side
Front
Mid Point 3¾
⅛
¼
½
⅓
1
7/8
3/8
½
1
⅓
⅛
1/3
1 5/8
3/4
1 3/8
¼
3/4
1
1 1/2
1 2/3
3/8
1/3
2
1
2/3
½
1 1/8
1 5/8
1 3/8
1 3/8
1 1/8
1/8
7/8
1 3/8
7/8
2/3
1

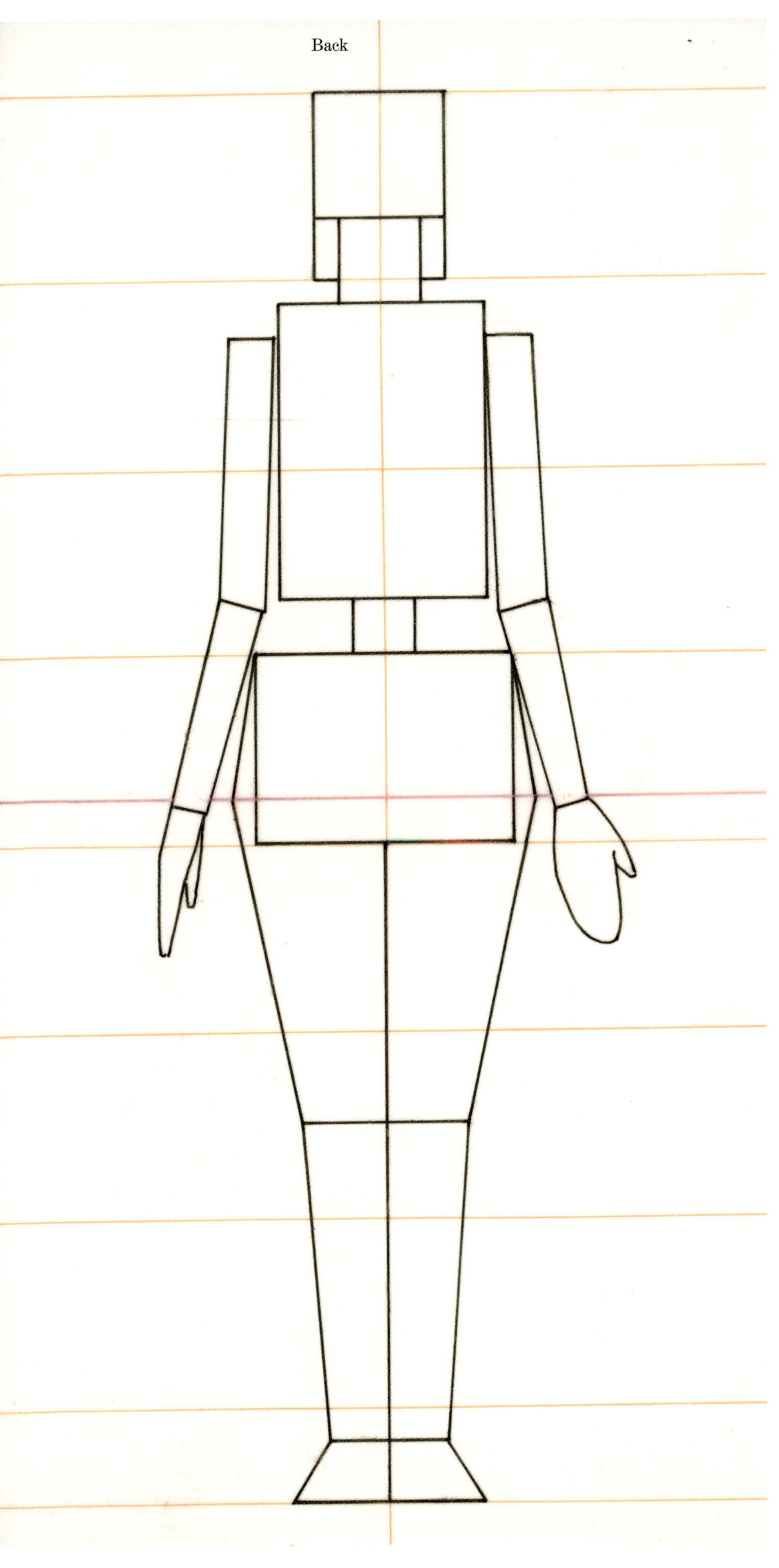

the various segments of the body without using awkward mathematical calculations that might hinder drawing. Use a divider or a compass to compare measurements.

In the stereometric rendition of the male proportions (previous pages), notice that while the ribcage and the hips have the same width in the front and back views of the body, the depth of the ribcage is greater than the depth of the hips in the side view. These are the typical proportional relationships between the ribcage and hips of the male skeleton. In the rendering of the female proportions, at left, the ribcage is narrower than the hips in the front and back views, but the depth of the ribcage is the same as the depth of the hips in the side view. Proportionally, men's ribcages are generally bigger than women's, and women's hips are generally bigger than men's.

STEREOMETRY OF THE FEMALE FIGURE

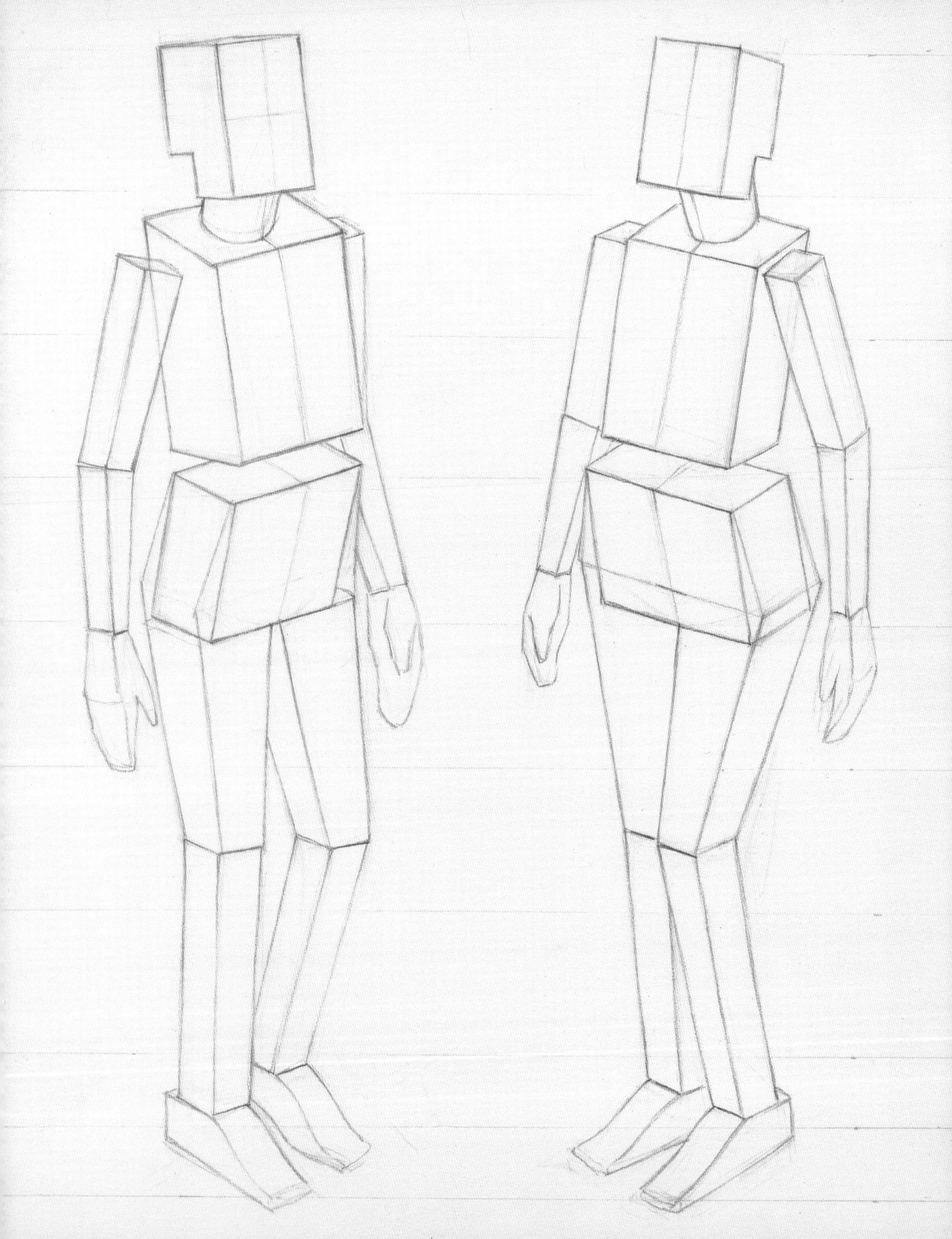

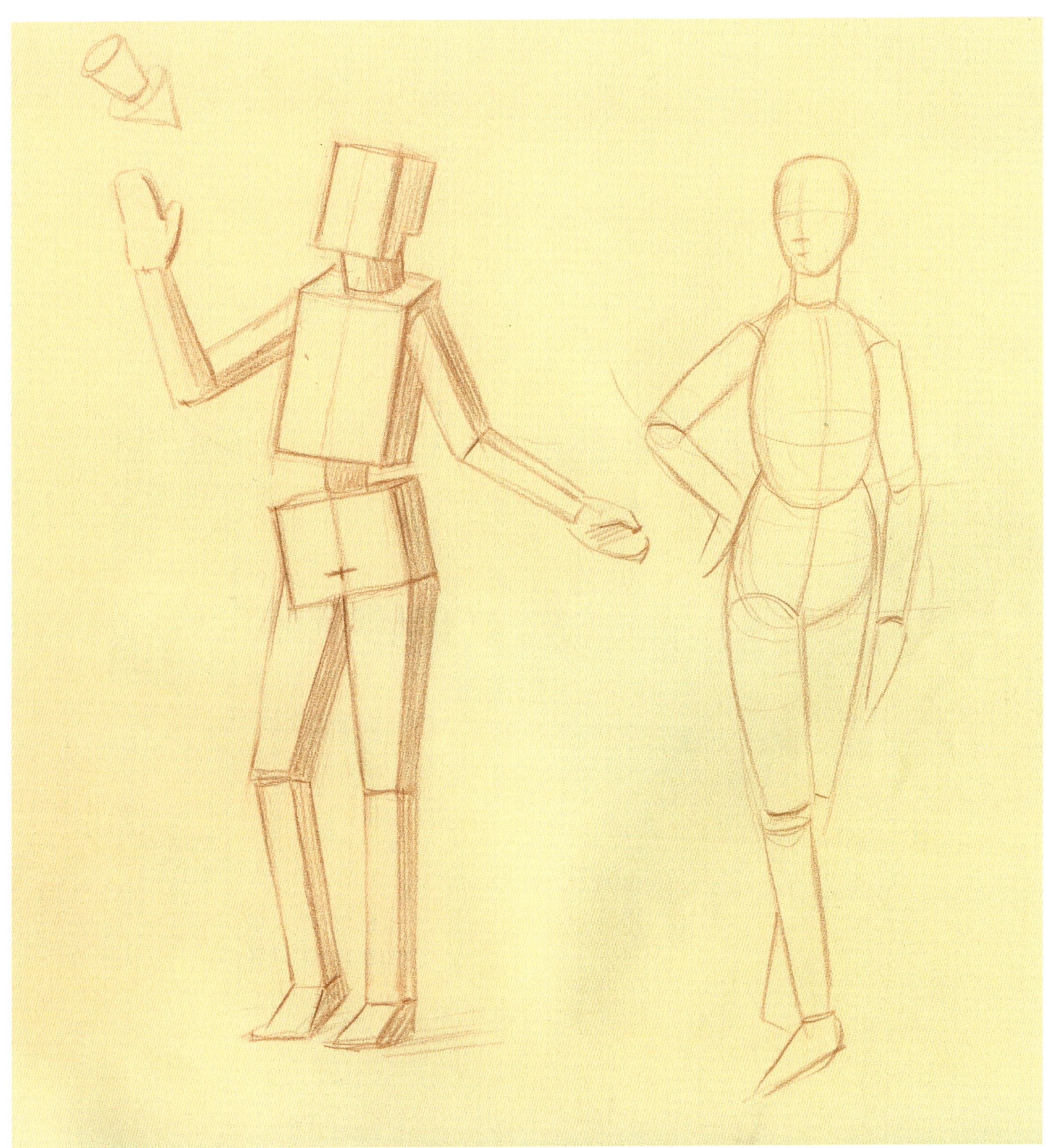

opposite
BASIC STEREOMETRIC RENDERINGS OF
MALE AND FEMALE BODIES
The distinctive difference between the genders can also be seen in
this drawing, which uses only the basic box shapes to depict male
and female figures in three-quarters views.

above
USING ANGULAR OR ROUNDED FORMS TO INDICATE GENDER
Gender differences can also be indicated by rendering the forms
of the male figure in a more angular way and the female figure in a
more rounded way.

A DIFFERENT HEAD-TO-BODY RATIO

Most of the drawings in this book are based on the head-to-body ratio of 1:7 ½, but the method I use can be applied to any system of proportions. The drawing shows, on the left, the proportions of a body based on a head-to-body ratio of 1:7 ½. On the right is a stereometric figure whose proportions are based on a ratio of 1:8. The background lines make it easy to compare the proportional relationships between the various segments of the body. The decision to use the 1:7 ½ or 1:8 or any other ratio is purely a personal choice, based on your aesthetic preferences or on specific artistic needs such as fashion design or creating characters for graphic novels or comics. Any set of proportions provides an excellent way to observe the body, to find the proportional relationships between the body's various segments, and to understand its essential forms. Eventually, you will want to move from the theoretical to the real, finding the specific proportions of the model you are portraying—1:7 ¼, 1:6 ¾, 1:8 ⅓, or whatever they may be.

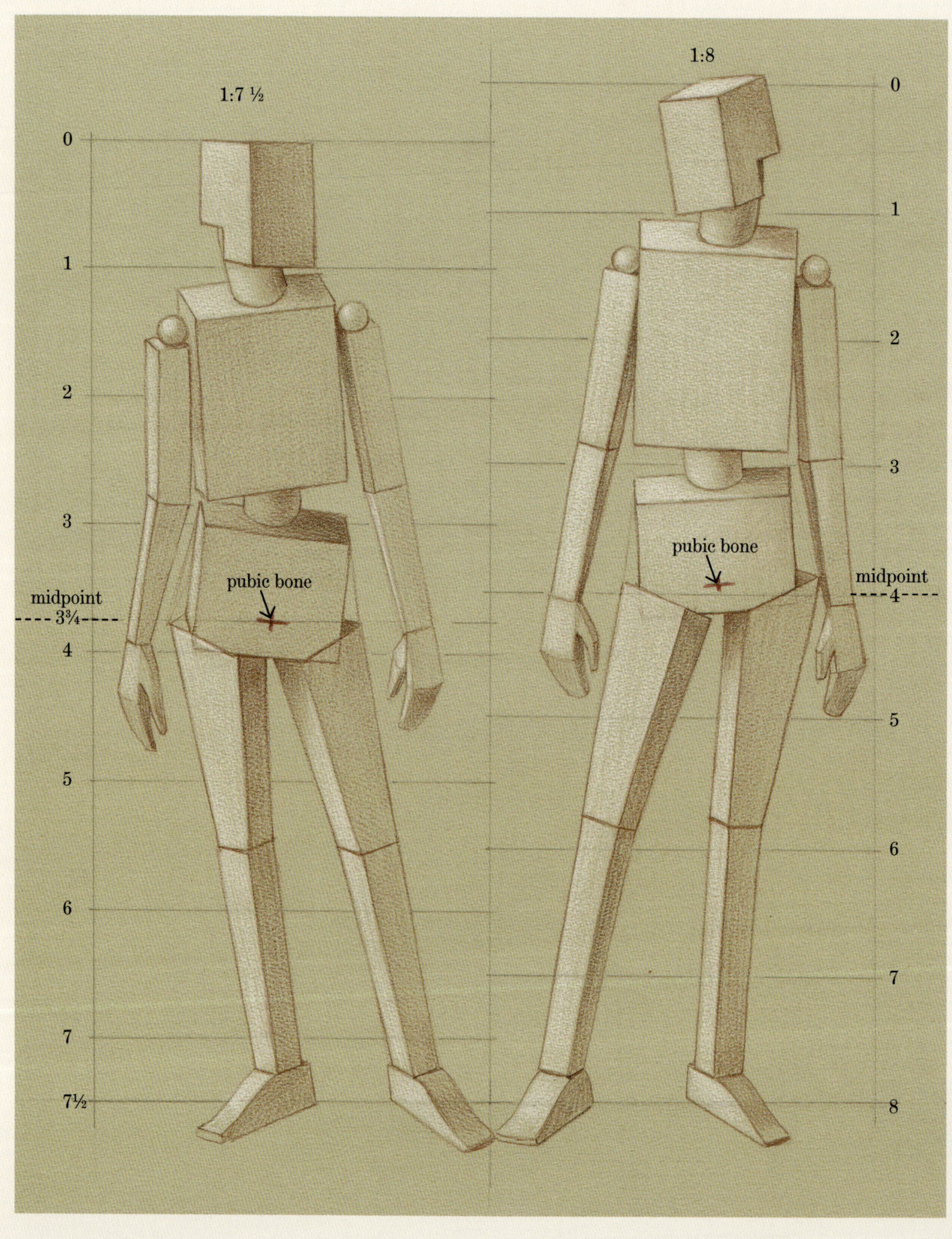

PROPORTIONS OF THE HEAD

Let's practice using the stereometric conceptualization of the figure by first focusing on just one segment—the head. The figure below gives you a thorough picture of the proportions of the head. When referring to it, remember that the measurements are proportional; "1" simply stands for the height of the head. Any element of the head is a fraction of that measure. Try to memorize the proportions. Even if you cannot recall them exactly, remember that the biggest measure of the head is always the height from top to bottom, that the depth is the second-biggest measure (almost the same as the height), and that the width is third biggest. Another measure you may want to memorize is the measure between the base of the skull and the bottom of the box of the head. It is one-third of 1.

Now try to imagine the blocks representing the head from as many different points of view as you can think of. Draw each of them freehand, trying to be as precise as possible regarding the proportional relationship of the various parts. Draw them as if you could see through them, as in the figure on page 24. This will help you think of the objects as three-dimensional and will improve your drawings.

STEREOMETRIC REPRESENTATION OF THE HEAD

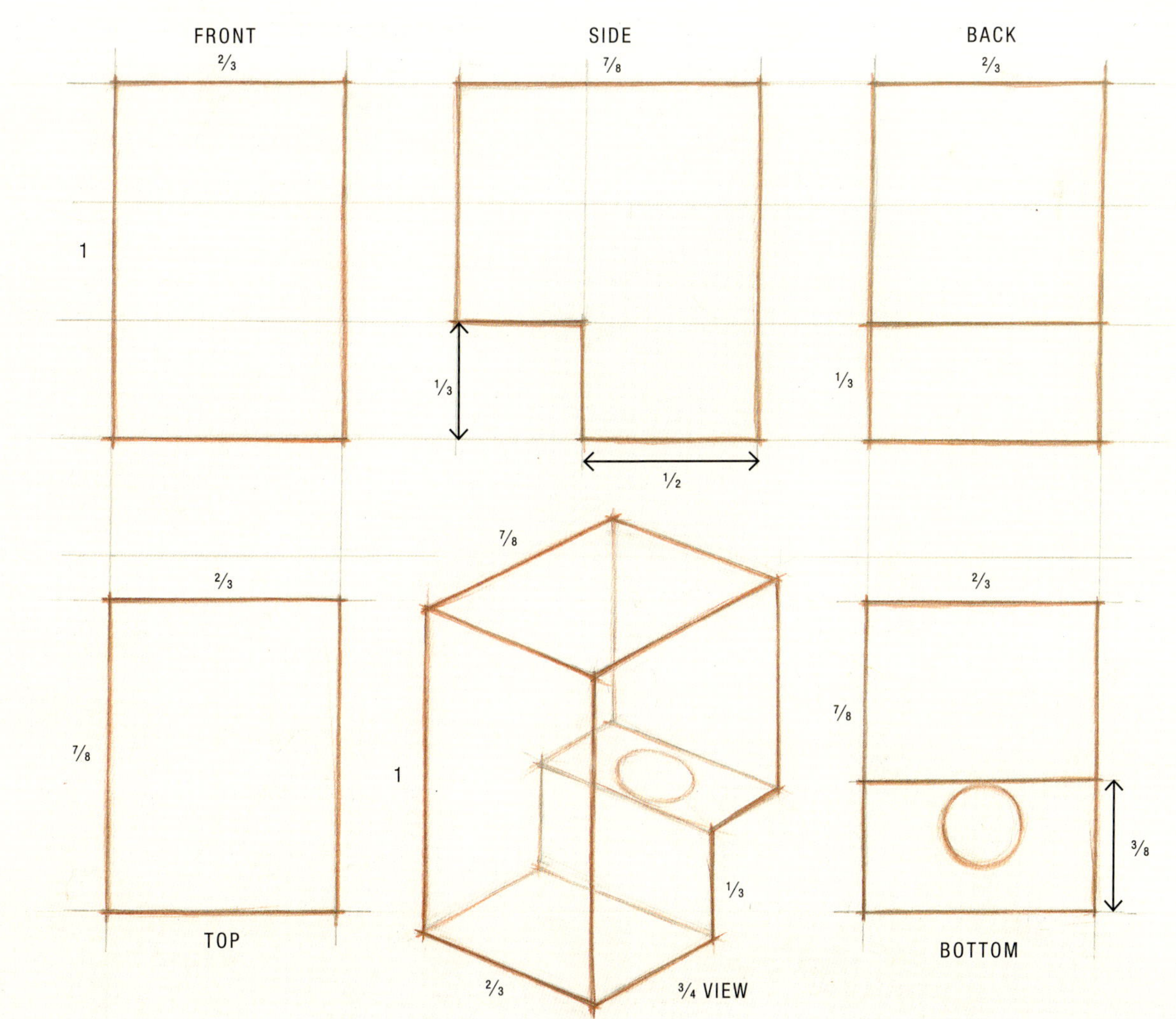

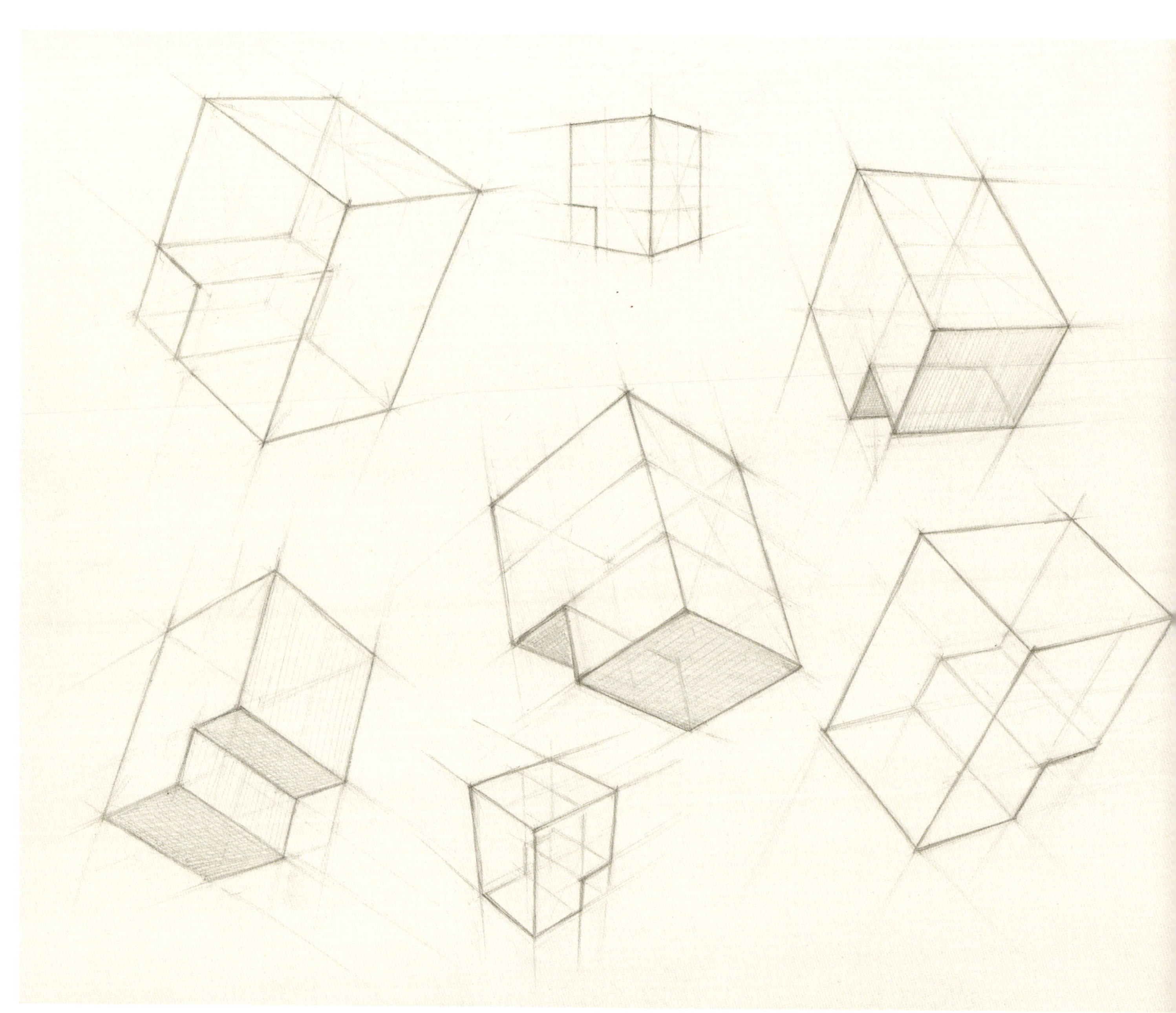

STEREOMETRIC REPRESENTATIONS OF THE HEAD FROM
VARIOUS ANGLES

CREATING A STEREOMETRIC CHART

To reiterate an important point: When we talk about the proportions of the body and say that the measure of the head is "1," we're *not* talking about an actual measurement but rather about the vertical length of the head *in relation to* the lengths of other parts of the body. In a given drawing, painting, or sculpture, a figure's head may measure 1 inch from crown to chin, or 13.6 centimeters, or 3 ½ feet, or whatever measure the artist decides on. The measures of all the other parts of the body will be established in relation to the measure of the head.

Now imagine the mathematical difficulty of having to determine the precise lengths of other body parts for a figure with a head that measures, say, 13 ⅝ inches. To find the correct proportion for the anterior measure of the torso, you would have to calculate the value of 1 ⅜ of 13 ⅝ inches. And then you'd have to do the same kind of calculation for all the other body parts. You can see how this would be a pretty uninspiring approach to drawing the figure!

A scale for the creation of a stereometric rendition of the body will solve this problem, permitting you to easily determine fractions and multiples of "1." To make one, you will need a pencil (grade H), a ruler, a triangle, and a proportional divider. (A compass can be used instead of a divider.) Draw your scale in the upper left corner of an 11 X 14-inch piece of illustration board (hot press or plate finish) as shown in the charts on pages 16–19. The figures below and on the following pages explain the process for creating a stereometric scale.

STEP 1: Begin with a line (A) that is the same height as the height of the head you will be drawing. For this demonstration, I am using a one-inch-long line (1 = 1 inch) to make the process easier, but the size of the

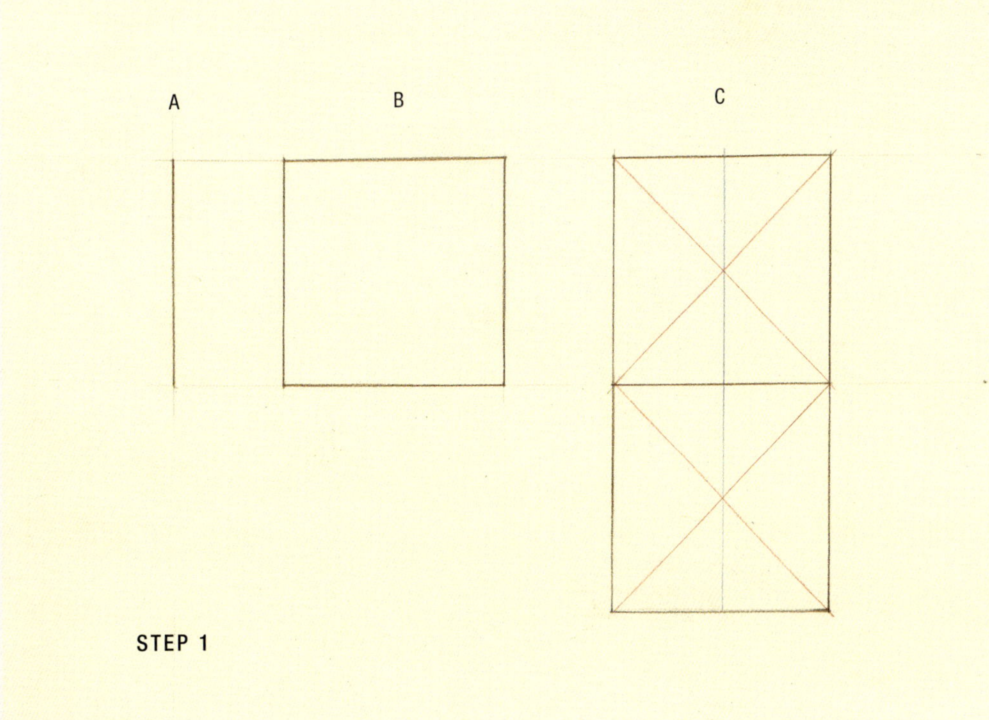

STEP 1

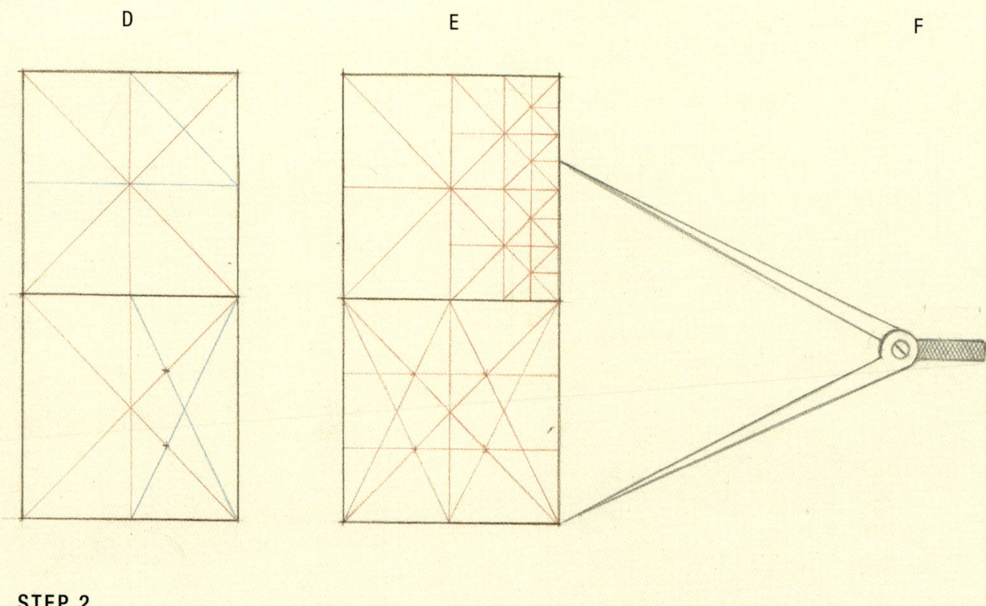

STEP 2

head can be any measure you choose. Using this measure, draw a square (*B*) and then another of the same size below the first one (*C*), drawing the diagonals (red lines) as shown and then dividing the two squares with a vertical line that goes through the centers determined by the diagonals (blue line).

STEP 2: Using a triangle and a ruler, divide the top square horizontally (horizontal blue line). You have now divided the original square into four smaller squares and determined the measure of ½. You can now keep subdividing the small squares into smaller

and smaller squares using the diagonals (*D*, upper square). Then divide the lower square with diagonals as shown in the image (blue lines). The point of intersection between the red diagonals and the blue diagonals will give you the measure of ⅓ (*D*, lower square). Diagram *E* shows the completed scale, with the upper square divided into smaller and smaller squares (½, ¼, ⅛) and the lower square divided into thirds. Using the divider or compass (*F*) you can use the scale to find the measure you need to determine the size of any segment of the body.

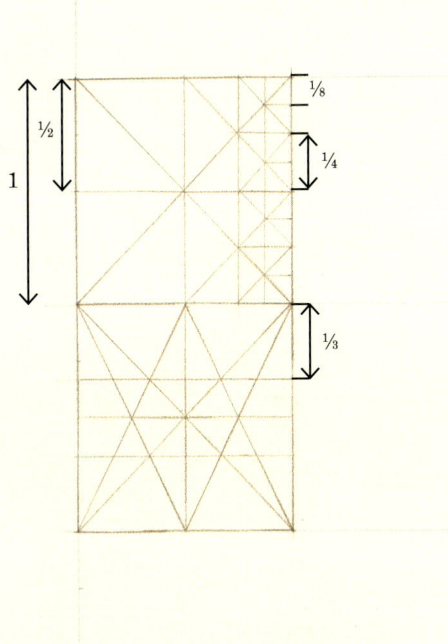

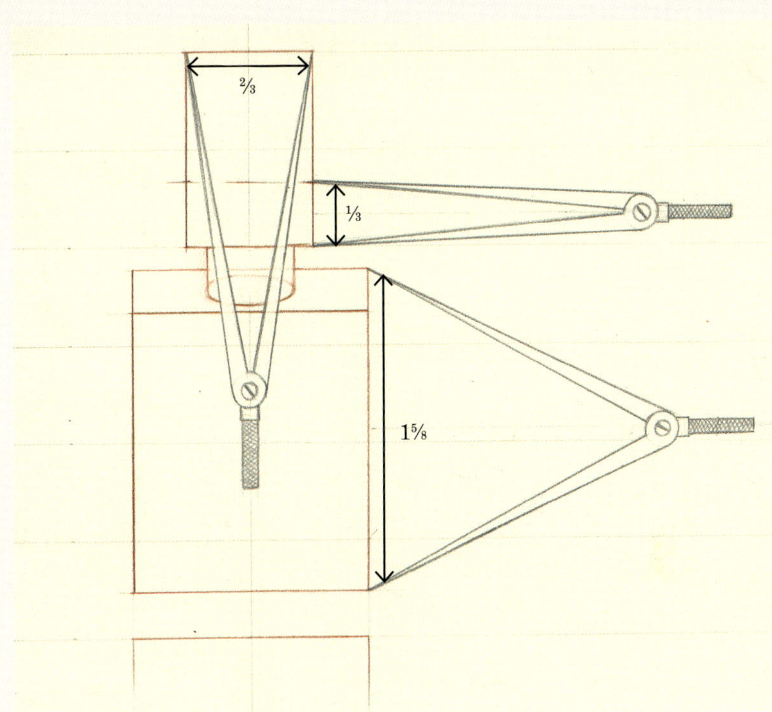

COMPLETED STEREOMETRIC SCALE

Now that you have built the scale, you can start drawing stereometric visualizations of the body, recreating the charts of male and female stereometric figures found on pages 16–19. For now, pick just one (male or female). To begin, draw an 8-inch vertical line about 2 inches from the left side of the illustration board. (Leave 1½ inches above the line and 1½ inches below the line.) Divide that line in eight segments of 1 inch each. Now divide the bottom segment in half and discard the lower half. You now have a line divided into eight segments: The first seven should each be 1 inch, and the bottom segment should be ½ inch. This line represents the 7 ½ heads ratio used throughout the book. Repeat the process, drawing the same line on the right side of the board and dividing it into eight segments and dividing the bottom segment in half. Using a ruler, now draw parallel horizontal lines connecting the marks on the two parallel vertical lines. This will give you a grid of nine parallel horizontal lines enclosed by the two parallel vertical lines on the sides.

USING THE PROPORTIONAL DIVIDER

Now, using the stereometric scale and the proportional divider, draw the complete stereometric figure. With the divider, take the measurement you need from the scale, as shown in diagrams *E* and *F* in step 2, opposite, and use it to establish the size of the various segments of the figure. Because the value of the head (1) here is equal to 1 inch, you can use a ruler to check whether you are doing a good job determining the proportions of the various segments of the body. Next, you can create a scale where the value "1" is any measurement you decide the height of the head should be.

USING FORMS THAT ARE MORE ORGANIC

Drawing the figure using the basic stereometric approach, which employs boxlike shapes, is useful when you are becoming acquainted with the proportional relationships of the various segments of the body. But using only box-shaped volumes can be slow and impractical. The figure below shows how you can create simpler conceptualizations of the body that are easier to draw and bring you closer to the organic forms of the human body. Note how the oviform shapes render the figures more humanlike and fluid. The figure on the far right shows how you can also start hinting at more specific volumes, such as the forms of the calves and the buttocks. The figure also shows how you can indicate gender-specific proportions: Whether you are using angular or rounded forms, make the ribcage and hips the same width when drawing a male form; when drawing a female form, make the hips wider than the ribcage.

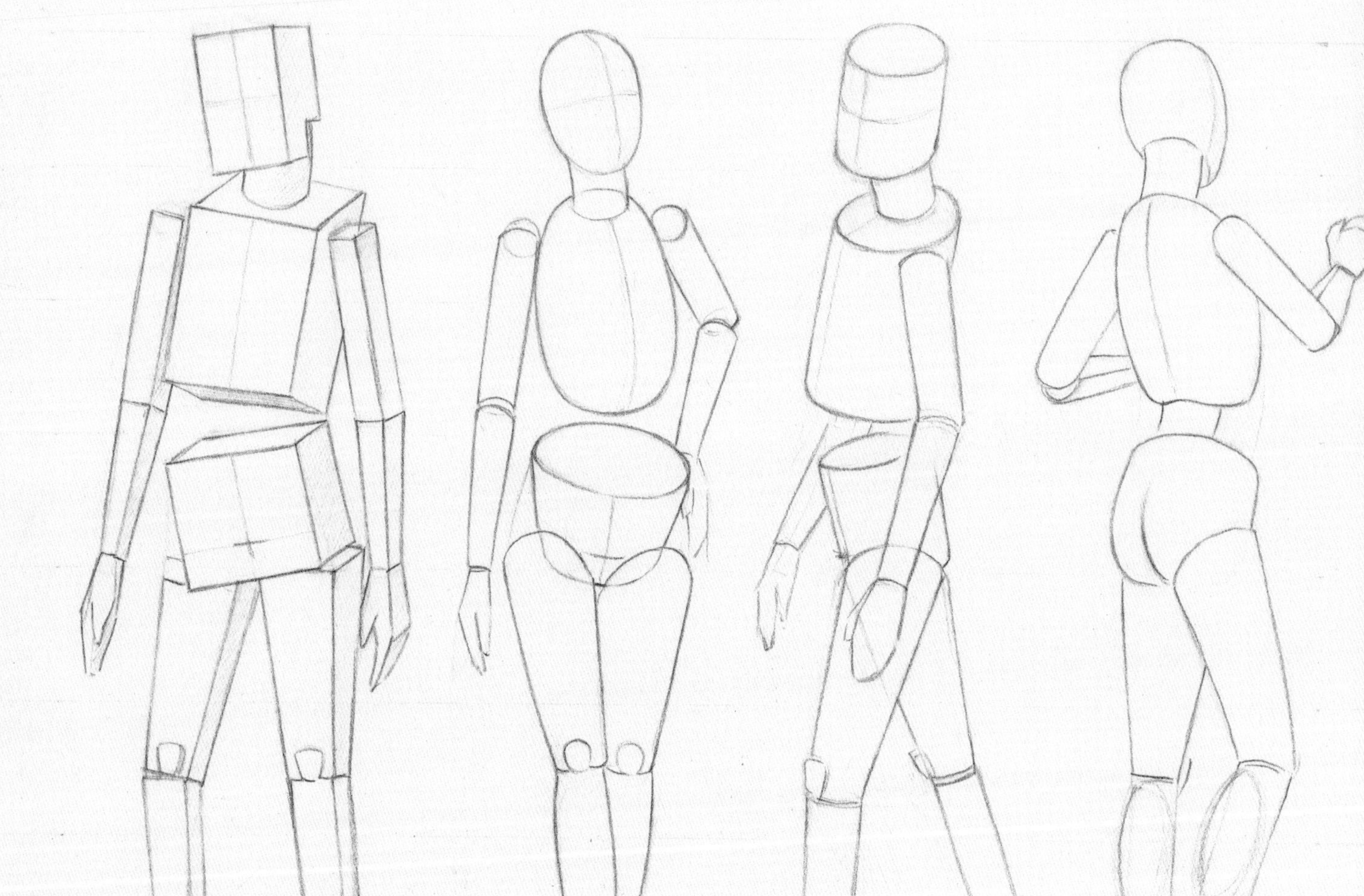

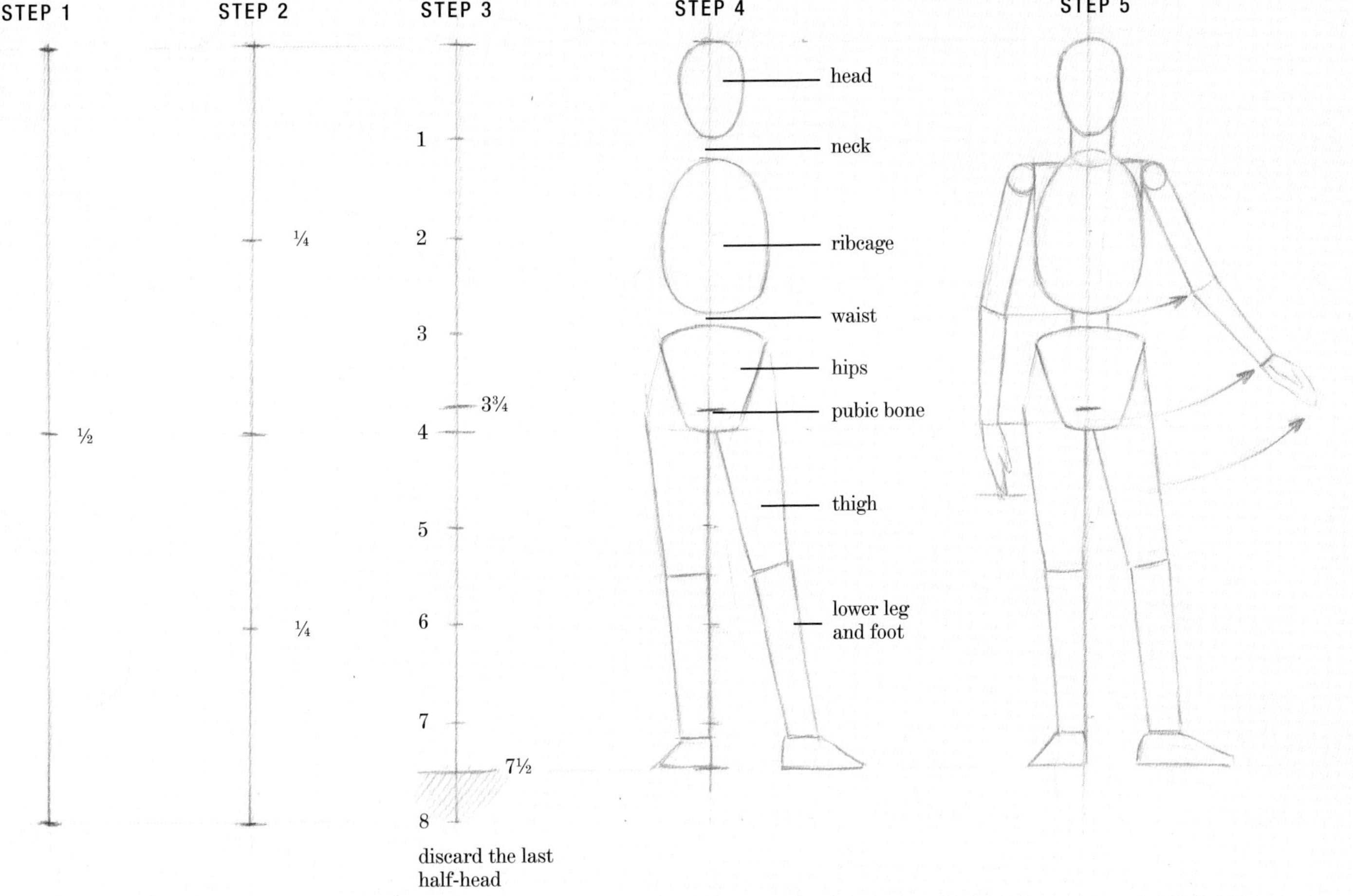

A SIMPLIFIED APPROACH TO RENDERING THE SEGMENTS OF THE BODY

To follow the sequence shown here, start by drawing a vertical line that represents the length of your figure and divide it in half (step 1). Then divide it in four equal segments (step 2), and then into eight segments. This will give you a set of proportions that you can use for the 1:8 heads scale. By erasing the bottom half of the last segment you obtain seven and a half segments (step 3). The midpoint of the 1:7 ½ figure (red line) corresponds to the pubic bone, which is at 3 ¾ heads, just above the line marking the fourth segment. (Note: The term *pubic bone* is conventionally used in artistic anatomy to designate the front part of the pelvis just above the genitals; in reality it is not a separate bone.)

As step 4 shows, you draw the head in the top segment using an oviform shape; the next two segments will be occupied by the ribcage, but not entirely, because you must leave some space for the neck and waist. Just remember that the neck and waist have to be carved out of the two segments assigned to the ribcage, making the ribcage only a little more than one and a half segments long. (Check the charts on pages 16–17 and 18–19 for the specific measures.) The hips are one segment long and occupy the fourth segment; the thighs are one and a half segments; and the lower legs and feet occupy two segments. Add the arms in the final step (5). The upper arms are the same length as the ribcage, the forearms reach slightly below the pubic bone, and the hands reach halfway down the length of the thighs.

TWO SIMPLIFIED APPROACHES

The figures here show a sequence that is more intuitive than the standard stereometric approach and that moves you toward a more creative rendering of the figure. To do this sequence yourself, you'll need drawing paper, pencils, an eraser, a pencil sharpener, and a proportional divider or compass. The proportional divider (or compass) will speed up your work, making it easier to transfer measurements from the stereometric scale explained in the sidebar on pages 25–27. The divider also allows you to divide a line into equal segments without using a ruler; you can simply compare the segments to each other to see if they are the same length.

The sequence below shows an alternative simplified approach to rendering body segments.

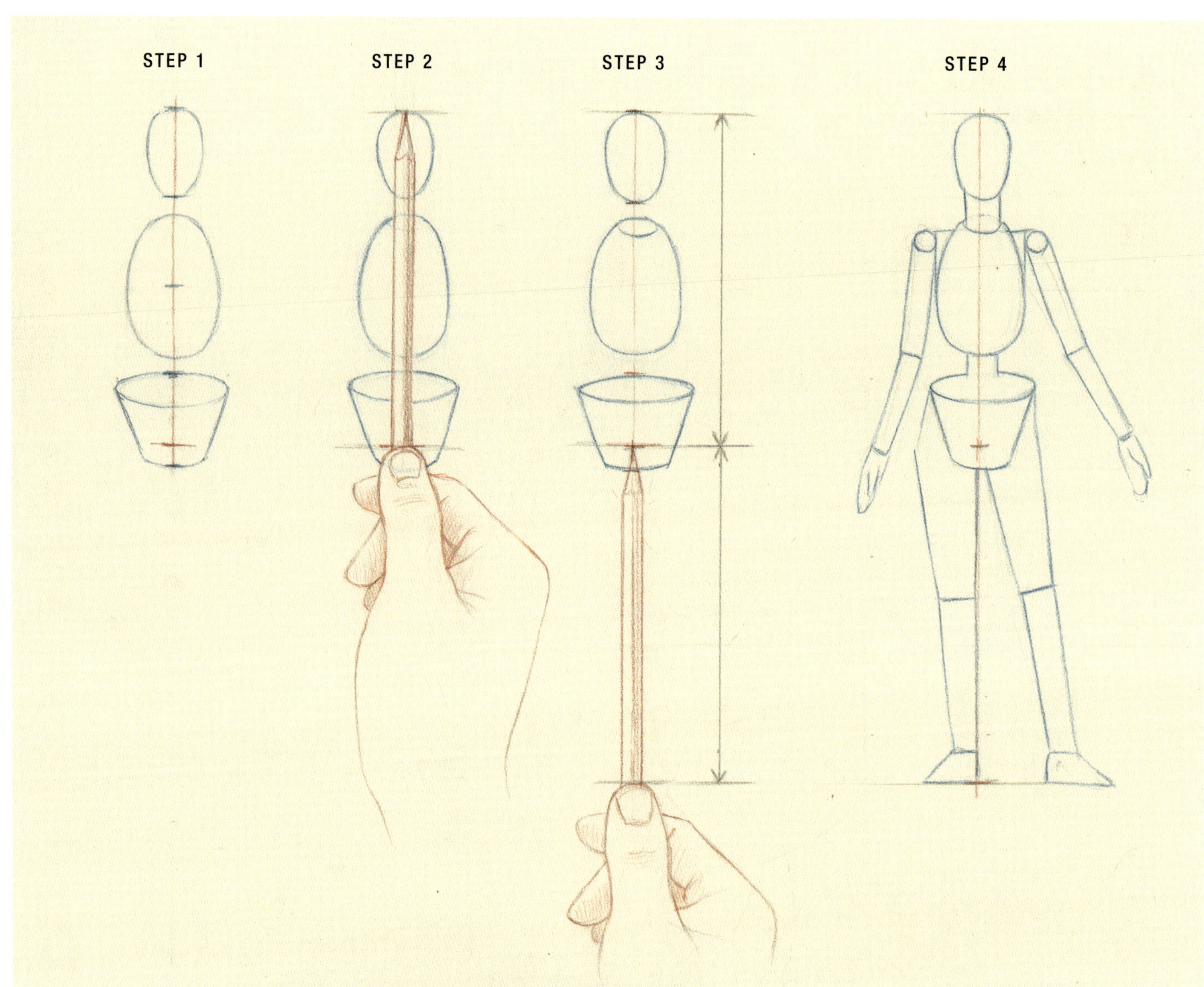

ANOTHER SIMPLIFIED APPROACH

In step 1, start with a line that will be divided into four equal segments—one for the head, two for the ribcage, and one for the hips—and then establish the position of the pubic bone, which is three-quarters of the way down the segment of the hips. The pubic bone is the midpoint of the body, so the measure between the top of the head and the midpoint is one-half of the body's total length. As shown in steps 2 and 3, you can use your pencil as a measuring device to determine the total length of the figure. Then finish the figure (step 4) by adding arms, hands, legs, and feet.

LANDMARKS OF THE BODY

The landmarks of the body are very important reference points. You can use them to measure the proportions of the body better and to read the posture of the figure more accurately, which will improve your drawings. Surface landmarks also give us clues about the skeleton beneath. The figure below shows only a few landmarks; more will be added in later chapters, where you will learn more specifically about using landmarks when drawing the figure.

A FEW ESSENTIAL LANDMARKS OF THE BODY

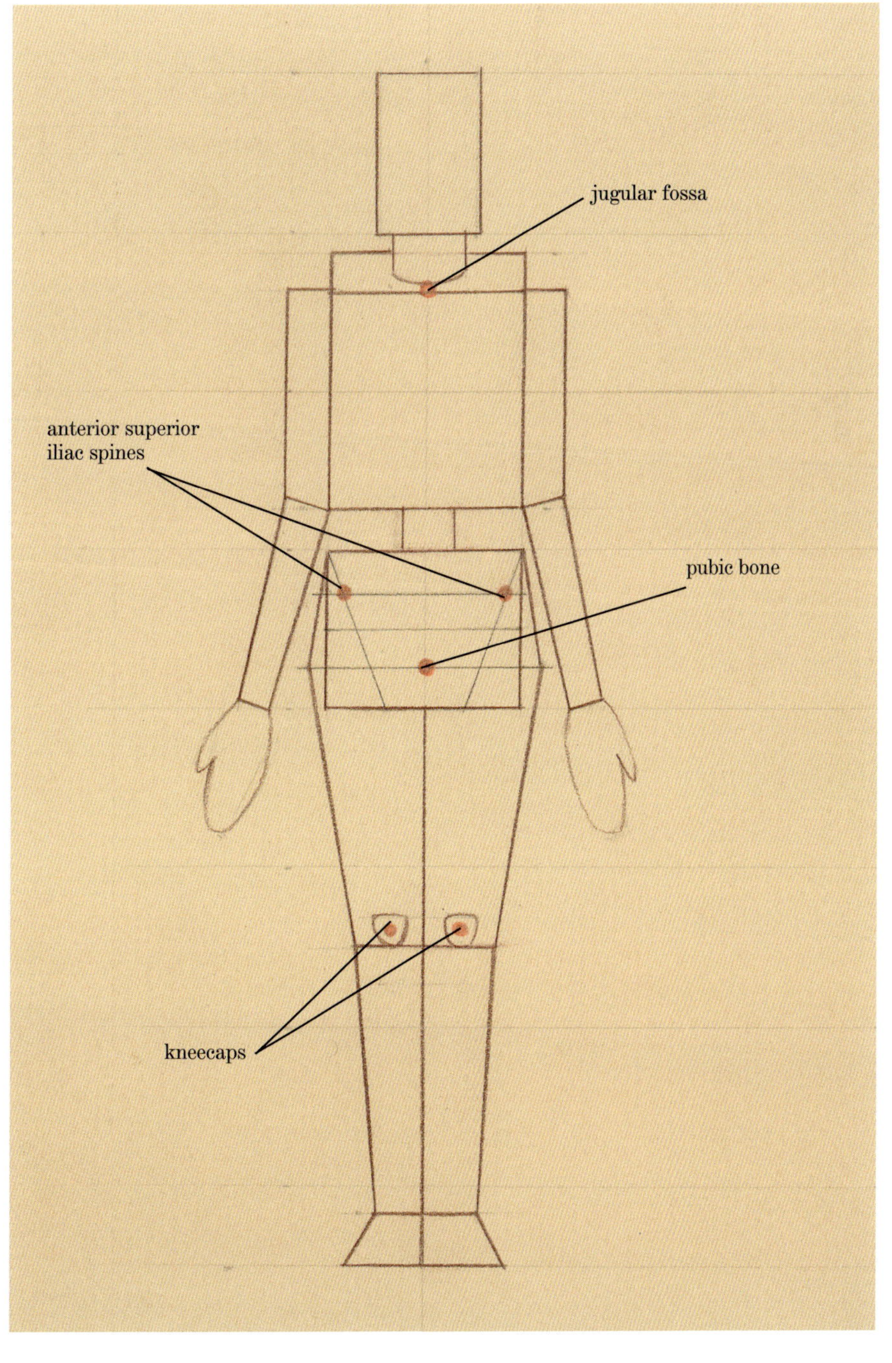

PRACTICAL BENEFITS OF THE STEREOMETRIC APPROACH

As mentioned earlier, the stereometric method of studying the human form was devised during the Renaissance. In the sixteenth century, the Italian Mannerist painter Luca Cambiaso created a great number of sketches and compositional studies using stereometric conceptualizations of the body. If you search for his work online, you will find a wealth of preparatory sketches and drawings, employing different levels of schematization. Cambiaso made these as studies for his paintings. Like the works of most painters of this period, Cambiaso's paintings were very big and therefore time-consuming and expensive to produce. Because each painting was such a complex project, he had to make sure that he had the composition right—and that both he and his client were satisfied with it—before beginning to paint.

Some of Cambiaso's stereometric studies are of figures in motion, demonstrating one benefit of the stereometric approach. Because a moving figure is such a challenging subject to draw or paint, it can be of great help to subdivide the figure into its various components and then reassemble them. When you divide the body into head, torso, hips, upper and lower arms, hands, thighs, lower legs, and feet, you gain a better understanding of the parts as joined, articulated segments. And if you have this mental image of the body, you can produce more dynamic, realistic, harmonious figures.

Once you understand how the segments of the body relate proportionally and how they are connected, you can start to create a variety of poses. The figures in this section show how stereometric renderings can be used for compositional purposes as well as for studying light and shadow and their effect on a composition.

Opposite, top
CONNECTING THE SEGMENTS OF THE BODY

Drawing 1 shows the axes of the three main segments of the body aligned along one central axis. Drawing 2 shows how you can position the segments at angles to each other. Drawing 3 goes further, showing how the segments can move at different angles *and* in different directions.

Opposite, bottom
APPLYING THE ANALYSIS OF THE SEGMENTS OF THE BODY AND THEIR AXES TO FIGURE DRAWING

These images demonstrate how to gradually include the limbs—at first just the upper segments of the arms and legs and then the whole limbs, including hands and feet. It greatly helps to draw the segments of the arm and leg as if they were cylinders, implying the volume and three-dimensionality of the forms and making it easier to show foreshortening.

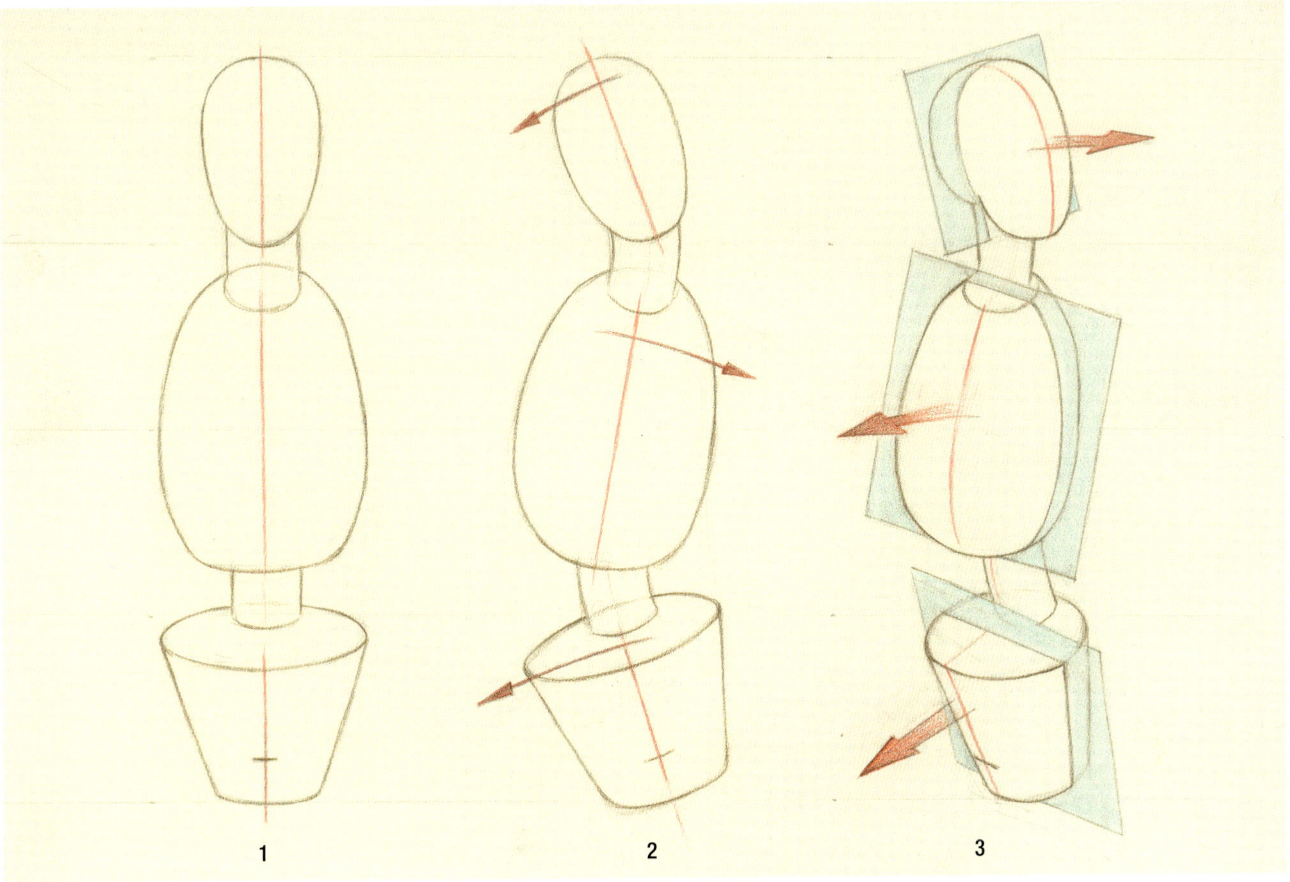

1
2
3

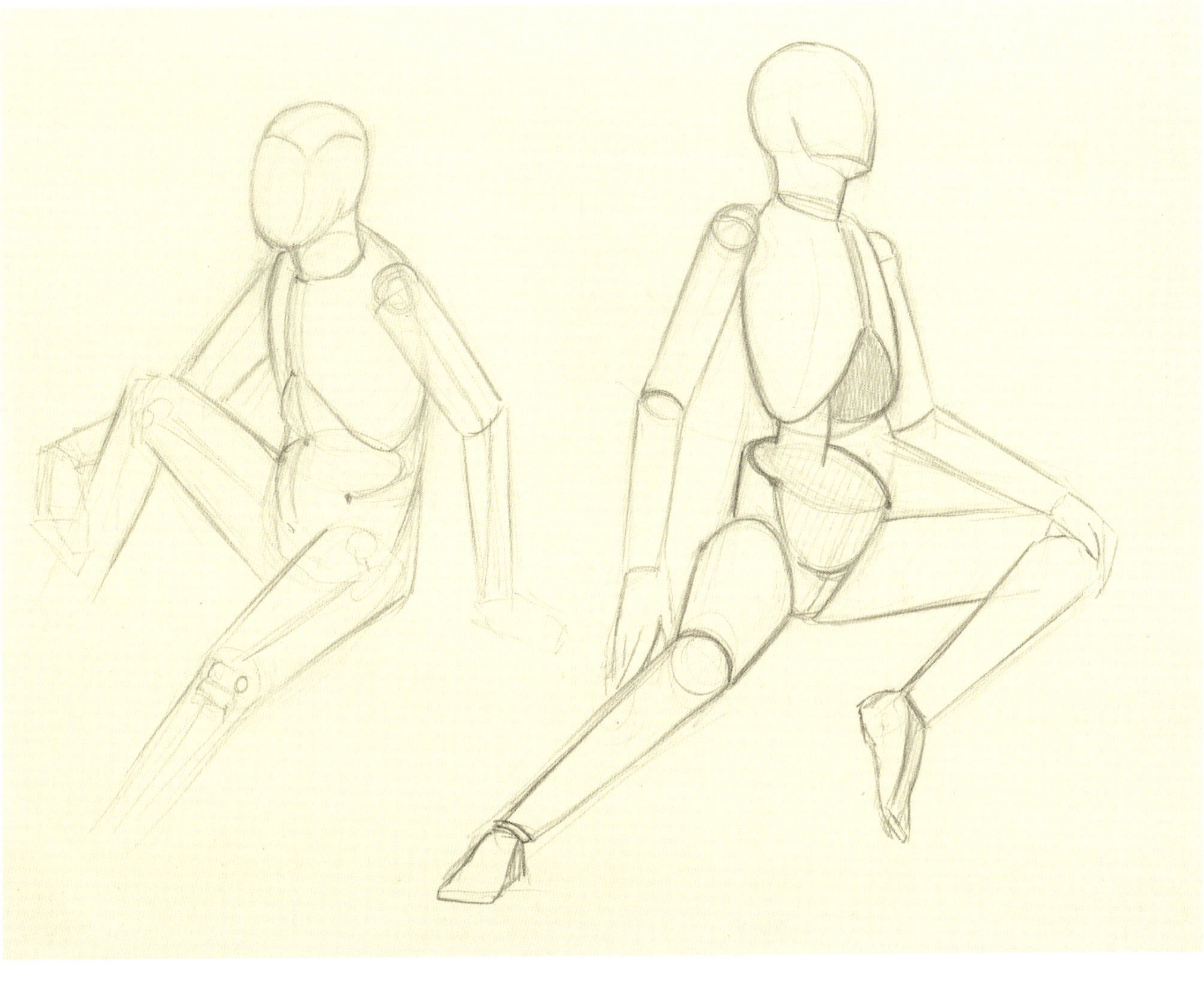

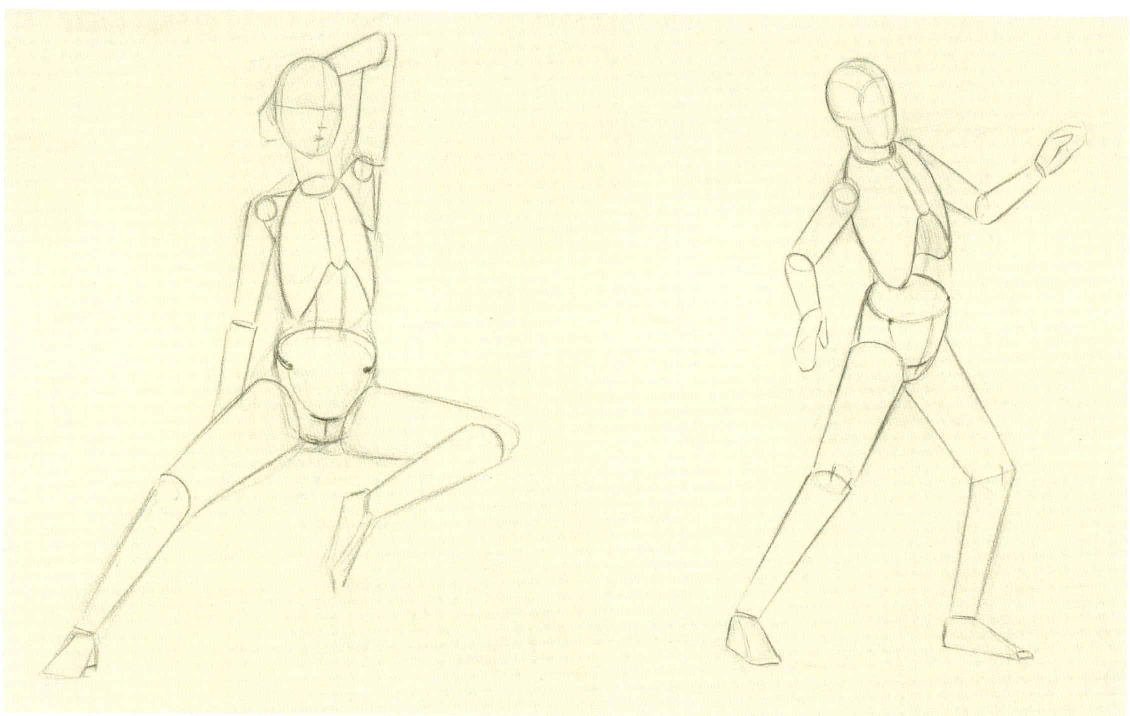

DYNAMIC POSES

In these two images, you can see how to experiment with moving the segments of the body and the limbs in various directions, imparting a sense of movement to the puppet figure.

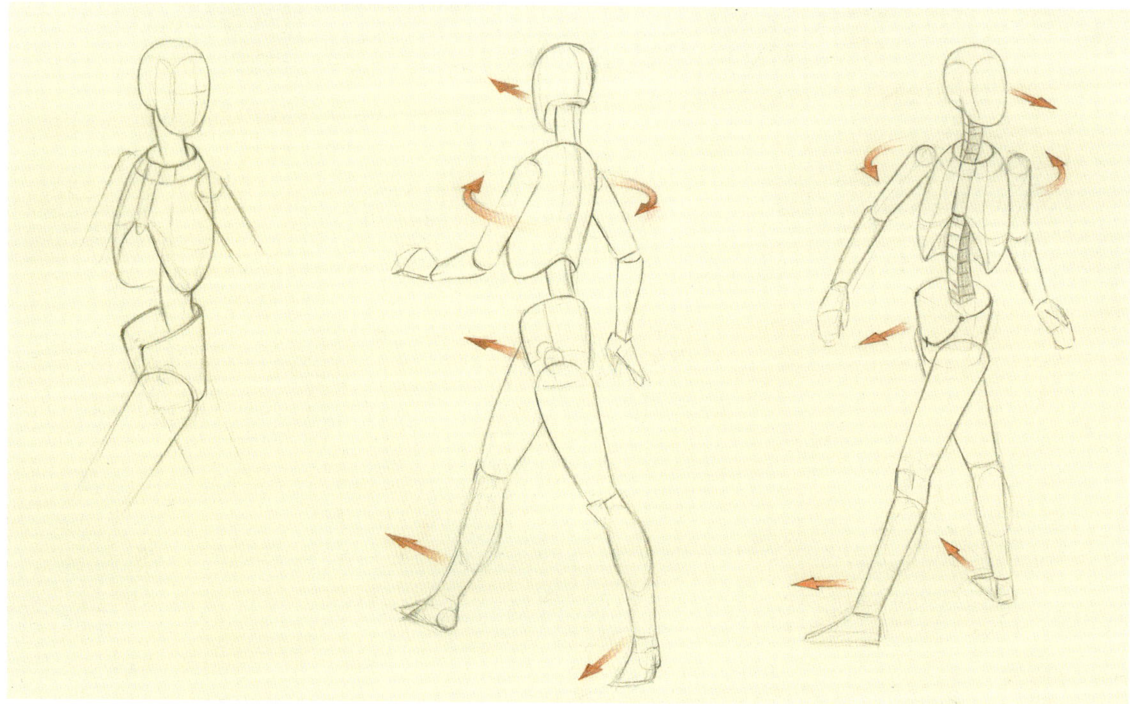

FIGURES IN MOVEMENT

You can draw figures that convey a sense of life by orienting the various volumes of the body in different directions while maintaining a fluid connection between them. In these drawings, note the movement created by a spiraling alignment of the body segments and their various orientations, as indicated by the arrows.

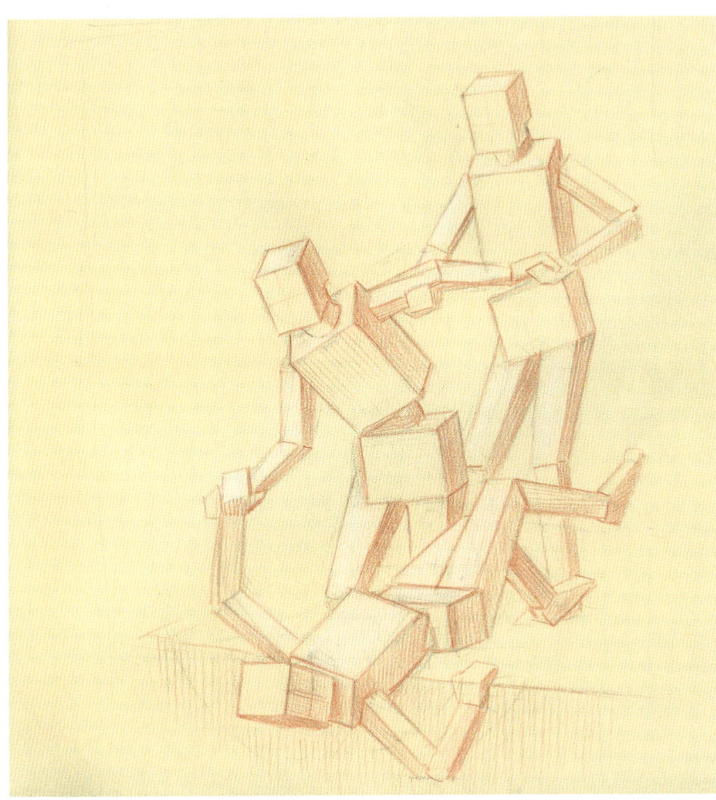

STEREOMETRIC STUDY FOR COMPOSITION

Stereometry is also very useful when preparing quick compositional sketches like this one. Such studies can be done from imagination or memory, without the use of a live model. You can visualize ideas and refine compositions, evaluating possible options and alternatives. Once you've done that, you can narrow the possible compositions to a couple of options that you can then further refine using live models and a larger format to create studies that are more complete.

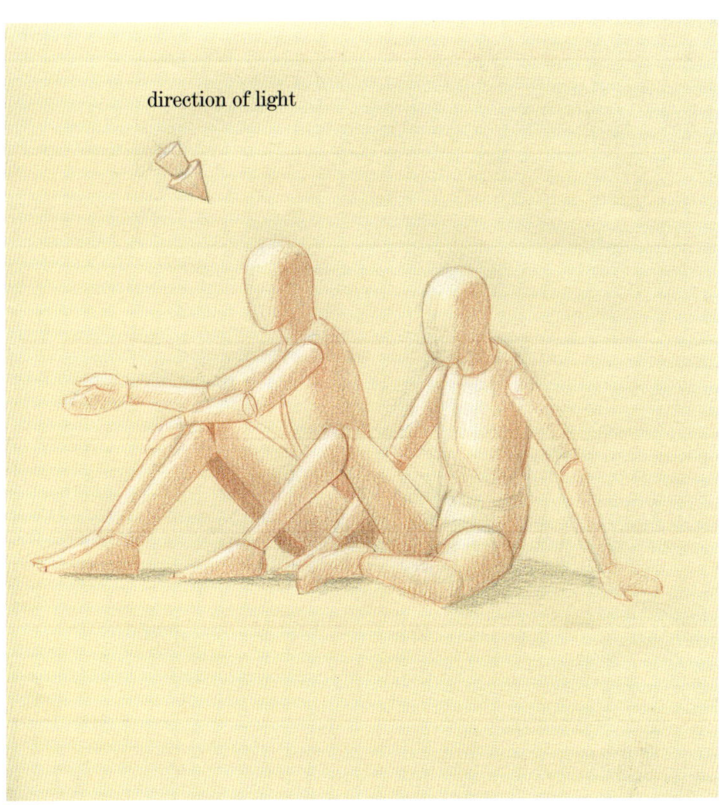

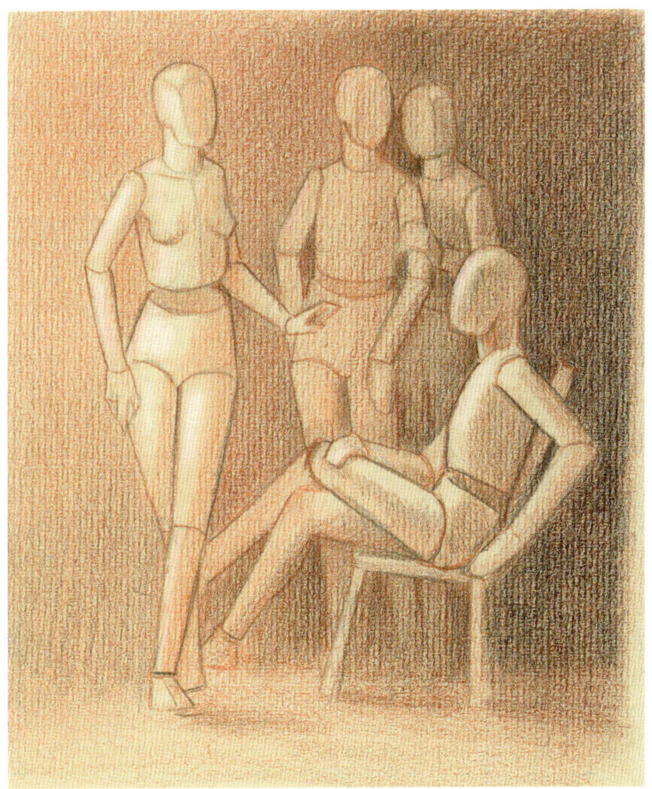

STUDIES OF LIGHT ON STEREOMETRIC FIGURES

These studies show another use for stereometric renderings—the study of light on figures (left) and of light on figures and the surrounding environment (right). Because the bodies are reduced to very simple forms, it is easy to imagine how light would hit them once you have established the light's direction.

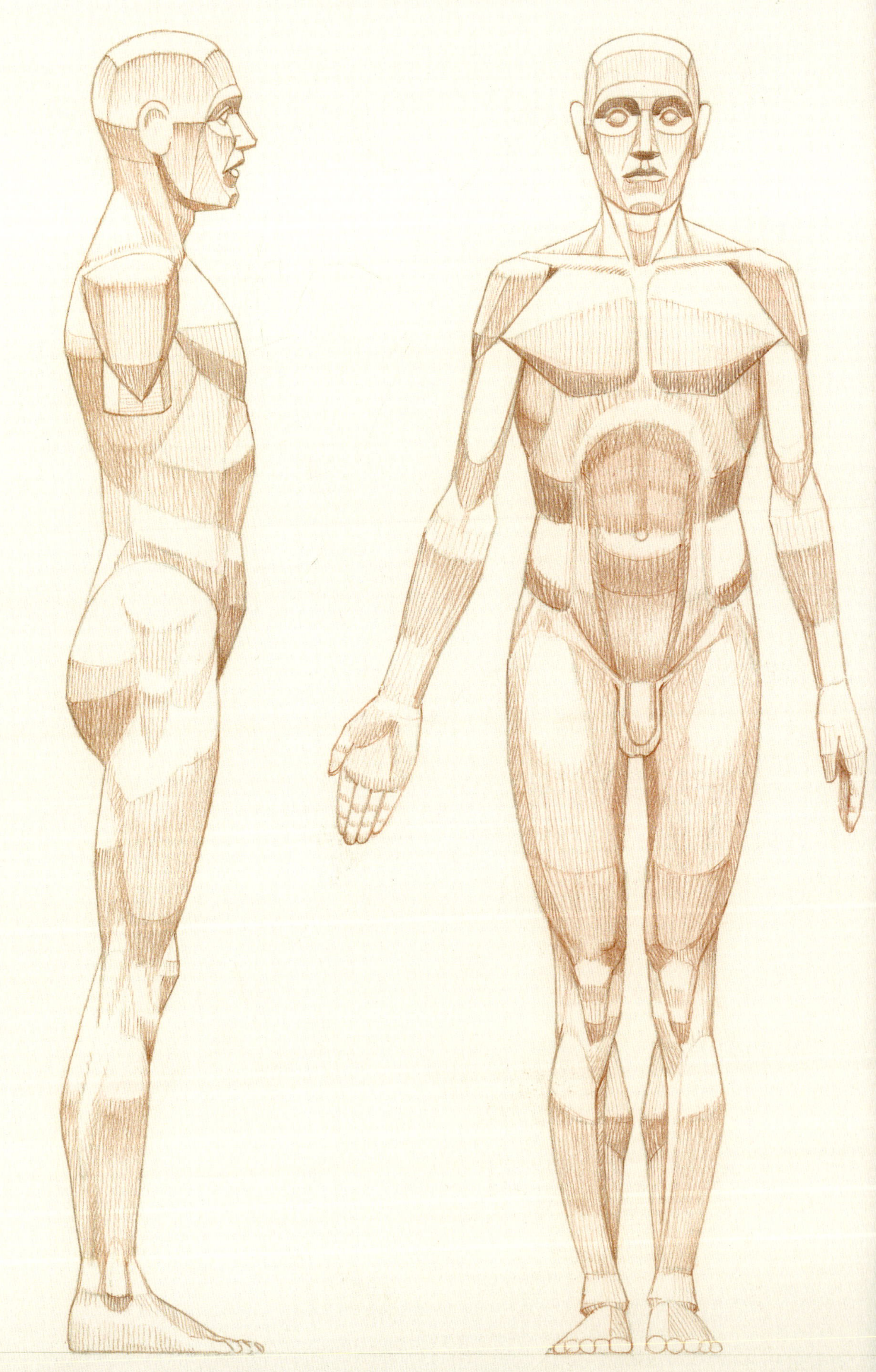

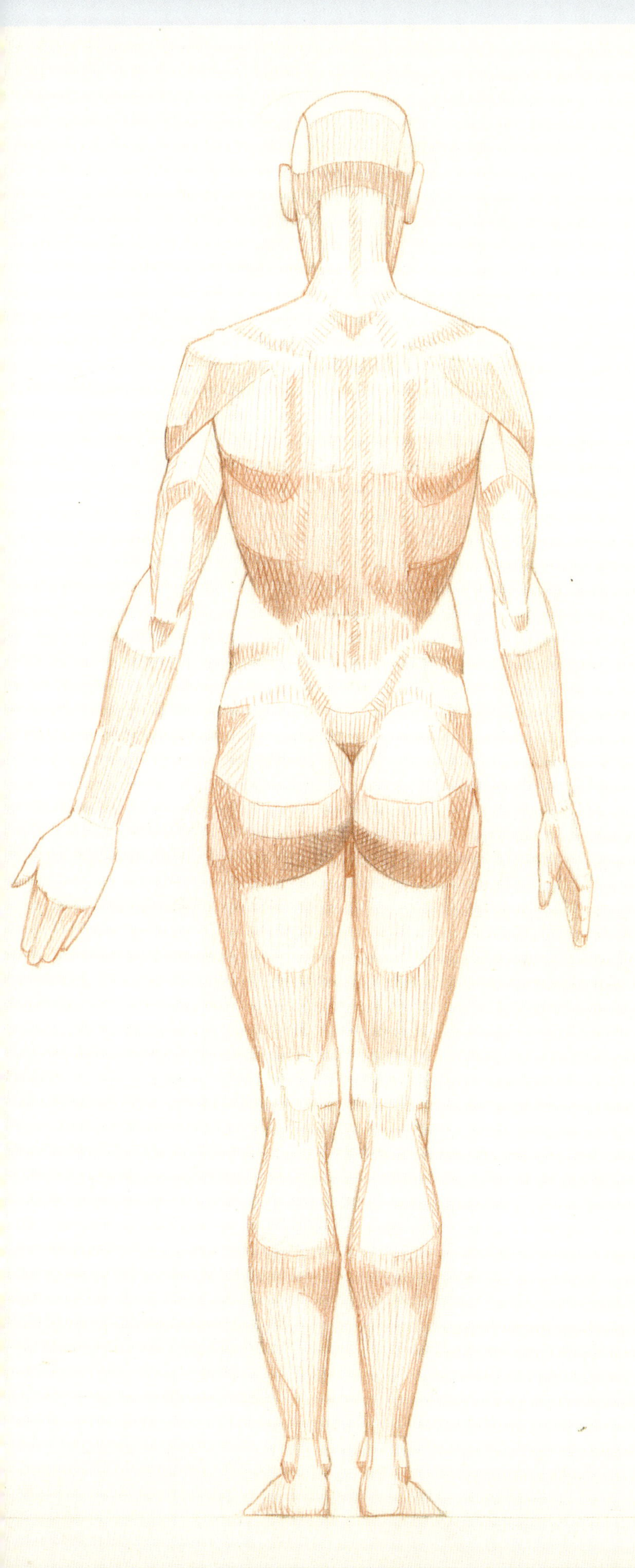

PLANES OF THE FIGURE

Another way of geometrically conceptualizing the figure is to reduce it to a series of planes, as shown here and on the following pages.

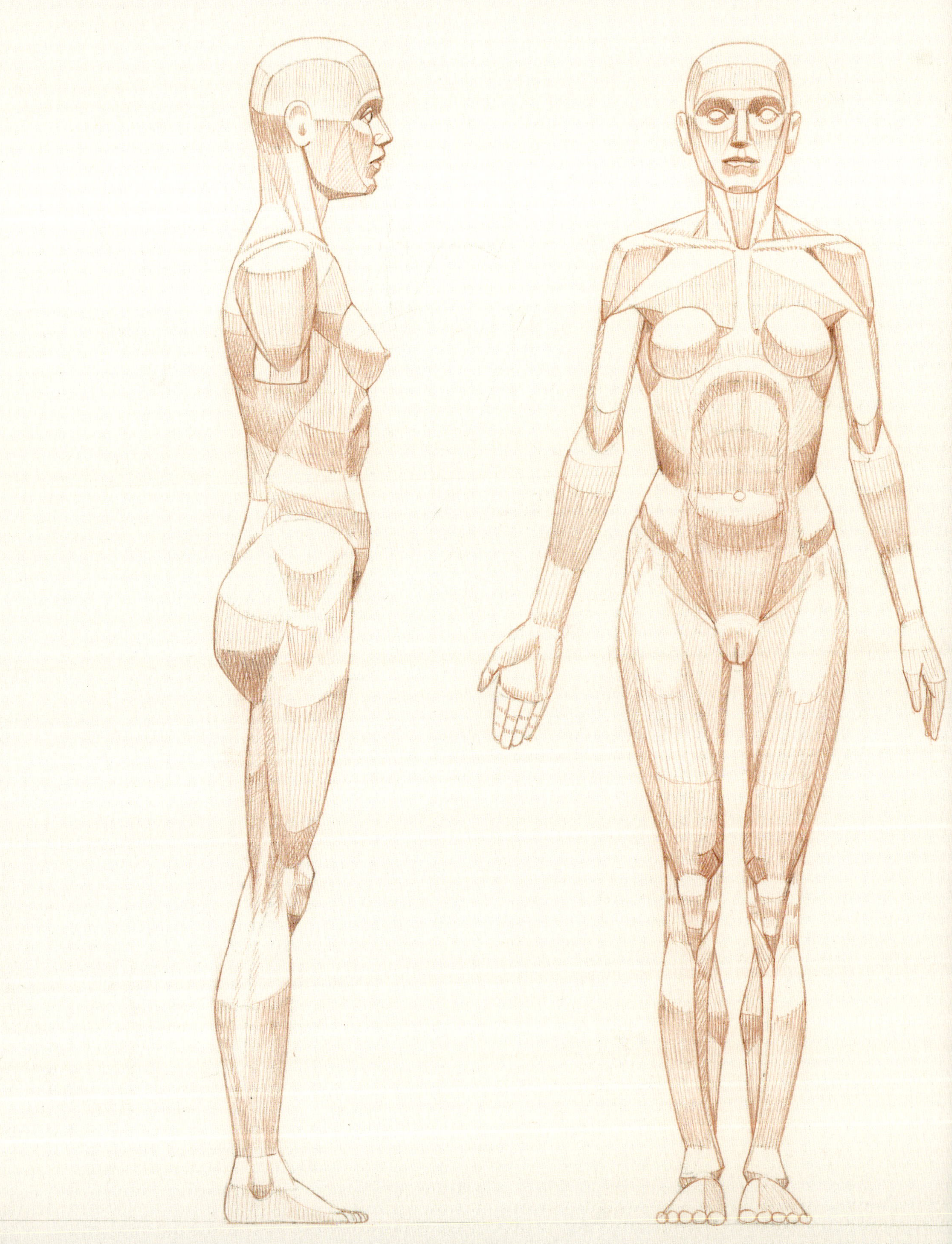

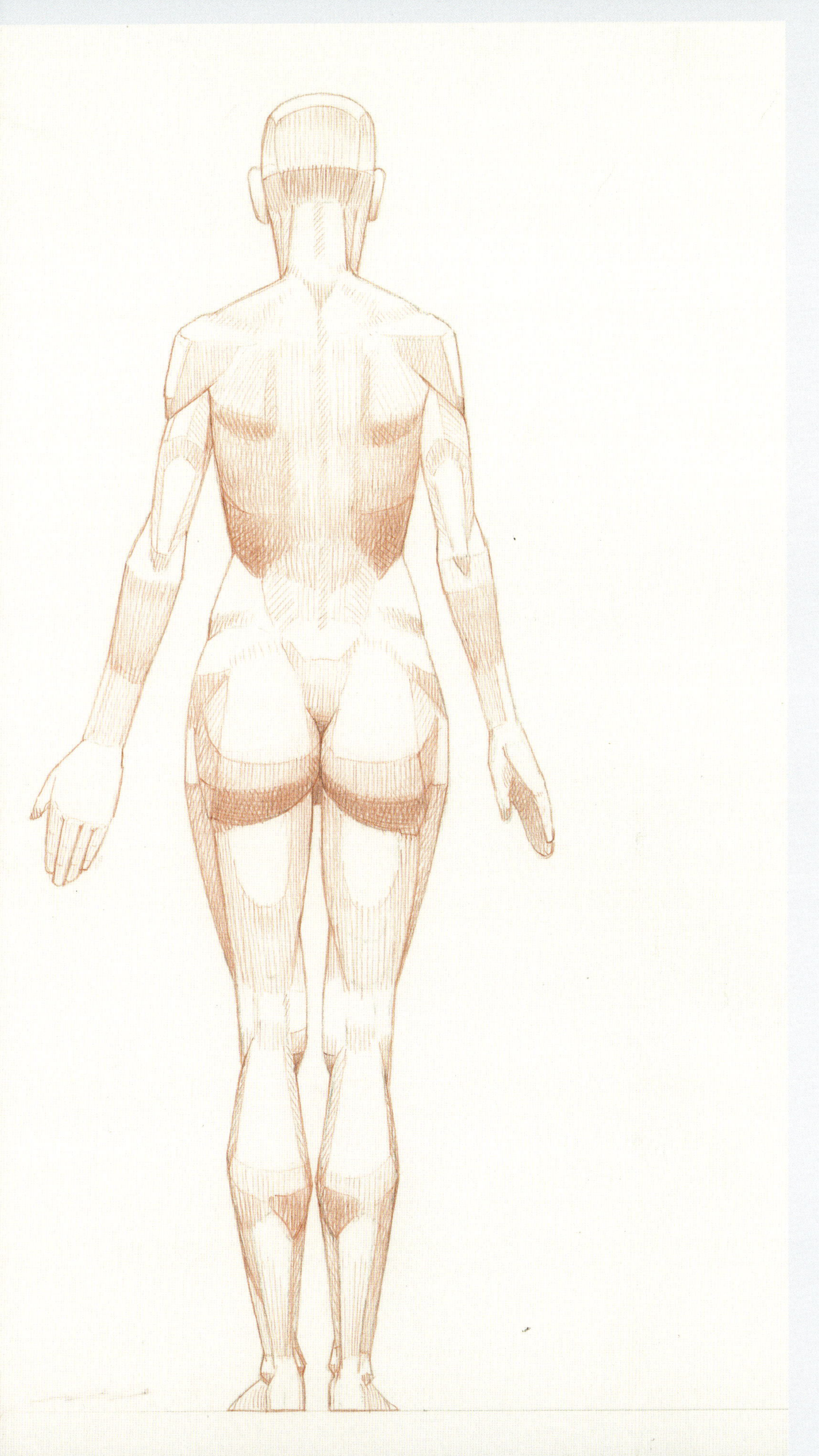

THE PLANES OF THE
FEMALE FIGURE

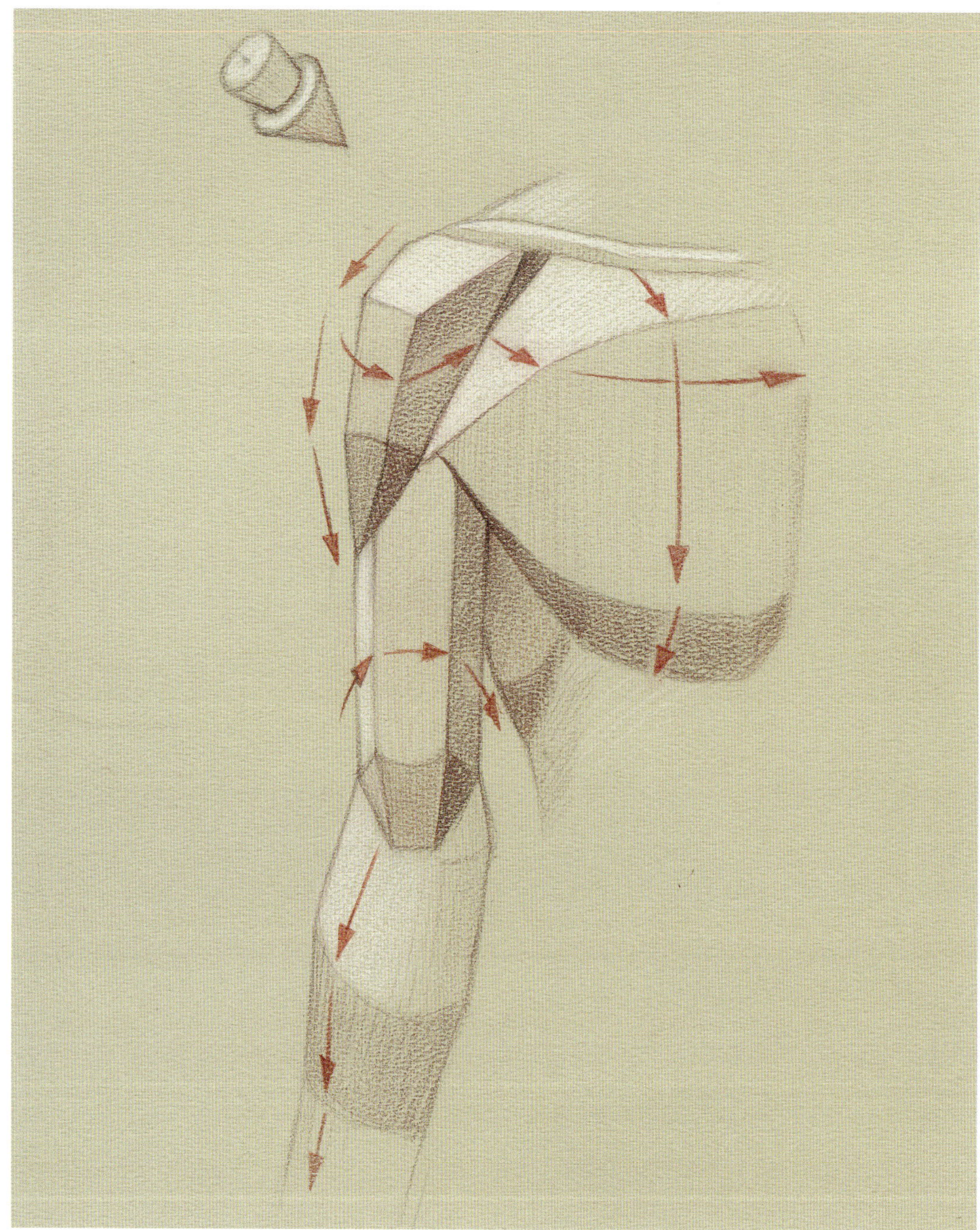

EXERCISES

For these exercises, you will need colored pencils (dark colors) or graphite pencils (grade HB or F), erasers, pencil sharpeners, and drawing paper (11 X 14 inches). Don't use newsprint if you can afford better quality paper. For exercises 2, 3, and 4, you might want to use magazine or newspaper photos of people in action. You can draw your stereometric studies directly on the photos, or you can place tracing paper over them. For exercise 5 you will need toned paper; use a medium value (more or less the value of a brown paper bag) and a neutral color—brown, gray, or blue-gray. You will also need a white colored pencil.

LIGHT ON THE PLANES OF THE BODY

This image shows the effect of the light on the body in relation to its main volumes. Understanding this correlation can help to achieve a greater three-dimensional effect.

EXERCISE 1: DRAW VOLUMES FROM DIFFERENT VIEWS

Practice drawing the stereometric volumes
of the head. First draw them in front, back,
side, top, bottom, and three-quarters views, as
shown in the figure at right, where you see
the basic views of the head. Then draw various
other possible views, as shown in the figure
below.

right
BASIC STEREOMETRIC VIEWS OF THE HEAD

below
STEREOMETRIC VIEWS OF THE HEAD FROM
VARIOUS ANGLES

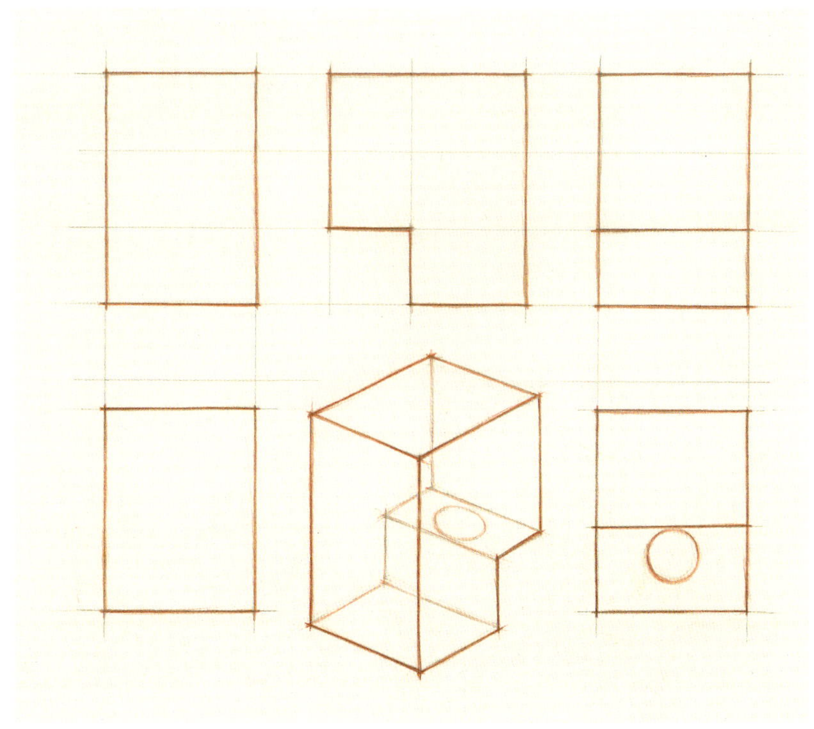

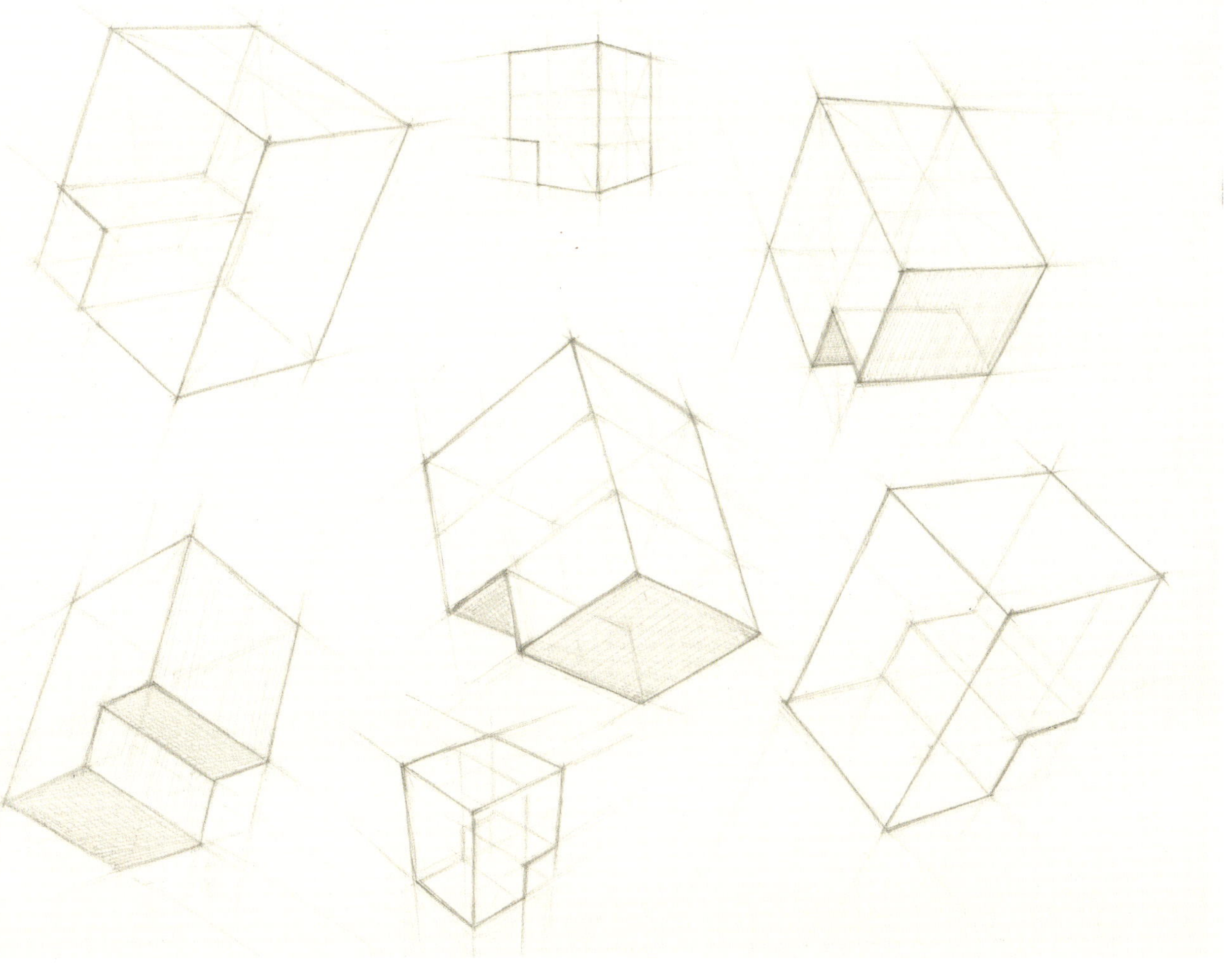

EXERCISE 2:
DRAW MALE AND FEMALE FIGURES

On a sheet of drawing paper, draw about
twenty stereometric renderings of male
and female figures in front, side, back, and
three-quarters views. Use a graphite or dark
brown, red earth, or blue colored pencil. Draw
the figures in various sizes so that you get
used to working at different scales. Do a few
pages of these until you feel confident about
your figures.

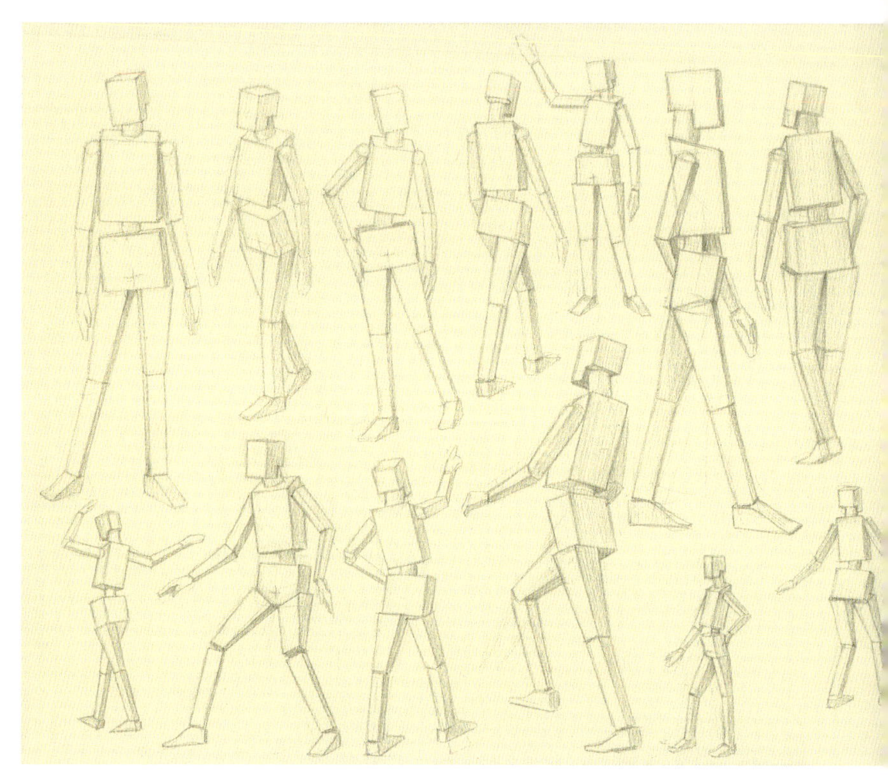

EXERCISE 3:
DRAW FIGURES IN ACTION POSES

Now, practice imparting movement to the
male and female figures by drawing a few
pages of them in various action poses. If you
wish, you can draw the stereometric "boxes"
over photographs from magazines or news-
papers. (Sports magazines and the sports
section of the newspaper are especially useful,
since they contain many photos of athletes in
action.)

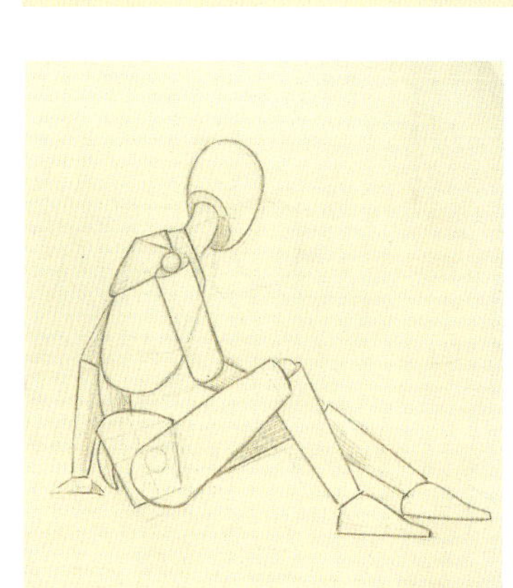

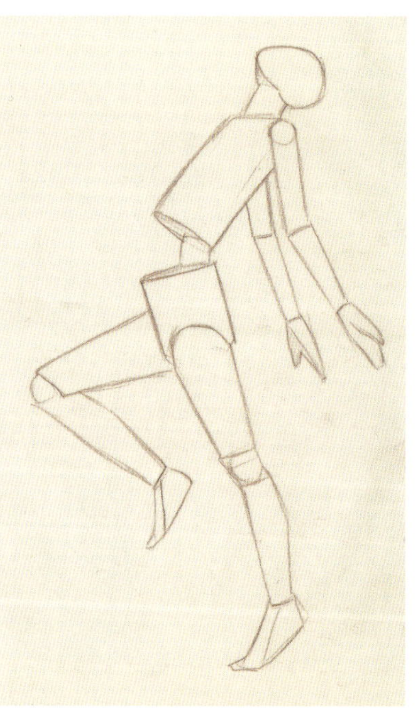

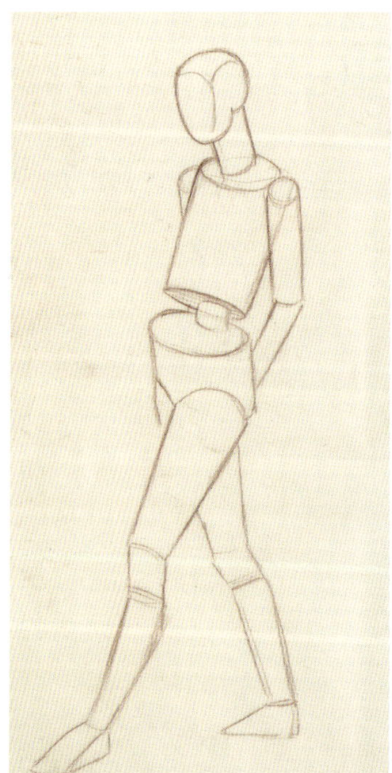

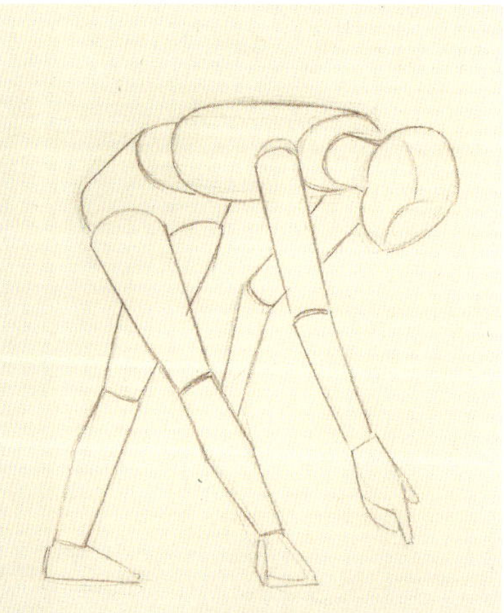

EXERCISE 4:
DRAW GROUPS OF INTERACTING FIGURES

Now, start practicing compositions in which figures interact with each other, as in the illustrations on page 35. Start with just two or three figures and then move on to more complex compositions that include more figures and movement.

EXERCISE 5:
SHOW LIGHT AND SHADOW

Before you start drawing on toned paper, do a practice run using the images you created in exercise 4. Imagine a light source for each composition, and draw the shadows on the figures. When you are ready, you can start drawing on toned paper. Draw a composition like one of those you did for exercise 4, then imagine the light source and define shadow masses with a graphite or dark colored pencil and the light masses with a white pencil. The mid values will be defined by the value of the toned paper. After this, draw another composition and include the light and shadows in the environment around the figures as well as on the figures themselves.

EXERCISE 6:
PRACTICE DRAWING THE EFFECTS OF A LIGHT SOURCE ON THE PLANES OF THE FIGURE

Using tracing paper, trace the drawings of the planes of the figure that appear on pages 36–37 and 38–39—drawing only the planes and not the shading. Now imagine a directional light source and draw the shadow masses, midtones, and highlights. Once you have traced the charts, you can scan your tracings and print copies for practicing the effects that different light sources have on the figures, as shown below.

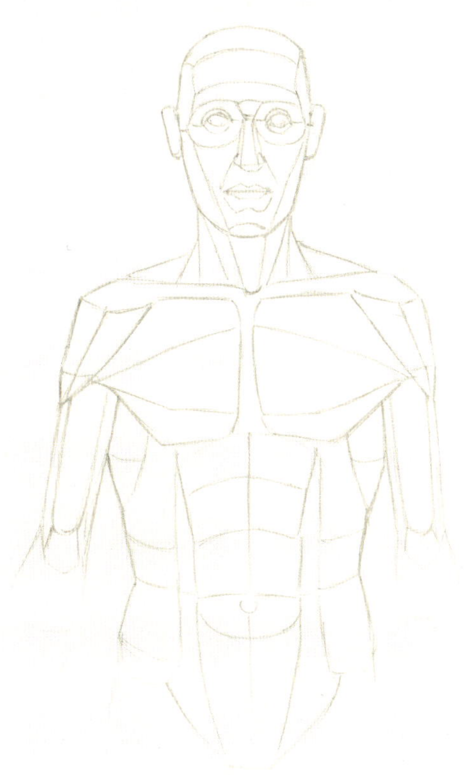

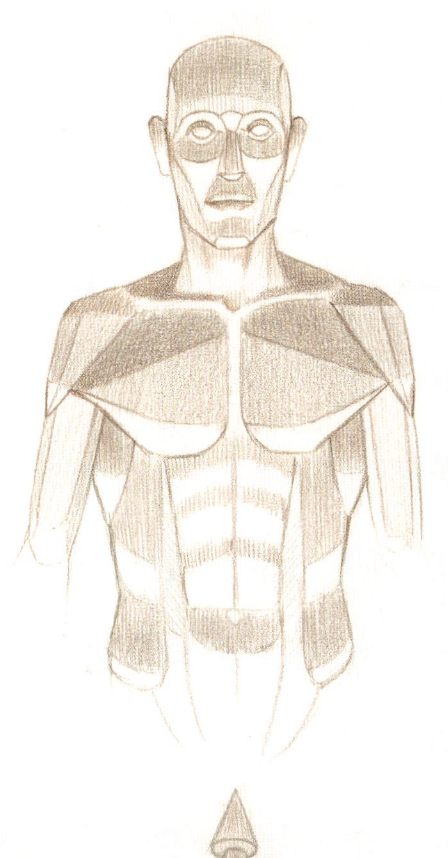

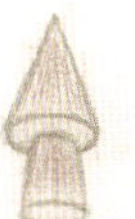

DO GESTURE DRAWINGS

As you study anatomy, you'll find gesture drawing to be rewarding and fun. In my opinion, the best gesture drawings are those that have very few lines—only the essential ones. Gesture drawings are done very quickly: Keep the poses short (between one and three minutes) so that the model can hold difficult, dynamic poses that he or she could not maintain in a twenty-minute pose. (But do try some static poses, too.) The short pose will force you to observe the model carefully and draw only the essential lines. Even if you draw quickly, however, you should stay away from simple lines; rather, find a way to create synthetic lines informed by your knowledge of the subject. For example, when you draw the legs, try to identify which muscles you are drawing and the characteristics of those muscles or muscle groups—the peaks of the forms, angles, directions, and so on. The examples here range from very simple to slightly more finished.

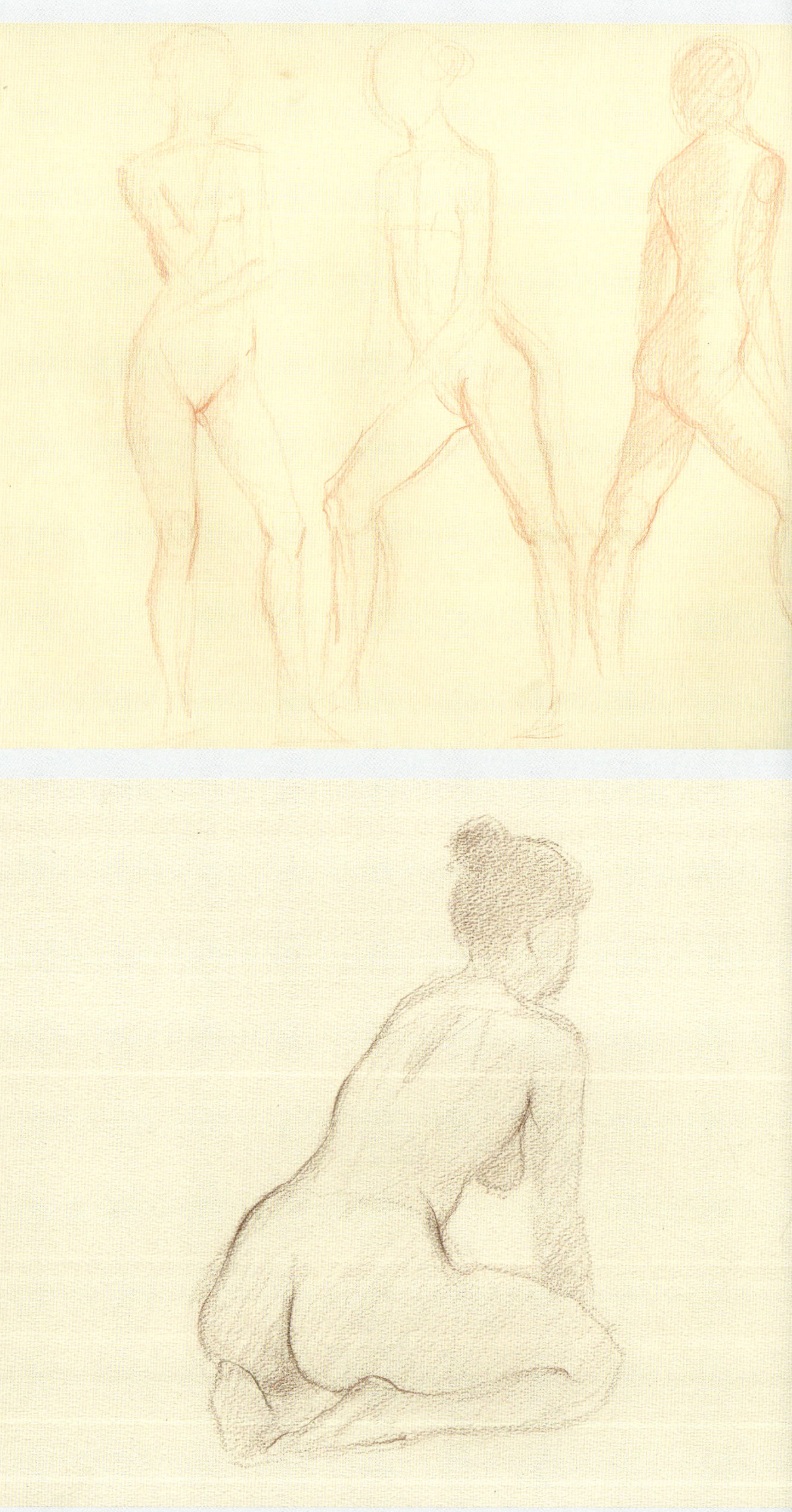

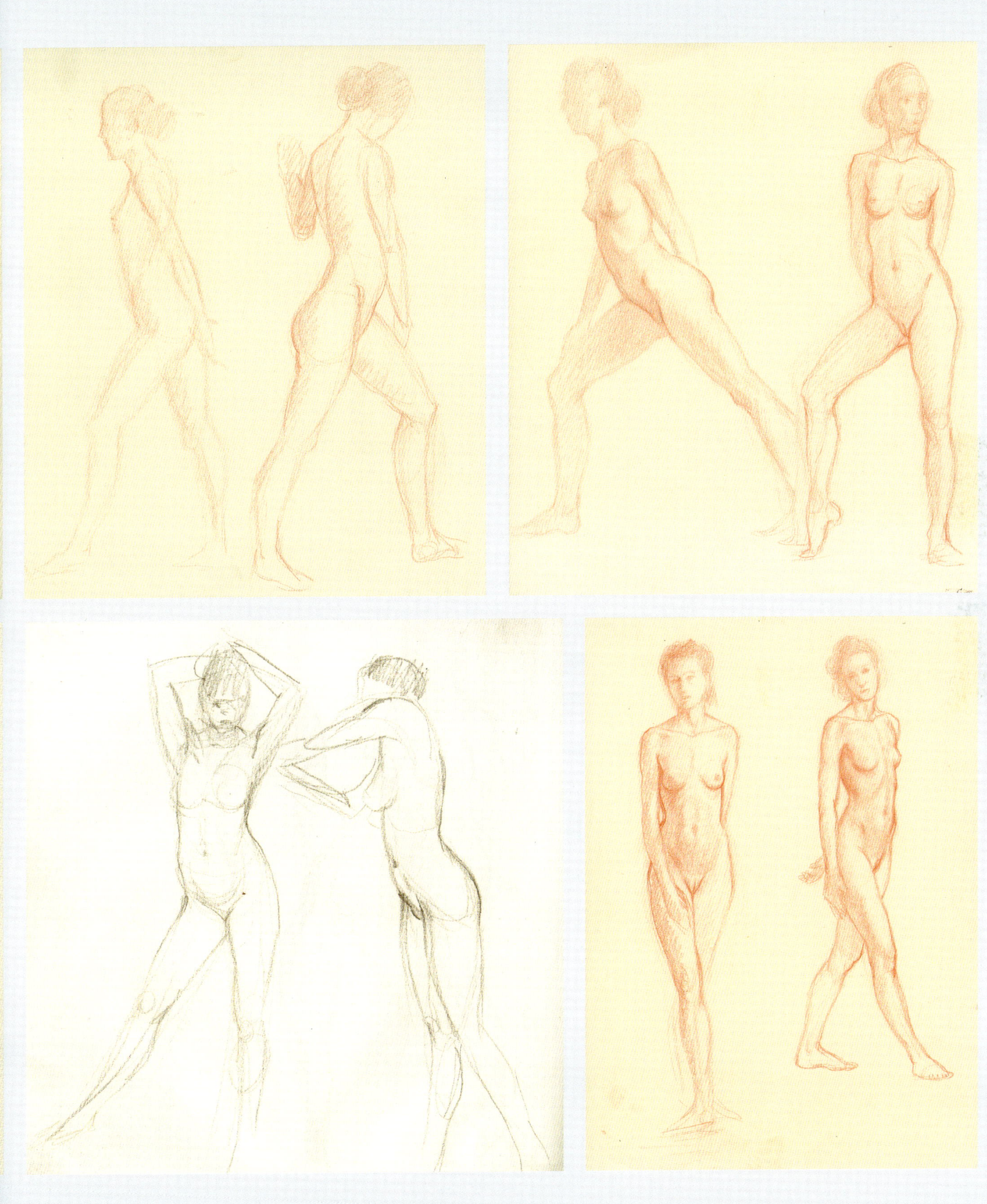

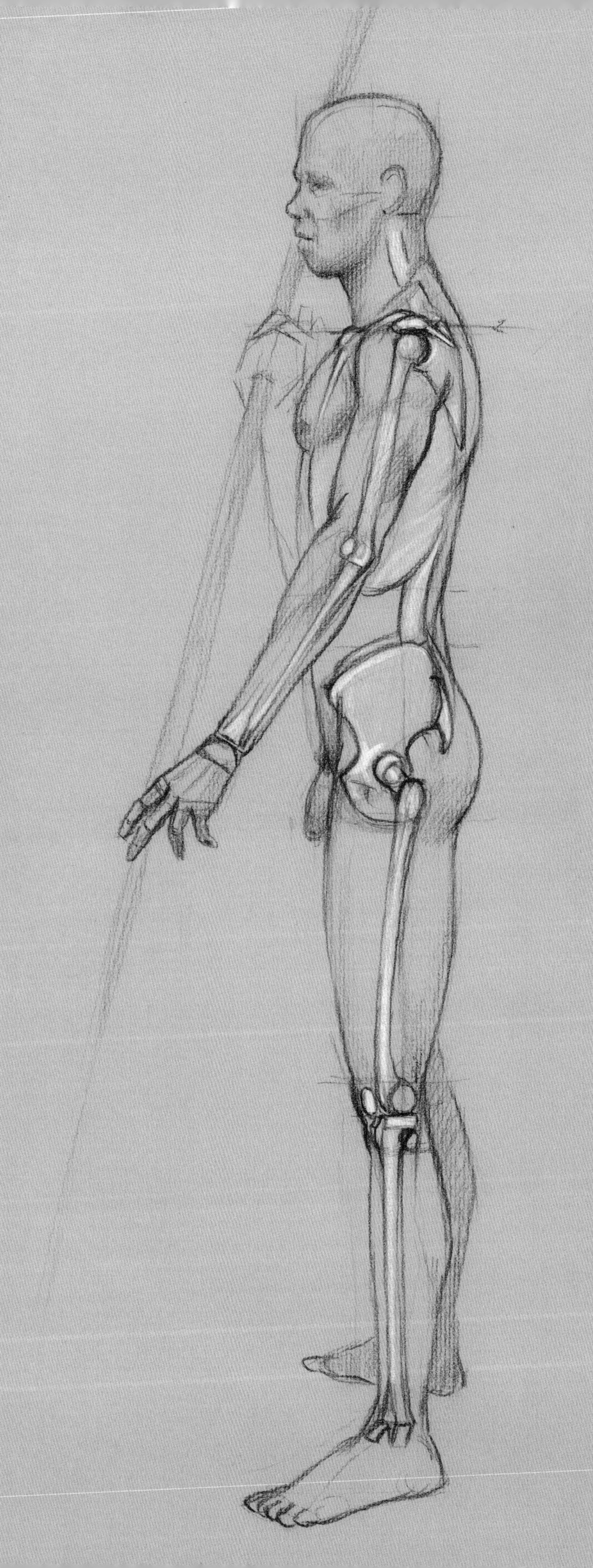

Chapter 2

THE STRUCTURAL SKELETON

Chapter 1 defined the stereometric approach, which reduces the body to basic geometric volumes. That method is very thorough and gives us very specific proportions for the various segments of the body. But although the stereometric approach is good for learning purposes, it is a little slow and cumbersome in practice. For this reason we gradually moved toward hybrid forms of the human figure that incorporate rounded forms more like the organic forms of the body. These hybrid conceptualizations offer advantages: They are easier and faster to draw, and they create more realistic figures.

In this chapter, I define in detail the basic structural characteristics of the skeleton. Conceptualizing the skeleton according to its basic structure gives us an idea of how it is built, how its parts are joined together, how it moves, and how the weight is carried and distributed. Defining this essential structure will make it much easier to add specific parts of the skeleton, which we will do in chapter 3.

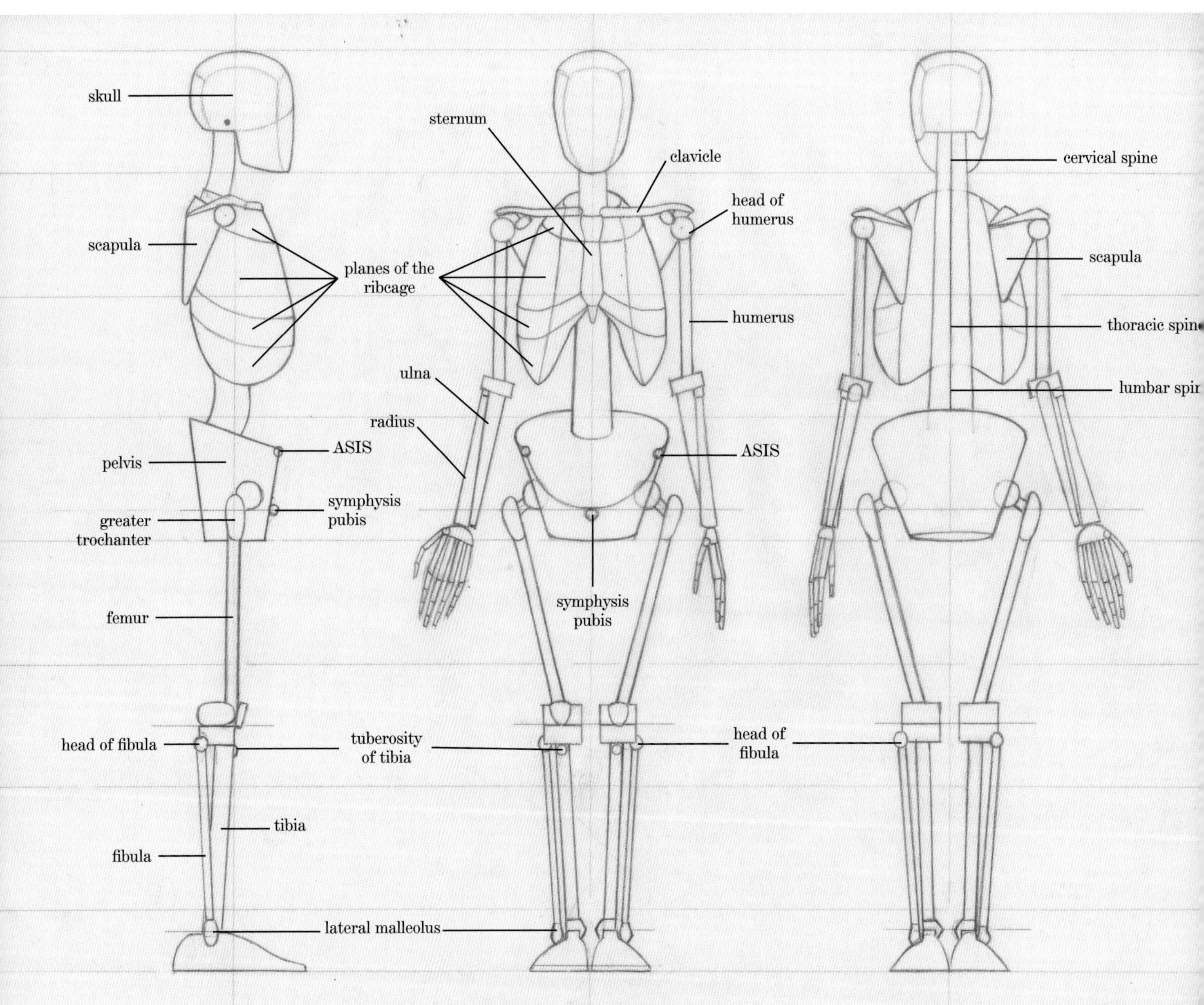

THE MALE STRUCTURAL SKELETON

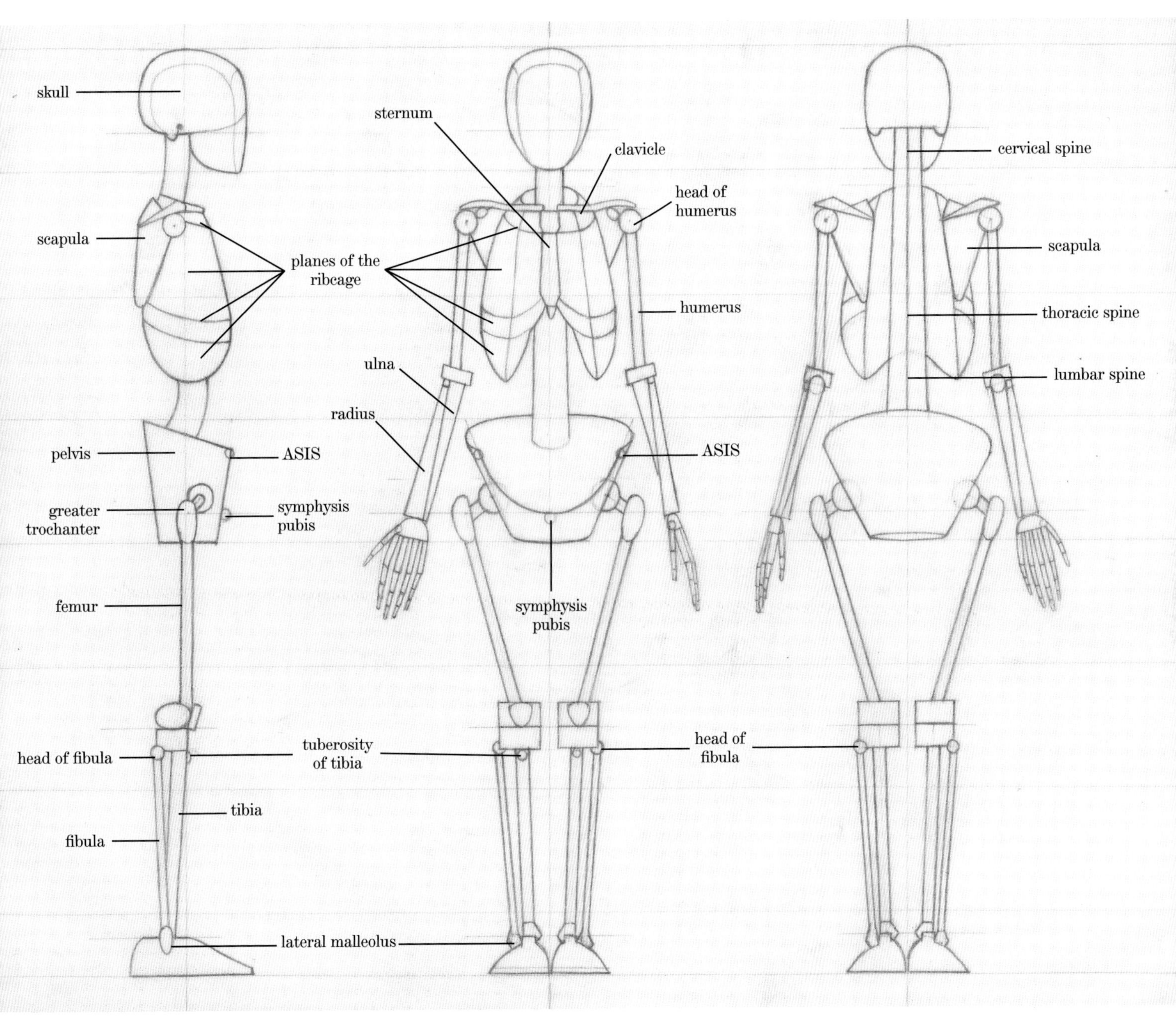

THE FEMALE STRUCTURAL SKELETON

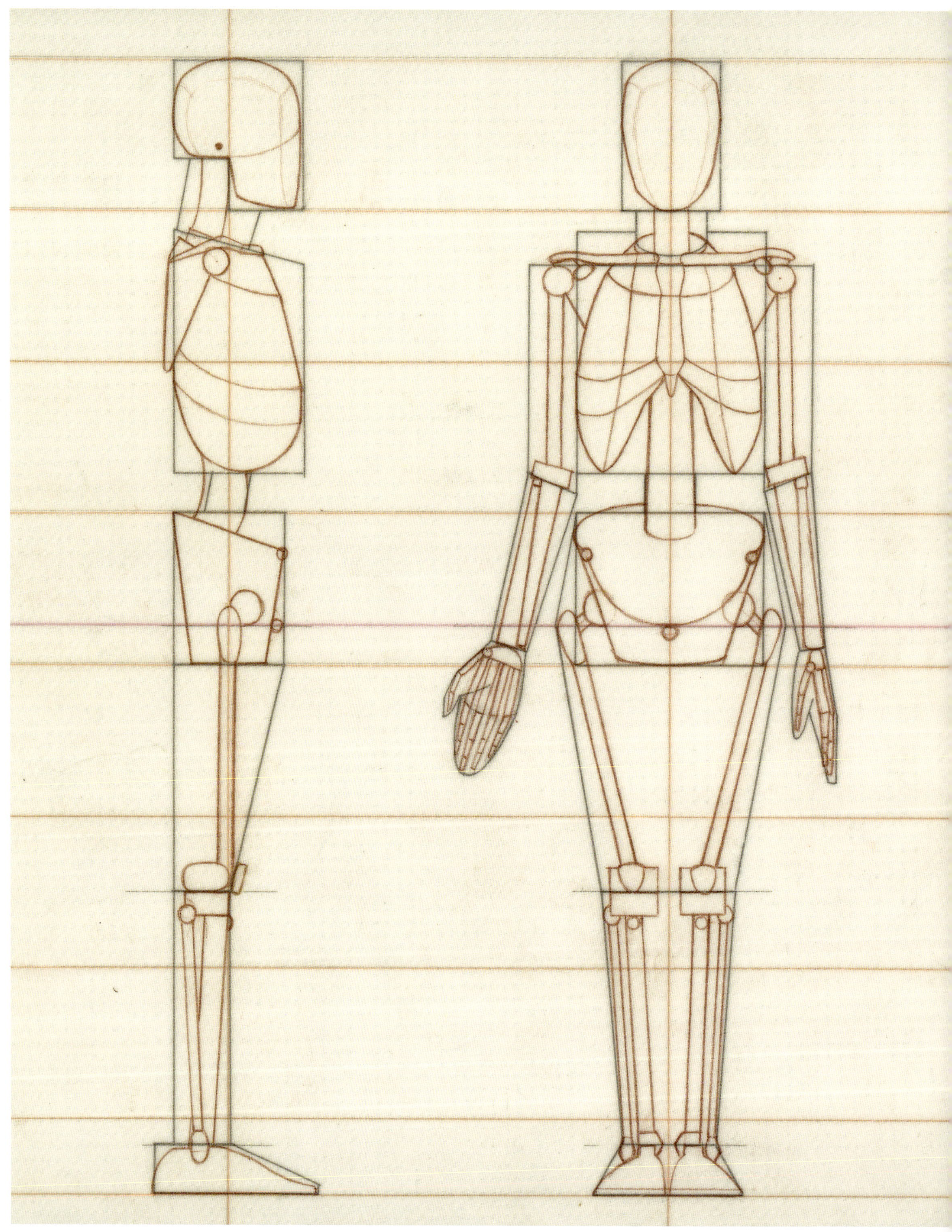

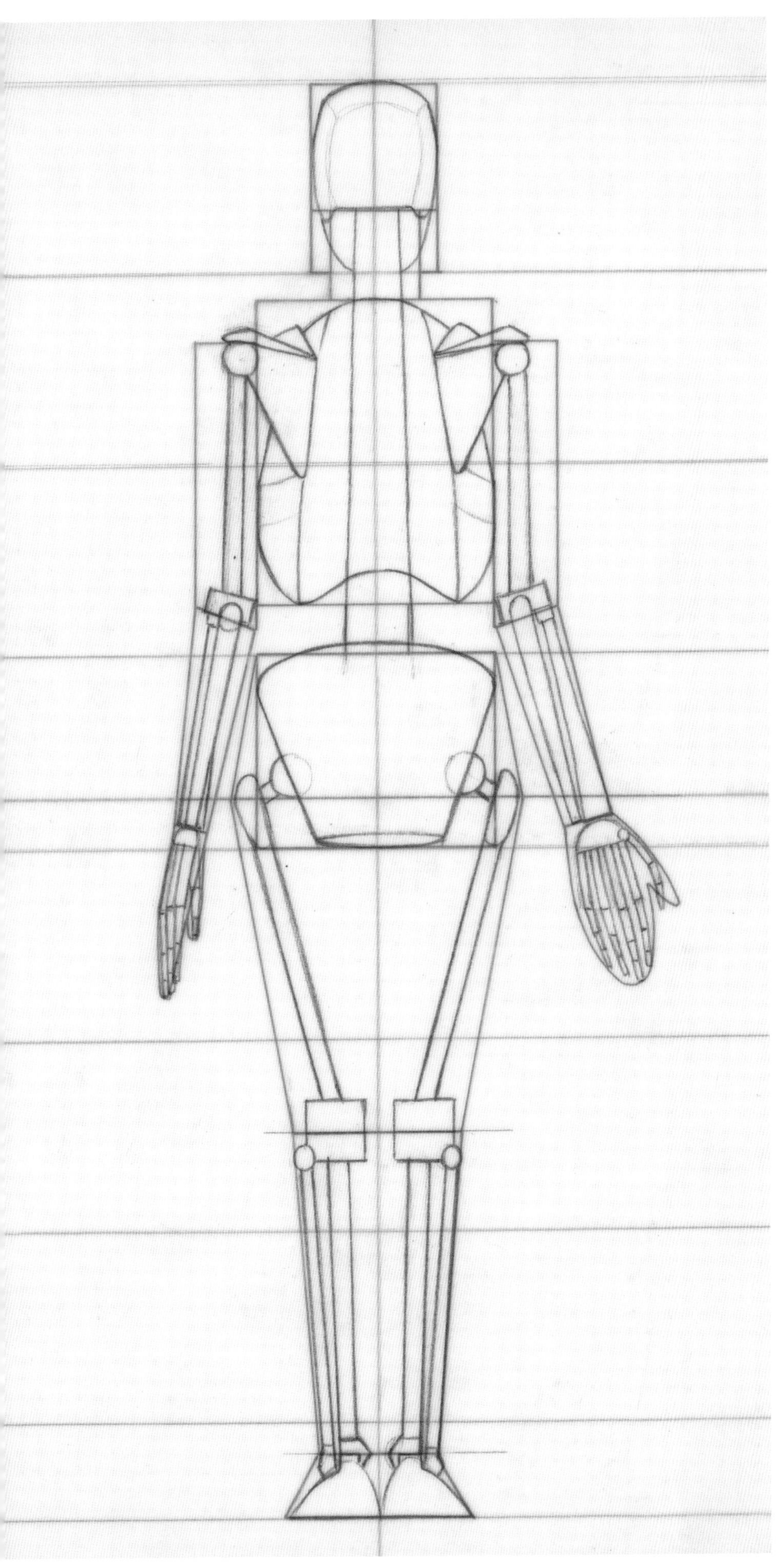

To better understand the structural aspects of the skeleton, we
reduce it to forms that are synthesized versions of parts of the actual,
organic skeleton. The figures on
the previous pages show male and
female structural skeletons, respectively, as seen from the side, front,
and back. Ovoid forms are used to
represent the volumes of the head
and ribcage, and the hips can be
synthesized as a truncated cone with
the wider base on top, or as a bucket
shape. This schematization, which
brings us closer to the organic forms
of the skeleton, makes it possible to
define a few more landmarks and
some specific characteristics of each
segment of the body, such as its
planes and angles.

The figure at left, showing
stereometric figures superimposed
on three views of the structural
skeleton, connects chapter 1 with
the material covered in this chapter.

THE INTUITIVE APPROACH TO THE STRUCTURAL SKELETON

Before diving into a detailed analysis of the structural skeleton, it is useful to practice drawing it in a more intuitive way. The figures here show a simplified, intuitive approach to drawing the structural skeleton. The steps outlined can be followed for creating a series of drawings or a three-dimensional figure in clay or other sculpting material.

STEP 1: Start by establishing the measures for head, ribcage, and hips as described in chapter 1. The volume of the head will be represented by an upside-down egg form, the ribcage by an upright egg, and the pelvis by a bucket shape. Please note that the side view of the head, far left, shows a notch removed to create the base of the skull and the jaw line.

STEP 2: Cut off the top and bottom of the ribcage to create the base of the neck and the bottom of the ribcage, as shown. Also cut a slice from

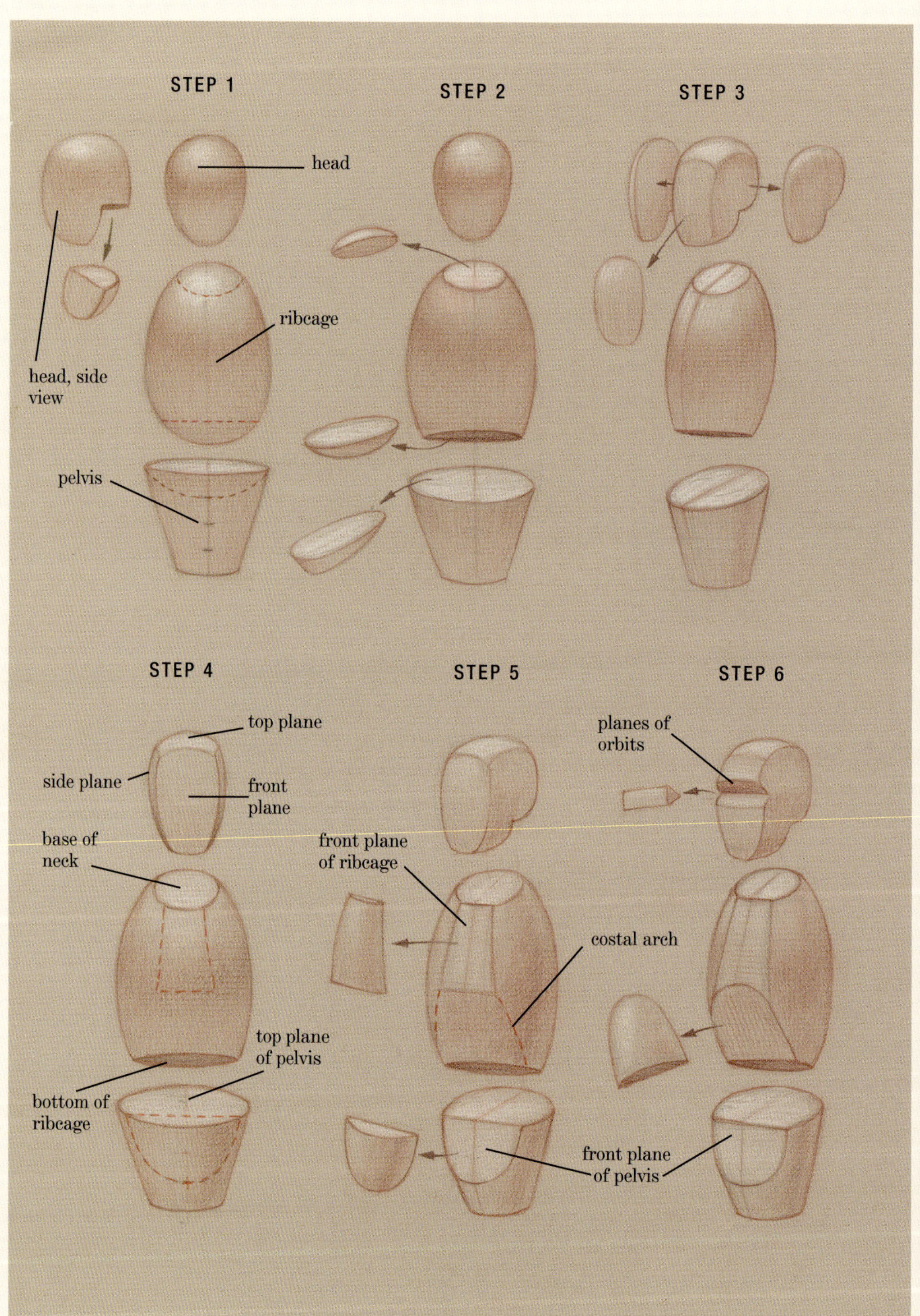

THE INTUITIVE APPROACH TO VOLUMES AND PLANES OF THE SKELETON

the bucket shape of the pelvis, moving from the back down toward the front, exiting at the upper quarter of the pelvis. (You can see the angle more clearly in the three-quarters view in step 3.)

STEP 3: Now cut three thin slices from the volume of the head—two from the sides and one from the front. These cuts help define the top, front, side, and back planes of the head more clearly.

STEP 4: Now you will make more cuts to further define the planes of the structural skeleton. Here, the planes have already been defined—the top, front, side, and back planes of the head; the base of the neck and bottom of ribcage; and the slanted plane of the top of the pelvis.

STEP 5: On the ribcage, cut a thin slice starting from the base of the neck and going halfway down the front of the ribcage. You have now created the flat plane defined by the sternum and the cartilage ribs above the costal arch (the arching shape that defines the abdomen), which is indicated with dotted red lines. On the pelvis, cut a thin slice from the front to create a flat frontal plane that starts at the top front of the pelvis and ends at the lower quarter, where the pubic bone is located.

STEP 6: Now, cut a wedge from the middle of the front plane of the head to create the margin of the eyebrows (above) and the upper margin of the zygomatic bone, or cheekbone (below). These two margins will frame the eye cavities. Then, starting from below the frontal plane of the torso, cut another slice down to the bottom of the ribcage, as shown. This creates the costal arch. (The top of the costal arch should be a little lower than the middle of the ribcage.)

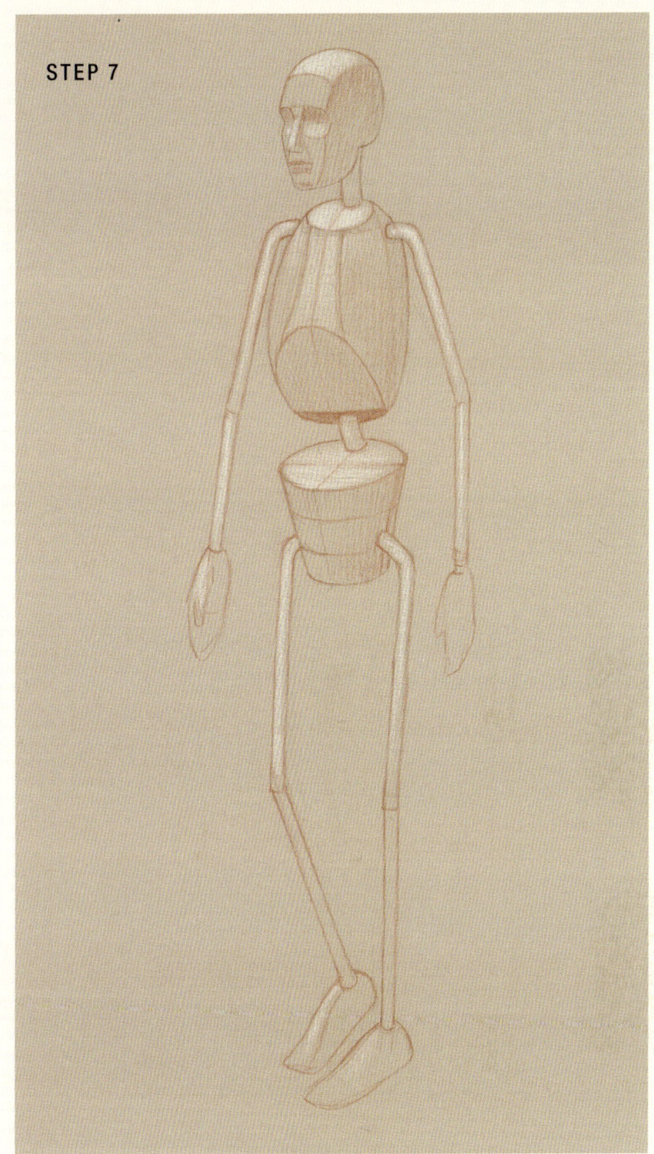

THE INTUITIVE APPROACH—FINAL FIGURE WITH ARMS AND LEGS

STEP 7: Now, connect the head and torso by drawing the neck (cervical spine), and connect the ribcage and pelvis by drawing the portion of the spine between the ribcage and the pelvis (lumbar spine). Add schematized arms, hands, legs, and feet as shown. You can check the limbs' proportions by referring to the charts of the male and female structural skeletons at the beginning of this chapter (pages 48–49).

PROPORTIONS OF THE STRUCTURAL SKELETON

The figures here compare the two most commonly used head-to-body proportions: 1:7 ½ (left) and 1:8 (right). Note the main differences between the two sets of proportions:

- In the 1:7 ½ figure, the midpoint (3 ¾ heads down) is located exactly at the pubic bone, whereas in the 1:8 figure the midpoint is 4 heads down, or just below the pubic bone.

- The articular plane of the knee (the plane at the joint between the end of the femur and the beginning of the tibia), is 2 heads from the bottom of the figure in the 1:7 ½ figure and 2 ¼ heads from the bottom in the 1:8 heads figure.

When studying these proportions, remember that they are generalizations. Actual proportions vary somewhat from person to person.

BASIC PROPORTIONS: 1:7 ½

BASIC PROPORTIONS: 1:8

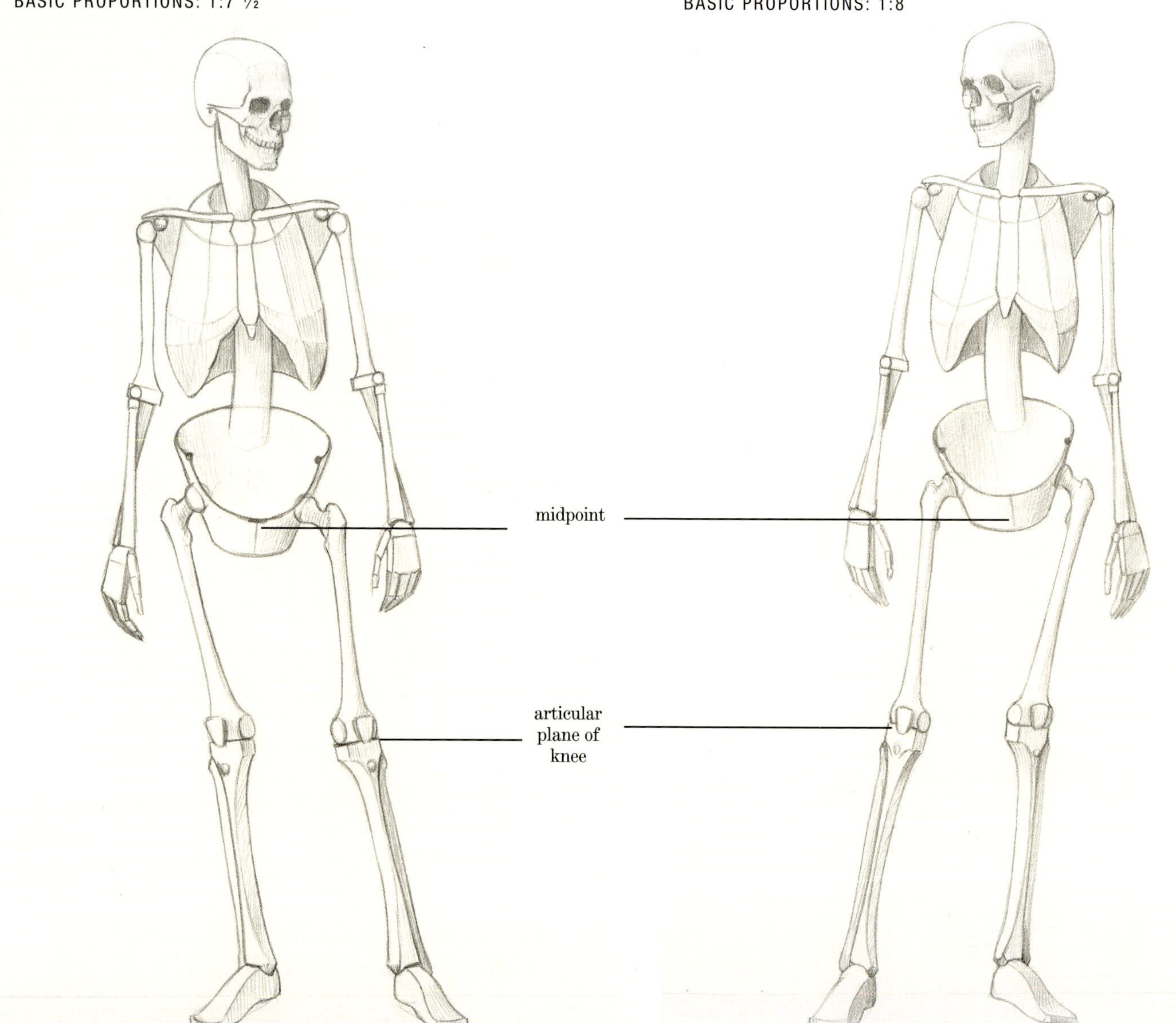

ALIGNMENT OF THE SEGMENTS OF THE BODY

In the figure below, you can see how the various segments of the body are ideally aligned along an axis that goes from the top of the head (not at the center of the cranium but slightly offset toward the back) down through the body and that exits at the soles of the feet. This axis is the line of the center of gravity. Notice how the line goes between the external acoustic meatus (earhole) and the jawline, then cuts through the front of the head of the humerus and, lower down, through the anterior half of the lumbar spine. Next, it divides the iliac crest in two equal halves and likewise divides the greater trochanter, then follows the length of the femur, either going through it lengthwise or tangent to (contiguous to) the front of the shaft of the femur. It then goes through the distal epiphysis of the femur and briefly exits the body at the level of the tuberosity of the tibia, running externally to the body until it enters the foot, more or less at the middle. Of course, this is an idealized posture—very rarely does anybody stand this upright!—but we need a starting point to appreciate all the possible postural variations.

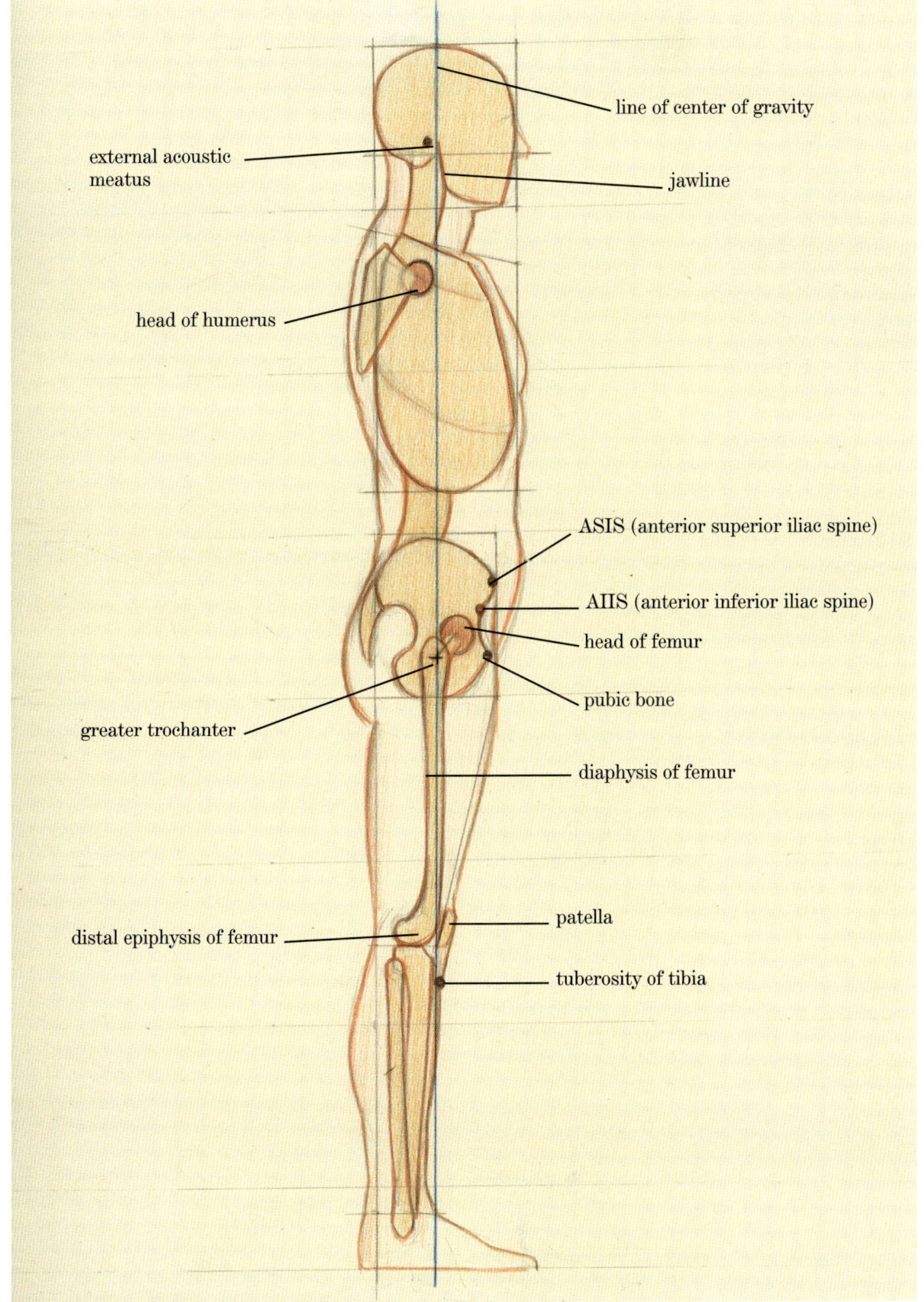

ALIGNMENT OF THE SEGMENTS OF THE BODY ALONG THE LINE OF THE CENTER OF GRAVITY

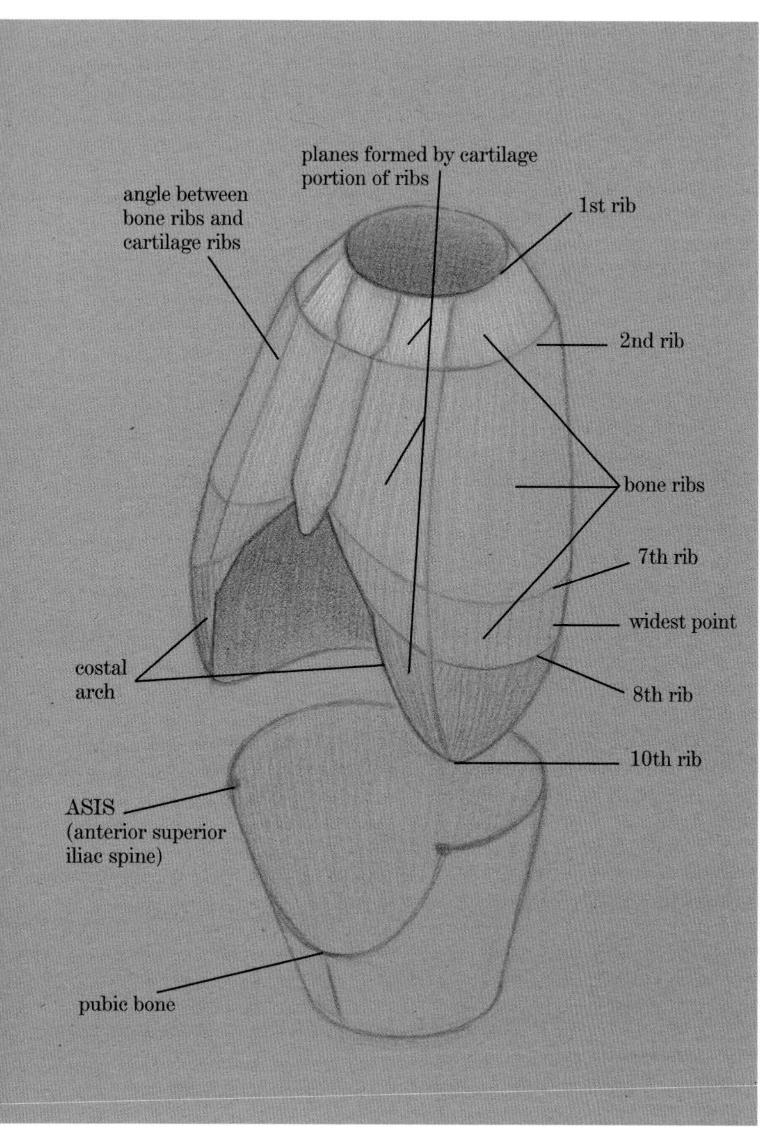

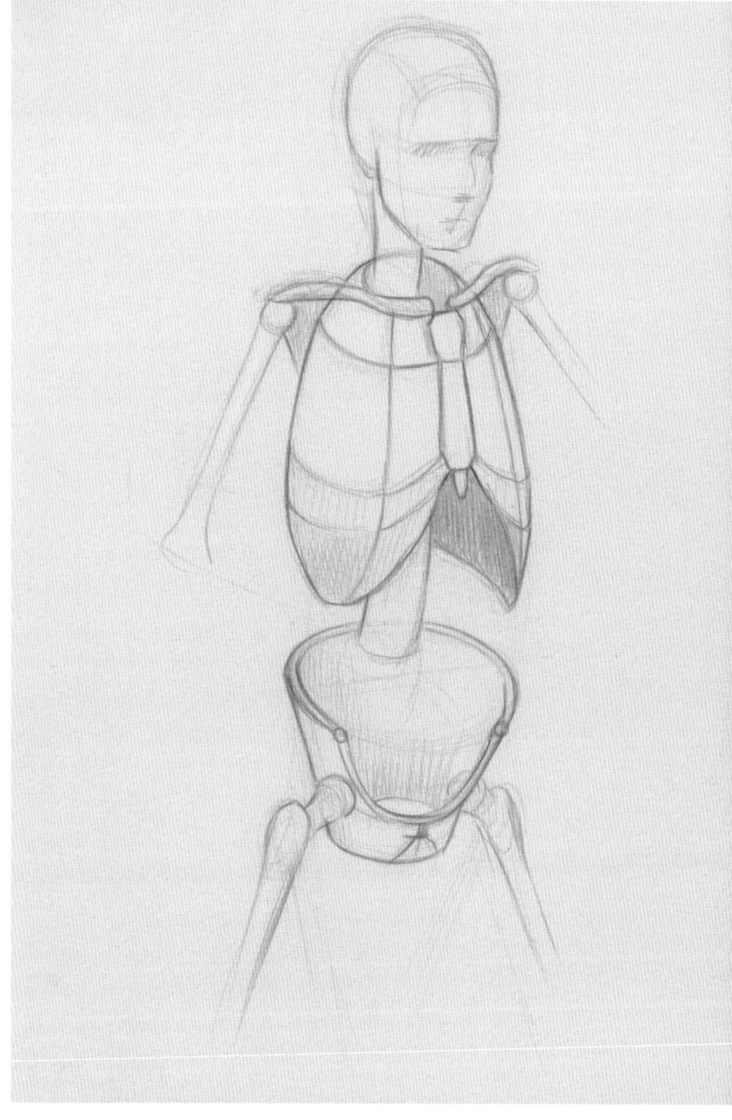

PLANES OF THE RIBCAGE

AXIAL SKELETON WITH THE PLANES OF THE RIBCAGE
DEFINED

The figure at left, above, describes specific planes of the ribcage. These planes are determined by anatomical structures such as the sternum, specific groups of ribs, and the cartilage portions of the ribs.

And the figure at right shows a more complete structural image of the ribcage as it connects with the neck, the shoulder joints, and the pelvis.

ANATOMICAL TERMINOLOGY

Many technical anatomical terms—terms that indicate direction, and names of body parts—are introduced in this and following chapters. Here are some definitions, as well as common English-language equivalents for some of the terms.

TERMS OF DIRECTION

ANTERIOR The front; can refer to the front side of the body or a body part or to a view of, or from, the front.

DISTAL Farther from the center of the body; the opposite of *proximal*.

DORSAL Refers to the back of the body, the back of the hand, or the top of the foot.

INFERIOR Lower or below; the opposite of superior.

INFRA- Prefix meaning "in between."

LATERAL The side; can refer to the outer side of the body or a body part or to a view of, or from, the outer side.

MEDIAL The middle; refers to a body part that faces toward the middle of the body (e.g., the medial malleolus, or inner ankle bone).

PALMAR Refers to the palm of the hand.

PLANTAR Refers to the sole of the foot.

POSTERIOR The back; can refer to the back side of the body or a body part or to a view of, or from, the back.

PROXIMAL Nearer the center of the body; the opposite of *distal*.

SUPERIOR Higher or above; the opposite of *inferior*.

SUPRA- Prefix meaning "above."

NAMES OF BODY PARTS

ACROMION A bony projection on the scapula.

ANTERIOR SUPERIOR ILIAC SPINE (ASIS) A bony projection on the ilium (the largest pelvic bone); an important surface landmark.

ARTICULAR PLANE OF THE ANKLE (APA) The plane between the articular surface of the talus and the distal articular surface of the tibia.

ARTICULAR PLANE OF THE KNEE (APK) The plane between the top of the head of the tibia and the distal epiphysis of the femur.

BONE RIBS The bone portion of the ribs (twelve pairs).

CARPUS The set of bones forming the wrist.

CARTILAGE RIBS The cartilage portion of the ribs that connects the first ten pairs of ribs with the sternum. (The 11th and 12th pairs of ribs, called the "floating" ribs, are not connected with the sternum.)

CERVICAL SPINE The neck portion of the spine.

CLAVICLE The collarbone.

CONDYLE A rounded protuberance at the end of some bones.

CORACOID PROCESS A beak-like projection on the scapula.

COSTAL ARCH The arching margin formed by the ribcage around the upper abdomen.

CONTINUED...

ANATOMICAL TERMINOLOGY, CONTINUED

DIAPHYSIS The shaft of a long bone (such as the humerus or femur).

EPICONDYLE A protuberance on the condyle of a long bone.

EPIPHYSIS The rounded end of a long bone.

EXTERNAL ACOUSTIC MEATUS The earhole, or ear canal.

FEMUR The thighbone.

FIBULA The smaller of the two bones of the lower leg.

GREATER TROCHANTER An eminence on the upper part of the femur, near the head of the femur.

HUMERUS The long bone of the upper arm.

ILIAC CREST The upper border of the wing of the ilium (the largest pelvic bone).

JUGULAR FOSSA A depression at the base of the neck defined at the bottom by the upper margin of the sternum and on the sides by the medial margins of the tendons of the sternocleidomastoid muscles at their origin on the sternum.

LATERAL MALLEOLUS The outer "ankle bone" (actually formed by the lower end of the fibula).

LUMBAR SPINE The lower portion of the spine, just above the sacrum, consisting of five vertebrae.

MANUBRIUM The upper part of the sternum.

MEDIAL MALLEOLUS The inner "ankle bone" (actually formed by the lower end of the tibia).

METACARPUS The bones of the hand between the carpus and phalanges.

METATARSUS The bones of the foot between the tarsus and the phalanges.

PATELLA The kneecap.

PELVIC BRIM The passage between the greater and lesser pelvis.

PHALANGES The bones of the fingers or toes (sing., phalanx).

PUBIC BONE Conventionally used to designate the part of the pelvis that is directly above the genitals. (The so-called pubic bone is not actually a separate bone.)

RADIUS One of the two long bones of the forearm (the one on the side of the thumb).

RAMUS A branch of a bone, such as the ramus of the ischium.

SACRUM The large triangular bone at the base of the spine.

SCAPULA The shoulder blade.

STERNUM The breastbone.

STYLOID PROCESS A pointed protrusion of a bone; serves as an attachment point for muscles.

TARSUS The set of seven bones of the foot between the lower ends of the tibia and fibula and the metatarsus.

THORACIC SPINE The portion of the spine in the region of the ribcage; consists of twelve vertebrae.

TIBIA The larger of the two bones of the lower leg.

TUBEROSITY A small eminence on a bone.

ULNA One of the two long bones of the forearm (the one on the side on the little finger).

ZYGOMATIC BONE The cheekbone.

STRUCTURAL ANALYSIS OF SKELETON SEGMENTS

Now that we have developed a good general understanding and mental image of the structural skeleton, we can examine its structure in greater detail. The figures in this section provide step-by-step structural analyses of the various segments that compose the skeleton. If you practice drawing them as you read, the material will be much easier to grasp and retain. Then, as soon as you can, start drawing these steps freehand and from memory. This will help you memorize them and understand them much more completely. Don't be intimidated by the apparent complexity of these steps; as you start drawing, you will see that these conceptualizations can be approached very intuitively.

RIBCAGE—ANTERIOR VIEW SEQUENCE

The first five figures give the sequence of steps you should follow when doing a structural analysis of the ribcage, as seen from the front (anterior view).

STEP 1: After drawing the boxes for the head, ribcage, and pelvis, divide each box in half both vertically and horizontally. Further divide the pelvis into four equal horizontal segments. Then draw the main volumes of each segment, using an upside-down egg for the head, an upright egg for the ribcage, and a bucket shape for the pelvis.

STEP 2: Following the measures in the image, mark the points of the jugular fossa (⅓ down from the chin), the end of the manubrium (¼ of 1), and the end of the sternum (just below the end of the second head). This will permit you to create the first and second pairs of ribs. About half a head up from the bottom of the ribcage mark

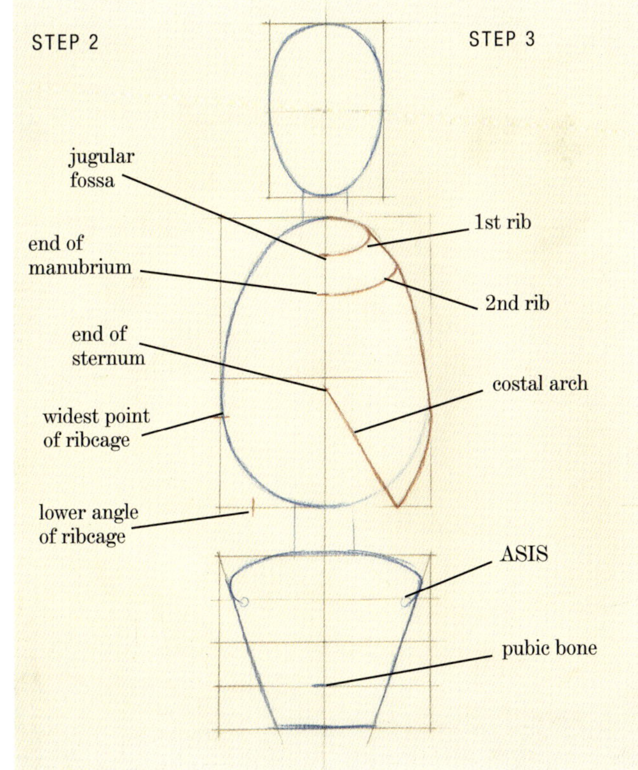

STRUCTURAL RIBCAGE SEQUENCE, ANTERIOR VIEW

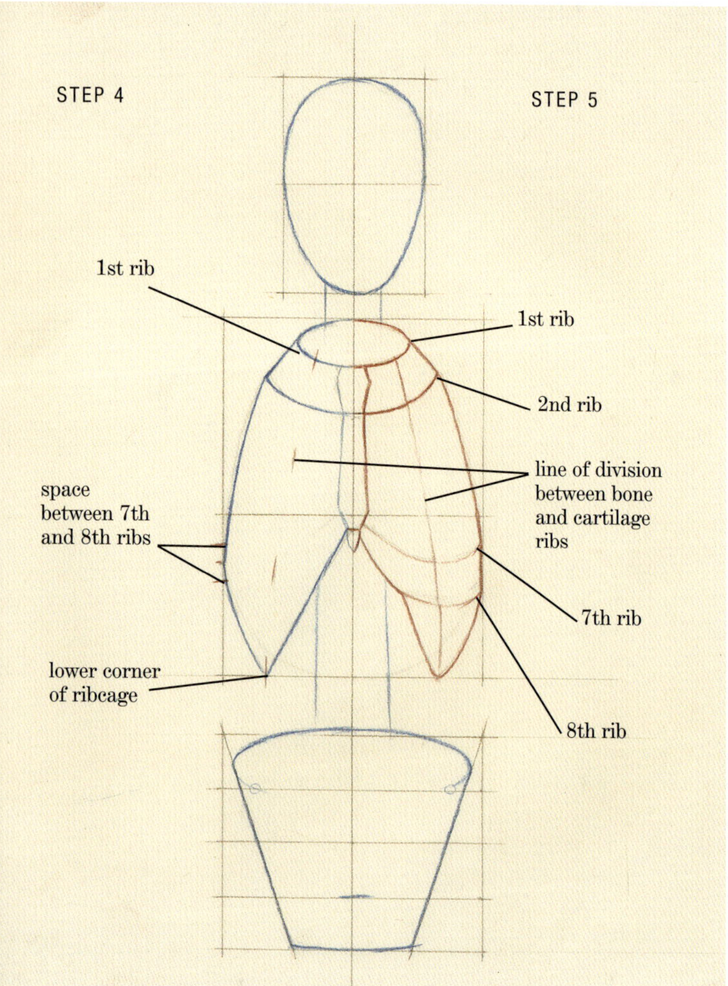

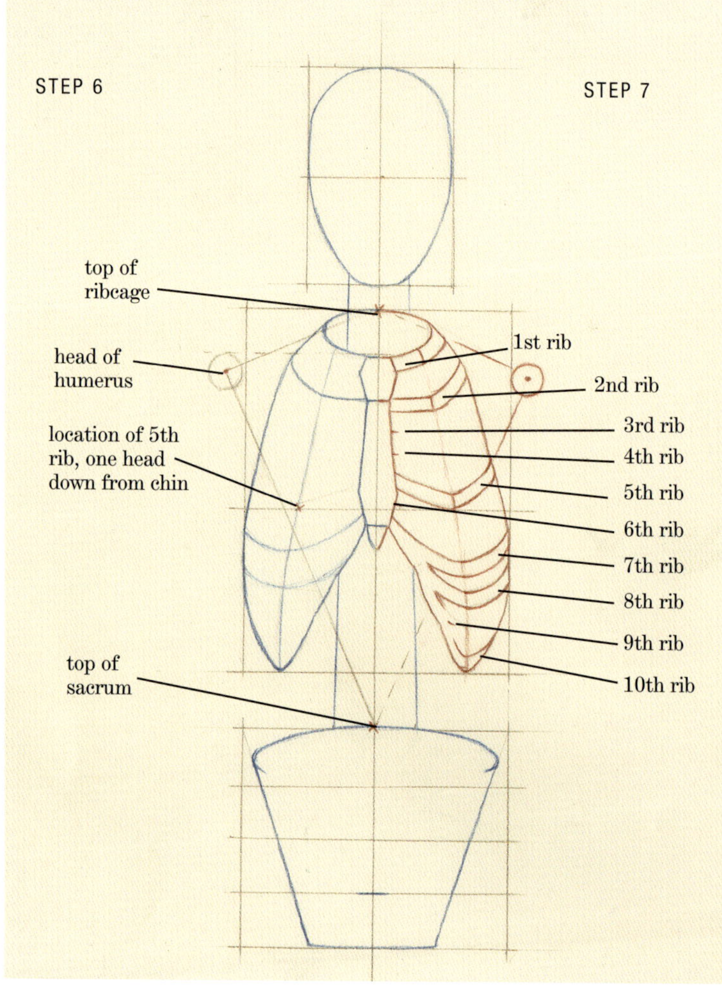

STRUCTURAL RIBCAGE SEQUENCE, ANTERIOR VIEW,
CONTINUED

the widest point of the ribcage, corresponding to the space between the 7th and 8th ribs. Then mark the lower angle of the ribcage.

STEP 3 (PREVIOUS PAGE): Using these reference points, create the rings of the 1st and 2nd ribs, the contour of the ribcage, and the costal arch (red lines). You can also mark the anterior superior iliac spine (ASIS) and the pubic bone in the hips.

STEP 4: Now draw the overall form of the ribcage and add the sternum. Starting from a point slightly above and a point slightly below the widest point of the ribcage, draw two lines to represent the 7th and 8th ribs. (The widest point of the ribcage is between the 7th and 8th ribs.) Mark a dotted line of division between the bone and cartilage of the ribs, starting from the middle of the 1st rib down to the lower corner of the ribcage, as shown.

STEP 5: Define the angles of the ribcage. Starting from the base of the neck (the first pair of ribs) draw a line that reaches the lower angle of the ribcage. This line, representing the division between

the bone and cartilage ribs, also defines the frontal plane of the ribcage. Now move down to the angles created by the 7th and 8th ribs and connect these points to the bottom of the sternum with two curved lines; these lines represent the 7th and 8th ribs and define the plane of the widest point of the ribcage.

STEP 6: Draw a circle representing the head of the humerus just outside the box of the ribcage and just below the level of the jugular fossa. Then, from the center of the head of the humerus, draw two lines that connect the top of the ribcage and the top of the hips. These lines will help you create the margins of the scapula. One head down from the chin, mark a point on the line of division between the ribs and the cartilage of the ribs. This point will help you position the 5th rib.

STEP 7: Now you have enough points of reference to position the 1st, 2nd, 5th, 7th, 8th, and 10th ribs. (I am excluding the last two ribs because they are barely visible from the front.)

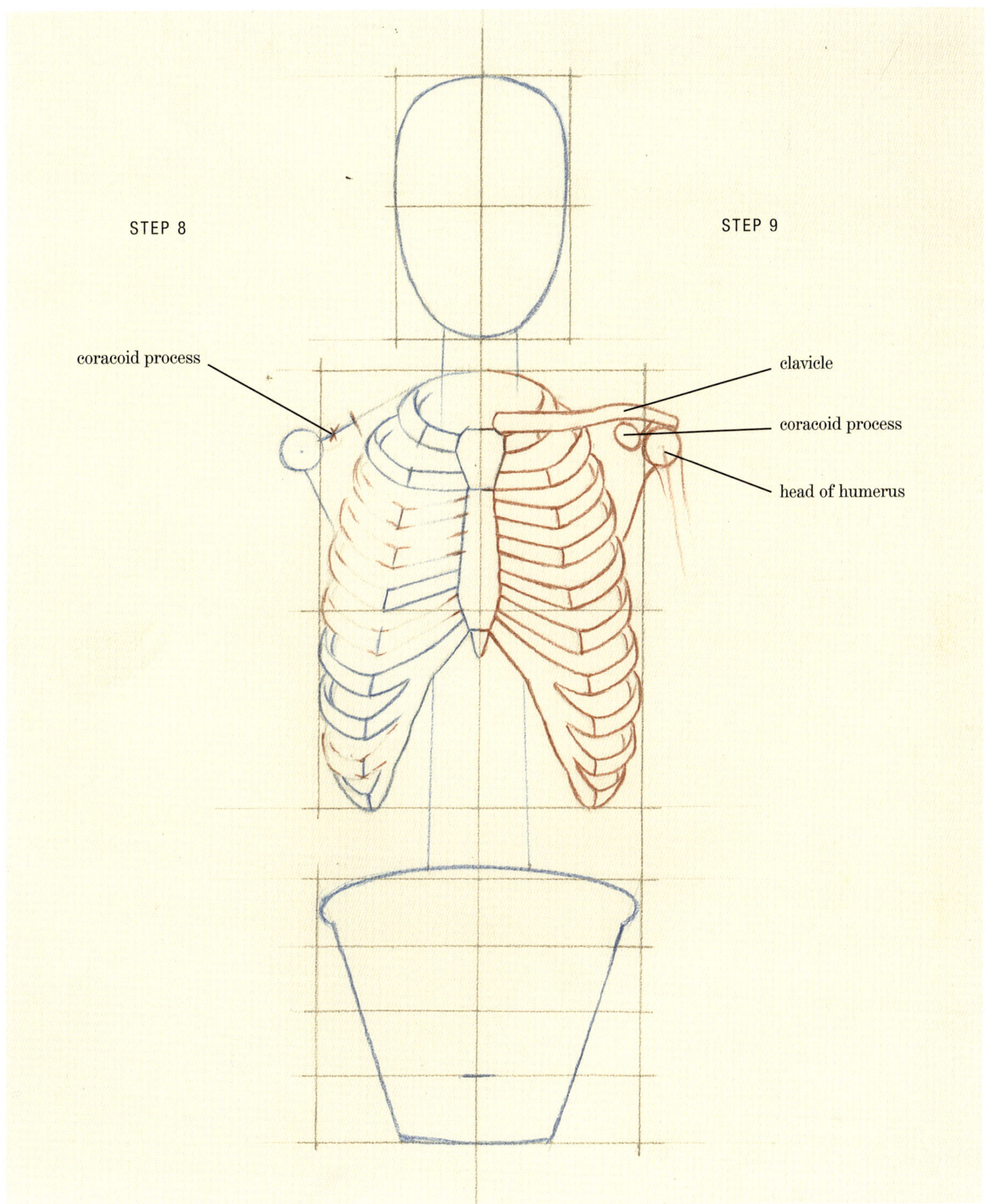

STEP 8: Mark the spot for the coracoid process and sketch in the remaining ribs, spacing them evenly between the ribs you have identified so far.

STEP 9: Draw the clavicle to connect the corner of the sternum with the scapula just above the head of the humerus. Add the coracoid process right next to the head of the humerus and below the clavicle. Fill in the remaining ribs, spacing them evenly.

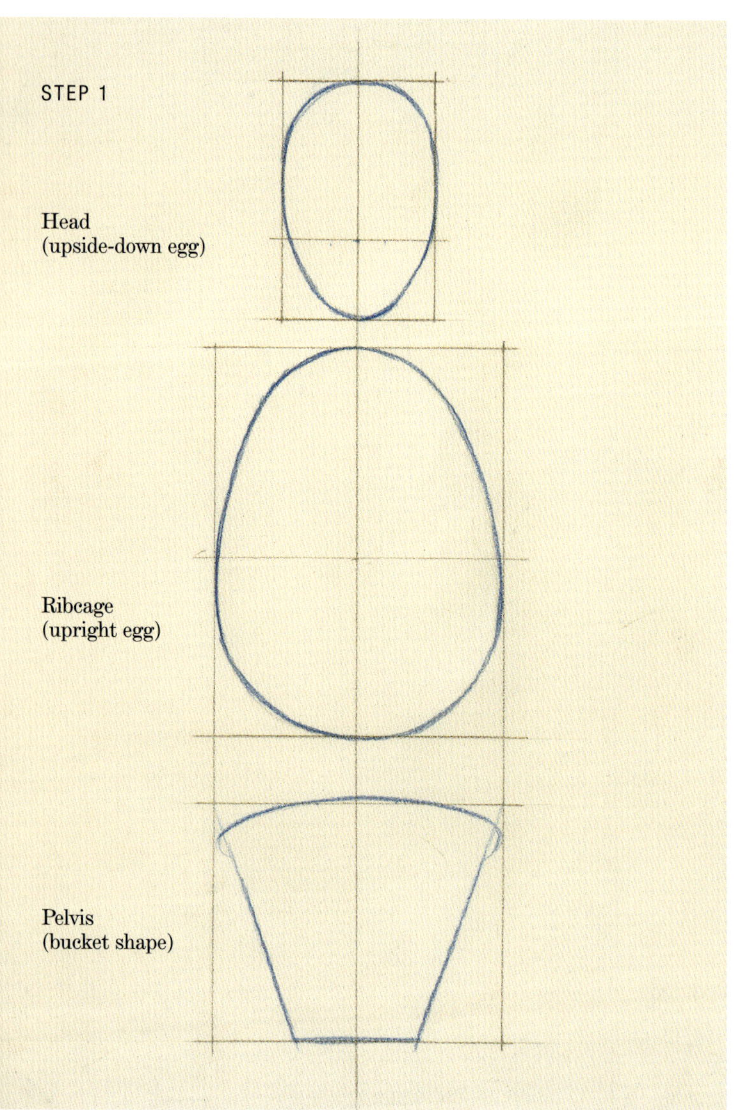

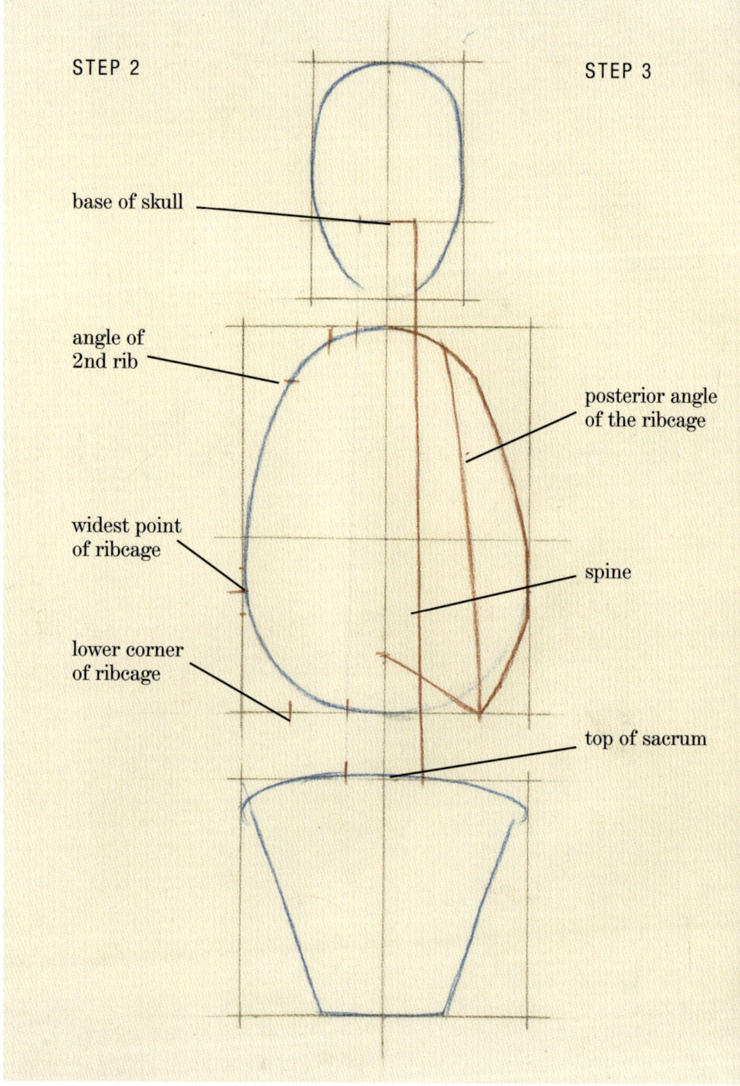

STRUCTURAL RIBCAGE SEQUENCE, POSTERIOR VIEW

RIBCAGE—POSTERIOR VIEW SEQUENCE

The four figures here demonstrate the sequence for structurally analyzing the ribcage from the back (posterior) view.

STEP 1: After drawing the boxes for the head, torso, and pelvis, draw the vertical center line. Then draw the main volumes of each segment, using an upside-down egg for the head, an upright egg for the ribcage, and a bucket shape for the pelvis.

STEP 2: Mark the base of the skull one-third of the way up from the bottom of the box of the head. Draw a vertical line connecting the base of the skull with the top of the pelvis, as shown; this line represents the side of the spine. Mark the lower corner of the ribcage and the widest point. About one-quarter of a head down from the top of the ribcage, mark the angle of the second rib.

STEP 3: Now define the profile of the ribcage, draw the profile of the spine, and indicate the posterior angle of the ribcage by drawing a line connecting the top of the ribcage with the bottom. When you draw the spine, make sure it gradually widens as it goes from the base of the skull to the top of the sacrum.

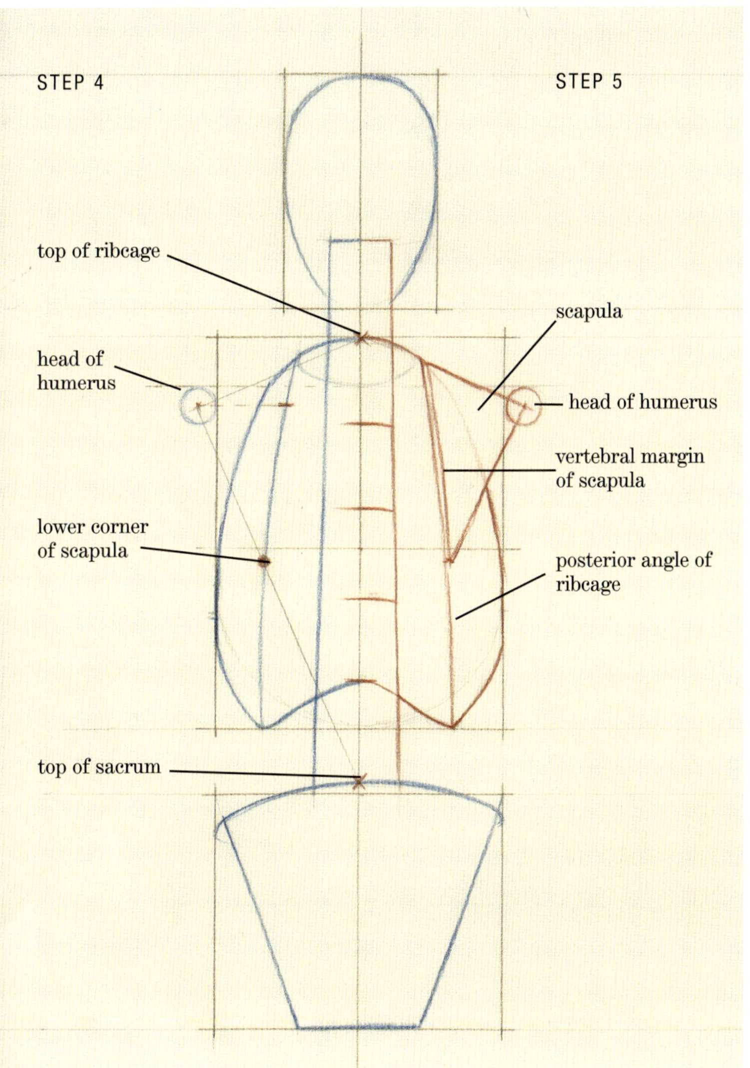

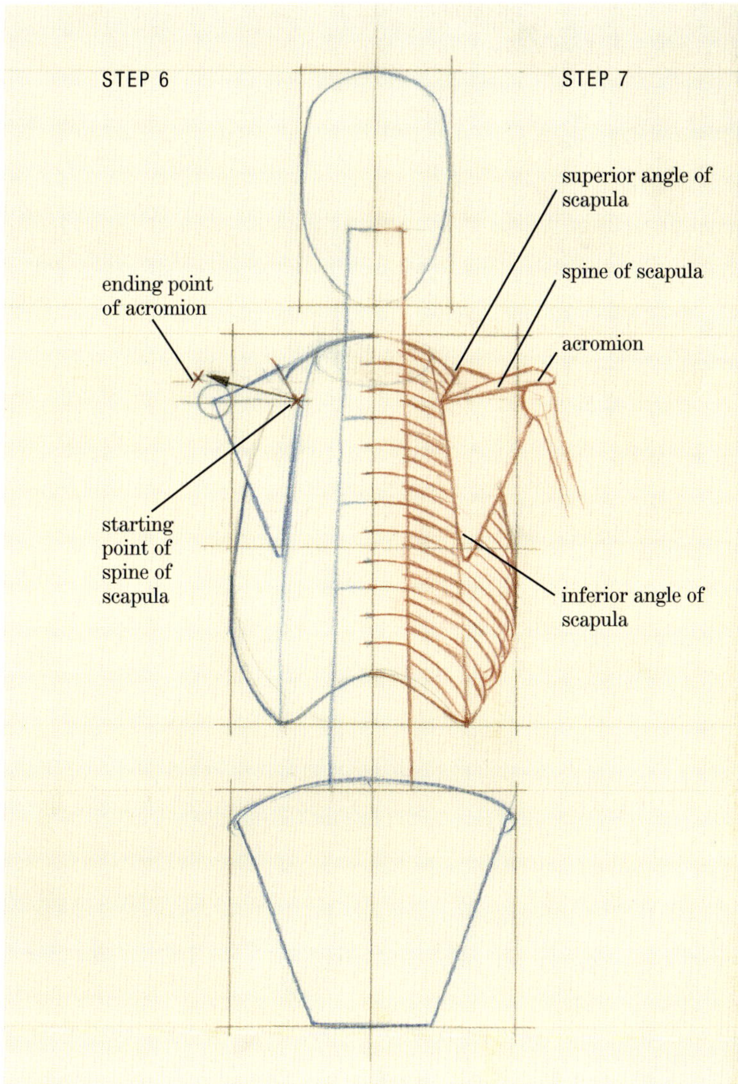

STEP 4: Mark the head of the humerus just outside the box of the torso and below the level of the sternal notch, just as you did for the front view. From the center of the head of the humerus, draw a line to connect it with the top of the ribcage and then another line to connect it with the top of the sacrum. The lower corner of the scapula is just below a measure of one head down from the chin, and the vertebral margin of the scapula is parallel to the line of the angle of the ribs.

STEP 5: Divide the thoracic spine in half and then into four segments. It will now be easy to divide each segment into three further segments to obtain the twelve thoracic vertebrae, as you will see in the next step. Draw a horizontal line from the center of the head of the humerus toward the spine. When the line encroaches the vertebral margin of the scapula, draw a line that goes diagonally to meet the upper margin of the scapula, defining its upper corner.

STEP 6: The spine of the scapula starts at the same level as the center of the humerus but along the vertebral margin of the scapula. Mark this point as shown in the image. Now mark the ending point of the acromion, just above the head of the humerus.

STEP 7: Draw the spine of the scapula and the acromion. Finish dividing the thoracic spine into twelve segments for the twelve thoracic vertebrae. Draw the ribs starting from the top of each vertebra and going down at an angle toward the side of the ribcage.

PELVIS AND THIGHS—ANTERIOR VIEW SEQUENCE

These figures show the steps for the pelvis and thighs,

from the front (anterior) view.

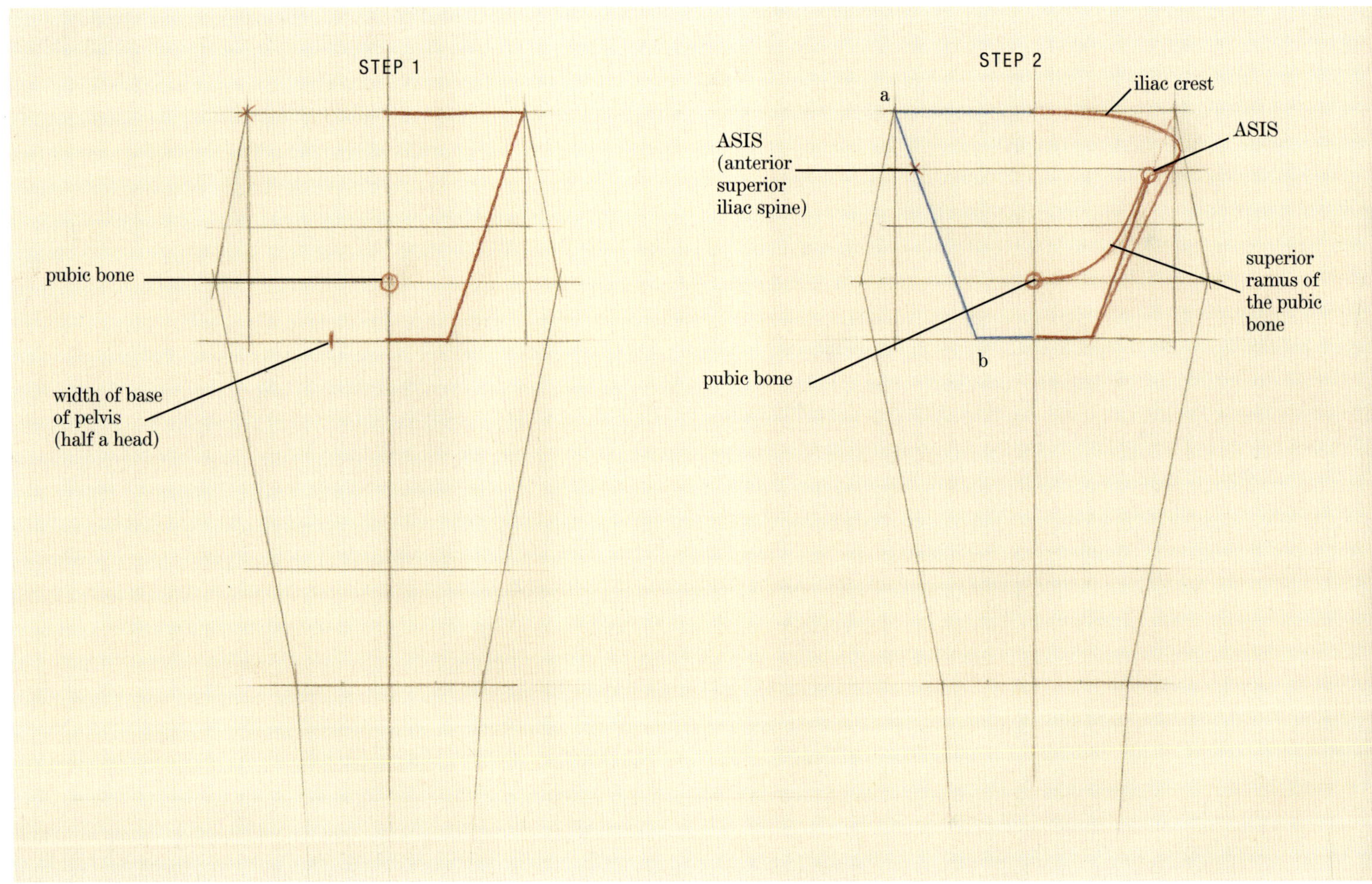

STRUCTURAL PELVIS AND THIGHS SEQUENCE, ANTERIOR VIEW

STEP 1: Draw stereometric boxes for the pelvis and thighs, including the width of the trochanters. Divide the pelvis into four equal segments and position the pubic bone at the lowest quarter (red circle). Mark the width of half a head at the base of the box of the pelvis, and then draw a line going from the upper corner of the box of the pelvis diagonally down to this point on the lower margin of the pelvis to define the profile of the pelvis (red line).

STEP 2: The point of intersection of the line *a–b* with the line of the upper quarter of the pelvis marks the anterior superior iliac spine, or ASIS. Draw the curve of the iliac crest at the top margin of the pelvis, then draw another curved line going from the ASIS to the pubic bone to define the superior ramus of the pubic bone.

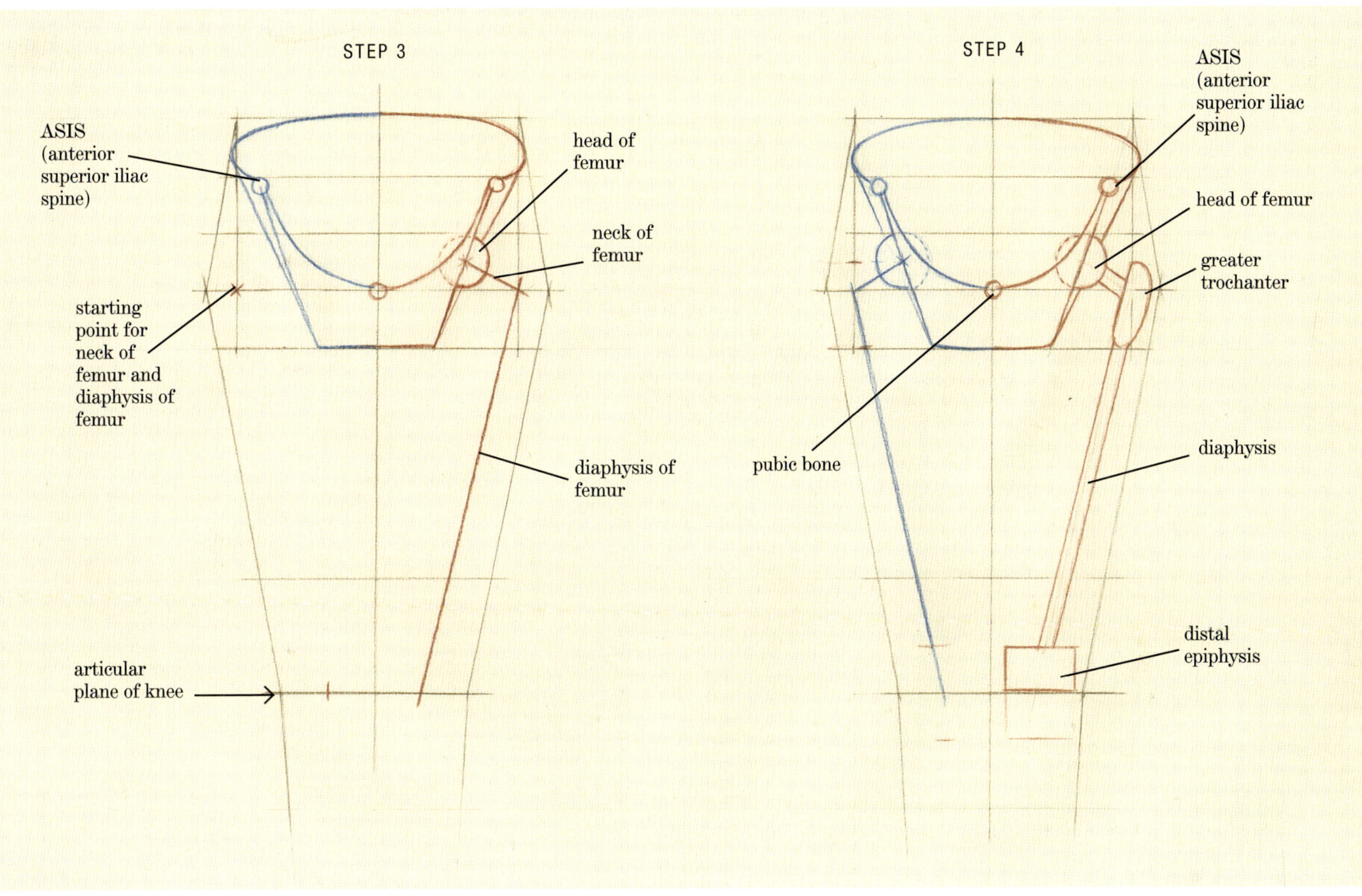

STEP 3: Draw a circle in the third segment of the box of the pelvis, half inside and half outside the volume of the pelvis. This circle represents the head of the femur. Remember that the head of the femur is just above the level of the pubic bone. From the center of the head of the femur, draw a line that reaches the intersection between the line of the width of the pelvis and the line of the lower quarter. This line approximately locates the neck of the femur. Then draw another line starting from the side of the hips and reaching down to the middle of the articular plane of the knee, creating the main axis (diaphysis) of the femur.

STEP 4: Finish the pelvis and femur by adding volume and specific parts, such as the greater trochanter and the distal epiphysis.

PELVIS AND THIGHS—LATERAL VIEW SEQUENCE

This figure demonstrates the steps for the pelvis and thighs, from a side (lateral) view. Note that the front of the body is to the right in these images.

STEP 1: Draw the boxes for the volumes of the pelvis and thigh. Divide the pelvis in four equal segments and mark the ASIS at the upper quarter and the pubic bone at the lower quarter. Draw the line that represents the center of gravity (red dotted line). This line divides the pelvis into two equal parts and is tangent, or contiguous, to the front of the lower leg.

STEP 2: Define the shape of the pelvis as shown in the figure by adding the iliac crest (the diagonal line red line at the top of the pelvis). Add a circle representing the head of the femur just above the line of the pubic bone and in front (to the right) of the dotted line of the center of gravity. Position the distal epiphysis of the femur (oval shape) above the articular plane of the knee (APK) and the head of the tibia (rectangular shape) below the APK. Both of these forms must be behind (to the left of) the line of the center of gravity.

STEP 3: Add the greater trochanter (upright oval shape) between the bottom of the box of the pelvis and, below it, a horizontal line going through the center of the head of the femur. The line of the center of gravity divides the trochanter into two equal parts.

STEP 4: Add the neck of the femur—a thin line that connects the slightly posterior trochanter to the slightly anterior head of the femur. Add the kneecap and refine the forms of the skeleton.

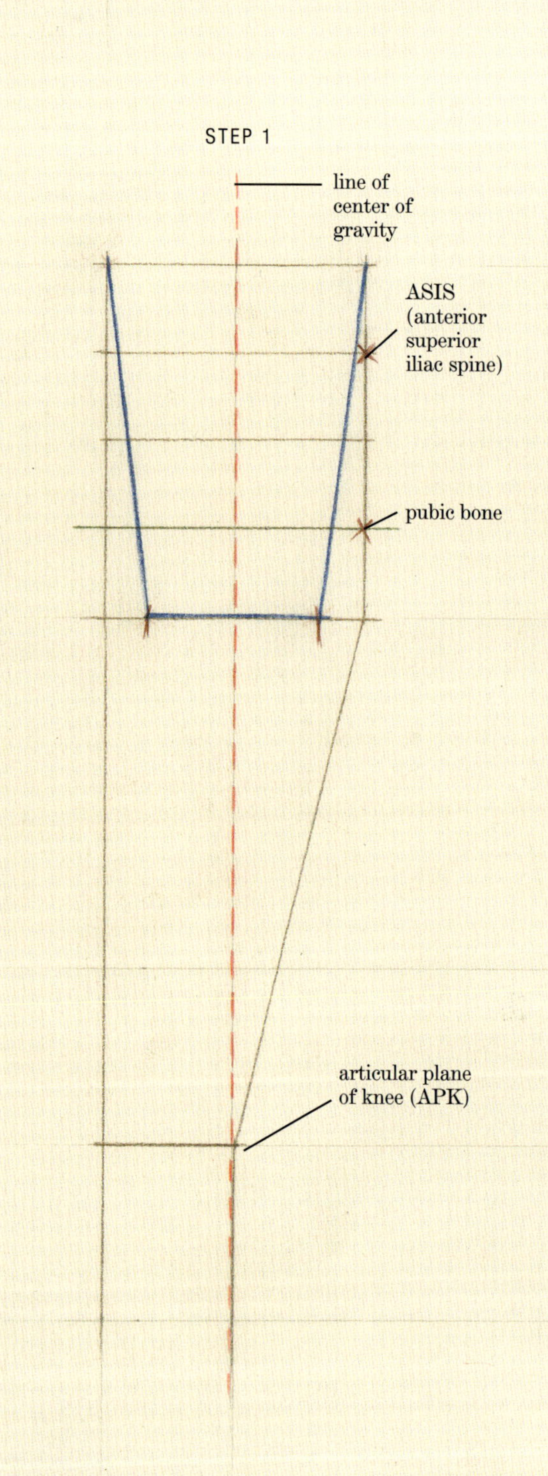

STRUCTURAL SEQUENCE FOR PELVIS AND THIGHS, LATERAL VIEW

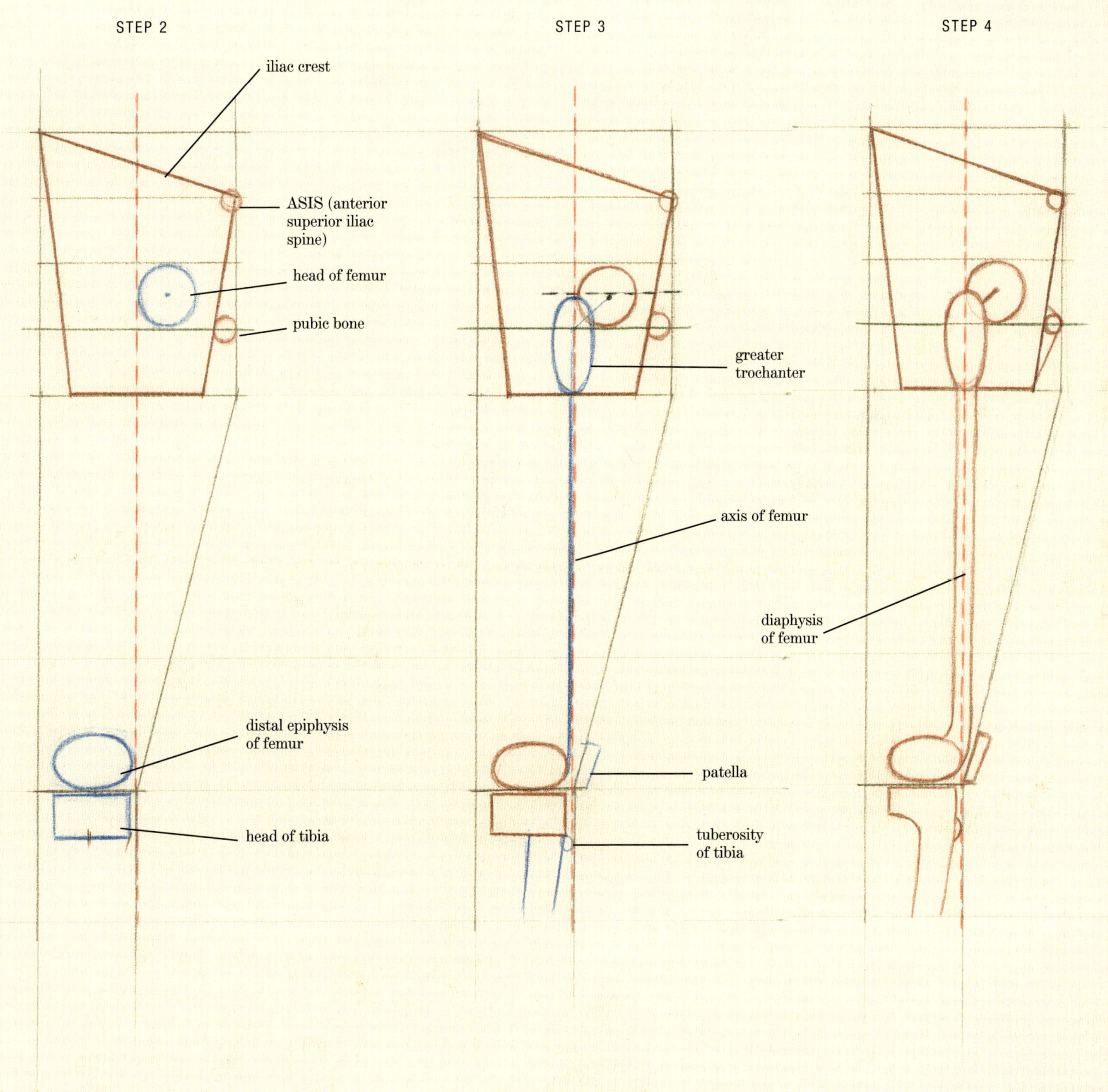

STEP 2
STEP 3
STEP 4
iliac crest
ASIS (anterior superior iliac spine)
head of femur
pubic bone
greater trochanter
axis of femur
diaphysis of femur
distal epiphysis of femur
patella
head of tibia
tuberosity of tibia

CHARACTERISTICS OF THE PELVIS

The pelvis can be described as the center, or fulcrum, of the body. As you can see from the schematic illustration at right, the pelvic structure is built to efficiently distribute the weight of the upper body (head and torso) down to the legs and feet and then to the ground.

The figure at top, opposite, is a further exploration of the characteristics of the pelvis, from a three-quarters view positioned above the pelvis. The drawings show a possible way of conceptualizing the pelvis's forms and help in creating a three-dimensional understanding of the forms. Once you understand the method of analyzing the body, you can come up with your own approach, so feel free to interpret it in the way that seems most natural to you.

The figure at bottom, opposite, shows a sequence of transformation from a highly schematic analysis of the pelvis, seen from a side view, toward a more organic set of forms.

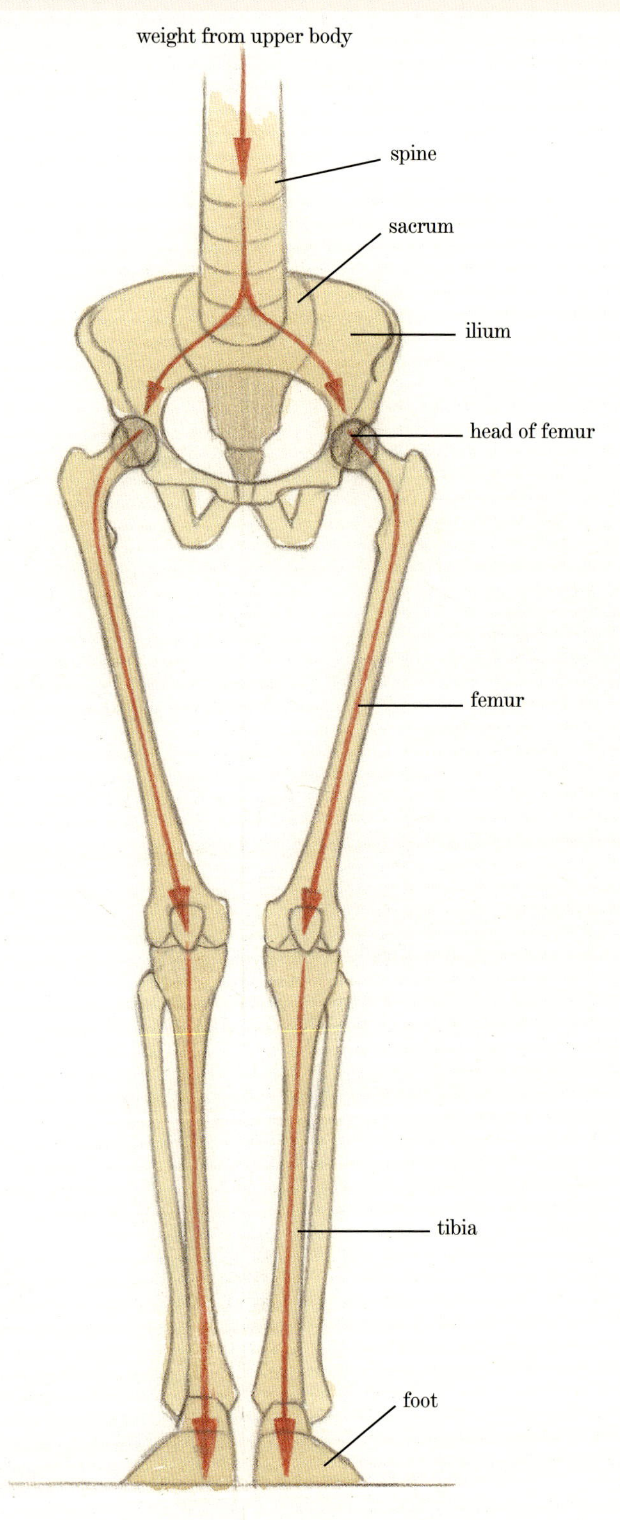

DISTRIBUTION OF THE WEIGHT OF THE UPPER BODY TO THE PELVIS AND THE GROUND

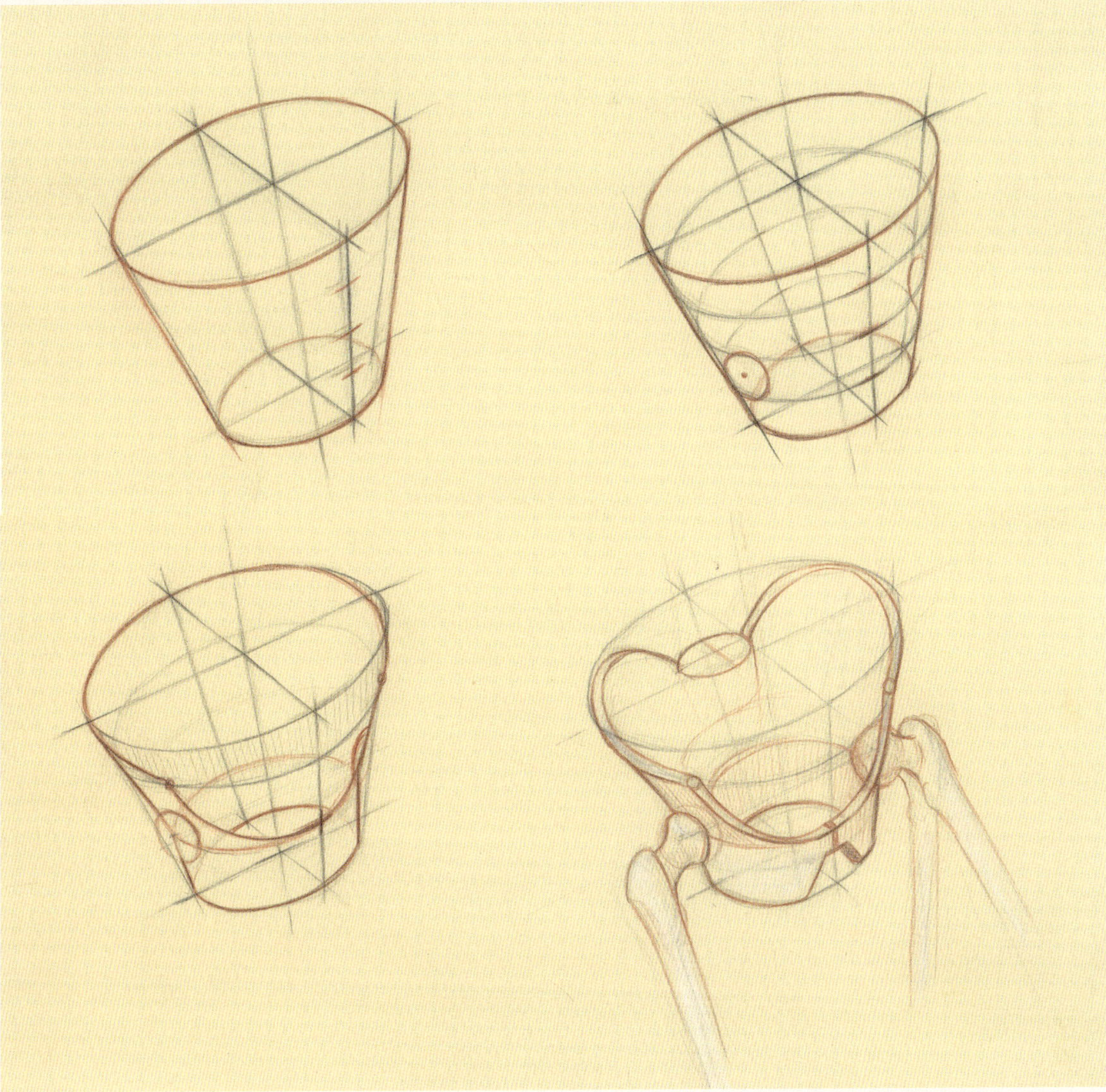

THE PELVIS AND HIPS—THREE-QUARTERS VIEW SEQUENCE

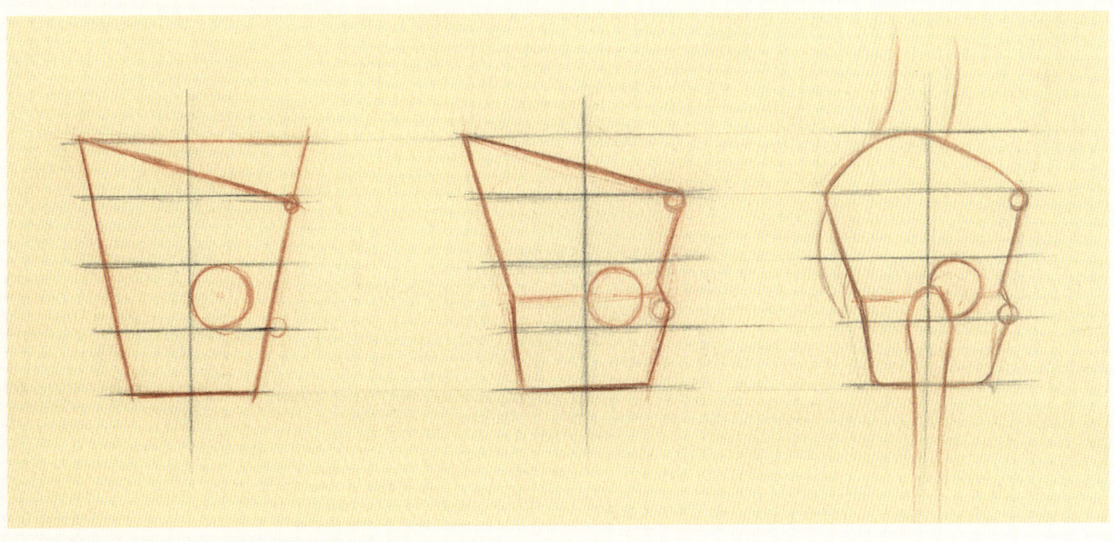

THE PELVIS AND HIPS, SIDE VIEW

ARM—ANTERIOR VIEW SEQUENCE

This figure shows the sequence of steps for the arm, from
a front (anterior) view.

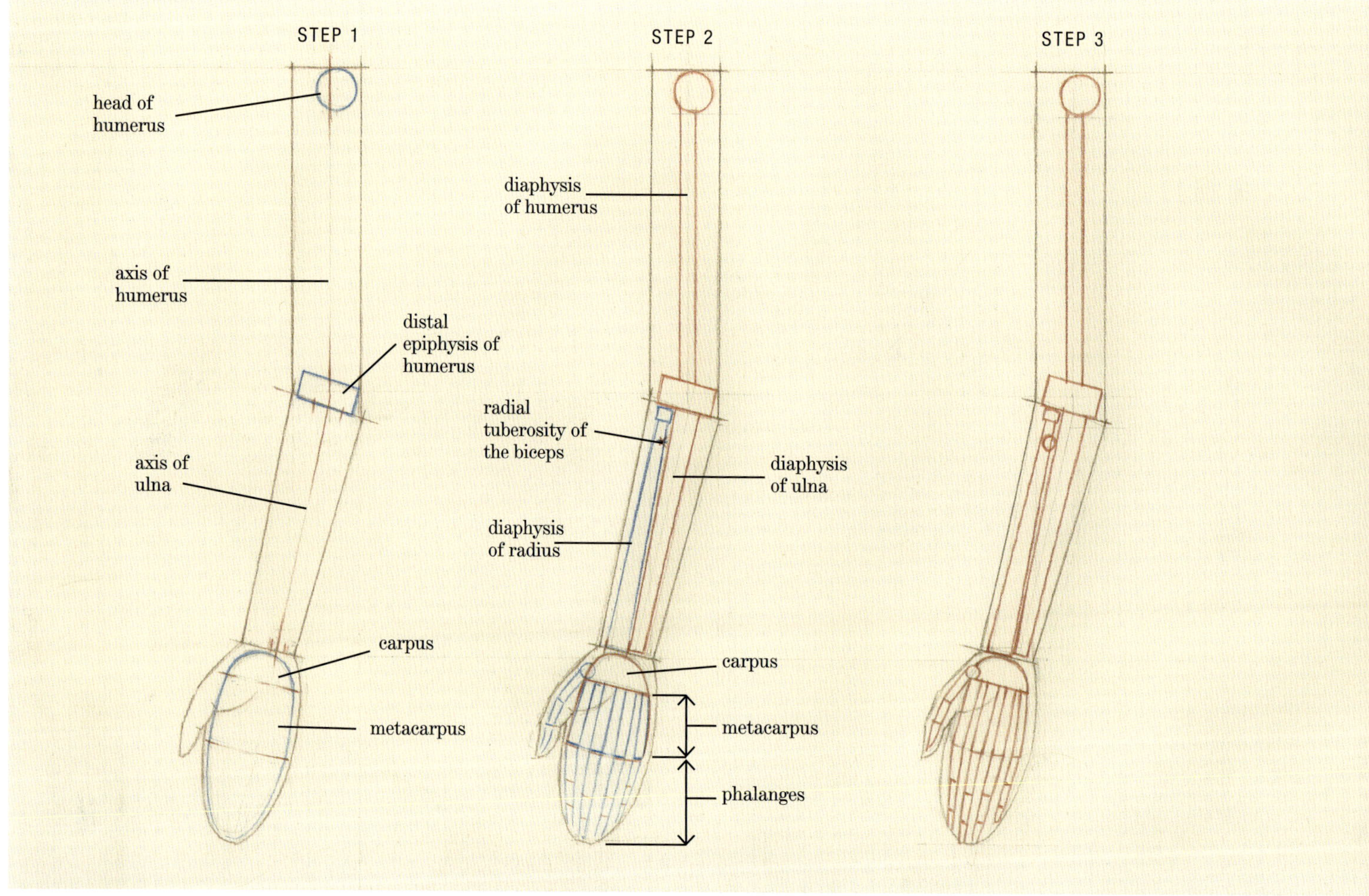

STRUCTURAL ARM SEQUENCE, ANTERIOR VIEW

STEP 1: Draw a circle representing the head of the humerus,
offsetting it slightly from the center of the stereometric box of the
upper arm. Then draw a rectangular shape, just above the line of
division between the upper and lower arm, to represent the distal
epiphysis of the humerus. Add the shape of the hand and connect
these three segments with two lines: a line that represents the
diaphysis (shaft) of the humerus and another line, going from the
elbow joint to the wrist, that represents the axis of the ulna.

STEP 2: Add volume to the diaphyses of the humerus and ulna,
then add the radius. Remember that the ulna is wider at the elbow
and narrower at the wrist, while the radius starts narrow at the
elbow and ends wide at the wrist. Add the carpus, metacarpus, and
phalanges (finger bones) inside the shape of the hand.

STEP 3: Refine the forms of the bones of the upper limb, adding
specific landmarks such as the radial tuberosity.

LOWER LEGS AND FEET—ANTERIOR VIEW SEQUENCE

This figure provides the steps for the lower legs and feet

from the front (anterior) view.

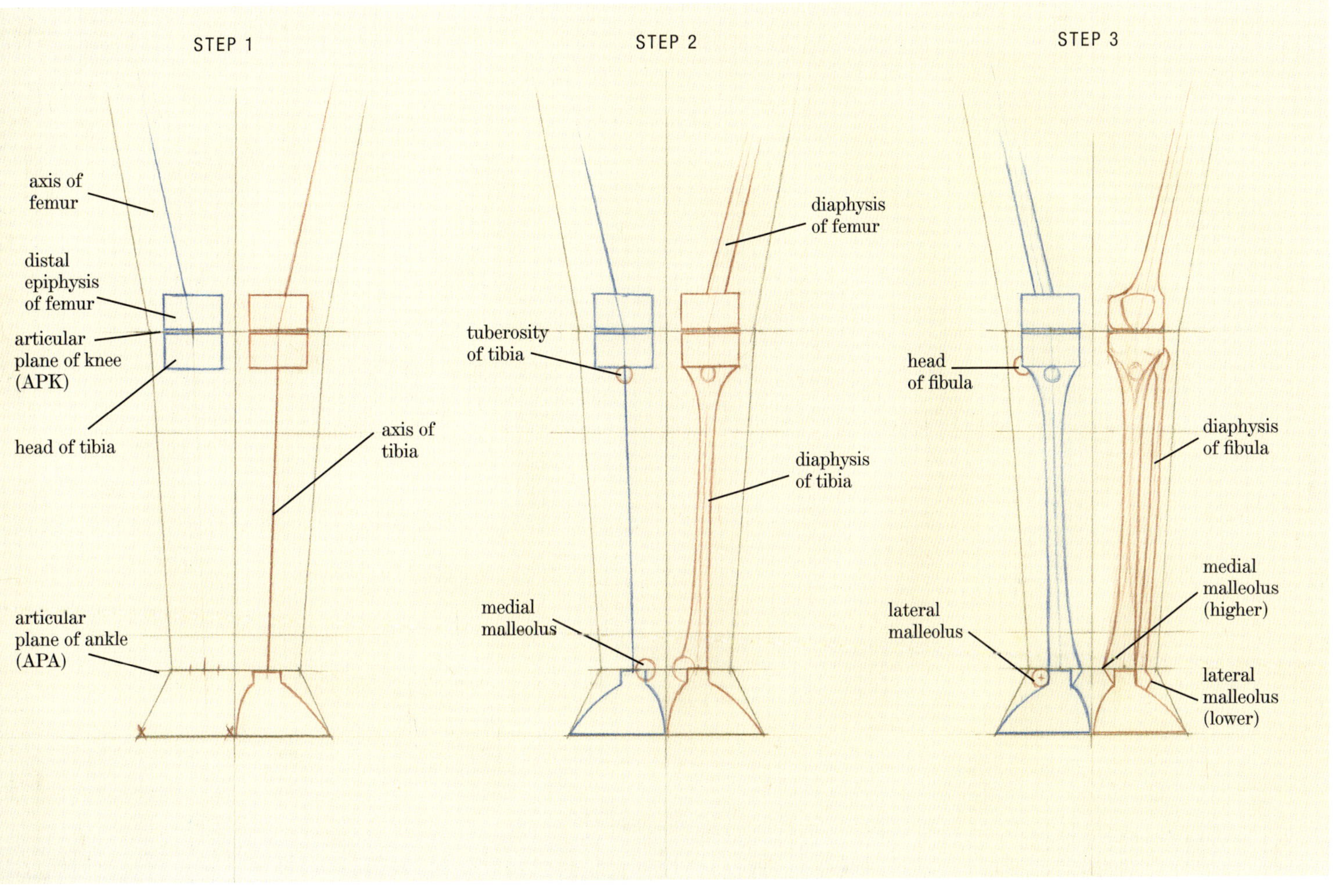

STRUCTURAL SEQUENCE FOR LEGS AND FEET, ANTERIOR VIEW

STEP 1: Draw the volumes for the lower leg and foot and part of the thigh. Mark the articular planes of the knee (APK) and ankle (APA), then draw two rectangular shapes, one above and one below the APK. These will represent the distal epiphysis of the femur and the head of the tibia, respectively. Draw a line from the center of the APK down to the center of the APA; this line will represent the diaphysis of the tibia. Draw the foot below the APA.

STEP 2: Position the tuberosity of the tibia just below the head of the tibia. Half above and half below the APA, draw a little circle on the medial (inner) side of the tibia, creating the medial malleolus. Add more volume to the femur and tibia.

STEP 3: Add a small circle on the lower margin of the lateral (outer) side of the head of the tibia; this will be the head of the fibula. Then add another little circle on the lateral side of the lower leg just below the APA; this will be the head of the lateral malleolus of the fibula. Merge the two circles with the body of the fibula, and add the patella above the APK. The medial malleolus will always be higher than the lateral malleolus and the kneecap will always be above the line of the APK.

LOWER LEGS AND FEET—LATERAL VIEW SEQUENCE

The steps for the lower leg and feet, as seen from a side (lateral) view of the right leg, are provided by the next figure.

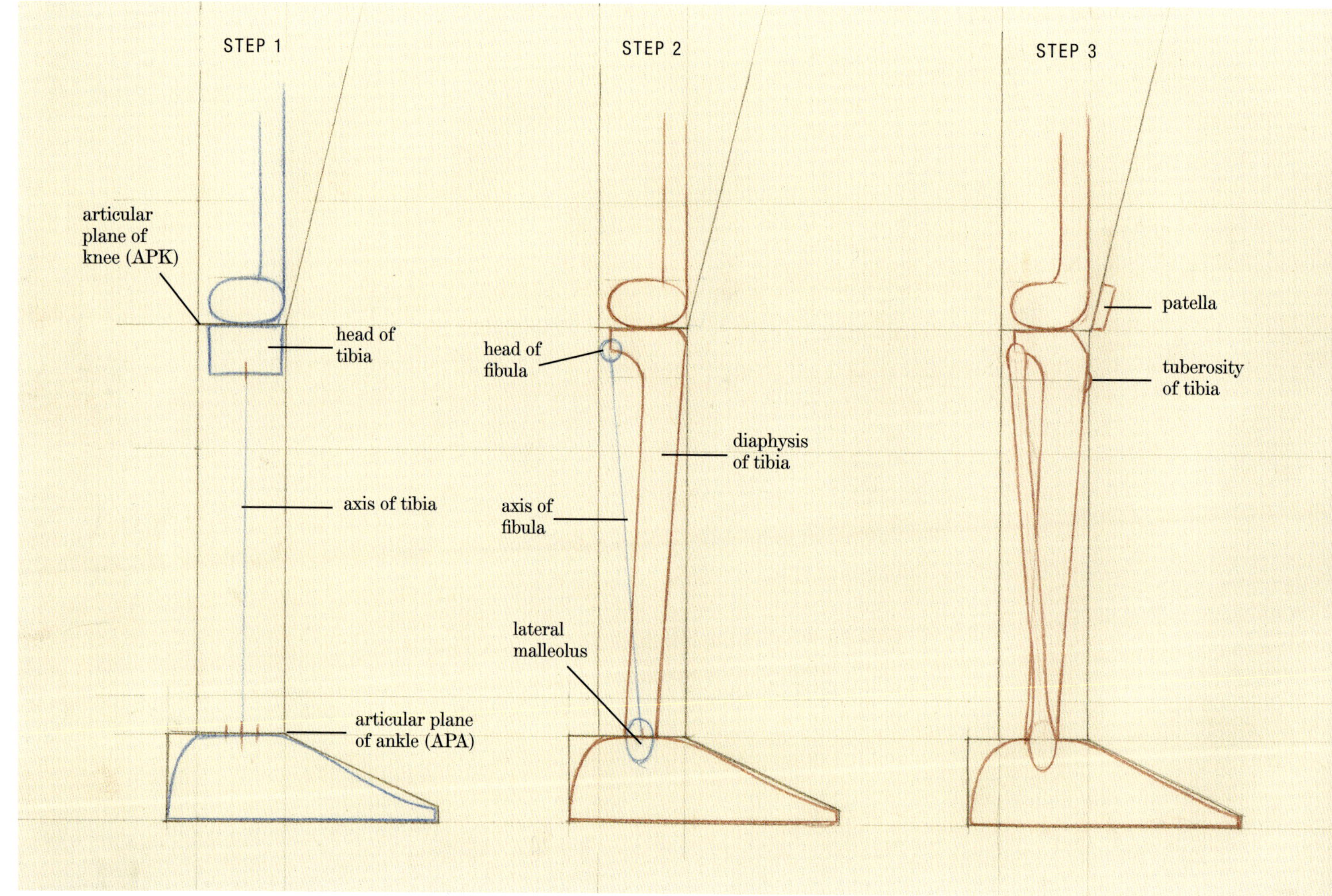

STRUCTURAL SEQUENCE FOR LOWER LEGS AND FEET, LATERAL VIEW

STEP 1: Draw a box for the head of the tibia inside the basic boxes of the lower leg. Then draw a line connecting the center of the head of the tibia with the center of the articular plane of the ankles (APA). Add the basic shape of the foot.

STEP 2: Draw a little circle at the posterior inferior (back bottom) margin of the head of the tibia and a little oval form at the APA, then connect them with a line that represents the shaft of the fibula. The fibula moves diagonally forward toward the ankle from its slightly posterior starting point.

STEP 3: This final step shows the relative positions of the tibia and fibula from a side view, with the fibula overlapping the tibia at the joint with the foot.

MALE AND FEMALE SKELETONS— STRUCTURAL DIFFERENCES

There are specific structural differences in the skeleton that are related to gender. The two figures here show the typical differences in the forms and angles of the male and female pelvis. The figure on the following page highlights differences in posture.

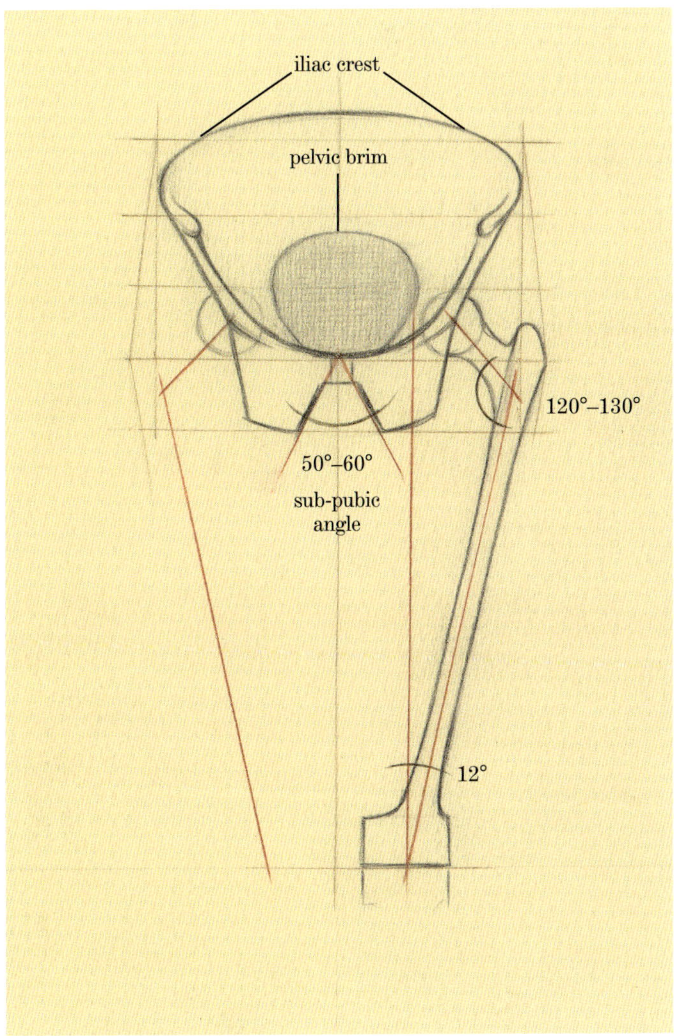

ANGLES OF THE MALE PELVIS

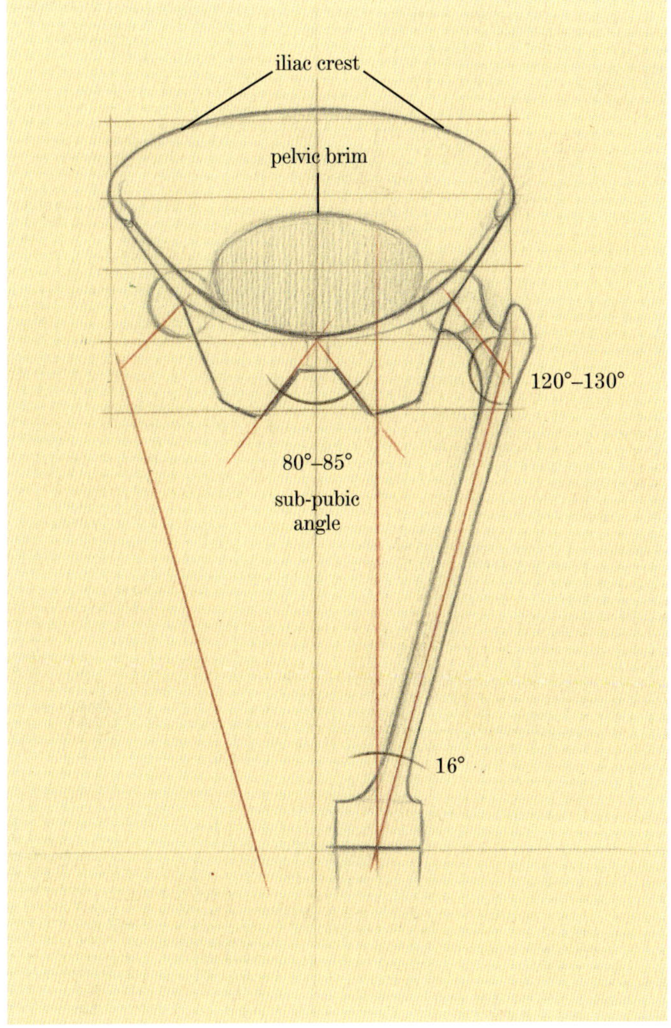

ANGLES OF THE FEMALE PELVIS

The rim created by the iliac crest tends to be narrower in the male than in the female pelvis. The angle at the articular plane of the knee (APK) between the axis of the femur and a vertical line going through the center of the APK is about 12 degrees. The sub-pubic angle is between 50 and 60 degrees in the male. The male pelvic brim tends to be narrower and more circular or heart-shaped than the female. The angle between the neck of the femur and the diaphysis is between 120 and 130 degrees.

The female pelvis is typically wider than the male pelvis, especially at the pelvic brim, which tends to have a more oval shape. The sub-pubic angle is between 80 and 85 degrees, and the angle between the axis of the femur and a vertical line that goes through the center of the articular plane of the knee is about 16 degrees. The rim of the iliac crest also tends to be wider.

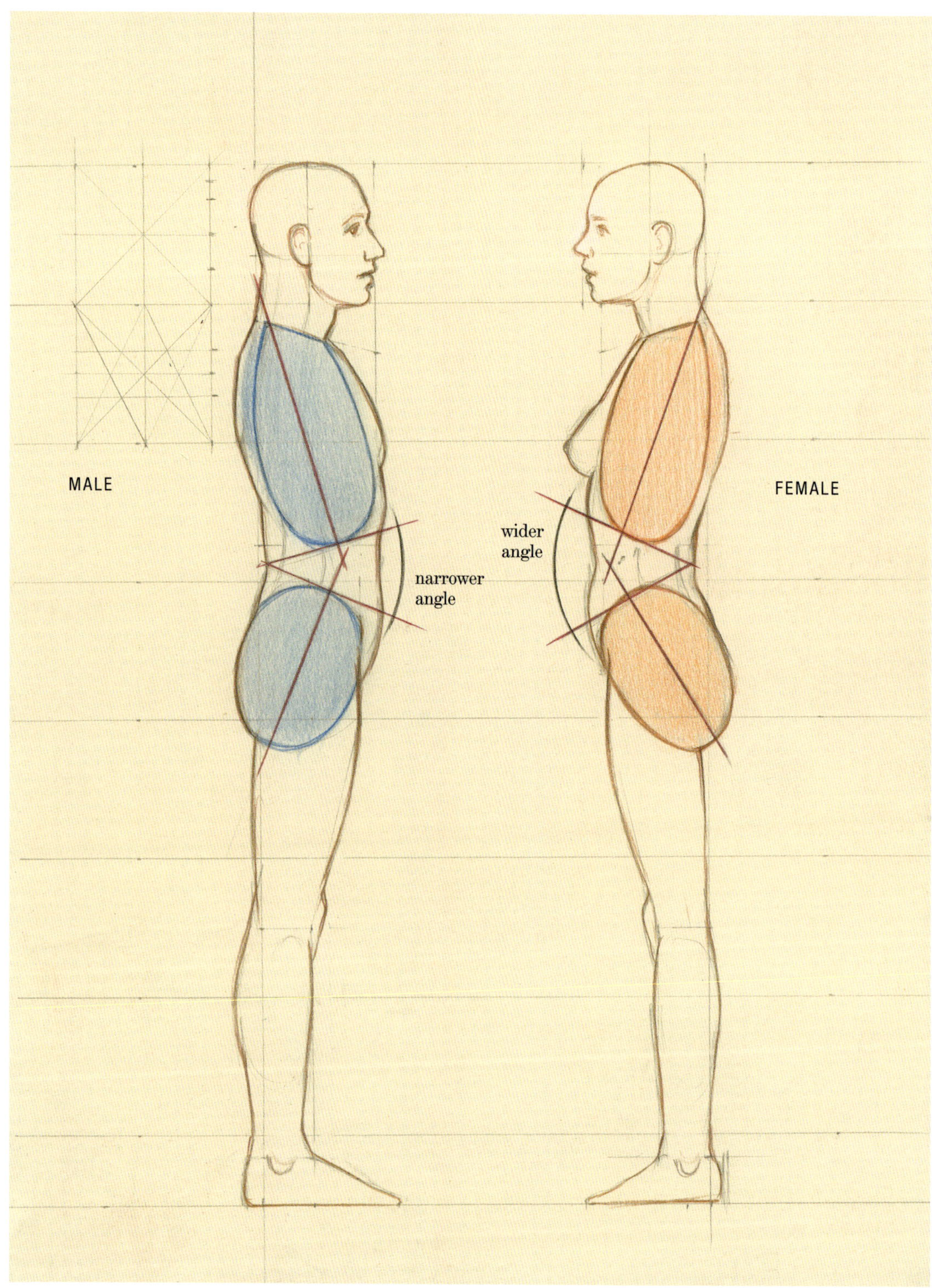

DIFFERENCES IN POSTURE

There are also typical differences in posture between the male and female figure. Note, especially, that the angle between the volumes of the ribcage and the pelvis is slightly wider in the female than in the male.

EXERCISES

Besides doing the exercises below, you should also practice drawing from life using the structural approach. When you do, make sure to identify the surface landmarks of the body, using them to "read" the skeleton inside. Most of the skeleton is, of course, invisible on the body's surface, but these few spots give you hints of it, and you can use these landmarks to extrapolate the skeleton. Your figures will become more solid, structurally sound, and harmonious as a result.

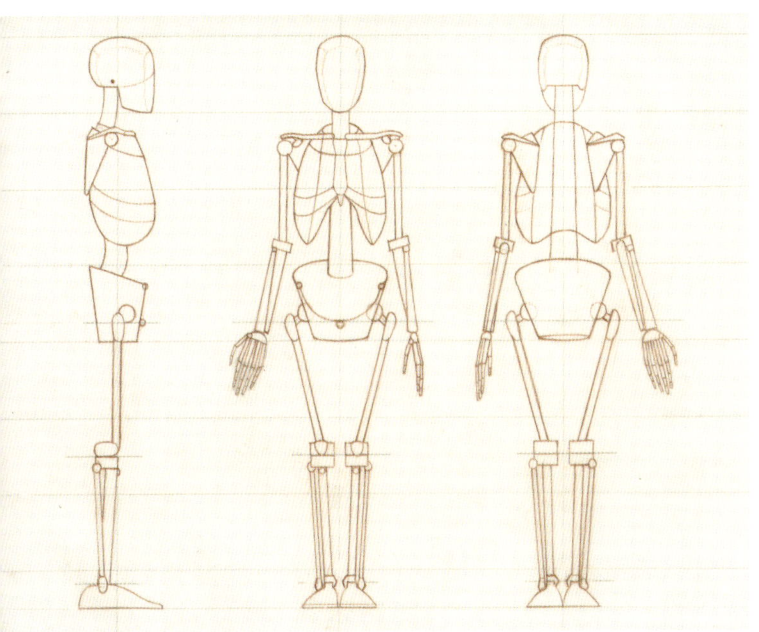

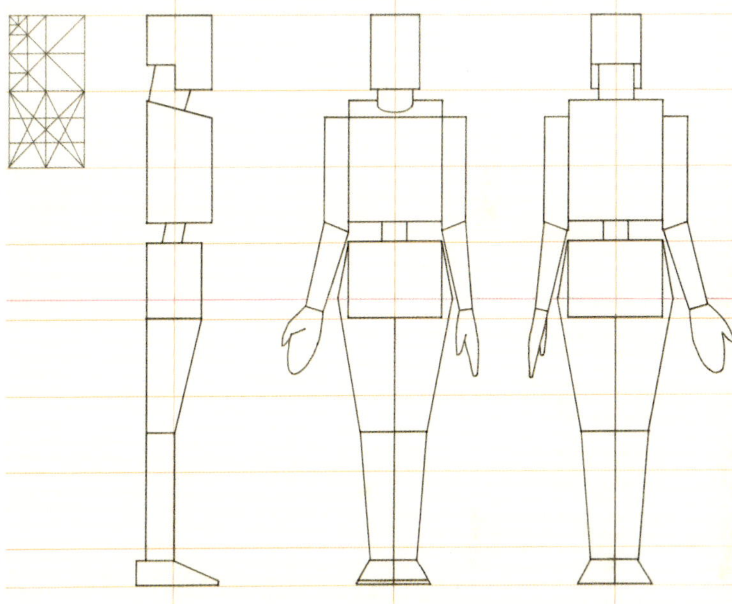

EXERCISE 1: DRAW THE STEREOMETRIC FIGURE AROUND THE STRUCTURAL SKELETON (AND VICE VERSA)

This exercise asks you to combine the conceptualizations of chapters 1 and 2. First, make photocopies of the figures on pages 48 and 49, then draw the boxes of the stereometric representation of the body around these schematic skeletons.

Then do the reverse: Using photocopies of the stereometric renditions of the body on pages 16–19, draw structural skeletons inside them. (If you wish, you may draw on tracing paper placed over the figures rather than making photocopies.) The figures here demonstrate the sequence.

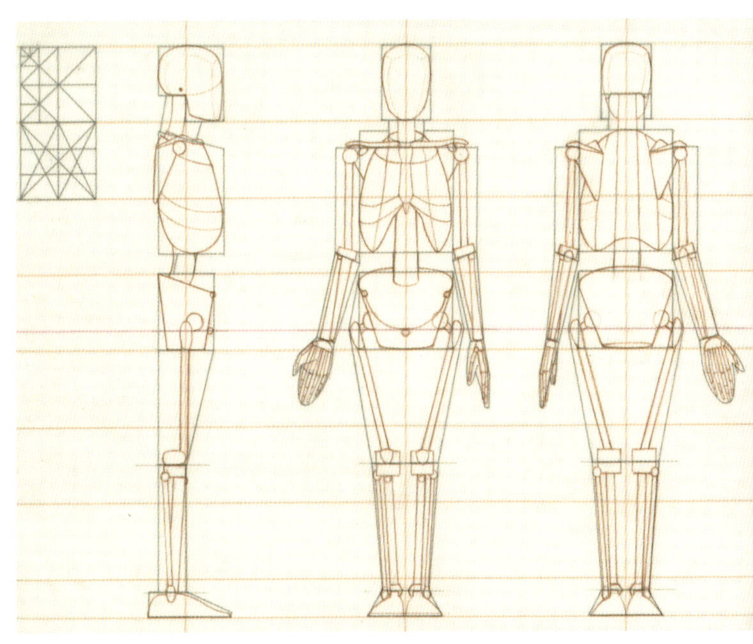

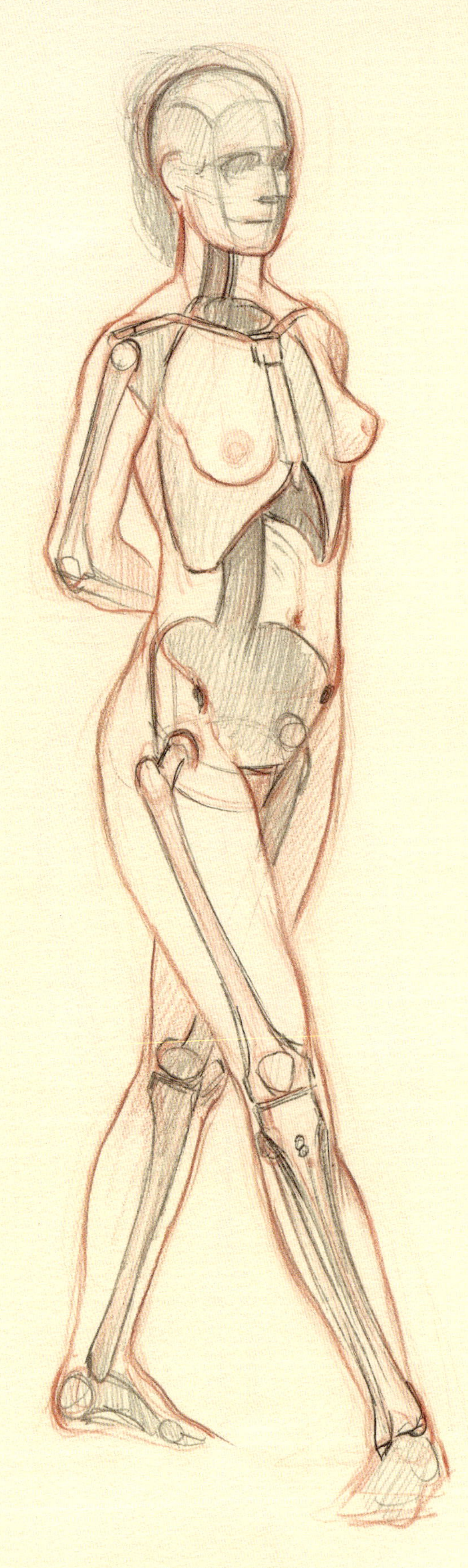

EXERCISE 2: DRAW THE STRUCTURAL SKELETON ON PHOTOS

For this exercise you need tracing paper, a pencil or marker, tape, and photos of nude models from magazines, the Internet, or other sources. (You can also use your own figure drawings as I did in the drawing opposite.) Tape some tracing paper over the photos and draw the structural skeleton inside the figures. Try this with a variety of poses so that you can develop a thorough understanding of the structural skeleton's forms.

EXERCISE 3: DRAW THE STRUCTURAL SKELETON WHILE WORKING WITH A LIVE MODEL

For this exercise you will need the help of a model: While the model is posing, draw his or her structural skeleton, extrapolating it by identifying the landmarks of the body, as in the figure below. Later, draw the soft parts on your studies to see whether there is a good correspondence between the way you perceived the skeleton and the way it really is. If parts of the skeleton are too big or small, this will become immediately evident as you add the external features of the model.

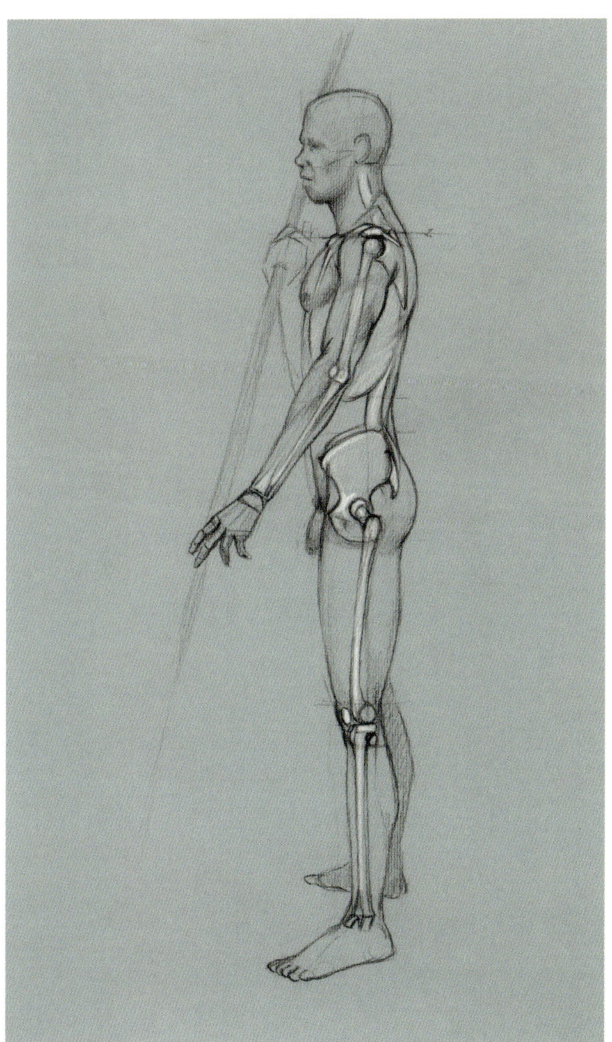

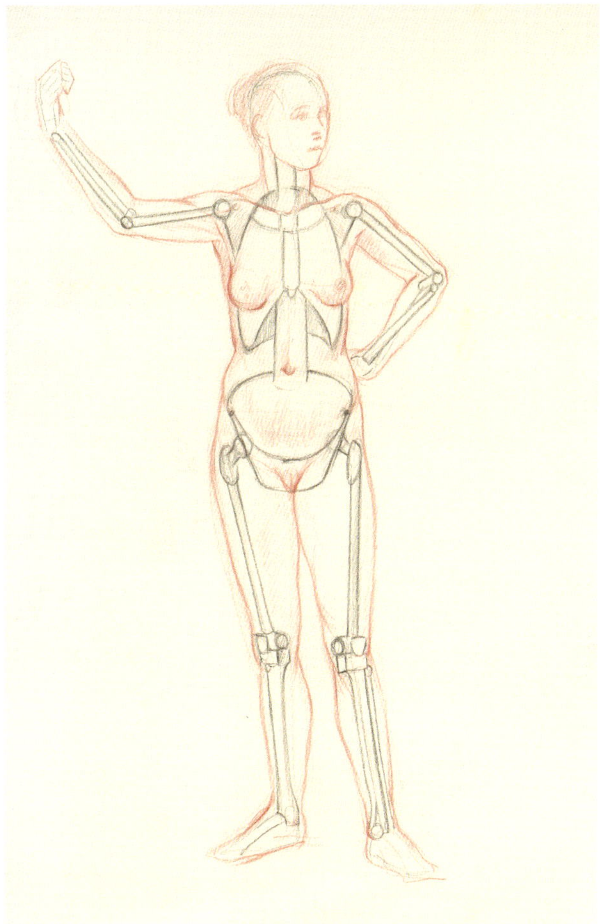

STUDIES OF THE STRUCTURAL SKELETON INSIDE LIVE MODELS

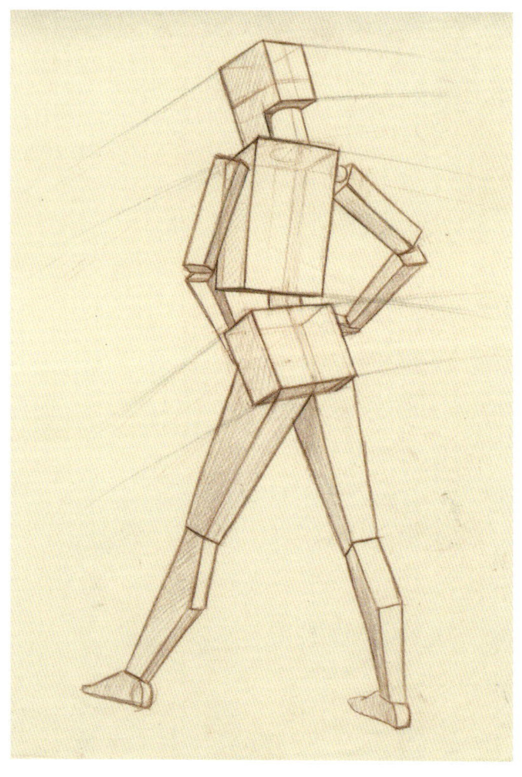

POSE RENDERED AS STEREOMETRIC FIGURE

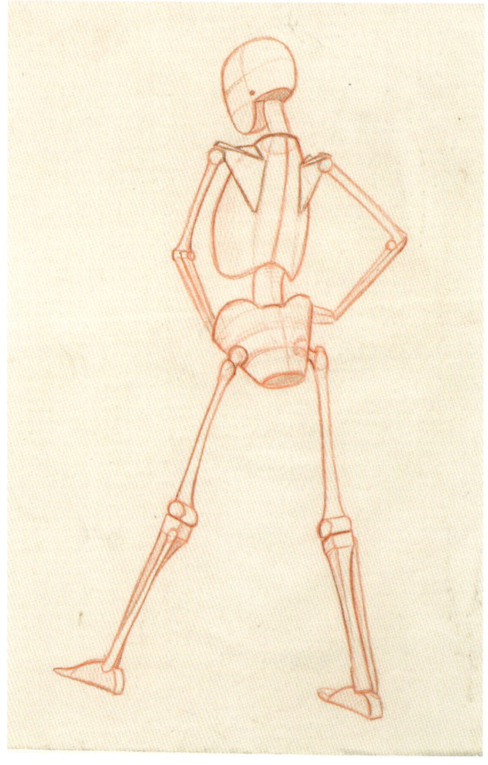

POSE RENDERED AS STRUCTURAL SKELETON

A related exercise is to draw the live model, reducing him or her to the basic stereometric and structural conceptualizations we have described so far, as in these figures. You may want to draw on tracing paper and then overlap the sheets to see how the various renditions of the figure line up.

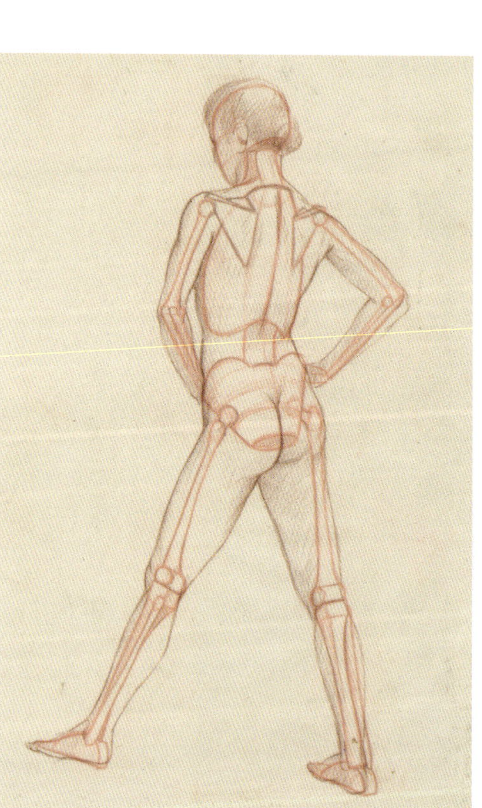

POSE RENDERED AS STRUCTURAL SKELETON AND STEREOMETRIC FIGURE

POSE RENDERED AS STRUCTURAL SKELETON AND ORGANIC FIGURE

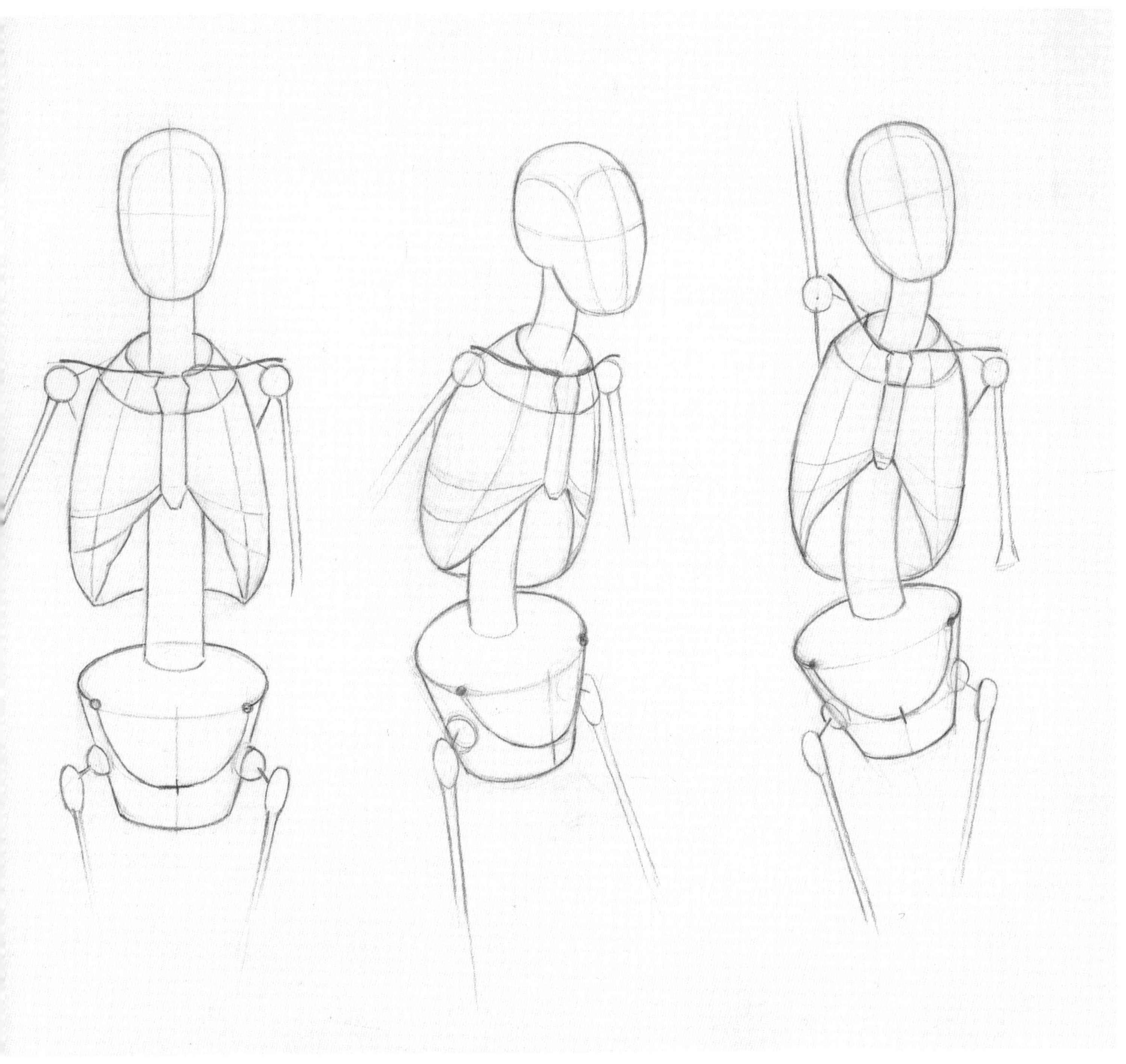

EXERCISE 4: DRAW THE STRUCTURAL SKELETON FROM MEMORY OR IMAGINATION

Finally, draw from memory or imagination several compositions that include multiple figures conceptualized as structural skeletons.

STRUCTURAL SKELETONS DRAWN FROM MEMORY

USE INK OR WATERCOLOR WASHES

Ink or watercolor washes allow you to study the effect of the light on the figure and provide a quick way of achieving an essential tonal rendering. For water-media (ink or watercolor), you will need a brush: Try a #12 round, which has a round belly to hold the ink or paint and a thin point for detail. I prefer synthetic brushes because they are cheap and do a good job, though their points splay fairly quickly and they don't hold as much paint as natural sable brushes. (Brushes made with Kolinsky sable are the best possible choice, but they are very expensive.) You will also need a tube or two of watercolors; start with black or a neutral tint and a red earth color such as Venetian, English, or Indian red. Buy the best quality watercolors you can afford. It is better to buy just a few tubes from a good maker, such as Winsor & Newton or Old Holland, than a cheap box of twenty-four colors of mediocre quality. Also get a ceramic or plastic dish to prepare the paint in, a bowl of water, and paper towels or cotton rags for blotting. Paper towels or cotton rags are essential for blotting your brush to eliminate excess paint and for immediately wiping away an accidental smudge or drop from your drawing. Use decent paper (at least 90 lb) from a good brand such as Arches, Fabriano, Canson, or Strathmore. A slightly textured cold press finish is a better choice than smoother hot press. Using cheap, thin paper is frustrating, because it will buckle or peel as you apply watermedia to it.

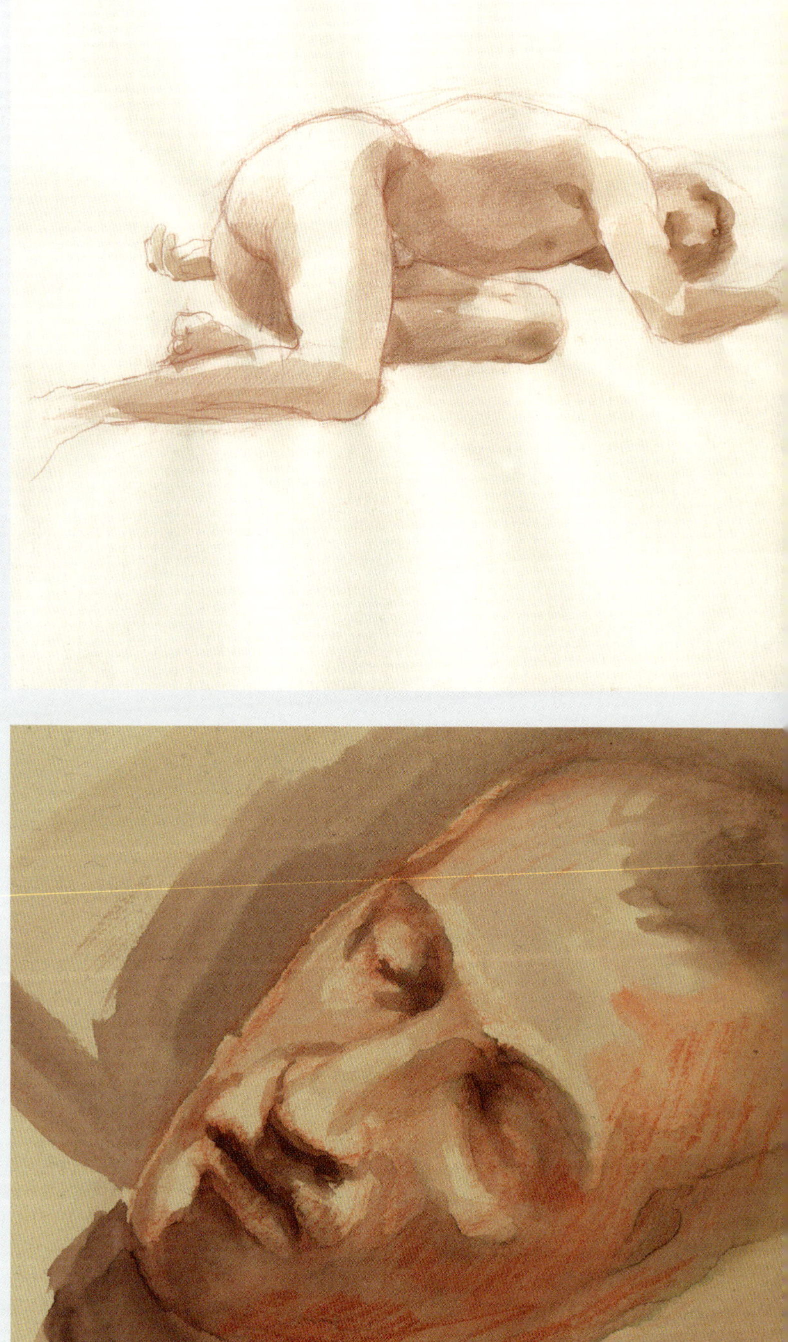

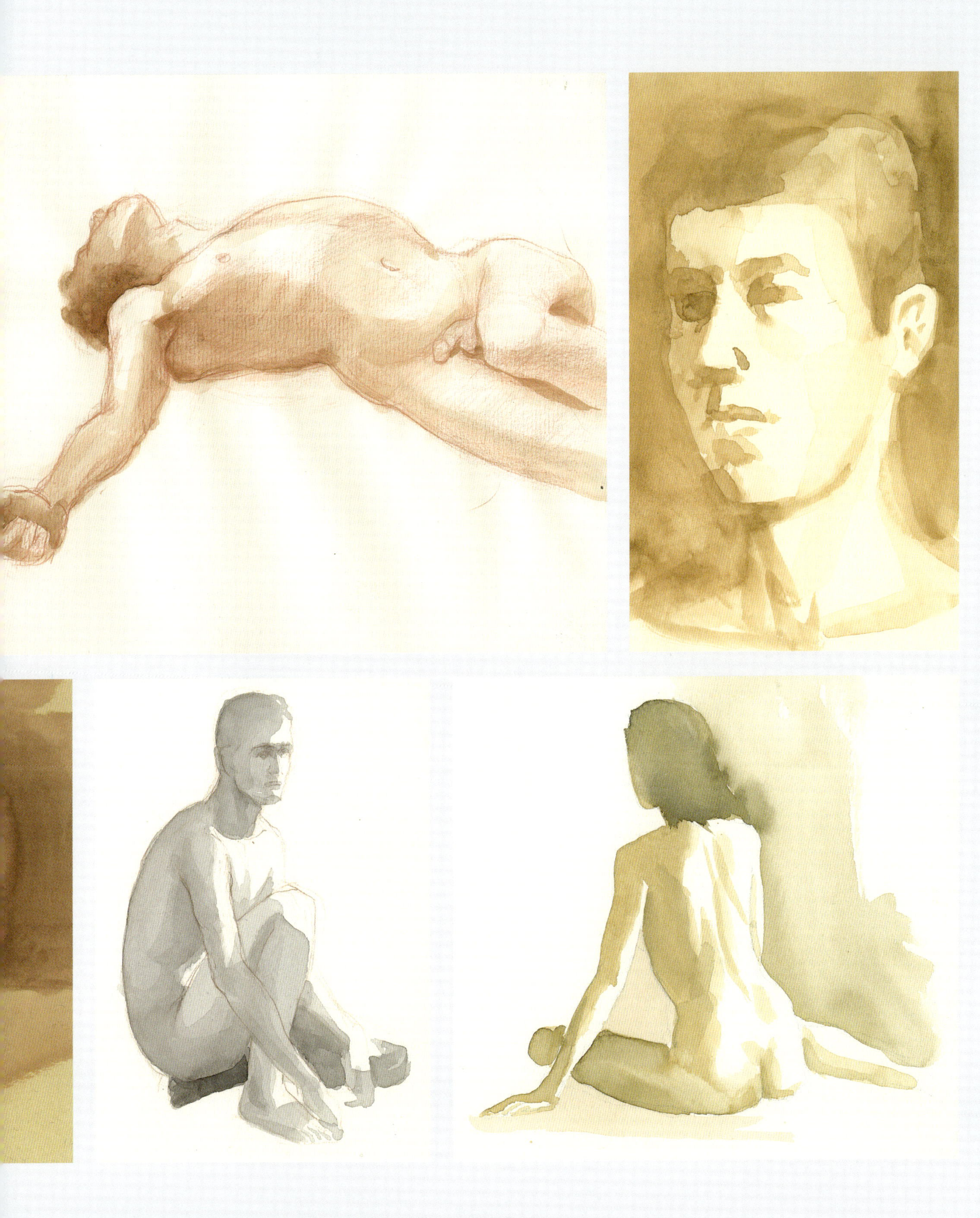

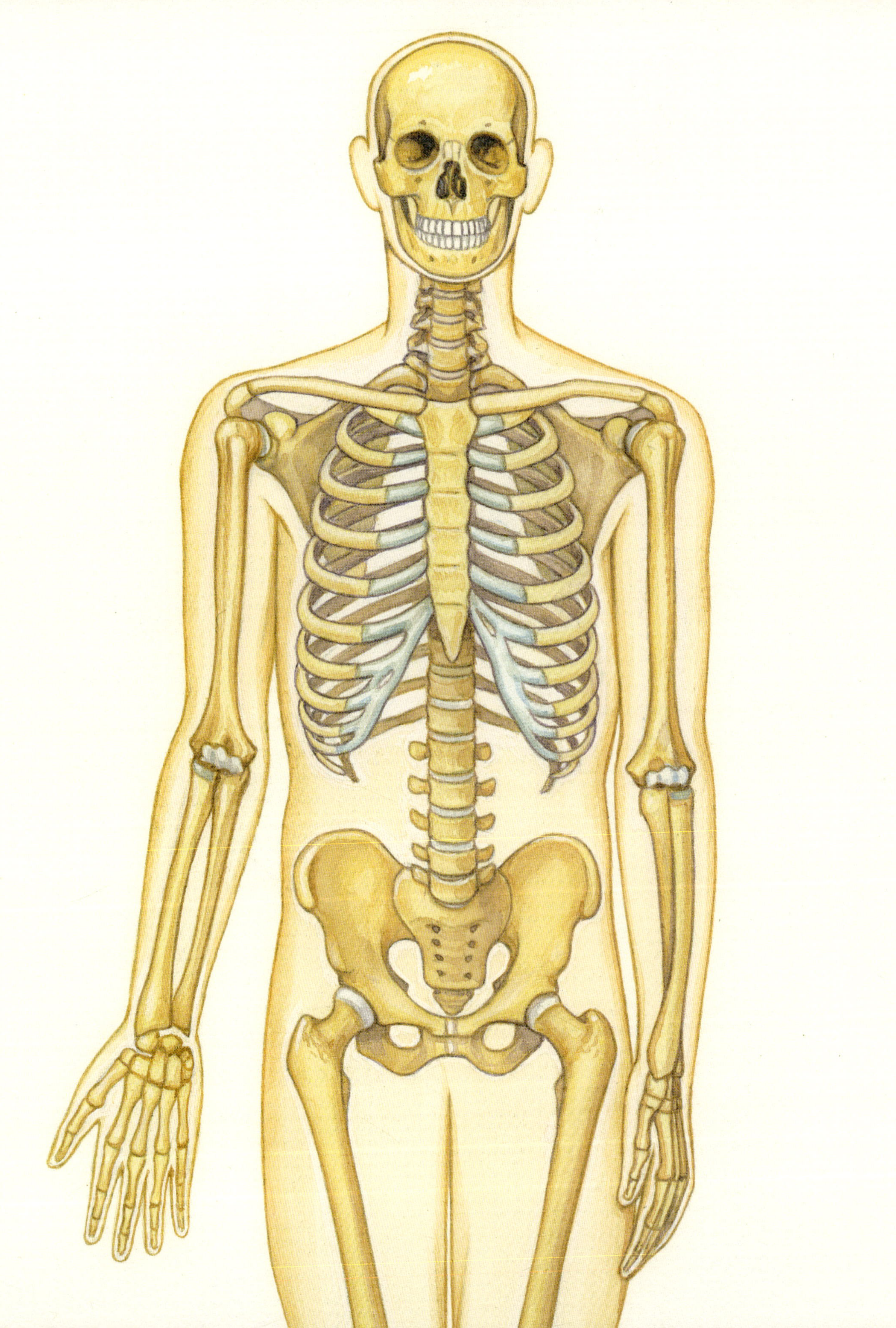

Chapter 3

ORGANIC FORMS OF THE SKELETON

In his 1435 book *On Painting*, Italian artist and philosopher Leon Battista Alberti laid the theoretical groundwork for an approach to figurative art in which the soft tissues are layered over a skeletal structure. This approach is architectural: The artist starts by drawing the skeleton—the deep structure of the body, equivalent to the foundation of a building—and then gradually builds it up, adding the muscles, the skin, and, eventually, clothes. Many preparatory sketches by artists such as Leonardo, Michelangelo, and Raphael bear witness to the use of this method by Renaissance artists.

The skeletal structure presented in the previous chapter is a very synthetic one, obtained by focusing on the basic volumes and landmarks of the skeleton and the main axes and joints. This

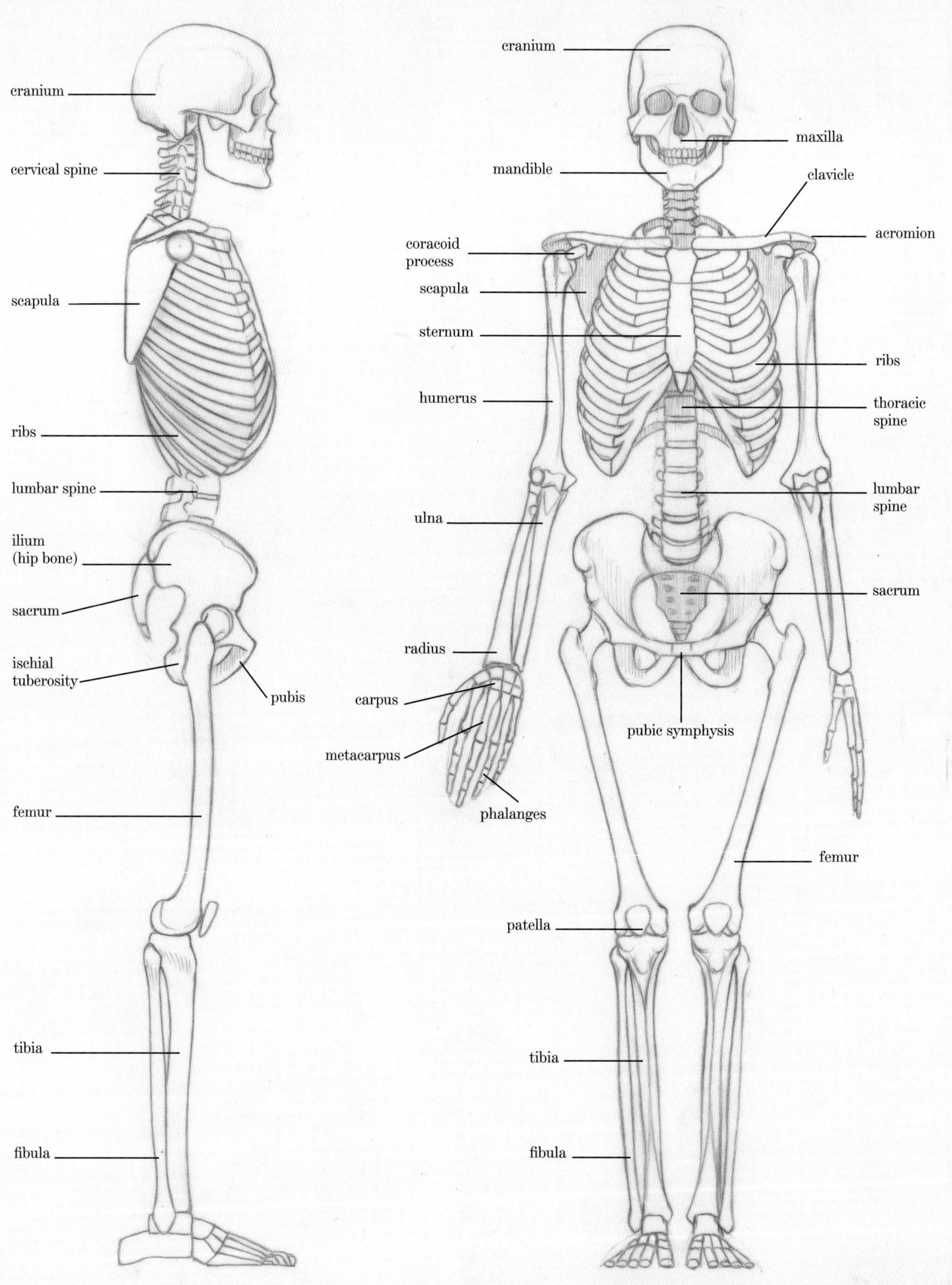

cranium
cervical spine
scapula
ribs
lumbar spine
ilium
(hip bone)
sacrum
ischial
tuberosity
pubis
femur
tibia
fibula
cranium
maxilla
mandible
clavicle
acromion
coracoid
process
scapula
sternum
ribs
humerus
thoracic
spine
ulna
lumbar
spine
sacrum
radius
carpus
metacarpus
pubic symphysis
phalanges
femur
patella
tibia
fibula

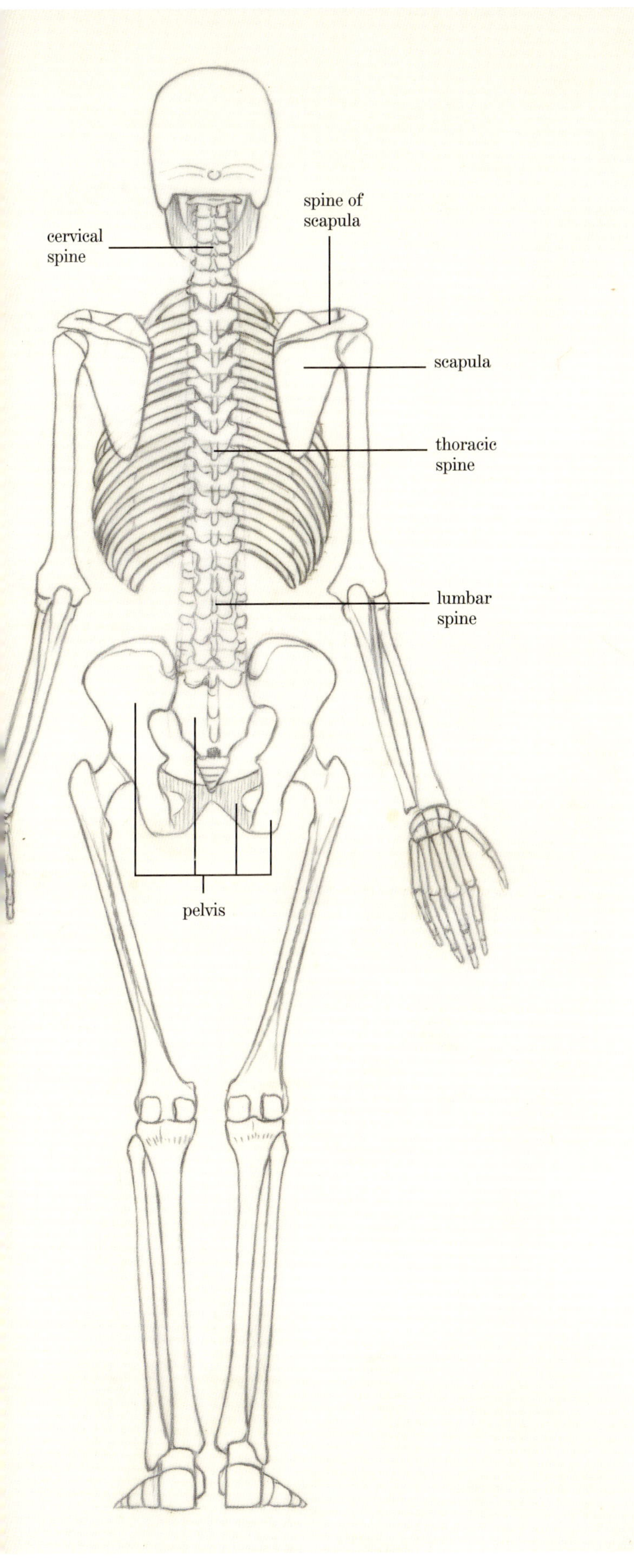

chapter adds the specific morphological aspects of the organic skeleton to that essential structural skeleton. These aspects are much easier to understand if you first master the characteristics of the structural skeleton as set out in chapter 2.

BONE STRUCTURES

As you look closely at the 206 bones that compose the adult human skeleton, you will notice that the surfaces of the various bones have all sorts of bumps, ridges, and rough areas. These formations—turberosities, spines, and so on—are not imperfections but have a purpose. All are places that muscles originate from or insert into, and their surfaces are rough so that the tendons of the muscles have more surface to hold onto.

The pelvic bone, for instance, has quite a few such points of muscle insertion: the four iliac spines (the anterior superior iliac spine, or ASIS; the anterior inferior iliac spine, or AIIS; the posterior superior iliac spine, or PSIS; and the posterior inferior iliac spine, or PIIS), iliac crest, pubic bone, linea pectinea, ischiatic tuberosity, and ischiatic spines. Becoming familiar with these structures and memorizing their names will help you understand the muscular structure from both a functional and an aesthetic point of view, enabling you to grasp the harmonies and rhythms of the body and the connections between various muscular forms that are distant from one another.

THE MALE SKELETON

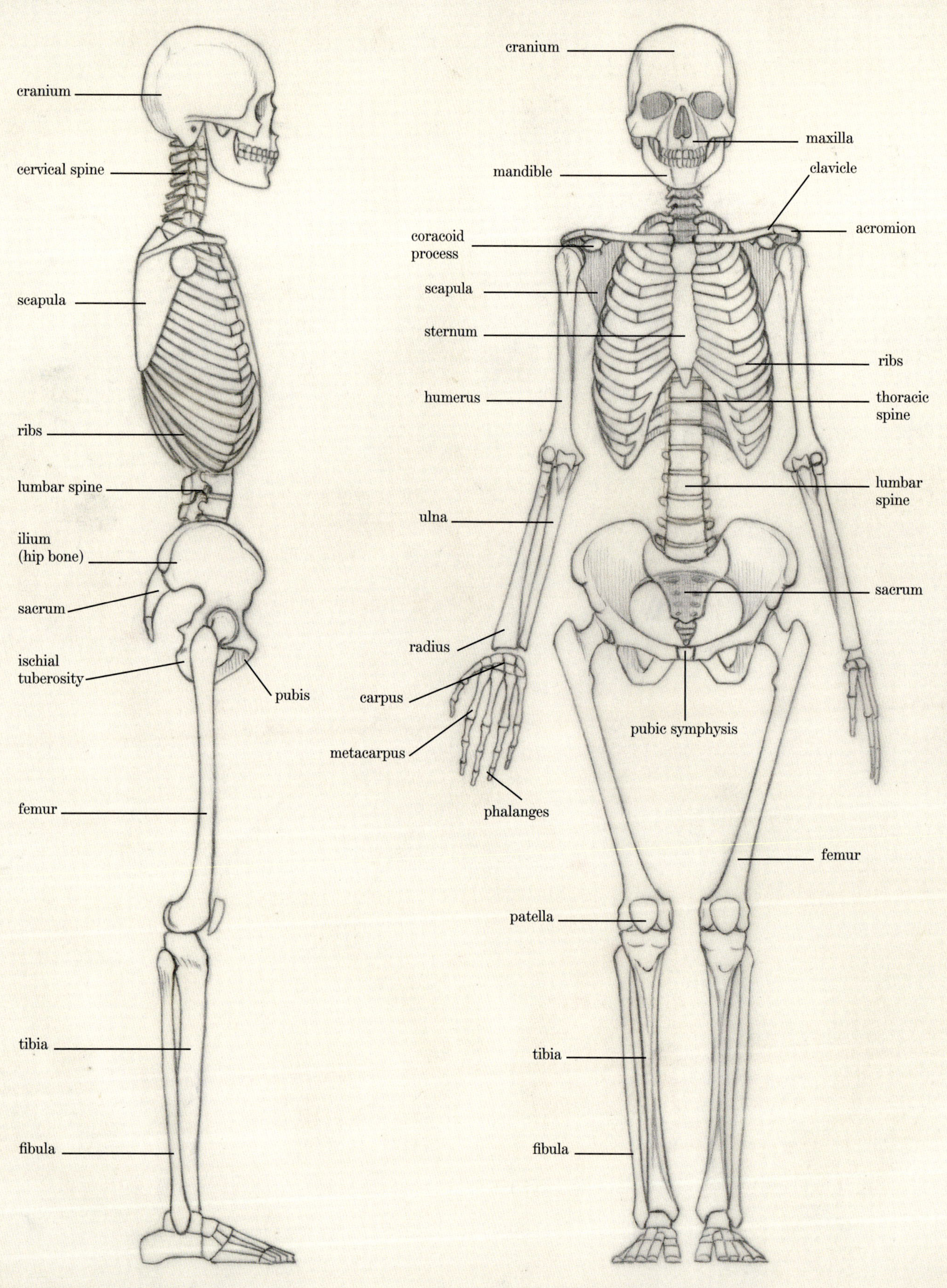

cranium
cervical spine
scapula
ribs
lumbar spine
ilium
(hip bone)
sacrum
ischial
tuberosity
pubis
femur
tibia
fibula
cranium
maxilla
mandible
clavicle
acromion
coracoid
process
scapula
sternum
ribs
humerus
thoracic
spine
lumbar
spine
ulna
sacrum
radius
carpus
metacarpus
pubic symphysis
phalanges
femur
patella
tibia
fibula

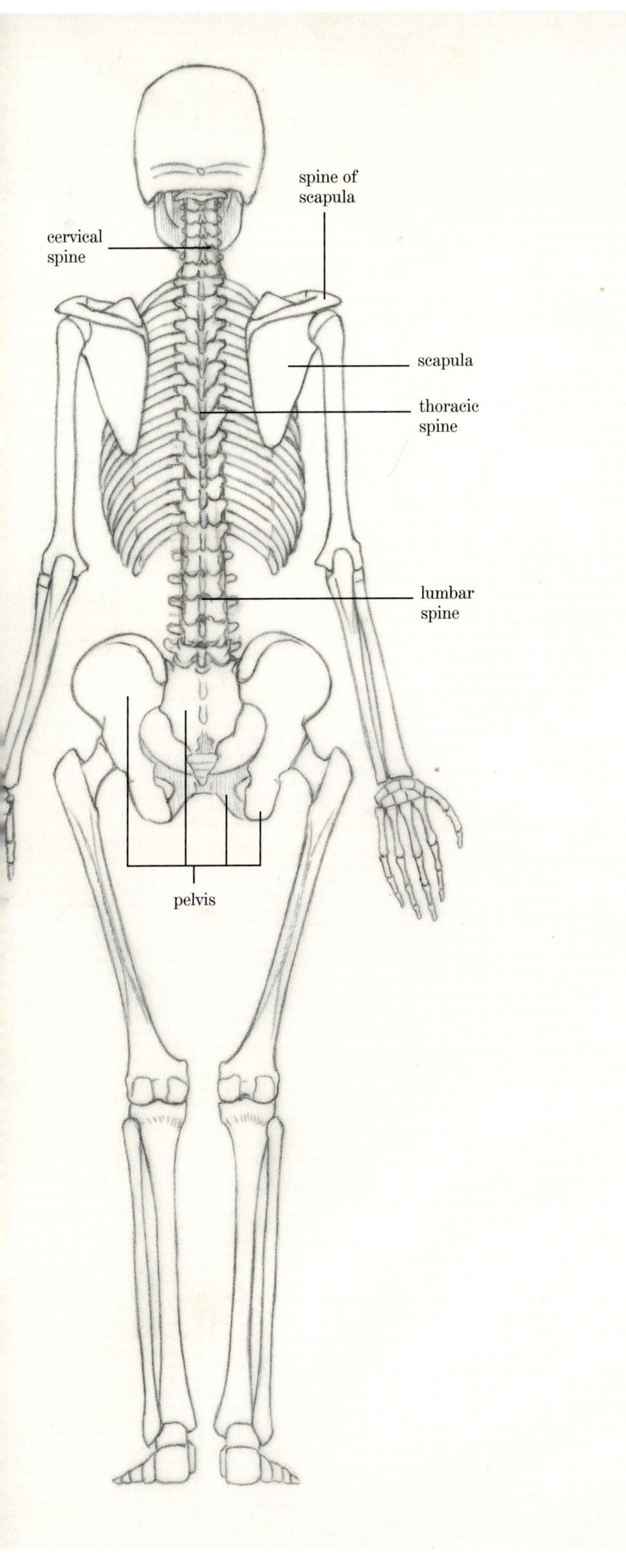

THE WHOLE SKELETON

Before moving to a detailed morphological description of the individual bones, let's take a look at the overall structure of the skeleton, male and female, the basic types of bones, and the nomenclature used for various parts of the bones.

The figures here and on the previous pages show the male and female skeletons in detail to help you better understand their morphological characteristics and see the gender differences. The figures on pages 88 and 89 will help you visualize the landmarks of the body. In the last chapter you became acquainted with the essential structural aspects of the skeleton; now you can look at the organic skeleton and appreciate its functional and morphological characteristics without being sidetracked by the many details of the actual skeleton. For example, when you look at the actual ribcage, you see an incredibly messy bunch of bones—very difficult to reproduce in a drawing. But if you understand the basic oviform structure of the ribcage and know its widest point, its angles, its planes, and how to extrapolate the positions of the ribs, you have the key for decoding this puzzling maze of bones. By knowing more about the skeleton, you can appreciate its incredible, beautiful complexity without being overwhelmed by it.

THE FEMALE SKELETON

LANDMARKS OF THE SKELETON

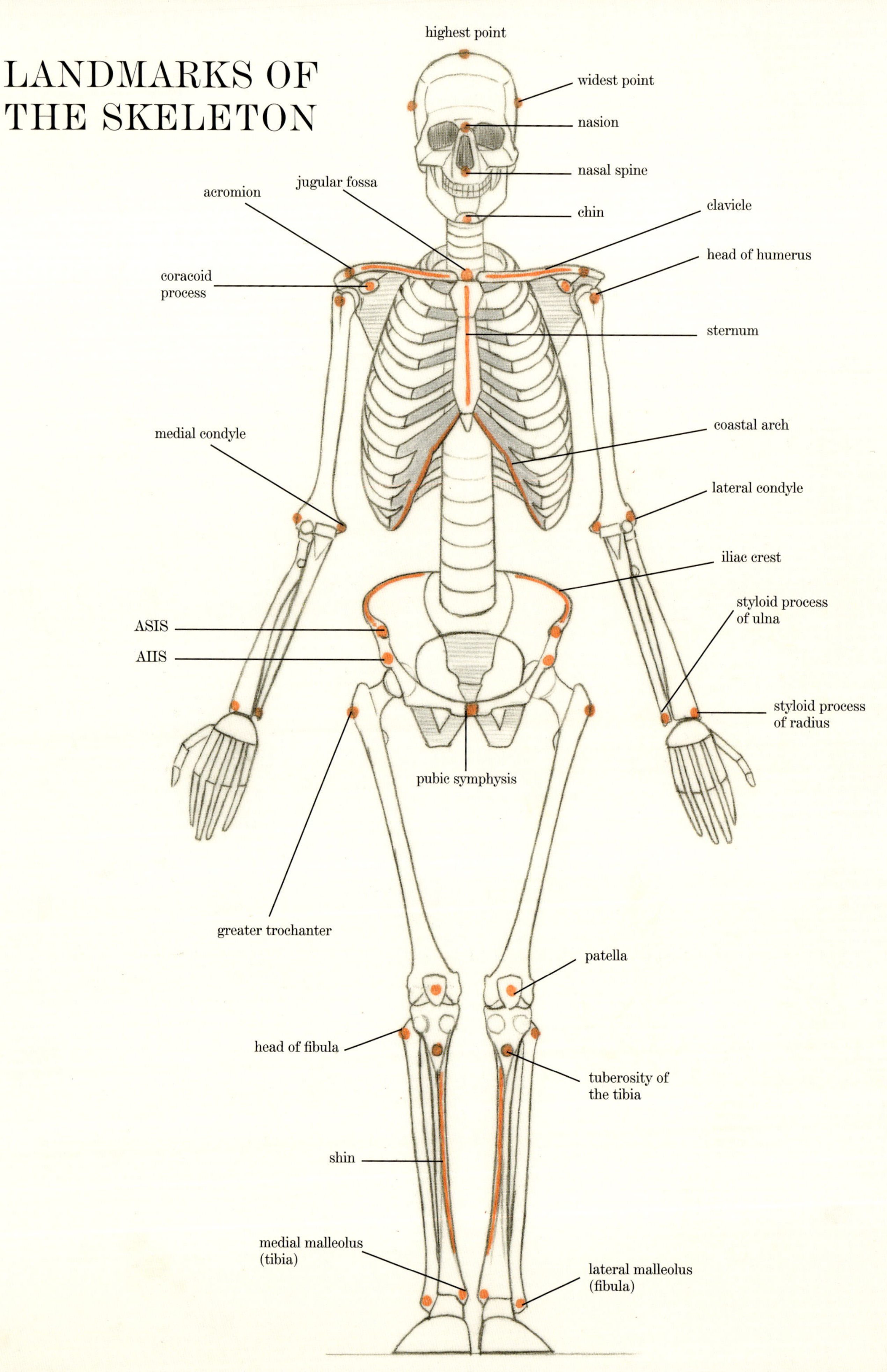

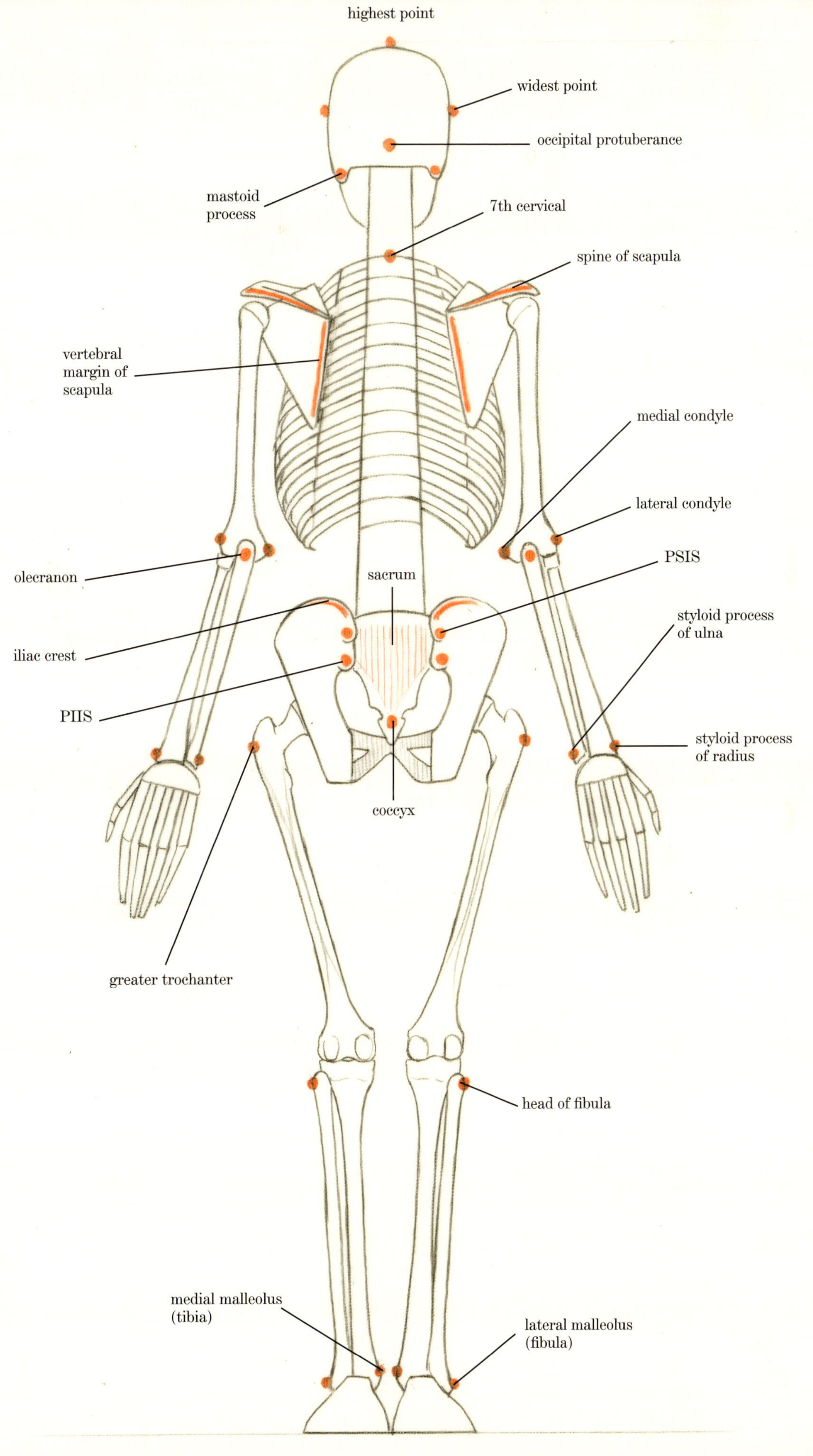

highest point
widest point
occipital protuberance
mastoid process
7th cervical
spine of scapula
vertebral margin of scapula
medial condyle
lateral condyle
olecranon
sacrum
PSIS
styloid process of ulna
iliac crest
PIIS
styloid process of radius
coccyx
greater trochanter
head of fibula
medial malleolus (tibia)
lateral malleolus (fibula)

TYPES OF BONES

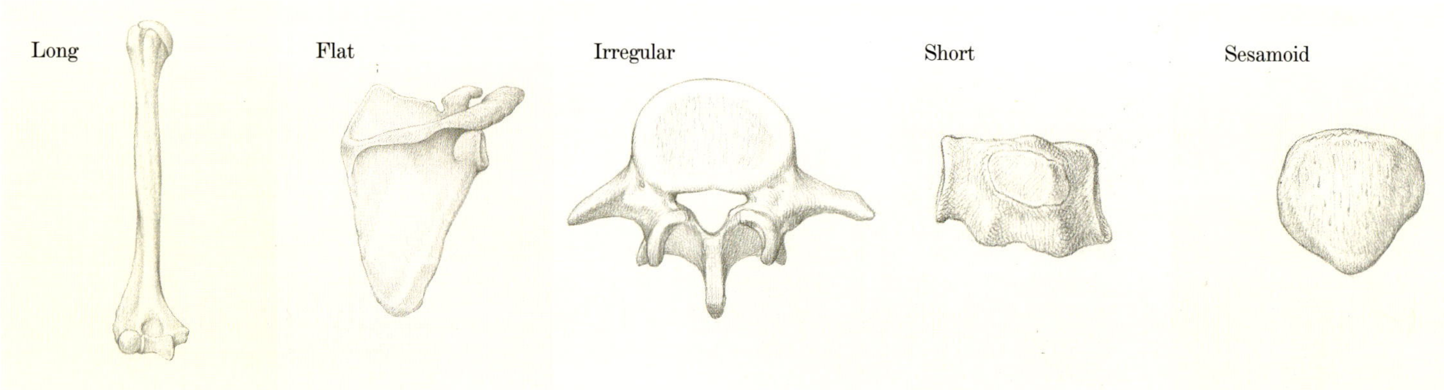

The figure above shows the five basic types of bones:

- Long (e.g., the femur, tibia, and humerus)
- Flat (e.g., the scapulae, sternum, iliac bone, and the bones of the cranium)
- Irregular (e.g., the vertebrae)
- Short (e.g., the tarsal bones and carpal bones)
- Sesamoid (e.g., the patella)

The figure at right shows the various parts of a long bone. This nomenclature can be applied to any long bone.

PARTS OF A LONG BONE

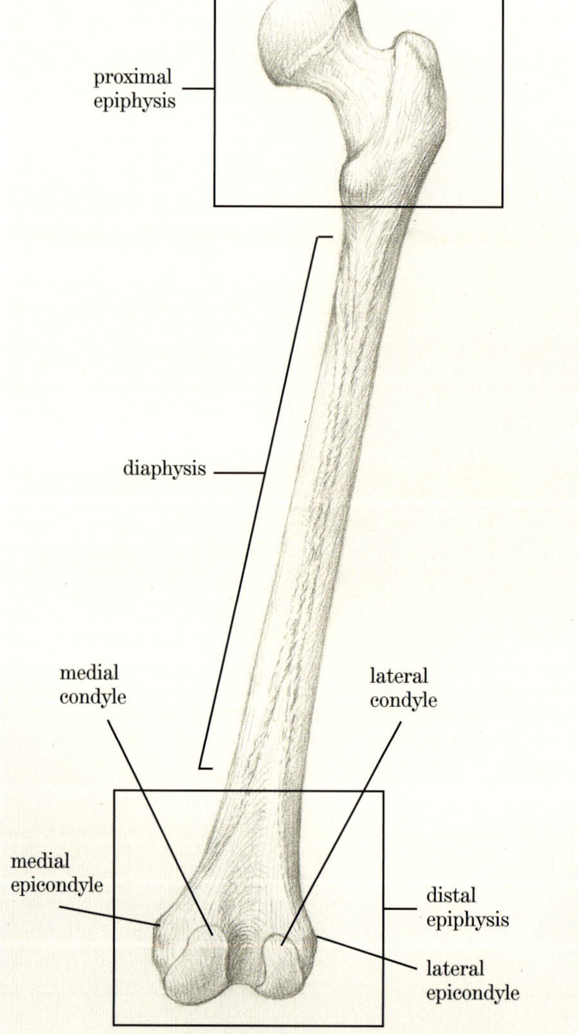

THE AXIAL AND APPENDICULAR SKELETONS

The skeleton can be subdivided in two basic parts: the axial skeleton and the appendicular skeleton, as shown below. The axial skeleton, composed of the head, torso, and spine (including the sacrum), represents the central axis of the body, while the appendicular skeleton is composed of the parts attached, or appended, to the axial skeleton: the arms (including the clavicle, scapula, humerus, radius, ulna, and hand) and the legs (including iliac wings, femur, tibia, fibula, and foot).

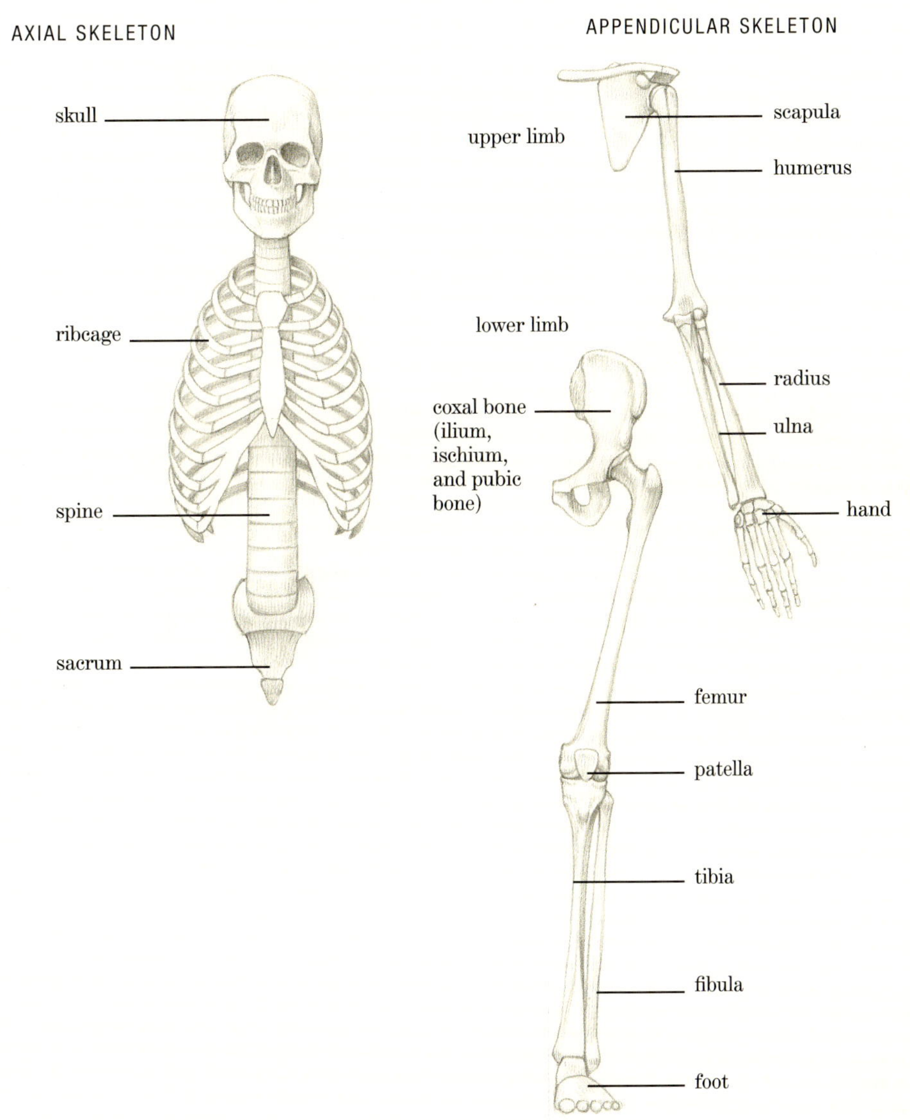

BONES OF THE AXIAL SKELETON AND PELVIS

Now we can look in detail at the specific characteristics of
the individual bones. The drawings in this section depict the
bones of the axial skeleton and the pelvis.

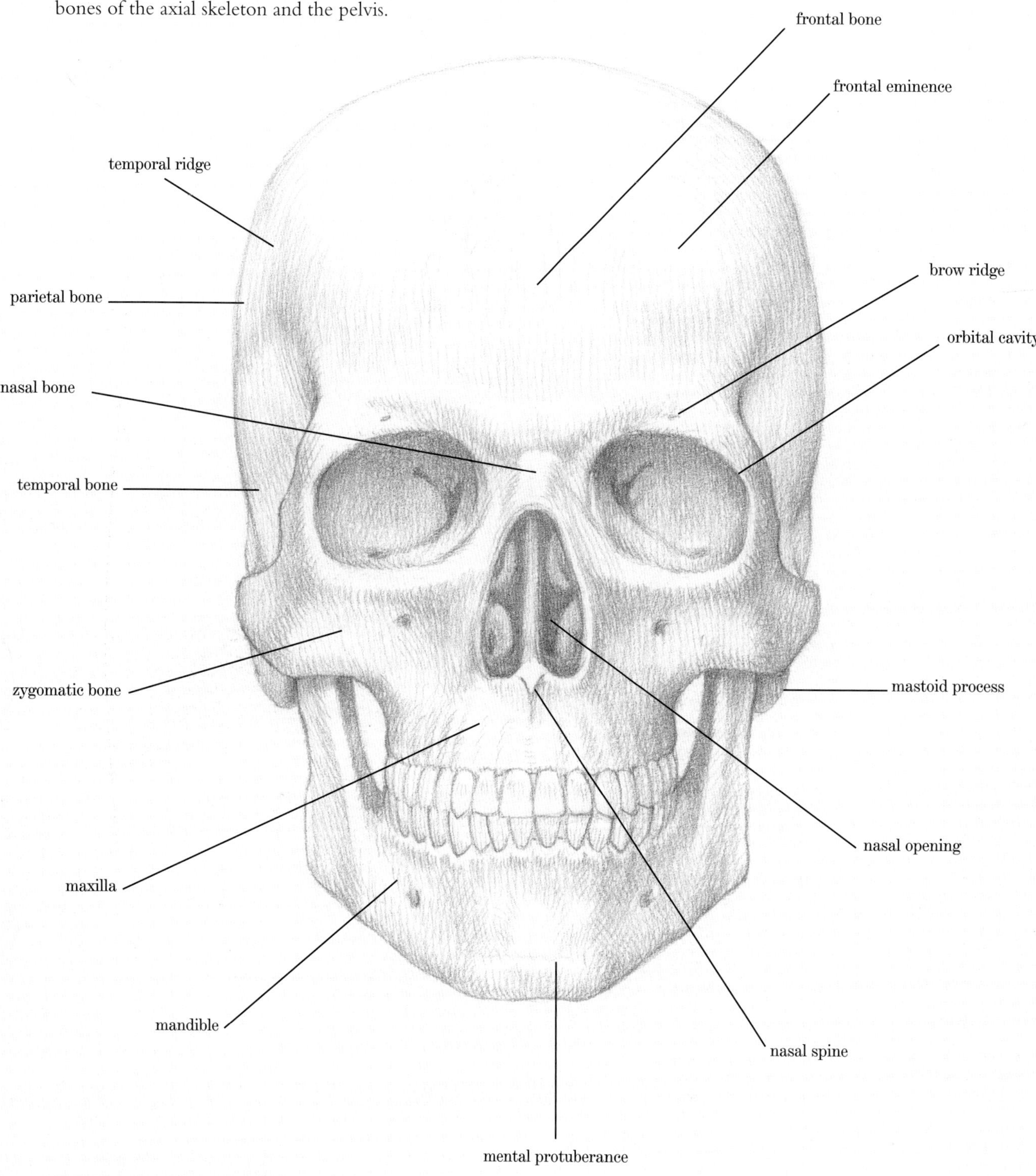

THE SKULL—ANTERIOR VIEW

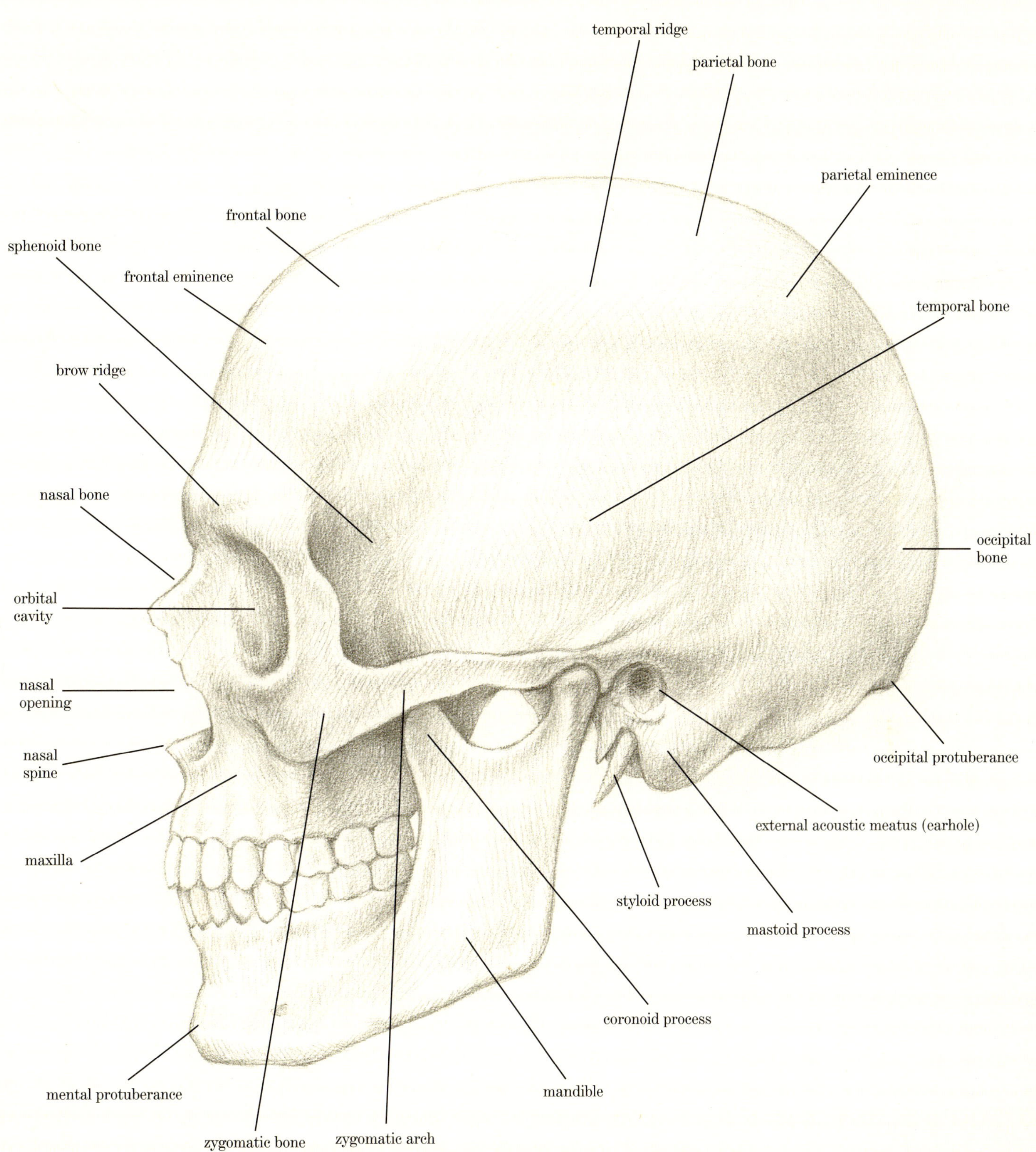

THE SKULL—LATERAL VIEW

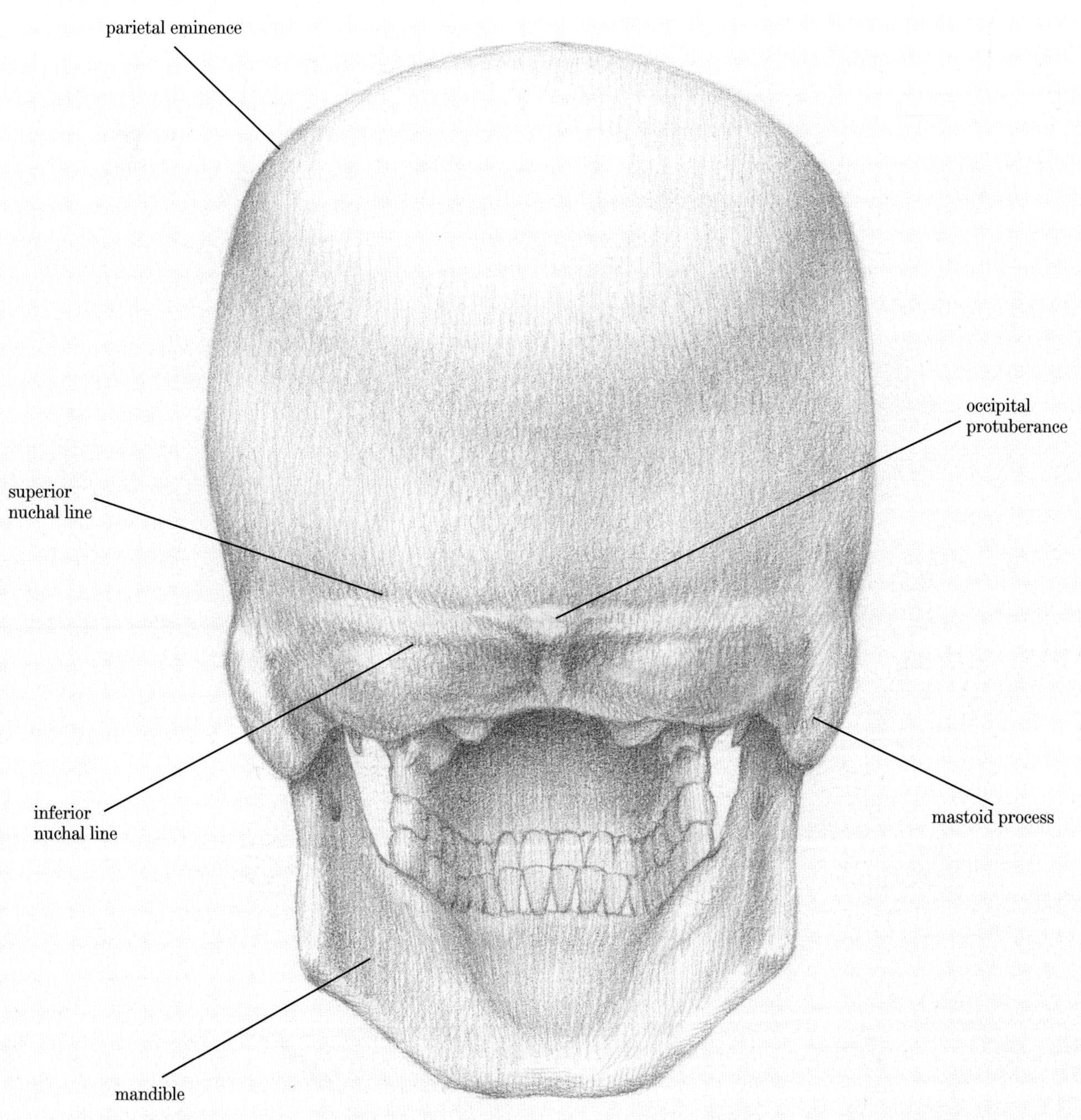

THE SKULL—POSTERIOR VIEW

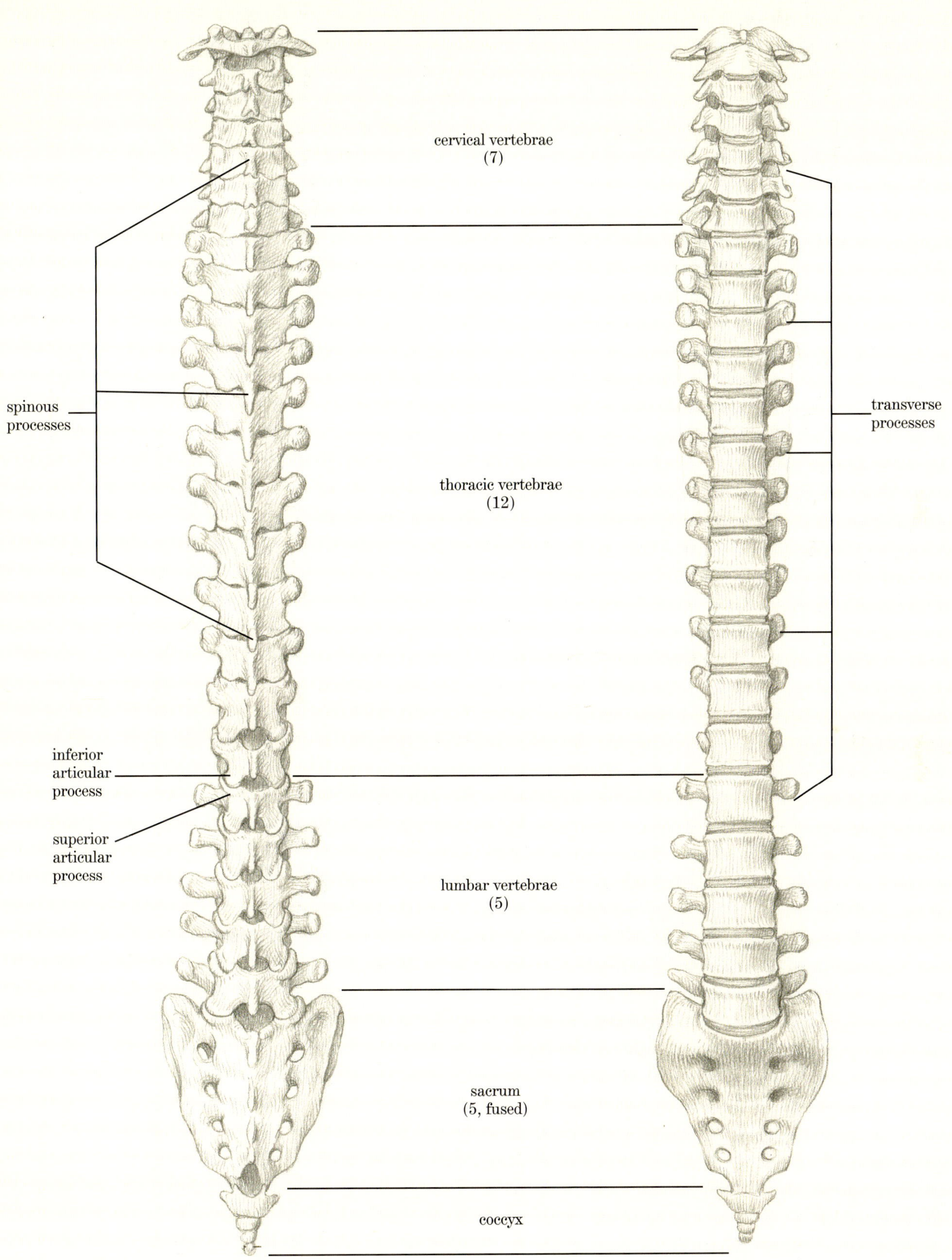

THE SPINE—ANTERIOR AND POSTERIOR VIEWS

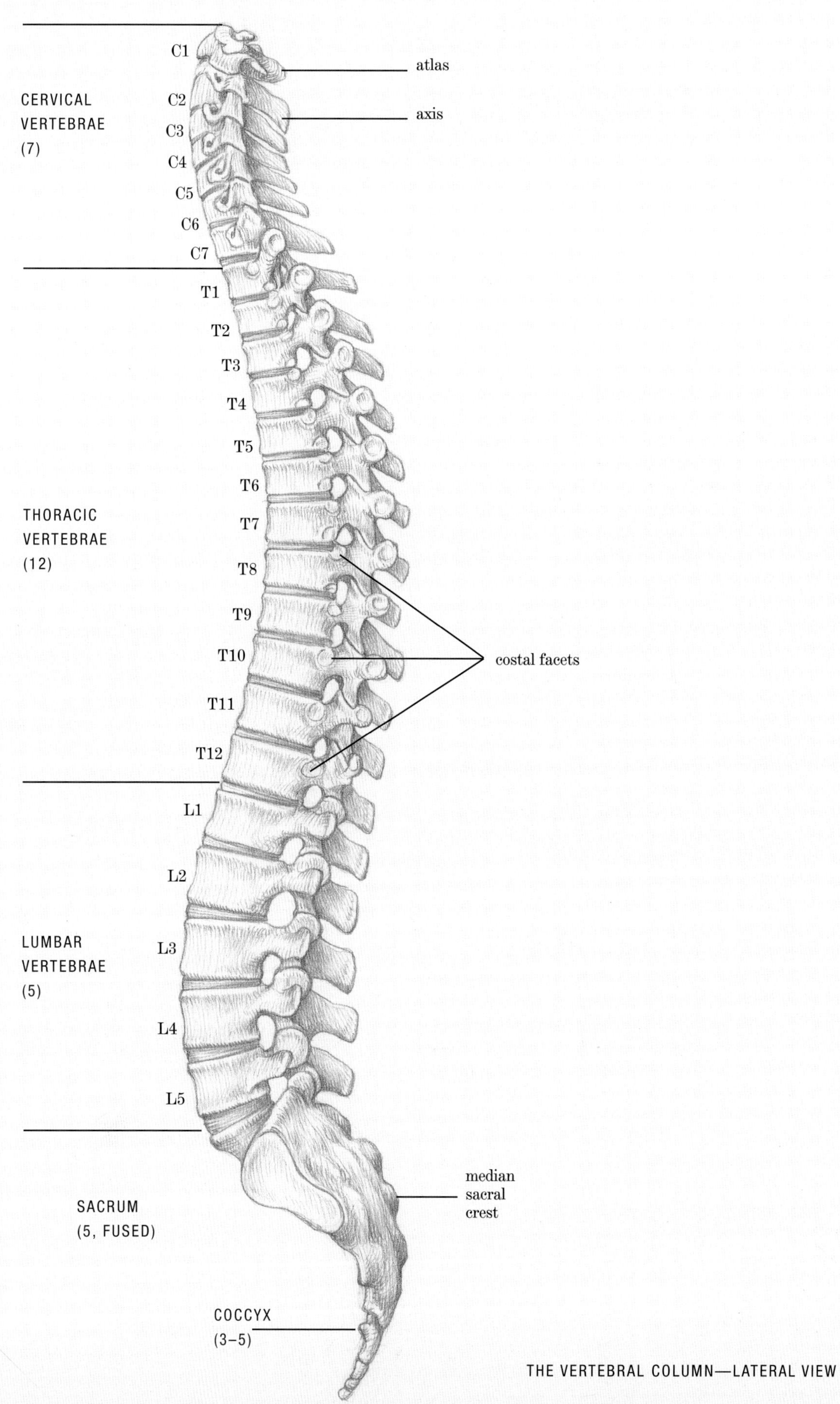

CERVICAL VERTEBRAE (7)
C1
C2
C3
C4
C5
C6
C7
atlas
axis
THORACIC VERTEBRAE (12)
T1
T2
T3
T4
T5
T6
T7
T8
T9
T10
T11
T12
costal facets
LUMBAR VERTEBRAE (5)
L1
L2
L3
L4
L5
SACRUM (5, FUSED)
median sacral crest
COCCYX (3–5)

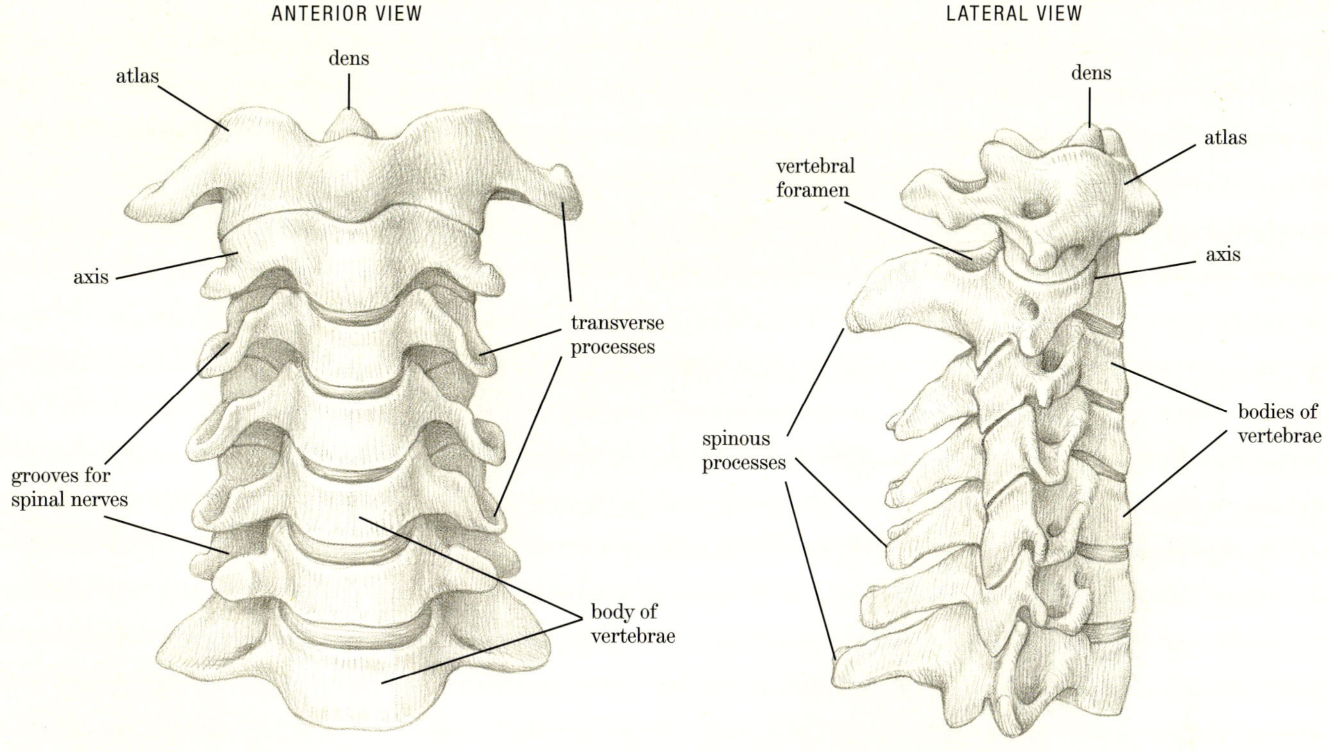

THE CERVICAL VERTEBRAE—ANTERIOR AND LATERAL VIEWS

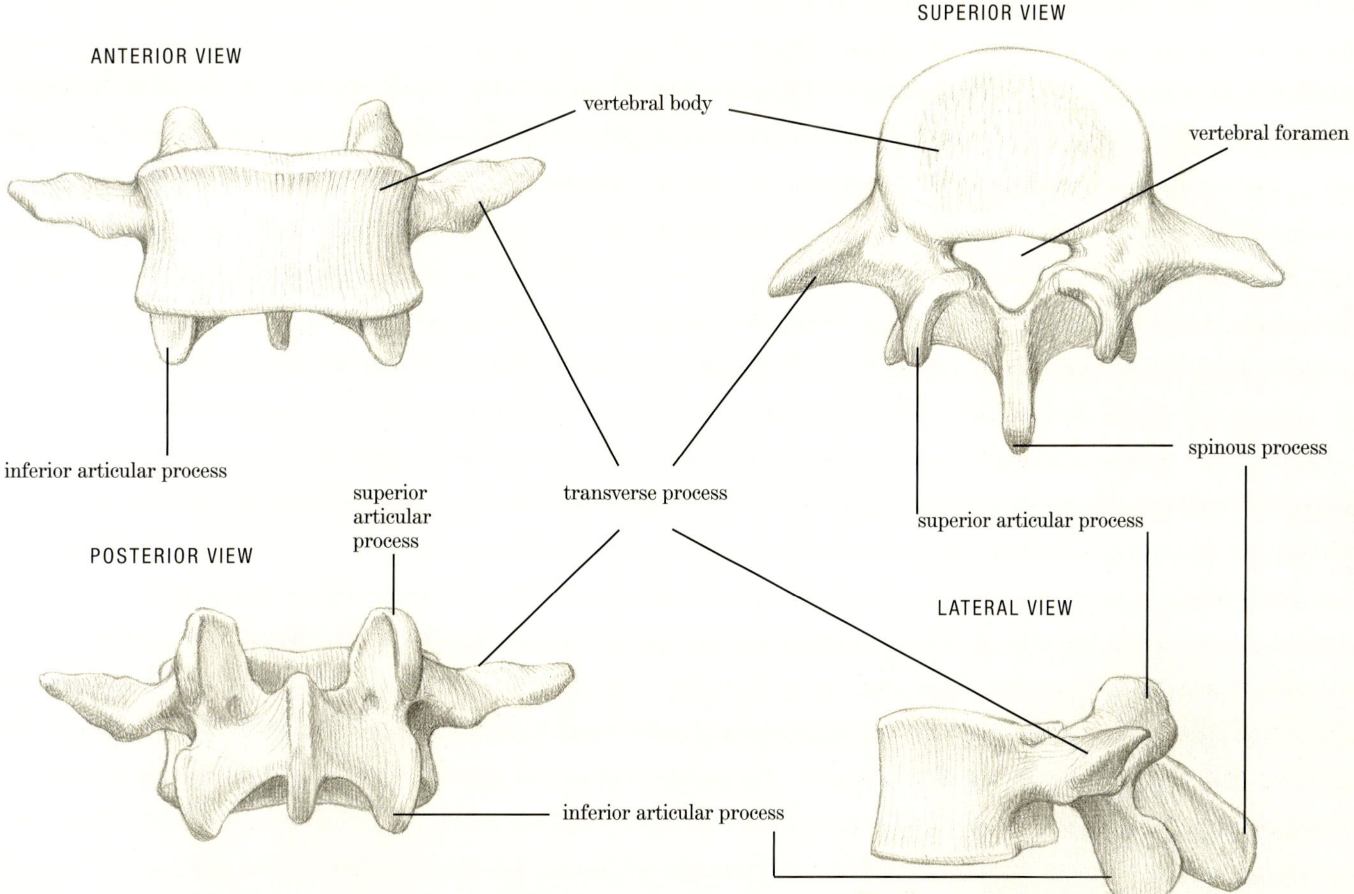

LUMBAR VERTEBRAE—ANTERIOR, SUPERIOR, POSTERIOR, AND LATERAL VIEWS

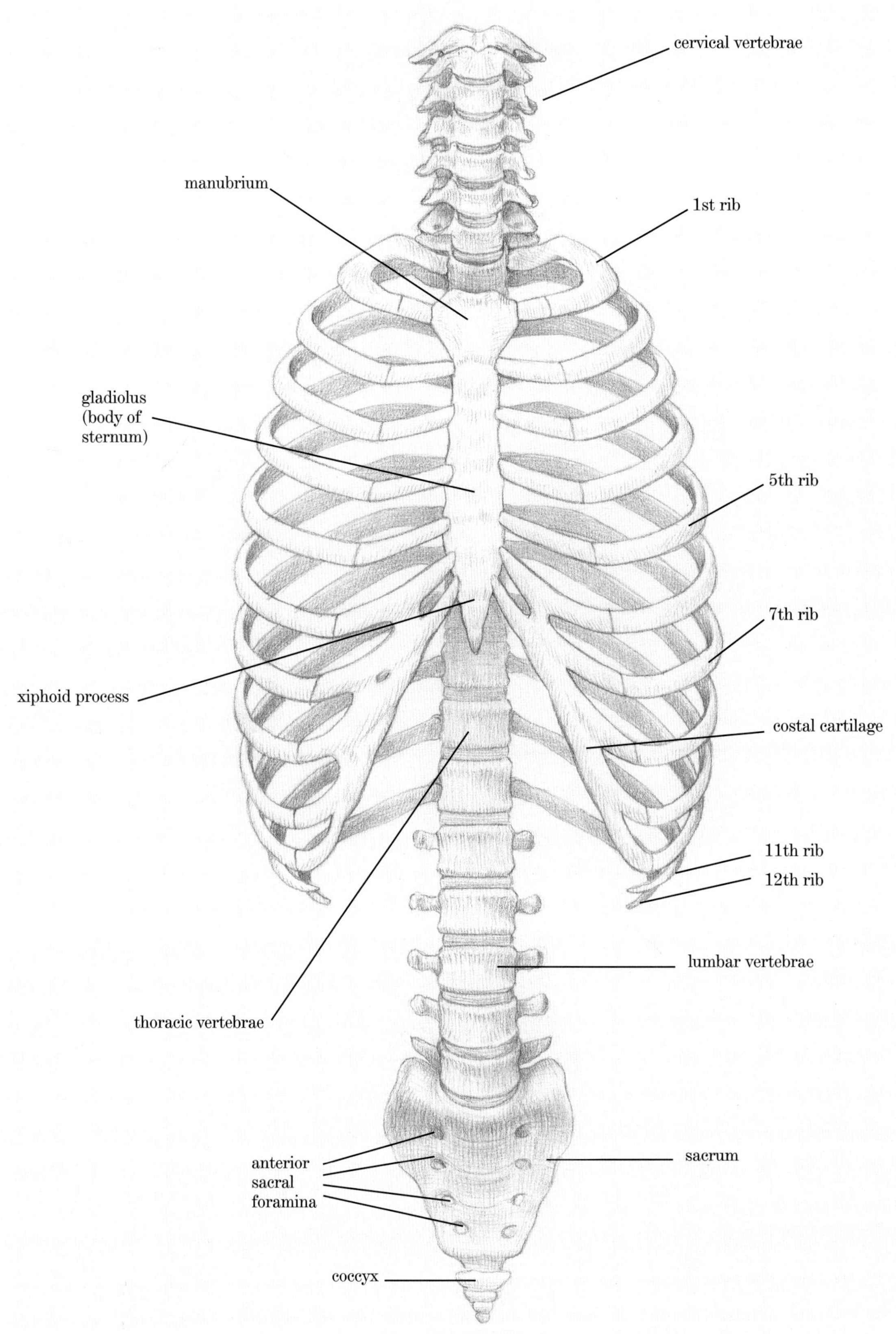

THE RIBCAGE AND SPINE—ANTERIOR VIEW

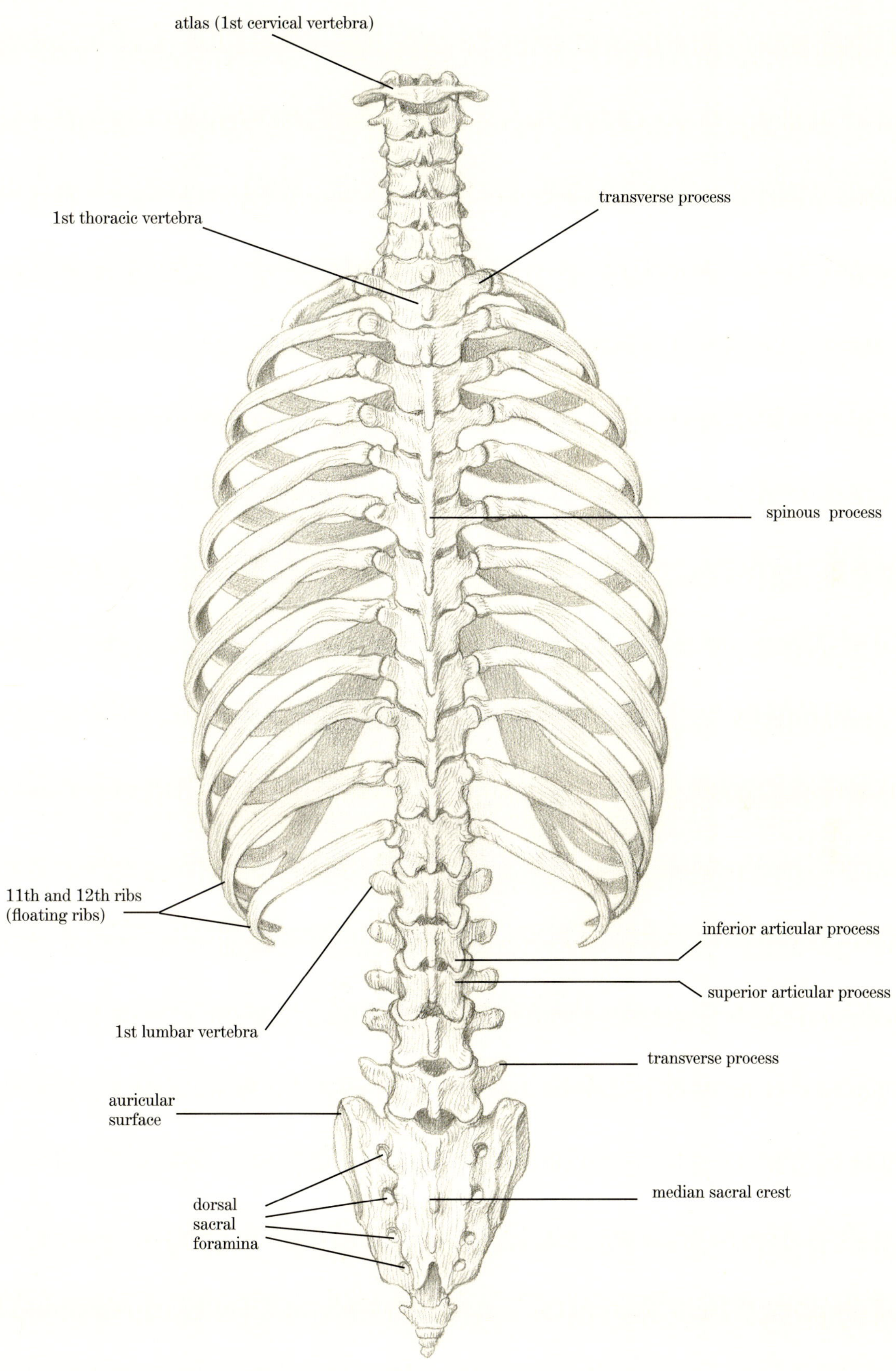

THE RIBCAGE AND SPINE—POSTERIOR VIEW

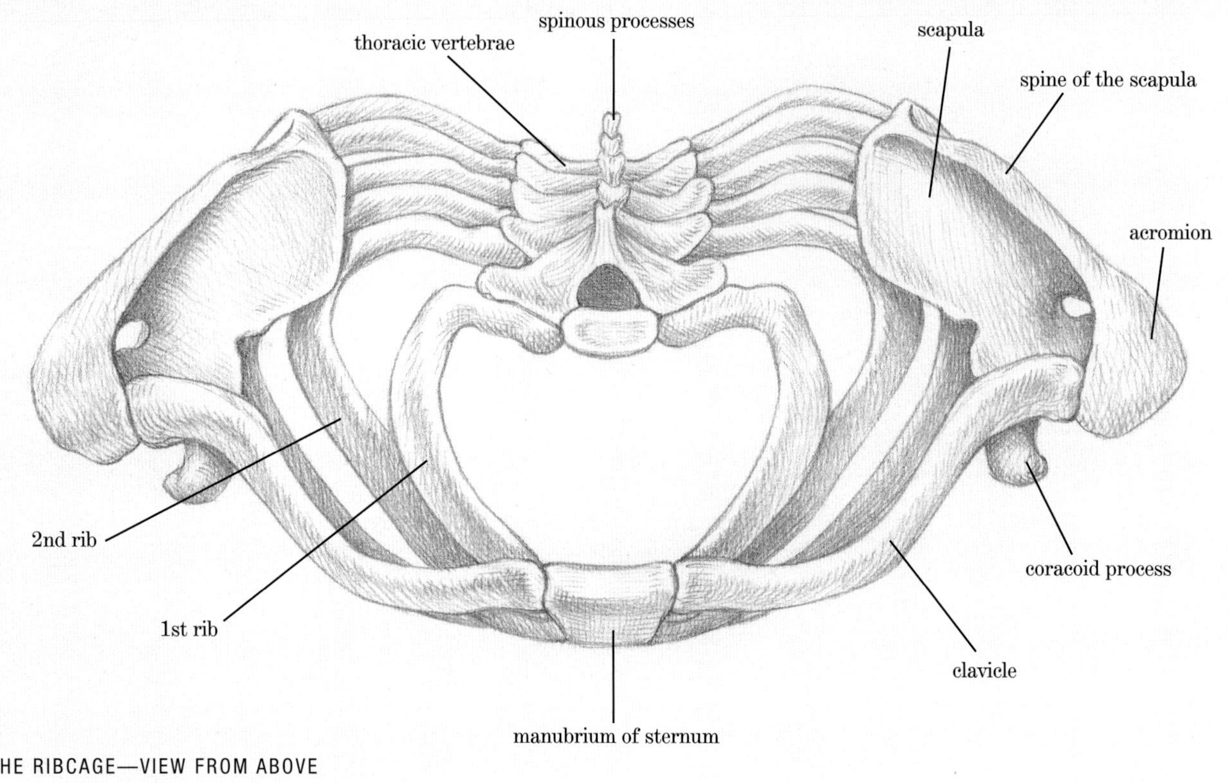

THE RIBCAGE—VIEW FROM ABOVE

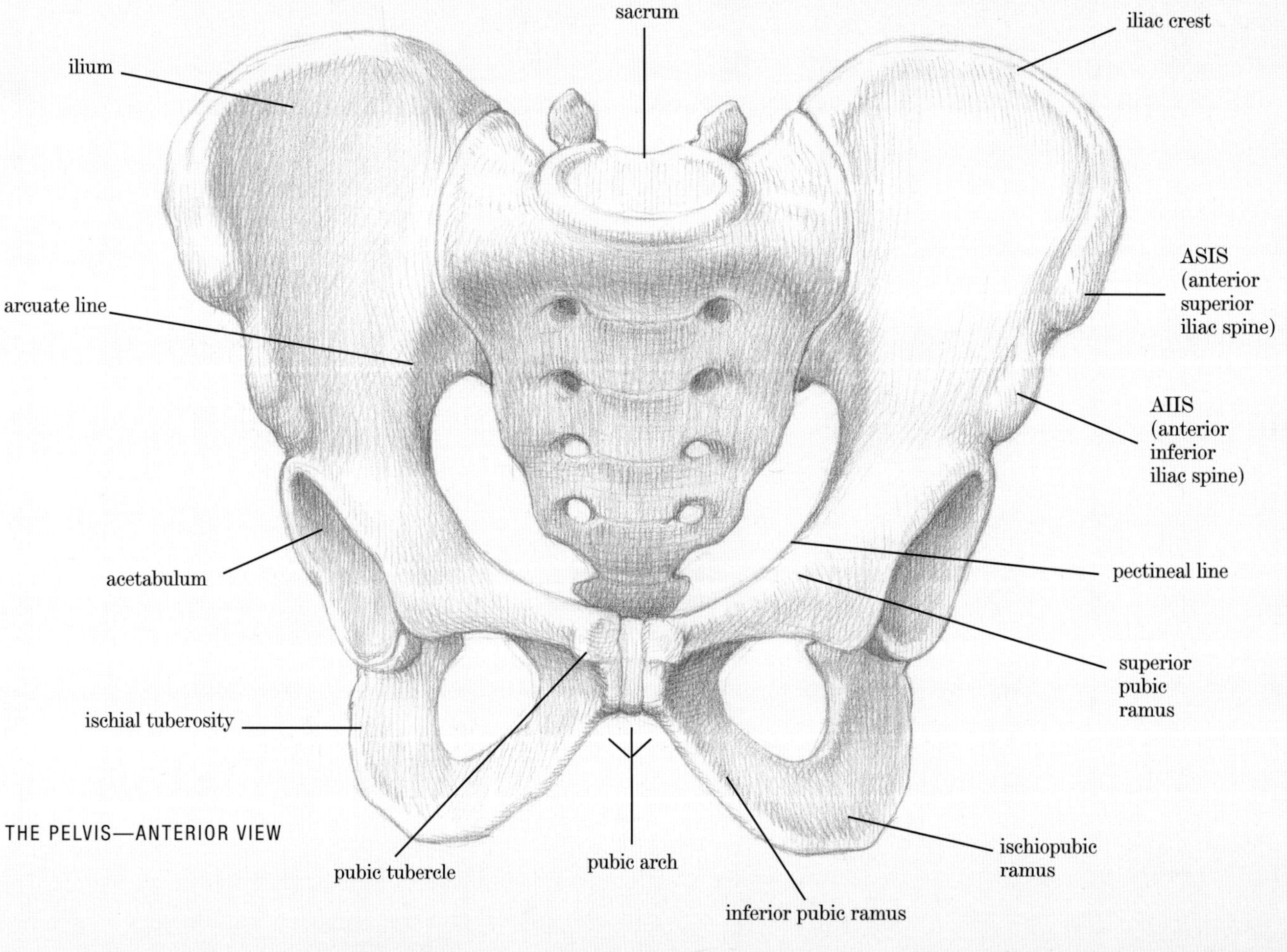

THE PELVIS—ANTERIOR VIEW

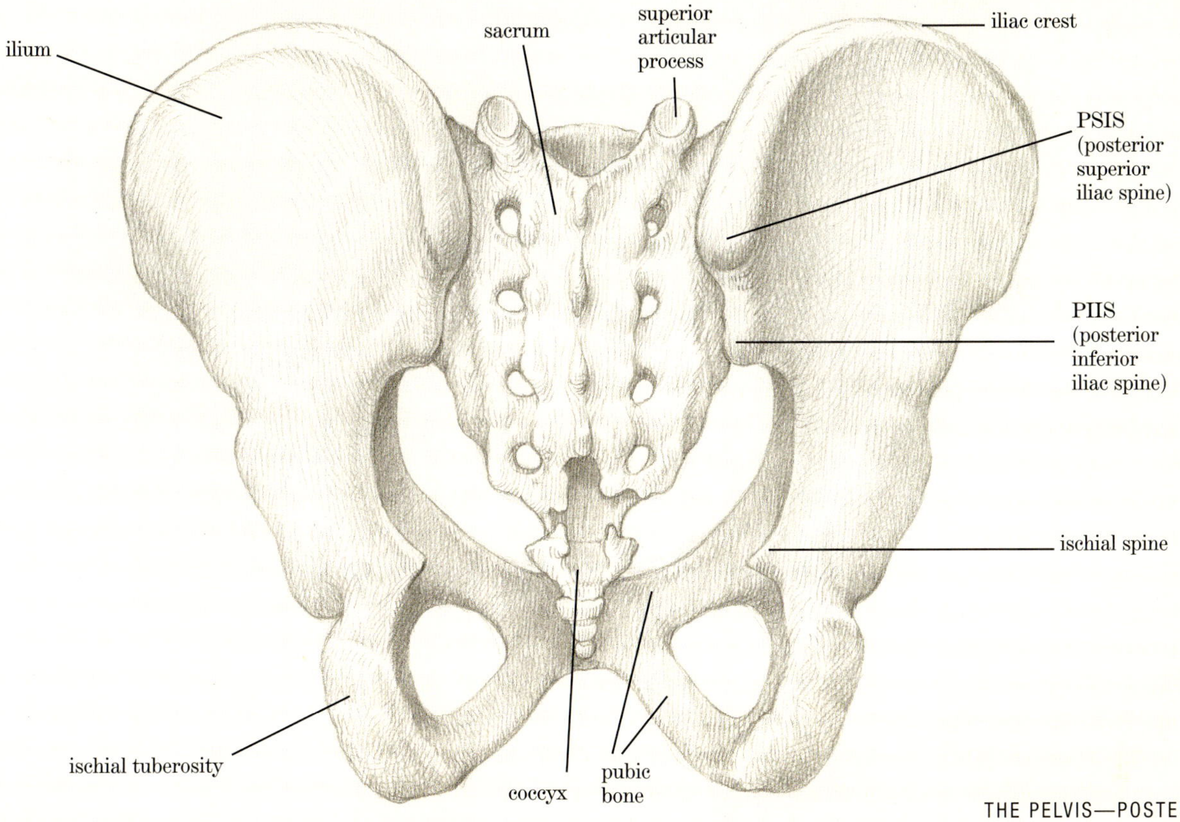

ilium

sacrum

superior
articular
process

iliac crest

PSIS
(posterior
superior
iliac spine)

PIIS
(posterior
inferior
iliac spine)

ischial spine

ischial tuberosity

coccyx

pubic
bone

THE PELVIS—POSTERIOR VIEW

THE PELVIS—LATERAL VIEW

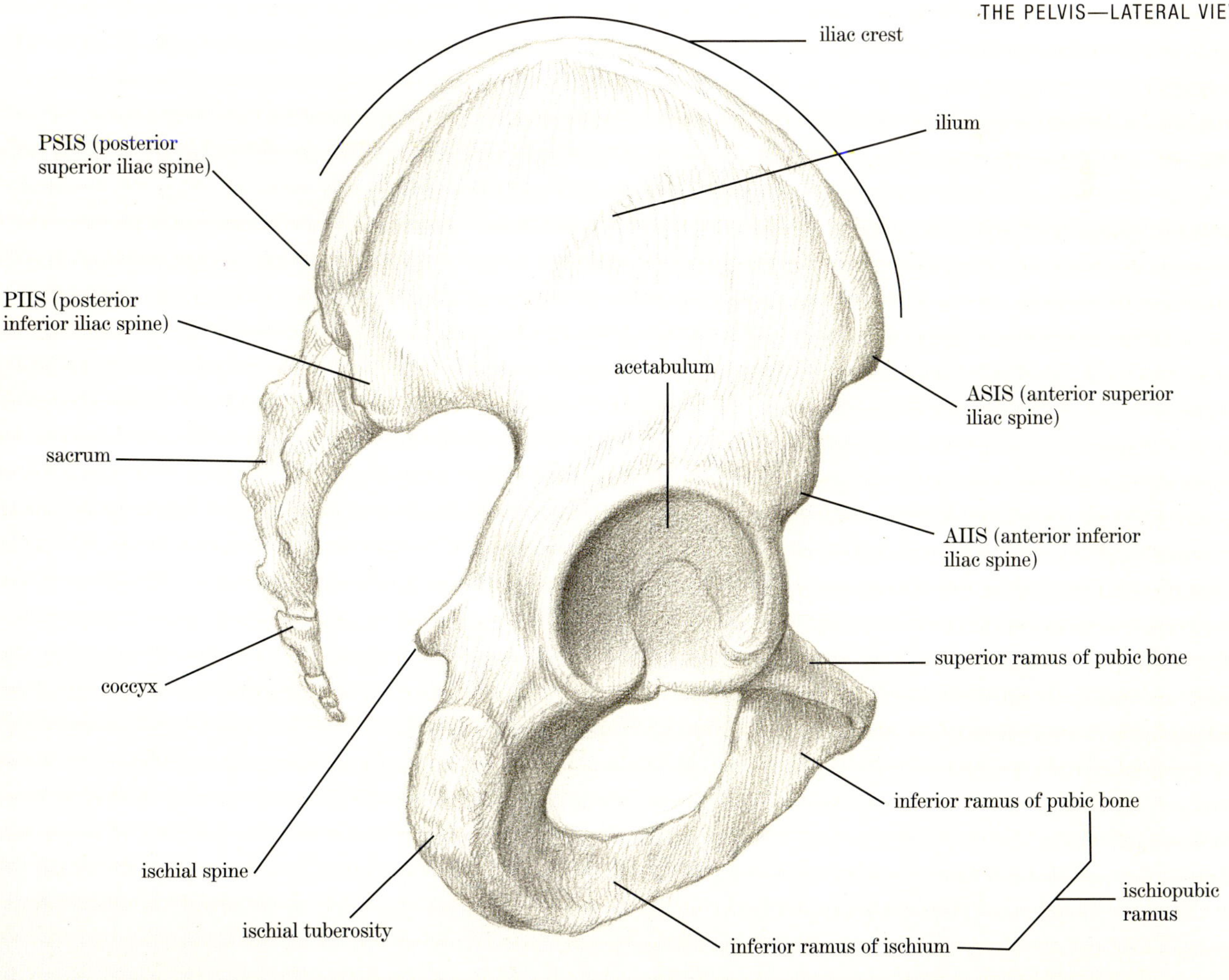

iliac crest

ilium

PSIS (posterior
superior iliac spine)

PIIS (posterior
inferior iliac spine)

acetabulum

ASIS (anterior superior
iliac spine)

sacrum

AIIS (anterior inferior
iliac spine)

coccyx

superior ramus of pubic bone

ischial spine

inferior ramus of pubic bone

ischiopubic
ramus

ischial tuberosity

inferior ramus of ischium

BONES OF THE APPENDICULAR SKELETON

The images in this section depict the bones of the appendicular skeleton. Remember that the bones of the upper limb include the clavicle (collarbone) and the scapula (shoulder blade).

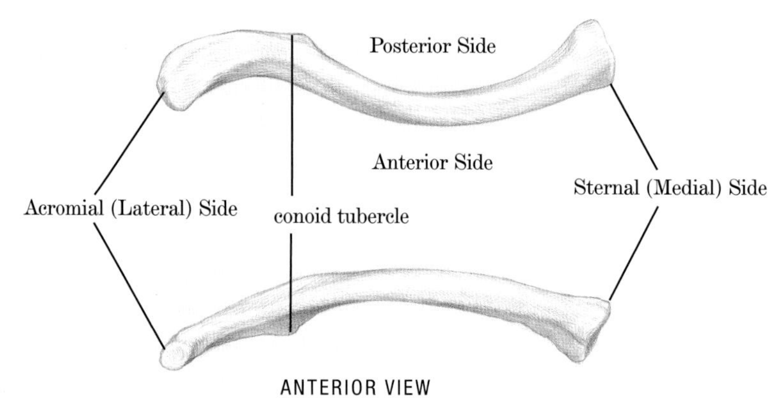

THE CLAVICLE—SUPERIOR AND ANTERIOR VIEWS
The right clavicle is depicted.

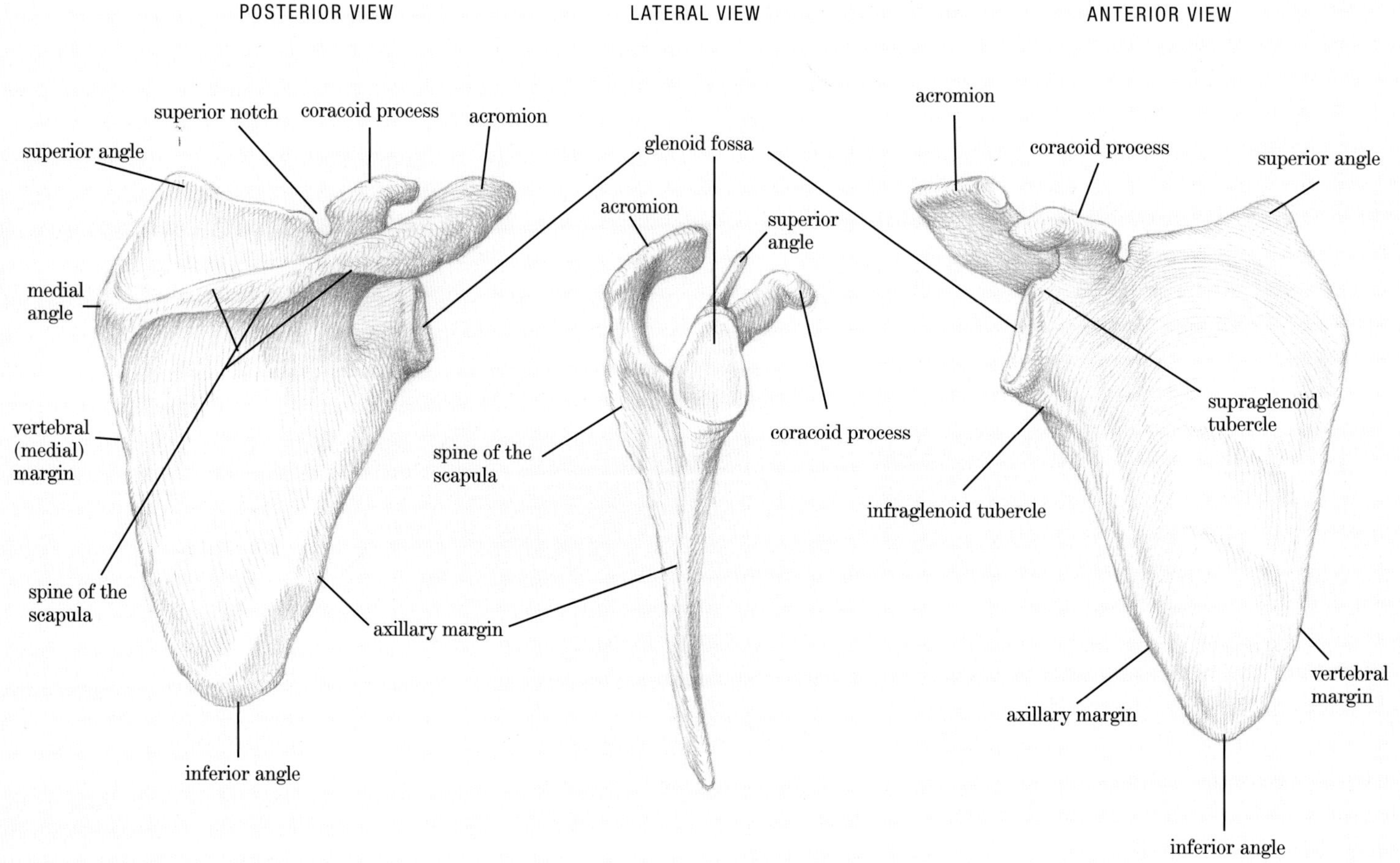

THE SCAPULA—POSTERIOR, LATERAL, AND ANTERIOR VIEWS
The right scapula is depicted.

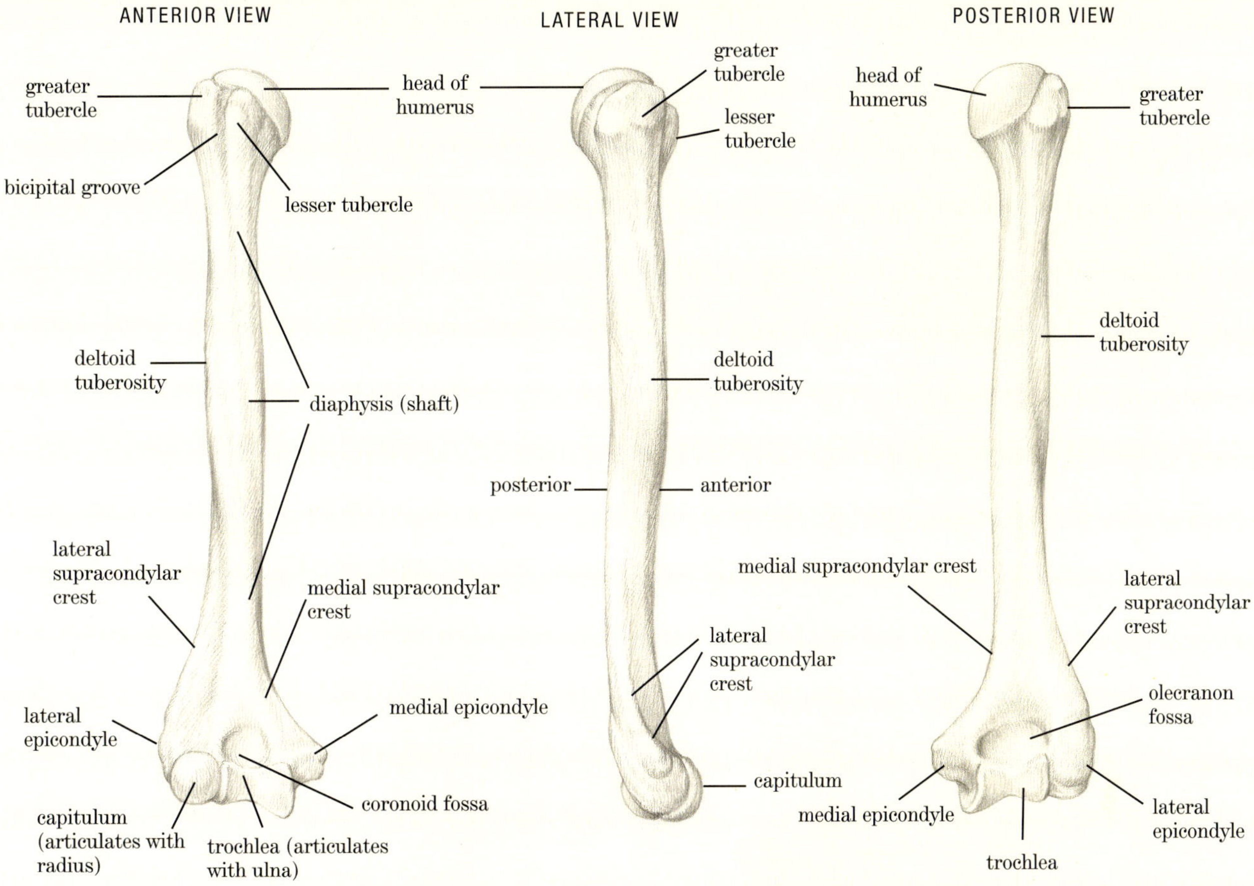

THE HUMERUS—ANTERIOR, LATERAL, AND POSTERIOR VIEW
The right humerus is depicted.

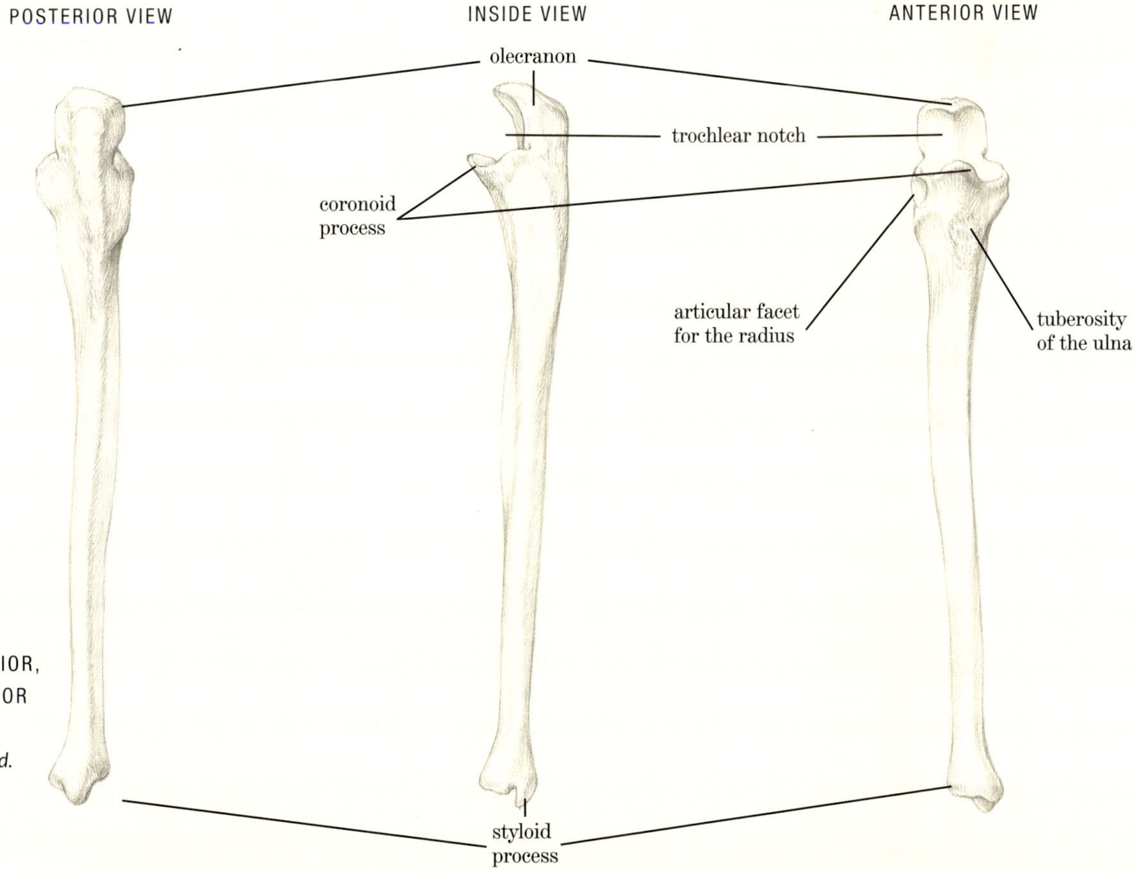

THE ULNA—POSTERIOR, INSIDE, AND ANTERIOR VIEWS
The right ulna is depicted.

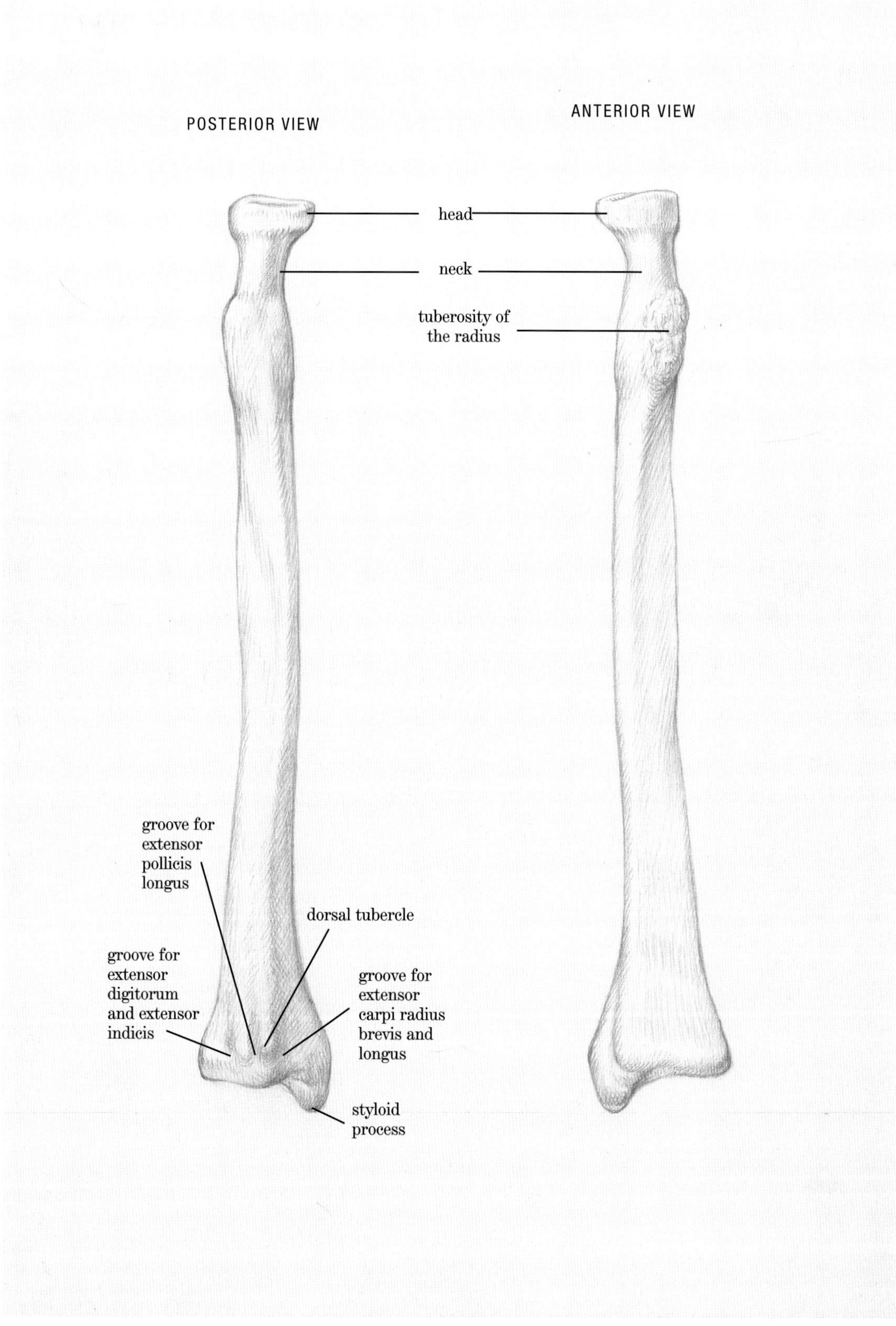

THE RADIUS—POSTERIOR AND ANTERIOR VIEWS

The right radius is depicted.

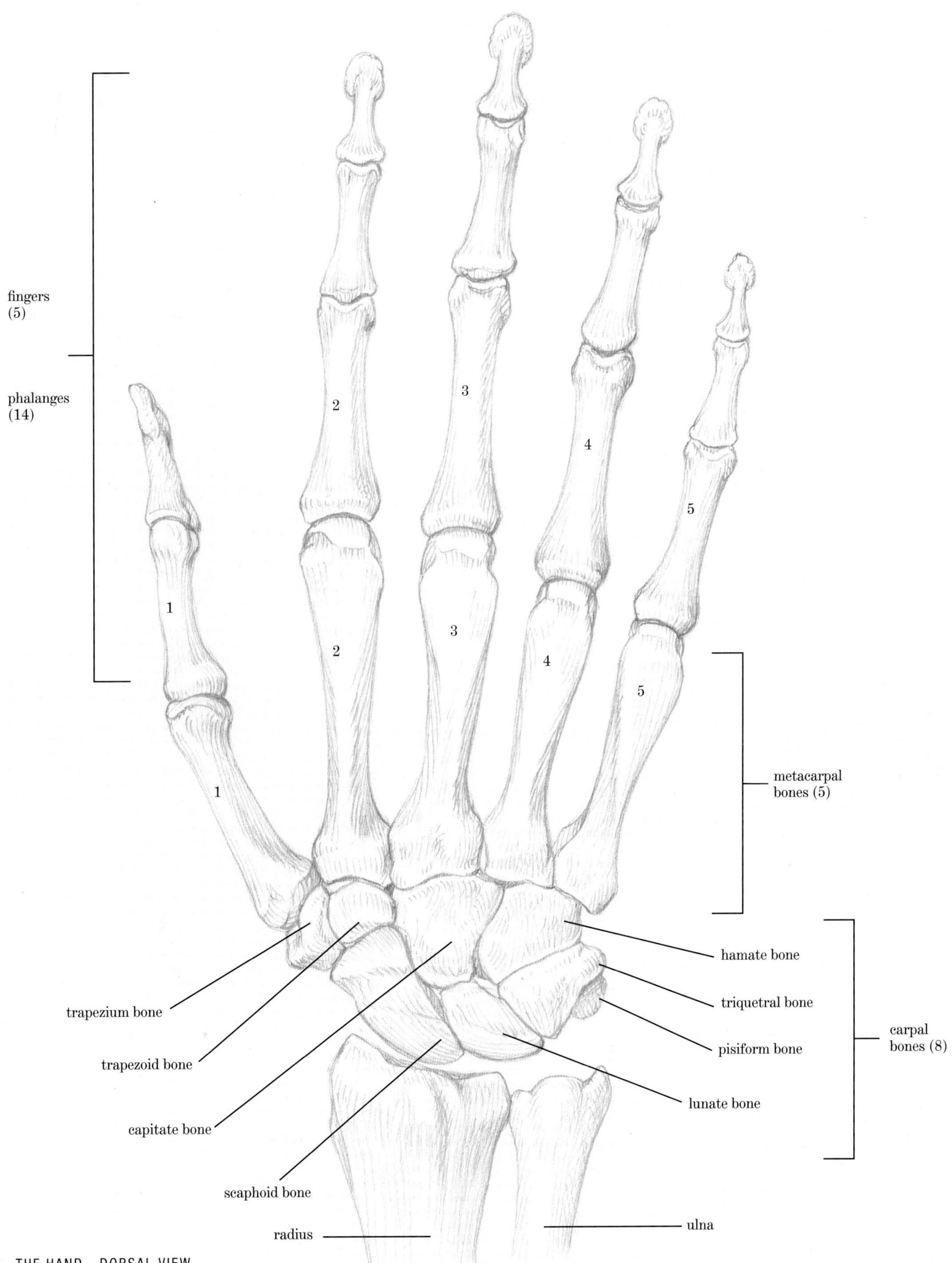

THE HAND—DORSAL VIEW

The right hand is depicted. Numbering indicates the standard way in which the finger bones, including those of the thumb, are identified.

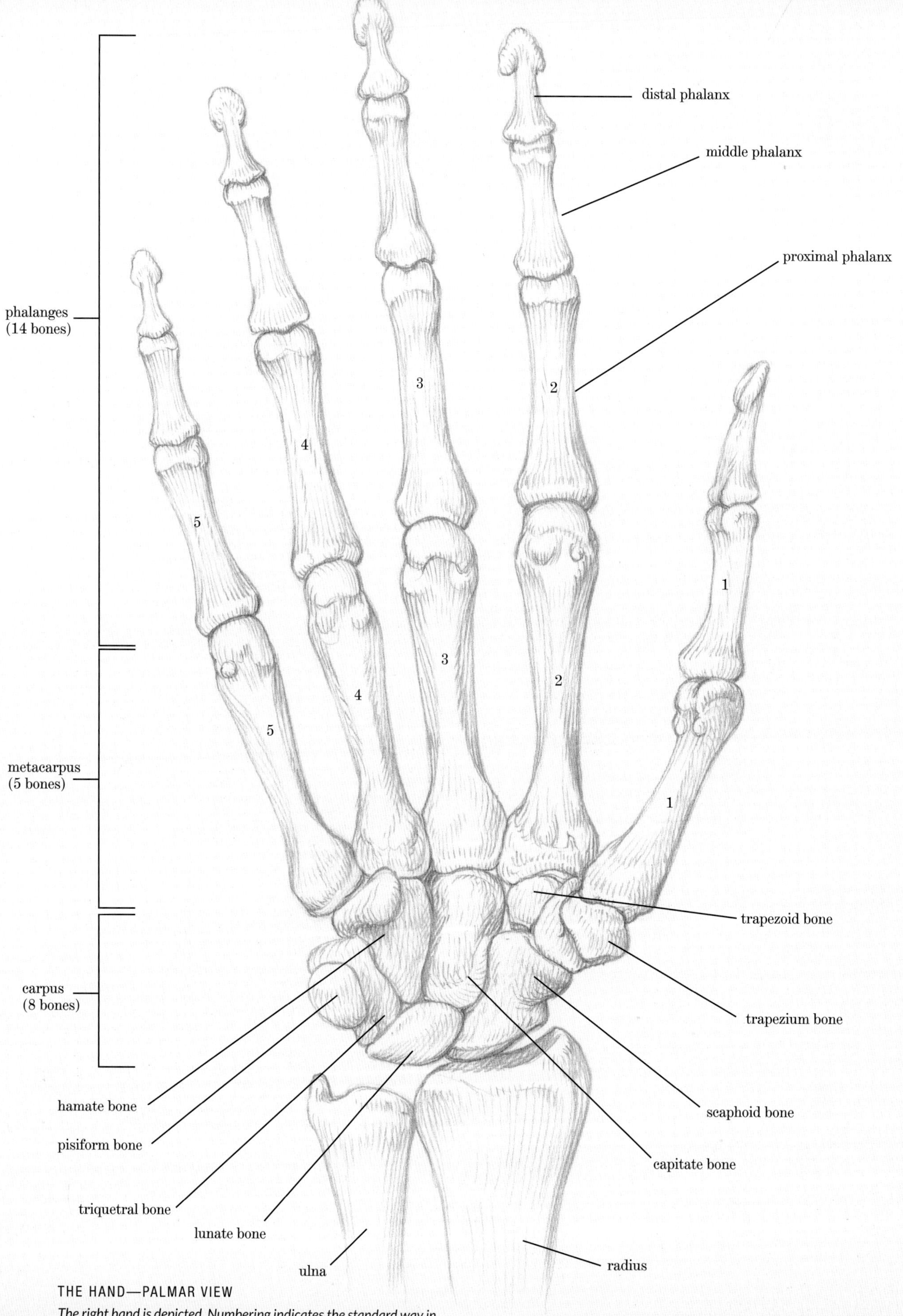

THE HAND—PALMAR VIEW

The right hand is depicted. Numbering indicates the standard way in which the finger bones, including those of the thumb, are identified.

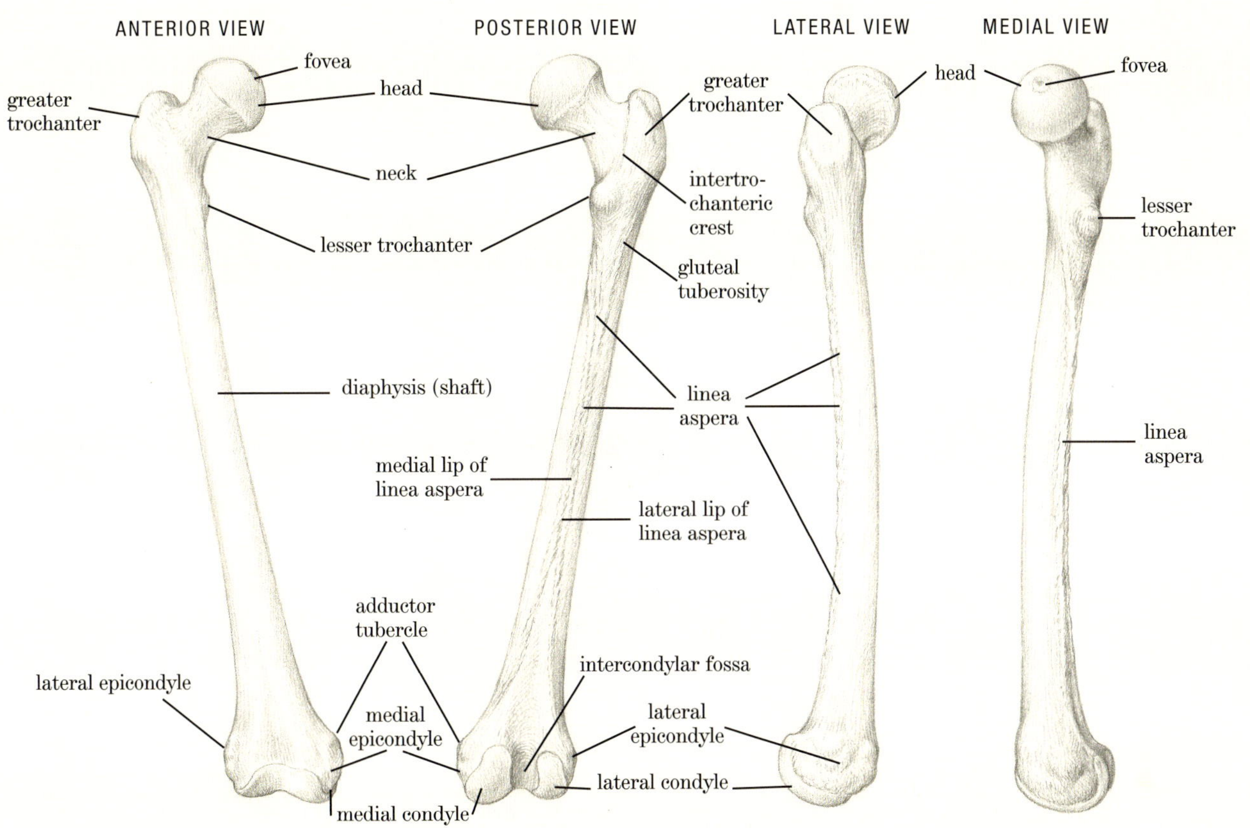

THE FEMUR—ANTERIOR, POSTERIOR, LATERAL, AND MEDIAL VIEWS

The right femur is depicted.

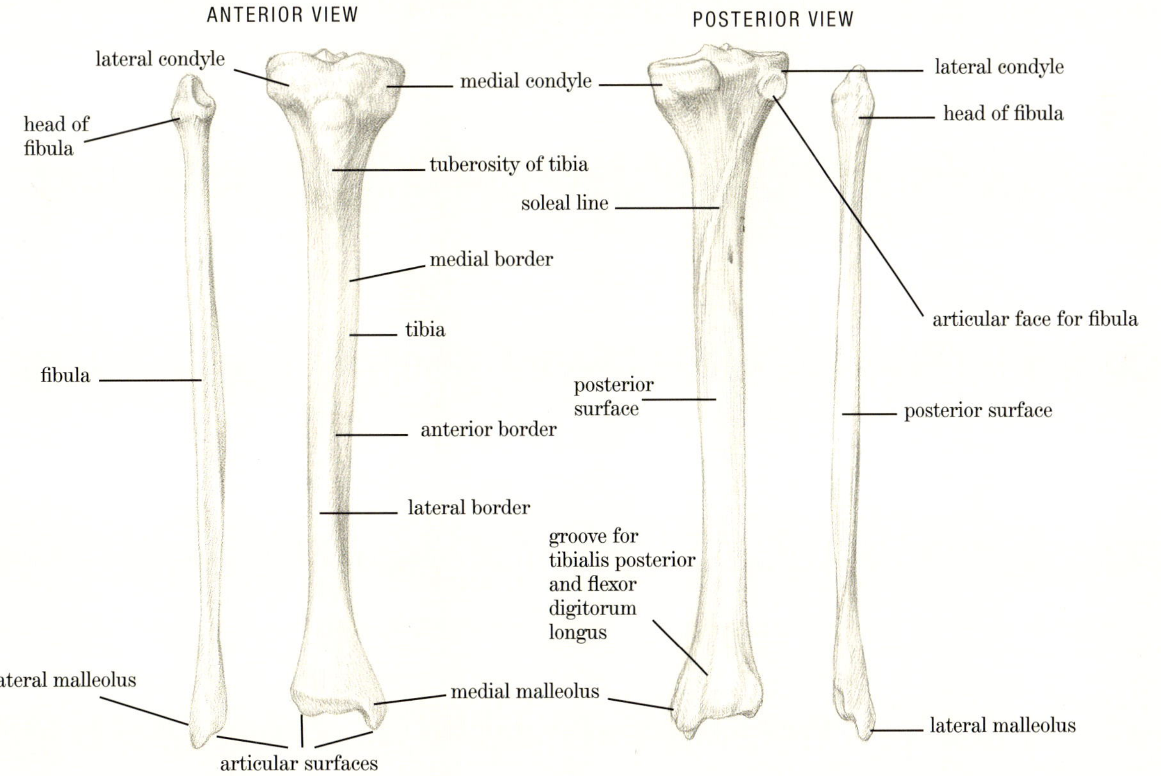

THE TIBIA AND FIBULA—ANTERIOR AND POSTERIOR VIEWS

The right tibia and fibula are depicted.

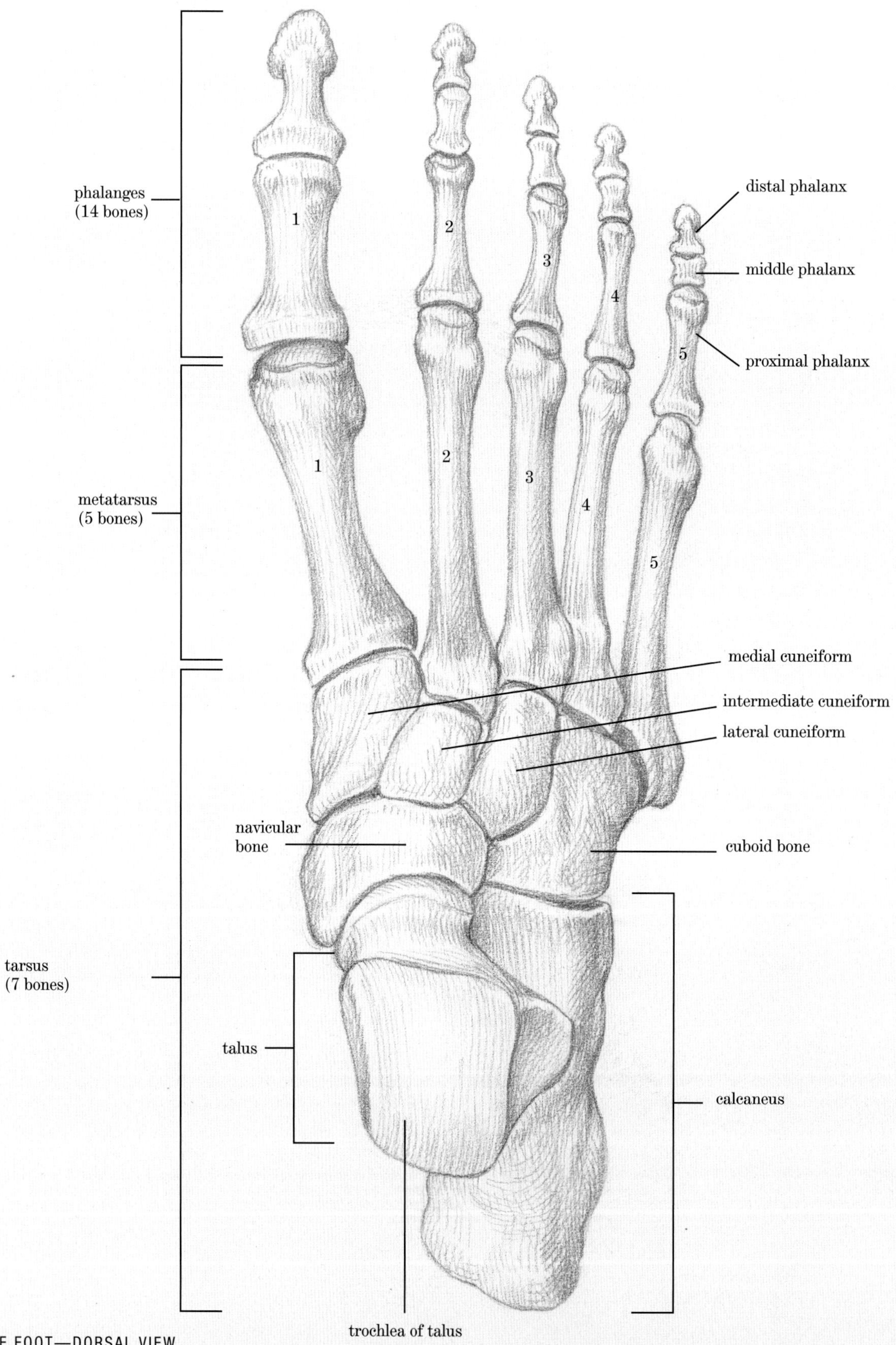

THE FOOT—DORSAL VIEW

The right foot is depicted. Numbering indicates the standard way in which the toe bones are identified.

THE FOOT—PLANTAR VIEW
The right foot is depicted.

phalanges
(14 bones)

metatarsus
(5 bones)

tarsus
(7 bones)

sesamoid bones

lateral cuneiform
medial cuneiform
intermediate cuneiform
navicular
talus
tuberosity of the calcaneus

tuberosity of the
5th metatarsal
cuboid
calcaneus

1
2
3
4
5

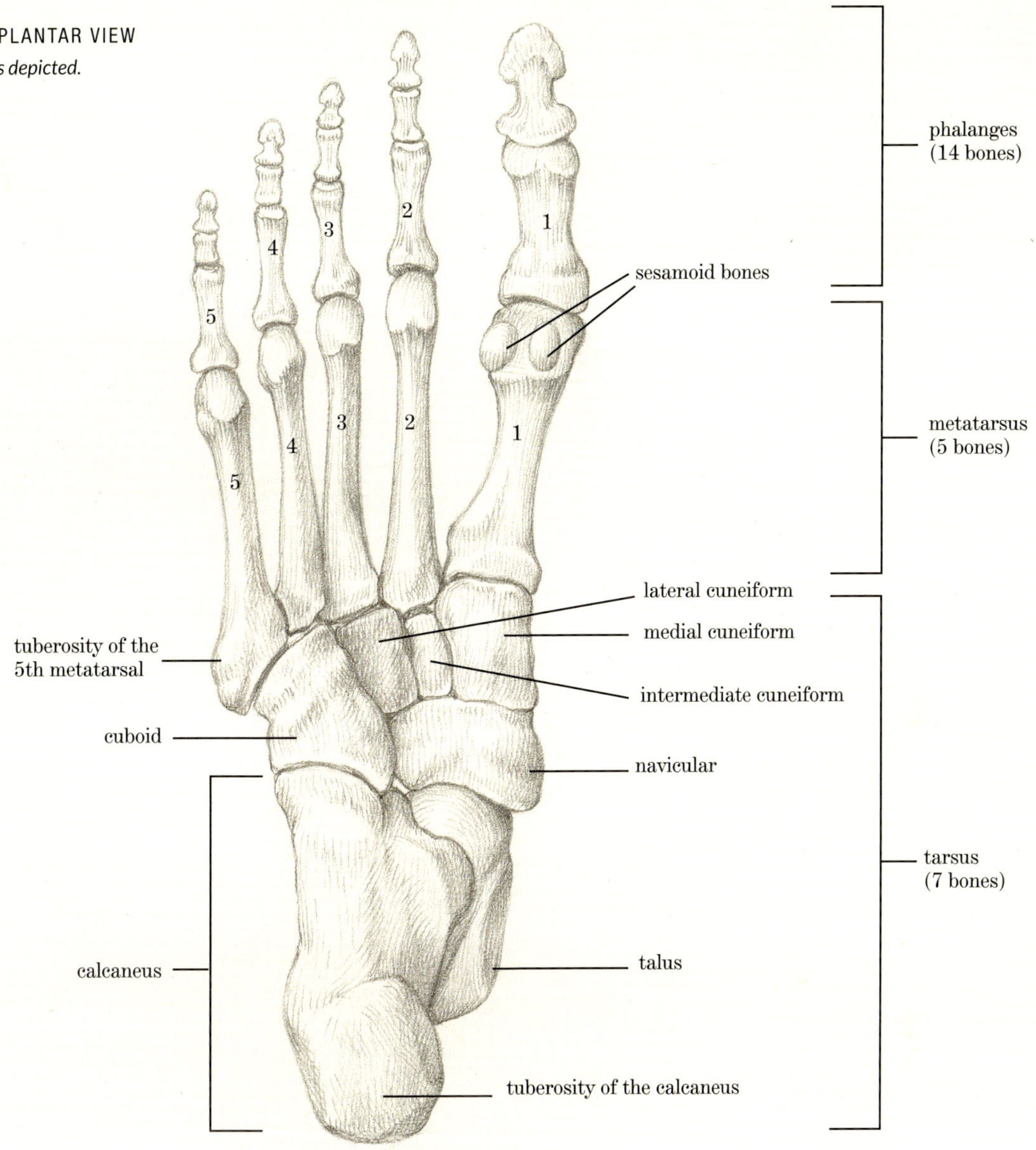

THE FOOT—LATERAL VIEW
The right foot is depicted.

tarsus
metatarsus
phalanges

talus
navicular
intermediate
cuneiform
metatarsal bones

trochlea

calcaneus
cuboid
lateral cuneiform

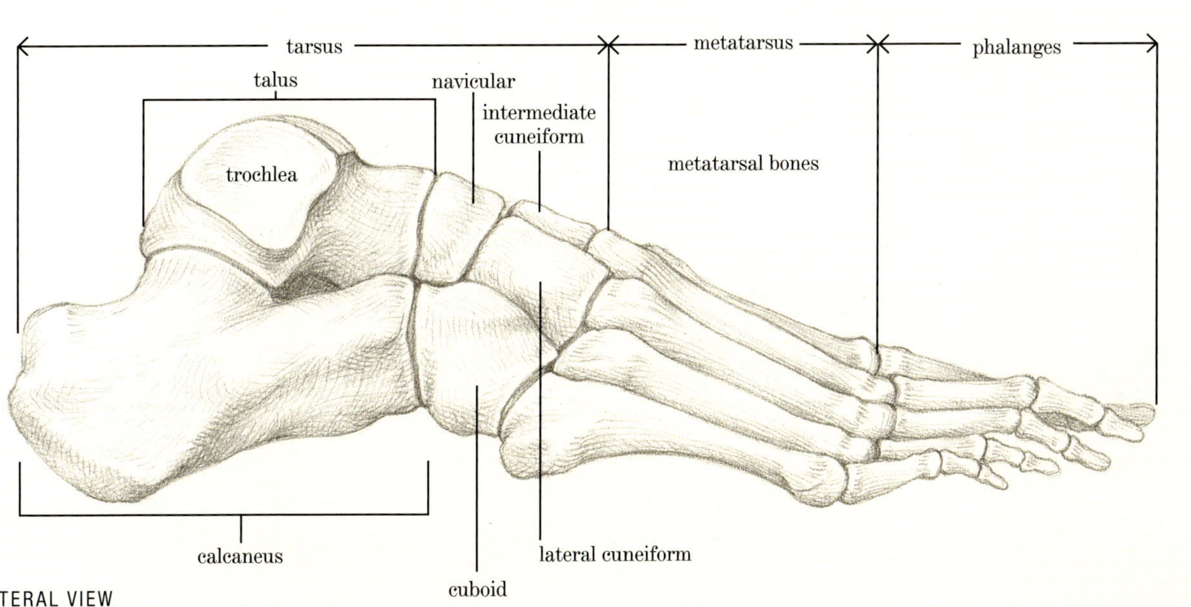

EXERCISES

The human skeleton can be an intimidating subject. Learning the names of the bones and reducing their complicated forms to essential patterns can help you master them.

EXERCISE 1: MEMORIZE THE BONES

Try memorizing the placement and names of all the bones of the human body. The figure shows an unlabeled skeleton (with a profile of the soft tissues that surround the bones). You can use this drawing for practice. Make a copy and label the bones, then compare your labels with those in the figures on pages 84–87.

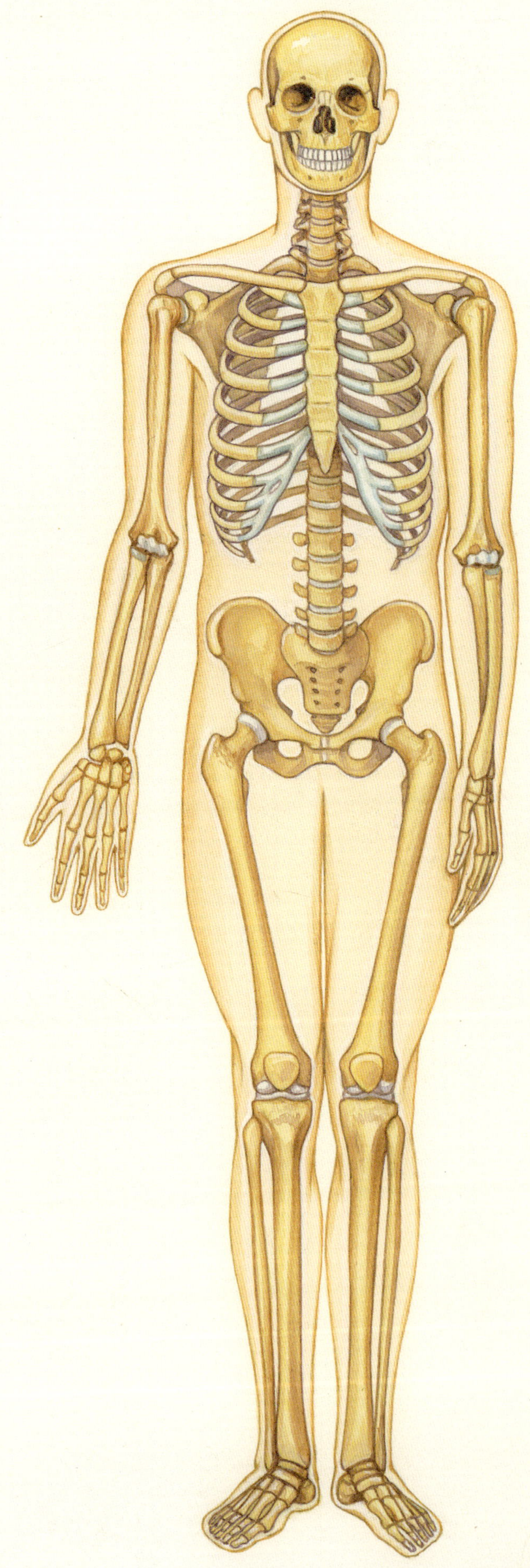

SKELETON FOR MEMORIZATION PRACTICE

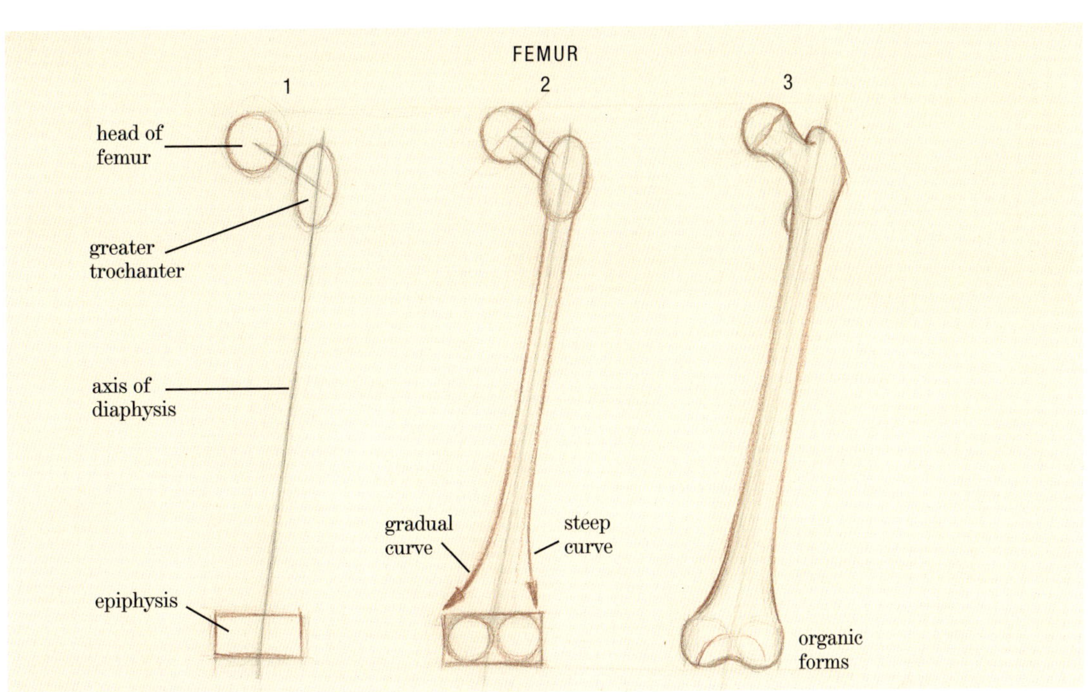

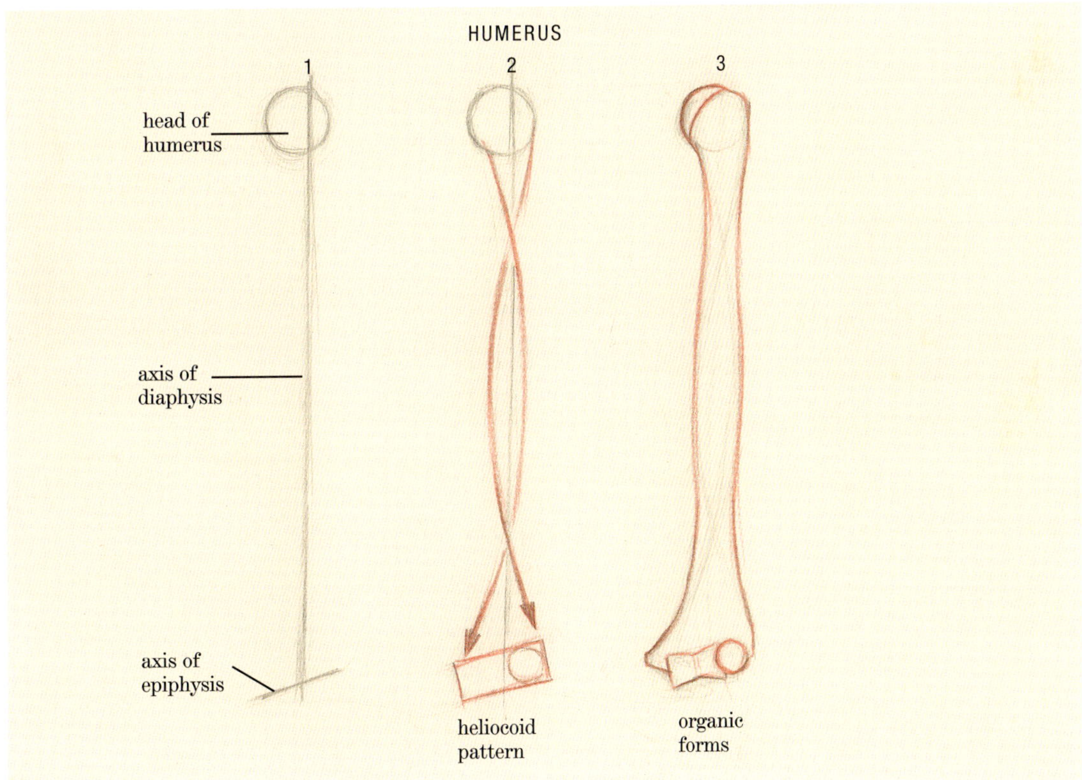

EXERCISE 2: PRACTICE DRAWING LONG BONES

The two images above show how you can approach analyzing and drawing long bones—specifically, the femur and humerus—by progressively describing their essential and specific characteristics: the angles of their axes, the proportions of their various parts, and specific rhythms such as the spiraling patterns of the bone ridges of the shaft of the humerus. Try following each of these progressions yourself.

above
LONG BONES: STRUCTURE, RHYTHMS, AND PATTERNS

USE A BLENDING STUMP

Drawing with a blending stump dipped in powdered pigment is a good way to transition from line drawing to tonal drawing, because the stump will not produce sharp lines. With the stump, you can start with a relatively thin line and end with a very wide line in one continuous stroke. You can quickly obtain powdered pigment by rubbing a conte crayon or colored pencil on a piece of sandpaper. The figures here show examples of the technique.

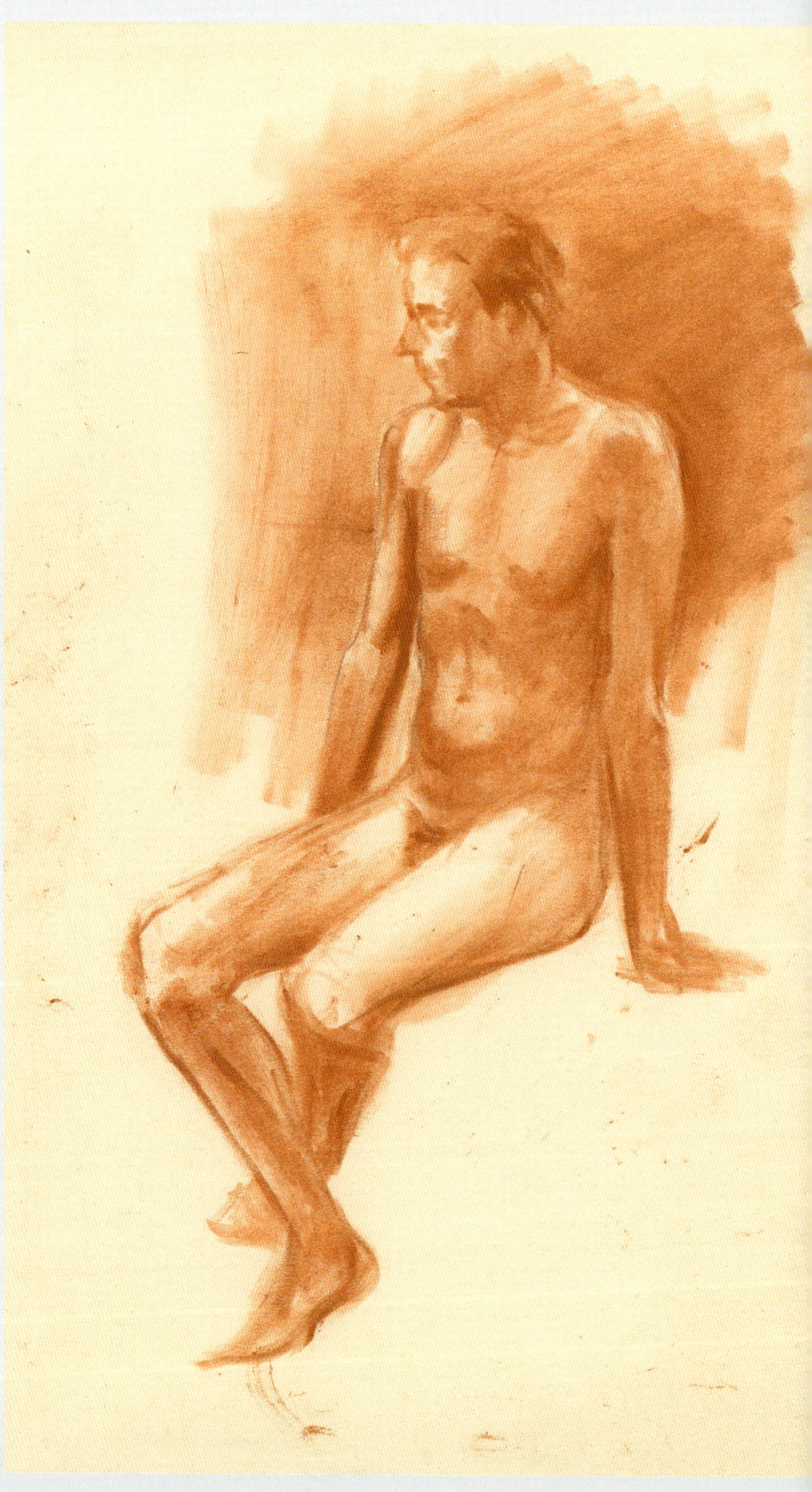

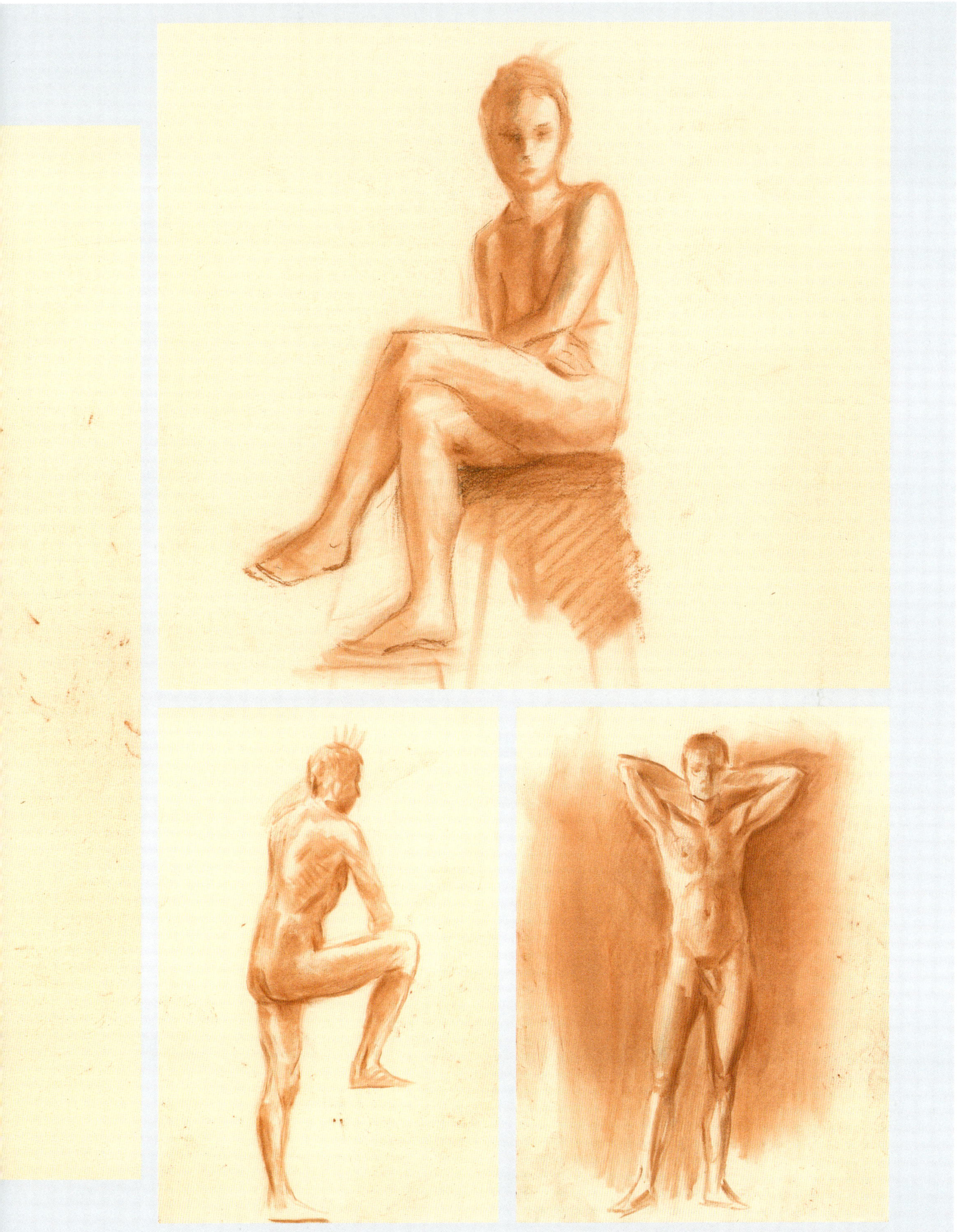

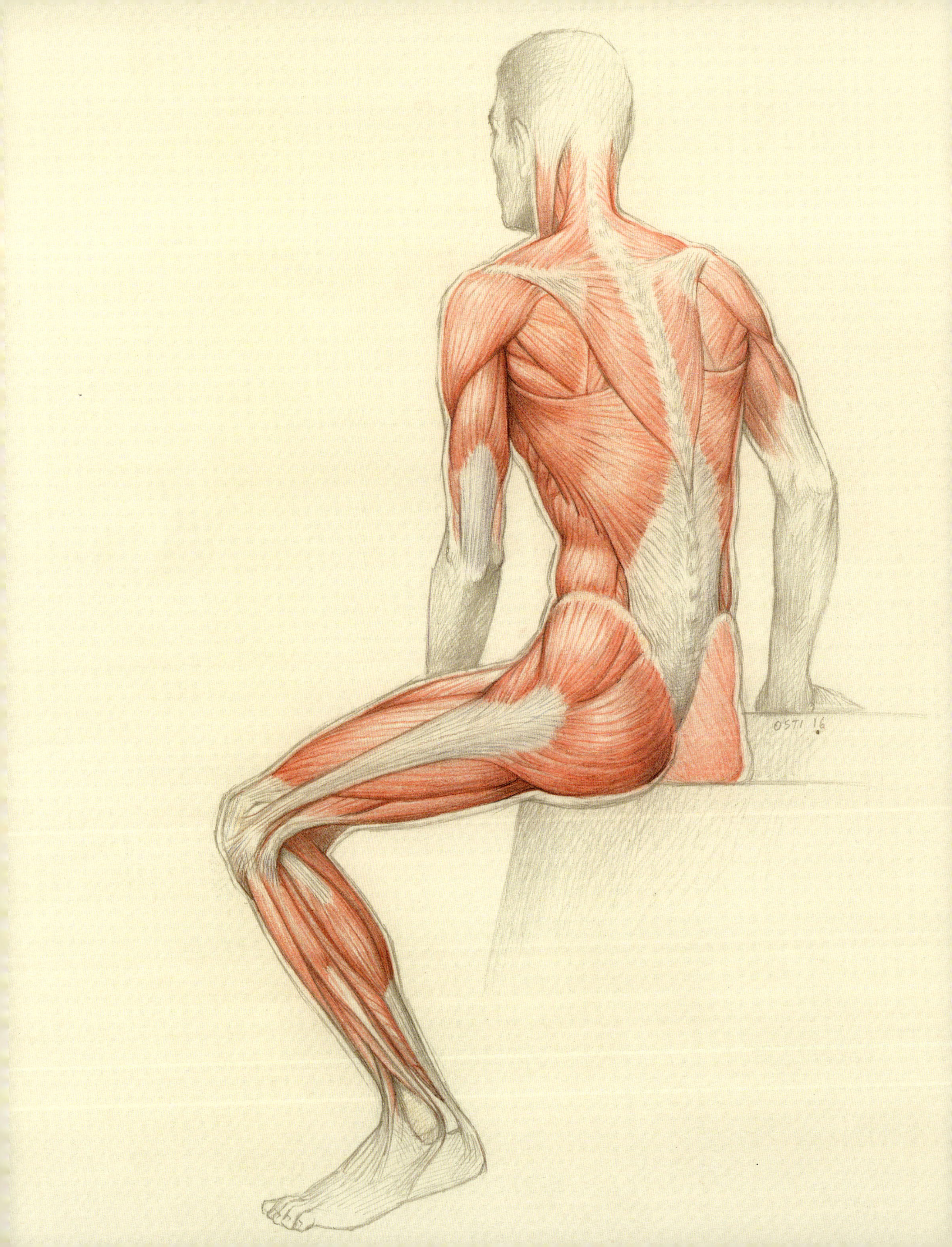
OSTI 16

Chapter 4

THE MUSCLES

For the purposes of this book, I have grouped muscles of the human body into three layers: the superficial layer, which are those muscles nearest the body's surface; the intermediate layer; and the deep layer. Generally, anatomical charts present the muscles in this order, which is comparable to a dissection process that starts with the more superficial muscles and gradually removes them to gain access to the layers below. But because I want to continue the additive process I've used in chapters 2 and 3, I've chosen the reverse approach, starting from the bare skeleton and gradually adding the deep muscles and then the intermediate and, finally, the superficial layers.

This method has distinctive advantages: It can, for example, be followed to create a three-dimensional écorché figure in clay or other plastic material. (An écorché figure is one from which the skin has been removed so that the muscles can be seen.) It will also help you to understand the deep connections of the muscles with the skeleton and how groups of muscles are organized. Finally, it shows you how deep muscles can have an influence on more superficial muscles. For instance, the form of a flat superficial muscle such as the latissimus dorsii (the broad muscle of the back, which bodybuilders call the "lats") is in part influenced by thicker, deeper muscles such as the teres major and the erector spinae. Understanding the complexity of the muscular forms will help you create more correct, three-dimensional, and beautiful drawings.

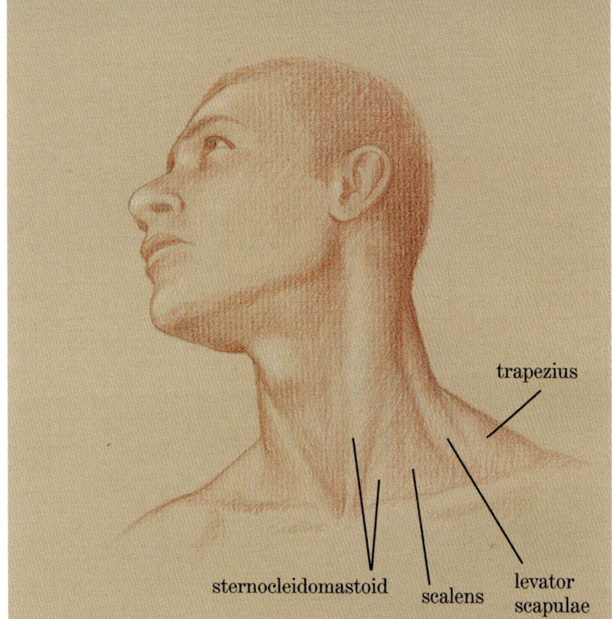

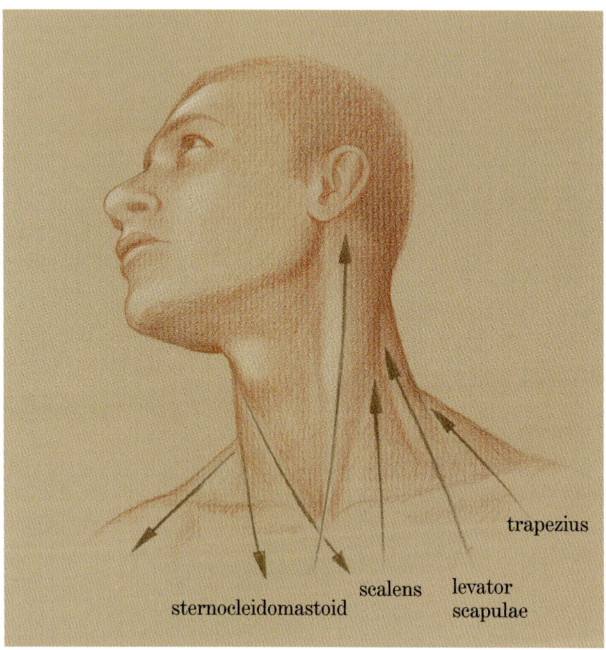

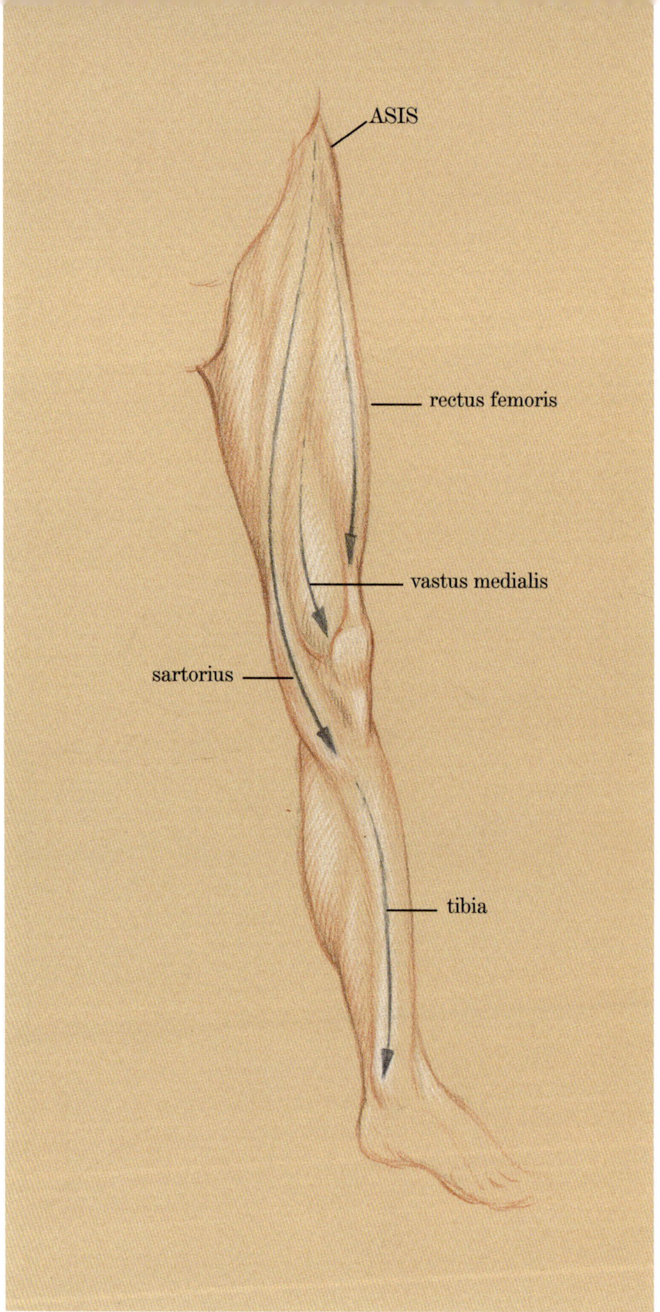

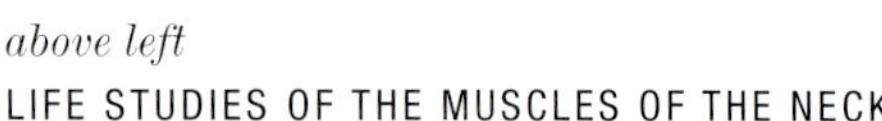

above left
LIFE STUDIES OF THE MUSCLES OF THE NECK

above right
THE RHYTHM OF MUSCULAR FORMS

Anatomists and figurative artists study the human body with different ends: The goal of the anatomist is to enhance medical science, but the artist "dissects" the body for aesthetic purposes—to understand its language, recognize the harmonies and rhythms created by contiguous groups of muscles, and to see the connections between forms that are distant from each other. For example, the drawings in the figure at left, above, show how the muscles and volumes of the neck create a beautiful spiraling pattern that is connected to function but that also illustrates a typical rhythm of the body that is of great interest to the artist.

That rhythmic interplay can also be seen in the drawing of the leg, above. And the drawings opposite show another characteristic of muscles that is of equal interest to the artist: Muscles are not flat structures but have three-dimensionality as they wrap around bones and other muscles.

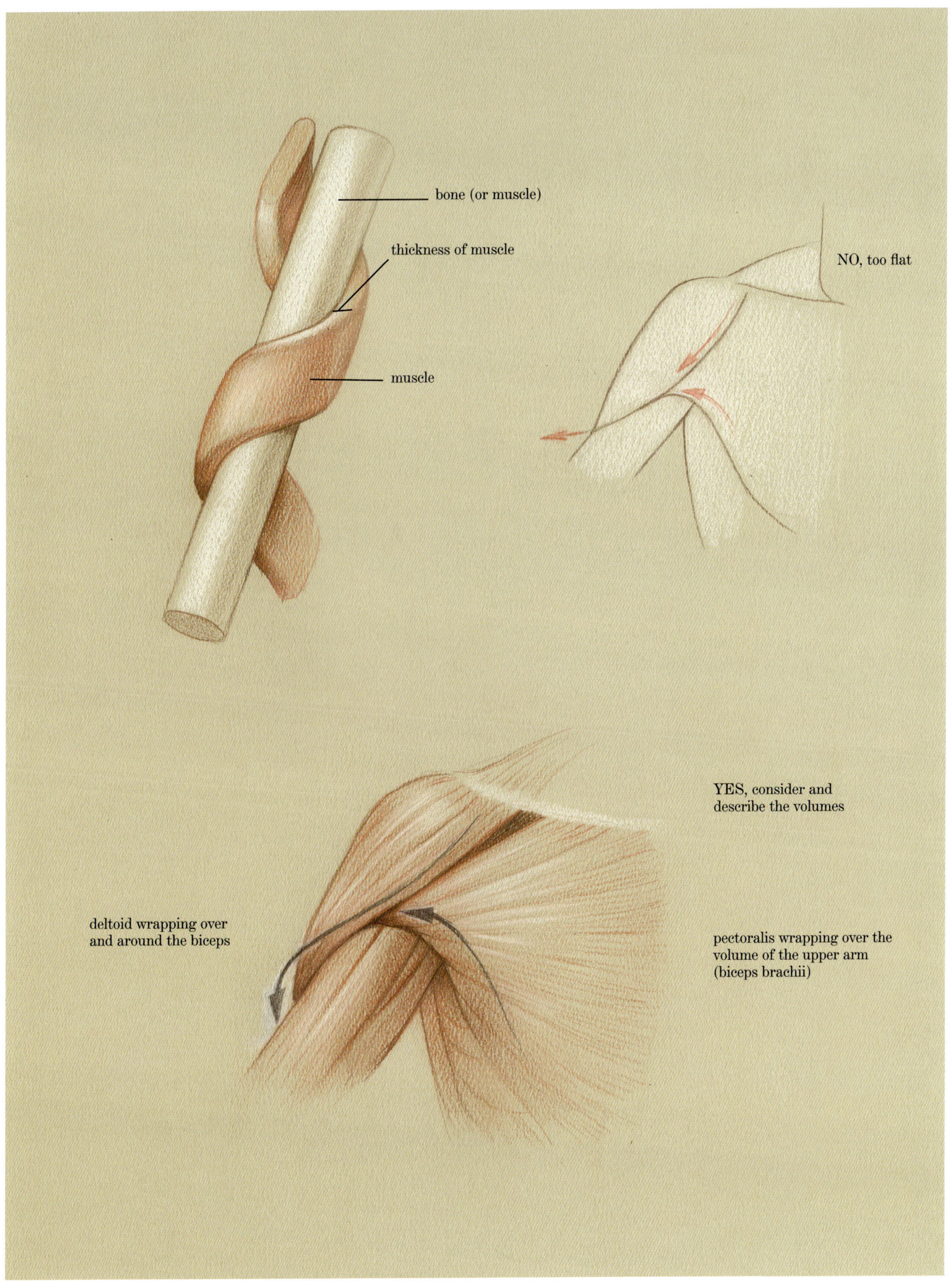

bone (or muscle)
thickness of muscle
muscle
NO, too flat
YES, consider and
describe the volumes
deltoid wrapping over
and around the biceps
pectoralis wrapping over the
volume of the upper arm
(biceps brachii)

SKELETAL AND MUSCULAR STRUCTURES

Unlike the number of bones in the human body, which can be easily counted, the number of muscles is very difficult to establish with precision. This difficulty has to do with individual variation to some extent, but it is mostly the result of disagreement among anatomists about how to organize the muscles. Depending on the anatomical authority, the human body contains anywhere from 320 pairs of muscles (i.e., 640 individual muscles) up to 420 pairs (840 individual muscles). The muscles described in this chapter do not represent all the muscles of the human body; I have omitted the deepest muscles as well as some others that do not produce a visible external volume. (The complex muscles of the head and face warrant separate treatment and are discussed in chapter 5.)

The figures on the following six pages, which show the superficial muscles of the male and female figure, are intended for a quick overall view of the muscles and their patterns and connections. Those are followed by three figures that show muscles and skeletal structures side by side to help you begin to connect the superficial muscular structure with the deep skeletal forms.

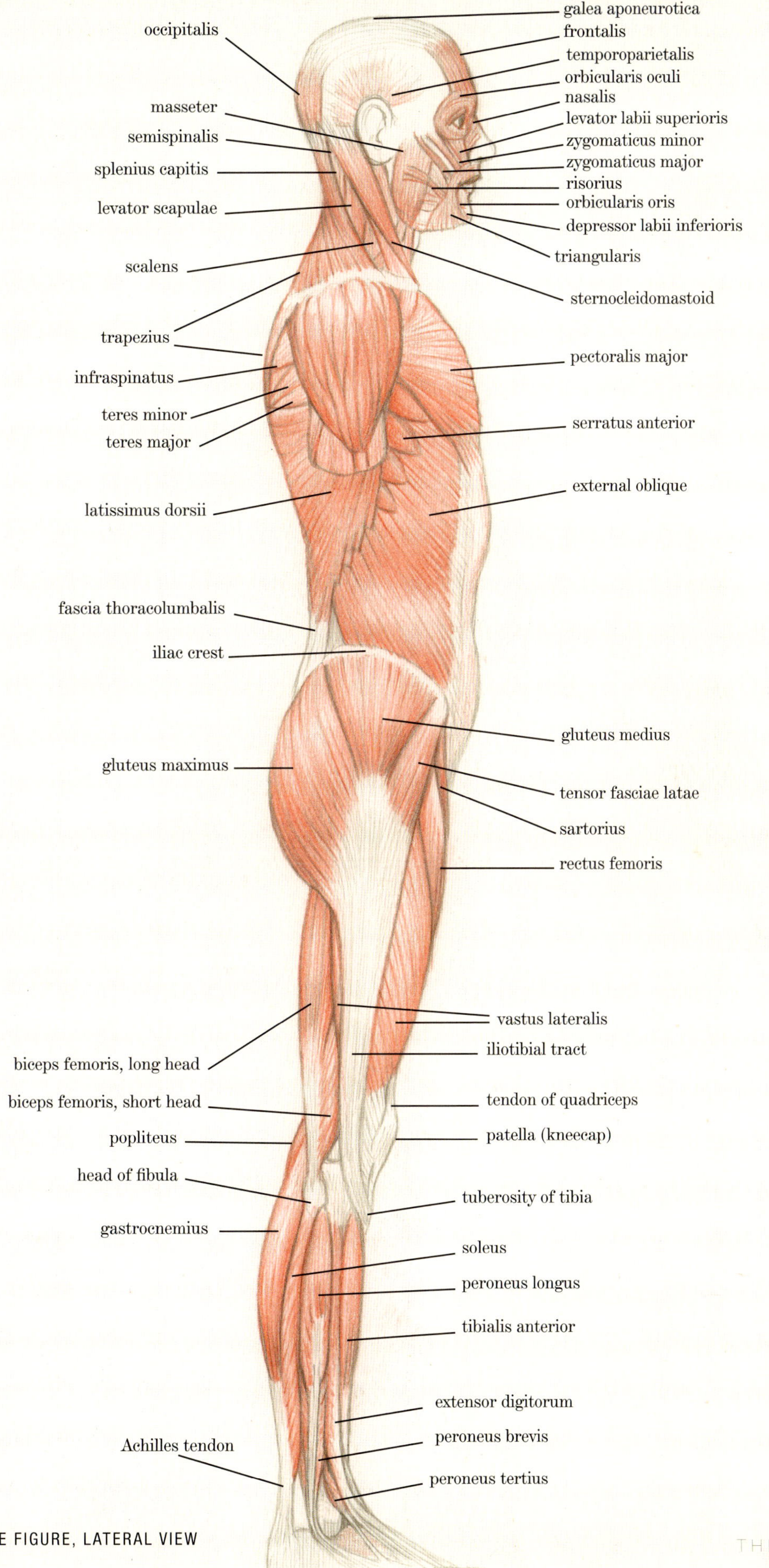

MUSCLES OF THE MALE FIGURE, LATERAL VIEW

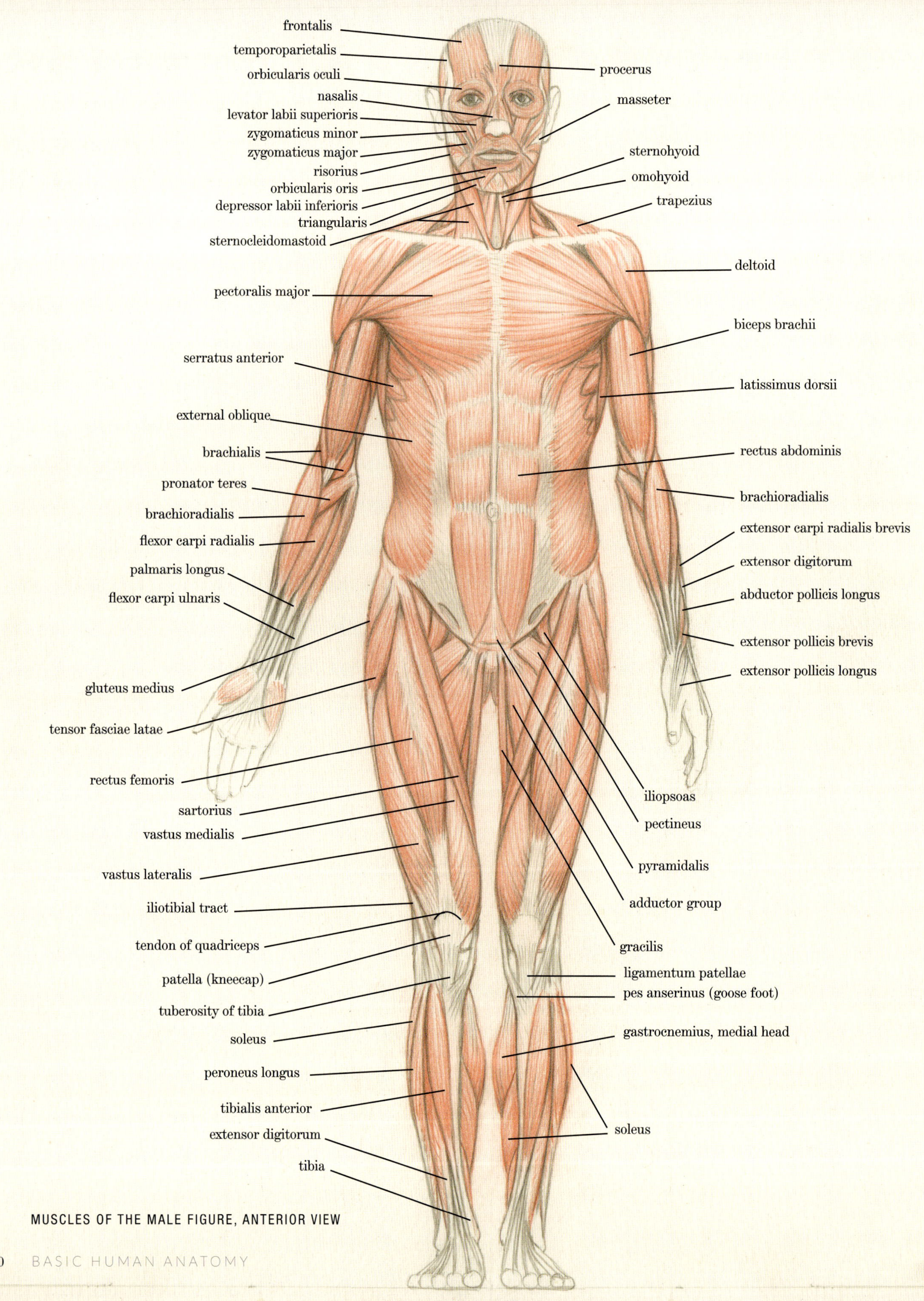

MUSCLES OF THE MALE FIGURE, ANTERIOR VIEW

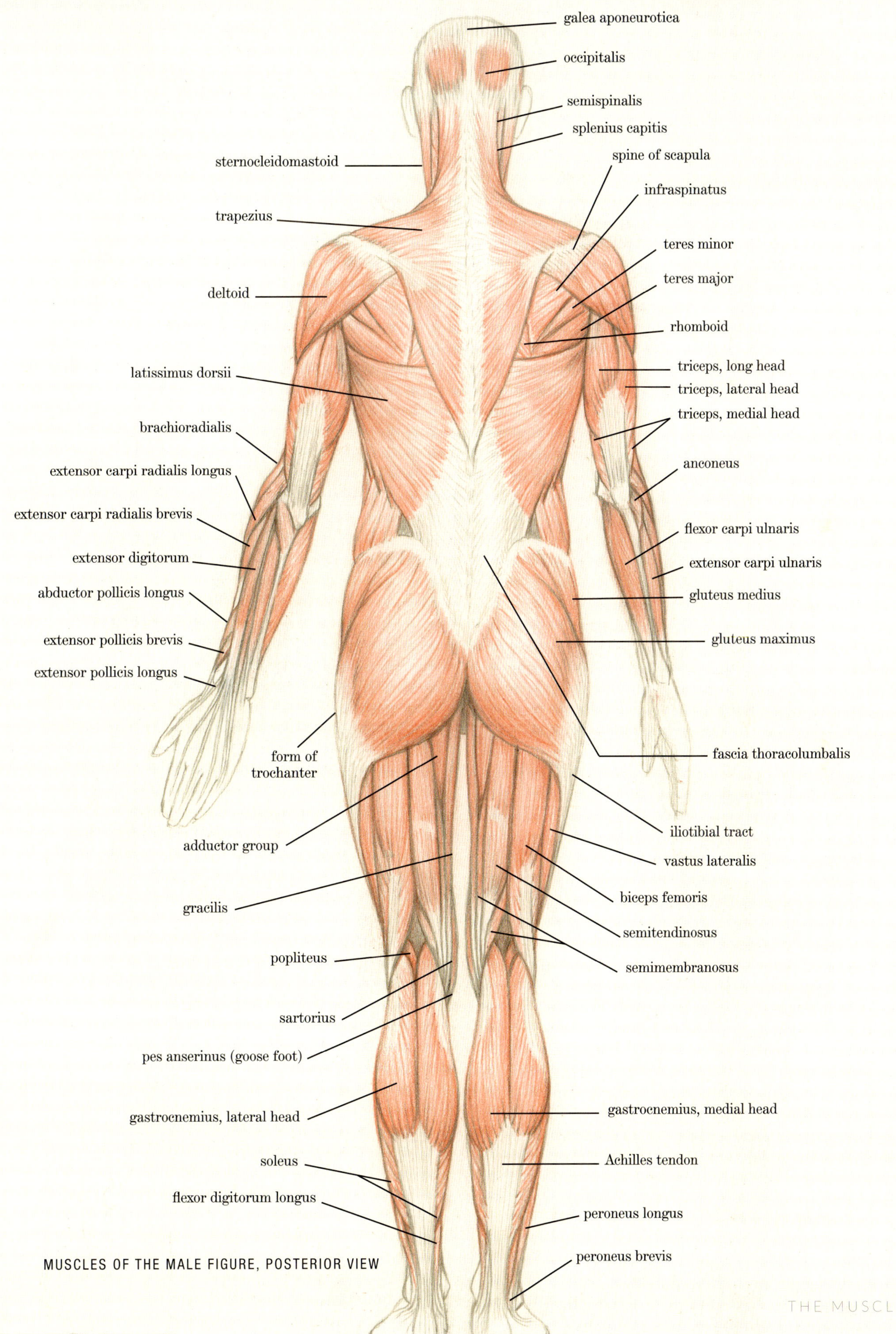

MUSCLES OF THE MALE FIGURE, POSTERIOR VIEW

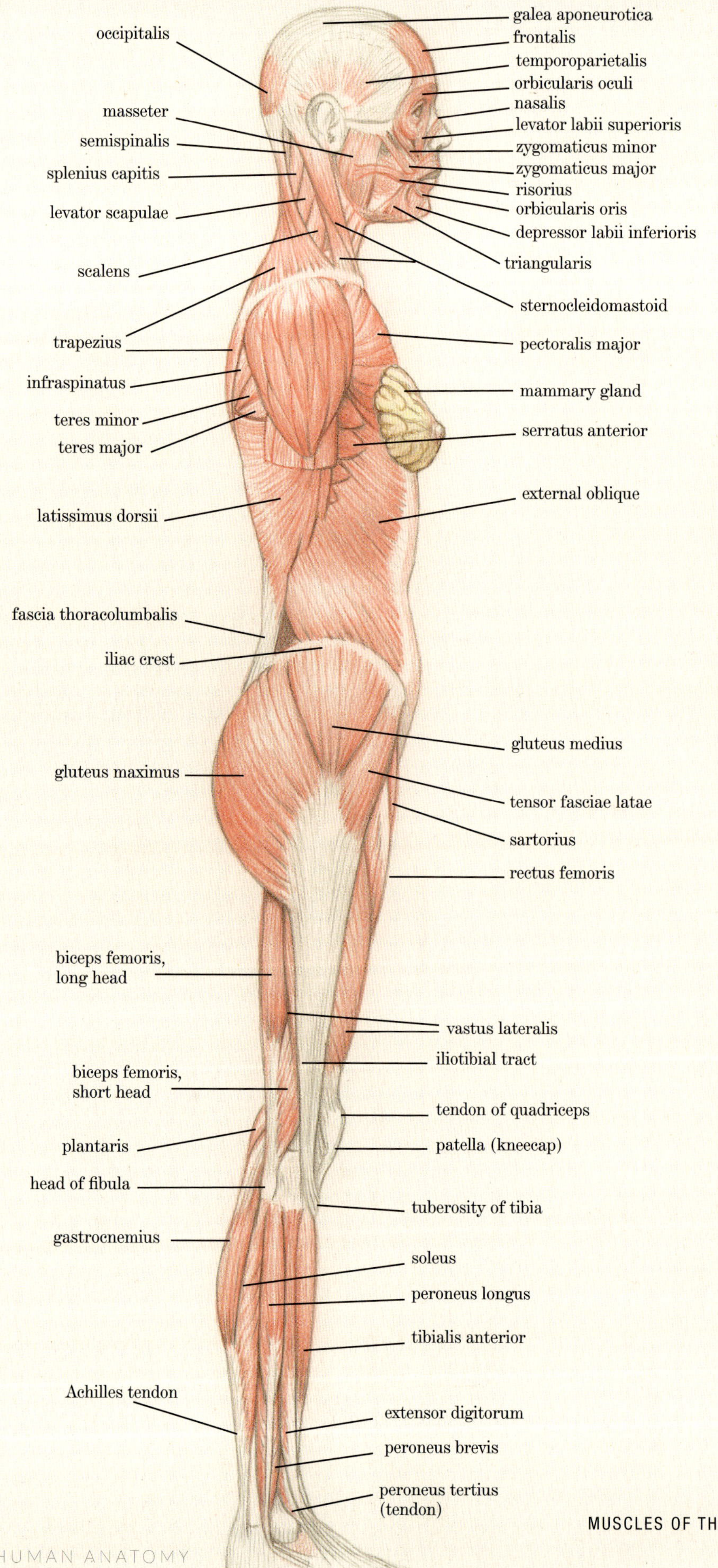

MUSCLES OF THE FEMALE FIGURE, LATERAL VIEW

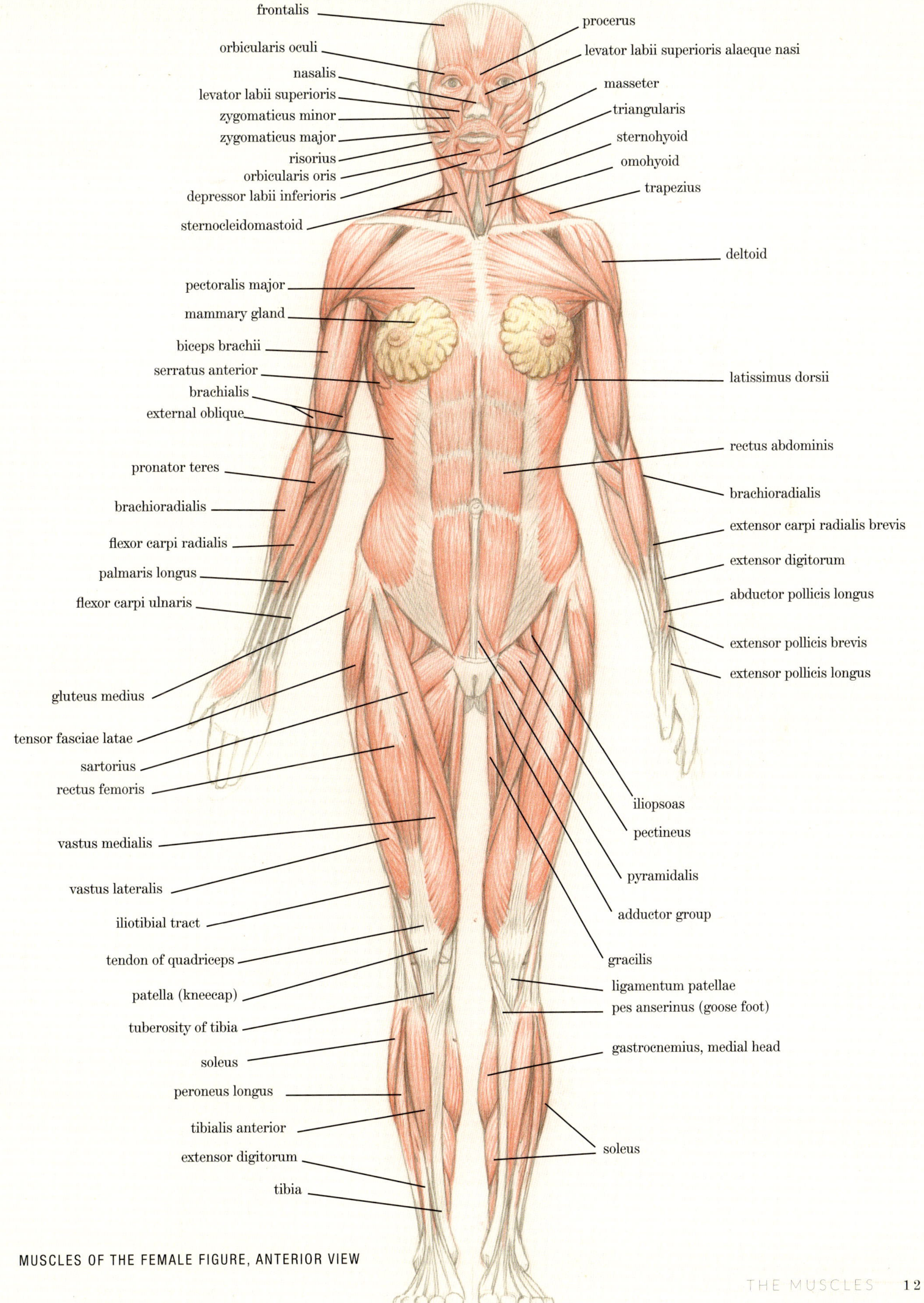

frontalis
orbicularis oculi
nasalis
levator labii superioris
zygomaticus minor
zygomaticus major
risorius
orbicularis oris
depressor labii inferioris
sternocleidomastoid
pectoralis major
mammary gland
biceps brachii
serratus anterior
brachialis
external oblique
pronator teres
brachioradialis
flexor carpi radialis
palmaris longus
flexor carpi ulnaris
gluteus medius
tensor fasciae latae
sartorius
rectus femoris
vastus medialis
vastus lateralis
iliotibial tract
tendon of quadriceps
patella (kneecap)
tuberosity of tibia
soleus
peroneus longus
tibialis anterior
extensor digitorum
tibia
procerus
levator labii superioris alaeque nasi
masseter
triangularis
sternohyoid
omohyoid
trapezius
deltoid
latissimus dorsii
rectus abdominis
brachioradialis
extensor carpi radialis brevis
extensor digitorum
abductor pollicis longus
extensor pollicis brevis
extensor pollicis longus
iliopsoas
pectineus
pyramidalis
adductor group
gracilis
ligamentum patellae
pes anserinus (goose foot)
gastrocnemius, medial head
soleus
MUSCLES OF THE FEMALE FIGURE, ANTERIOR VIEW
THE MUSCLES   123

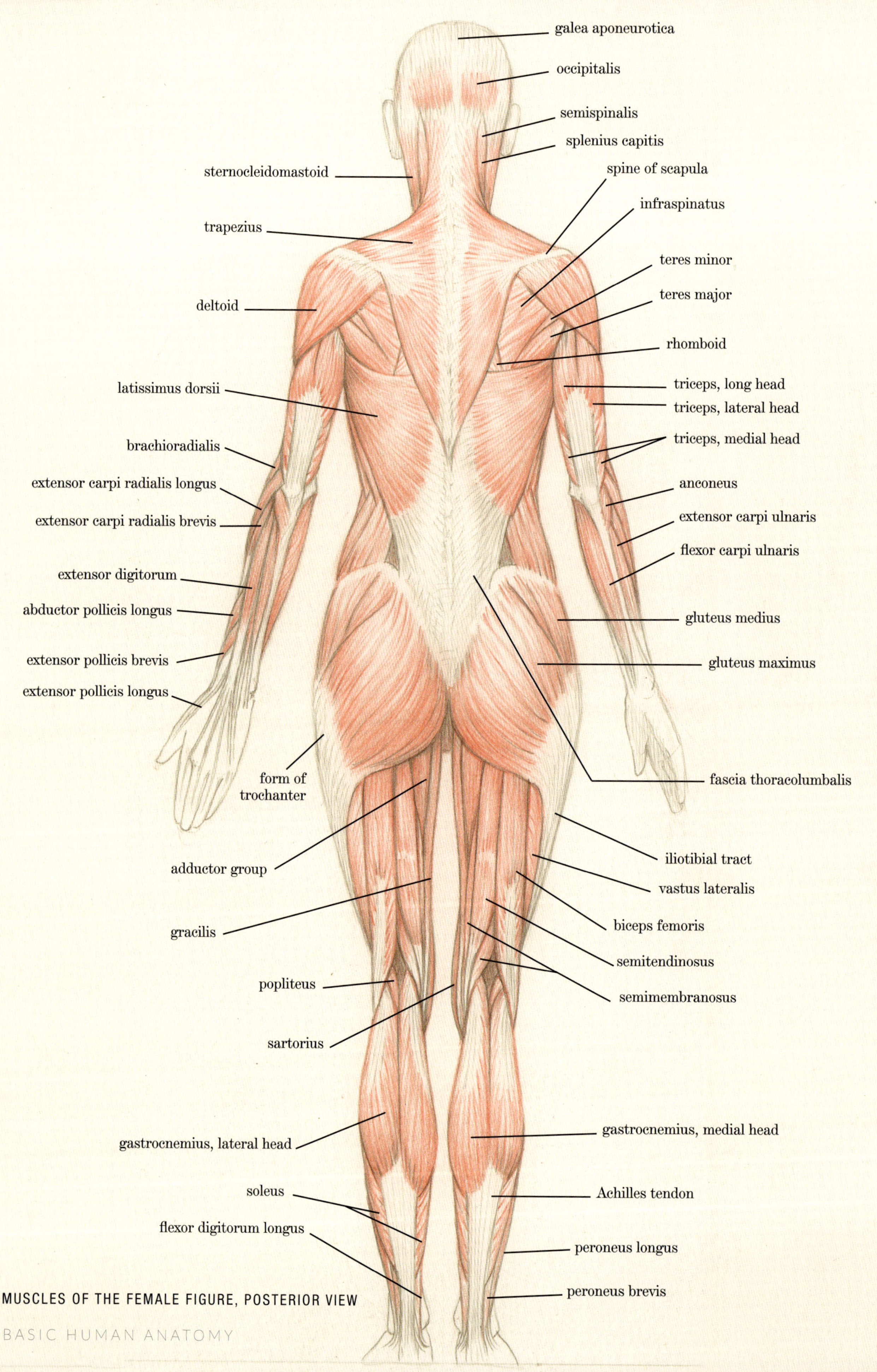

MUSCLES OF THE FEMALE FIGURE, POSTERIOR VIEW

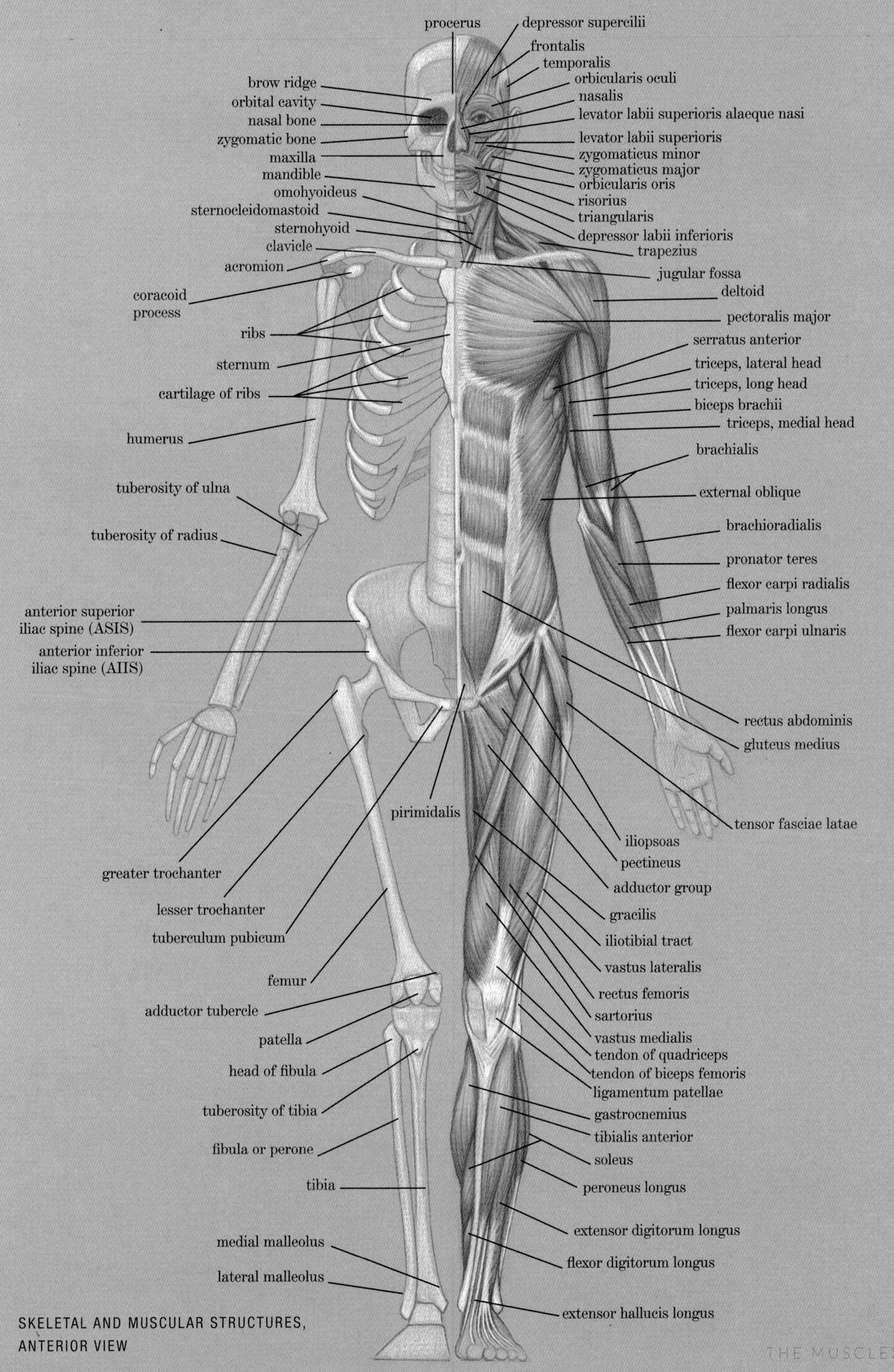

SKELETAL AND MUSCULAR STRUCTURES, ANTERIOR VIEW

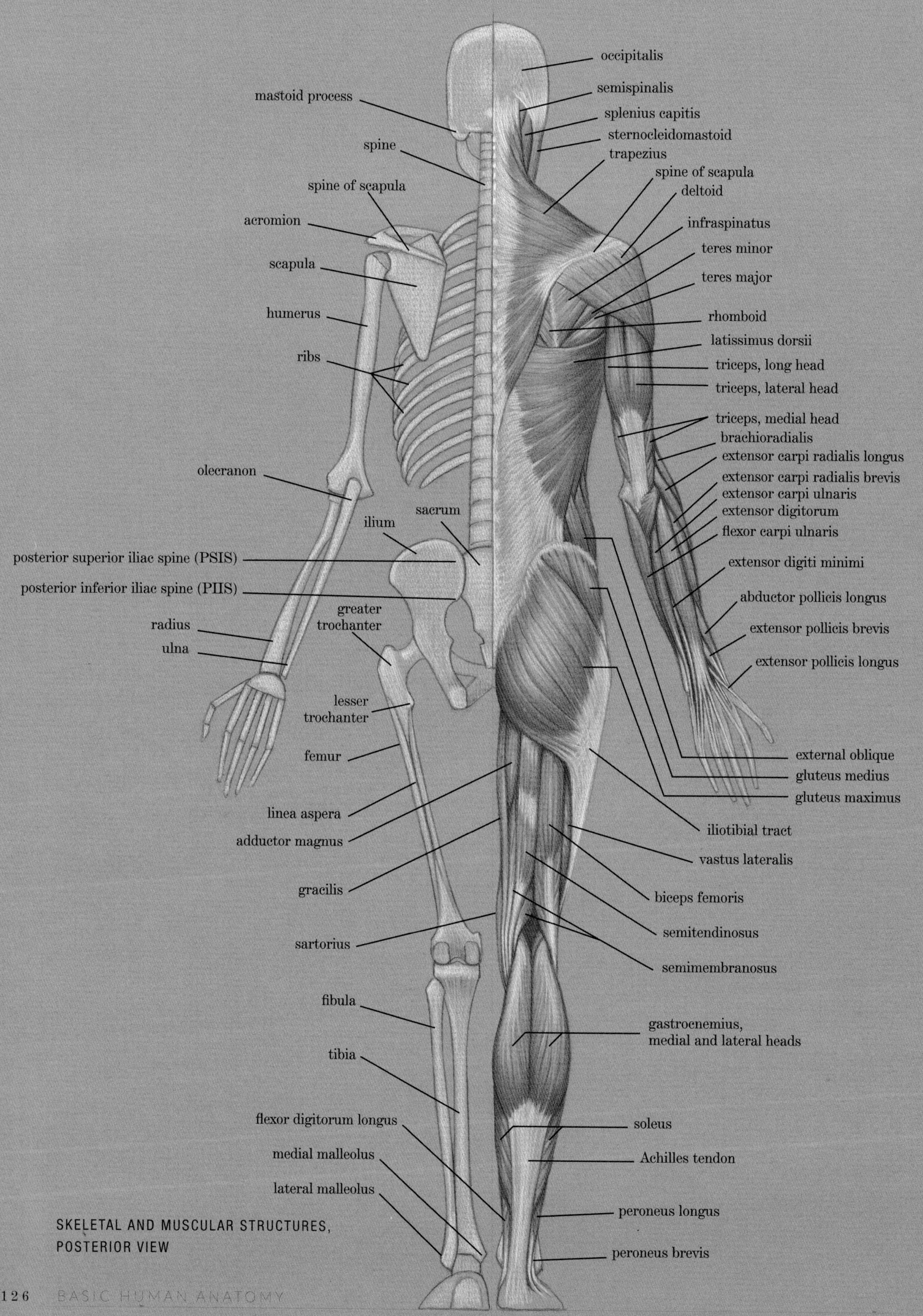

mastoid process
spine
spine of scapula
acromion
scapula
humerus
ribs
olecranon
ilium
sacrum
posterior superior iliac spine (PSIS)
posterior inferior iliac spine (PIIS)
greater trochanter
radius
ulna
lesser trochanter
femur
linea aspera
adductor magnus
gracilis
sartorius
fibula
tibia
flexor digitorum longus
medial malleolus
lateral malleolus
occipitalis
semispinalis
splenius capitis
sternocleidomastoid
trapezius
spine of scapula
deltoid
infraspinatus
teres minor
teres major
rhomboid
latissimus dorsii
triceps, long head
triceps, lateral head
triceps, medial head
brachioradialis
extensor carpi radialis longus
extensor carpi radialis brevis
extensor carpi ulnaris
extensor digitorum
flexor carpi ulnaris
extensor digiti minimi
abductor pollicis longus
extensor pollicis brevis
extensor pollicis longus
external oblique
gluteus medius
gluteus maximus
iliotibial tract
vastus lateralis
biceps femoris
semitendinosus
semimembranosus
gastrocnemius, medial and lateral heads
soleus
Achilles tendon
peroneus longus
peroneus brevis
SKELETAL AND MUSCULAR STRUCTURES, POSTERIOR VIEW

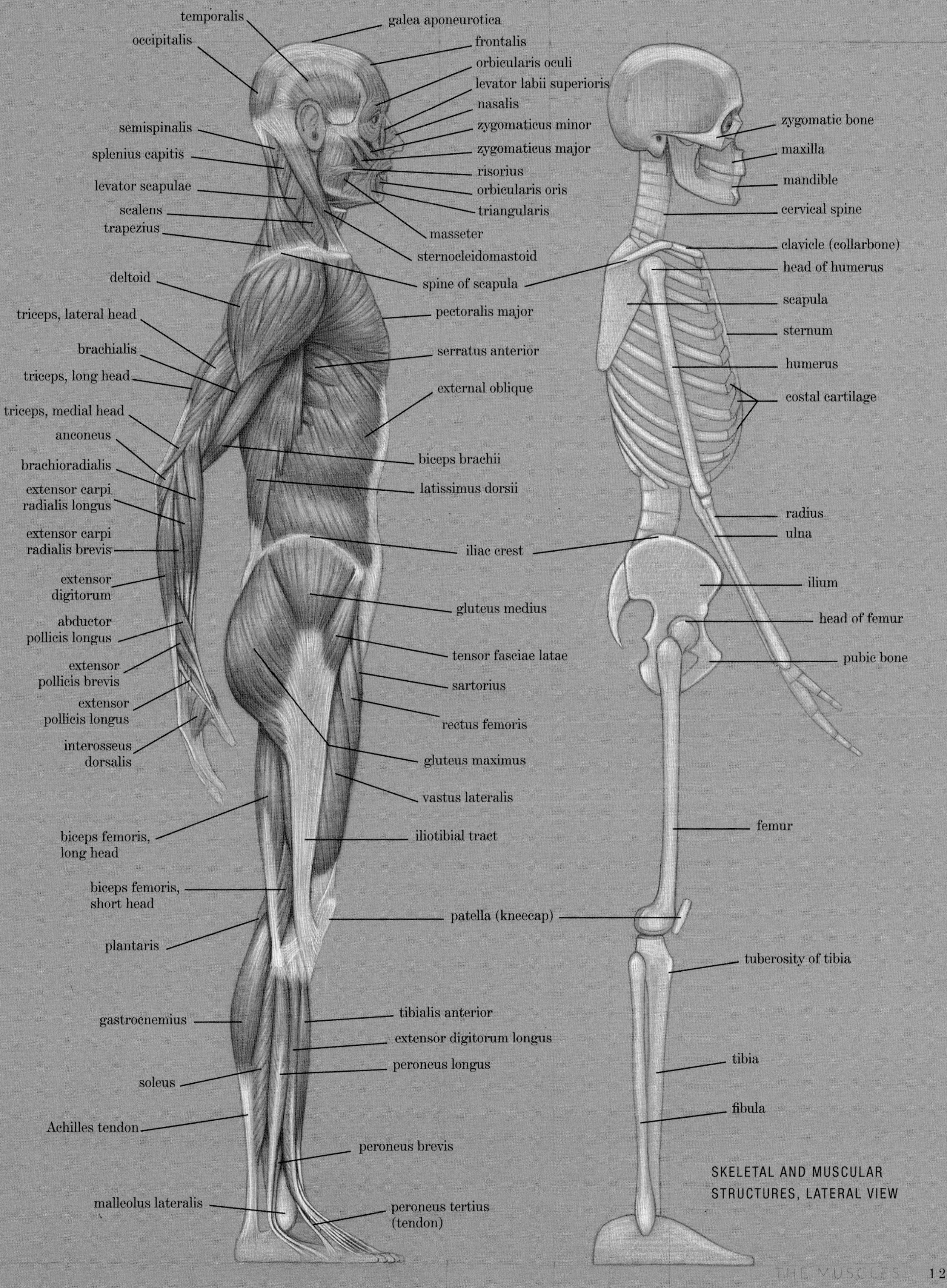

temporalis
occipitalis
galea aponeurotica
frontalis
orbicularis oculi
levator labii superioris
nasalis
zygomaticus minor
zygomaticus major
risorius
orbicularis oris
triangularis
masseter
sternocleidomastoid
spine of scapula
semispinalis
splenius capitis
levator scapulae
scalens
trapezius
deltoid
triceps, lateral head
brachialis
triceps, long head
triceps, medial head
anconeus
brachioradialis
extensor carpi radialis longus
extensor carpi radialis brevis
extensor digitorum
abductor pollicis longus
extensor pollicis brevis
extensor pollicis longus
interosseus dorsalis
pectoralis major
serratus anterior
external oblique
biceps brachii
latissimus dorsii
iliac crest
gluteus medius
tensor fasciae latae
sartorius
rectus femoris
gluteus maximus
vastus lateralis
iliotibial tract
biceps femoris, long head
biceps femoris, short head
plantaris
gastrocnemius
tibialis anterior
extensor digitorum longus
peroneus longus
soleus
Achilles tendon
peroneus brevis
malleolus lateralis
peroneus tertius (tendon)
patella (kneecap)
zygomatic bone
maxilla
mandible
cervical spine
clavicle (collarbone)
head of humerus
scapula
sternum
humerus
costal cartilage
radius
ulna
ilium
head of femur
pubic bone
femur
tuberosity of tibia
tibia
fibula
SKELETAL AND MUSCULAR STRUCTURES, LATERAL VIEW

ANALYSIS OF MUSCLES
AND MUSCLE GROUPS

The next group of figures examines in detail all the muscles of interest to the artist, showing the muscles' origin and insertion points as well as each muscle's action. Knowing the muscles' origins and insertions is essential to appreciating the connections and interactions between the various forms of the body, which lead to the creation of specific patterns. The origin point is where a muscle begins; the insertion point typically moves toward the origin point during the action of the muscle. The figures are ordered in layers, from the deepest (layer 1) up through the more superficial layers, permitting you to understand the relations between adjacent muscles.

ORIGIN AND INSERTION

ACTION

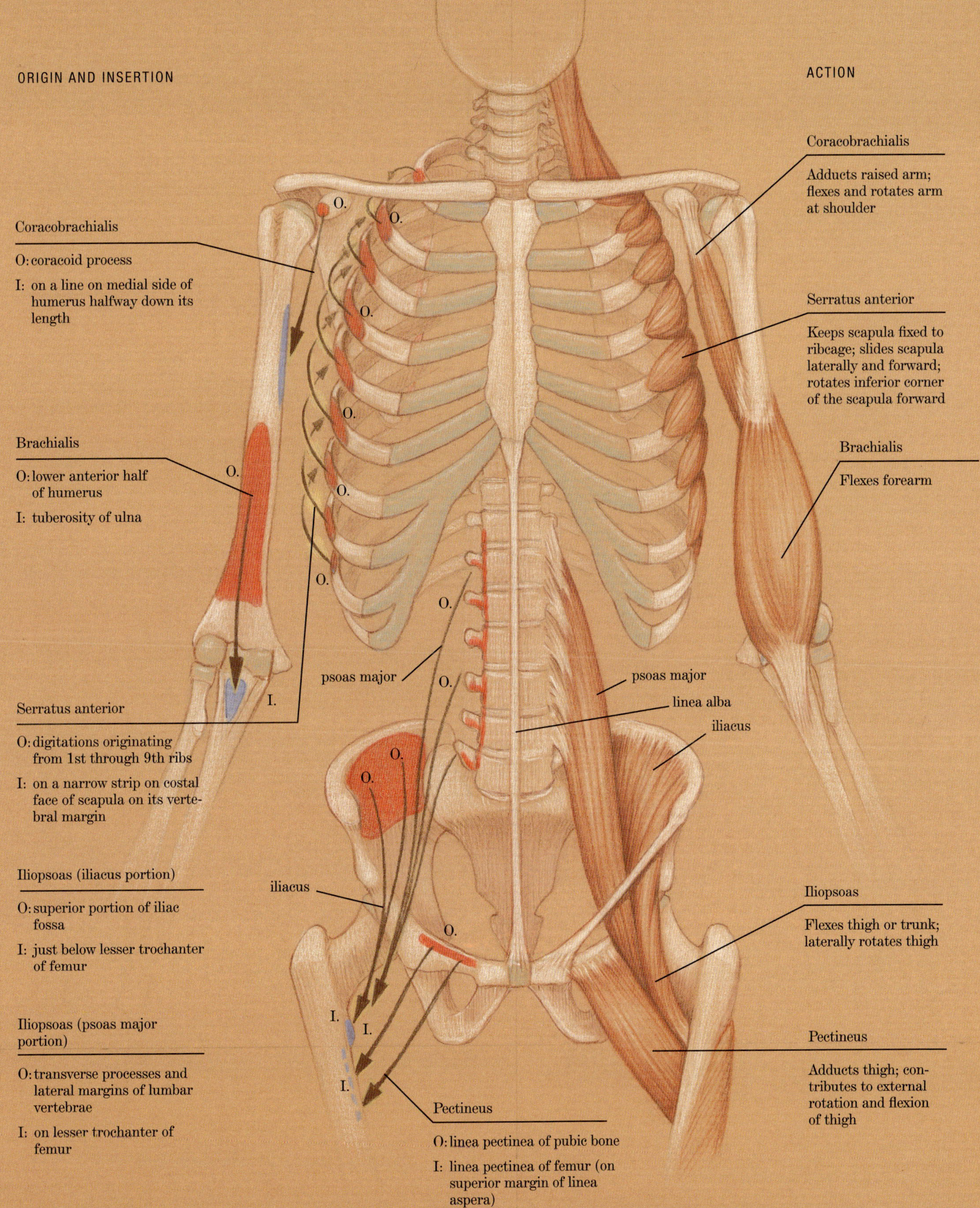

Coracobrachialis

O: coracoid process

I: on a line on medial side of humerus halfway down its length

Brachialis

O: lower anterior half of humerus

I: tuberosity of ulna

Serratus anterior

O: digitations originating from 1st through 9th ribs

I: on a narrow strip on costal face of scapula on its vertebral margin

Iliopsoas (iliacus portion)

O: superior portion of iliac fossa

I: just below lesser trochanter of femur

Iliopsoas (psoas major portion)

O: transverse processes and lateral margins of lumbar vertebrae

I: on lesser trochanter of femur

Pectineus

O: linea pectinea of pubic bone

I: linea pectinea of femur (on superior margin of linea aspera)

Coracobrachialis

Adducts raised arm; flexes and rotates arm at shoulder

Serratus anterior

Keeps scapula fixed to ribcage; slides scapula laterally and forward; rotates inferior corner of the scapula forward

Brachialis

Flexes forearm

Iliopsoas

Flexes thigh or trunk; laterally rotates thigh

Pectineus

Adducts thigh; contributes to external rotation and flexion of thigh

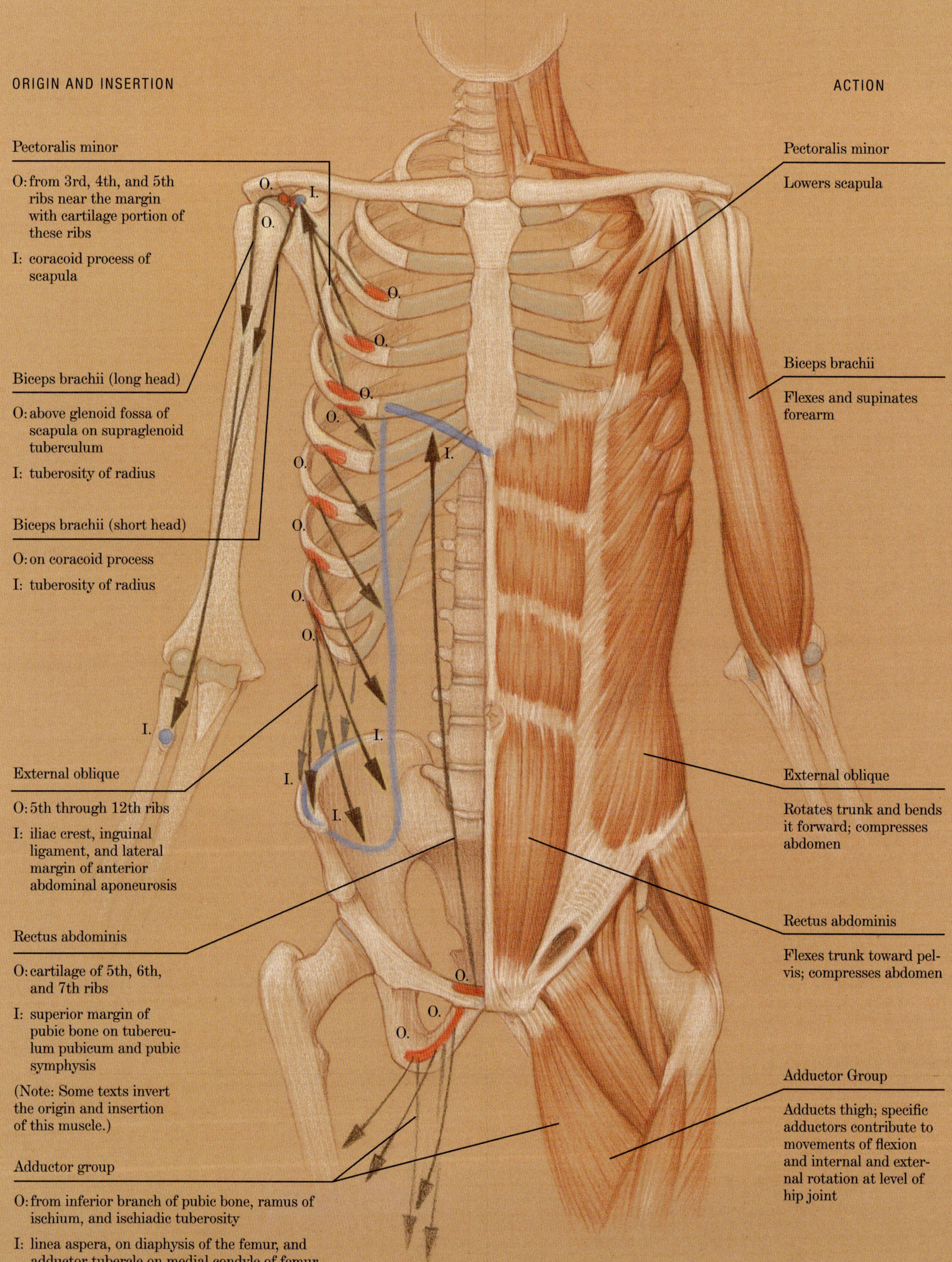

ORIGIN AND INSERTION

Pectoralis minor

O: from 3rd, 4th, and 5th ribs near the margin with cartilage portion of these ribs

I: coracoid process of scapula

Biceps brachii (long head)

O: above glenoid fossa of scapula on supraglenoid tuberculum

I: tuberosity of radius

Biceps brachii (short head)

O: on coracoid process

I: tuberosity of radius

External oblique

O: 5th through 12th ribs

I: iliac crest, inguinal ligament, and lateral margin of anterior abdominal aponeurosis

Rectus abdominis

O: cartilage of 5th, 6th, and 7th ribs

I: superior margin of pubic bone on tuberculum pubicum and pubic symphysis

(Note: Some texts invert the origin and insertion of this muscle.)

Adductor group

O: from inferior branch of pubic bone, ramus of ischium, and ischiadic tuberosity

I: linea aspera, on diaphysis of the femur, and adductor tubercle on medial condyle of femur

ACTION

Pectoralis minor

Lowers scapula

Biceps brachii

Flexes and supinates forearm

External oblique

Rotates trunk and bends it forward; compresses abdomen

Rectus abdominis

Flexes trunk toward pelvis; compresses abdomen

Adductor Group

Adducts thigh; specific adductors contribute to movements of flexion and internal and external rotation at level of hip joint

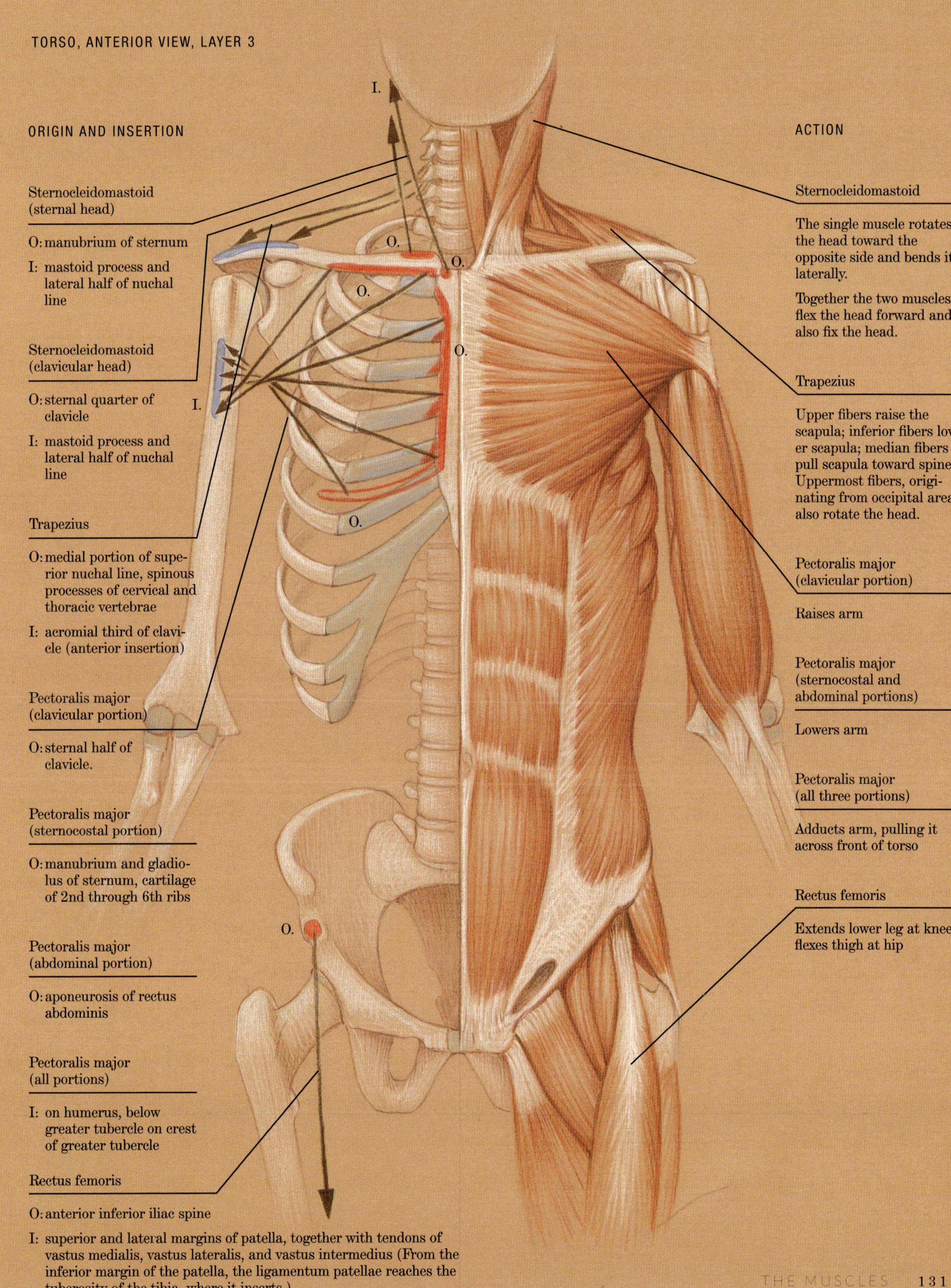

ORIGIN AND INSERTION

Sternocleidomastoid (sternal head)

O: manubrium of sternum

I: mastoid process and lateral half of nuchal line

Sternocleidomastoid (clavicular head)

O: sternal quarter of clavicle

I: mastoid process and lateral half of nuchal line

Trapezius

O: medial portion of superior nuchal line, spinous processes of cervical and thoracic vertebrae

I: acromial third of clavicle (anterior insertion)

Pectoralis major (clavicular portion)

O: sternal half of clavicle.

Pectoralis major (sternocostal portion)

O: manubrium and gladiolus of sternum, cartilage of 2nd through 6th ribs

Pectoralis major (abdominal portion)

O: aponeurosis of rectus abdominis

Pectoralis major (all portions)

I: on humerus, below greater tubercle on crest of greater tubercle

Rectus femoris

O: anterior inferior iliac spine

I: superior and lateral margins of patella, together with tendons of vastus medialis, vastus lateralis, and vastus intermedius (From the inferior margin of the patella, the ligamentum patellae reaches the tuberosity of the tibia, where it inserts.)

ACTION

Sternocleidomastoid

The single muscle rotates the head toward the opposite side and bends it laterally.

Together the two muscles flex the head forward and also fix the head.

Trapezius

Upper fibers raise the scapula; inferior fibers lower scapula; median fibers pull scapula toward spine. Uppermost fibers, originating from occipital area, also rotate the head.

Pectoralis major (clavicular portion)

Raises arm

Pectoralis major (sternocostal and abdominal portions)

Lowers arm

Pectoralis major (all three portions)

Adducts arm, pulling it across front of torso

Rectus femoris

Extends lower leg at knee; flexes thigh at hip

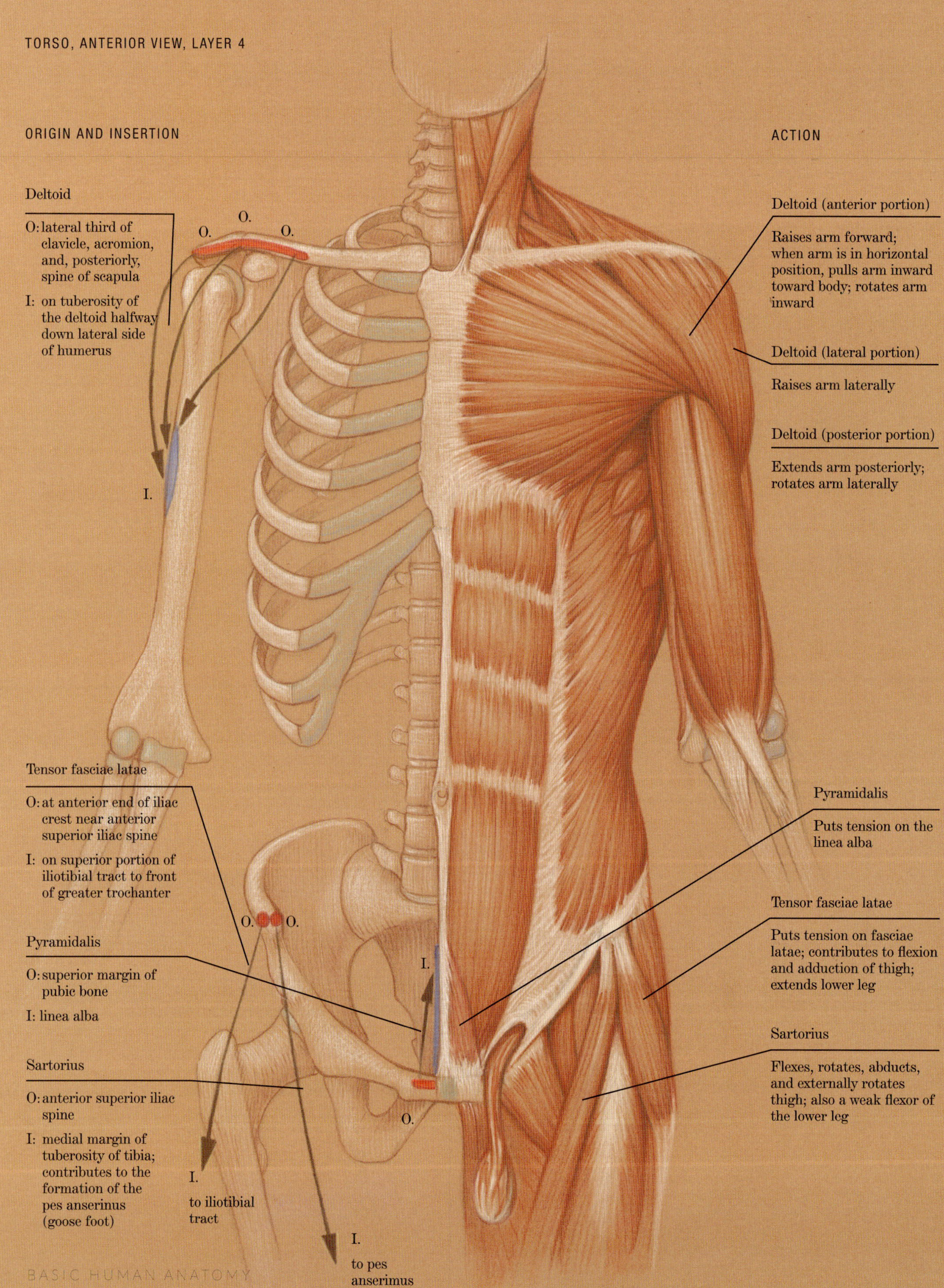

ORIGIN AND INSERTION

ACTION

Deltoid

O: lateral third of clavicle, acromion, and, posteriorly, spine of scapula

I: on tuberosity of the deltoid halfway down lateral side of humerus

O.
O.
O.
I.

Deltoid (anterior portion)

Raises arm forward; when arm is in horizontal position, pulls arm inward toward body; rotates arm inward

Deltoid (lateral portion)

Raises arm laterally

Deltoid (posterior portion)

Extends arm posteriorly; rotates arm laterally

Tensor fasciae latae

O: at anterior end of iliac crest near anterior superior iliac spine

I: on superior portion of iliotibial tract to front of greater trochanter

Pyramidalis

O: superior margin of pubic bone

I: linea alba

Sartorius

O: anterior superior iliac spine

I: medial margin of tuberosity of tibia; contributes to the formation of the pes anserinus (goose foot)

O.
O.
I.
O.
I.
to iliotibial tract
I.
to pes anserinus

Pyramidalis

Puts tension on the linea alba

Tensor fasciae latae

Puts tension on fasciae latae; contributes to flexion and adduction of thigh; extends lower leg

Sartorius

Flexes, rotates, abducts, and externally rotates thigh; also a weak flexor of the lower leg

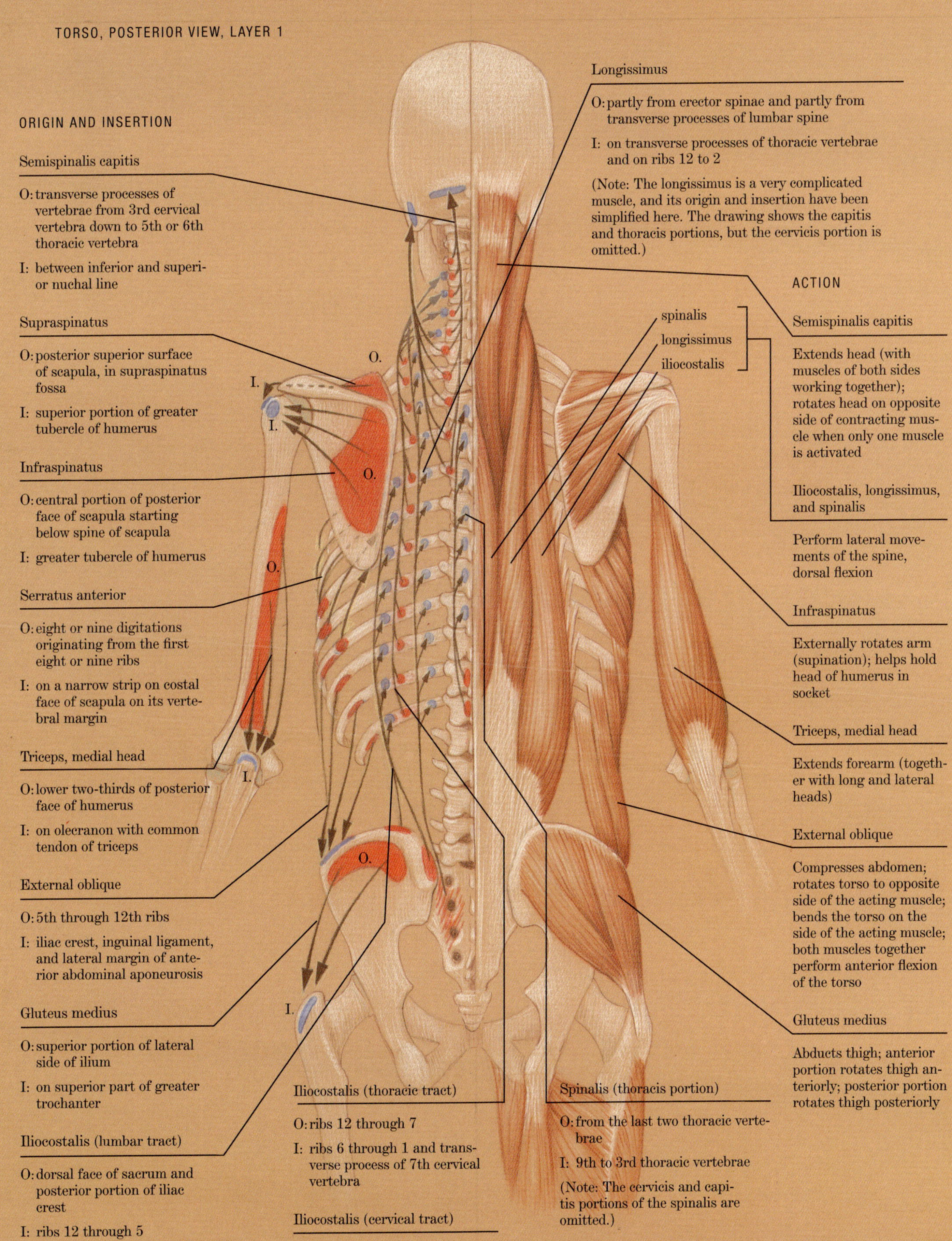

ORIGIN AND INSERTION

Semispinalis capitis

O: transverse processes of vertebrae from 3rd cervical vertebra down to 5th or 6th thoracic vertebra

I: between inferior and superior nuchal line

Supraspinatus

O: posterior superior surface of scapula, in supraspinatus fossa

I: superior portion of greater tubercle of humerus

Infraspinatus

O: central portion of posterior face of scapula starting below spine of scapula

I: greater tubercle of humerus

Serratus anterior

O: eight or nine digitations originating from the first eight or nine ribs

I: on a narrow strip on costal face of scapula on its vertebral margin

Triceps, medial head

O: lower two-thirds of posterior face of humerus

I: on olecranon with common tendon of triceps

External oblique

O: 5th through 12th ribs

I: iliac crest, inguinal ligament, and lateral margin of anterior abdominal aponeurosis

Gluteus medius

O: superior portion of lateral side of ilium

I: on superior part of greater trochanter

Iliocostalis (lumbar tract)

O: dorsal face of sacrum and posterior portion of iliac crest

I: ribs 12 through 5

Iliocostalis (thoracic tract)

O: ribs 12 through 7

I: ribs 6 through 1 and transverse process of 7th cervical vertebra

Iliocostalis (cervical tract)

O: upper and middle ribs

I: median cervical vertebrae

O.
I.
I.
O.
O.
I.
O.
I.

Longissimus

O: partly from erector spinae and partly from transverse processes of lumbar spine

I: on transverse processes of thoracic vertebrae and on ribs 12 to 2

(Note: The longissimus is a very complicated muscle, and its origin and insertion have been simplified here. The drawing shows the capitis and thoracis portions, but the cervicis portion is omitted.)

spinalis
longissimus
iliocostalis

ACTION

Semispinalis capitis

Extends head (with muscles of both sides working together); rotates head on opposite side of contracting muscle when only one muscle is activated

Iliocostalis, longissimus, and spinalis

Perform lateral movements of the spine, dorsal flexion

Infraspinatus

Externally rotates arm (supination); helps hold head of humerus in socket

Triceps, medial head

Extends forearm (together with long and lateral heads)

External oblique

Compresses abdomen; rotates torso to opposite side of the acting muscle; bends the torso on the side of the acting muscle; both muscles together perform anterior flexion of the torso

Gluteus medius

Abducts thigh; anterior portion rotates thigh anteriorly; posterior portion rotates thigh posteriorly

Spinalis (thoracis portion)

O: from the last two thoracic vertebrae

I: 9th to 3rd thoracic vertebrae

(Note: The cervicis and capitis portions of the spinalis are omitted.)

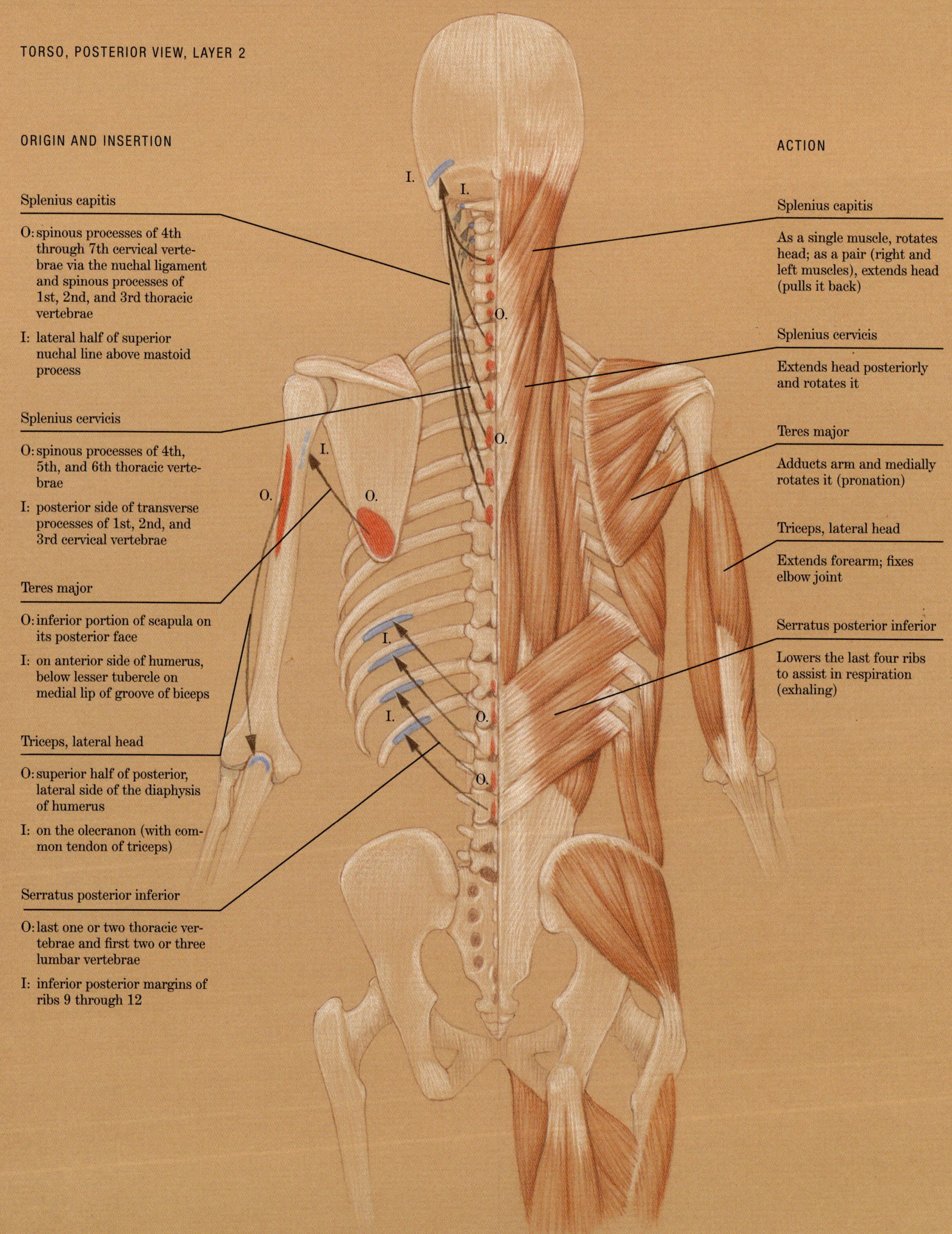

ORIGIN AND INSERTION

ACTION

Splenius capitis

O: spinous processes of 4th through 7th cervical vertebrae via the nuchal ligament and spinous processes of 1st, 2nd, and 3rd thoracic vertebrae

I: lateral half of superior nuchal line above mastoid process

Splenius cervicis

O: spinous processes of 4th, 5th, and 6th thoracic vertebrae

I: posterior side of transverse processes of 1st, 2nd, and 3rd cervical vertebrae

Teres major

O: inferior portion of scapula on its posterior face

I: on anterior side of humerus, below lesser tubercle on medial lip of groove of biceps

Triceps, lateral head

O: superior half of posterior, lateral side of the diaphysis of humerus

I: on the olecranon (with common tendon of triceps)

Serratus posterior inferior

O: last one or two thoracic vertebrae and first two or three lumbar vertebrae

I: inferior posterior margins of ribs 9 through 12

Splenius capitis

As a single muscle, rotates head; as a pair (right and left muscles), extends head (pulls it back)

Splenius cervicis

Extends head posteriorly and rotates it

Teres major

Adducts arm and medially rotates it (pronation)

Triceps, lateral head

Extends forearm; fixes elbow joint

Serratus posterior inferior

Lowers the last four ribs to assist in respiration (exhaling)

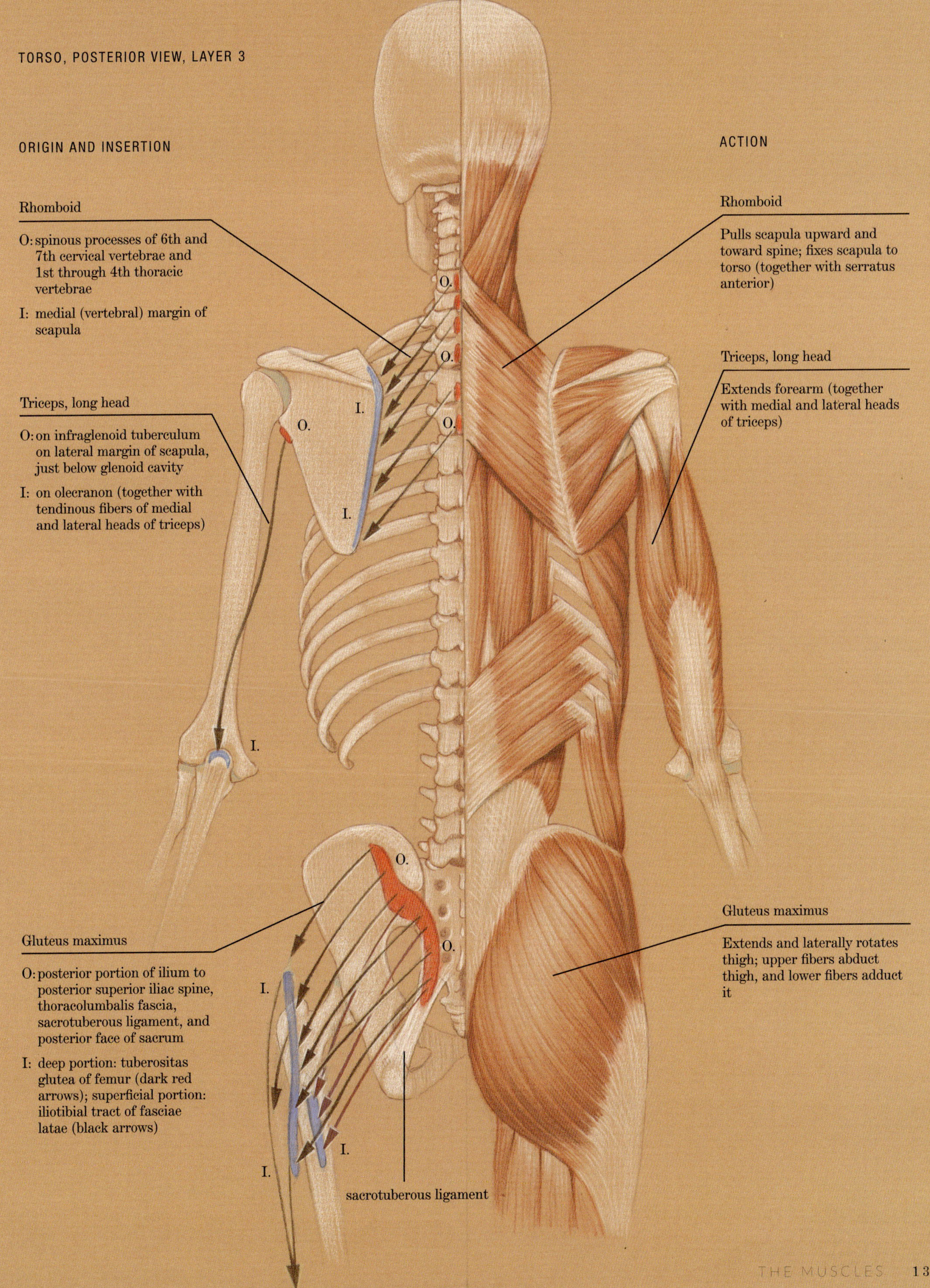

ORIGIN AND INSERTION

ACTION

Rhomboid

O: spinous processes of 6th and 7th cervical vertebrae and 1st through 4th thoracic vertebrae

I: medial (vertebral) margin of scapula

Rhomboid

Pulls scapula upward and toward spine; fixes scapula to torso (together with serratus anterior)

Triceps, long head

O: on infraglenoid tuberculum on lateral margin of scapula, just below glenoid cavity

I: on olecranon (together with tendinous fibers of medial and lateral heads of triceps)

Triceps, long head

Extends forearm (together with medial and lateral heads of triceps)

Gluteus maximus

O: posterior portion of ilium to posterior superior iliac spine, thoracolumbalis fascia, sacrotuberous ligament, and posterior face of sacrum

I: deep portion: tuberositas glutea of femur (dark red arrows); superficial portion: iliotibial tract of fasciae latae (black arrows)

Gluteus maximus

Extends and laterally rotates thigh; upper fibers abduct thigh, and lower fibers adduct it

sacrotuberous ligament

O.
I.

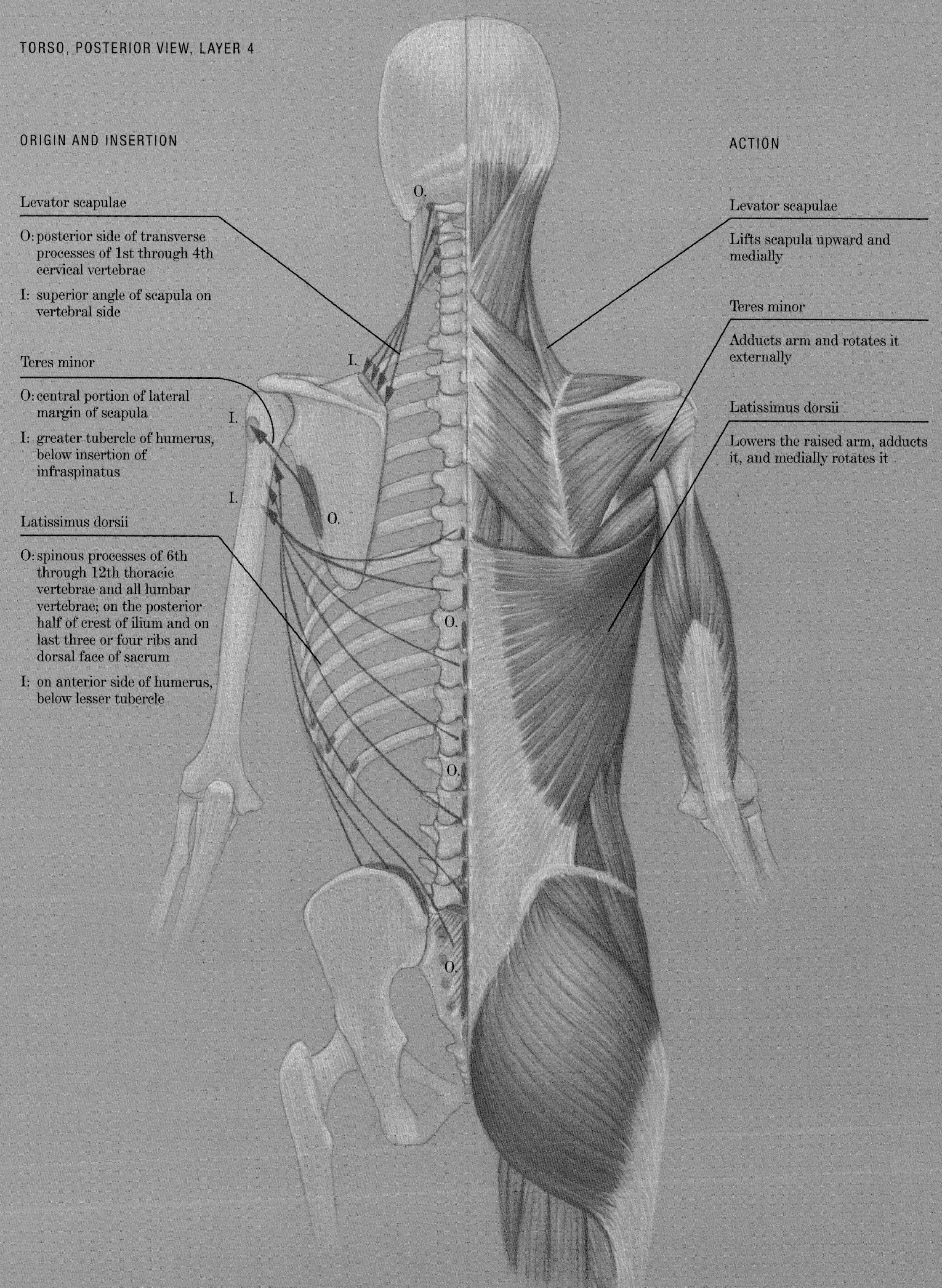

ORIGIN AND INSERTION

Levator scapulae

O: posterior side of transverse processes of 1st through 4th cervical vertebrae

I: superior angle of scapula on vertebral side

Teres minor

O: central portion of lateral margin of scapula

I: greater tubercle of humerus, below insertion of infraspinatus

Latissimus dorsii

O: spinous processes of 6th through 12th thoracic vertebrae and all lumbar vertebrae; on the posterior half of crest of ilium and on last three or four ribs and dorsal face of sacrum

I: on anterior side of humerus, below lesser tubercle

ACTION

Levator scapulae

Lifts scapula upward and medially

Teres minor

Adducts arm and rotates it externally

Latissimus dorsii

Lowers the raised arm, adducts it, and medially rotates it

O.
I.
I.
I.
O.
O.
O.
O.

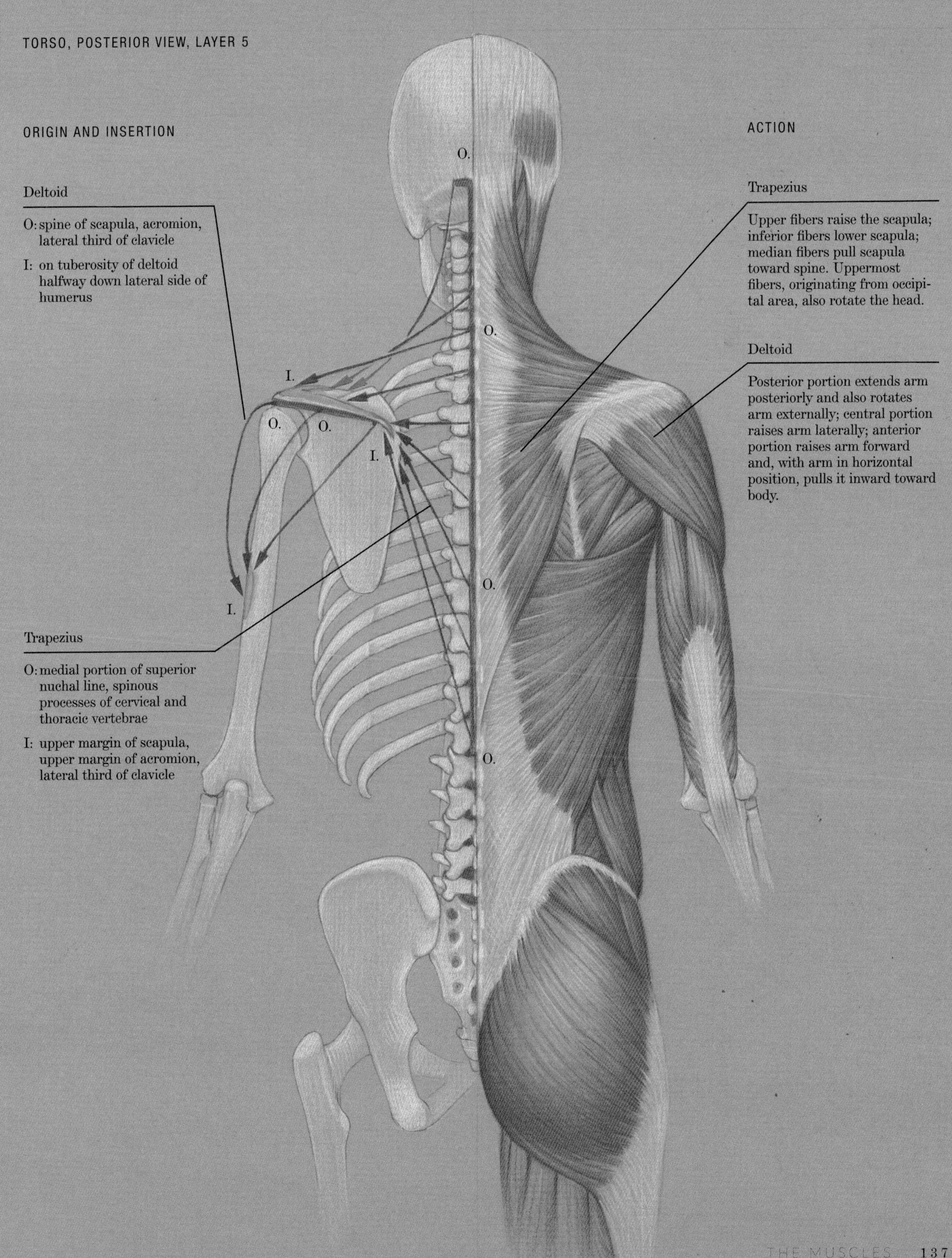
ORIGIN AND INSERTION

ACTION

Deltoid

O: spine of scapula, acromion, lateral third of clavicle

I: on tuberosity of deltoid halfway down lateral side of humerus

Trapezius

O: medial portion of superior nuchal line, spinous processes of cervical and thoracic vertebrae

I: upper margin of scapula, upper margin of acromion, lateral third of clavicle

Trapezius

Upper fibers raise the scapula; inferior fibers lower scapula; median fibers pull scapula toward spine. Uppermost fibers, originating from occipital area, also rotate the head.

Deltoid

Posterior portion extends arm posteriorly and also rotates arm externally; central portion raises arm laterally; anterior portion raises arm forward and, with arm in horizontal position, pulls it inward toward body.

O.
O.
I.
O.
O.
I.
O.
I.
O.
O.

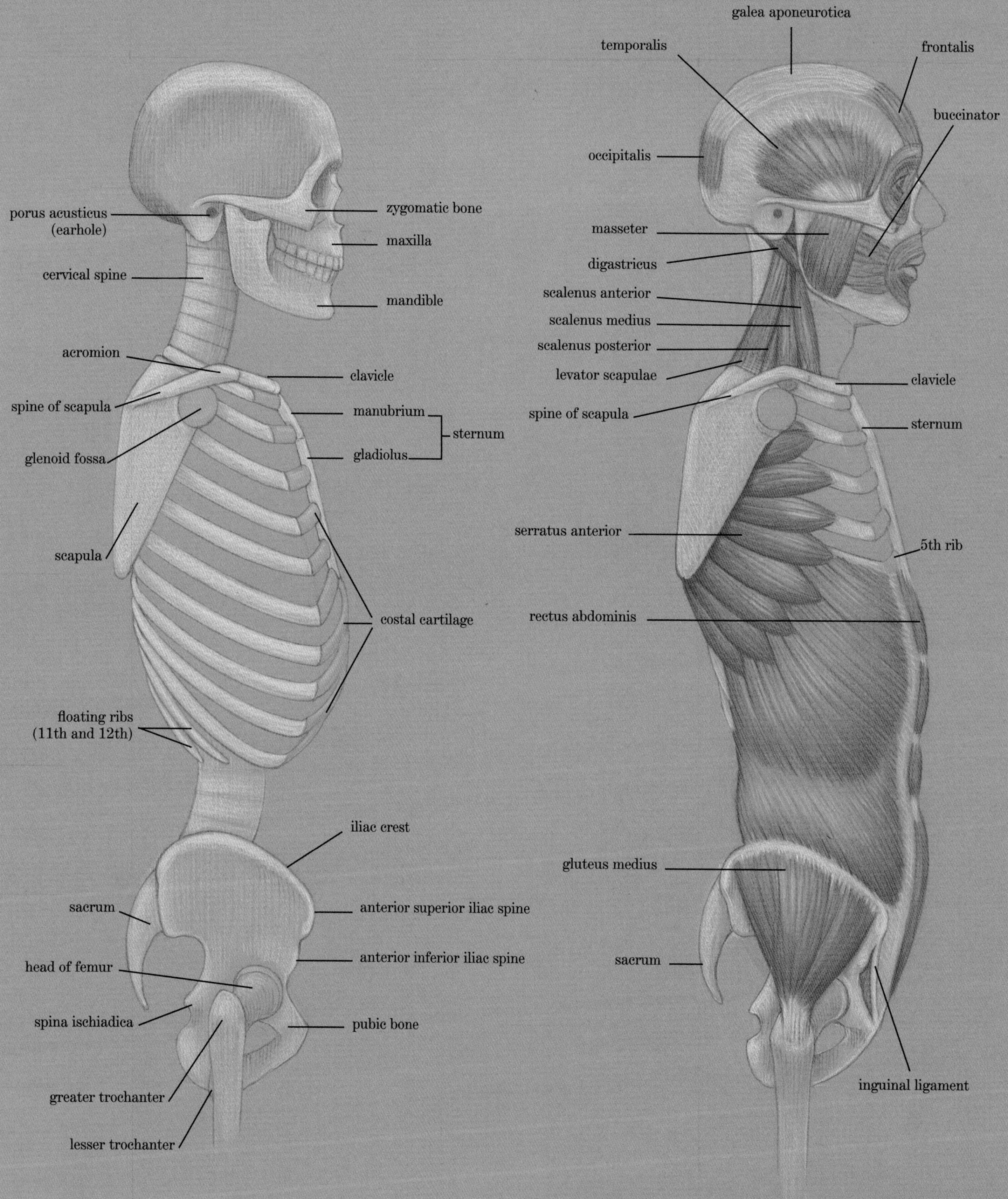

HEAD AND TORSO, LATERAL VIEW, LAYER 1 (THE SKELETON)

HEAD AND TORSO, LATERAL VIEW, LAYER 2

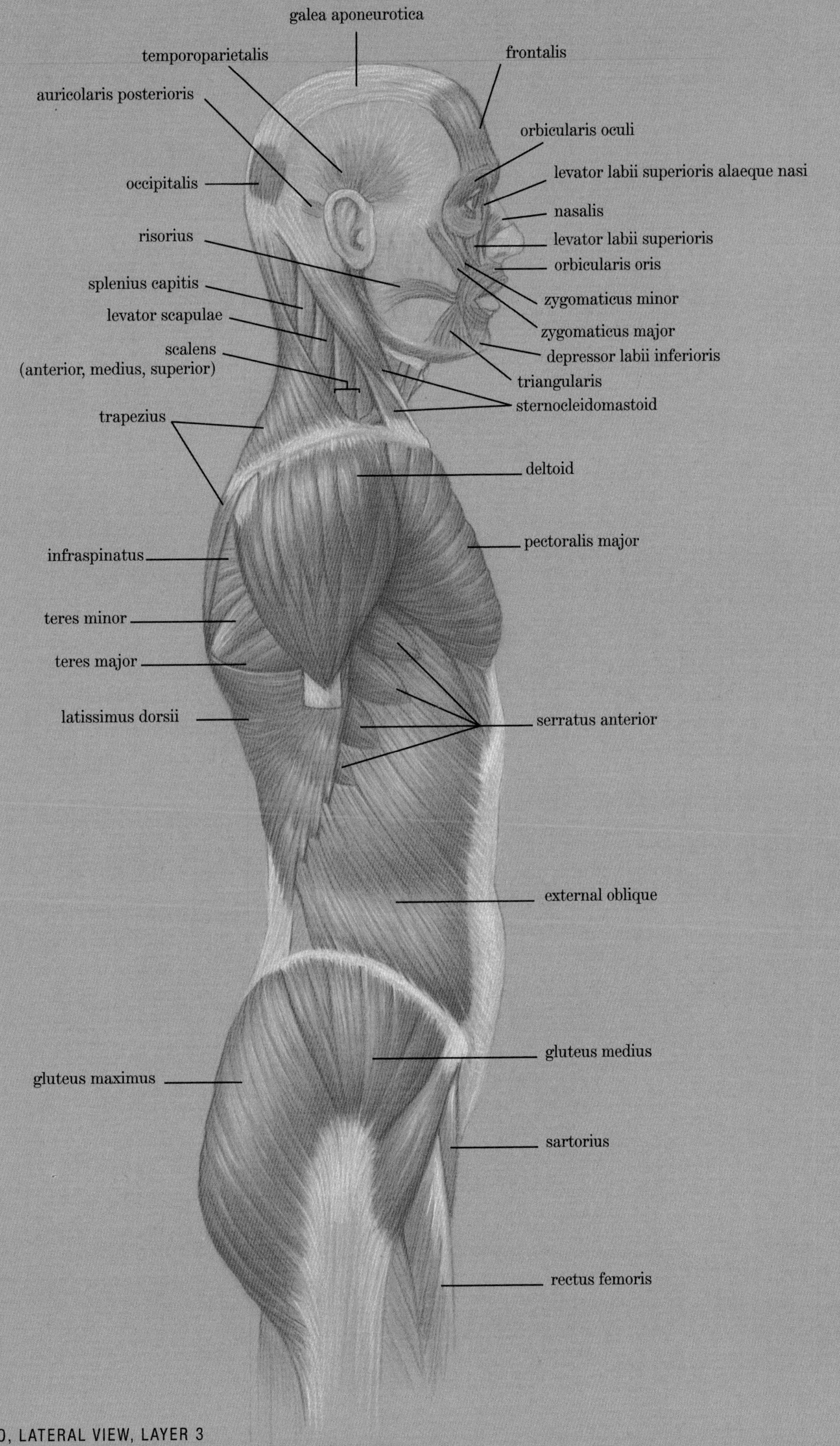

galea aponeurotica
temporoparietalis
frontalis
auricolaris posterioris
orbicularis oculi
levator labii superioris alaeque nasi
occipitalis
nasalis
levator labii superioris
risorius
orbicularis oris
splenius capitis
zygomaticus minor
levator scapulae
zygomaticus major
scalens
(anterior, medius, superior)
depressor labii inferioris
triangularis
trapezius
sternocleidomastoid
deltoid
pectoralis major
infraspinatus
teres minor
teres major
latissimus dorsii
serratus anterior
external oblique
gluteus medius
gluteus maximus
sartorius
rectus femoris
HEAD AND TORSO, LATERAL VIEW, LAYER 3

ORIGIN AND INSERTION

ACTION

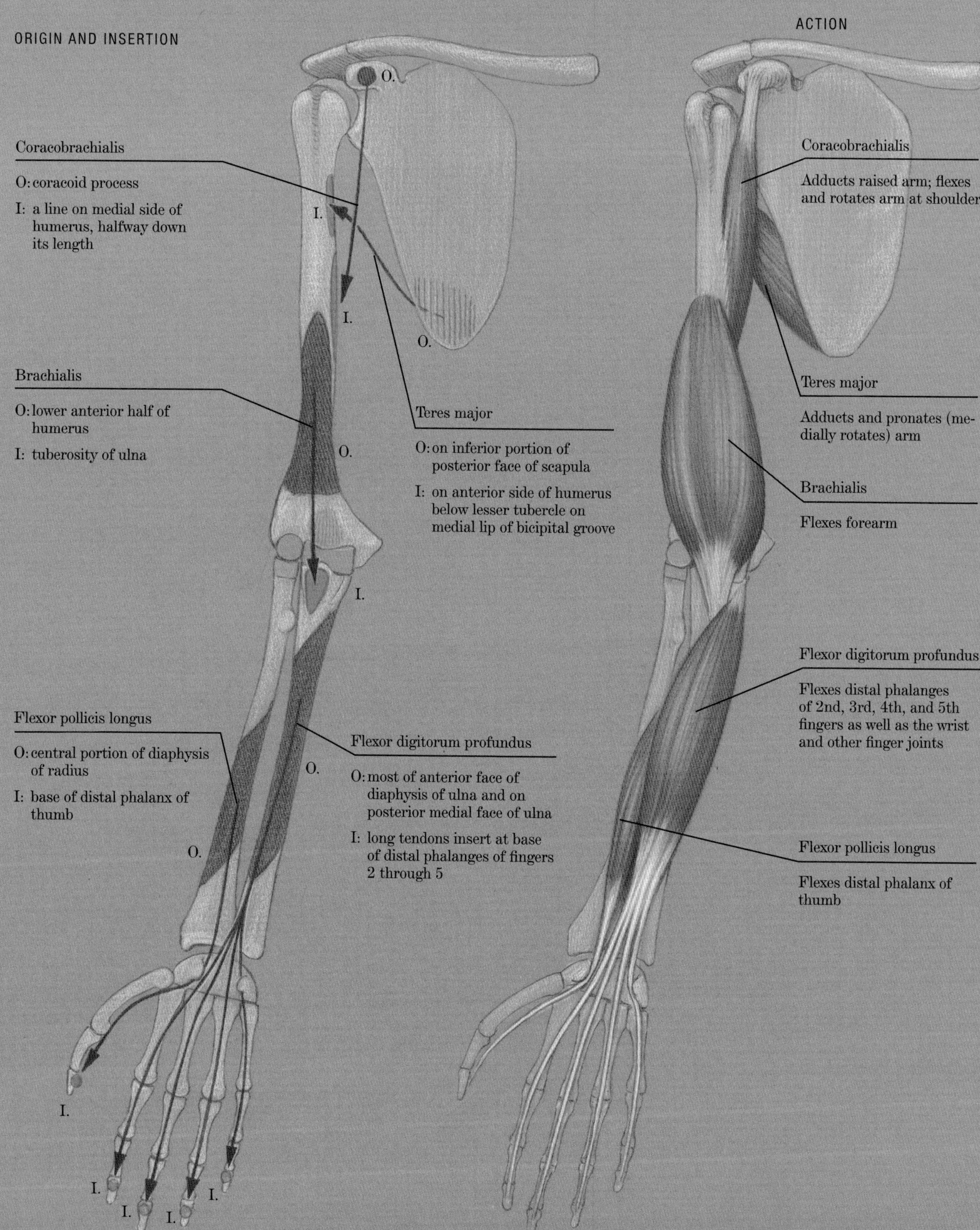

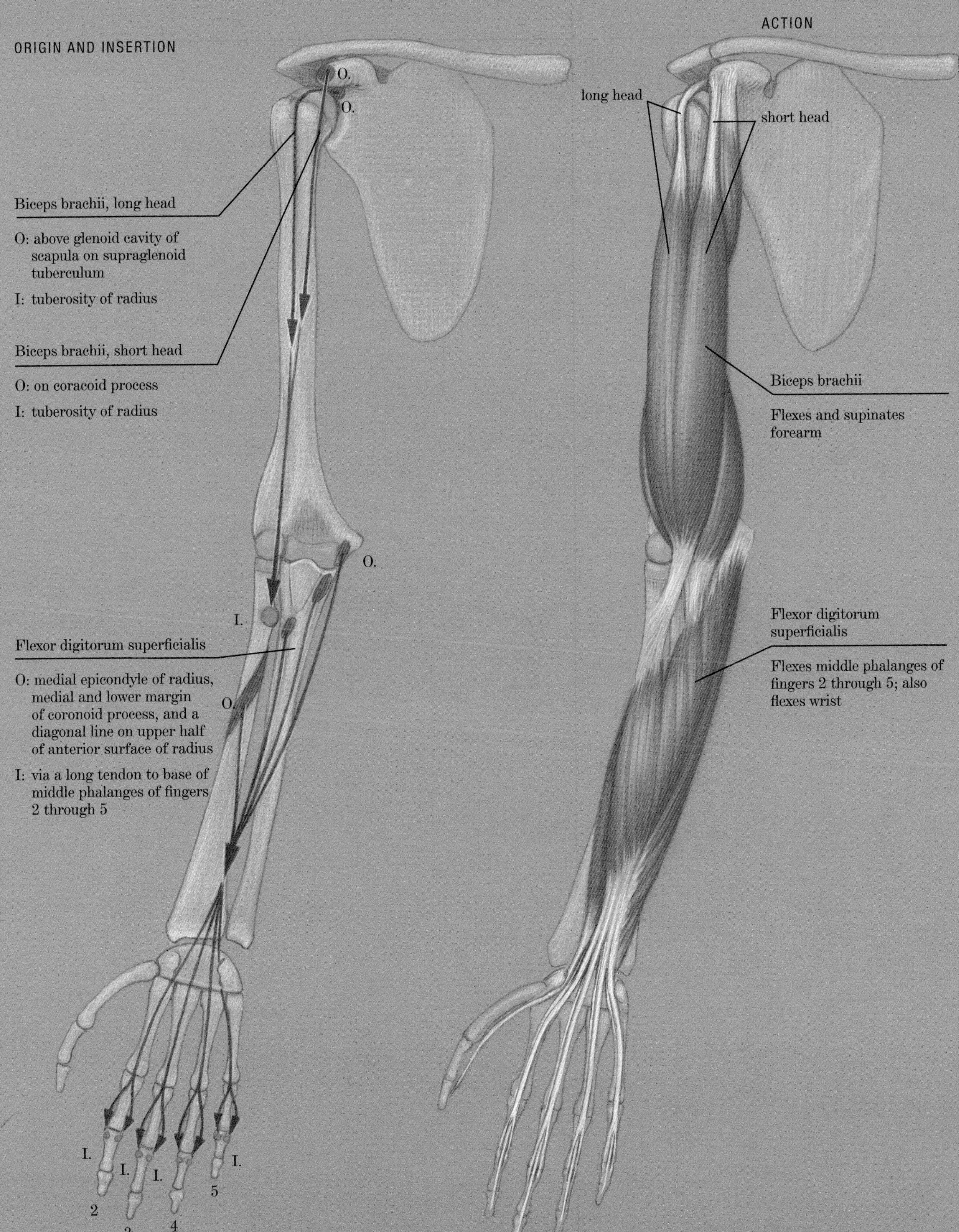
ORIGIN AND INSERTION
ACTION
O.
O.
long head
short head
Biceps brachii, long head
O: above glenoid cavity of
scapula on supraglenoid
tuberculum
I: tuberosity of radius
Biceps brachii, short head
O: on coracoid process
I: tuberosity of radius
Biceps brachii
Flexes and supinates
forearm
O.
I.
Flexor digitorum superficialis
O: medial epicondyle of radius,
medial and lower margin
of coronoid process, and a
diagonal line on upper half
of anterior surface of radius
I: via a long tendon to base of
middle phalanges of fingers
2 through 5
O.
Flexor digitorum
superficialis
Flexes middle phalanges of
fingers 2 through 5; also
flexes wrist
I.
I.
I.
I.
2
3
4
5

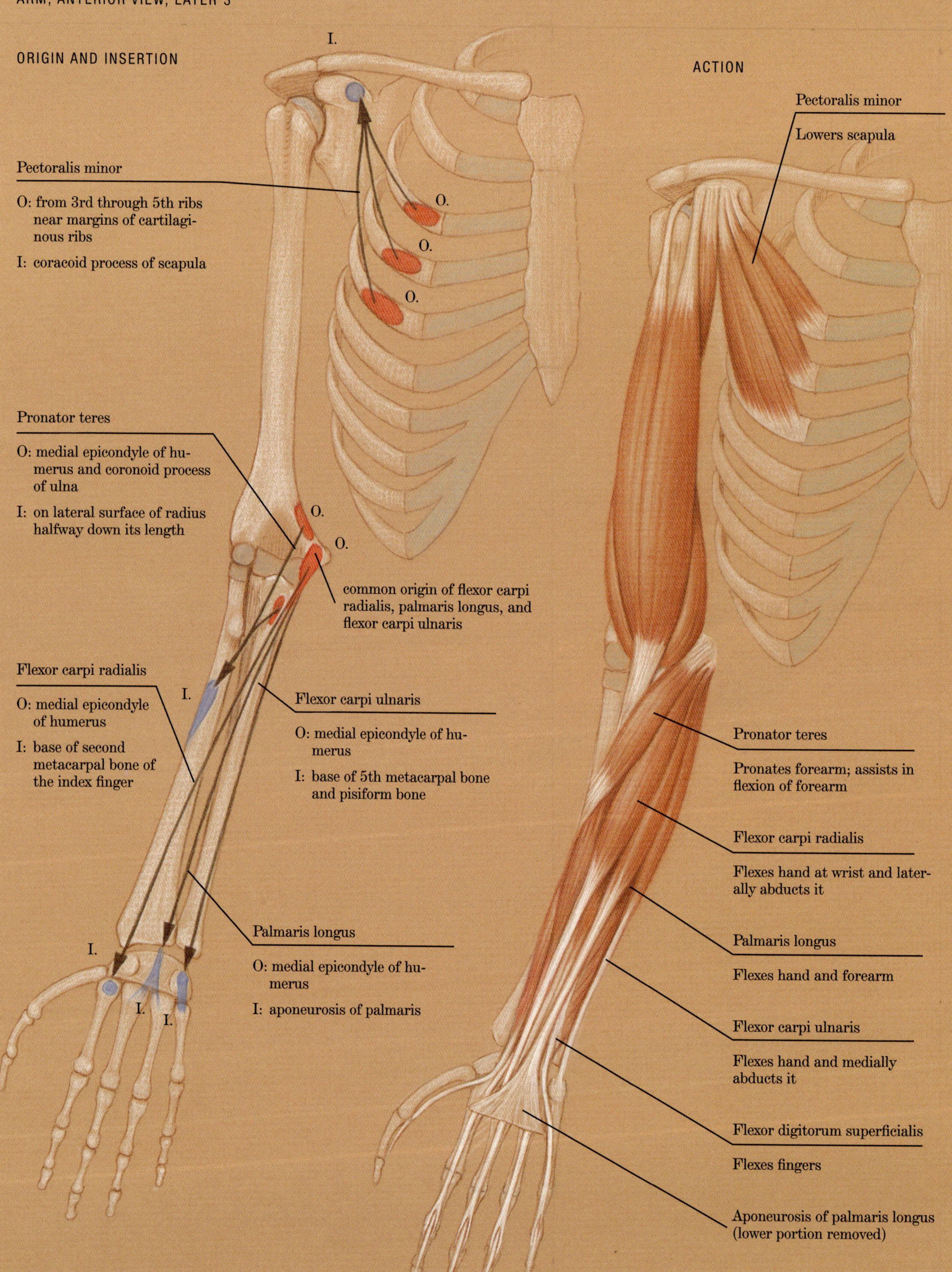
ORIGIN AND INSERTION

ACTION

I.

O.
O.
O.

Pectoralis minor

O: from 3rd through 5th ribs
near margins of cartilagi-
nous ribs

I: coracoid process of scapula

Pronator teres

O: medial epicondyle of humerus and coronoid process
of ulna

I: on lateral surface of radius
halfway down its length

O.
O.
I.

common origin of flexor carpi
radialis, palmaris longus, and
flexor carpi ulnaris

Flexor carpi radialis

O: medial epicondyle
of humerus

I: base of second
metacarpal bone of
the index finger

I.

Flexor carpi ulnaris

O: medial epicondyle of humerus

I: base of 5th metacarpal bone
and pisiform bone

I.
I. I.

Palmaris longus

O: medial epicondyle of humerus

I: aponeurosis of palmaris

Pectoralis minor

Lowers scapula

Pronator teres

Pronates forearm; assists in
flexion of forearm

Flexor carpi radialis

Flexes hand at wrist and laterally abducts it

Palmaris longus

Flexes hand and forearm

Flexor carpi ulnaris

Flexes hand and medially
abducts it

Flexor digitorum superficialis

Flexes fingers

Aponeurosis of palmaris longus
(lower portion removed)

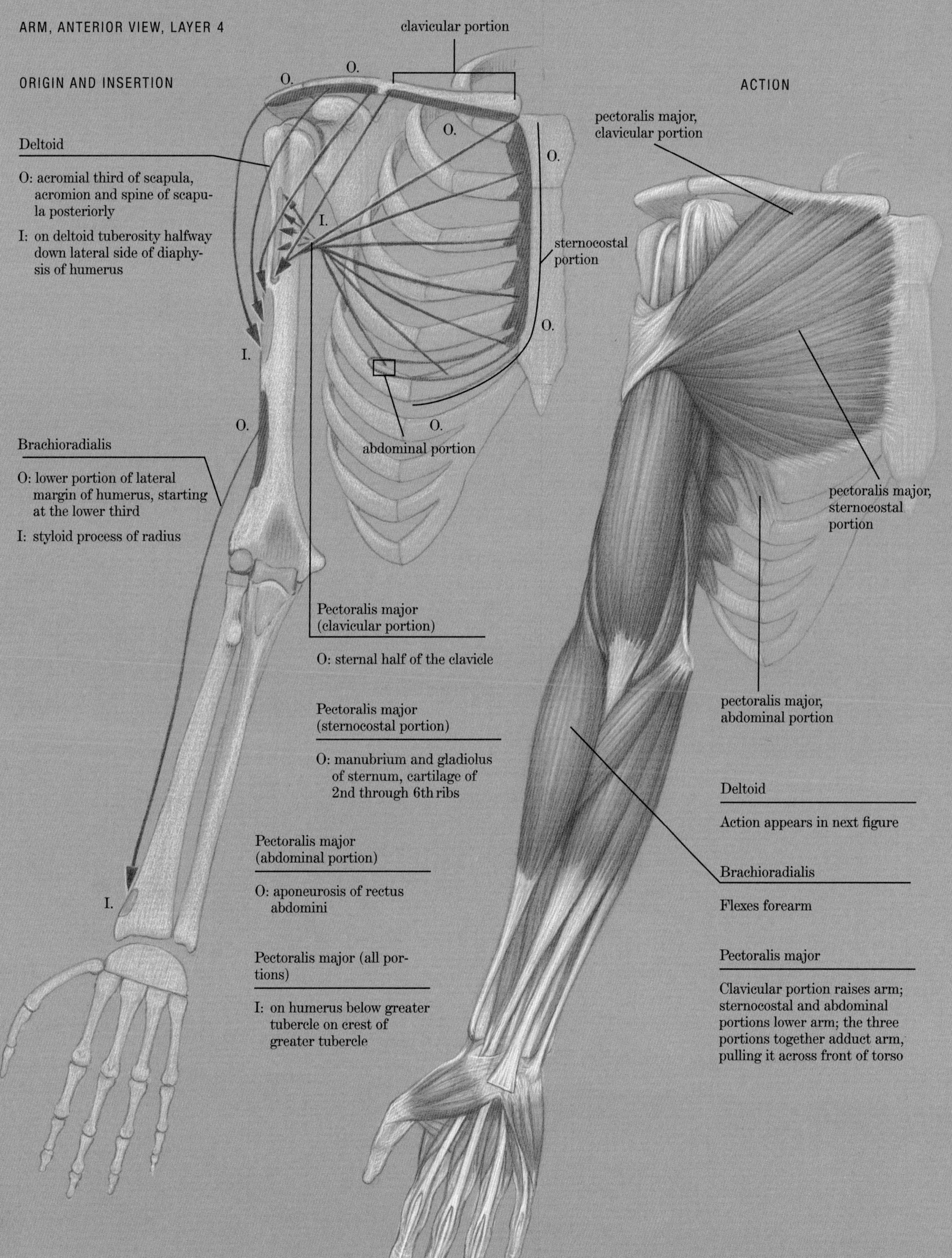
ORIGIN AND INSERTION

ACTION

clavicular portion

O.
O.
O.
O.
O.
O.
O.

sternocostal portion

I.

abdominal portion

Deltoid

O: acromial third of scapula, acromion and spine of scapula posteriorly

I: on deltoid tuberosity halfway down lateral side of diaphysis of humerus

I.
O.

Brachioradialis

O: lower portion of lateral margin of humerus, starting at the lower third

I: styloid process of radius

I.

Pectoralis major (clavicular portion)

O: sternal half of the clavicle

Pectoralis major (sternocostal portion)

O: manubrium and gladiolus of sternum, cartilage of 2nd through 6th ribs

Pectoralis major (abdominal portion)

O: aponeurosis of rectus abdomini

Pectoralis major (all portions)

I: on humerus below greater tubercle on crest of greater tubercle

pectoralis major, clavicular portion

pectoralis major, sternocostal portion

pectoralis major, abdominal portion

Deltoid

Action appears in next figure

Brachioradialis

Flexes forearm

Pectoralis major

Clavicular portion raises arm; sternocostal and abdominal portions lower arm; the three portions together adduct arm, pulling it across front of torso

ACTION

Deltoid

Anterior portion raises arm
forward and, with arm in horizontal position, pulls it inward
toward the body; anterior
portion also rotates the arm
inward; lateral portion raises
arm laterally; posterior portion
extends arm posteriorly and
also rotates it externally

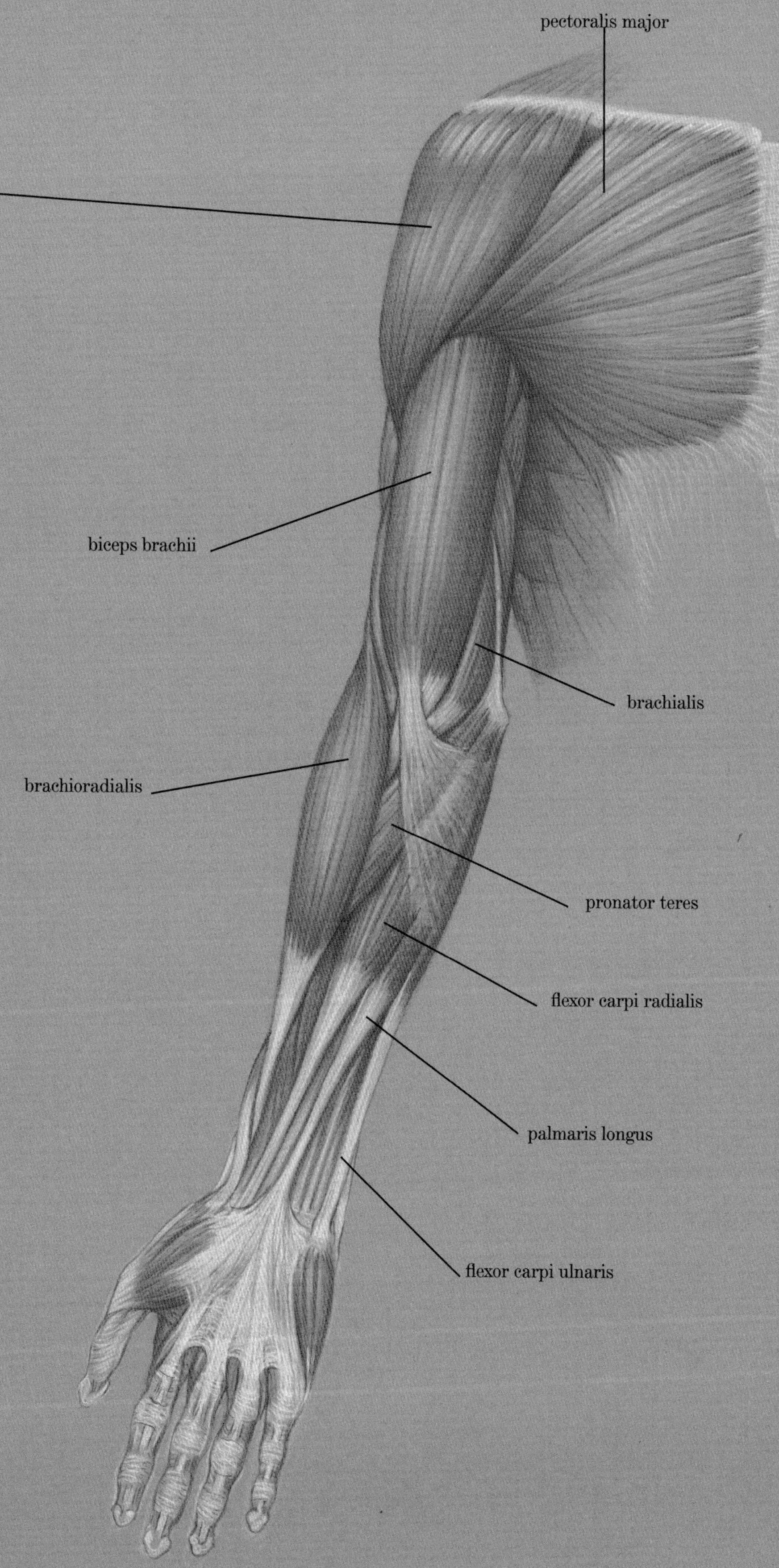

ACTION

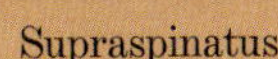

Supraspinatus

O: fossa supraspinata of
scapula

I: greater tubercle of
humerus

Teres major

O: inferior portion of scapula
on its posterior face

I: on anterior side of humerus,
below lesser tubercle on
medial lip of groove of biceps

Brachioradialis

O: lower part of lateral
margin of humerus

I: styloid process of
radius

**Extensor carpi radialis
longus**

O: lower portion of lateral
margin of humerus

I: dorsal side of 2nd metacarpal

Anconeus

O: lateral condyle of humerus

I: posterior side of ulna, just
below olecranon

Extensor carpi radialis brevis

O: lateral epicondyle of humerus

I: dorsal side of 3rd metacarpal

Supraspinatus

Abducts (lifts) arm

Teres major

Adducts arm and pronates
(medially rotates) it

Brachioradialis

Flexes forearm

**Extensor carpi
radialis longus**

Extends hand,
abducts hand at
wrist

**Extensor carpi
radialis brevis**

Extends hand,
abducts hand at
wrist

Anconeus

Extends forearm;
stabilizes forearm

ORIGIN AND INSERTION

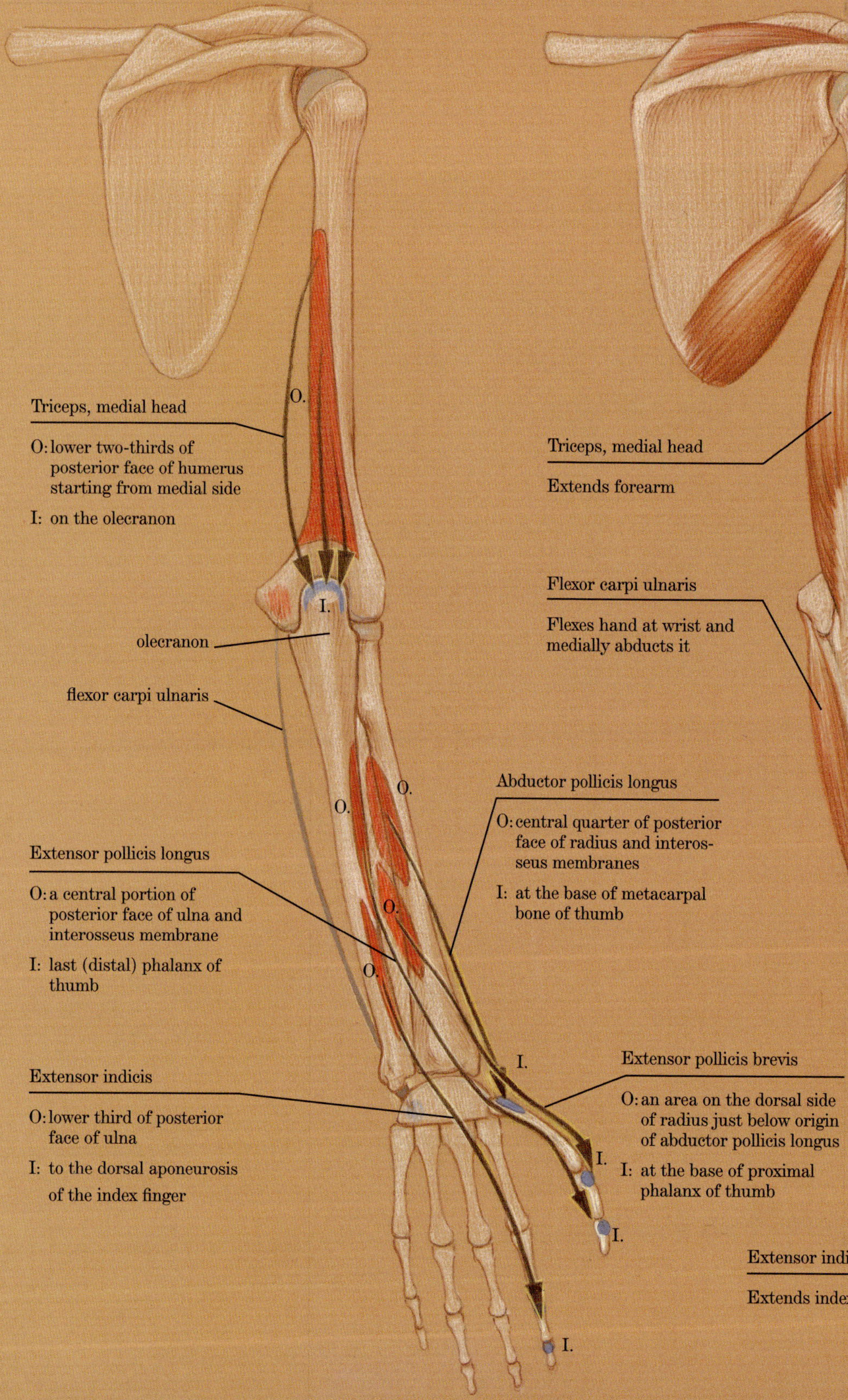

ACTION

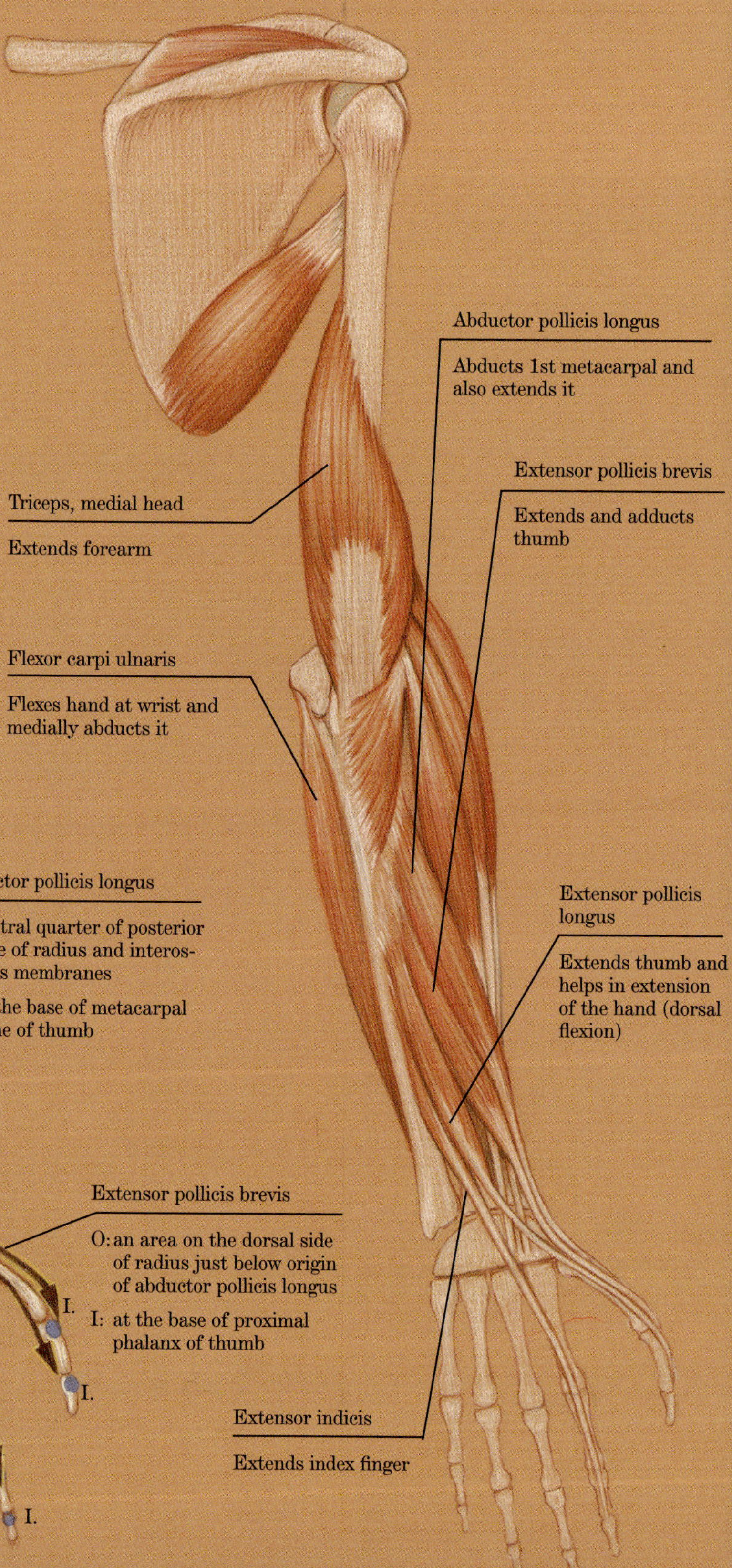

Triceps, medial head

O: lower two-thirds of posterior face of humerus starting from medial side

I: on the olecranon

olecranon

flexor carpi ulnaris

Extensor pollicis longus

O: a central portion of posterior face of ulna and interosseus membrane

I: last (distal) phalanx of thumb

Extensor indicis

O: lower third of posterior face of ulna

I: to the dorsal aponeurosis of the index finger

Abductor pollicis longus

O: central quarter of posterior face of radius and interosseus membranes

I: at the base of metacarpal bone of thumb

Extensor pollicis brevis

O: an area on the dorsal side of radius just below origin of abductor pollicis longus

I: at the base of proximal phalanx of thumb

Triceps, medial head

Extends forearm

Flexor carpi ulnaris

Flexes hand at wrist and medially abducts it

Abductor pollicis longus

Abducts 1st metacarpal and also extends it

Extensor pollicis brevis

Extends and adducts thumb

Extensor pollicis longus

Extends thumb and helps in extension of the hand (dorsal flexion)

Extensor indicis

Extends index finger

ORIGIN AND INSERTION

ACTION

glenoid fossa

infraglenoid tuberculum

O.

O.

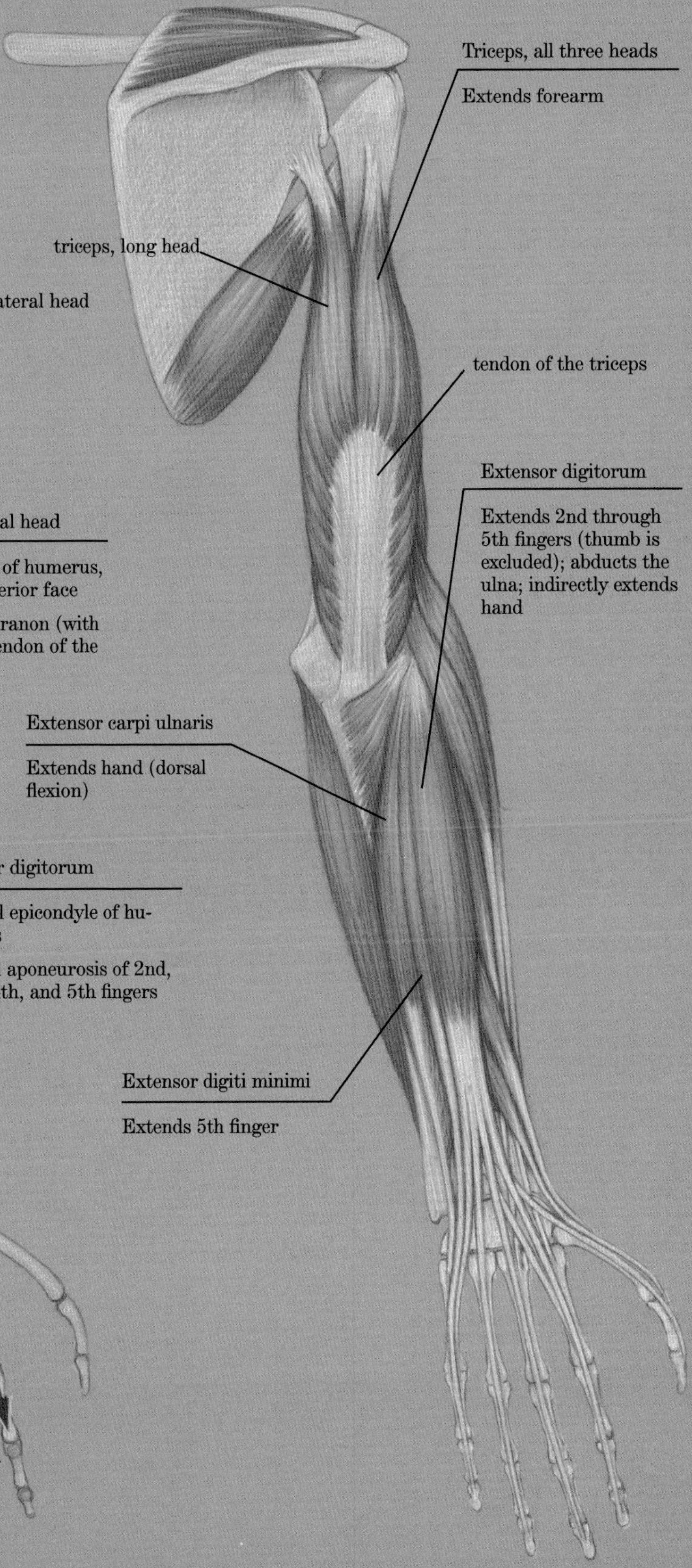

Triceps, all three heads

Extends forearm

triceps, long head

triceps, lateral head

tendon of the triceps

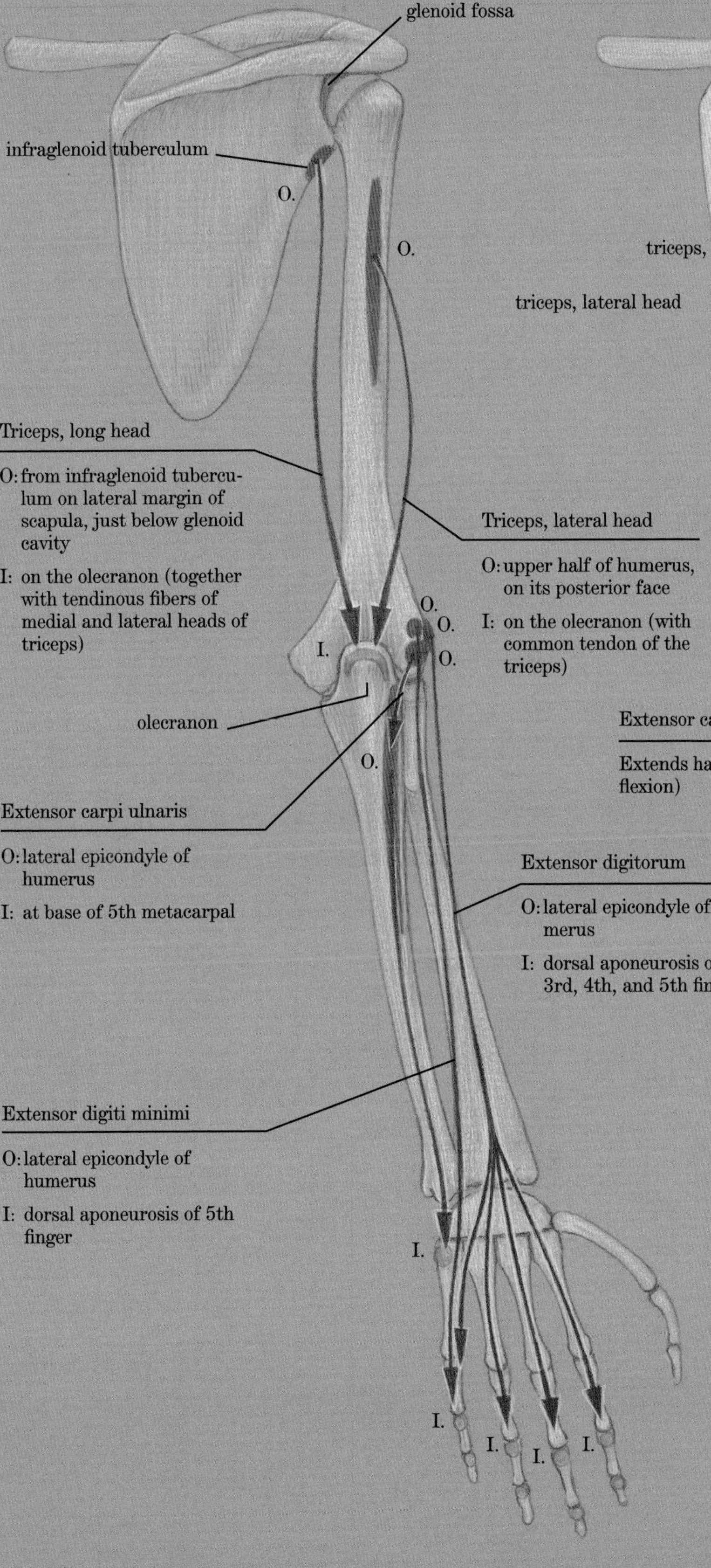

Triceps, long head

O: from infraglenoid tuberculum on lateral margin of
scapula, just below glenoid
cavity

I: on the olecranon (together
with tendinous fibers of
medial and lateral heads of
triceps)

olecranon

Triceps, lateral head

O: upper half of humerus,
on its posterior face

I: on the olecranon (with
common tendon of the
triceps)

Extensor digitorum

Extends 2nd through
5th fingers (thumb is
excluded); abducts the
ulna; indirectly extends
hand

Extensor carpi ulnaris

O: lateral epicondyle of
humerus

I: at base of 5th metacarpal

Extensor carpi ulnaris

Extends hand (dorsal
flexion)

Extensor digitorum

O: lateral epicondyle of humerus

I: dorsal aponeurosis of 2nd,
3rd, 4th, and 5th fingers

Extensor digiti minimi

O: lateral epicondyle of
humerus

I: dorsal aponeurosis of 5th
finger

Extensor digiti minimi

Extends 5th finger

ORIGIN AND INSERTION

ACTION

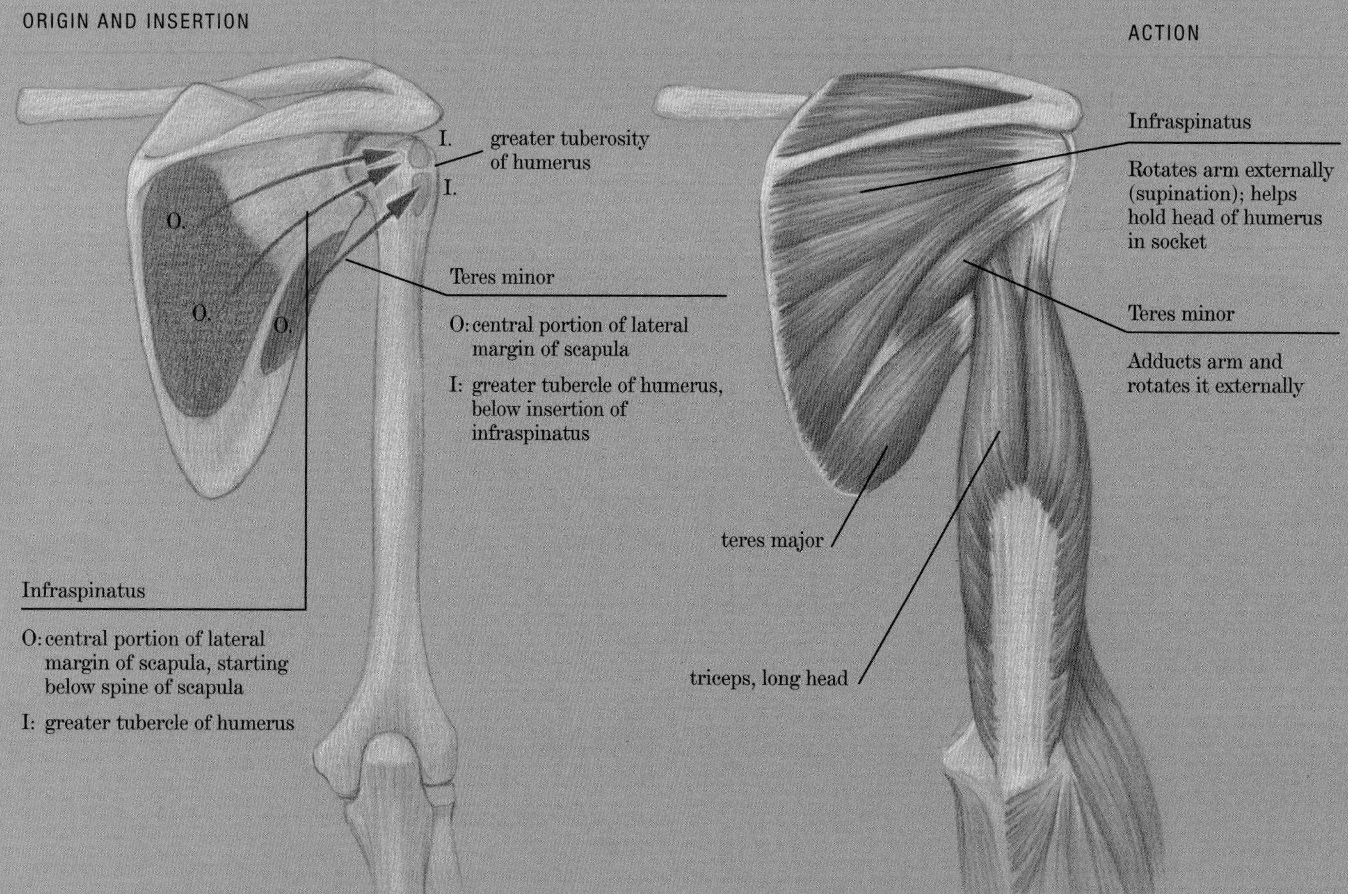

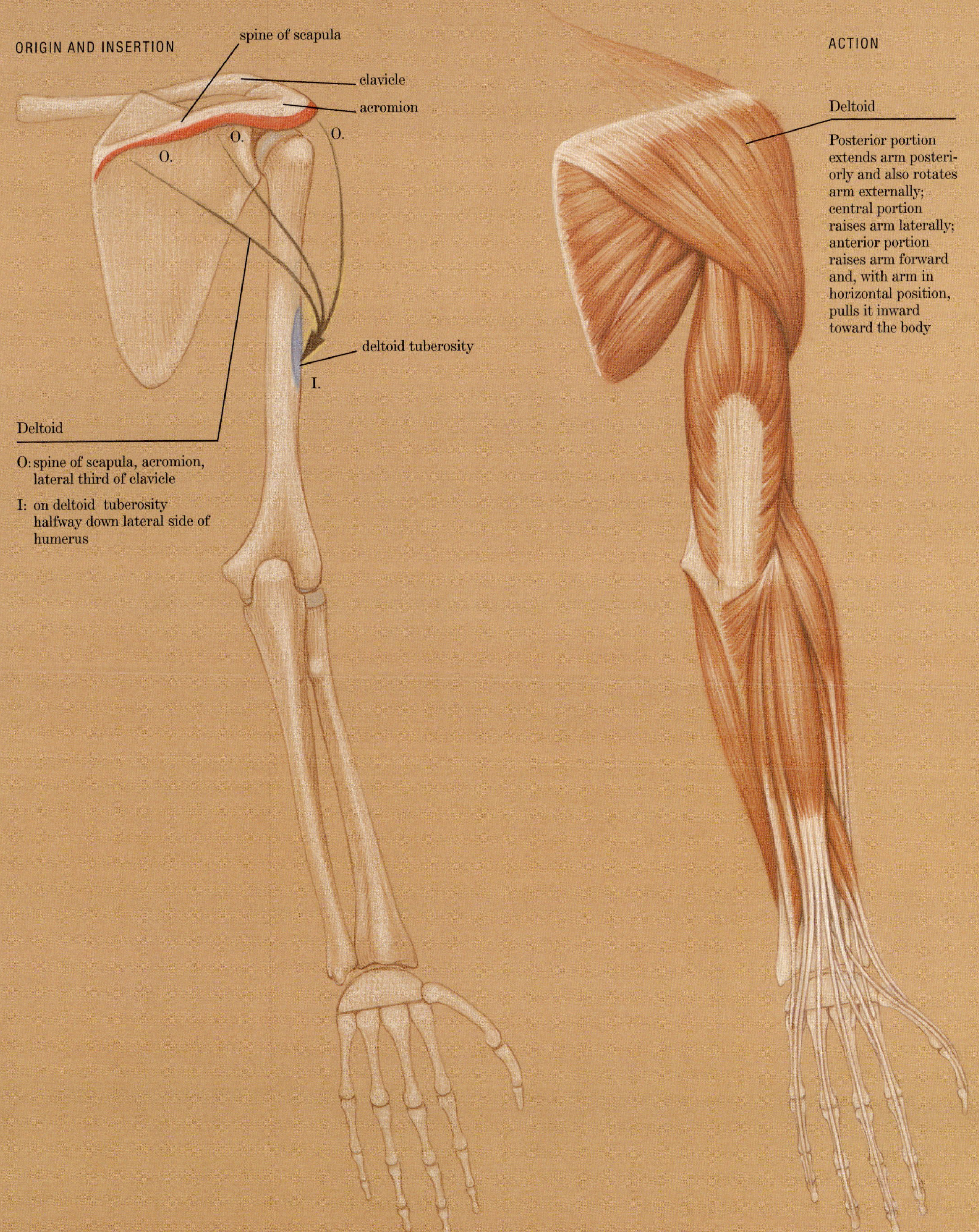
ORIGIN AND INSERTION
spine of scapula
clavicle
acromion
O.
O.
O.
deltoid tuberosity
I.
Deltoid
O: spine of scapula, acromion, lateral third of clavicle
I: on deltoid tuberosity halfway down lateral side of humerus
ACTION
Deltoid
Posterior portion extends arm posteriorly and also rotates arm externally; central portion raises arm laterally; anterior portion raises arm forward and, with arm in horizontal position, pulls it inward toward the body

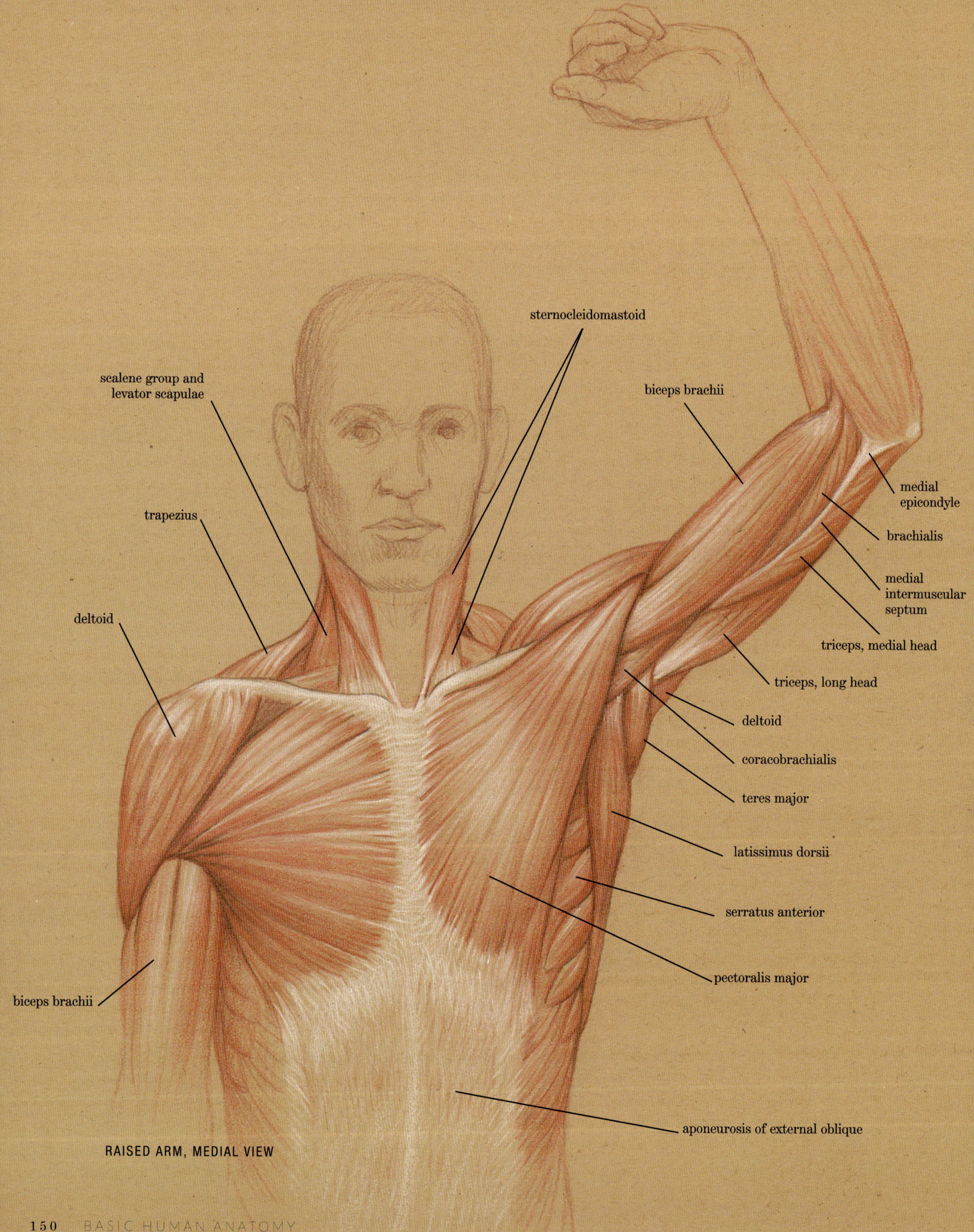

sternocleidomastoid
scalene group and
levator scapulae
biceps brachii
medial
epicondyle
brachialis
trapezius
medial
intermuscular
septum
triceps, medial head
triceps, long head
deltoid
deltoid
coracobrachialis
teres major
latissimus dorsii
serratus anterior
biceps brachii
pectoralis major
aponeurosis of external oblique
RAISED ARM, MEDIAL VIEW

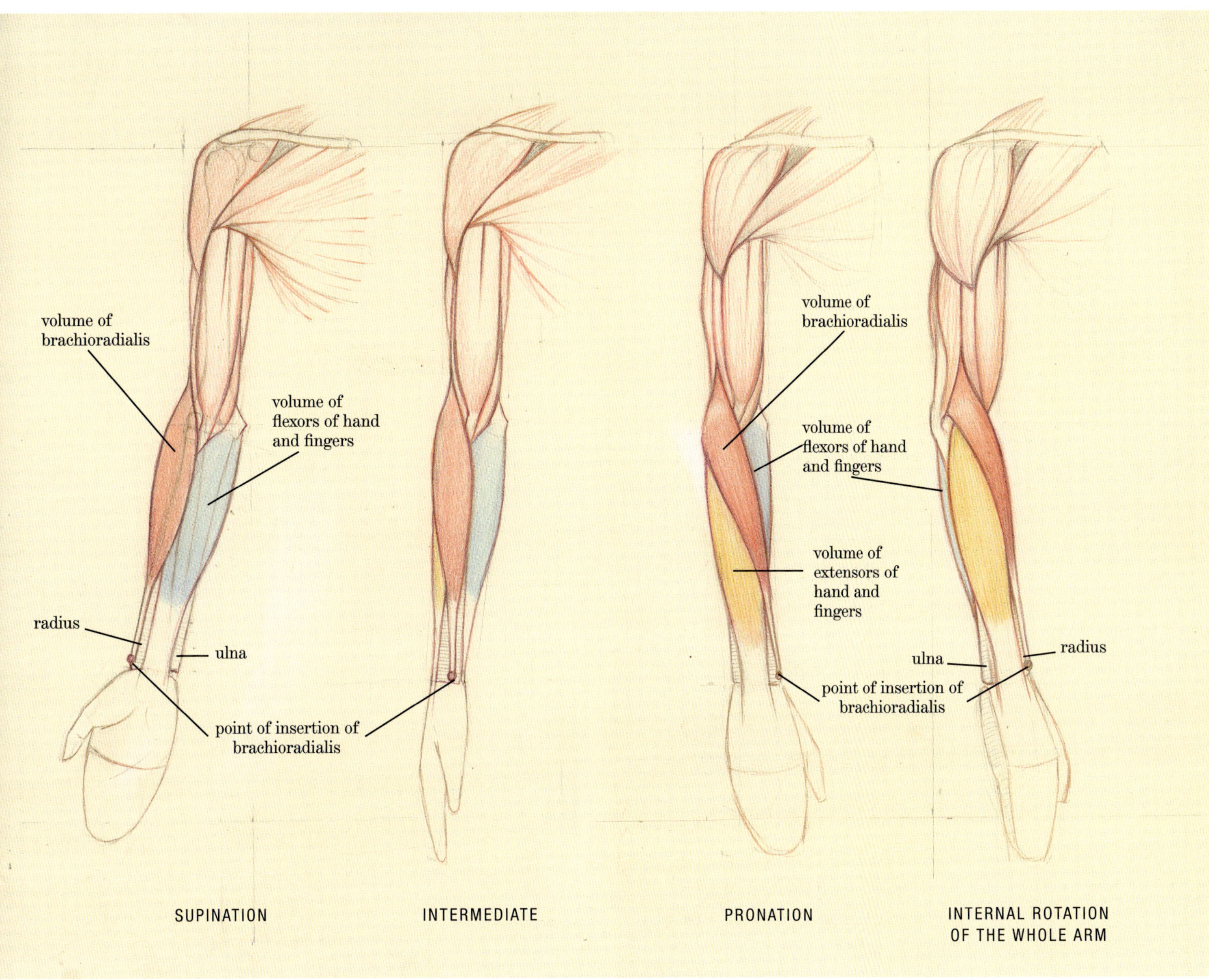

SUPINATION

Supination is the outward rotation of the hand, with the thumb moving away from the body. In this position the radius and ulna are parallel to each other.

PRONATION

Pronation is the inward rotation of the hand, with the thumb moving toward the body. In this position the radius crosses over the ulna.

ORIGIN AND INSERTION

Gluteus medius

O: superior portion of lateral side of ilium

I: on superior lateral part of greater trochanter

Iliopsoas (iliacus portion)

O: superior portion of iliac fossa

I: just below lesser trochanter of femur

Iliopsoas (psoas major portion)

O: transverse processes and lateral margins of lumbar vertebrae

I: on lesser trochanter of femur

Pectineus

O: linea pectinea of pubic bone

I: linea pectinea of femur (on superior margin of linea aspera)

Adductor group

O: from superior and inferior branches of pubic bone, ramus of ischium, and ischial tuberosity

I: linea aspera, on diaphysis of the femur, and adductors tubercle on medial condyle of femur

Peroneus brevis

O: inferior half of anterior margin of fibula

I: tuberosity of 5th metacarpal bone

Extensor hallucis longus

O: inferior half of lateral-anterior margin of fibula and interosseus membrane

I: dorsal surface of hallucis

ACTION

Gluteus medius

Abducts thigh; anterior portion rotates thigh anteriorly; posterior portion rotates thigh posteriorly

Iliopsoas

Flexes thigh and trunk; rotates thigh laterally

Pectineus

Adducts thigh; contributes to external rotation and flexion of thigh

Adductor group

Adducts thigh; specific adductors contribute to movements of flexion and internal and external rotation at level of hip joint

Peroneus brevis

Raises lateral margin of foot (pronation)

Extensor hallucis longus

Extends hallucis

ADDUCTOR GROUP

For the sake of clarity, the adductor muscles are grouped together as if they were a single muscle. In reality, the adductors are four separate muscles: adductor magnus, adductor longus, adductor brevis, and adductor minimus. Adductor minimus is often considered a segment of adductor magnus rather than a separate muscle. (The pectineus is also an adductor, but I describe it separately because it originates from the superior branch of the pubic bone, unlike the other adductors, which originate from the inferior portion of the pubic bone.)

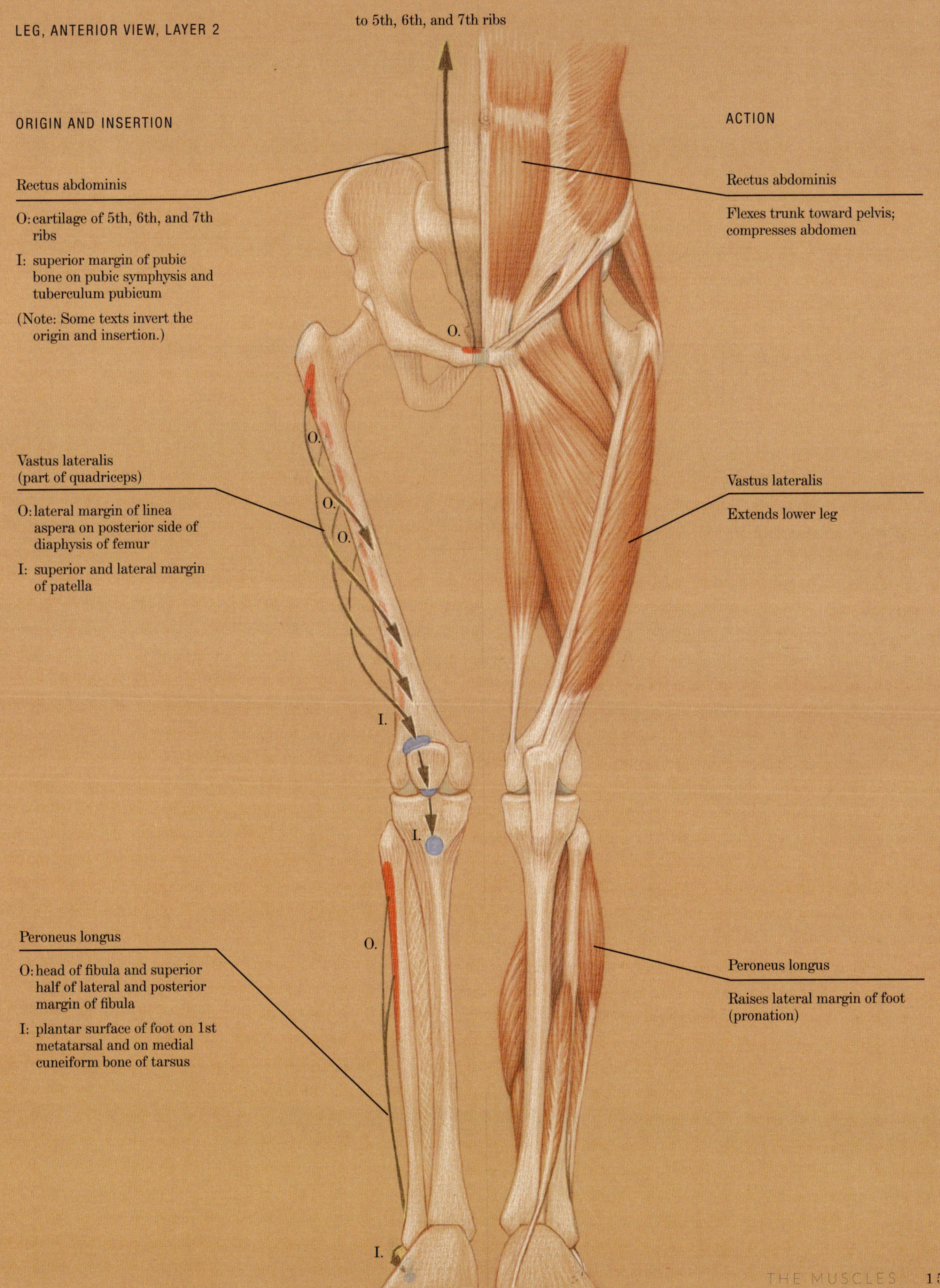

LEG, ANTERIOR VIEW, LAYER 2

ORIGIN AND INSERTION

Rectus abdominis

O: cartilage of 5th, 6th, and 7th ribs

I: superior margin of pubic bone on pubic symphysis and tuberculum pubicum

(Note: Some texts invert the origin and insertion.)

Vastus lateralis (part of quadriceps)

O: lateral margin of linea aspera on posterior side of diaphysis of femur

I: superior and lateral margin of patella

Peroneus longus

O: head of fibula and superior half of lateral and posterior margin of fibula

I: plantar surface of foot on 1st metatarsal and on medial cuneiform bone of tarsus

ACTION

Rectus abdominis

Flexes trunk toward pelvis; compresses abdomen

Vastus lateralis

Extends lower leg

Peroneus longus

Raises lateral margin of foot (pronation)

I.
to 5th, 6th, and 7th ribs

O.
O.
O.
O.
I.
I.
O.
I.

ORIGIN AND INSERTION

ACTION

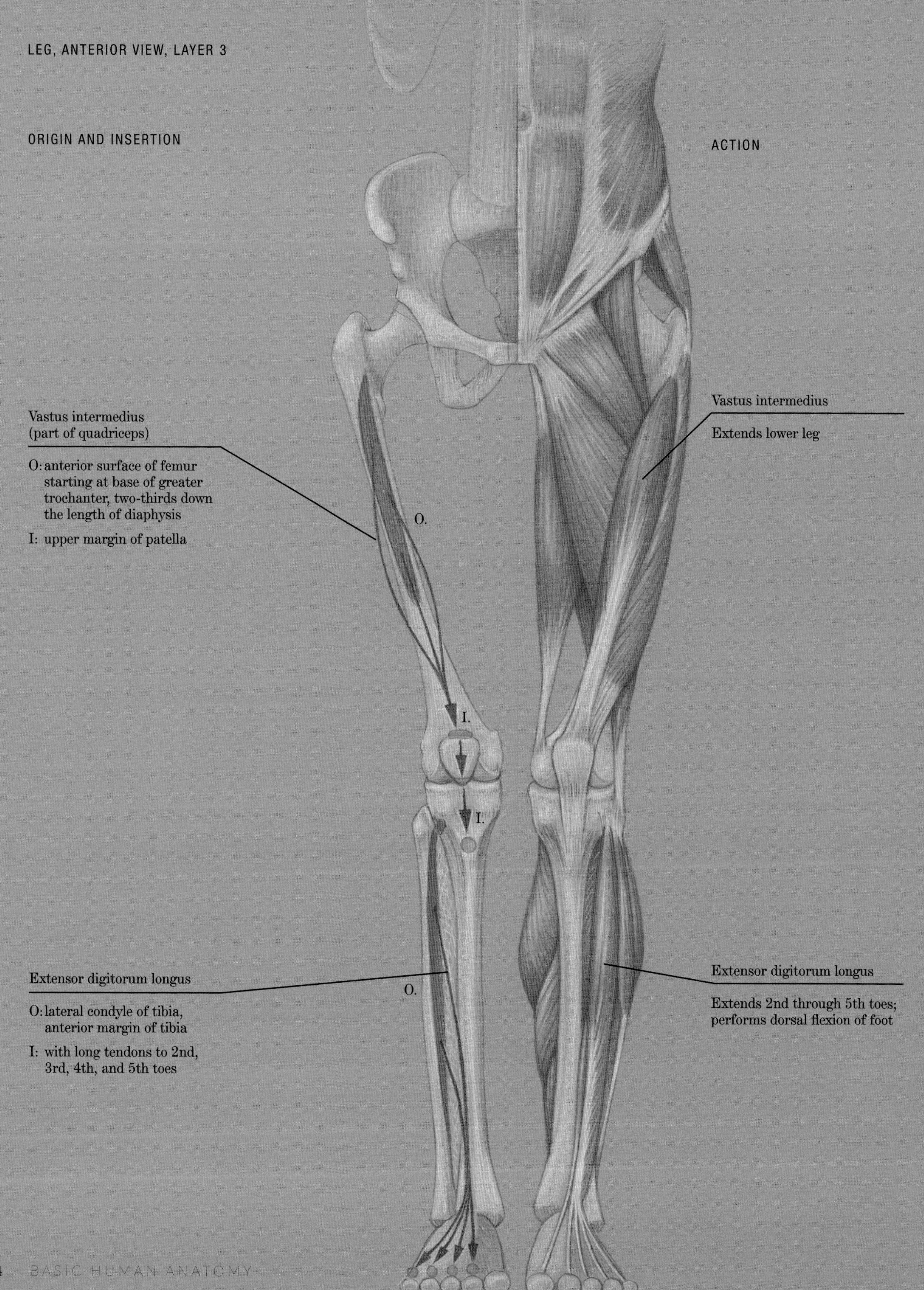

ORIGIN AND INSERTION

ACTION

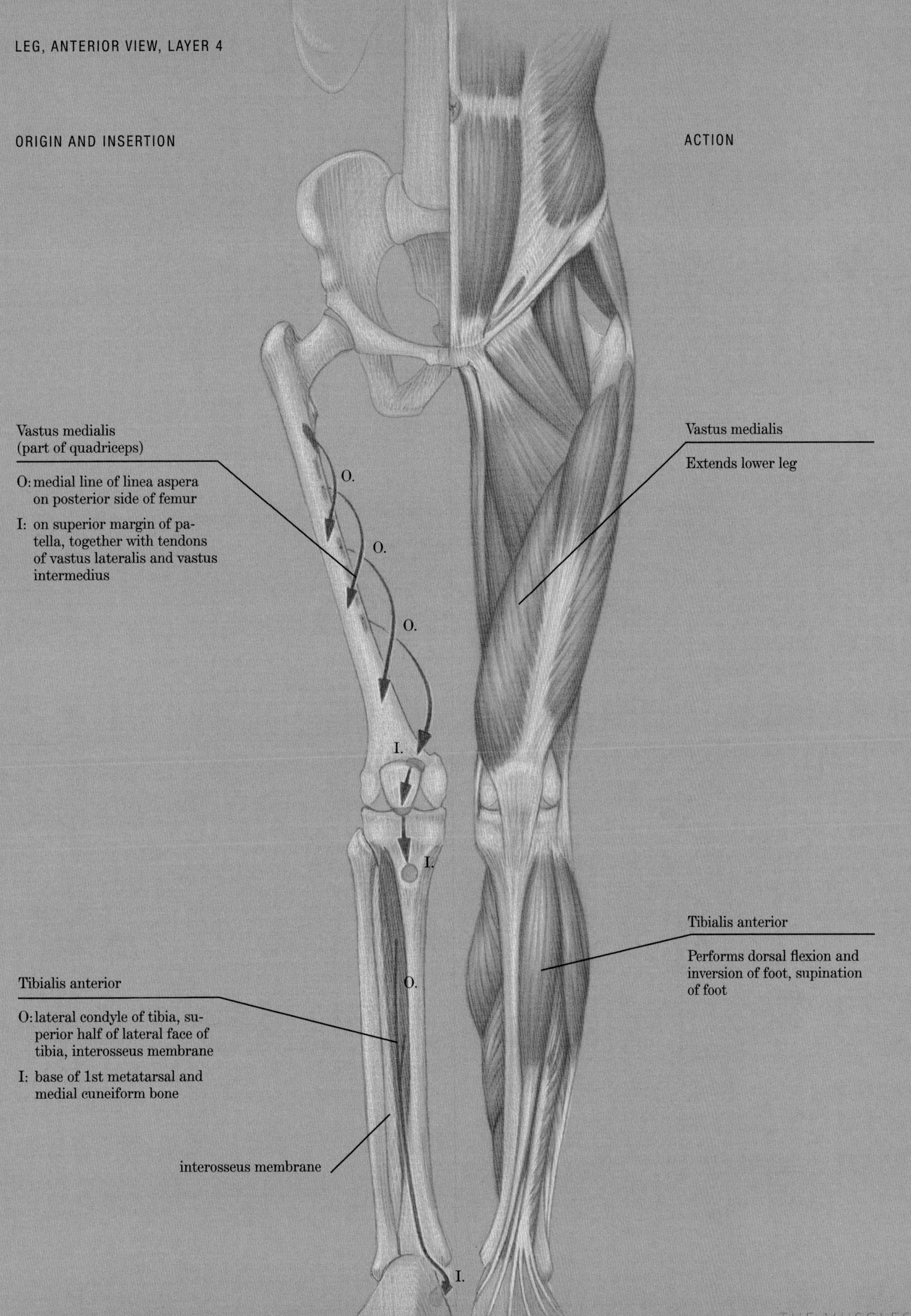

ORIGIN AND INSERTION

ACTION

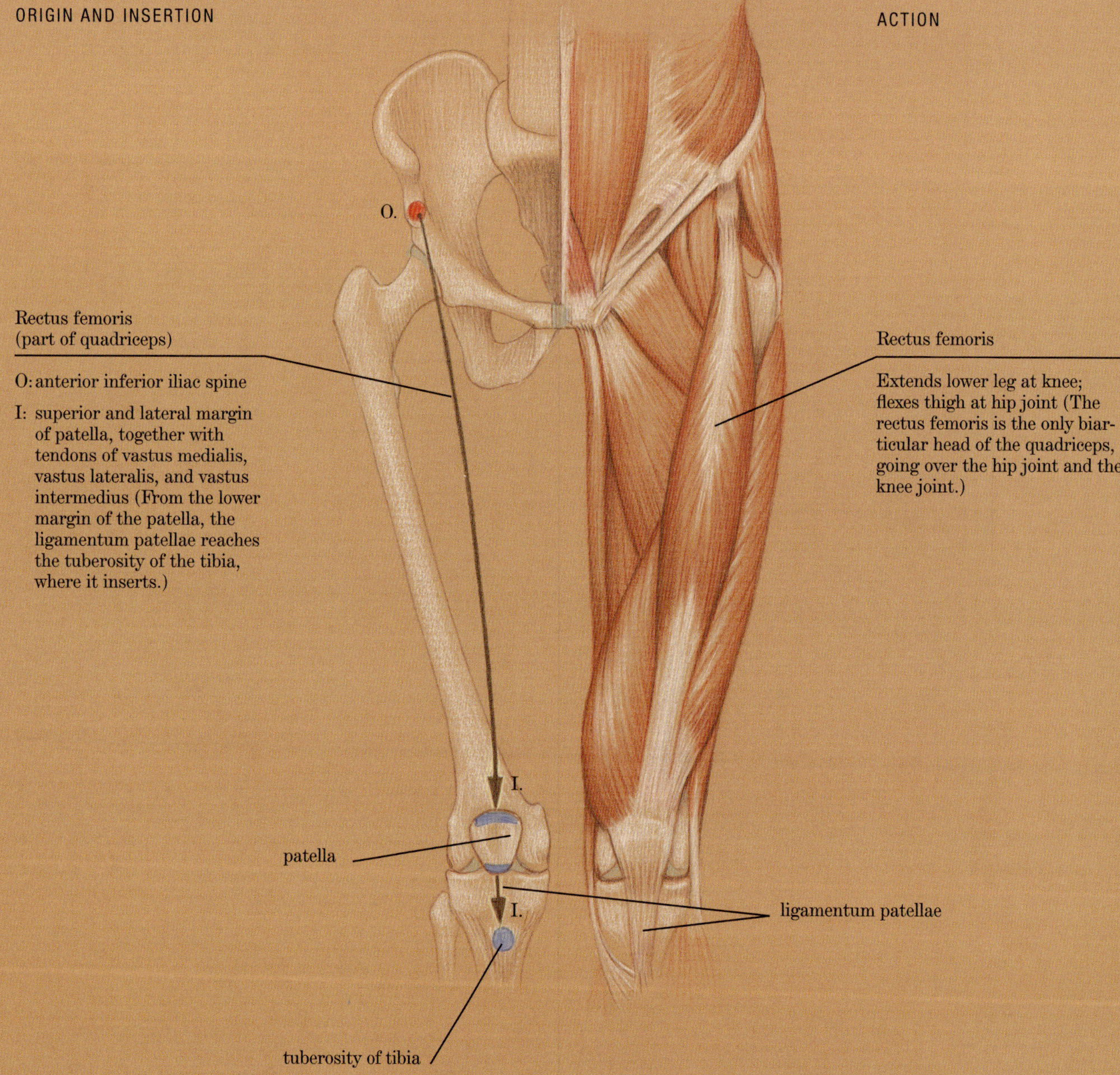

Rectus femoris
(part of quadriceps)

O: anterior inferior iliac spine

I: superior and lateral margin
of patella, together with
tendons of vastus medialis,
vastus lateralis, and vastus
intermedius (From the lower
margin of the patella, the
ligamentum patellae reaches
the tuberosity of the tibia,
where it inserts.)

Rectus femoris

Extends lower leg at knee;
flexes thigh at hip joint (The
rectus femoris is the only biar-
ticular head of the quadriceps,
going over the hip joint and the
knee joint.)

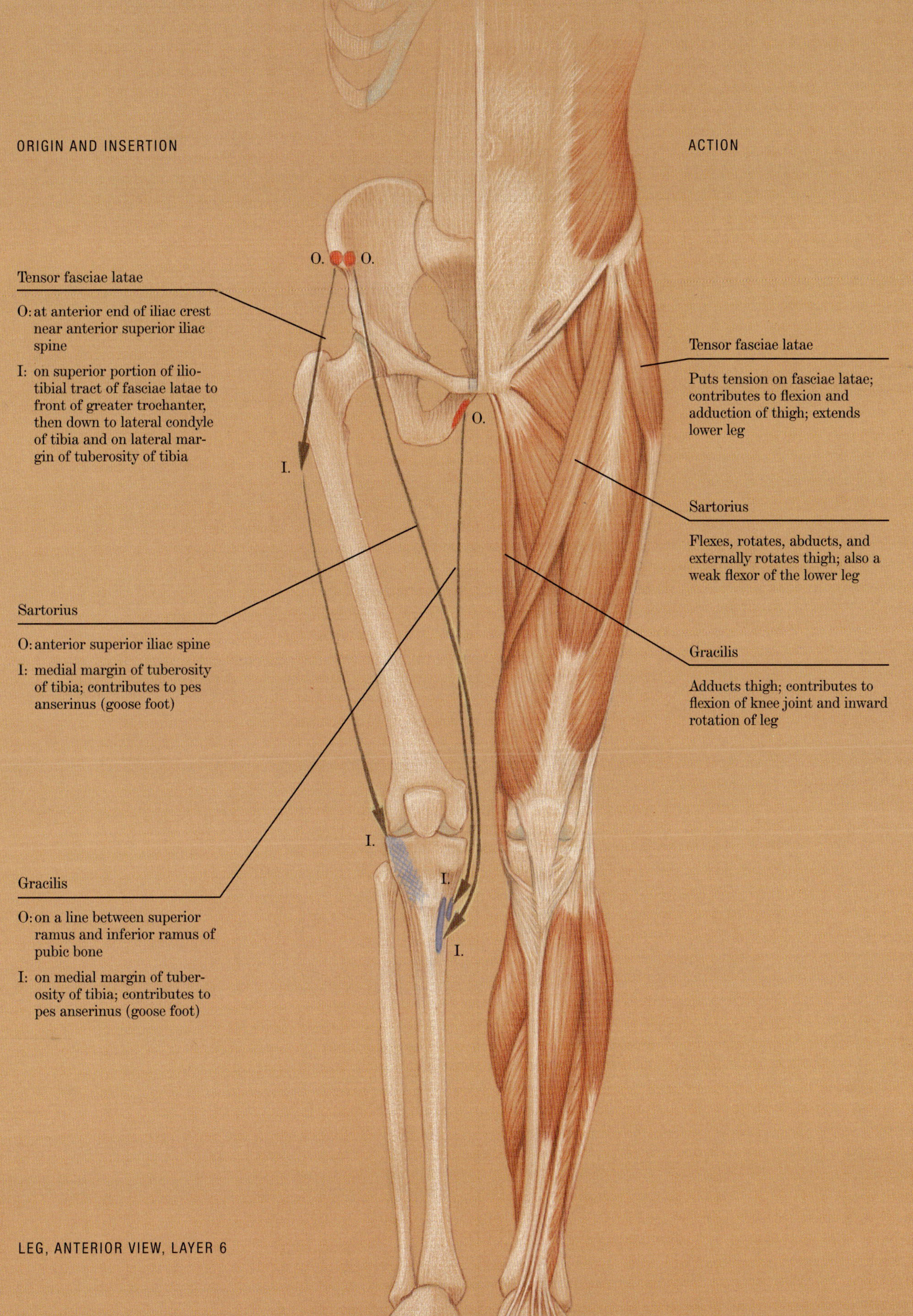
Tensor fasciae latae
O: at anterior end of iliac crest near anterior superior iliac spine
I: on superior portion of ilio-tibial tract of fasciae latae to front of greater trochanter, then down to lateral condyle of tibia and on lateral margin of tuberosity of tibia
Sartorius
O: anterior superior iliac spine
I: medial margin of tuberosity of tibia; contributes to pes anserinus (goose foot)
Gracilis
O: on a line between superior ramus and inferior ramus of pubic bone
I: on medial margin of tuberosity of tibia; contributes to pes anserinus (goose foot)
O. O.
O.
I.
I.
I.
I.
Tensor fasciae latae
Puts tension on fasciae latae; contributes to flexion and adduction of thigh; extends lower leg
Sartorius
Flexes, rotates, abducts, and externally rotates thigh; also a weak flexor of the lower leg
Gracilis
Adducts thigh; contributes to flexion of knee joint and inward rotation of leg
LEG, ANTERIOR VIEW, LAYER 6

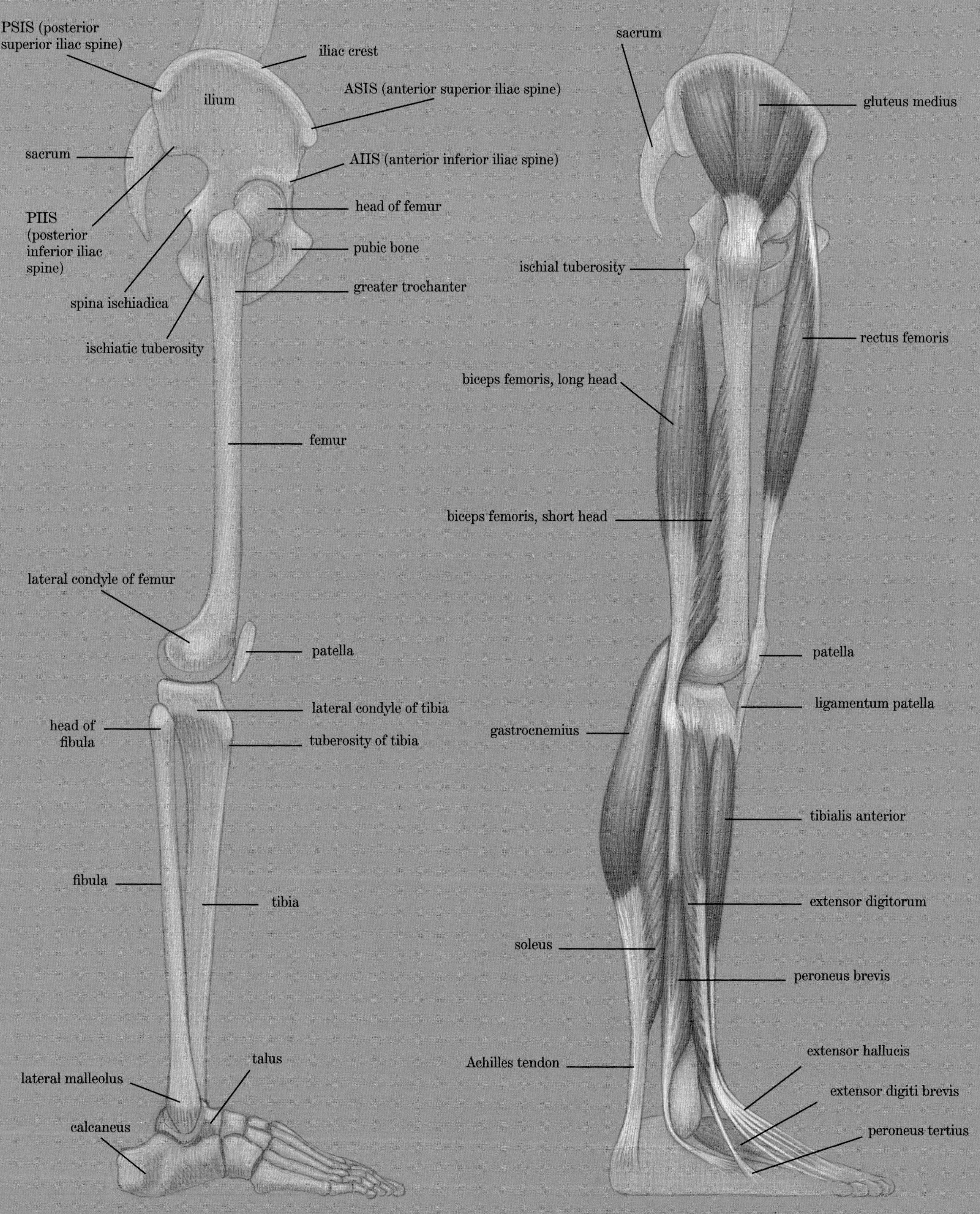

LEG, LATERAL VIEW, LAYER 1 (THE SKELETON)

LEG, LATERAL VIEW, LAYER 2

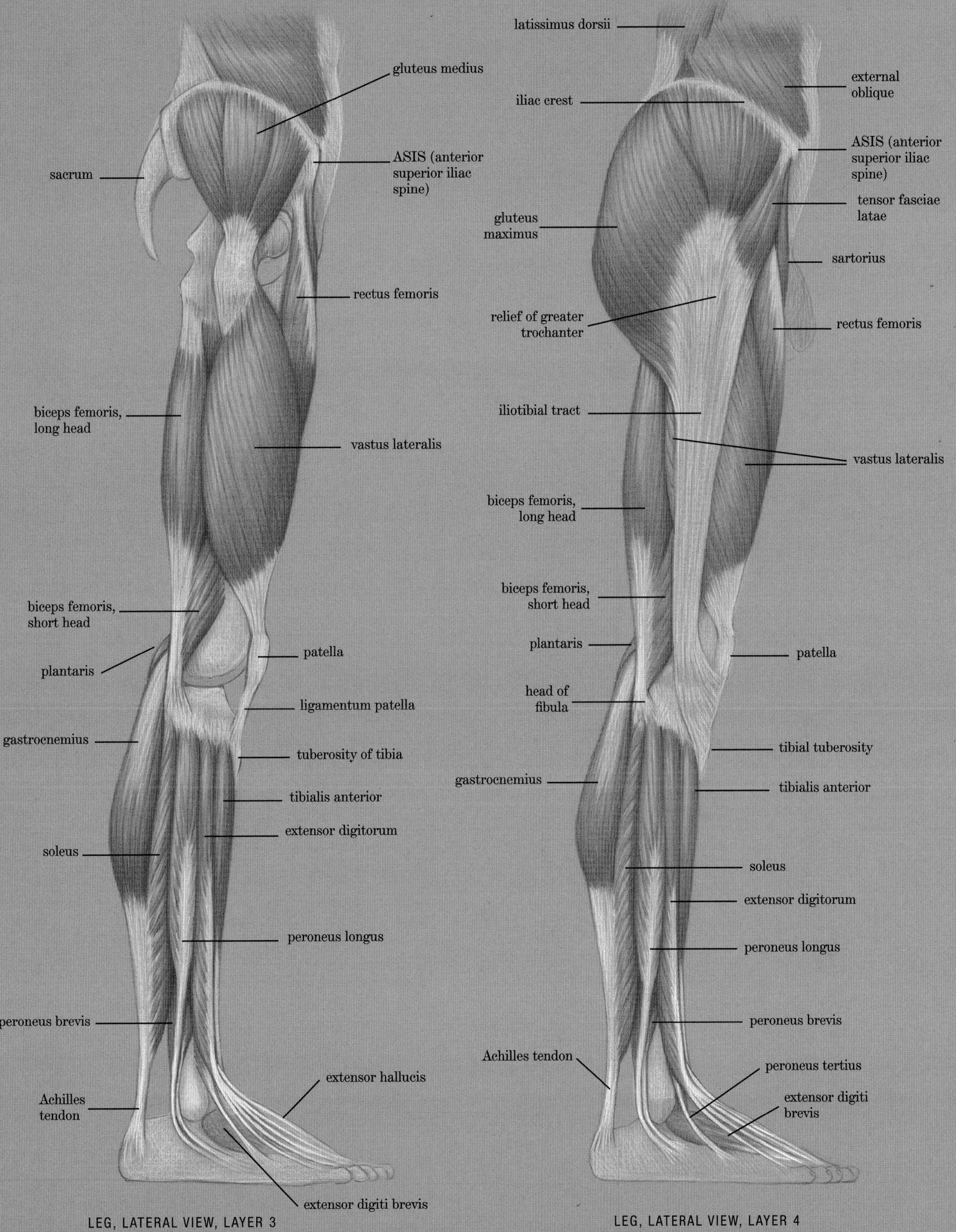

gluteus medius
sacrum
ASIS (anterior superior iliac spine)
rectus femoris
biceps femoris, long head
vastus lateralis
biceps femoris, short head
plantaris
patella
ligamentum patella
gastrocnemius
tuberosity of tibia
tibialis anterior
extensor digitorum
soleus
peroneus longus
peroneus brevis
extensor hallucis
Achilles tendon
extensor digiti brevis
LEG, LATERAL VIEW, LAYER 3
latissimus dorsii
iliac crest
external oblique
ASIS (anterior superior iliac spine)
gluteus maximus
tensor fasciae latae
sartorius
relief of greater trochanter
rectus femoris
iliotibial tract
vastus lateralis
biceps femoris, long head
biceps femoris, short head
plantaris
patella
head of fibula
tibial tuberosity
gastrocnemius
tibialis anterior
soleus
extensor digitorum
peroneus longus
peroneus brevis
Achilles tendon
peroneus tertius
extensor digiti brevis
LEG, LATERAL VIEW, LAYER 4

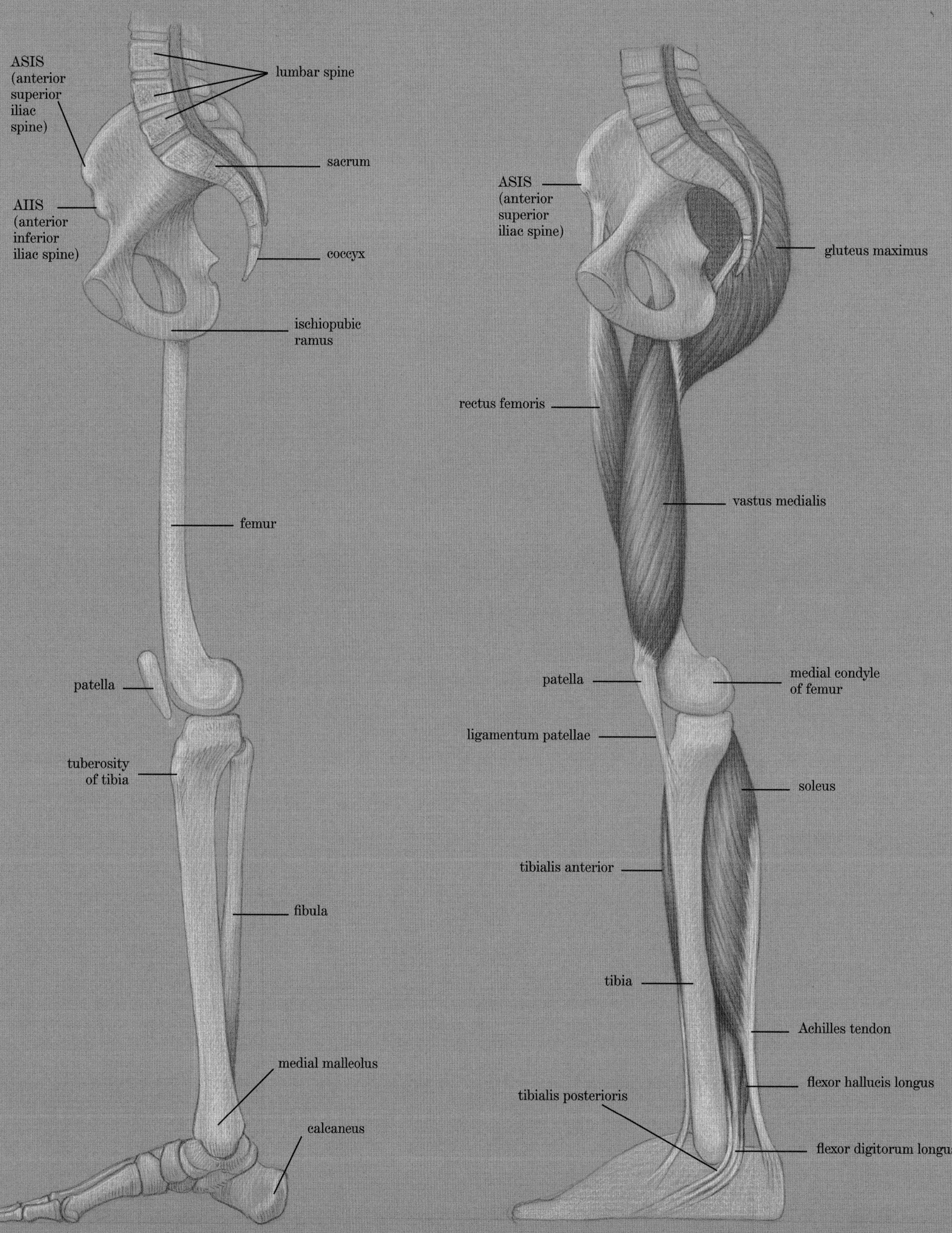

ASIS
(anterior
superior
iliac
spine)
lumbar spine
sacrum
AIIS
(anterior
inferior
iliac spine)
coccyx
ischiopubic
ramus
femur
patella
tuberosity
of tibia
fibula
medial malleolus
calcaneus
LEG, MEDIAL VIEW, LAYER 1 (THE SKELETON)
ASIS
(anterior
superior
iliac spine)
gluteus maximus
rectus femoris
vastus medialis
patella
medial condyle
of femur
ligamentum patellae
soleus
tibialis anterior
tibia
Achilles tendon
flexor hallucis longus
tibialis posterioris
flexor digitorum longus
LEG, MEDIAL VIEW, LAYER 2

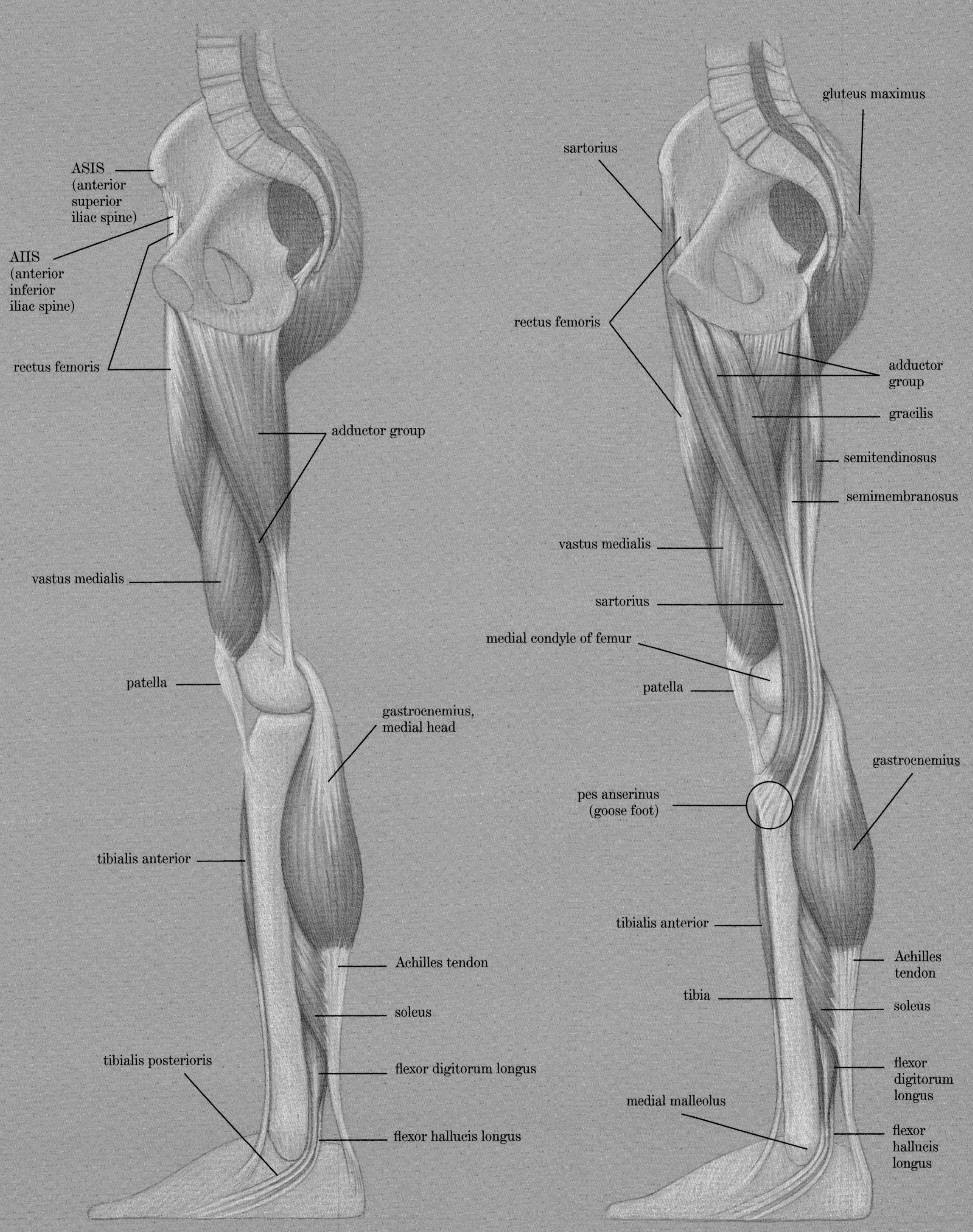

ASIS
(anterior
superior
iliac spine)
AIIS
(anterior
inferior
iliac spine)
rectus femoris
adductor group
vastus medialis
patella
gastrocnemius,
medial head
tibialis anterior
Achilles tendon
soleus
tibialis posterioris
flexor digitorum longus
flexor hallucis longus
gluteus maximus
sartorius
rectus femoris
adductor
group
gracilis
semitendinosus
semimembranosus
vastus medialis
sartorius
medial condyle of femur
patella
gastrocnemius
pes anserinus
(goose foot)
tibialis anterior
tibia
Achilles
tendon
soleus
flexor
digitorum
longus
medial malleolus
flexor
hallucis
longus
LEG, MEDIAL VIEW, LAYER 3
LEG, MEDIAL VIEW, LAYER 4

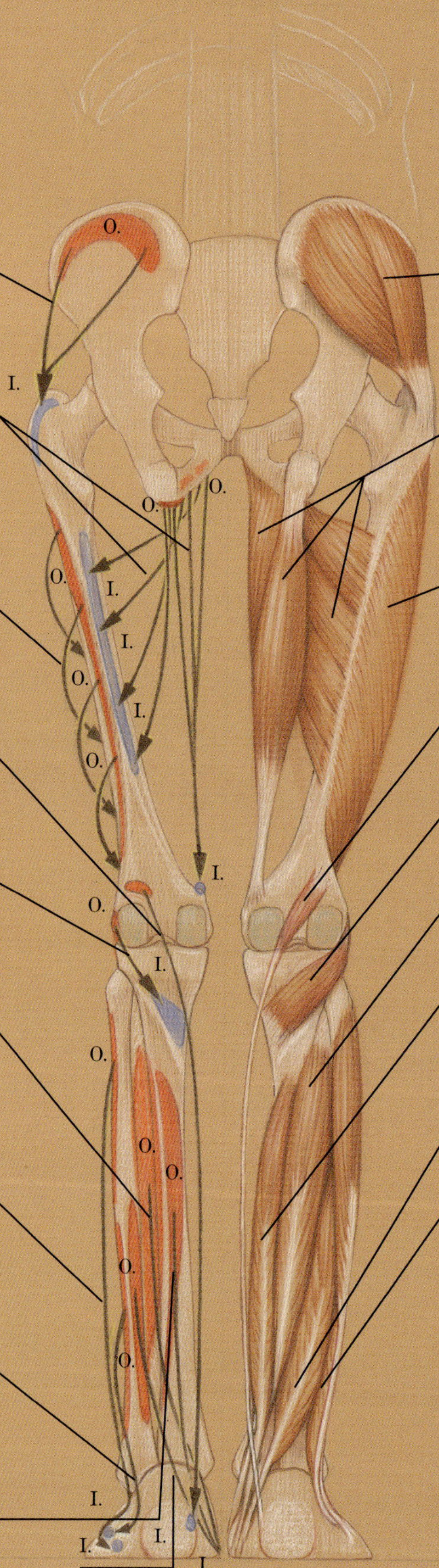

ORIGIN AND INSERTION

Gluteus medius

O: superior portion of lateral side of ilium

I: on superior-lateral part of greater trochanter

Adductor group

O: from inferior branch of pubic bone, ramus of ischium, and ischial tuberosity

I: linea aspera, on diaphysis of the femur, and adductors tubercle on medial condyle of femur

Vastus lateralis (part of quadriceps)

O: lateral margin of linea aspera on posterior side of diaphysis of femur

I: superior and lateral margin of patella

Plantaris

O: lateral epicondyle of femur

I: Achilles tendon

Popliteus

O: lateral epicondyle of femur

I: posterior face of tibia above origin of soleus (linea solei)

Tibialis posterioris

O: posterior face of tibia and interosseus membrane

I: to plantar surface of foot on tarsal and metatarsal bones

Peroneus longus

O: from superior half or two-thirds of lateral and posterior margins of fibula

I: plantar surface of foot on 1st metatarsal and medial cuneiform bone of tarsus

Peroneus brevis

O: inferior half of lateral and anterior margin of fibula

I: tuberosity of 5th metatarsal

Flexor digitorum longus

O: on posterior face of diaphysis of tibia

I: base of last (distal) phalanges of 2nd, 3rd, 4th, and 5th toes

Flexor hallucis longus

O: posterior face and medial margin of fibula

I: last phalanx of hallucis

ACTION

Gluteus medius

Abducts thigh; anterior portion rotates thigh anteriorly; posterior portion rotates thigh posteriorly

Adductor group

Adducts thigh; specific adductors contribute to movements of flexion and internal and external rotation at level of hip joint

Vastus lateralis (part of quadriceps)

Extends lower leg

Plantaris

Performs plantar flexion of foot

Popliteus

Flexes lower leg

Tibialis posterioris

Performs flexion and inversion of foot

Flexor digitorum longus

Flexes extremities of toes (except hallucis); supinates and adducts foot

Flexor hallucis longus

Flexes the hallucis

Peroneus longus and peroneus brevis

Raise lateral margin of foot (pronation)

ORIGIN AND INSERTION

ACTION

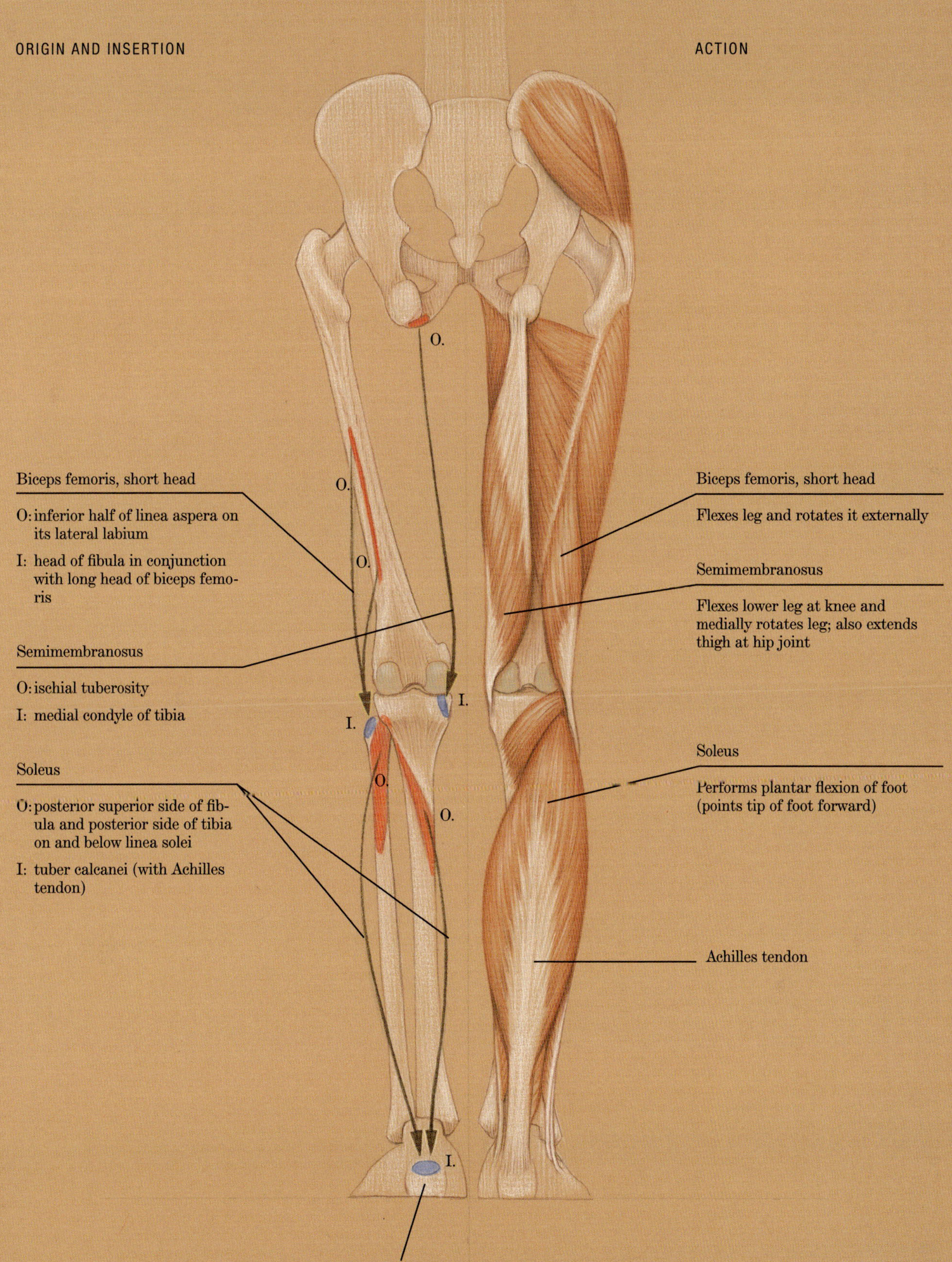

Biceps femoris, short head

O: inferior half of linea aspera on its lateral labium

I: head of fibula in conjunction with long head of biceps femoris

Semimembranosus

O: ischial tuberosity

I: medial condyle of tibia

Soleus

O: posterior superior side of fibula and posterior side of tibia on and below linea solei

I: tuber calcanei (with Achilles tendon)

Biceps femoris, short head

Flexes leg and rotates it externally

Semimembranosus

Flexes lower leg at knee and medially rotates leg; also extends thigh at hip joint

Soleus

Performs plantar flexion of foot (points tip of foot forward)

Achilles tendon

tuber calcaneus

ORIGIN AND INSERTION

ACTION

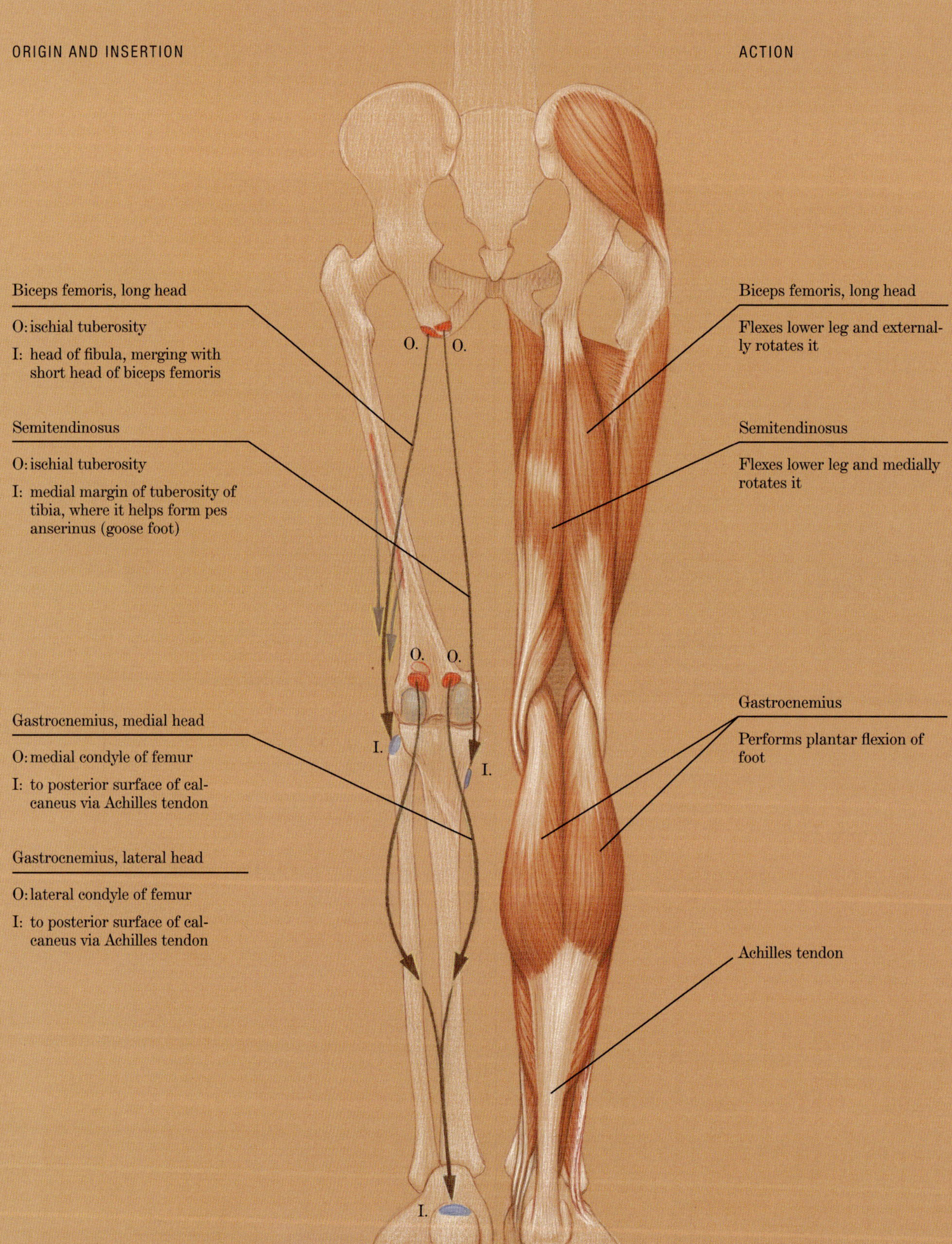

ORIGIN AND INSERTION

Gluteus Maximus

O: posterior portion of ilium to posterior superior iliac spine, thoracolumbalis fascia, sacrotuberosus ligament, and posterior face of sacrum

I: deep portion: tuberositas glutea of femur (dark red arrows); superficial portion: iliotibial tract of fasciae latae (black arrows)

Gracilis

O: on a line between superior ramus and inferior ramus of pubic bone

I: on medial margin of tuberosity of tibia, contributing to the pes anserinus (goose foot)

ACTION

Gluteus maximus

Extends and laterally rotates thigh; upper fibers abduct thigh, and lower fibers adduct it

Gracilis

Adducts thigh; contributes to flexion of knee joint; rotates leg inward

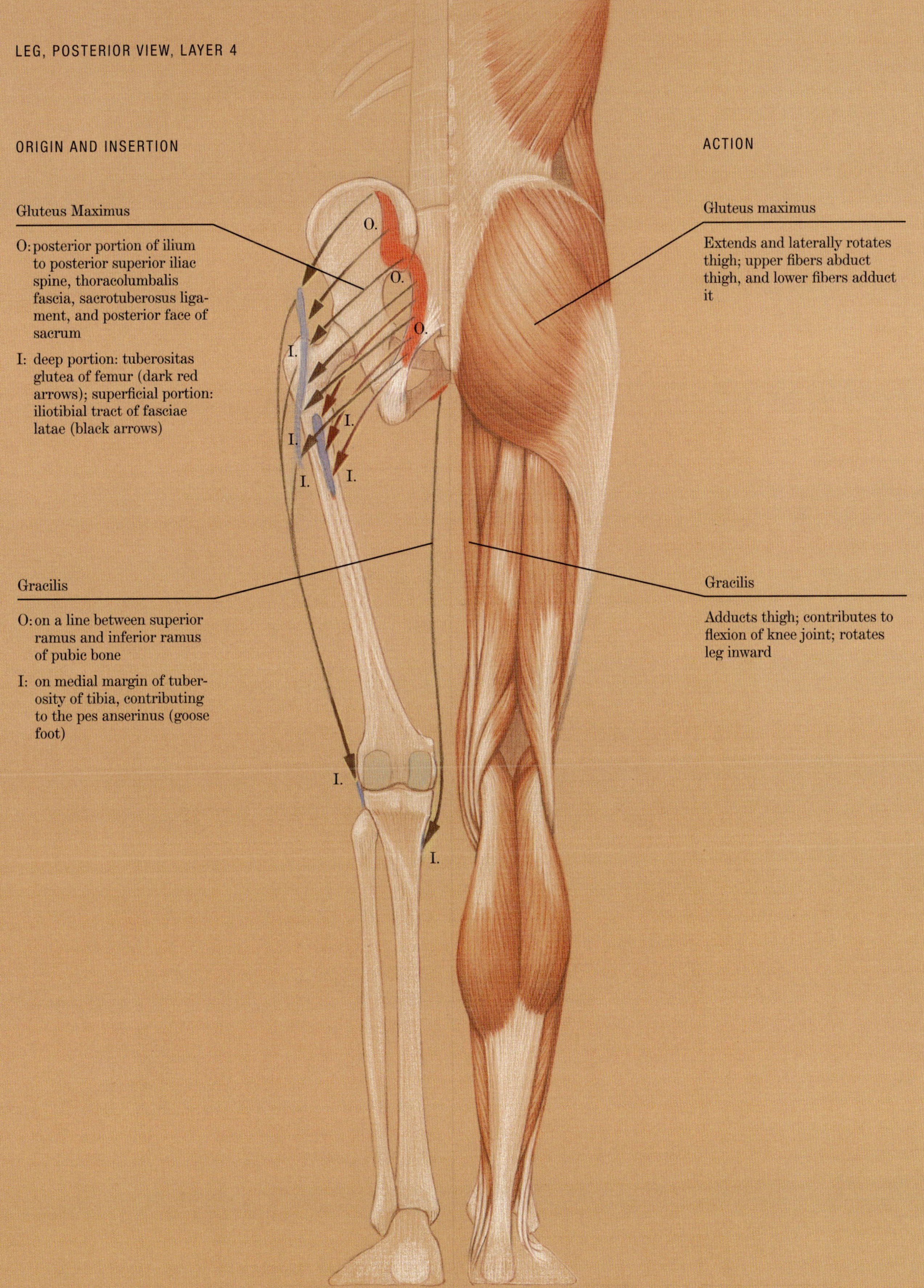

TRANSFORMING SCHEMATIC VOLUMES INTO ORGANIC MUSCLE FORMS

This section leads you through a metamorphic process from conceptual to organic form. The metamorphosis can be used as a mnemonic device by the artist: Starting from a stereometric rendition of the body, you will add more volumes and anatomical details, making it easier to remember them all. Each of the drawings in this section guides you through a series of steps that show how you can transform the essential volumes of the muscles into organic forms.

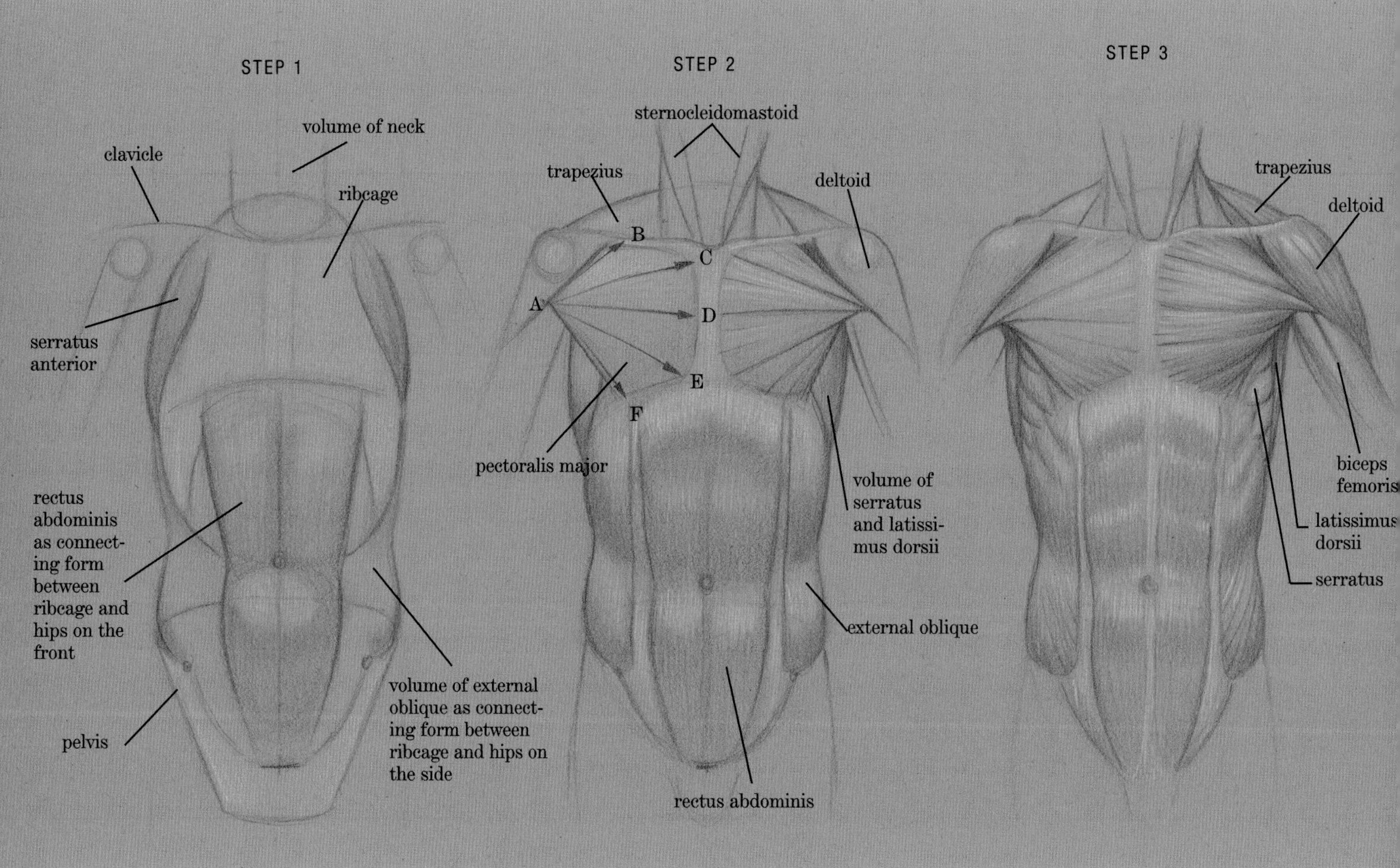

SCHEMATIC TO ORGANIC: THE TORSO, ANTERIOR VIEW

STEP 1: Draw the volumes of the ribcage and the hips. Add the heads of the humeri. As shown, draw the form of the rectus abdomini, starting from just below the lower margin of the pectoralis, at the vertical halfway point of the ribcage, and reaching down to the pubic bone. Add the forms of the serratus anterior (without the digitations).

STEP 2: Draw the pectoralis major with lines that start from point *A* (a little below the head of the humerus) and reaching points *B*, *C*, *D*, *E*, and *F*, as shown. The lines will define the specific sections of the pectoralis.

STEP 3: Refine the drawing by adding more anatomical details, making the figure more realistic.

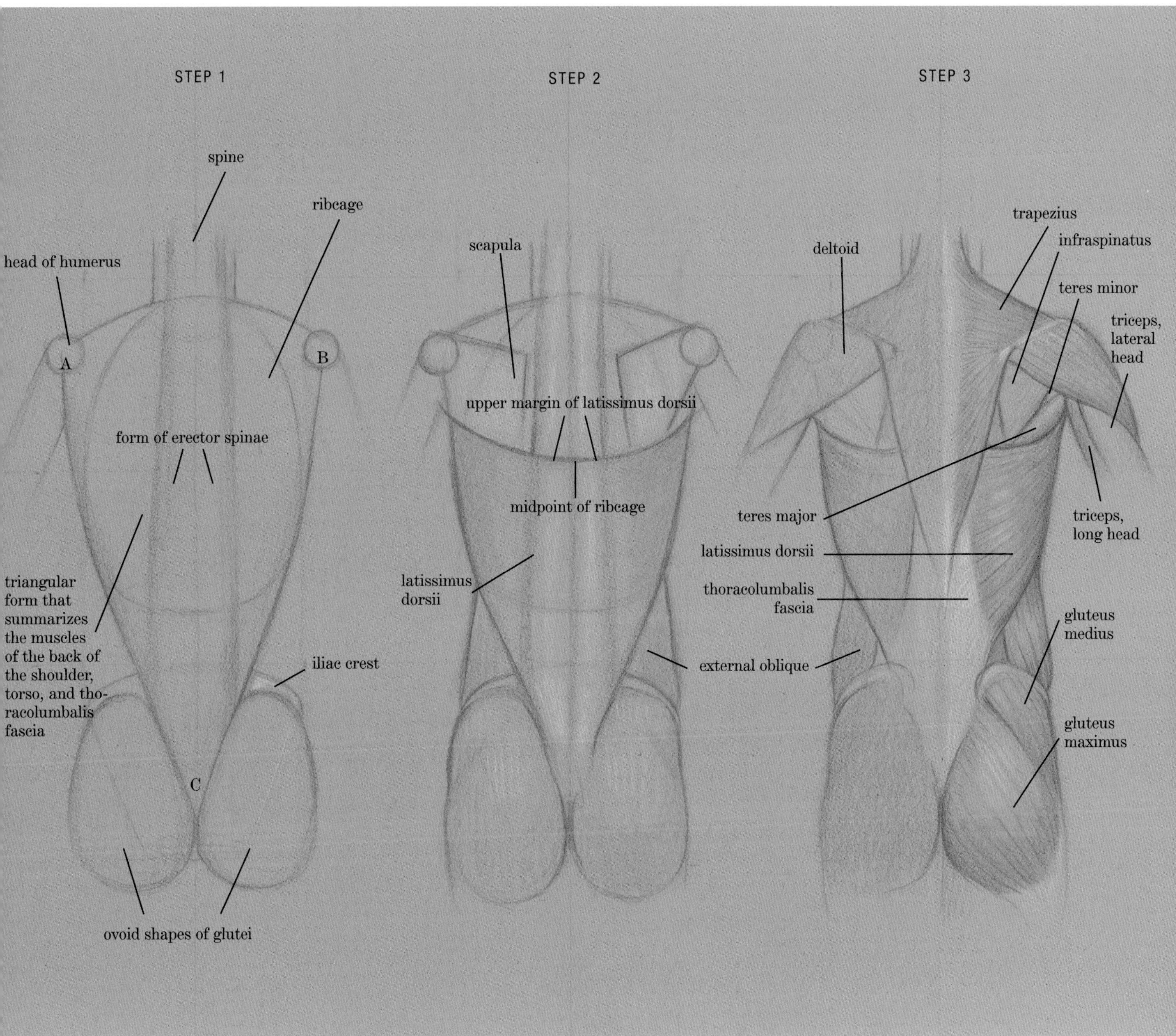

SCHEMATIC TO ORGANIC: THE TORSO, POSTERIOR VIEW

STEP 1: Draw the volumes of the ribcage and hips, then the shoulders and a hint of neck. Define the generic shape of the back by drawing a line that merges the heads of the humeri (*A–B*) and two lines that go from the humeri to the bottom of the sacrum (*A–C, B–C*). Draw the forms of the glutei as two standing eggs, starting from below the iliac crest and going past the bottom of the hips below the ischia. Draw the columnar forms of the erector spinae.

STEP 2: Draw the top margin of the latissimus dorsii from armpit to armpit, going through the vertical midpoint of the ribcage (corresponding to the 6th thoracic vertebra). The shape of the latissimus dorsii is like that of a corset. Add the scapulae and the triangular shapes of the external oblique, as shown.

STEP 3: Finally, add the deltoid and the trapezius. The trapezius resembles a kite.

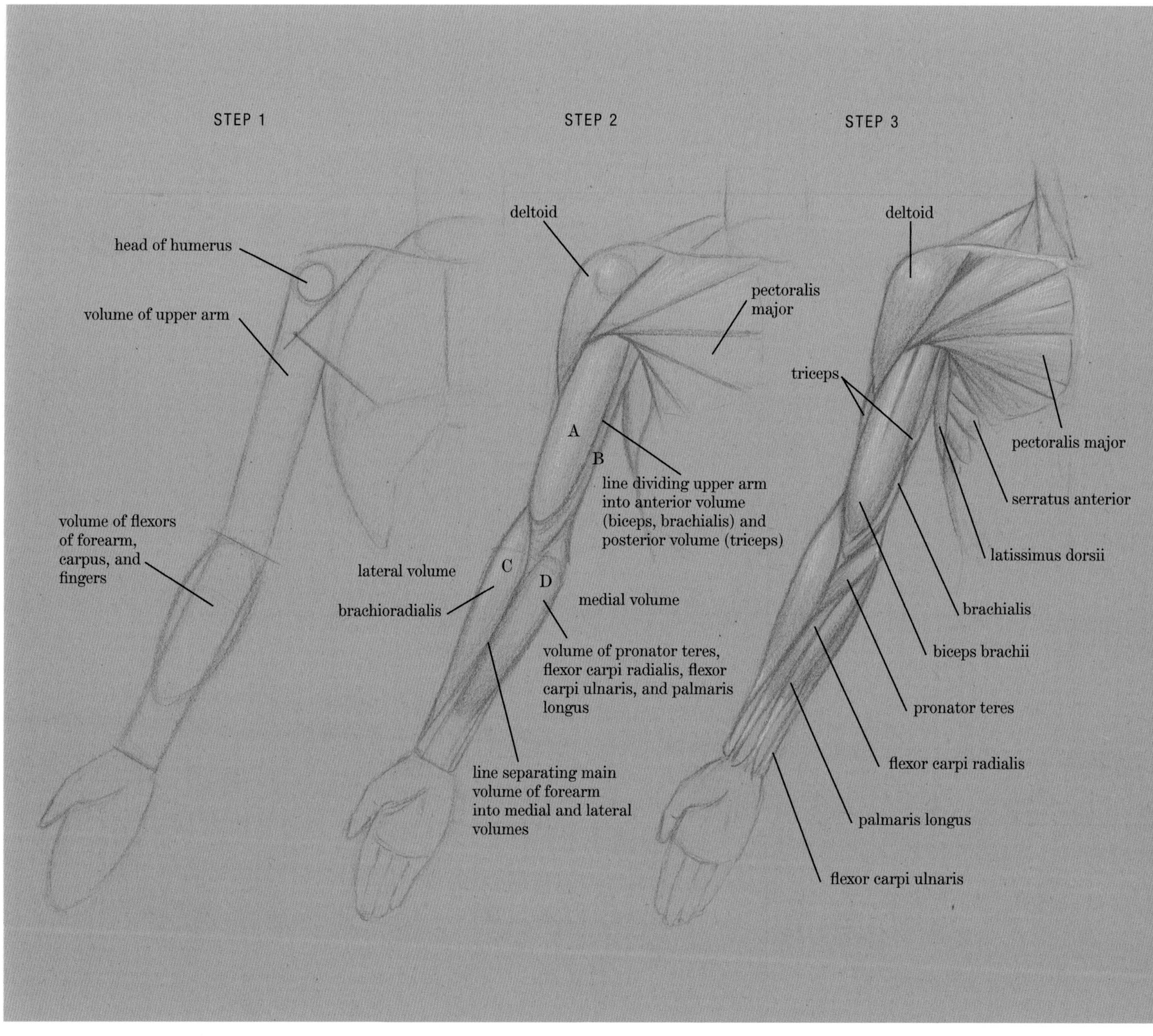

SCHEMATIC TO ORGANIC: THE ARM, ANTERIOR VIEW

STEP 1: To the basic volumes of the arm, add the volume of the forearm and the pectoralis, and cut a corner at the shoulder that will represent the deltoid.

STEP 2: Divide the form of the upper arm into anterior and posterior volumes. Then divide the form of the forearm into lateral and medial volumes.

STEP 3: Further subdivide the forms in the specific muscles: A is subdivided into the forms of the biceps brachii and brachialis; B contains the medial and long head of the triceps; C contains the brachioradialis; and D contains the pronator teres and the flexors (flexor carpi radialis, palmaris longus, and flexor carpi ulnaris).

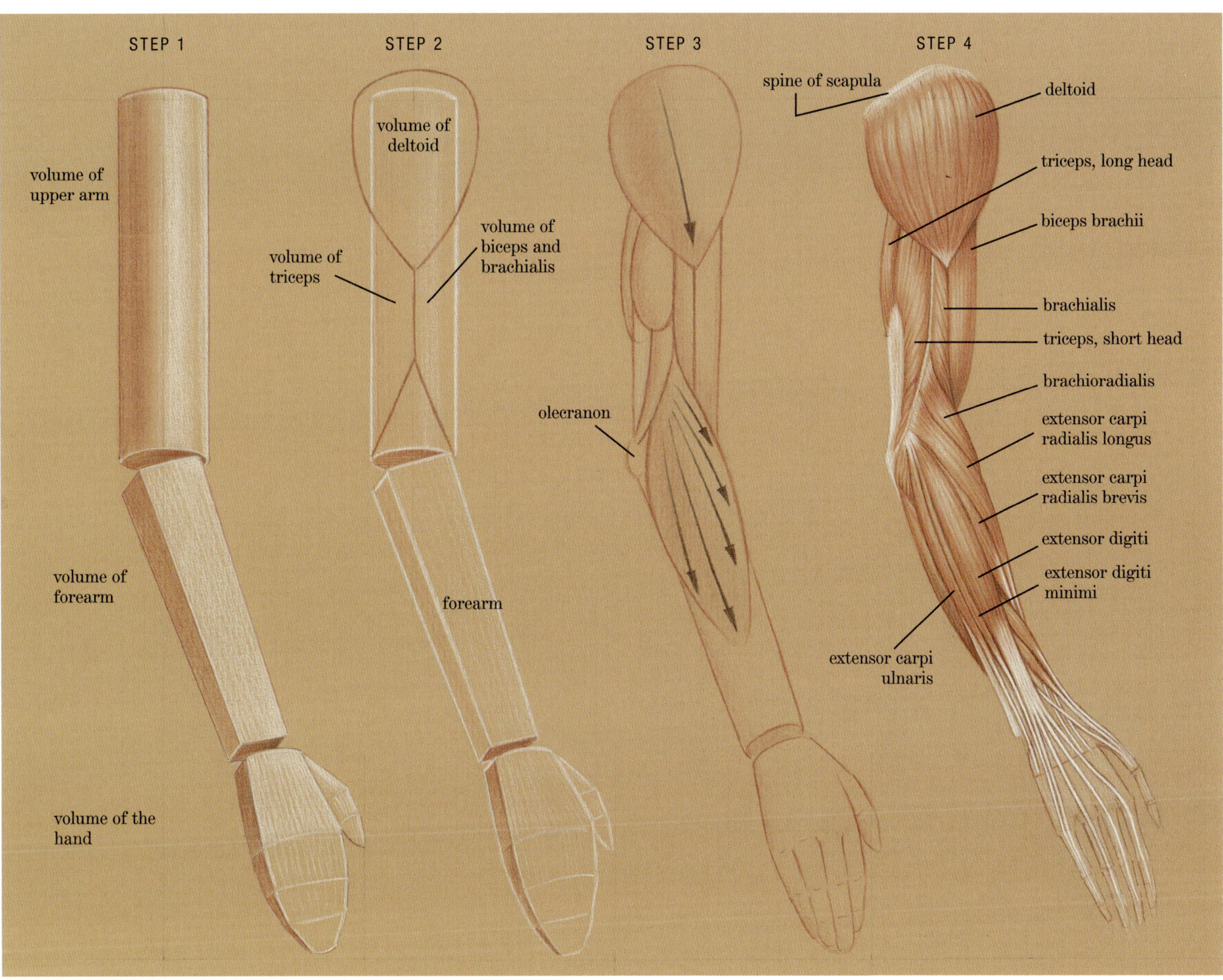

SCHEMATIC TO ORGANIC: THE ARM, LATERAL VIEW

STEP 1: Draw the volumes of the arm as simple geometric forms—a cylinder and a rectangular prism for the upper arm and forearm, respectively, and a paddle-like form for the hand.

STEP 2: Add the volume of the deltoid, starting from slightly above the volume of the upper arm and going down to the middle of the upper arm. Then draw a line that divides the portion of the upper arm below the deltoid into anterior and posterior sections. As you approach the lower third of the upper arm, split the line in two; one line will go to the front end of the upper arm and the other to the posterior end. This triangular shape is the starting point of the volume of the forearm.

STEP 3: Subdivide the anterior half of the upper arm into biceps brachii and brachialis. Draw the lateral and long heads of the triceps and the triceps tendon in the posterior half of the upper arm, and add the olecranon. Draw a radiating pattern on the volume of the forearm to indicate the directions of the muscles of the forearm. Note how the volume of the deltoid is now slightly angled forward and ends above the brachialis muscle.

STEP 4: In the last step, define all the muscles of the arm and forearm, as shown.

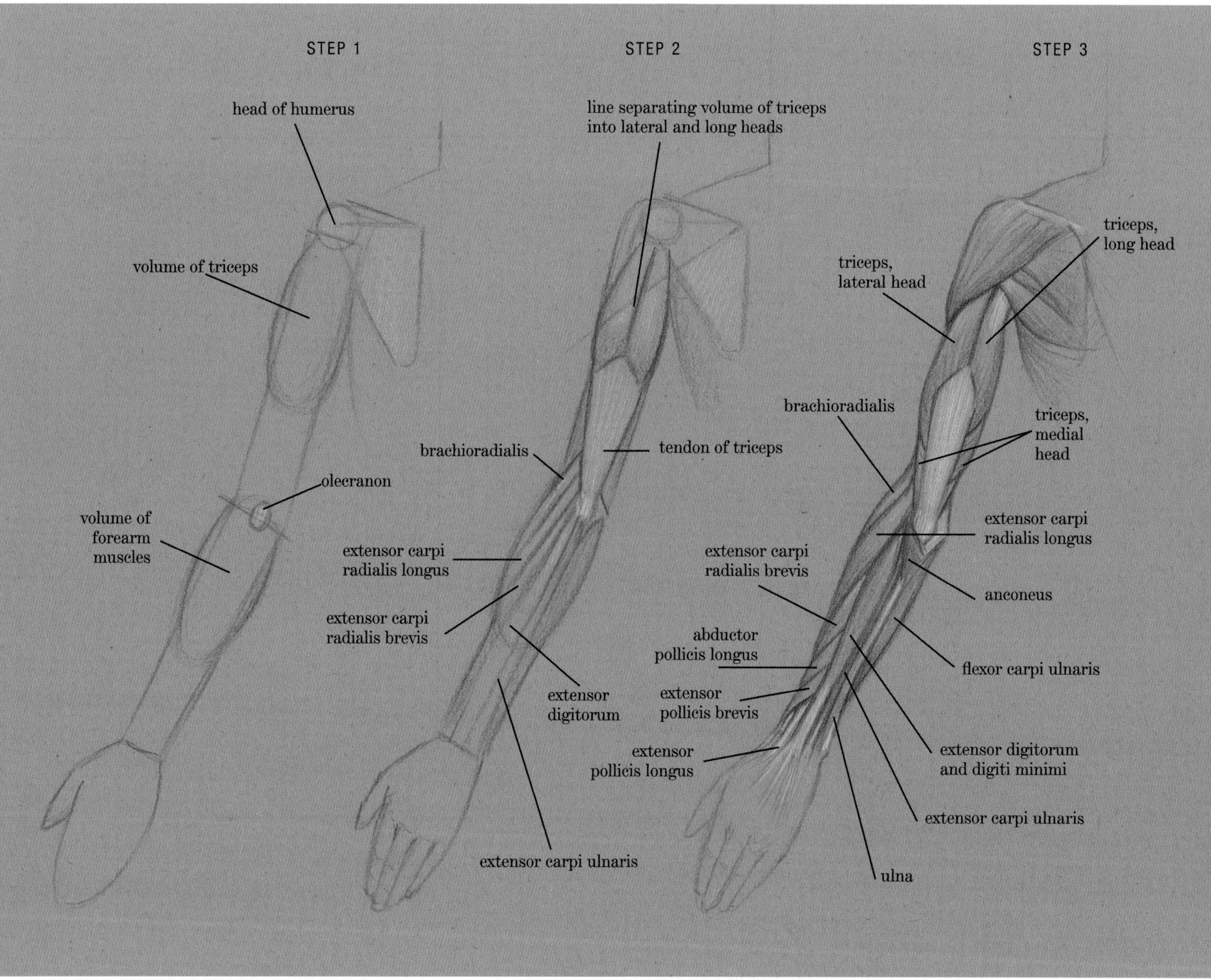

SCHEMATIC TO ORGANIC: THE ARM, POSTERIOR VIEW

STEP 1: Draw the two basic oviform volumes of the upper arm and forearm—one for the triceps and one for the extensors of the forearm. Draw the olecranon at the elbow joint.

STEP 2: Divide the volume of the triceps group lengthwise to determine the long head of the triceps medially and the lateral head next to it. Draw the triangle of the tendon of the triceps that goes from the lower margin of the triceps to the olecranon. Divide the volume of the extensors into five segments radiating away from the olecranon; these five segments correspond to the muscles of the forearm as labeled in the figure.

STEP 3: Complete the anatomy of the arm, adding the deltoid, the muscles of the scapula, and, in the forearm, the extensor digiti minimi and the anconeus.

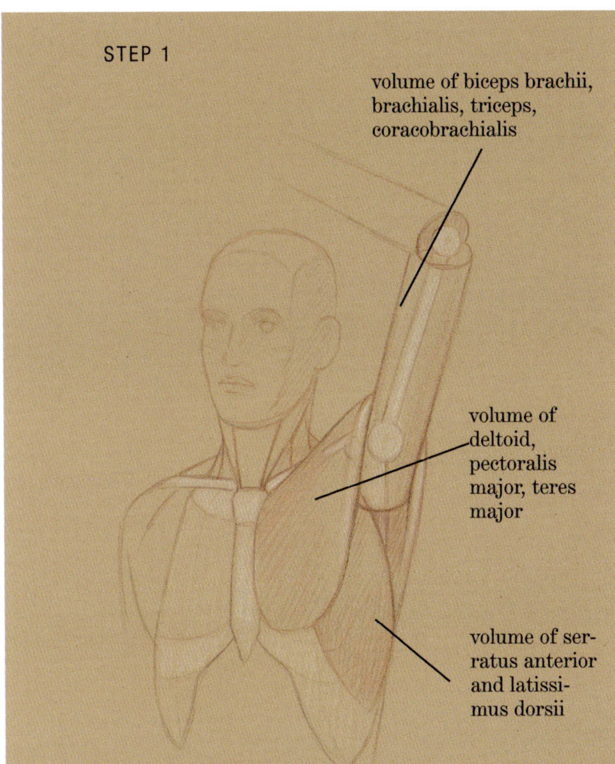

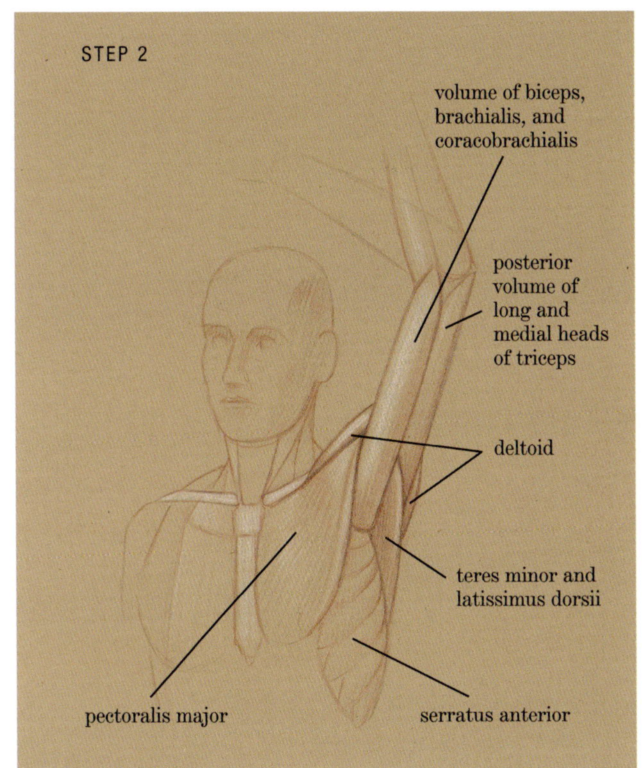

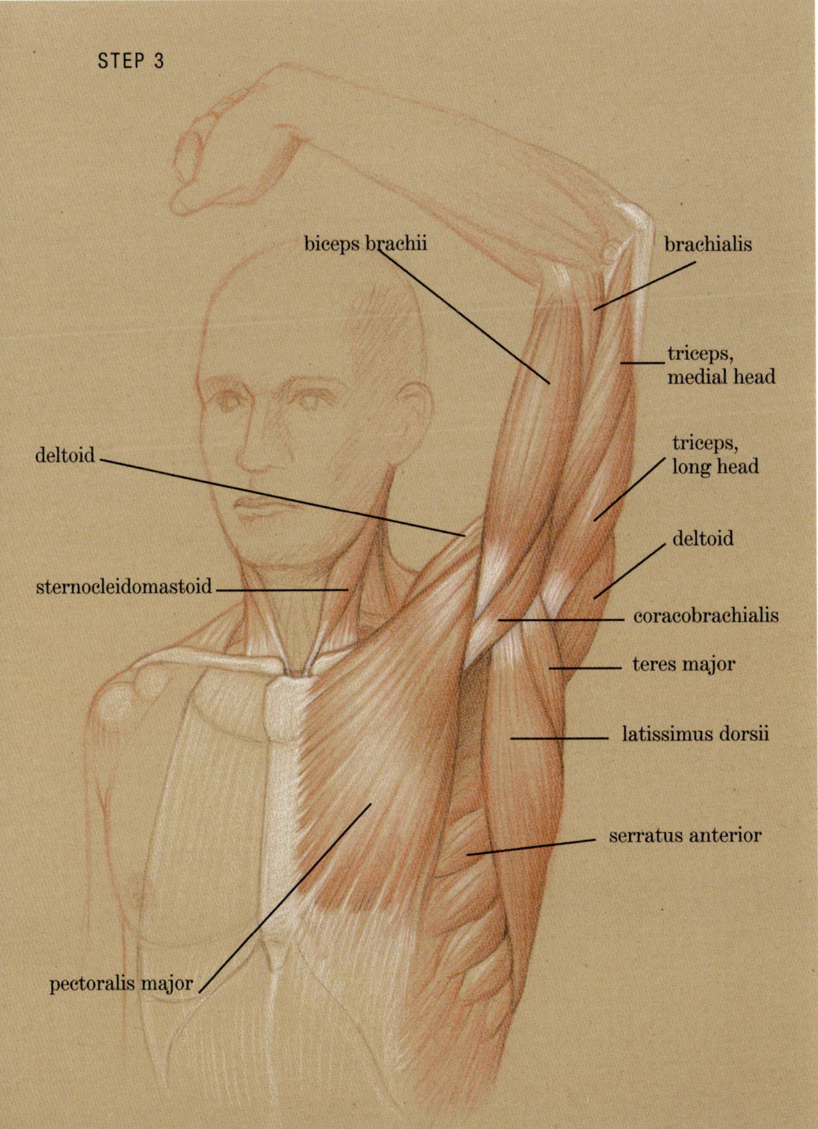

SCHEMATIC TO ORGANIC: THE RAISED ARM AND AXILLA (ARMPIT)

STEP 1: Reduce the muscles to basic volumes, each grouping together several muscles. This simplification makes it easier to identify the main masses and remember the basic patterns that they create. The cylindrical volume of the arm includes the triceps, biceps, brachialis, and coracobrachialis; the form that wraps over the shoulder is made up of the deltoid, pectoralis, and teres major, and the form on the side of the ribcage includes the serratus anterior and the latissimus dorsii.

STEP 2: Subdivide the upper arm into anterior and posterior portions. Also subdivide the form that wraps over the shoulder into more components. Wedge a form representing the teres major and the latissimus dorsii between the anterior and posterior volumes of the upper arm. Hint at the digitations of the serratus.

STEP 3: Complete the anatomy of the axilla, rendering all the muscles of the armpit region.

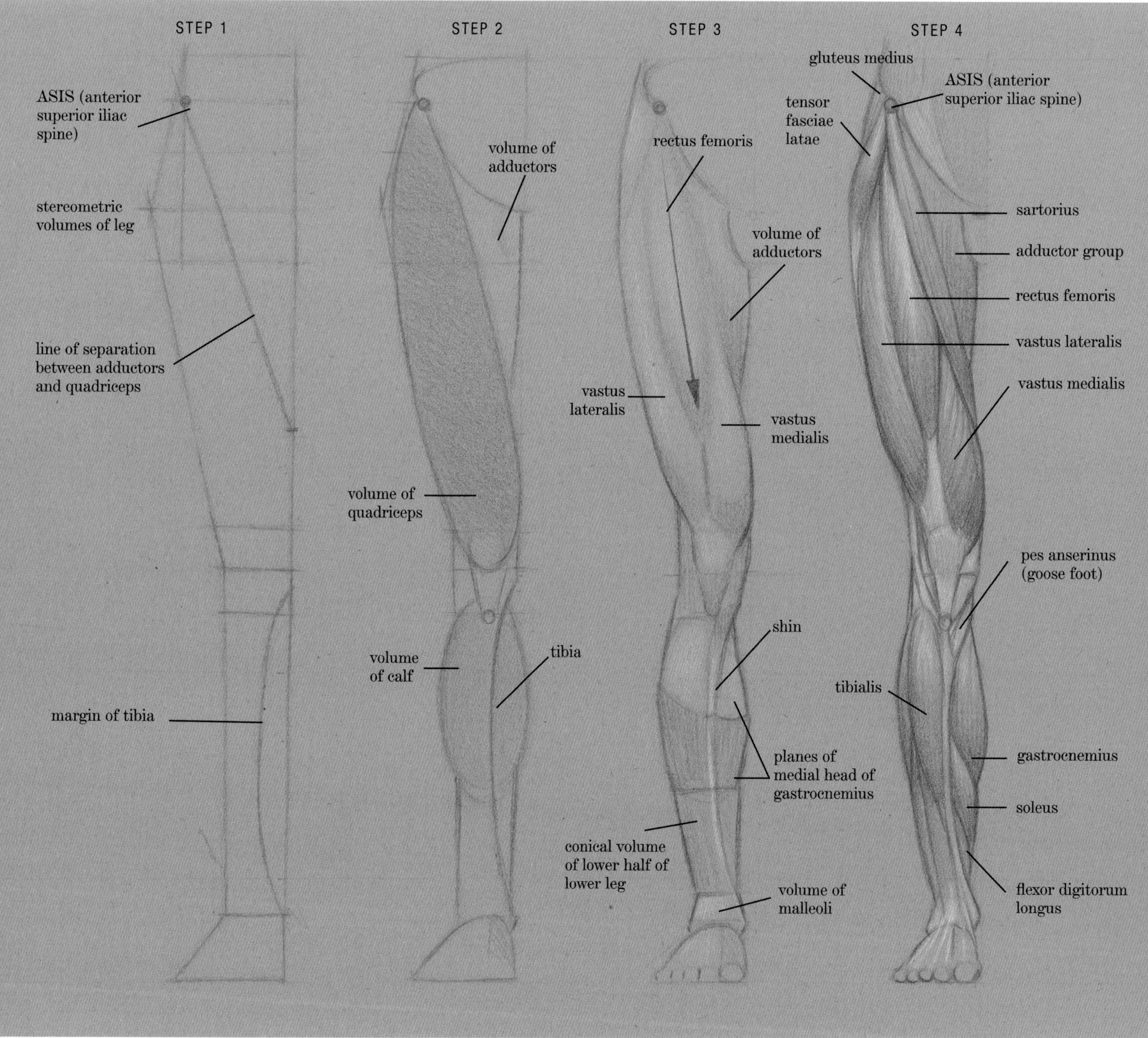

SCHEMATIC TO ORGANIC: THE LEG, ANTERIOR VIEW

STEP 1: Divide the volumes of the thigh with a diagonal line starting from the ASIS and going to the lower medial third of the thigh. This diagonal line corresponds to the sartorius; to its left is the volume of the quadriceps, and to its right the volume of the adductors.

STEP 2: Define the volumes of the quadriceps (red) and of the calf (blue), as indicated.

STEP 3: Draw the volume of the rectus femoris along the median line of the quadriceps (arrow). By doing so, you automatically define the vastus medialis and the vastus lateralis.

STEP 4: Add the sartorius and tensor fasciae latae and refine the muscles. Define the peaks of the calf.

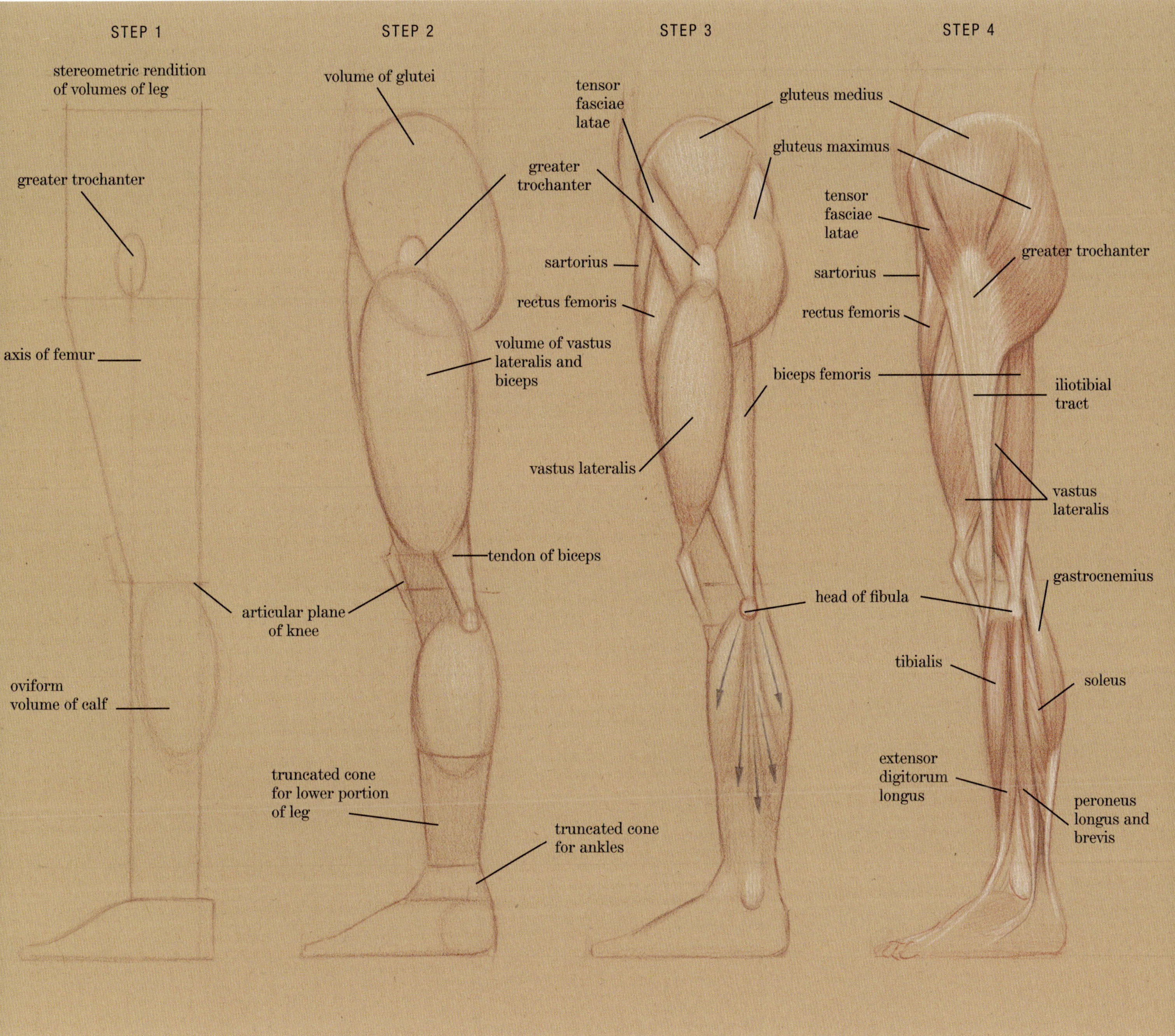

SCHEMATIC TO ORGANIC: THE LEG, LATERAL VIEW

STEP 1: Draw the basic volumes of the leg; draw the calf; and add the trochanter.

STEP 2: Draw the forms of the glutei. Add the box of the knee and the tendon of the biceps femoris. Draw the cones of the lower part of the lower leg and the ankles.

STEP 3: Subdivide the main volume of the thigh, defining its muscles. In the lower leg, note the radiating pattern of the muscles starting from the head of the fibula and moving outward, as indicated by the arrows.

STEP 4: Add the iliotibial tract, and define all the muscles of the leg.

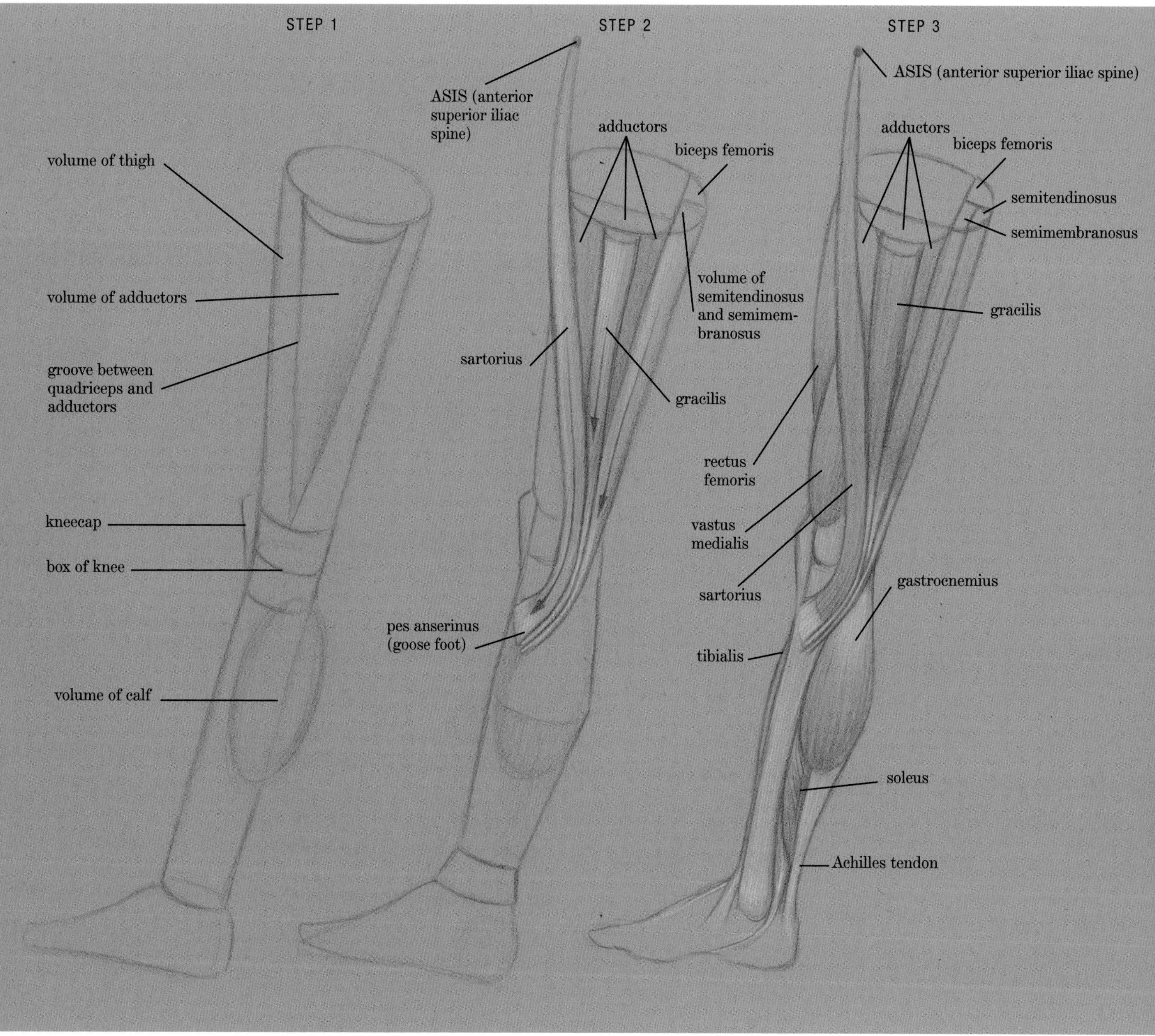

SCHEMATIC TO ORGANIC: THE LEG, MEDIAL VIEW

The right leg is depicted.

STEP 1: Draw the basic volumes of the thigh and lower leg, adding the foot, kneecap, adductor group, and calf.

STEP 2: Draw the sartorius, starting from the front, at the ASIS, and moving down along the anterior groove between the adductor group and the quadriceps. The sartorius will cover the posterior half of the knee. Past the knee, the sartorius moves forward toward the tibial tuberosity. Then draw the gracilis, which runs down the medial side of the thigh just over the peak of the form of the adductor group. Finally, draw the volume of the semitendinosus and semimembranosus as one volume and make it merge with the tendons of sartorius and gracilis. As indicated by the arrows, these muscles converge to create the pes anserinus (goose foot).

STEP 3: Finish the leg by defining all the muscular masses, as shown.

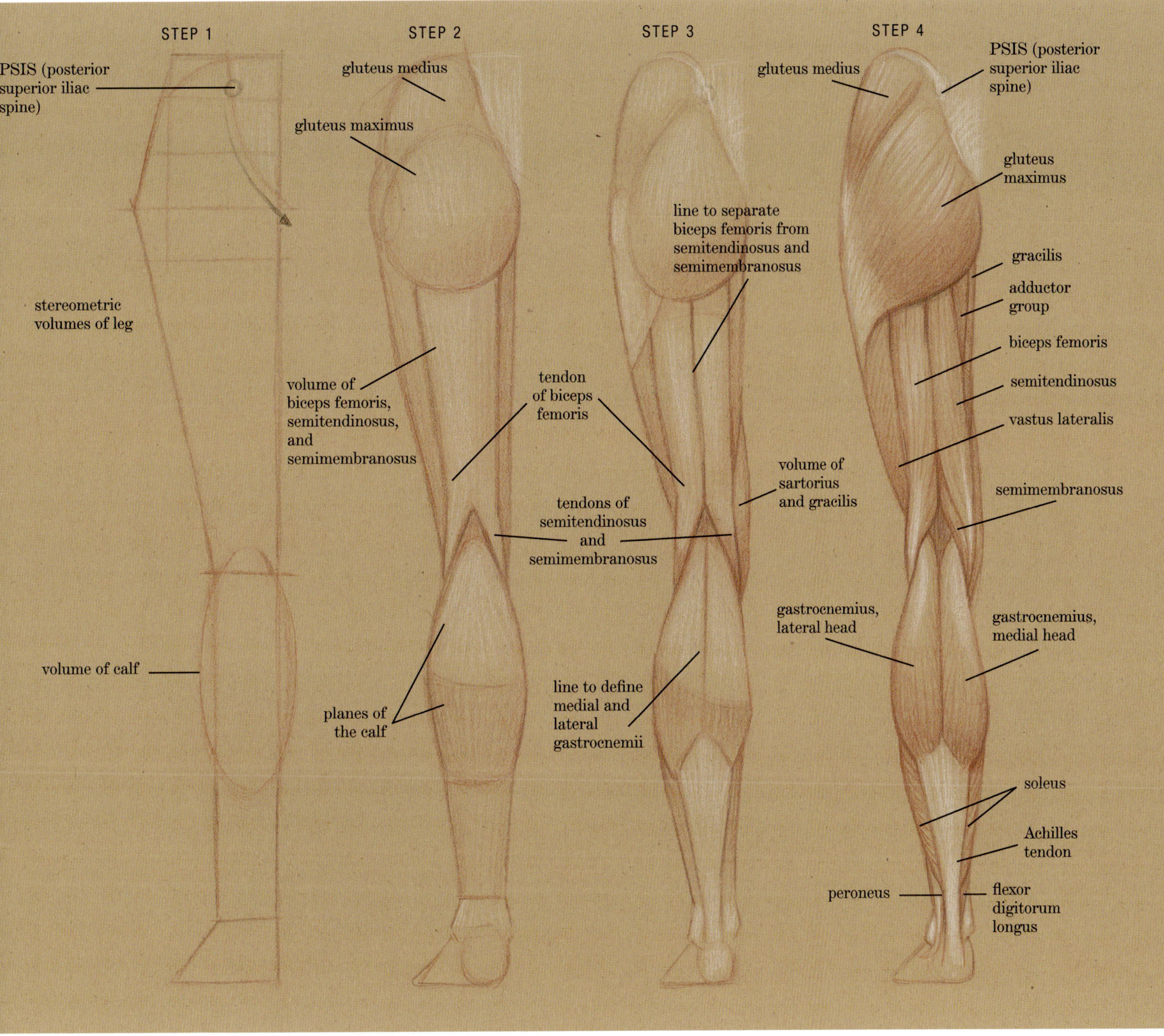

SCHEMATIC TO ORGANIC: THE LEG, POSTERIOR VIEW

STEP 1: Over the basic forms of the legs and hips, draw the profile of the sacrum using a curved line that goes from the posterior superior iliac spine (PSIS), at the upper quarter of the hips, down to the tip of the sacrum at the lower quarter of the hips.

STEP 2: As you add the glutei, remember that the lower margin of the glutei has to be lower than the bottom of the hips. Add the cylindrical form of the biceps femoris, semitendinosus, and semi-membranosus, taking care to divide the form at the bottom into the tendons that go to the sides of the leg. Shape the lower leg into slightly more organic forms, as shown.

STEP 3: Shape the glutei into two main volumes: gluteus maximus and gluteus medius. Define the volumes of the biceps femoris and the semitendinosus and semimembranosus. Divide the calf into the medial and lateral heads of the gastrocnemius. Finally, add the volume of the muscles that create the pes anserinus (goose foot).

STEP 4: Finish the leg by refining the muscles of the leg as shown.

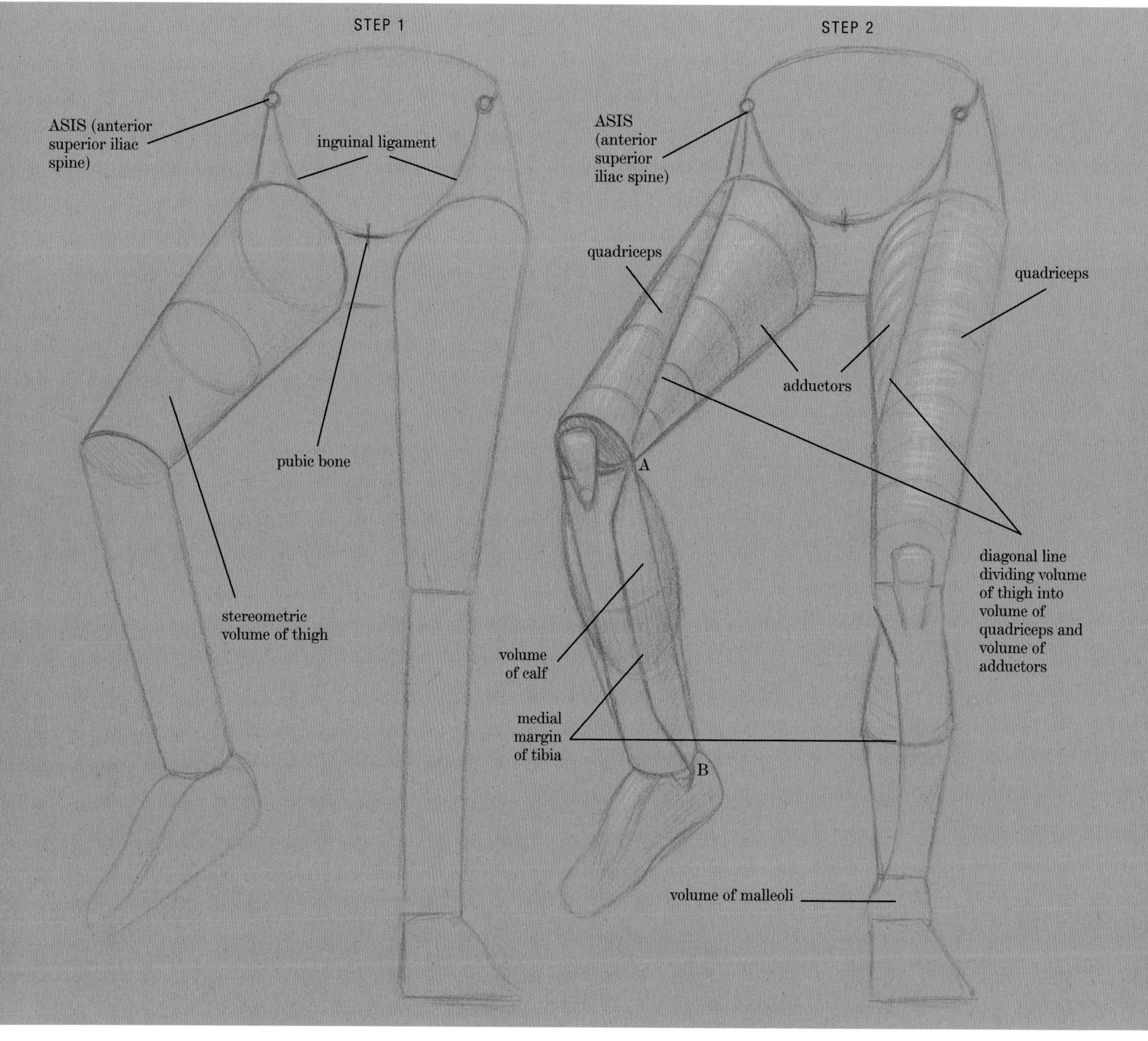

SCHEMATIC TO ORGANIC: THE LEGS, FLEXED, THREE-QUARTER VIEW

STEP 1: Draw the volumes of the leg in a slightly flexed and foreshortened position, as shown. Mark the ASIS and pubic bone. Hint at the volumes of the thigh and lower leg using curving cross-sections, as indicated; this will help you to render the leg more volumetrically. Draw a line connecting the iliac spines with the pubic bone to represent the inguinal ligament and the lower limit of the abdomen.

STEP 2: Draw a line that corresponds to the path of the sartorius muscle and goes from ASIS to point A on the medial side of the head of the tibia, as shown. This line separates the thigh into two distinct parts: One describes the volume of the quadriceps, the other the volume of the adductor group. (It is much easier to understand the form of the adductor muscles if they are reduced to one big volume.) The line going lengthwise across the medial side of the tibia from point A to point B (the medial malleolus of the tibia) describes the path of the tibia.

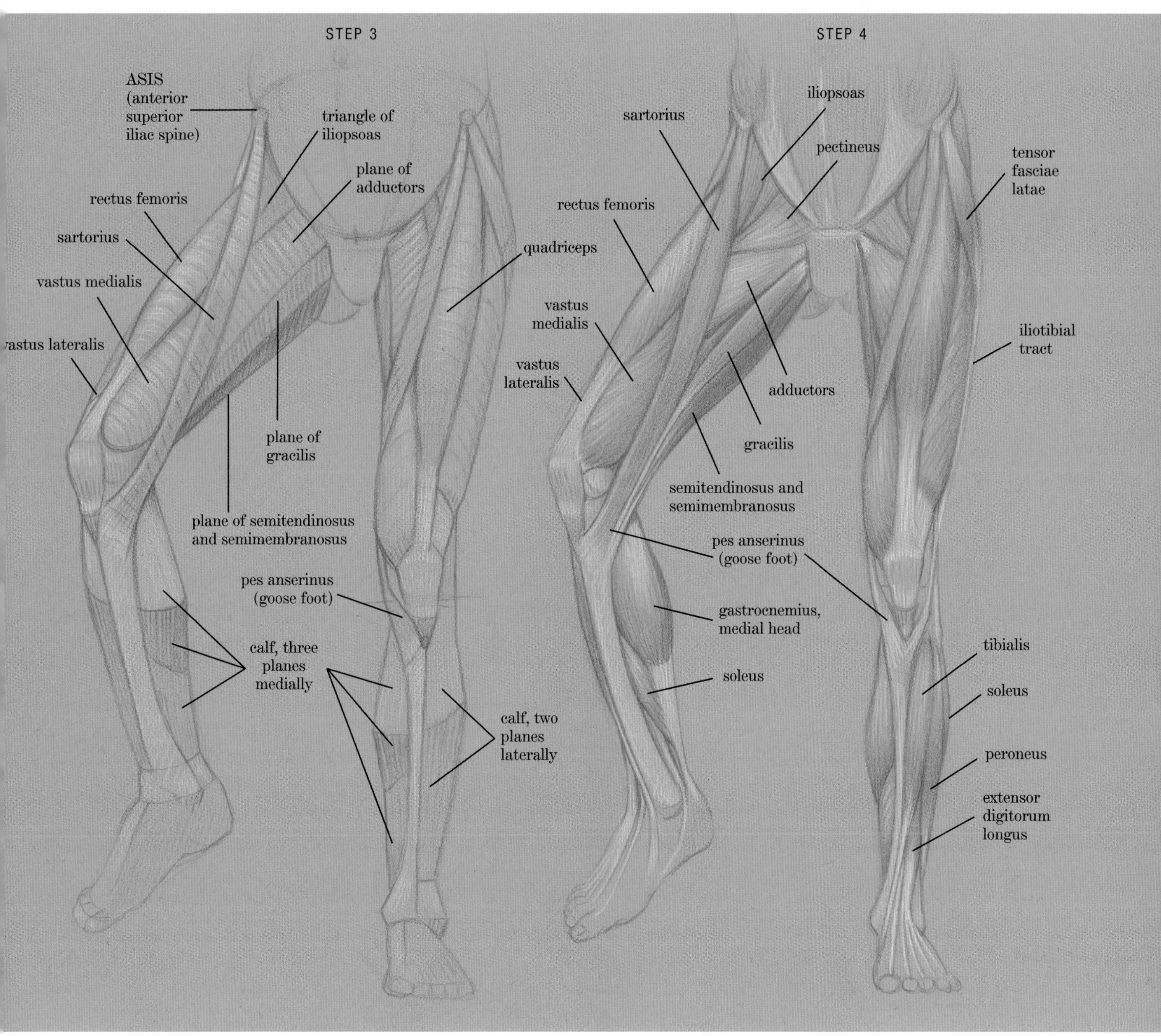

SCHEMATIC TO ORGANIC: THE LEGS, FLEXED, FRONT VIEW

STEP 3: Subdivide the quadriceps volume into its components: the rectus femoris, vastus medialis, and vastus lateralis. Define the planes of the adductors group. (Note how, in the drawing, the planar characteristics of the adductor group are emphasized by the areas of light and shadow.) The sartorius muscle runs in the groove between the quadriceps and the adductor group, starting from the ASIS and going down to the medial portion of the head of the tibia, where it contributes to forming the pes anserinus, or goose foot.

Now render the form of the calves more accurately by defining the three changes of plane on the medial side of each calf and the two planes on the lateral side, as indicated.

STEP 4: Finish the leg, rendering its organic forms and adding all the specific muscles.

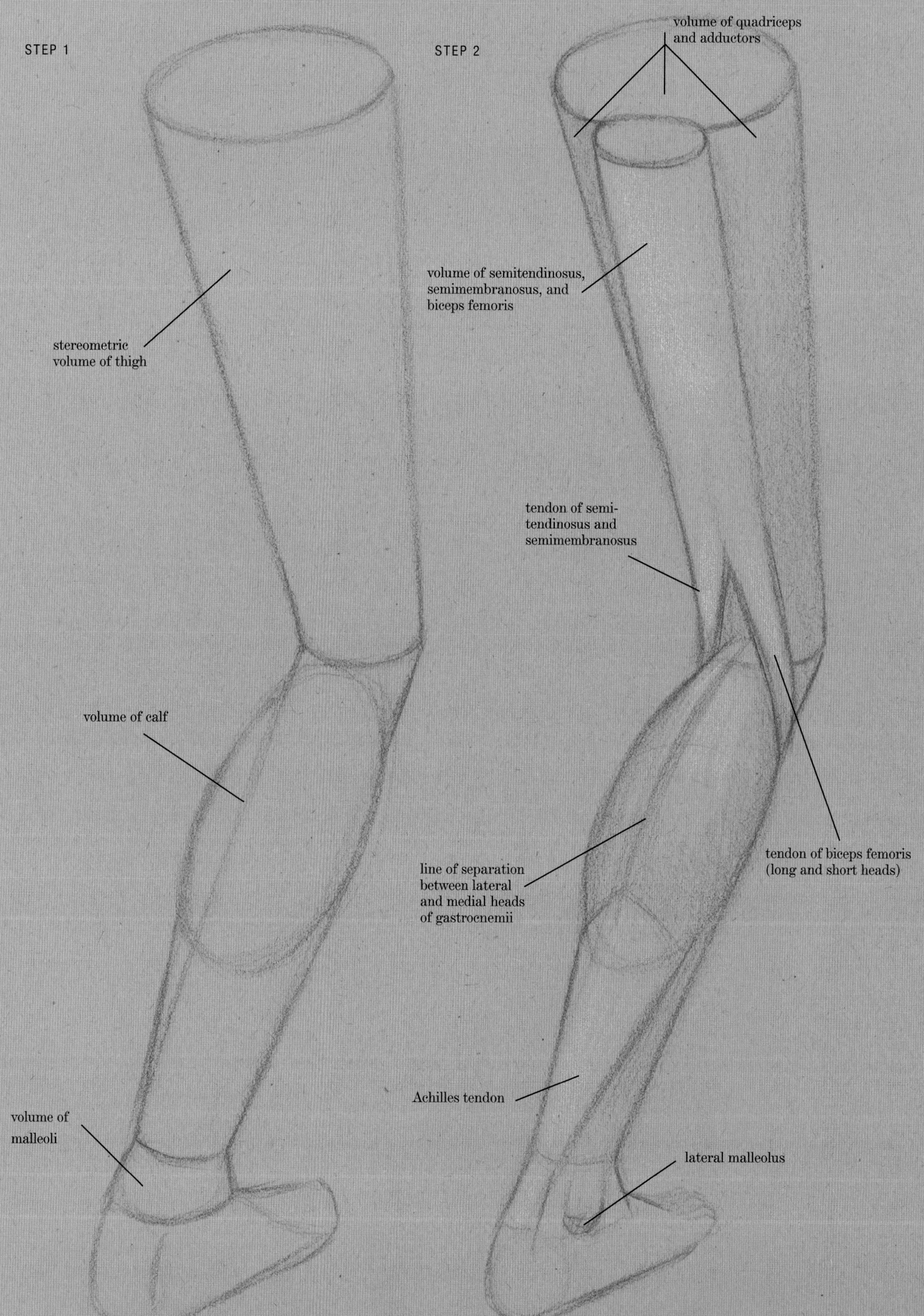

STEP 1
STEP 2
volume of quadriceps
and adductors
stereometric
volume of thigh
volume of semitendinosus,
semimembranosus, and
biceps femoris
tendon of semi-
tendinosus and
semimembranosus
volume of calf
line of separation
between lateral
and medial heads
of gastrocnemii
tendon of biceps femoris
(long and short heads)
Achilles tendon
volume of
malleoli
lateral malleolus

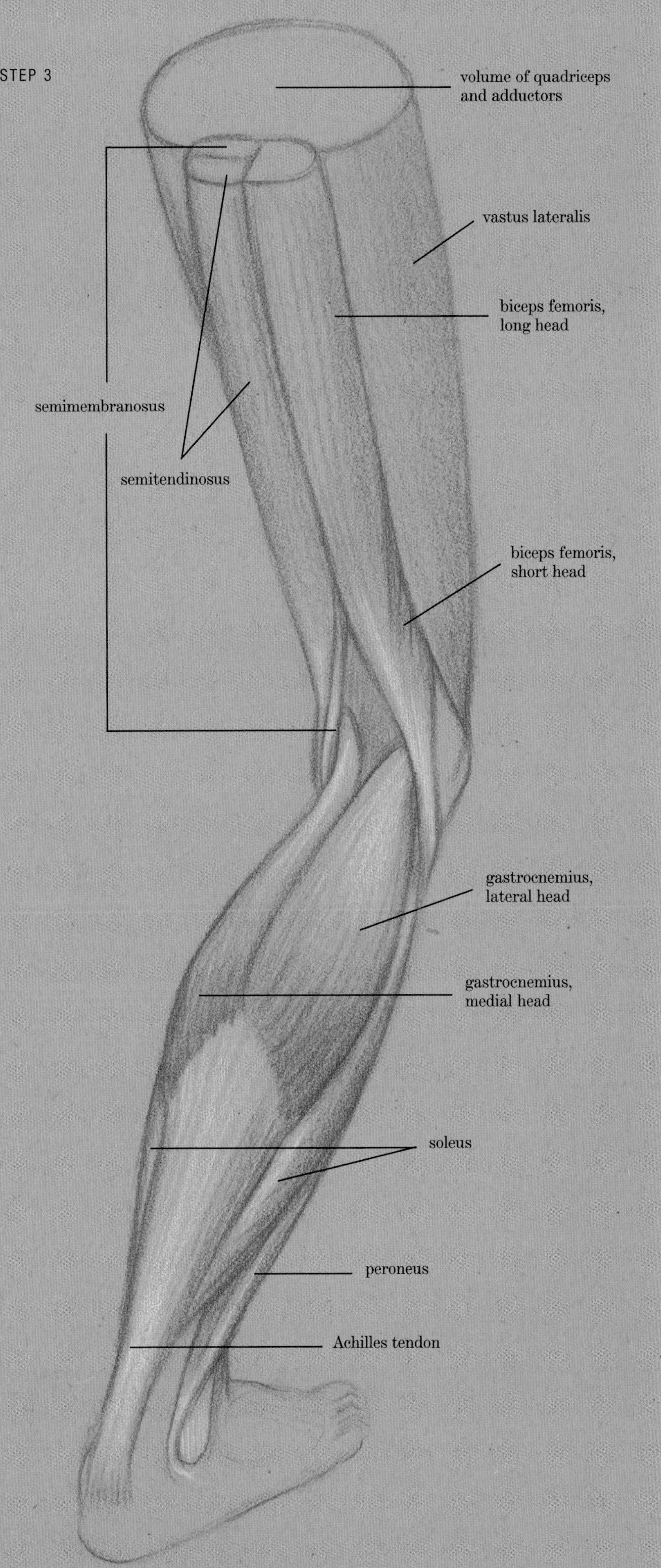

SCHEMATIC TO ORGANIC: THE LEG, POSTERIOR THREE-QUARTERS VIEW, LEG FLEXED

STEP 1: To the basic volumes of the leg, add the volume of the calf, the cone below it, and the cone of the ankles.

STEP 2: Add the conical form of the hamstrings (the semimembranosus, semitendinosus and biceps femoris) behind the thigh. As this form reaches the knee, it splits into two heads that reach toward the sides of the leg. Draw the line of the soleus as shown.

STEP 3: Define the muscles of the thigh and lower leg as shown.

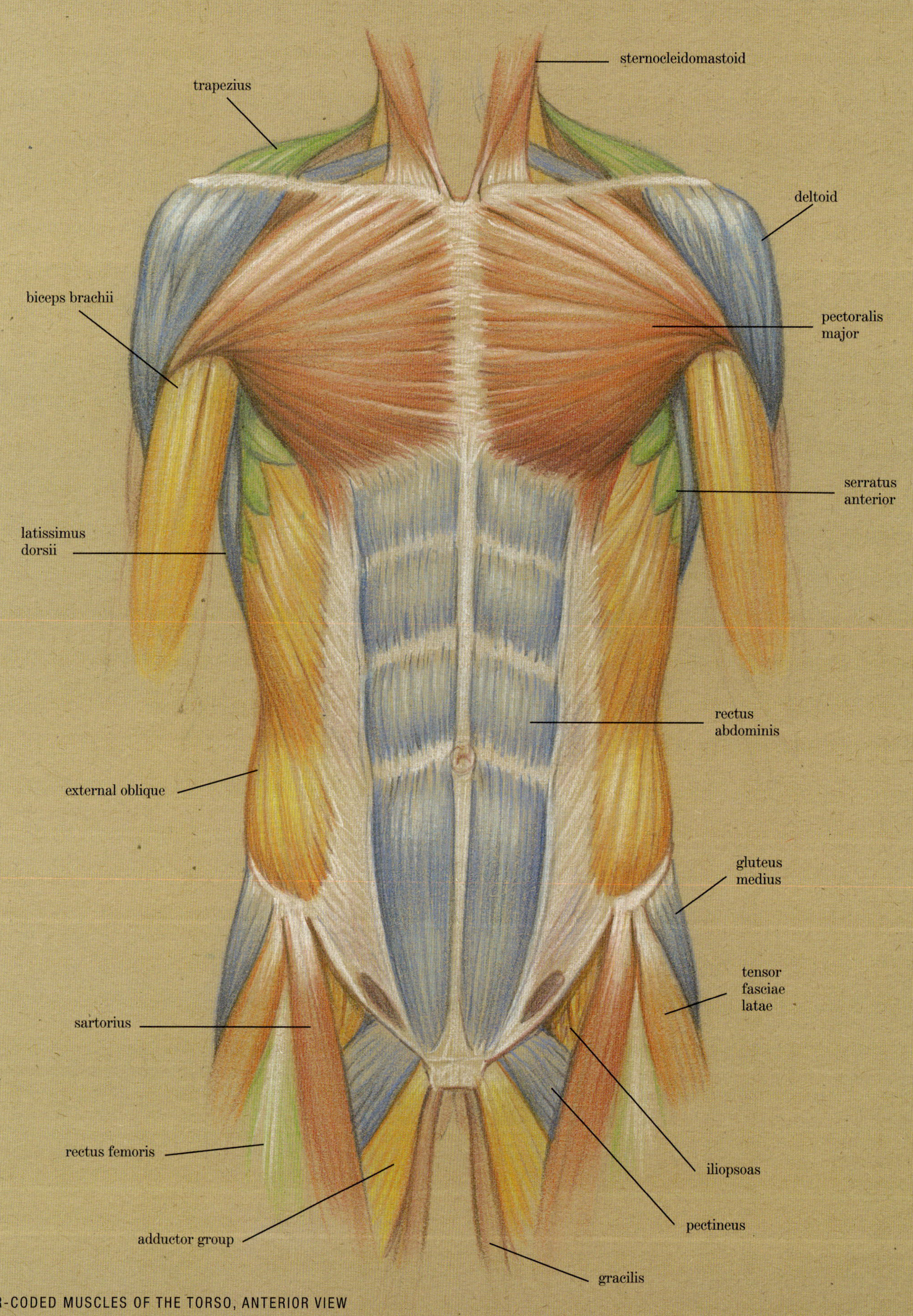

COLOR-CODED MUSCLES OF THE TORSO, ANTERIOR VIEW

INDIVIDUATING MUSCLES BY COLOR-CODING

Color-coding is an excellent way to individuate the muscles. By clarifying their specific shapes, boundaries, and other characteristics, you can start comparing their forms to objects to help you remember them. For example, looking at the back of the torso, you see that the trapezius could be compared to a kite, that the latissimus dorsii resembles a corset, and that the deltoid has a delta shape. The triangular form between the latissimus dorsii, the trapezius, and the deltoid may remind you of a slice of pie or pizza. The figures in this section show the various sections of the body with their muscles color-coded.

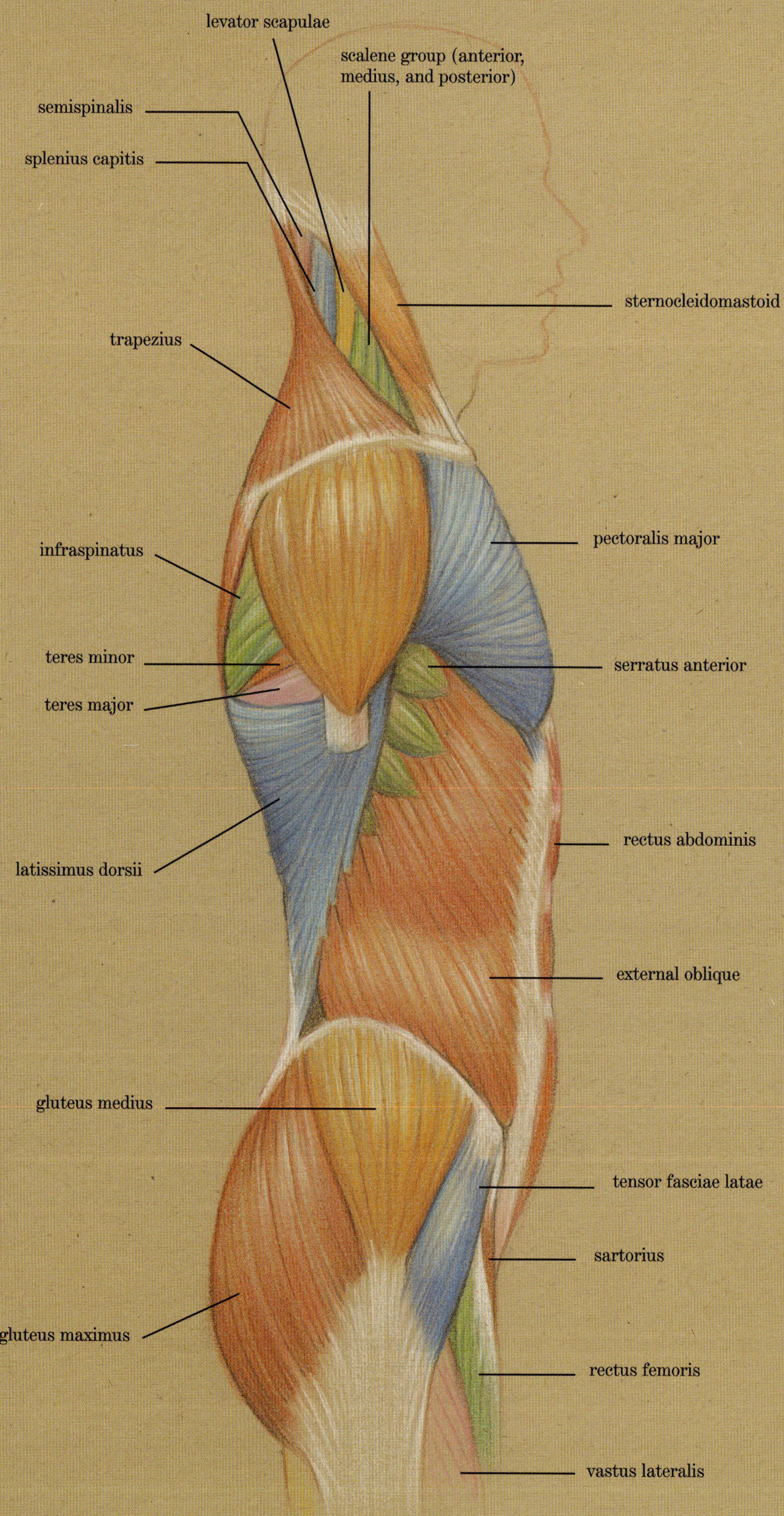

COLOR-CODED MUSCLES OF THE TORSO, LATERAL VIEW

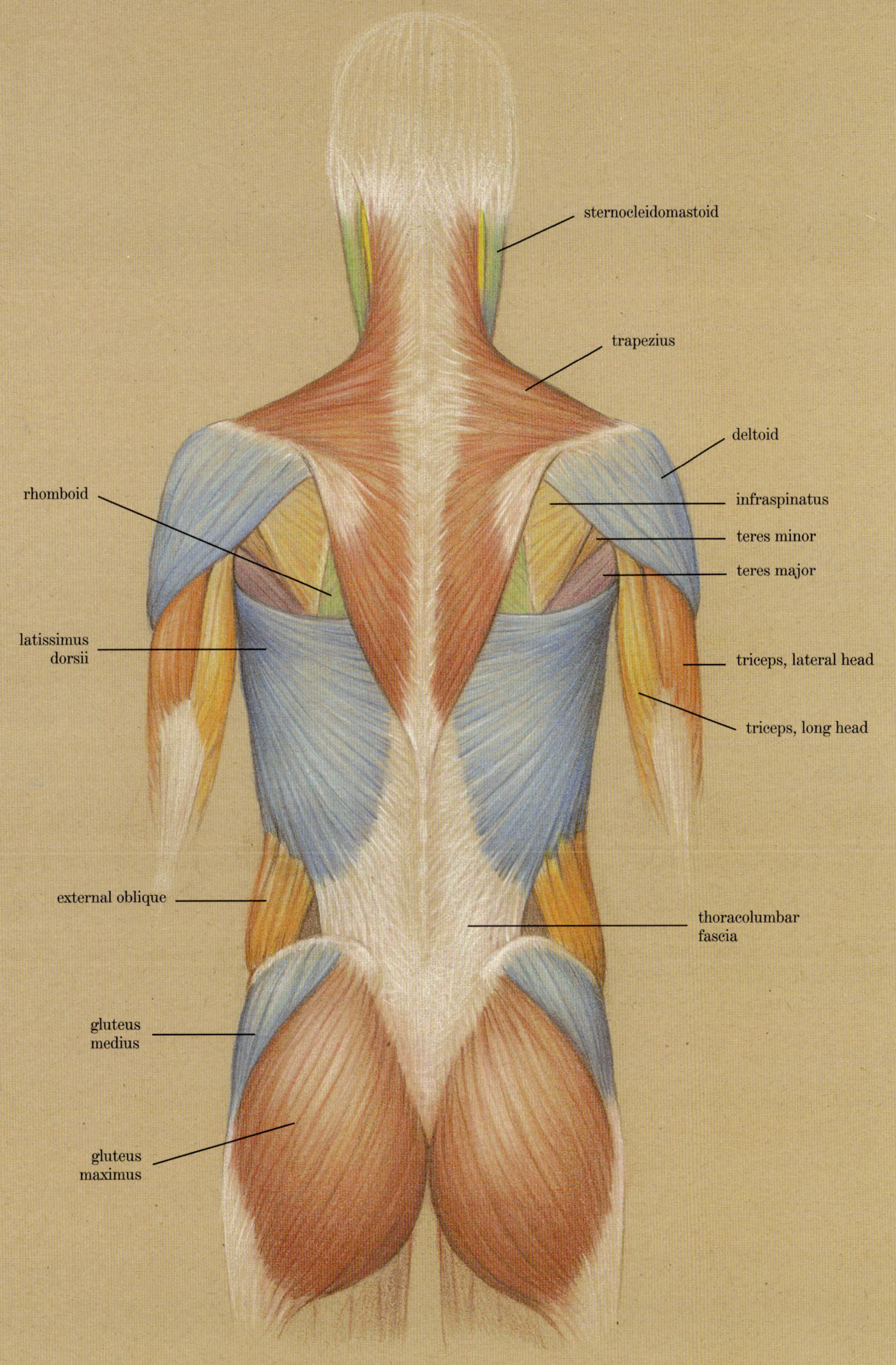

COLOR-CODED MUSCLES OF THE TORSO, POSTERIOR VIEW

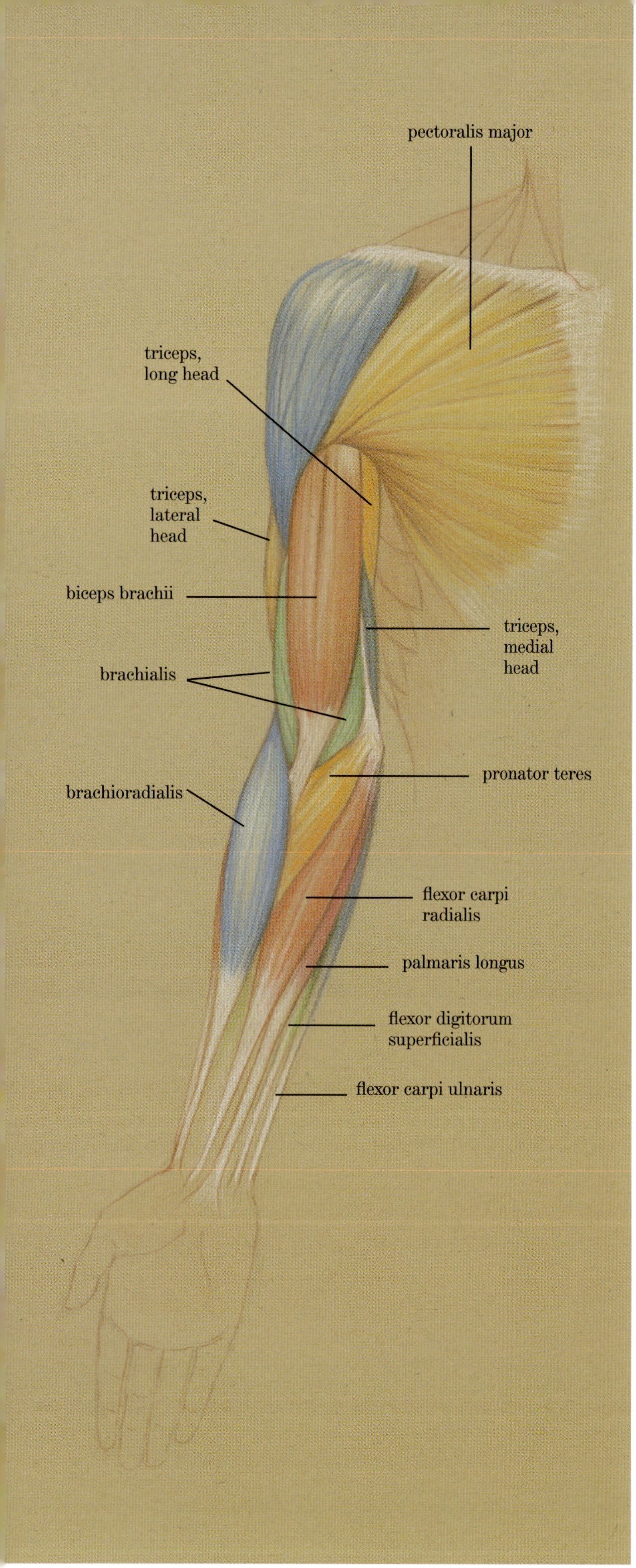

COLOR-CODED MUSCLES OF THE ARM, ANTERIOR VIEW

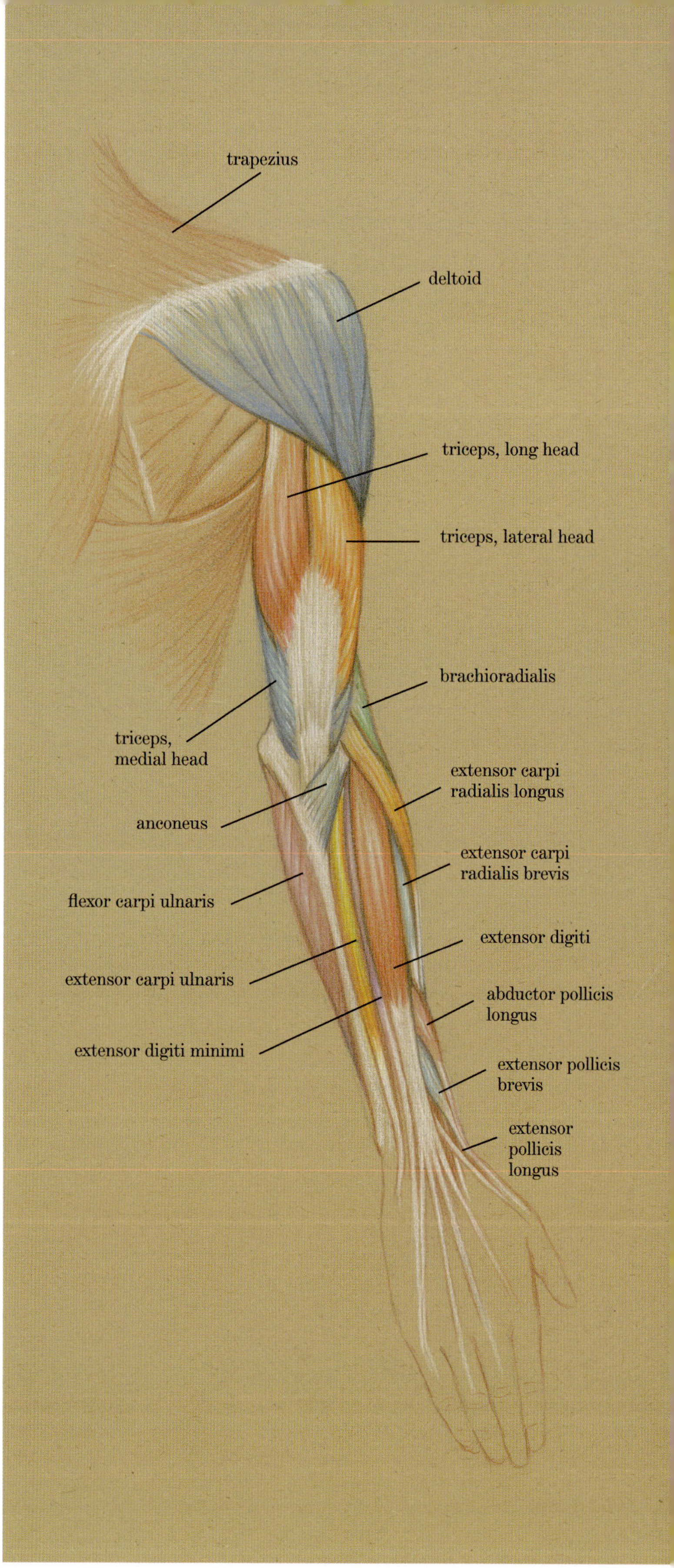

COLOR-CODED MUSCLES OF THE ARM, POSTERIOR VIEW

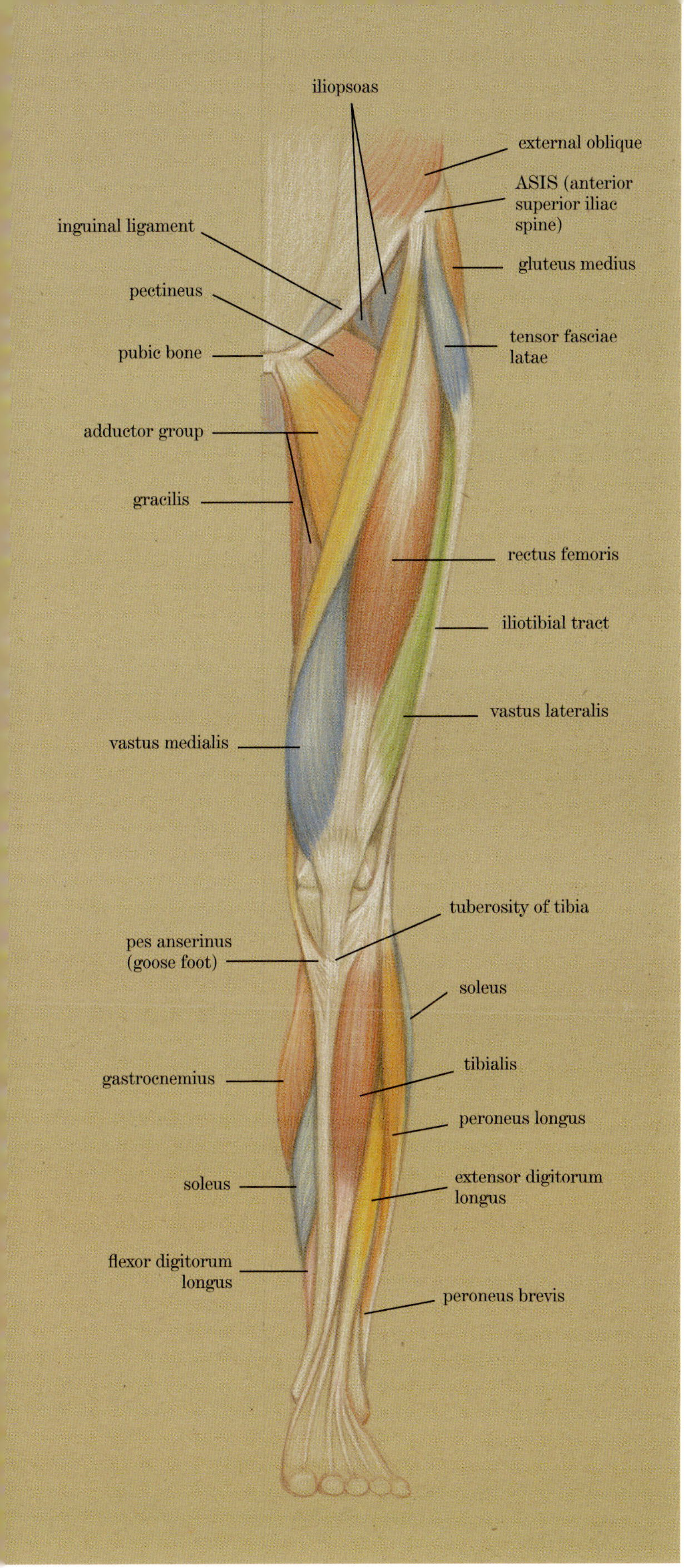

COLOR-CODED MUSCLES OF THE LEG, ANTERIOR VIEW

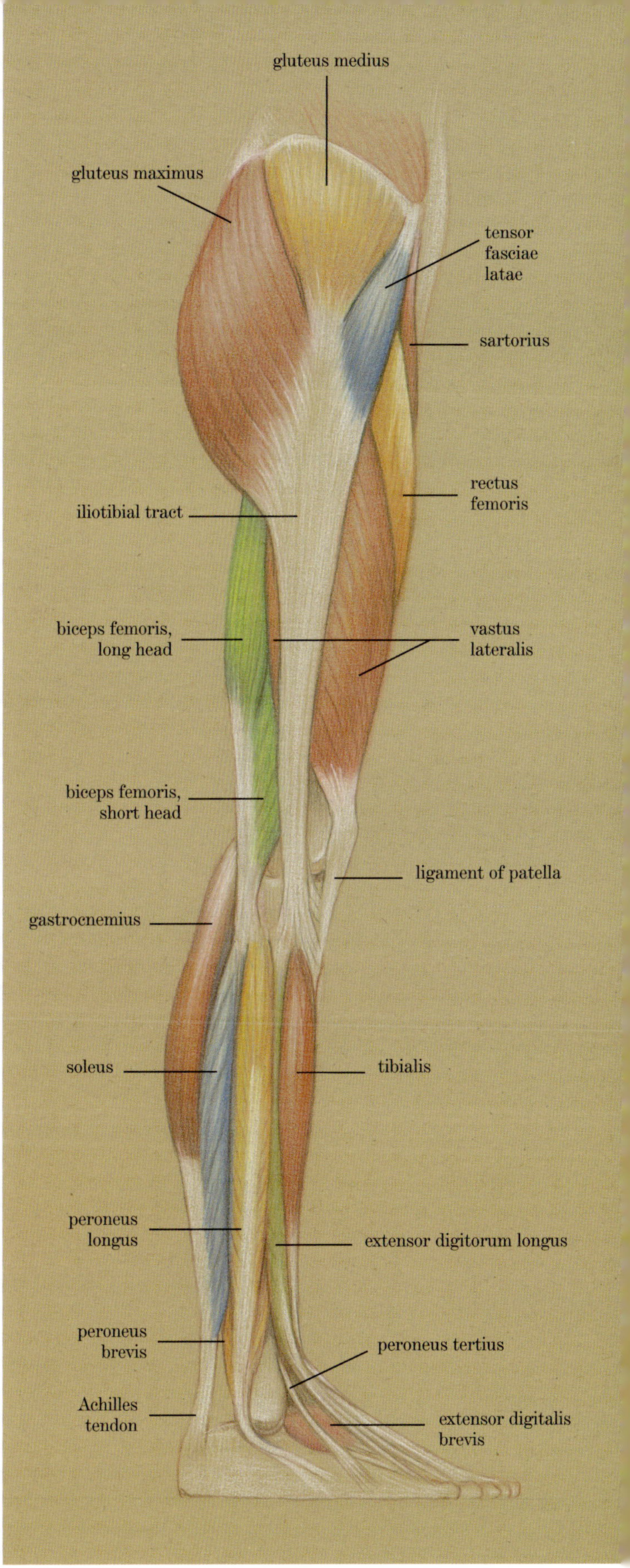

COLOR-CODED MUSCLES OF THE LEG, LATERAL VIEW

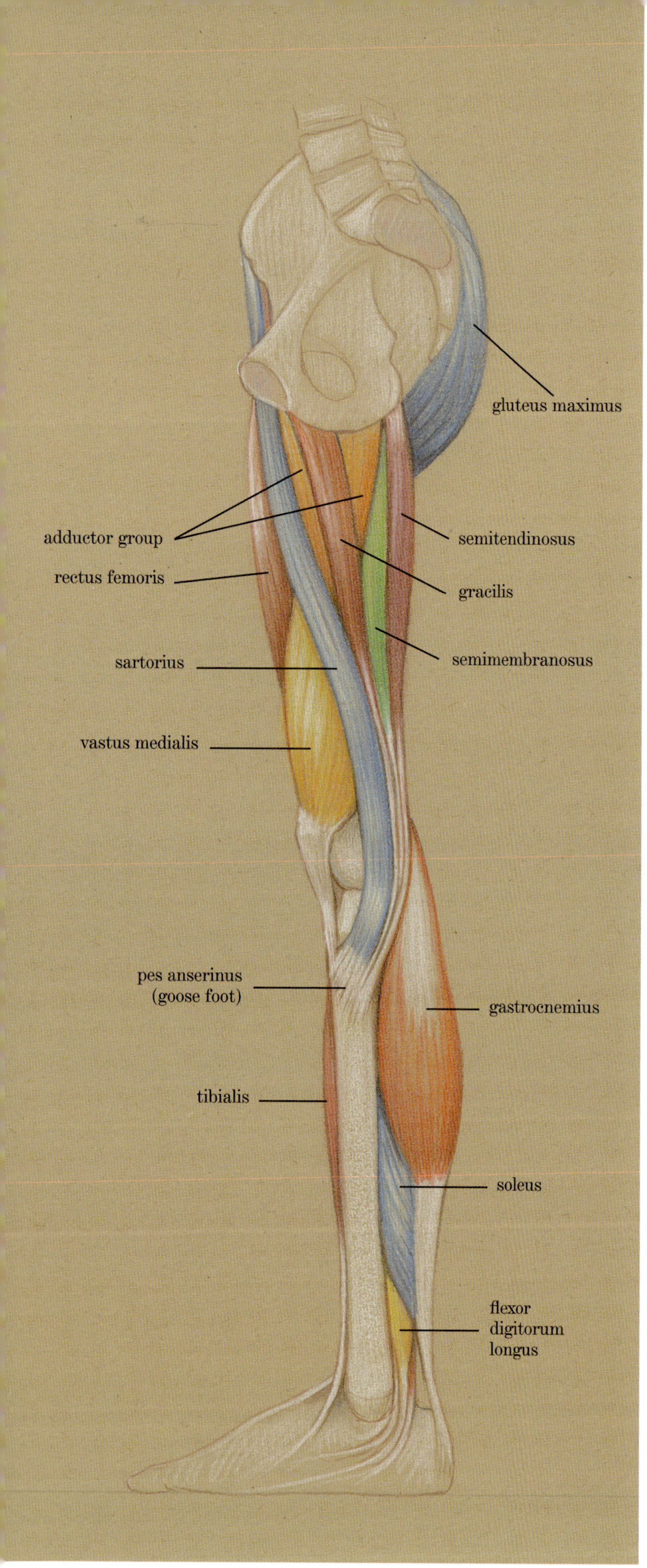

COLOR-CODED MUSCLES OF THE LEG, MEDIAL VIEW

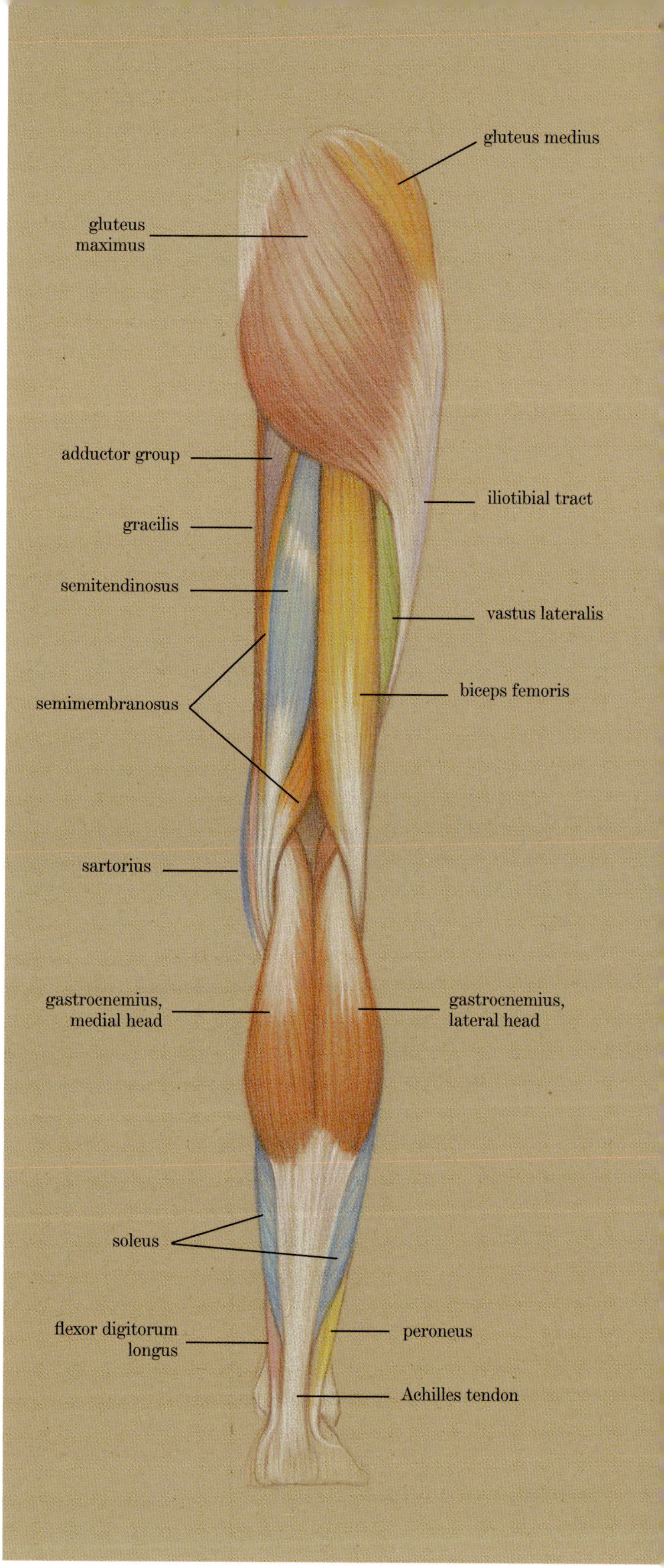

COLOR-CODED MUSCLES OF THE LEG, POSTERIOR VIEW

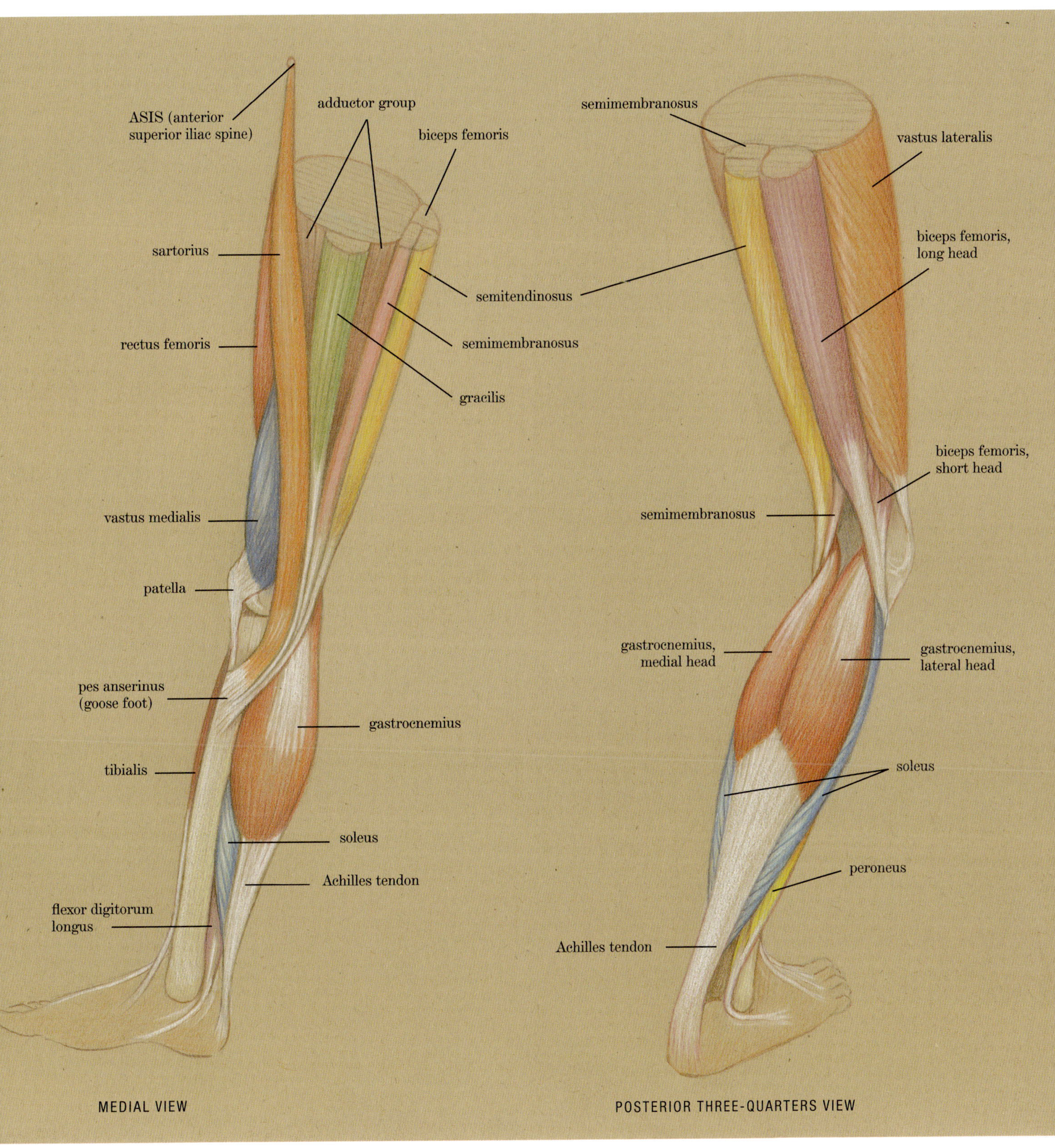

COLOR-CODED MUSCLES OF THE LEG, MEDIAL AND POSTERIOR THREE-QUARTERS VIEWS

LANDMARKS OF THE BODY

The landmarks of the body—places where parts of bones or other structures are visible beneath the skin—give very important clues for extrapolating the skeleton that underlies the figure. Being able to recognize and locate these landmarks, and therefore to visualize the skeleton, helps you create more solid, three-dimensional figures. The figures here show correlations between the most important landmarks of the body on the structural skeleton, the flayed figure (a figure from which the skin has been removed to show the muscles clearly), and the nude figure.

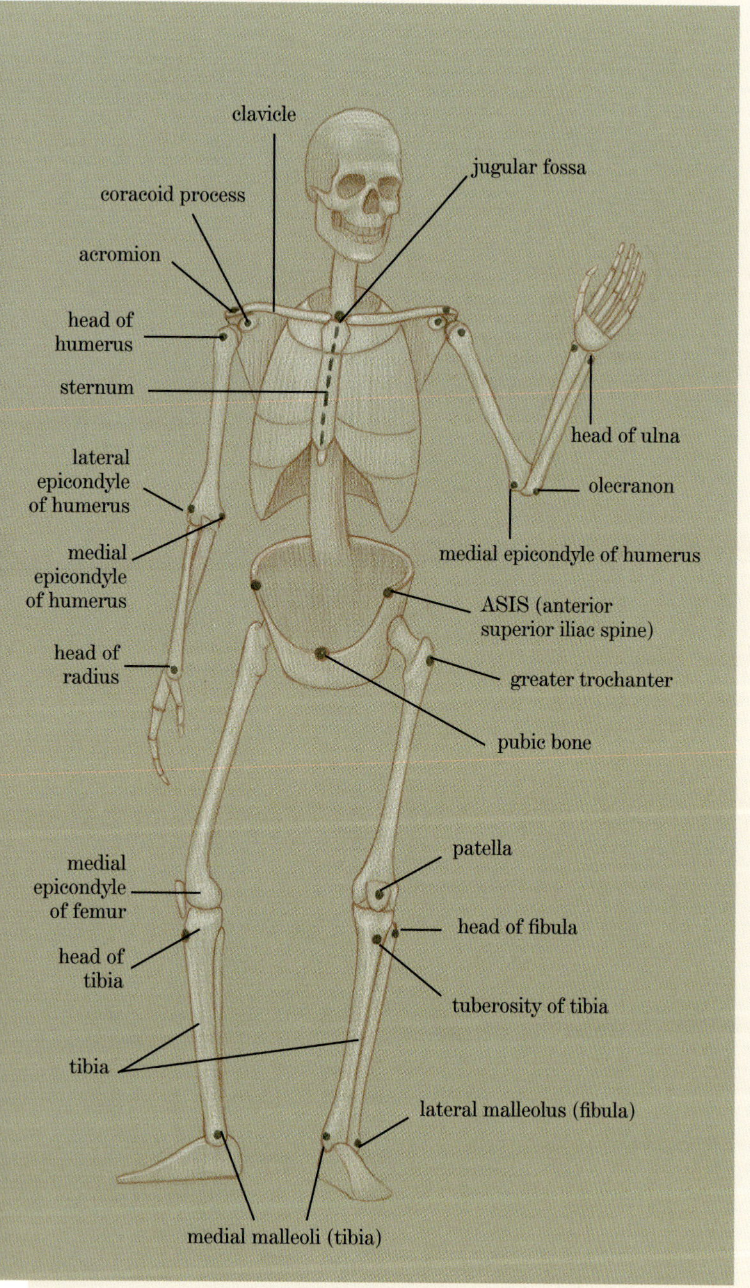

LANDMARKS ON THE STRUCTURAL SKELETON

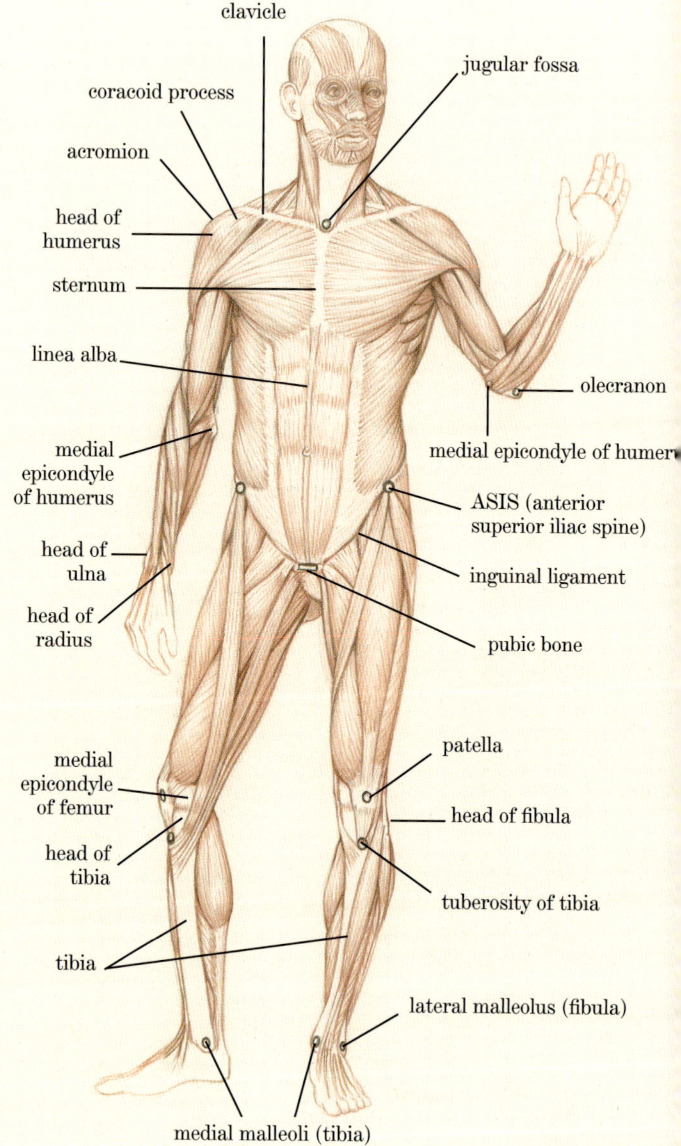

LANDMARKS ON THE FLAYED FIGURE

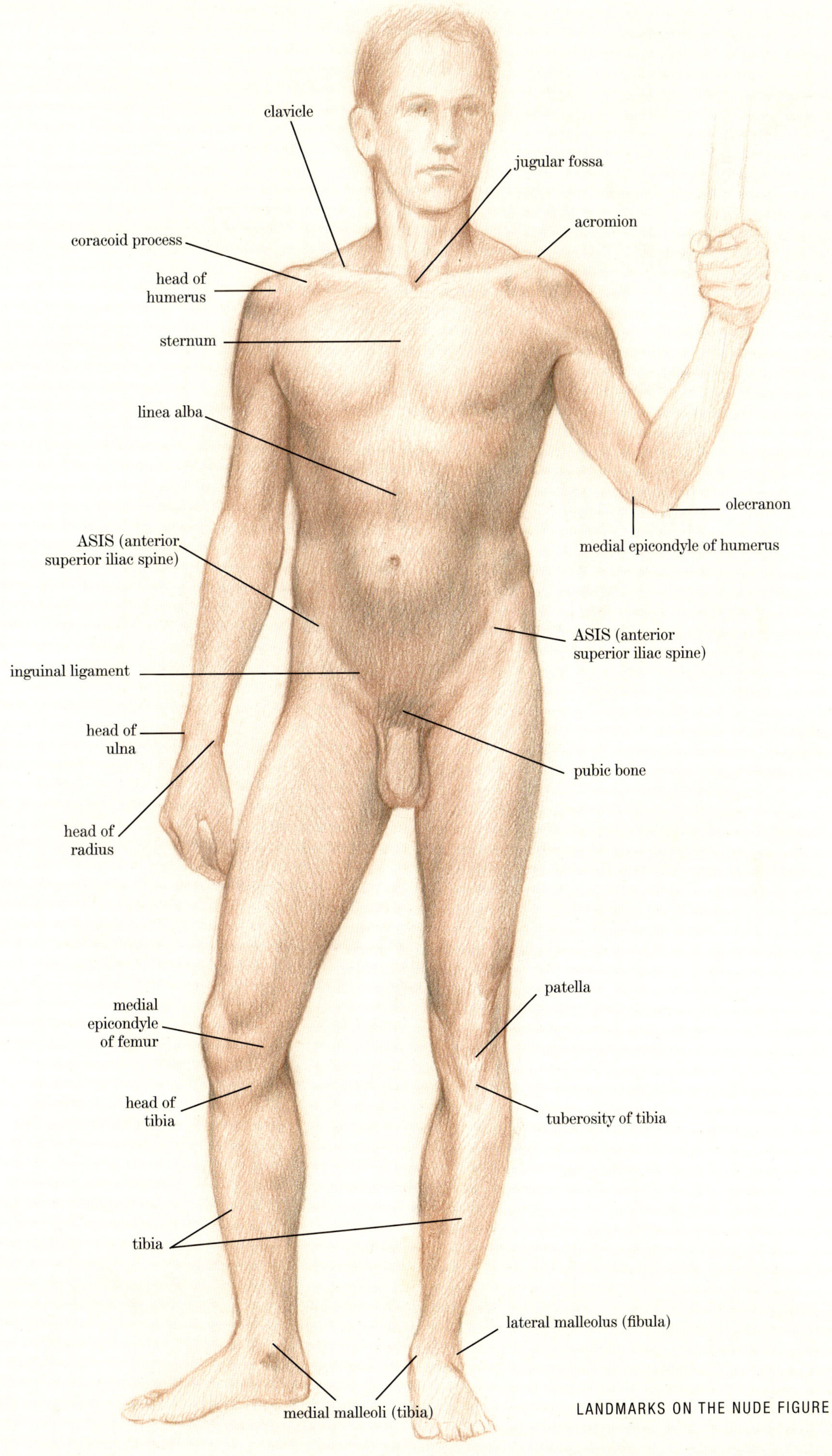

clavicle
jugular fossa
acromion
coracoid process
head of humerus
sternum
linea alba
olecranon
medial epicondyle of humerus
ASIS (anterior superior iliac spine)
ASIS (anterior superior iliac spine)
inguinal ligament
head of ulna
head of radius
pubic bone
medial epicondyle of femur
patella
head of tibia
tuberosity of tibia
tibia
lateral malleolus (fibula)
medial malleoli (tibia)
LANDMARKS ON THE NUDE FIGURE

EXERCISES

Now you can start analyzing your figure drawings from an anatomical point of view, which will help you to better assimilate the material we have studied so far, conferring the practical benefit of enabling you to draw more precise and beautiful pictures.

EXERCISE 1: DO AN ANATOMICAL STUDY OF A BODY PART

After drawing a figure from life, do a study of the anatomy of a specific body part, as in the figure on this page. You can also create more complete studies directly over the drawing of the figure, as shown in the figure opposite.

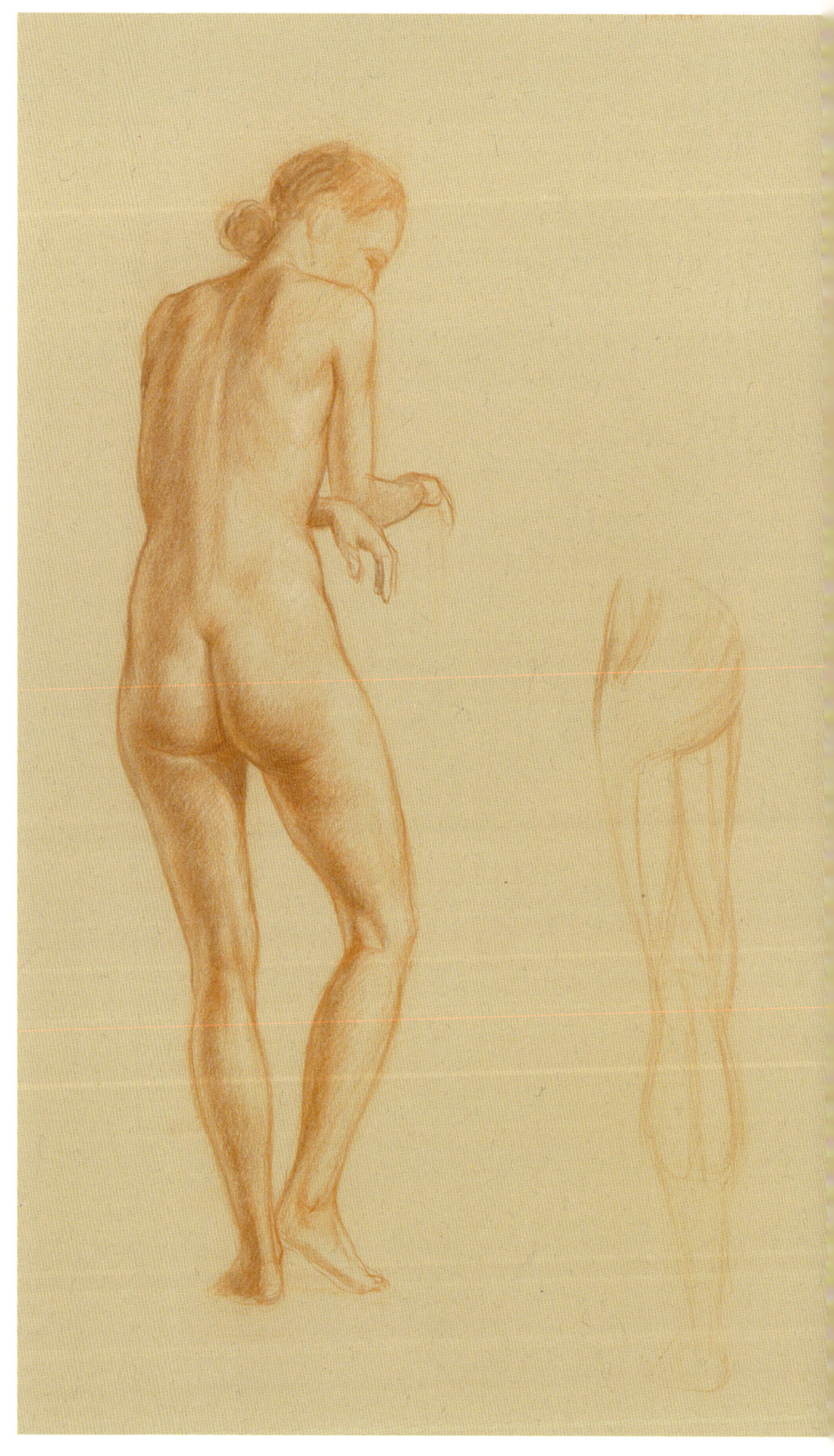

FIGURE DRAWING WITH ANATOMICAL STUDY OF LEG

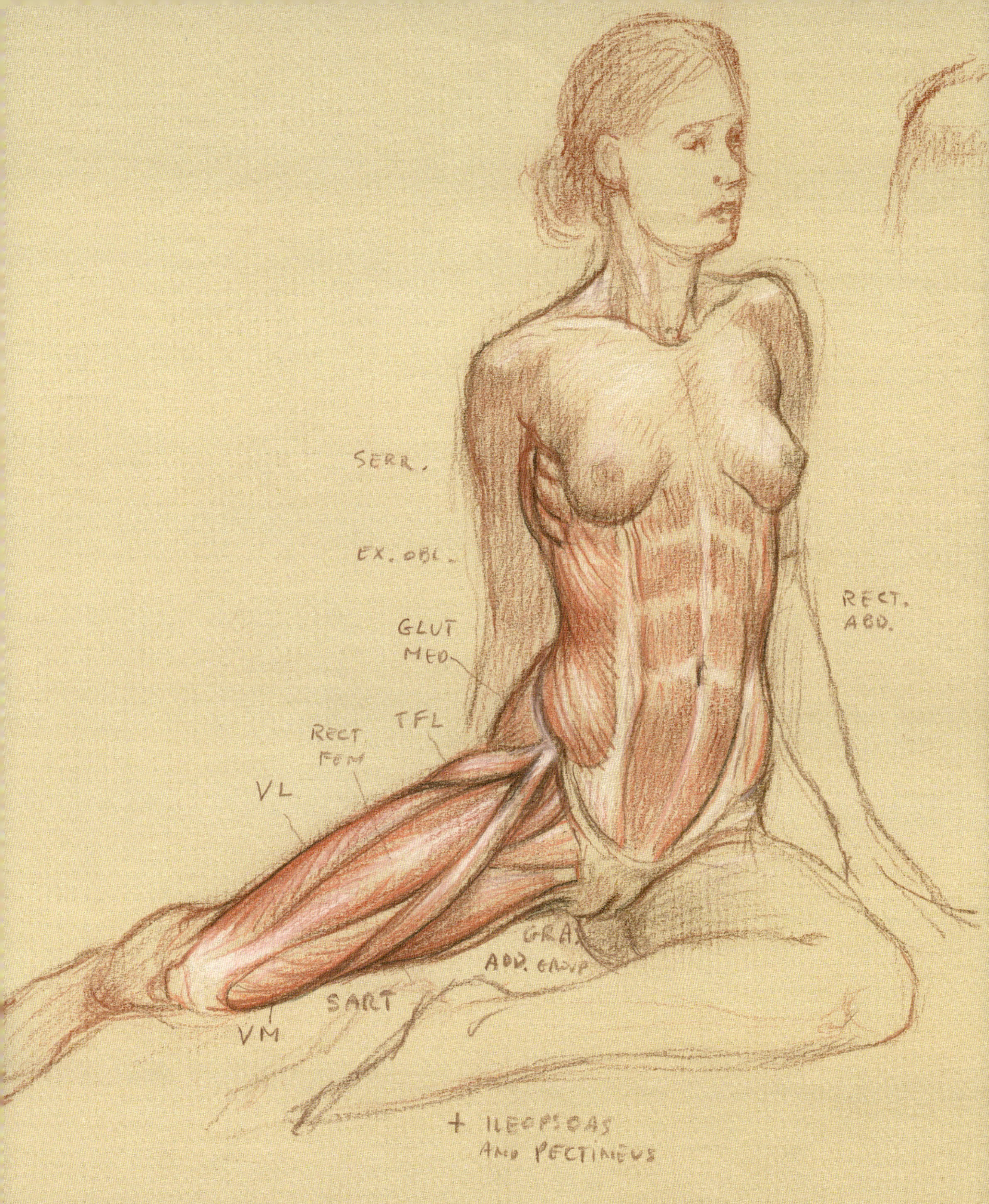

LIFE DRAWING INCORPORATING ANATOMICAL STUDY

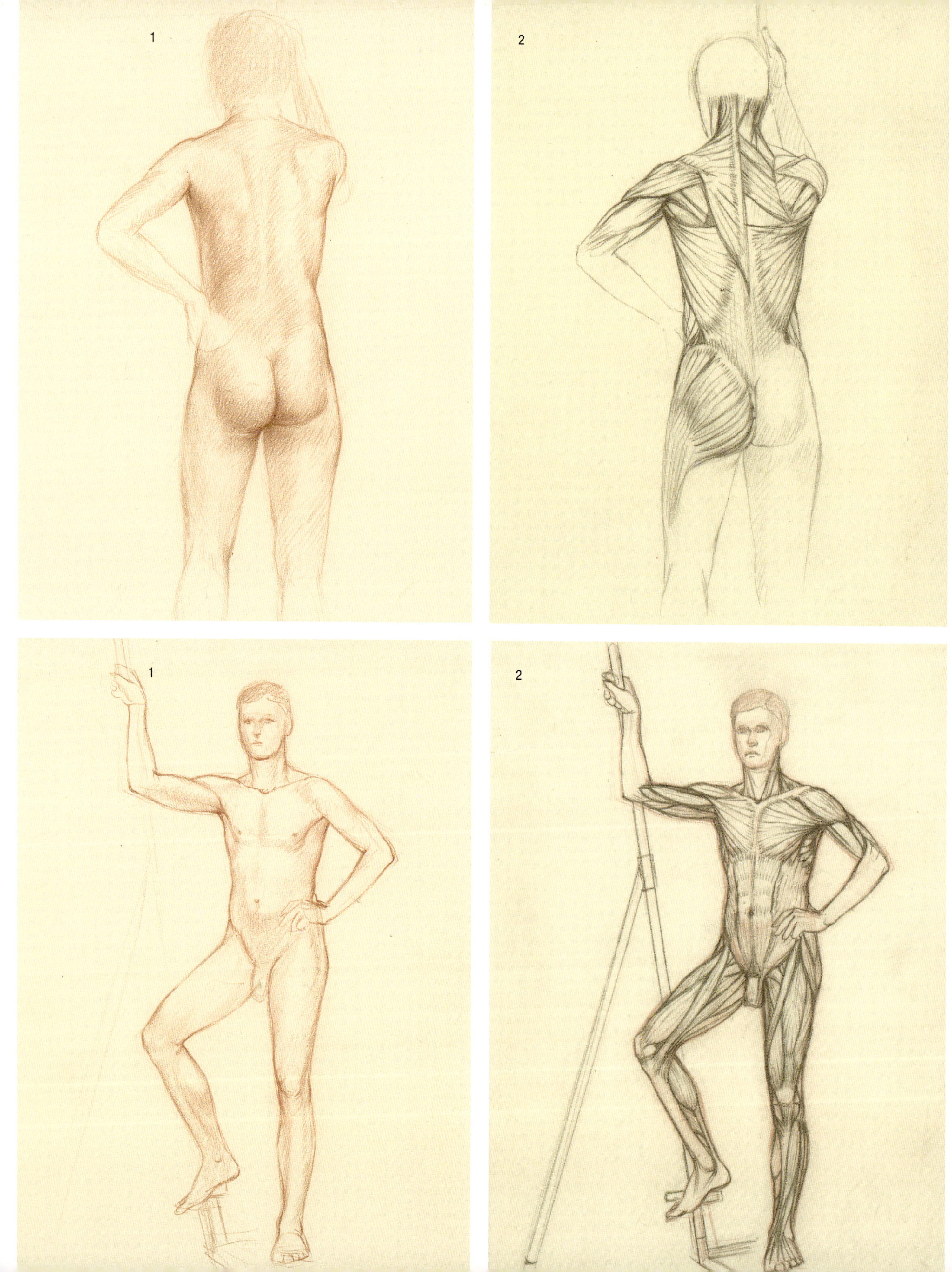

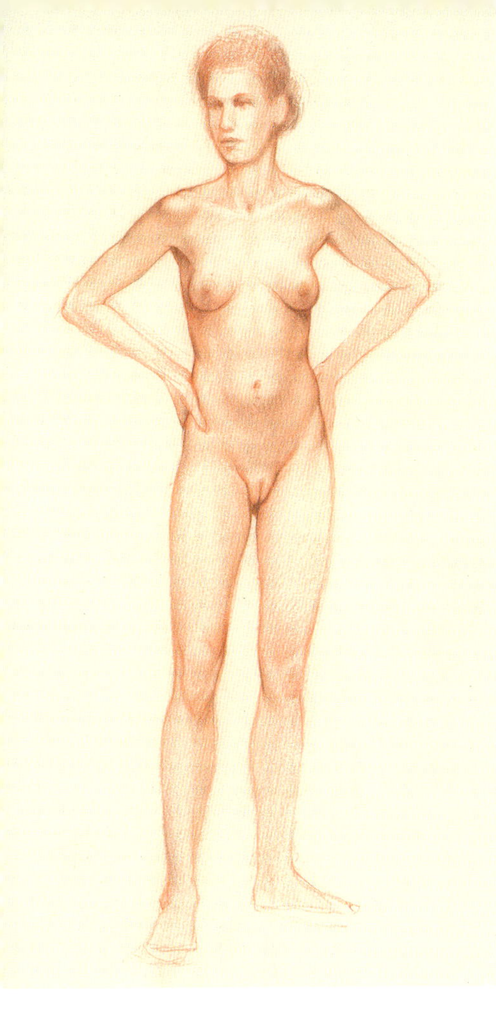

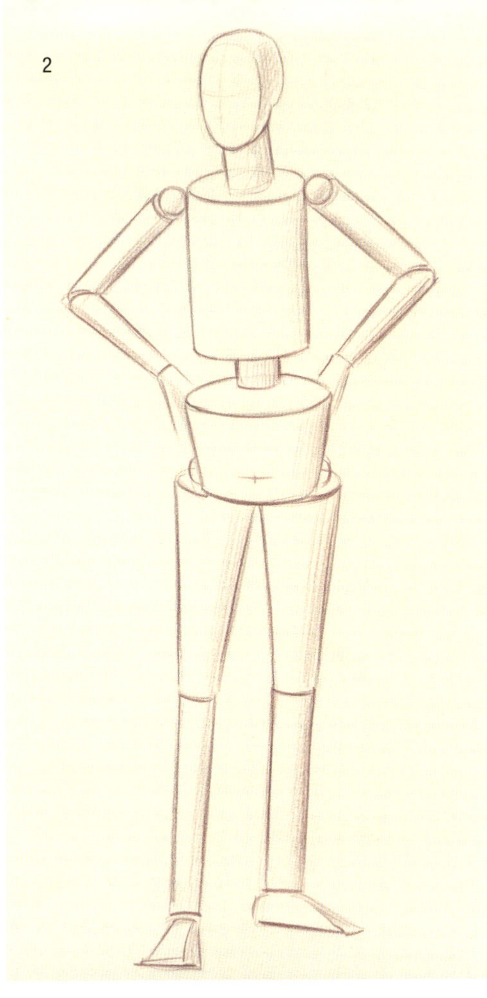

EXERCISE 2: DO ANATOMICAL OVERLAYS USING TRACING PAPER

Layer a sheet of tracing paper over one of your figure drawings and, using the muscle charts in this chapter for reference, draw muscles over it, as shown in figures opposite. (If you wish, you may use photos of nude models instead of your own drawings.) You can also create two layers: one for the skeleton and one overtop it for the muscles.

EXERCISE 3: CREATE A MULTILAYERED DRAWING

To review all the material covered in this book so far, create a multilayered drawing: Start with a fairly accurate drawing (you may use a photograph instead) and, using tracing paper, draw the various levels of schematization we have studied, starting with a stereometric rendition, then the skeleton (either schematic or organic), and then the muscles. The figures here show you how to create such a sequence.

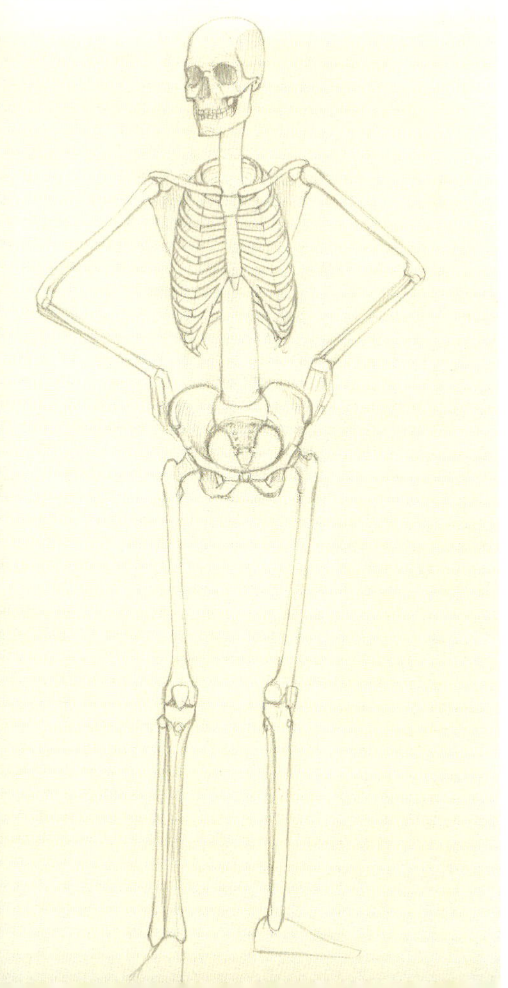

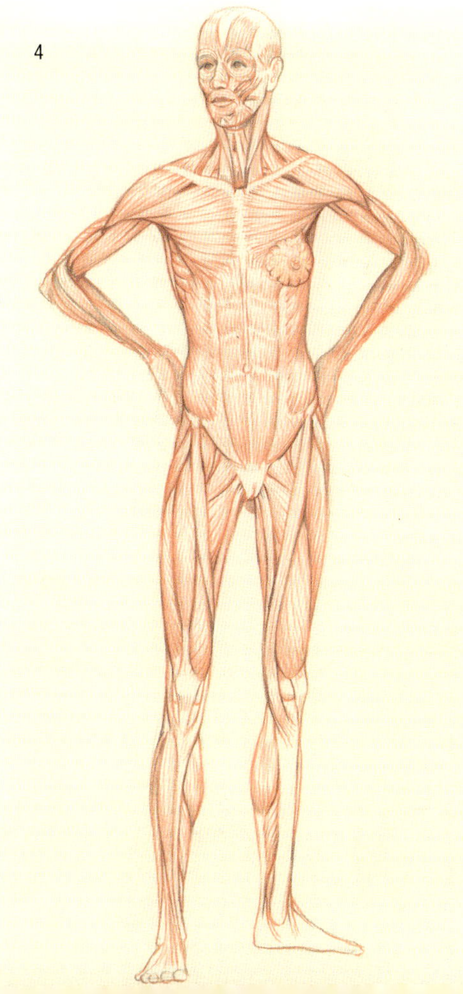

opposite, top
STUDY OF FIGURE WITH TRACING PAPER
OVERLAY SHOWING ANATOMY

opposite, bottom
STUDY OF MALE FIGURE WITH TRACING
PAPER OVERLAY SHOWING ANATOMY

left
A MULTILAYERED SEQUENCE

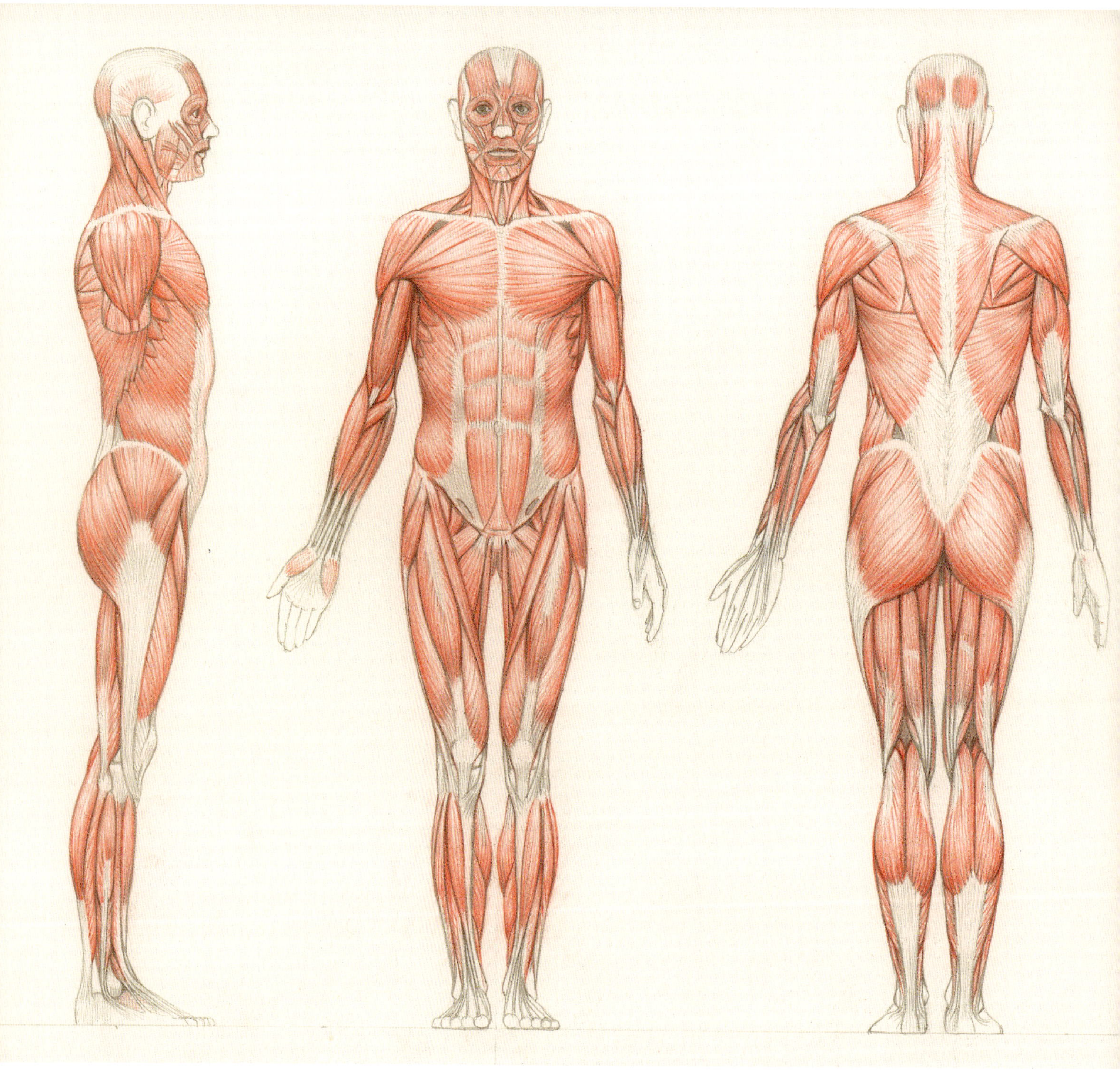

EXERCISE 4: DRAW MUSCLES
OVER SKELETONS

Working from life or imagination, draw skeletons in various poses, then draw the muscles over them. To begin with, use the anatomical charts in this and the previous chapter as references, but then try drawing the muscles from memory. Drawing from memory will tell you what you know and what you don't know. When you can't remember which muscle goes where, look it up. Practice this exercise until you remember all the muscles.

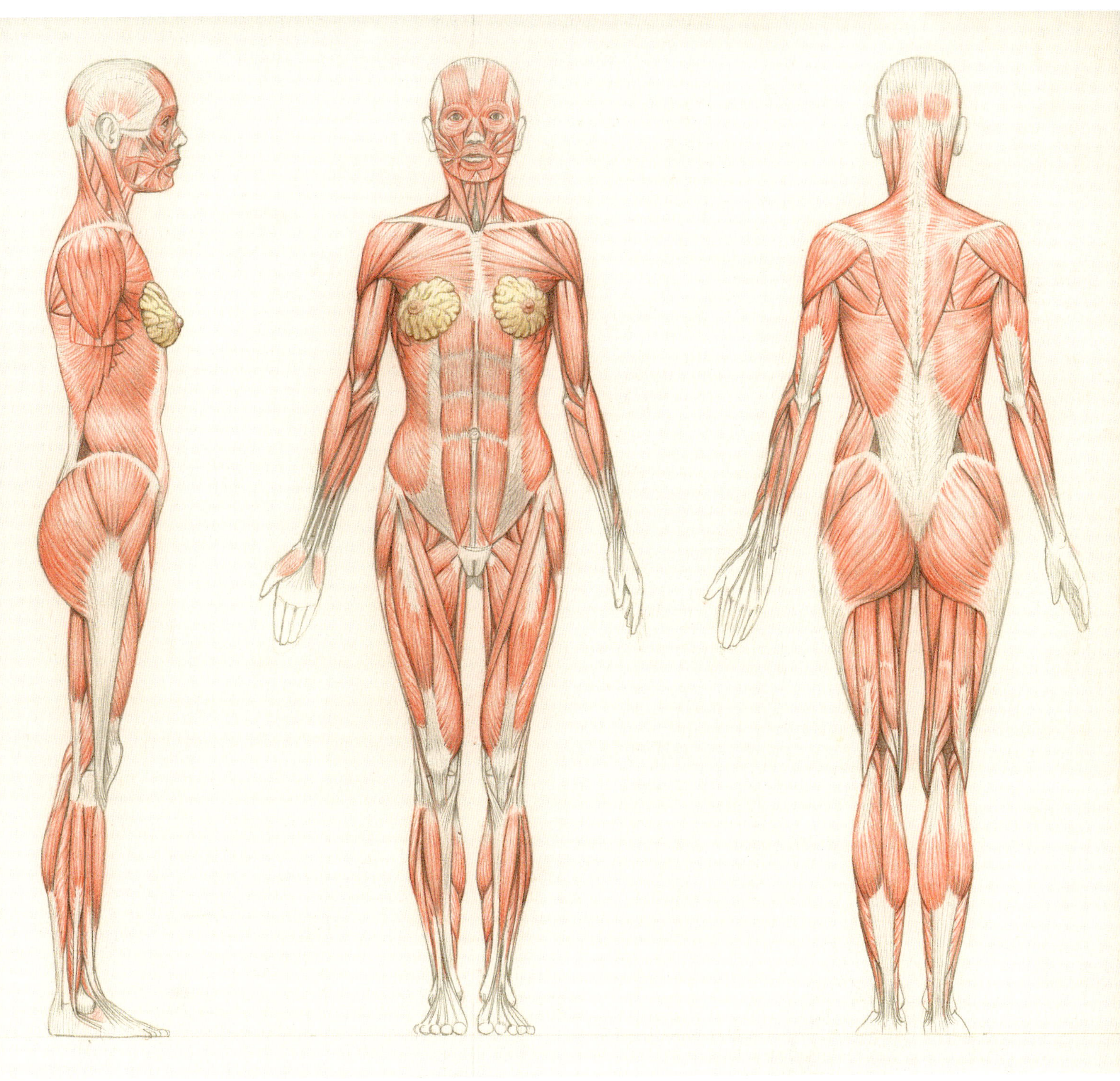

EXERCISE 5: CREATE COLOR-CODED
MUSCLE CHARTS FOR THE WHOLE BODY

Make black-and-white photocopies of the drawings of the
muscles of the male and female figures above and opposite
and, using colored pencils, create color-coded charts for
the whole body, labeling the muscles as you go.

opposite
MUSCLES OF THE MALE FIGURE

above
MUSCLES OF THE FEMALE FIGURE

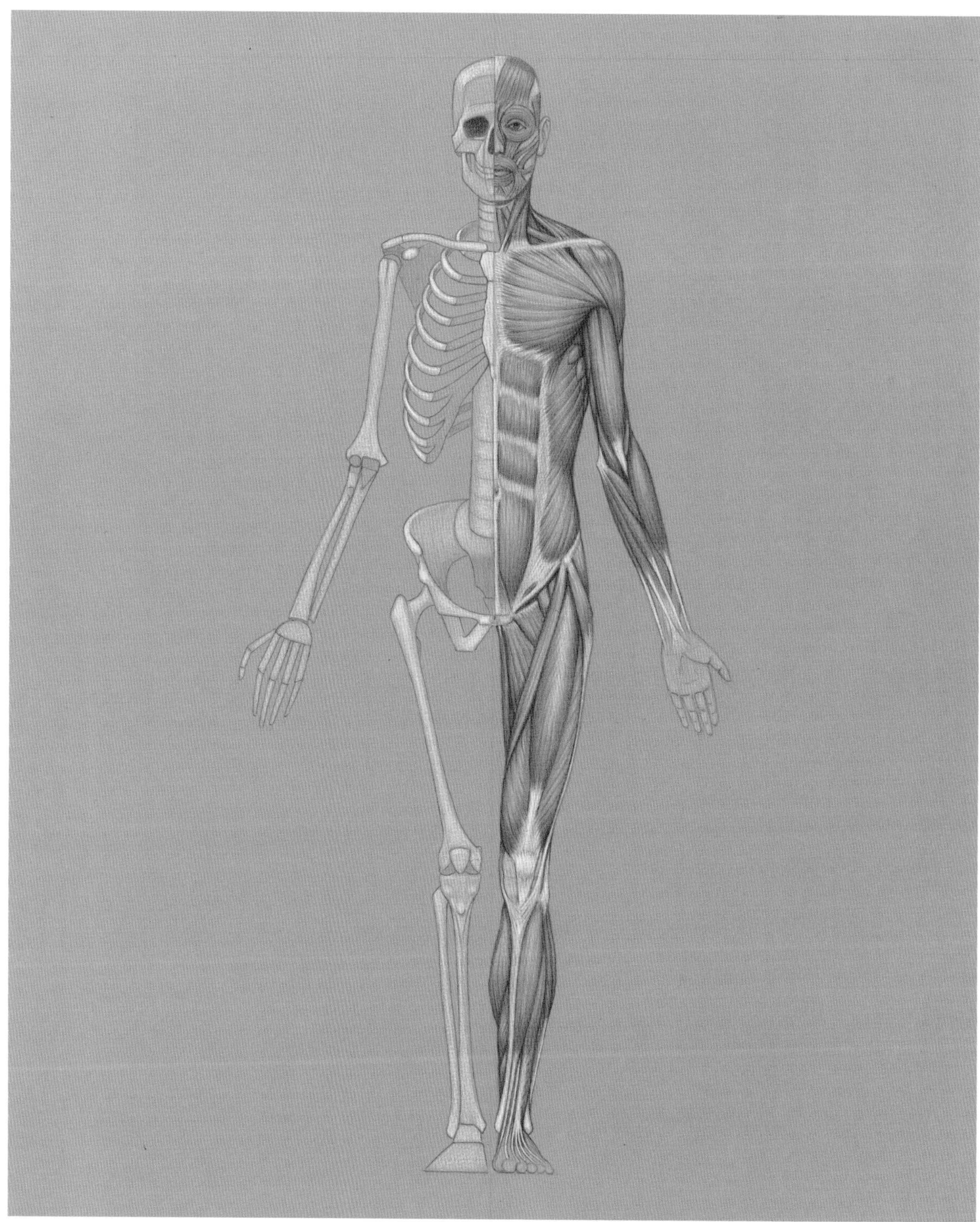

EXERCISE 6: REVIEW AND MEMORIZE THE BONES AND MUSCLES

Photocopy or scan and print these figures and, from memory, label the various bones and muscles of the human body. Do this as many times as you need to until you have memorized the all the bones' and muscles' names and locations. My students often print these images and carry them around with them so that they can work on memorization during their commutes to and from school. Whenever you get stuck, refer back to the labeled versions of these charts on pages 125–127.

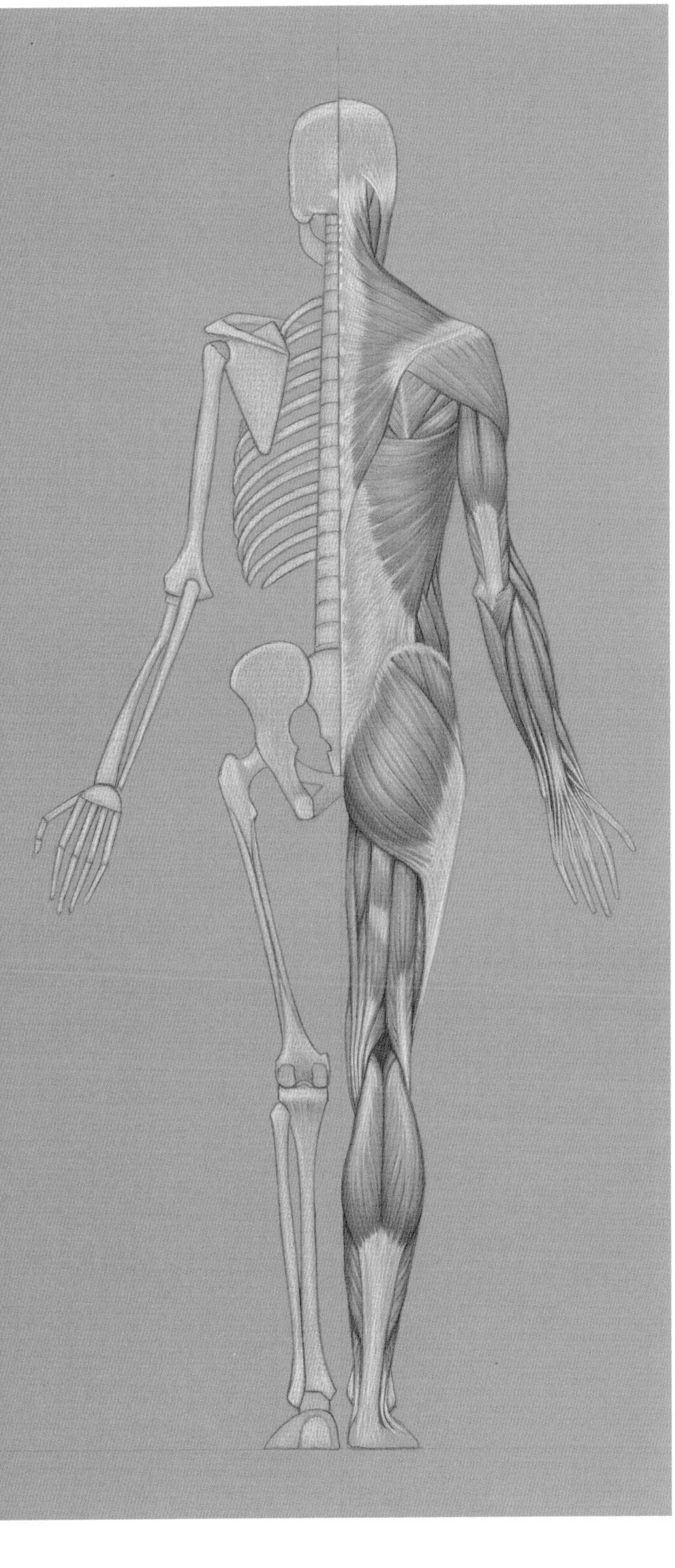

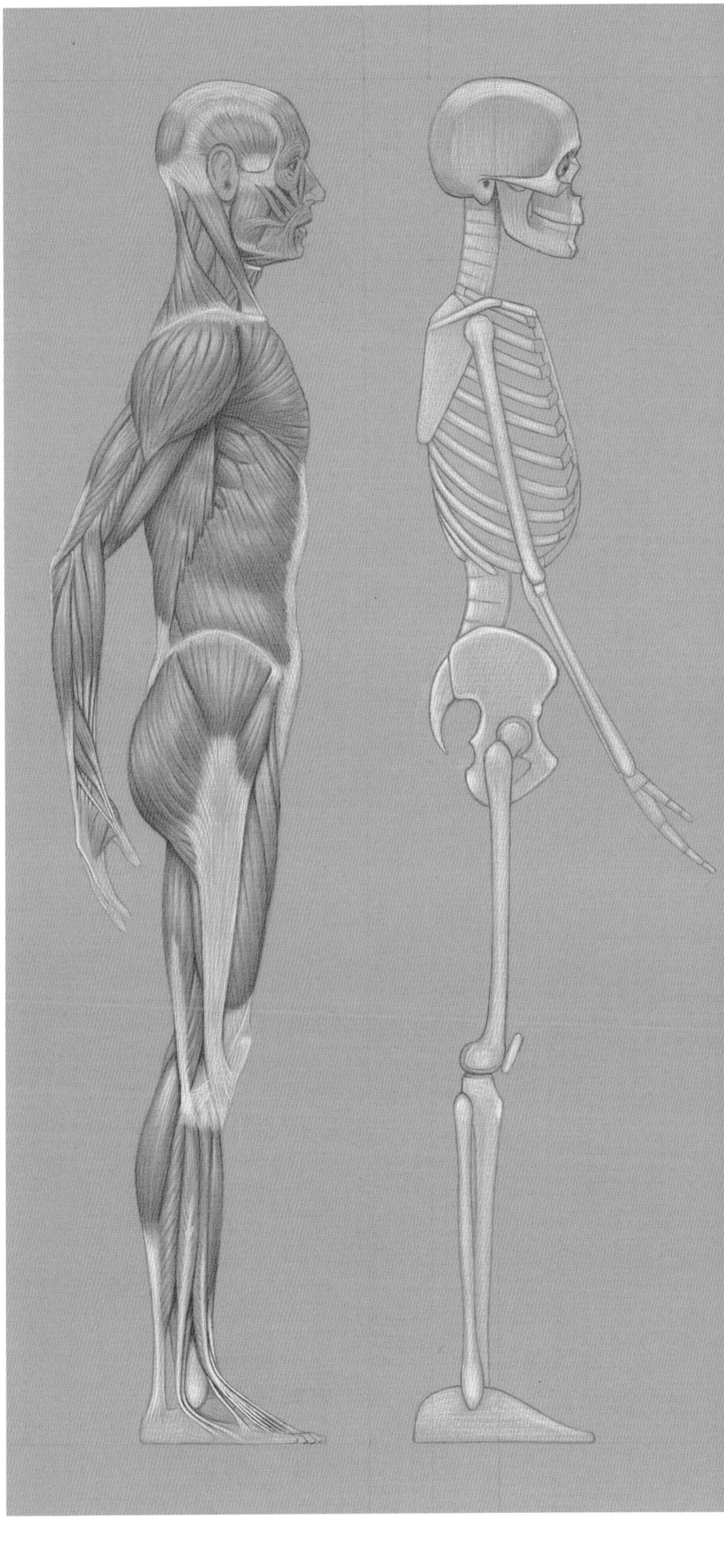

opposite
BONES AND MUSCLES, ANTERIOR VIEW
above left
BONES AND MUSCLES, POSTERIOR VIEW
above right
BONES AND MUSCLES, LATERAL VIEW

MIX TONE AND LINE

You might try drawing with a pastel or a colored pencil whose tip is sanded flat lengthwise to make it longer and wider. (If you are using a colored pencil, shave the wood off the casing to obtain about one to one and a half inches of free lead.) First, block in the volumes and tonal aspects of the figure with the pastel or free lead. Then, using a well-sharpened colored pencil, draw the essential lines of the figure, as shown in the figures here.

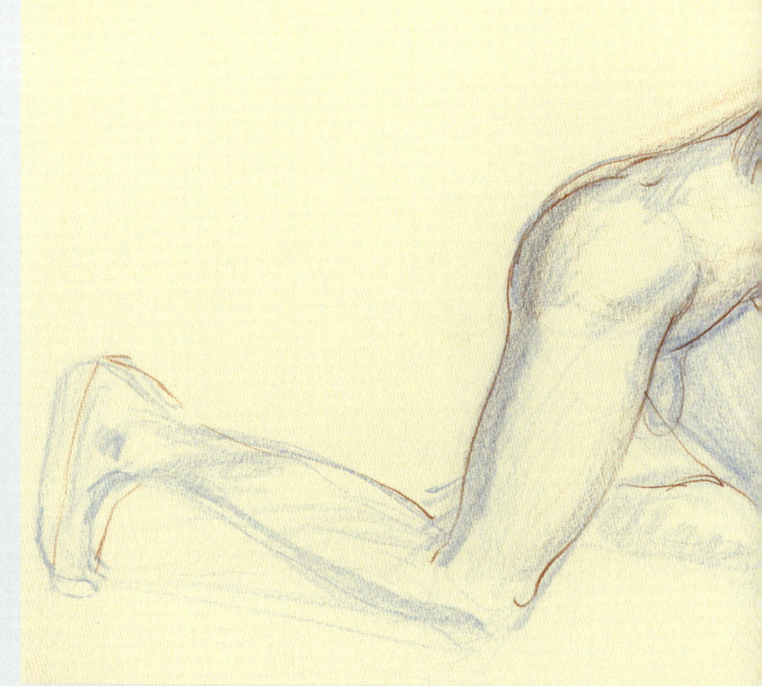

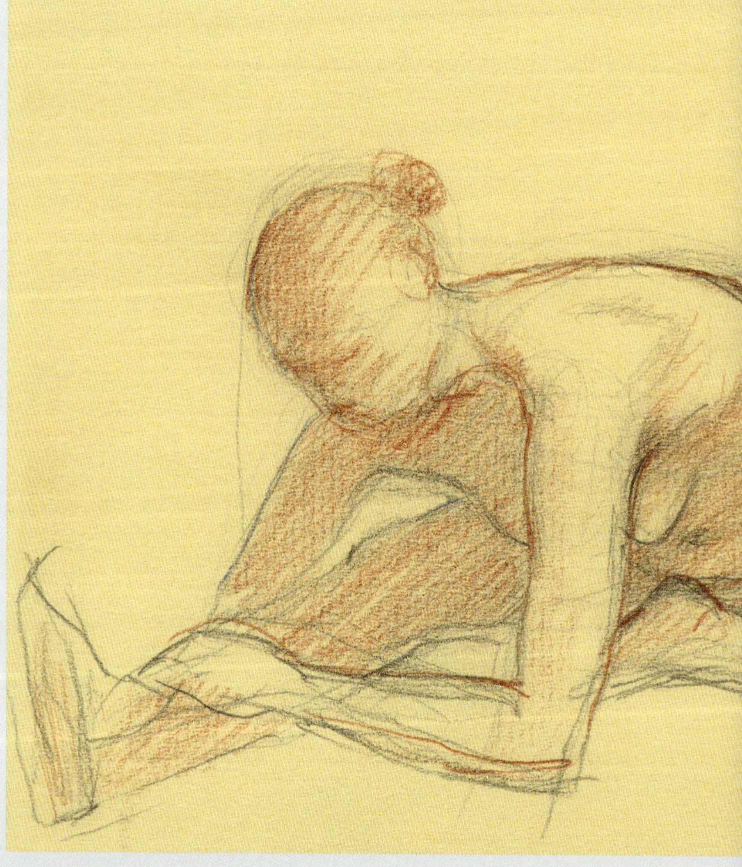

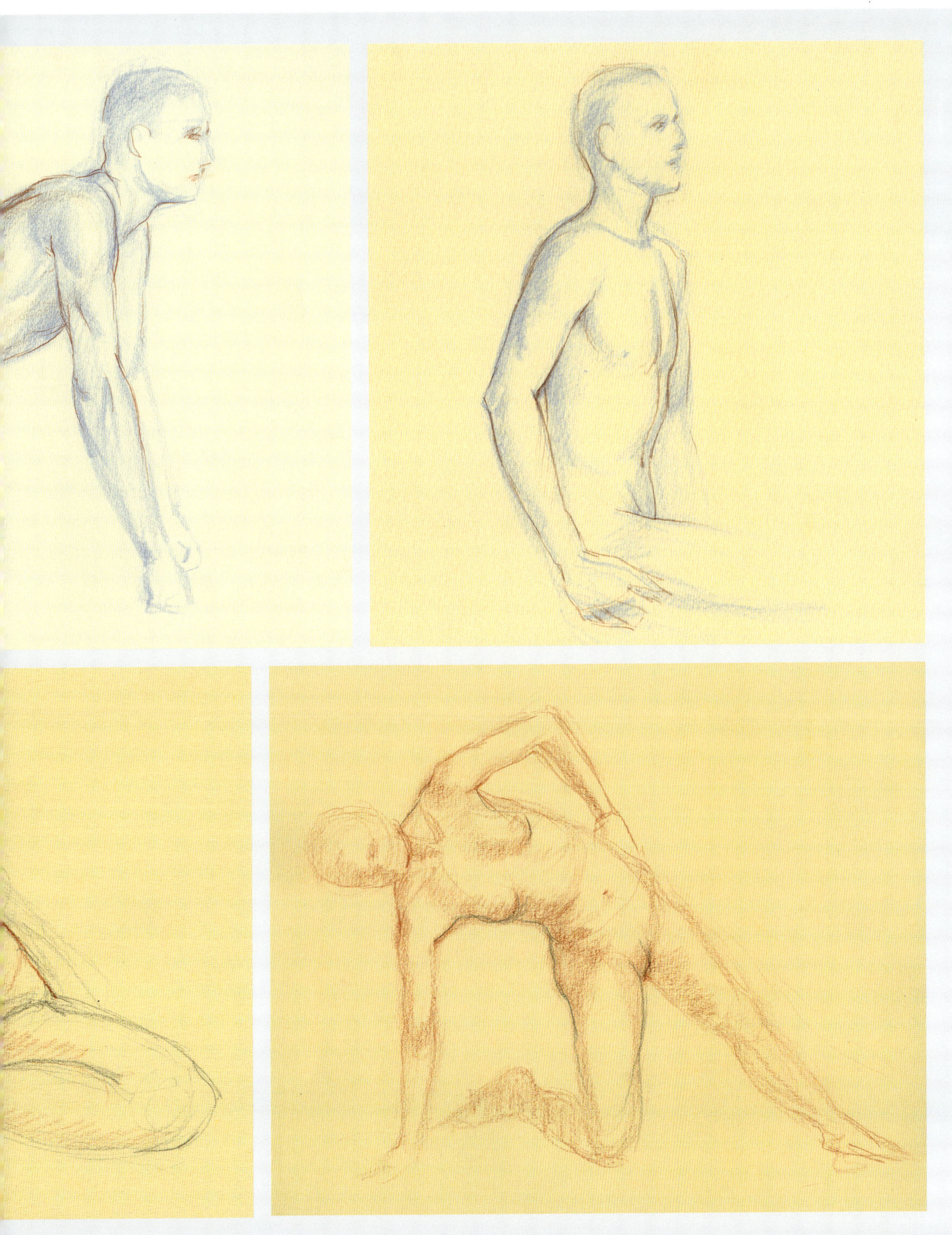

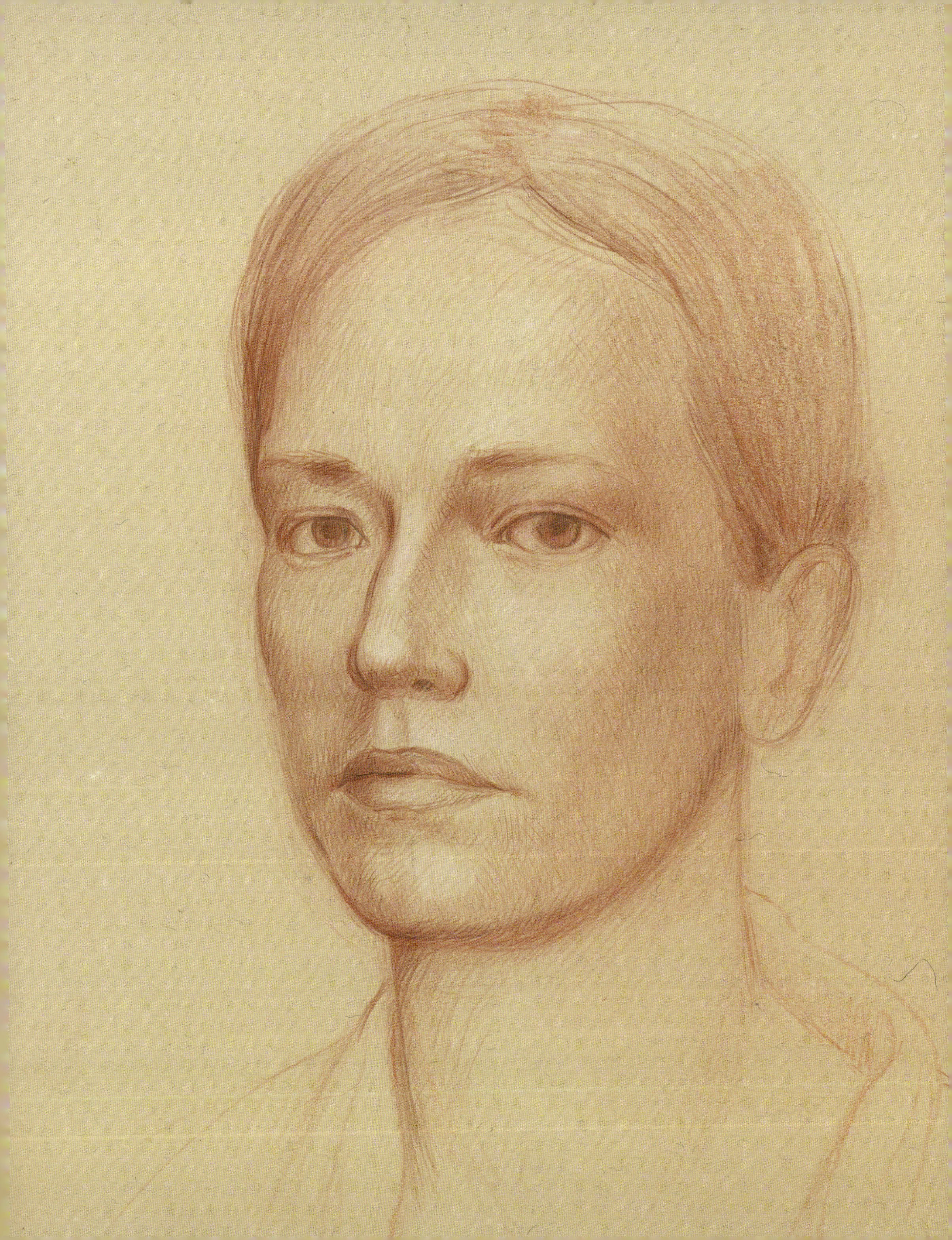

Chapter 5

THE HEAD AND NECK

Have you ever wondered why it is so difficult to draw a portrait that looks just like your sitter—one that captures his or her physiognomic traits accurately, as well as the mood of the face? When looking at a depiction of a human face, you will immediately notice small mistakes or slight anomalies: a nose that is too long, eyes that are too close to each other or too far apart, a forehead that's too small or big. Often, you cannot identify the specific anomaly—you just feel that there is something wrong about the nose or the ears without being able to pinpoint the problem exactly. You're aware of the defect in an instinctual way.

The recognition of the facial features is so important to humans that areas in our brain evolved specifically for this purpose. But we read human faces and expressions through two filters, cultural as well as biological, and this makes us very discerning when interpreting people's faces, including their intentions or moods.

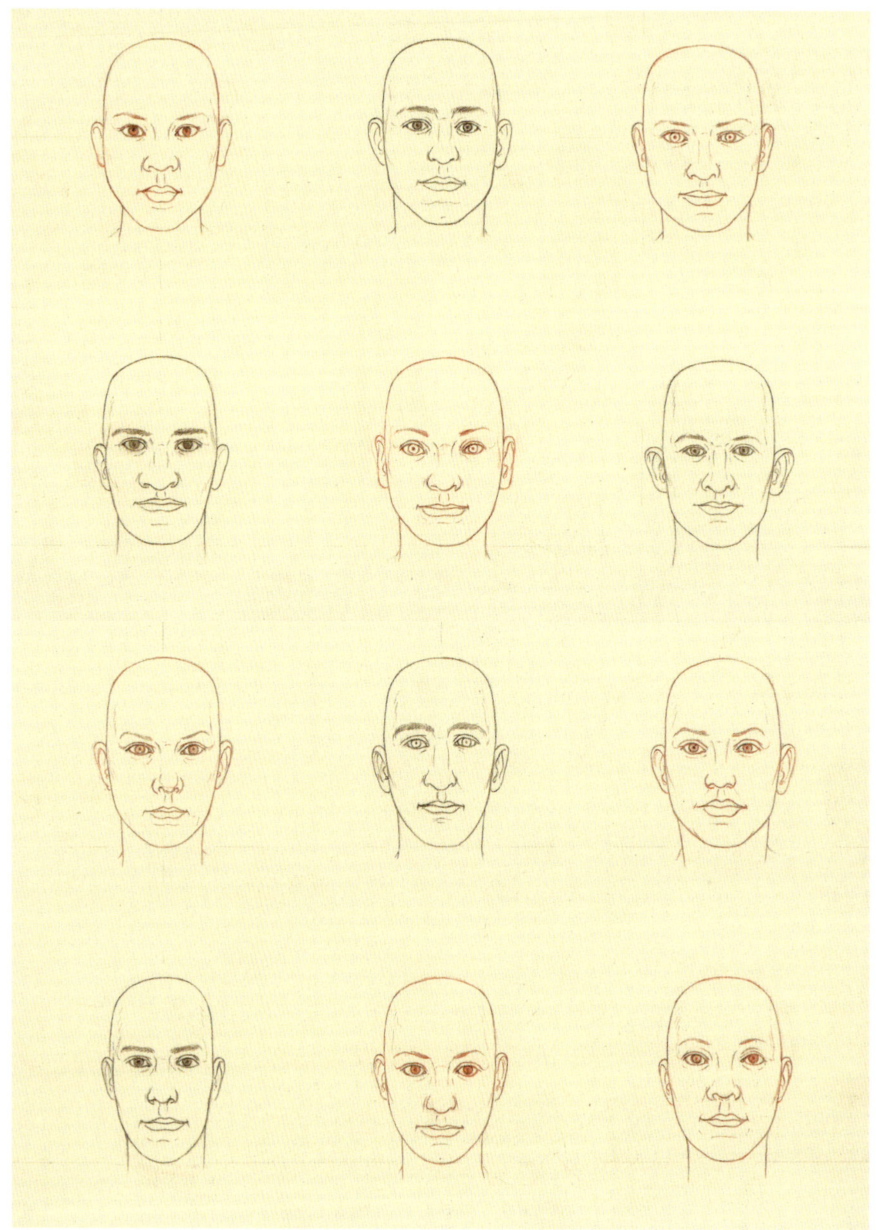

VARIETIES OF FACIAL FEATURES

Human facial features exhibit more variety than those of any other animal. For example, a person's nose might be wide or narrow, long or short, upturned or aquiline, straight or bulbous, and so on. Leonardo da Vinci studied facial features and expressions in depth to better convey human emotions and narrative in his paintings. He also devised a systematic approach to the study of human facial features, classifying ten basic types of noses, for example. But Leonardo's observations of the nose and other features were limited mostly if not exclusively to European and Mediterranean Basin types. You can imagine how many more types of noses could be identified if his research were extended to the whole human species. Add in differences in gender, age, body weight, and so on, and you can imagine how great—if not infinite—the number of possible variations of the human face can be. The variety of faces shown in the figure above gives you some idea of the variety of facial traits.

FACIAL PROPORTIONS AND PLANES

Despite the enormous individual variation in human faces, an artist who wants to do figure studies and portraits needs to become aware of certain proportions that are statistically true for the majority of the human population. You will find that most people's facial proportions, with some minimal variation, are very close to the basic measures discussed here. Please note that the facial proportions I propose in this chapter are not intended to be seen as "ideal" but rather as pragmatic. They are not selected as paradigmatic proportions or canons of beauty but just as statistical measurements to be used as a general guide and that carry no moral or aesthetic value.

My intention is to describe a grid that is not canonical but constitutes an adaptable diagram that can help you draw facial features more accurately and quickly. The image at right shows how to create this grid, with which you can create an "undifferentiated" face that reflects basic anthropometric measurements on which you can superimpose the specific facial features of the individual you are portraying.

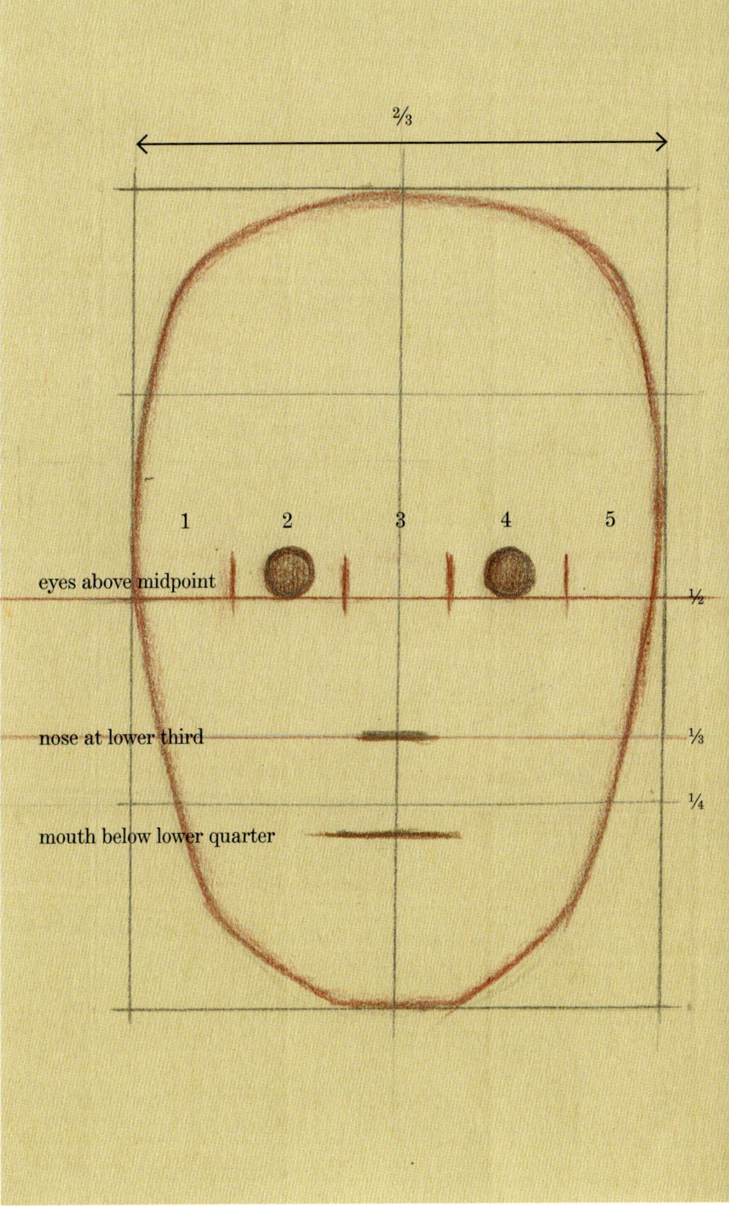

right

BASIC PROPORTIONS OF THE FACE

In this generalized facial diagram, the irises are just above the median line that divides the head in two equal portions horizontally. The base of the nasal opening is two-thirds of the way down from the top of the head (or one-third up from the chin), and the mouth is a little bit above the midline between the tip of the nose and the chin. The width of one eye is approximately one-fifth of the width of the face. The advantage of becoming acquainted with these parameters is that they allow you to block-in a generic, undifferentiated face. After doing so, you can then observe and define the specific physiognomic characteristics of your subject.

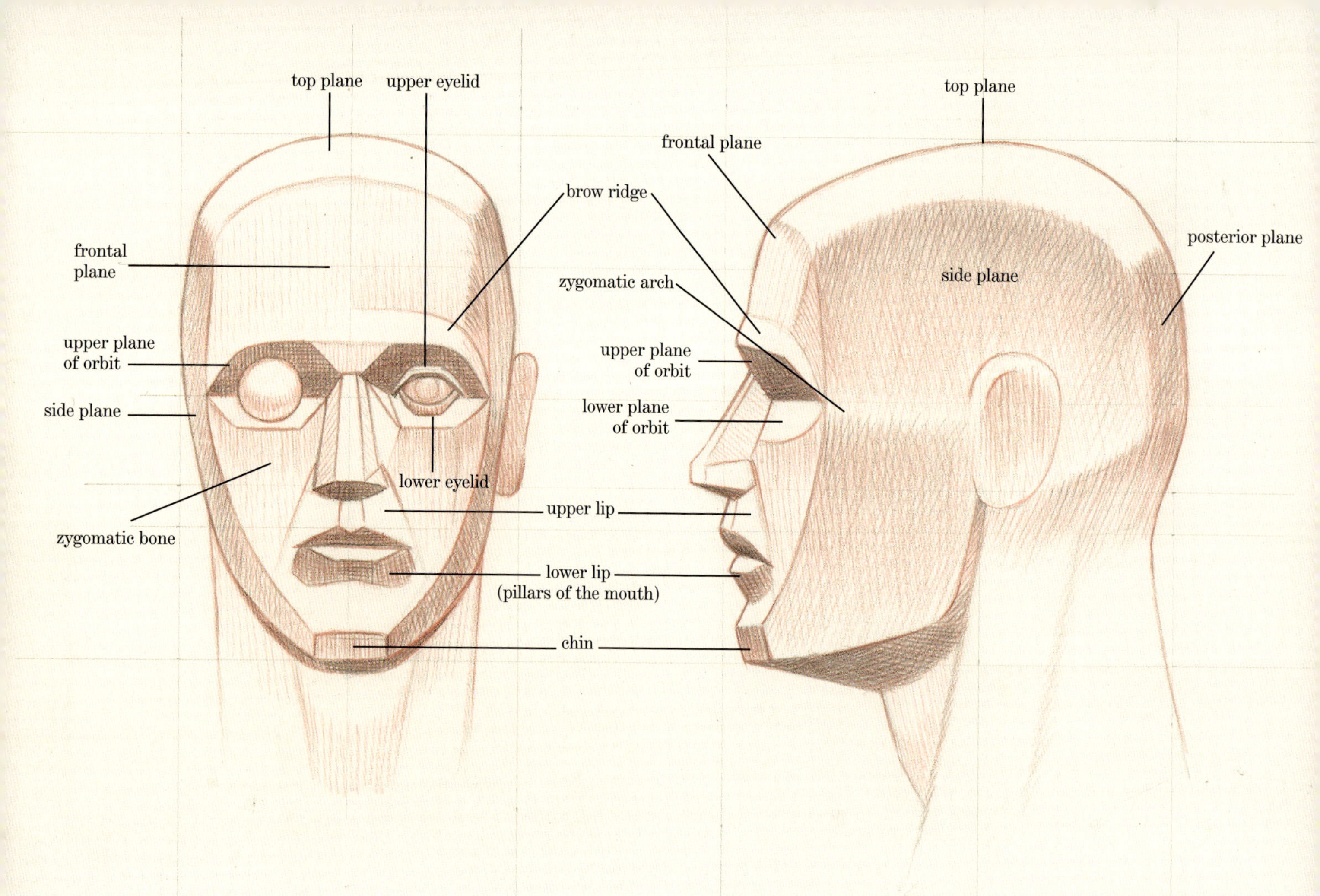

above
PLANES OF THE HEAD, ANTERIOR AND LATERAL VIEWS

right
PLANES OF THE HEAD, THREE-QUARTERS VIEW

Having established the basic facial proportions, let's turn our attention to the planes of the head. The figure above shows the planes of the head from anterior and lateral views; in the anterior view, the left side of the face is rendered with fewer planes, while a more complete description of the planes of the head appears on the right. The figure at right shows a three-quarters view, which provides a better understanding of the three-dimensional aspects of the head.

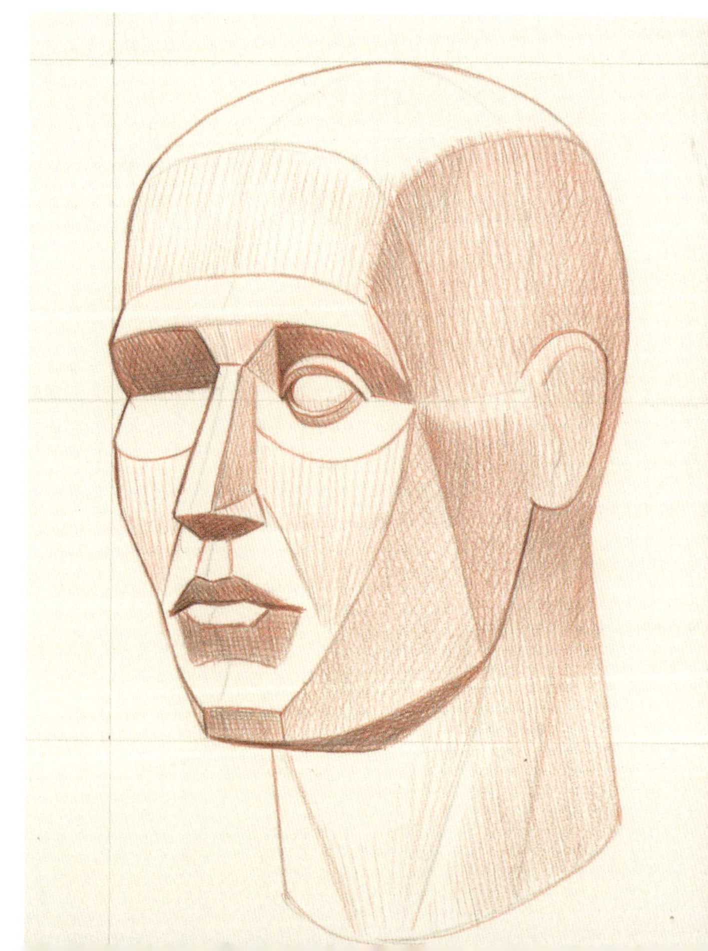

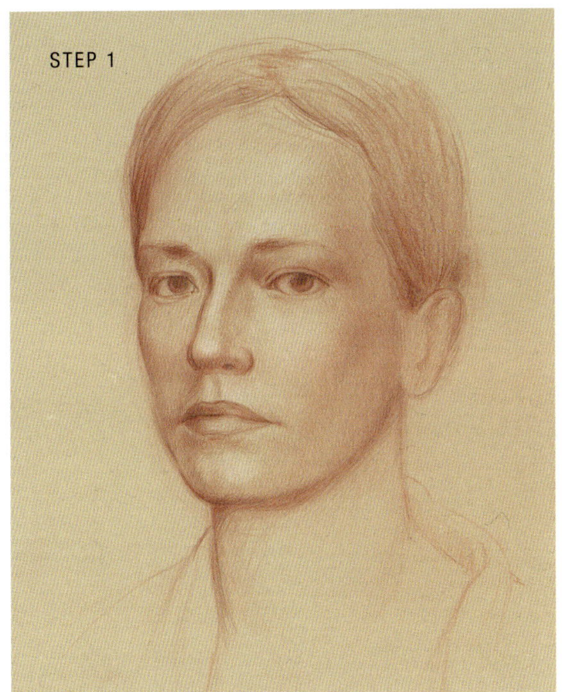

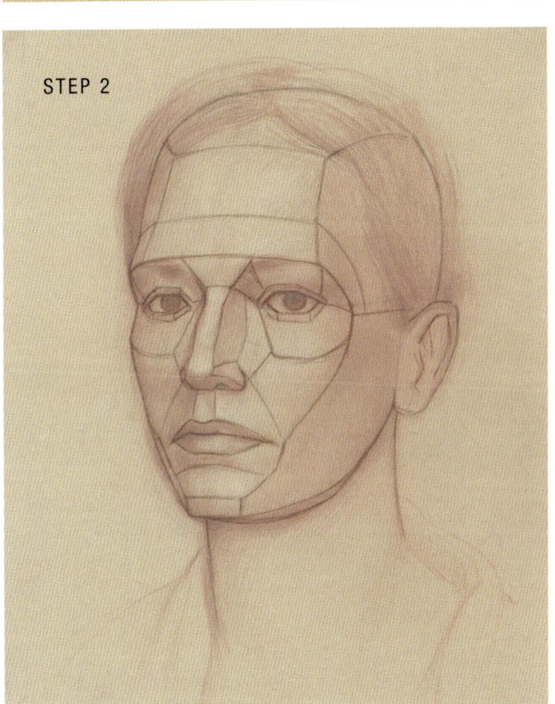

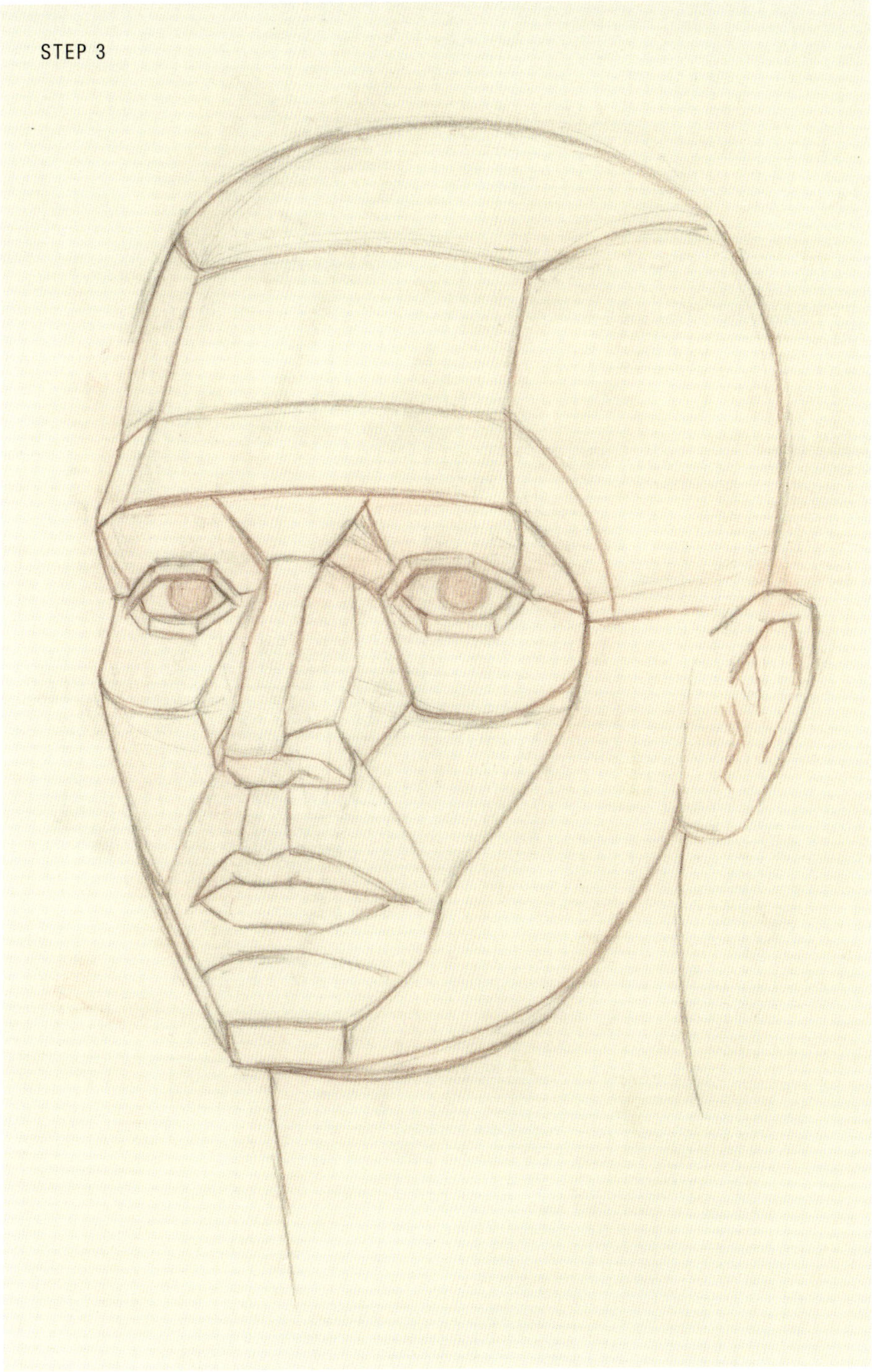

The series of drawings above shows how, starting from a drawing or photograph, you can identify the planes of the head.

IDENTIFYING THE PLANES OF THE HEAD

First, choose a drawing (or photograph) of a head that has strong directional light that clearly shows the planes of the head (step 1). Then lay a sheet of tracing paper over the drawing and trace the planes of the head that you see (step 2). When you remove the tracing paper (step 3), you have a planar rendering of the model's head that you can use to practice the effect of light and shadow on the forms.

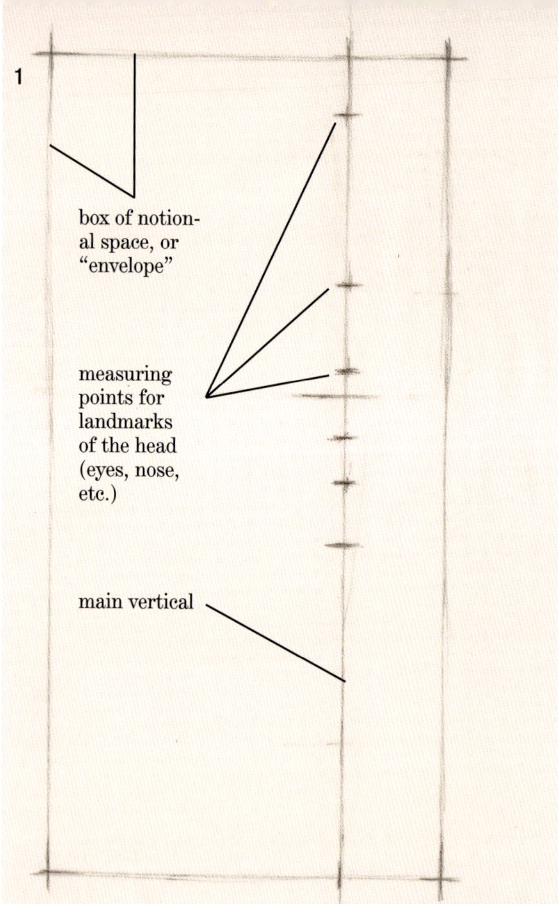

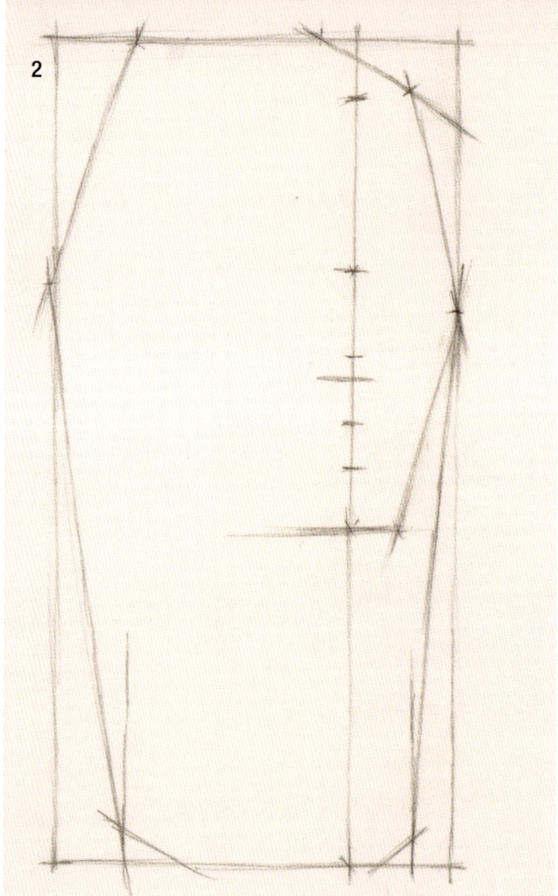

PLANES OF THE HEAD, STEP 1

First, I drew a notional space determined by the height and the width of the mannequin I was using and established the main vertical line along which I placed a few measurement marks corresponding to landmarks of the face and neck.

PLANES OF THE HEAD, STEP 2

Then I identified other measuring points and started defining the "envelope," or frame, that contains the outline of the main volumes of the head and neck.

PLANES OF THE HEAD, STEP 3

I continued to find additional measuring points, enabling me to describe more of the mannequin's features and details.

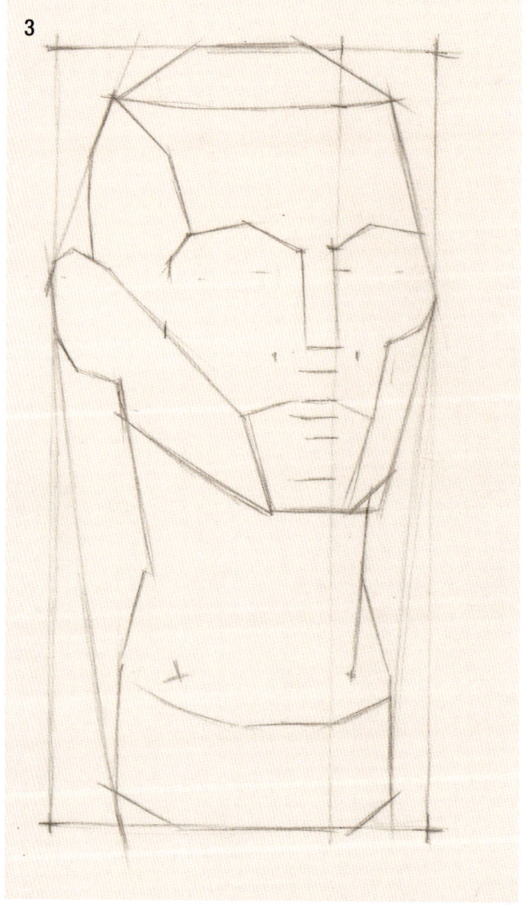

To develop the sequence of drawings here, I used the Planes of the Head mannequin. As you can see from the sequence, it is important that you start by defining the overall form and then gradually identify smaller and smaller forms. This way, you will always maintain a correct proportional relationship between the whole form and the smaller forms. Try copying my sequence, and then replicate it using any realistic sculpture of the head or a living model.

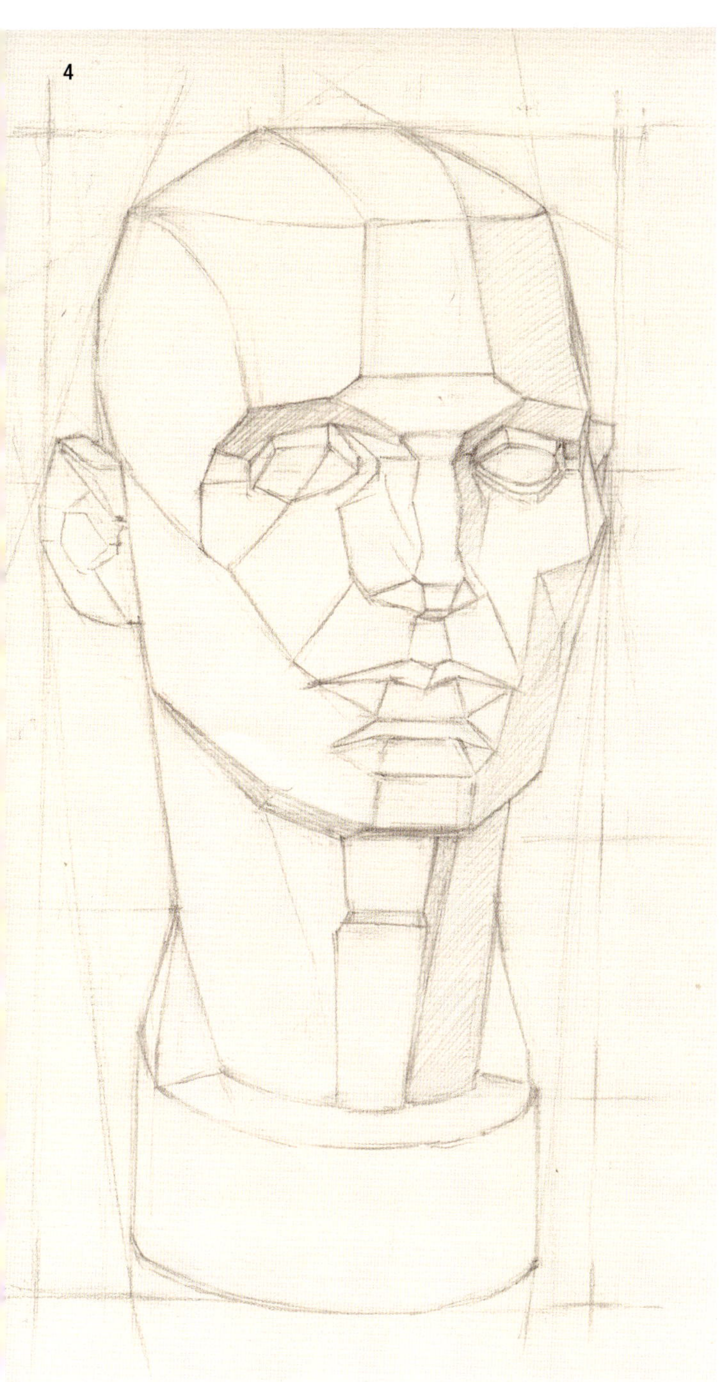

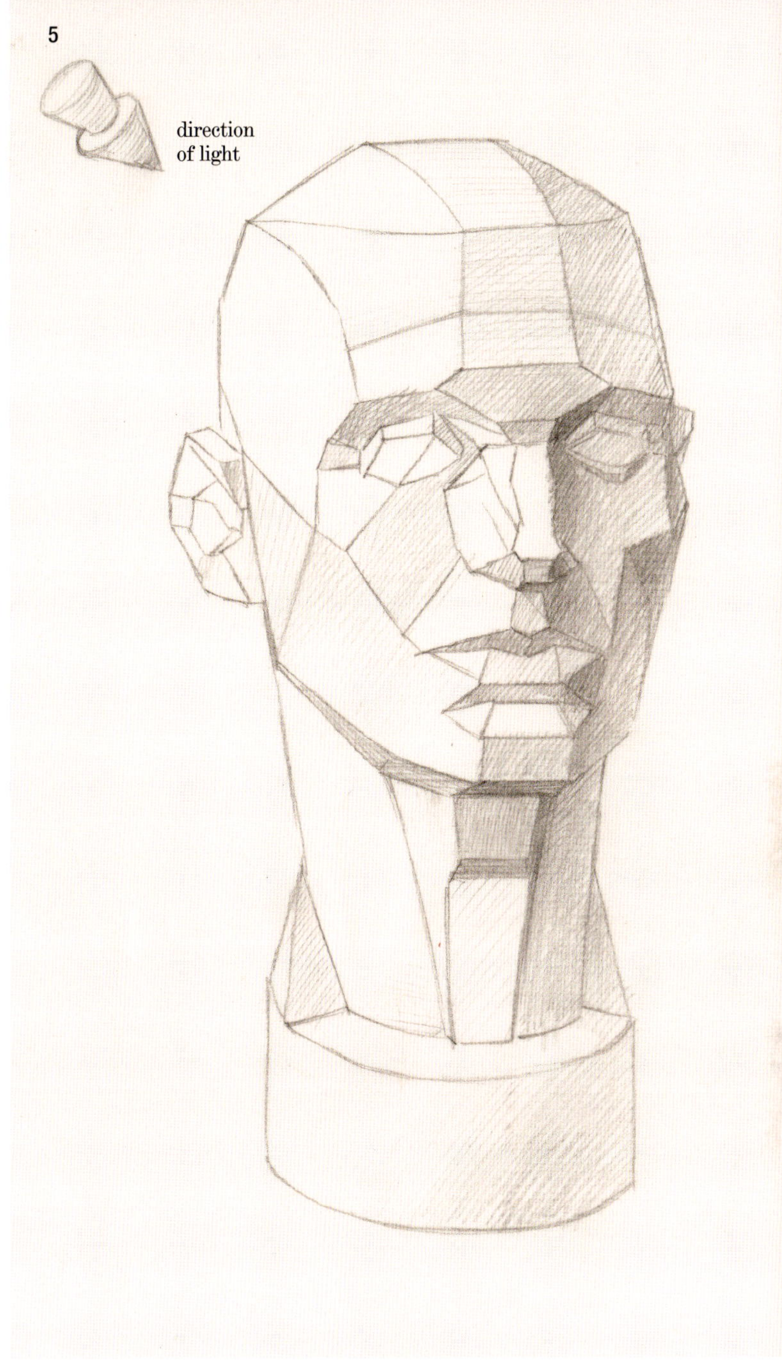

PLANES OF THE HEAD, STEP 4

I then developed the drawing tonally, adding the shadow masses. The clearly distinct planes of the mannequin made it easier to render the various planes of the head tonally.

PLANES OF THE HEAD—ADDING LIGHT AND SHADOWS FROM IMAGINATION, STEP 5

This last image in the sequence shows an exercise you can perform to practice drawing the light and shadows from your imagination. You can repeat this exercise, imagining the light coming from different directions. Because you are not working from life, you will be forced to imagine the effects of the light on the form and all the shadows and the tonal developments it will produce.

THE SKULL

Now, we are going to analyze the head starting from the deep layers and gradually moving on to the more superficial. Because the skeletal layer is the deepest layer that concerns the artist, we will start with the skull.

THE SKULL—SCHEMATIC RENDERING

Conceptualizing the skull schematically makes it easier to understand its structure and master its complex forms. The figures below offer schematic views of the skull from the front and side and from a three-quarters view.

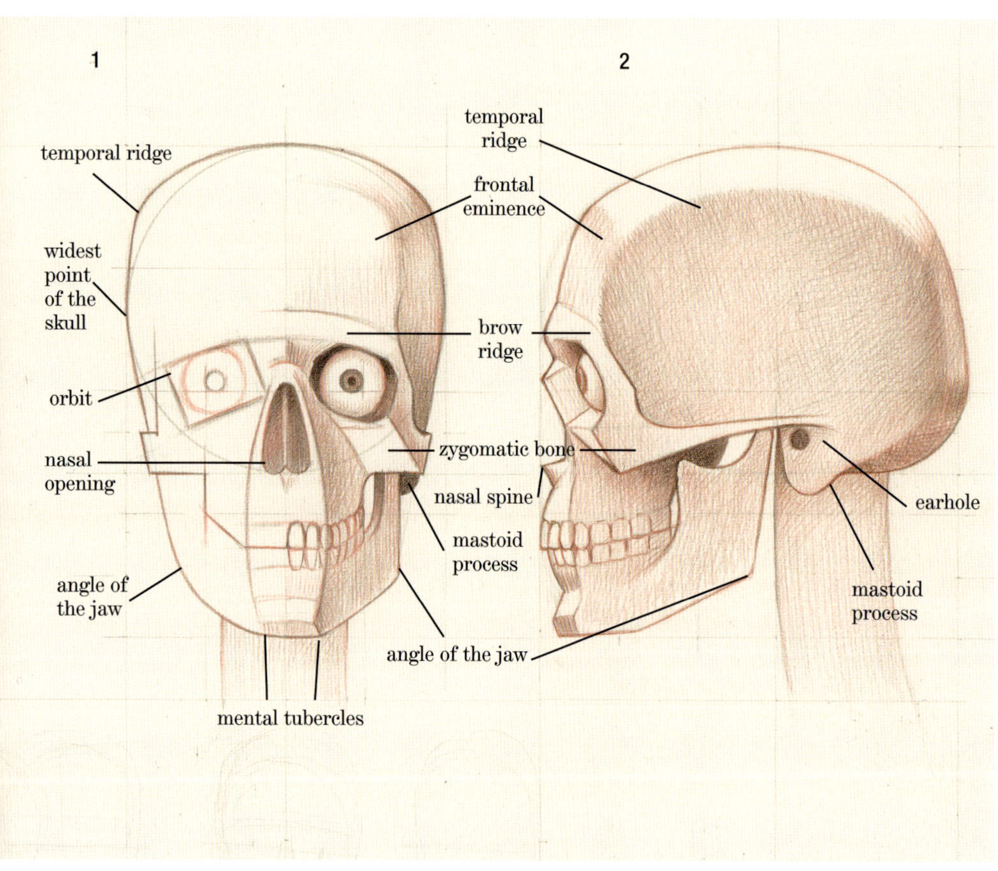

ANTERIOR AND LATERAL SCHEMATIC VIEWS OF THE SKULL

The anterior view of the skull (1) shows two stages of schematization: On the left half is a more linear, two-dimensional initial stage; on the right half, the forms have been developed. In the lateral view (2), note the positions of the parts of the skull that cannot be seen, or fully seen, from the front, including the zygomatic bone and earhole.

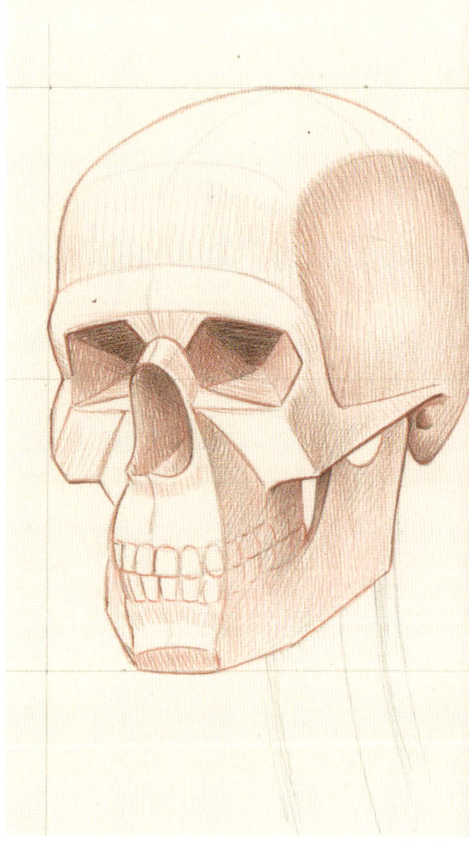

THREE-QUARTERS SCHEMATIC VIEW OF THE SKULL

From this three-quarters view, you can gain a better visualization of the three-dimensional form of the skull.

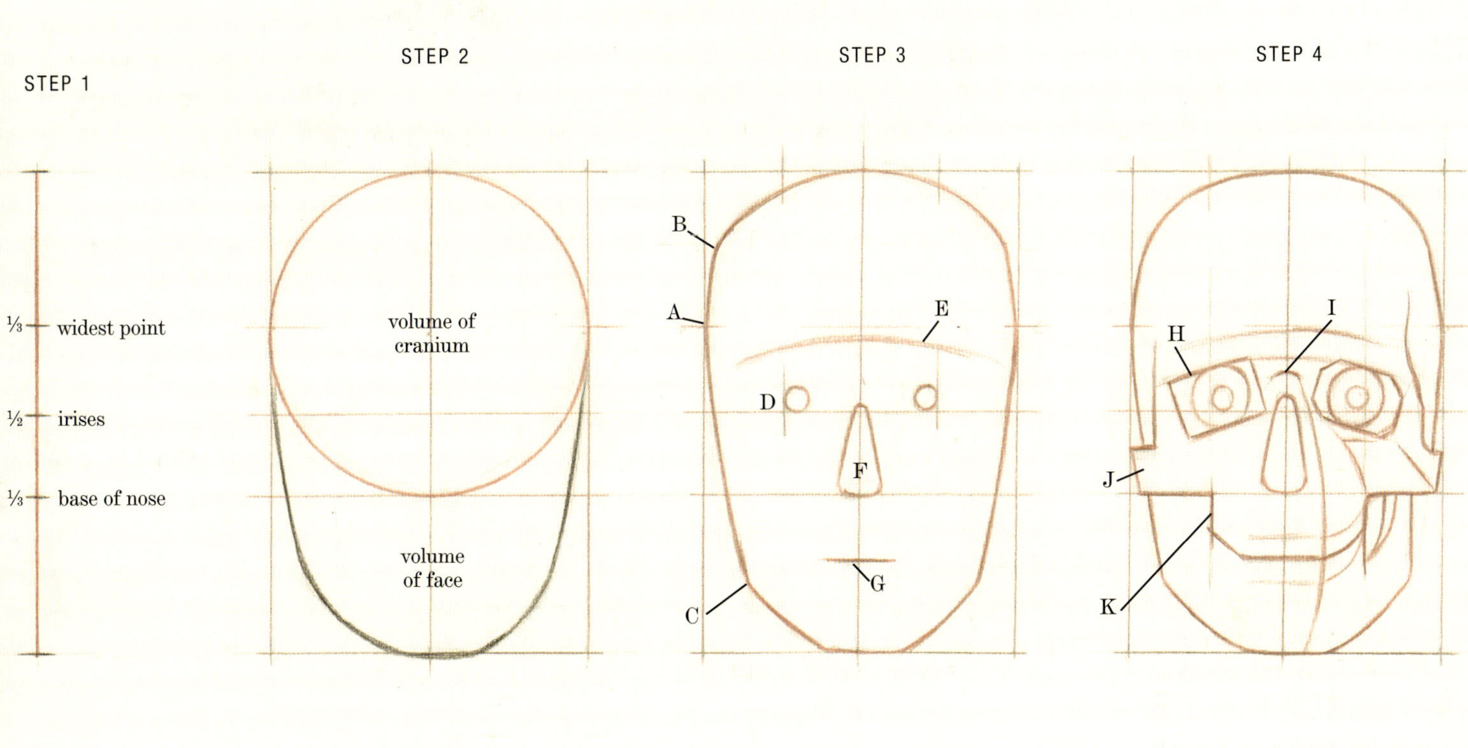

DRAWING A SCHEMATIC SKULL, ANTERIOR VIEW

The figures above present a four-step sequence for drawing schematic anterior and lateral views of the skull. As you practice these steps, remember that their purpose is strictly didactic; once you have assimilated the schematization, you will draw the skull freehand using a more intuitive approach.

STEP 1: Establish the main measurements by drawing a line that represents the height of the skull and then dividing it into halves and thirds.

STEP 2: Establish the volume of the cranium drawing a circle (red in the diagram) that has a diameter corresponding to the width of the head, which is two-thirds of the height. Then draw the volume of the face (black), creating a masklike shape.

STEP 3: Establish the angles of the head as marked: The widest point (A) is about at the upper third. The temporal ridge (B) is more or less between the top of the head and the widest point.

The angle of the jawline (C) can vary noticeably from person to person and from male to female, but, as a general rule, you can position it at the lower one-sixth of the head. Now define the face by positioning the irises (D) resting on the horizontal midline and on the medial side of the line that divides each side of the face into halves. Draw the brow ridge (E) as a slightly curved line that tops at the upper third of the face. Add the nasal opening (F) between the horizontal midline and the lower third of the face. Last, add a line for the mouth (G) positioned between the bottom of the nasal opening and the chin, but closer to the nasal opening.

STEP 4: Add the orbits (H). Putting the eyeballs inside the orbits will help you tell whether the orbits are the appropriate size and will also help you position the nasion (I), which is just above the level of the irises. Now you can define the zygomatic bones (J), which are between the line of the lower third of the face and a point halfway up toward the horizontal midline. The line of the maxilla (K) corresponds to the line that helps us position the iris. The right half of the step 4 drawing shows a more detailed definition of the planes of the skull.

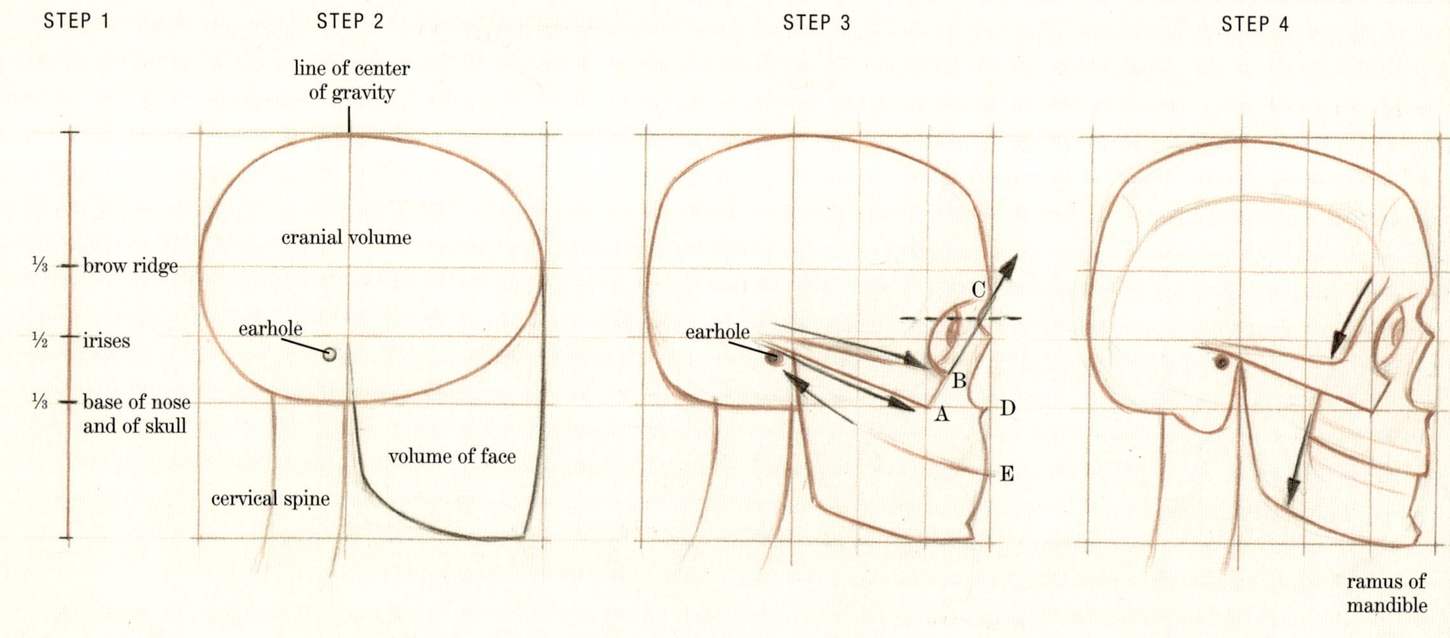

DRAWING A SCHEMATIC SKULL, LATERAL VIEW

STEP 1: The first step for the lateral (side) view is similar to the first step for the anterior view: Draw a line and divide it into halves and thirds. But you also have to find the width, which corresponds to seven-eighths of the height. To determine the width, divide the height of the skull into halves, then quarters, and then eighths; by subtracting the last eighth you get the seven-eighths measurement.

STEP 2: Once you have determined the envelope for the head, mark the horizontal midline and the lines demarcating the lower and upper thirds. Draw the line of the center of gravity, which divides the box in two unequal portions; the anterior portion is one-half of a head. Now draw the volume of the cranium (red oval) between the top of the box and the lower third. (The cranial volume looks like an egg on its side, with the pointy end toward the front of the skull.) Add the facial volume (black line) in the anterior half of the head between the jawline and the front of the face. Also add the earhole, an important landmark situated a little bit below the horizontal midline and to the rear of the line of the center of gravity.

STEP 3: Create a grid over the anterior portion of the skull, dividing it into three equal vertical segments and retaining the horizontal midline and lines marking the thirds. Now you can position the lower angle of the zygomatic bone (A) and its upper margin (B) halfway between the horizontal midline and the line marking the lower third—where the lower margin of the zygomatic bone, the base of the skull, and the nasal spine (D) are also positioned. Now describe the zygomatic arch by drawing a line going from above the earhole down to A and another that goes from the earhole to B. The lateral margin of the orbit, shaped like the letter C, lies behind the line A–C, which merges the lower corner of the zygomatic bone and the upper margin of the orbit. The straight line will also help you to position the eyeball, which does not protrude past it. The iris is slightly above the midline, and the nasion (root of the nose) is slightly above the pupil. Finish this step by drawing a gently curved line whose curve points to a spot just below the earhole; this represents the line between the teeth (E).

STEP 4: Now draw the posterior margin of the orbit, which is a line just behind and roughly parallel to the margin of the orbit. Continue this line down past the zygomatic bone to describe the anterior margin of the ramus of the mandible.

THE SKULL—REALISTIC RENDERING

Now that you have a good structural understanding of the skull it should be much easier for you to draw it realistically. The figures in this section demonstrate a sequence of steps showing you how to obtain a realistic rendering of the skull.

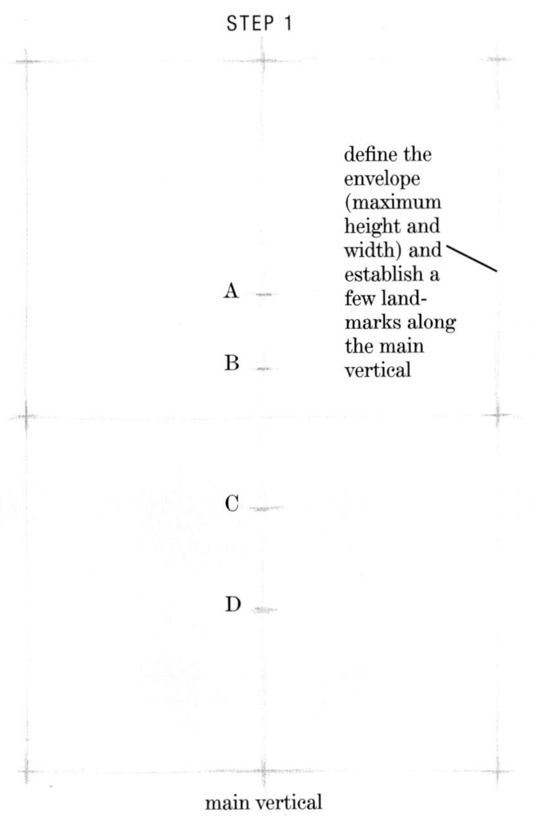

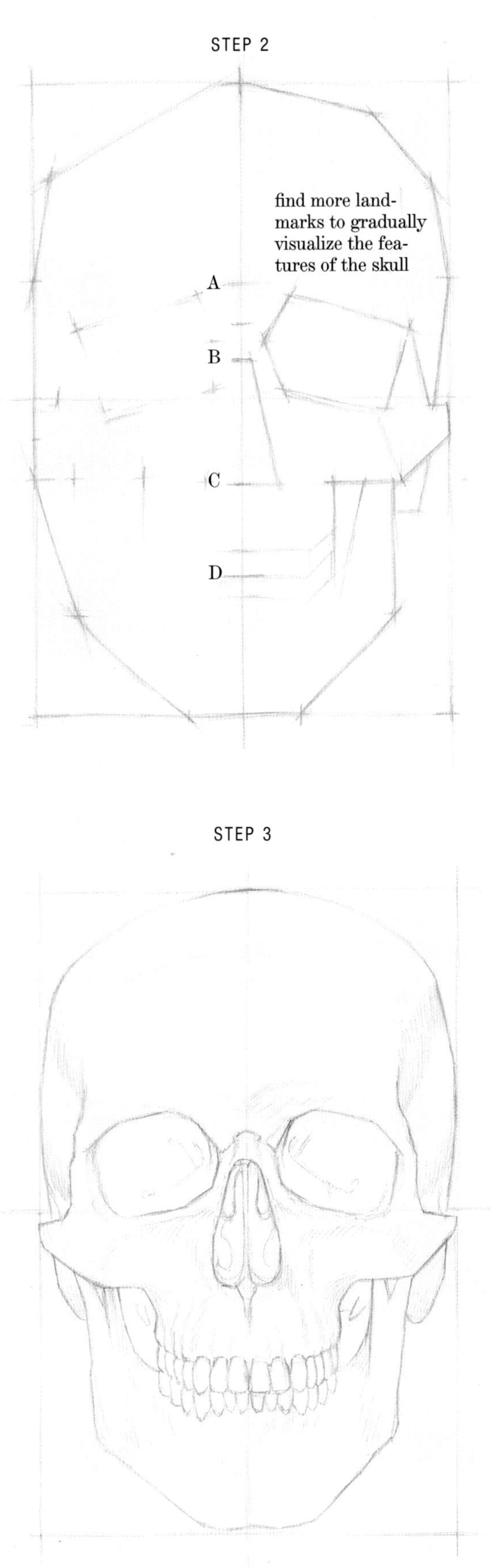

DRAWING A REALISTIC SKULL, STEP 1

Start the drawing by establishing the height and width of the skull; in this case, the "envelope" for your rendering is a rectangular shape whose sides are the maximum height and width of the skull. Now establish the main vertical line and mark the position of the landmarks (eyes, nose, mouth, etc.) on it.

DRAWING A REALISTIC SKULL, STEP 2

Once you have established the overall outline, start finding additional points to define yet more structures on the skull. In this

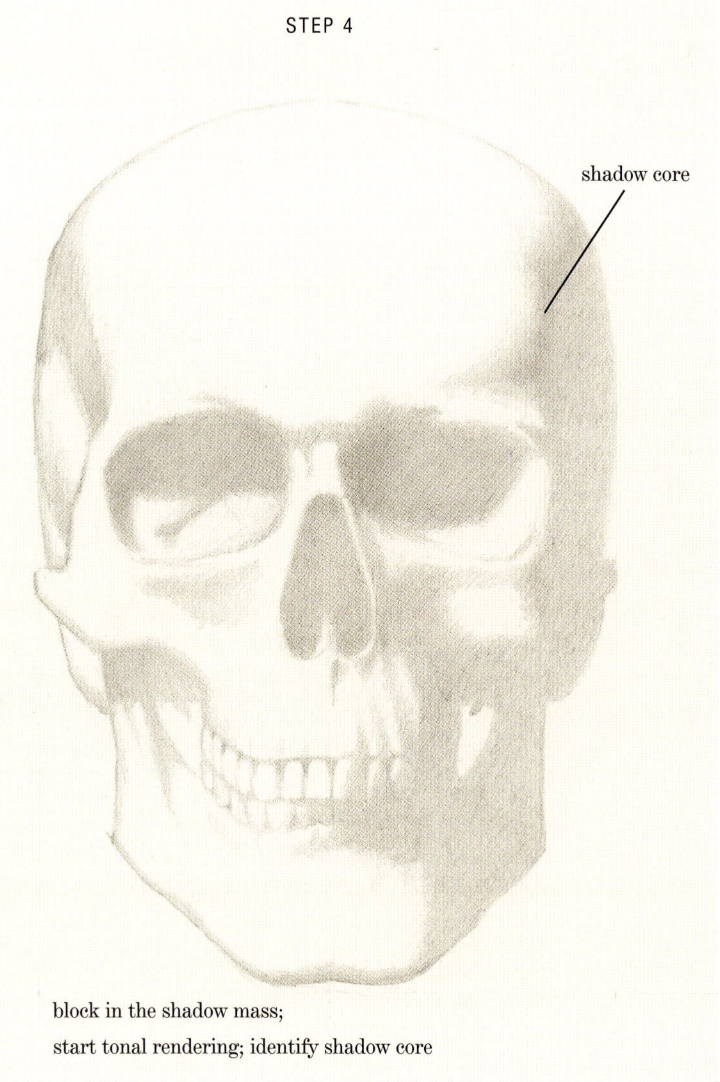

block in the shadow mass;
start tonal rendering; identify shadow core

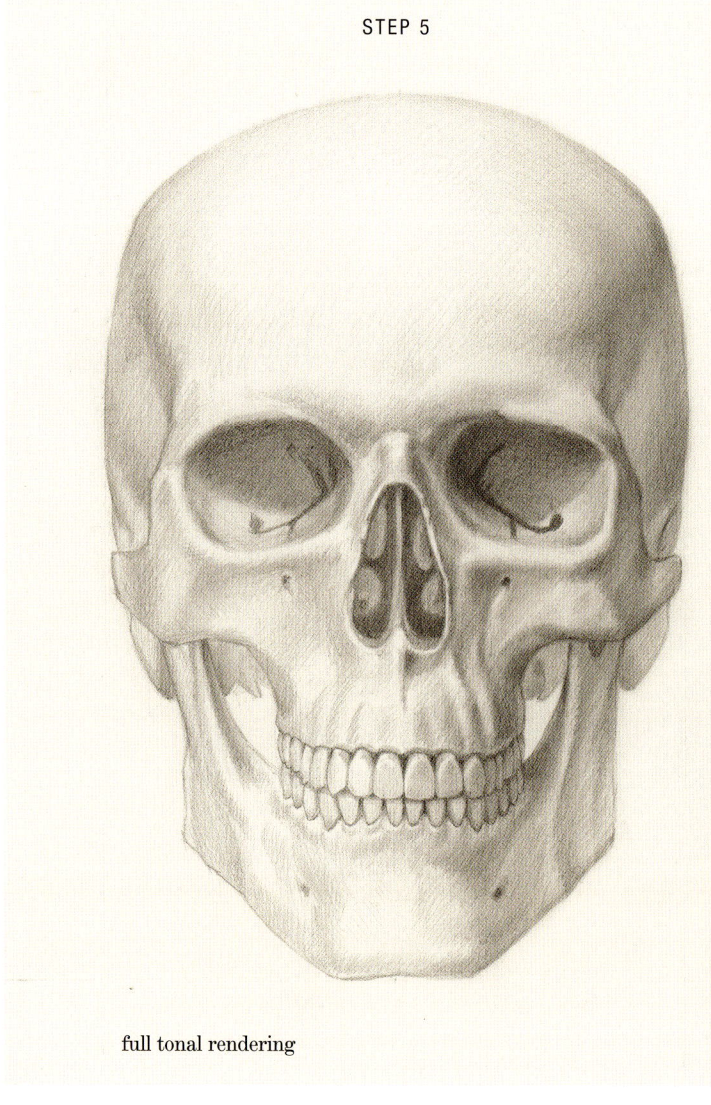

full tonal rendering

image you see various stages of the development of the drawing, as you move from the measuring points (left side) to the features of the skull (right). It is important that you progress from the overall shape of the skull and then start defining gradually smaller shapes. This way, you will maintain control of the overall proportions of the skull.

DRAWING A REALISTIC SKULL, STEP 3 (PREVIOUS PAGE)

Next, create a precise line drawing. This permits you to better understand the volumes, forms, and three-dimensionality of the skull. At this stage there is no shading to hide details of the form.

DRAWING A REALISTIC SKULL, STEP 4

Block in the shadow mass, beginning with the lightest value.

Blocking in the shadows will automatically define the light mass (left half). Now, introduce the shadow core, the area of darker value between the light mass and the shadow mass (right half). The shadow core defines the peaks of the form and begins to create the illusion of three-dimensionality.

DRAWING A REALISTIC SKULL, STEP 5 (FULL TONAL RENDERING)

In the final stage, develop the skull tonally, using as many different values as possible. The more values you can find, the more realistic and three-dimensional your work will be. It is very important that you start from the lightest values and gradually build your way down to the darkest one. Here, you can see a progression in tonal rendering from the left side (less developed) to the right (more developed).

THE BONES OF THE SKULL

Although it may appear that the human skull is composed of just two bones—the cranial mass and the mandible (jaw bone)—it actually has twenty-two bones: eight for the cranium and fourteen for the face. Except for the movable mandible, however, all of the skull's bones are fused. I will not describe all the bones here, as our main concern is the external morphology of the cranium as a whole. The figures below show color-coded maps of the bones of the skull from front and side views.

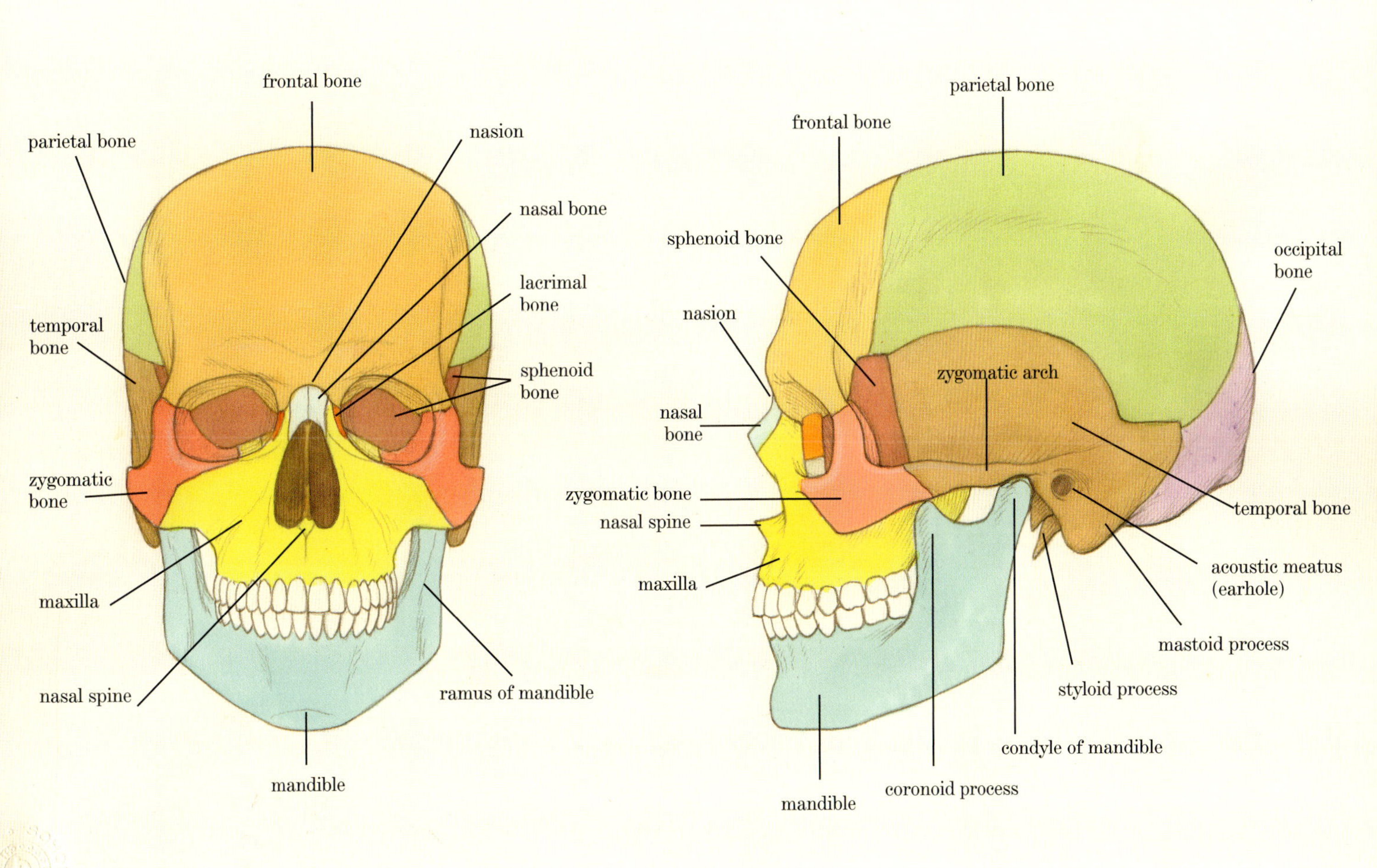

COLOR-CODED DIAGRAM OF THE BONES OF THE SKULL, ANTERIOR VIEW

COLOR-CODED DIAGRAM OF THE BONES OF THE SKULL, LATERAL VIEW

The forms of the head and face are created or influenced by the underlying skeletal and muscular structures. The illustrations below show the correspondences between the skeleton and the external features of the face.

As you can see in the figures opposite, there are subtle differences between male and female skulls. The male skull is more angular overall. The brow ridge and frontal eminence are more pronounced, and the jaw is often (but

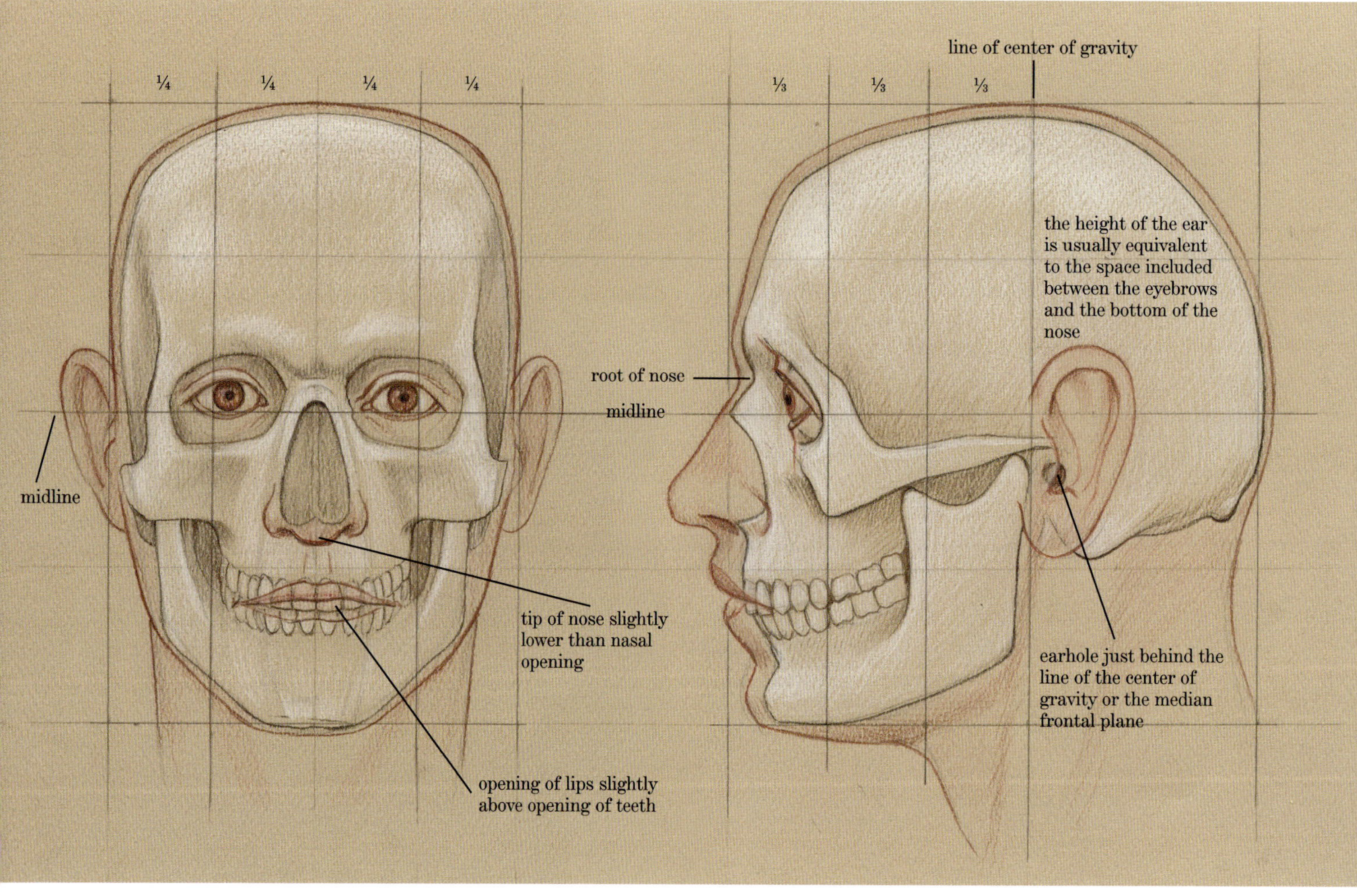

RELATION BETWEEN THE SKULL AND THE EXTERNAL FEATURES OF THE FACE, ANTERIOR VIEW

The tip of the nose is slightly lower than the nasal opening. The opening of the mouth (the lips) is slightly above the opening of the teeth. Dividing the width of the face into equal vertical parts shows that the lateral margins of the irises lie against the lines that divide each side of the face in half and rest above the horizontal midline. Note, too, that the width of one eye is one-fifth of the total width of the head (excluding the ears).

RELATION BETWEEN THE SKULL AND THE EXTERNAL FEATURES OF THE FACE, LATERAL VIEW

The nasion (root of the nose) is usually a little bit above the irises. The height of the ears is generally equivalent to the space between the eyebrows and the bottom of the nose. The grid on the front half of the head that goes from the jaw line to the tip of the nasal bone divides the face in three equal segments vertically and helps you locate the earhole, which lies just behind the line of the center of gravity. The jawline runs right in front of it, and the lateral margin of the orbit is at the line marking the first third of the grid.

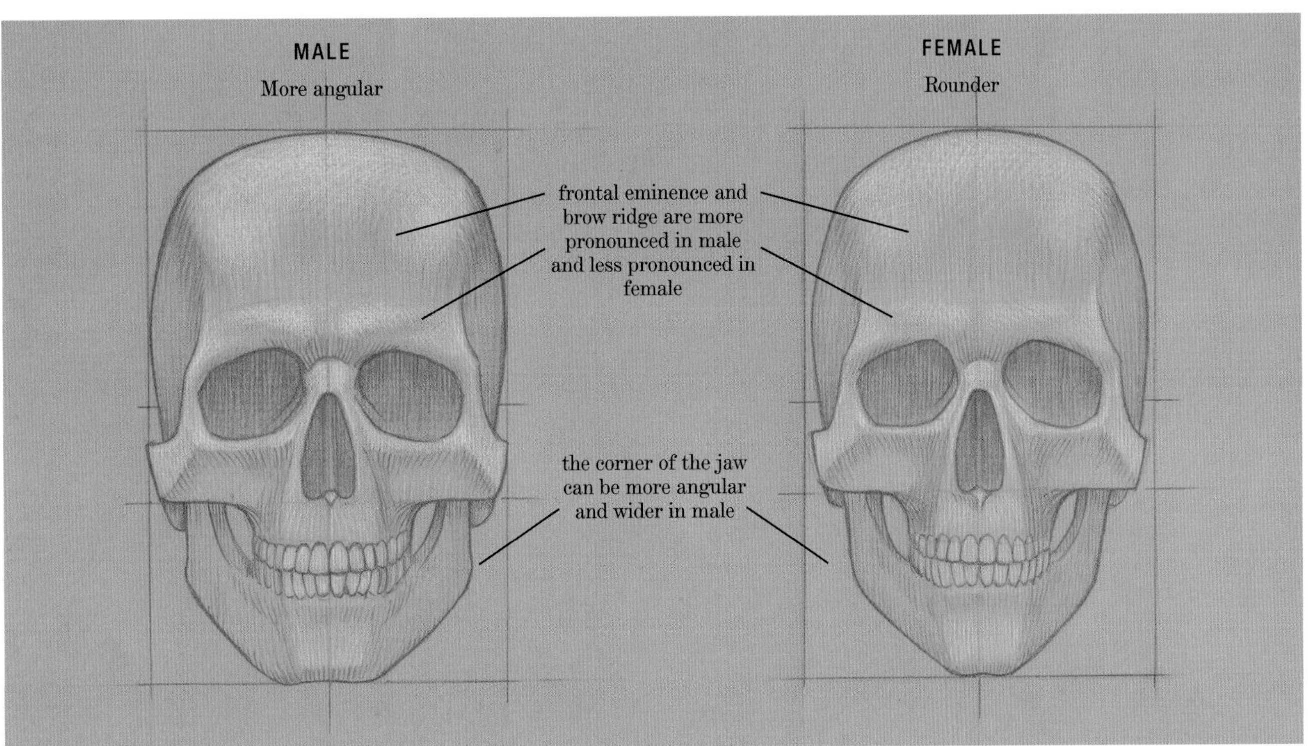

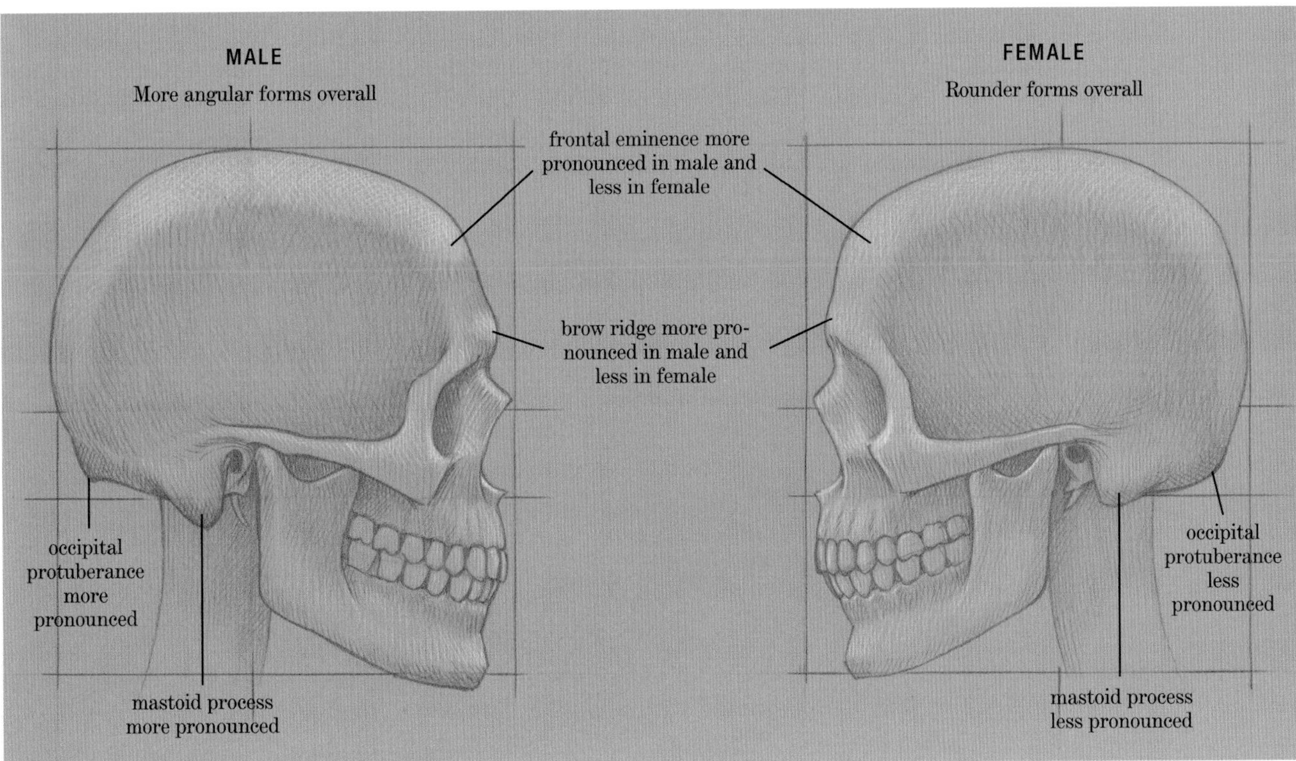

not always) wider and more angular. The female skull's overall forms are rounder, and the frontal eminences and brow ridge are not so pronounced. As is especially clear in the lateral, or profile, views, the forehead is more sloping on the male skull. The mastoid process is bigger, and the occiput bone is also more pronounced, as is the occip-ital protuberance. On the female skull, the forehead is straighter, and the occiput and the occipital protuberance are smaller, as is the mastoid process.

DIFFERENCES BETWEEN MALE AND FEMALE SKULLS, ANTERIOR AND LATERAL VIEWS

MUSCLES OF THE HEAD AND NECK

The numerous muscles of the face can be very difficult to remember. For this reason, I created the "Muscle Mask" shown here, which reduces the muscles of the face to simple patterns so that you can better understand their action. The patterns of movement are indicated by the arrows.

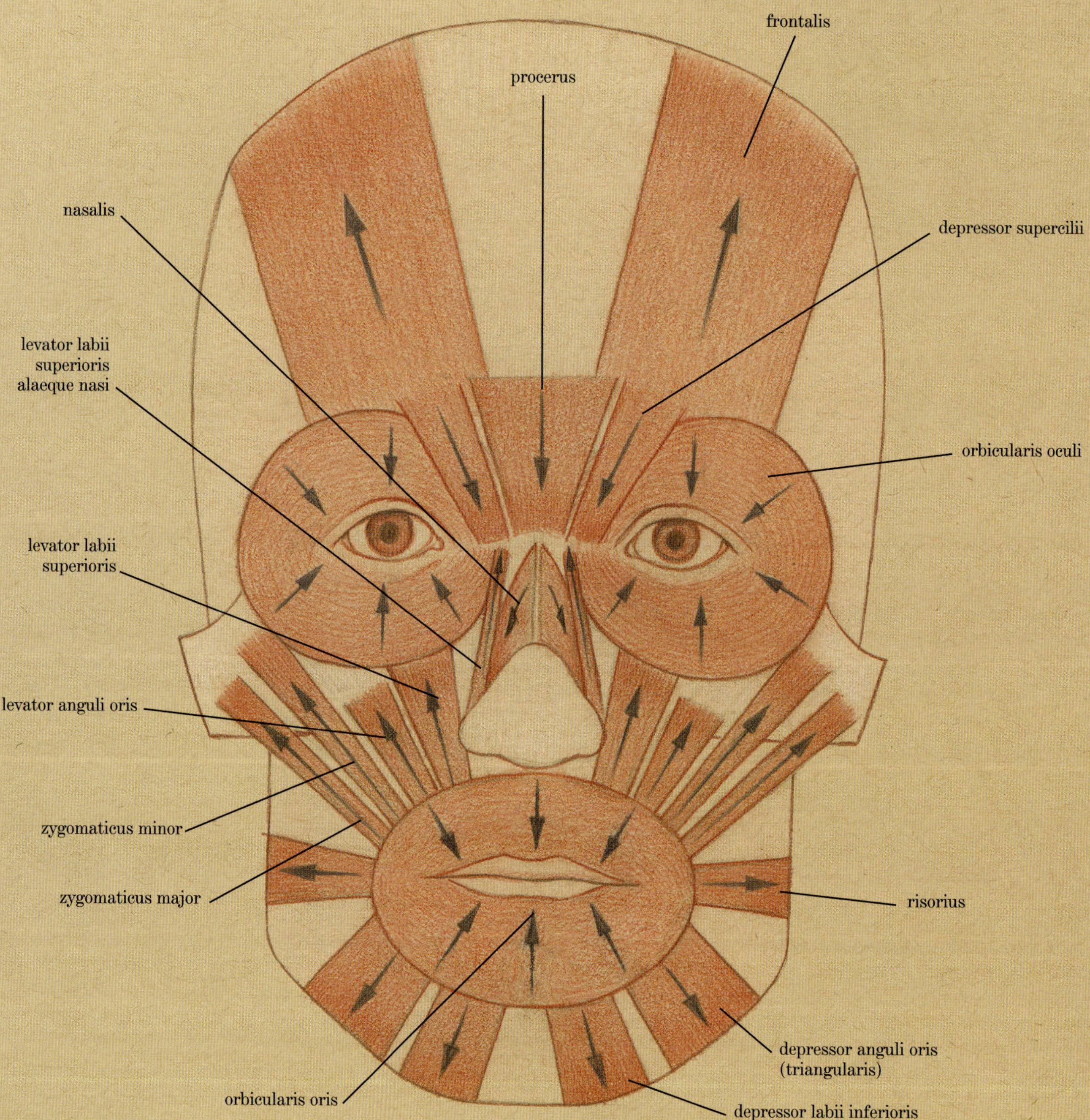

"MUSCLE MASK"

The concentric fibers of the muscle that encircles the mouth, the orbicularis oris, close the mouth and pucker the lips. The muscles that radiate from the outer margin of orbicularis oris have an antagonistic (opposite) action, moving the lips away from the opening of the mouth and creating all sorts of facial expressions.

The frontalis muscles that go from the top of the forehead to the brow ridge lift the eyebrows and also open the eyes wide, while the muscles going from the root of the nose to the glabella lower the eyebrows, creating various frowning expressions.

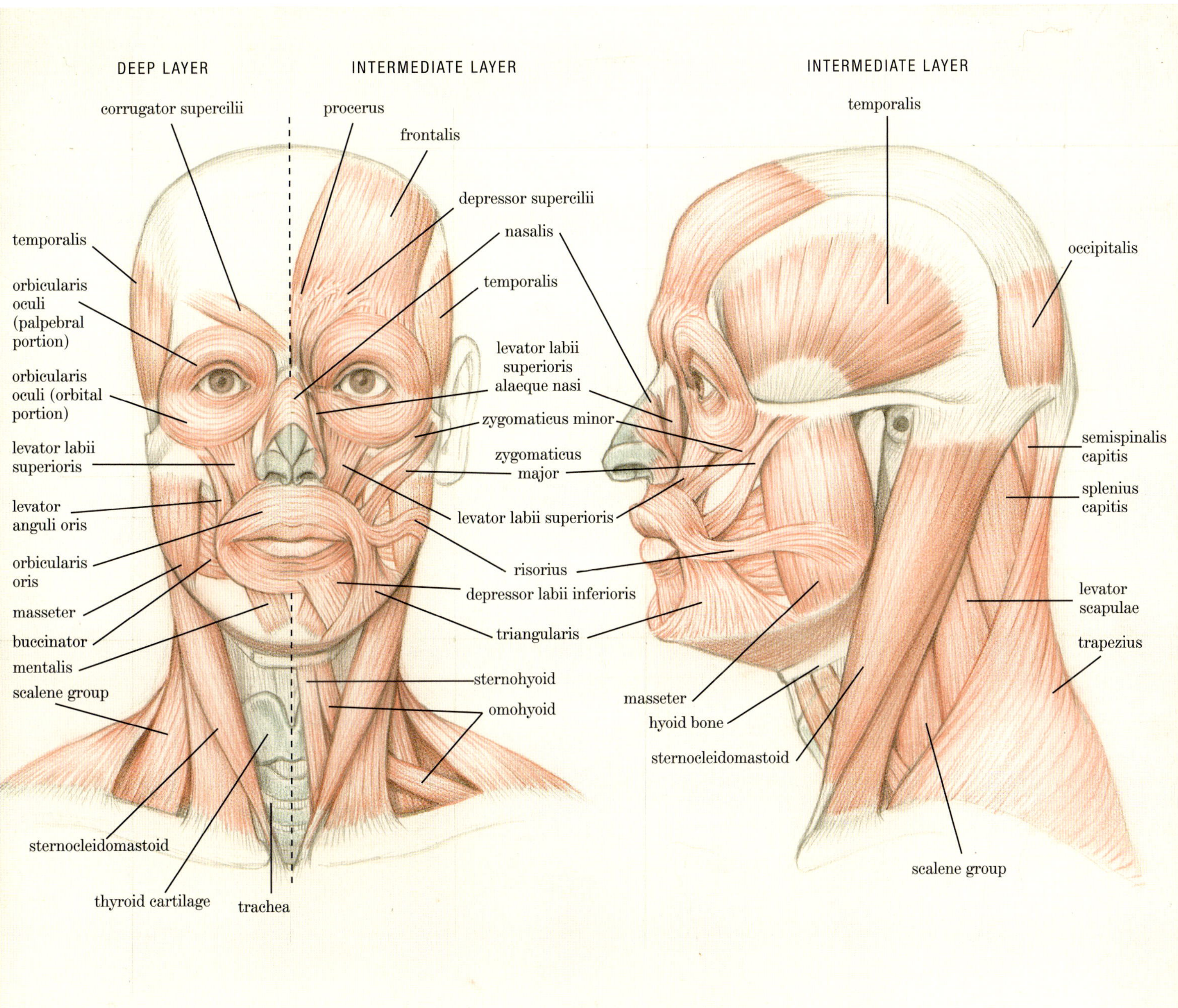

DEEP AND SUPERFICIAL MUSCLE LAYERS

Having looked at the general patterns of the facial muscles and their actions, we can now move to a more realistic rendering of the muscles of the face, as shown in the figures here and on the following page.

The front view shows the deep muscles of the face on the left side and intermediate-layer muscles on the right side, excluding the platysma. The side view shows the superficial muscles, excluding even more superficial ones such as the temporoparietalis, the auricolaris, and the platysma, which are shown in the next figure.

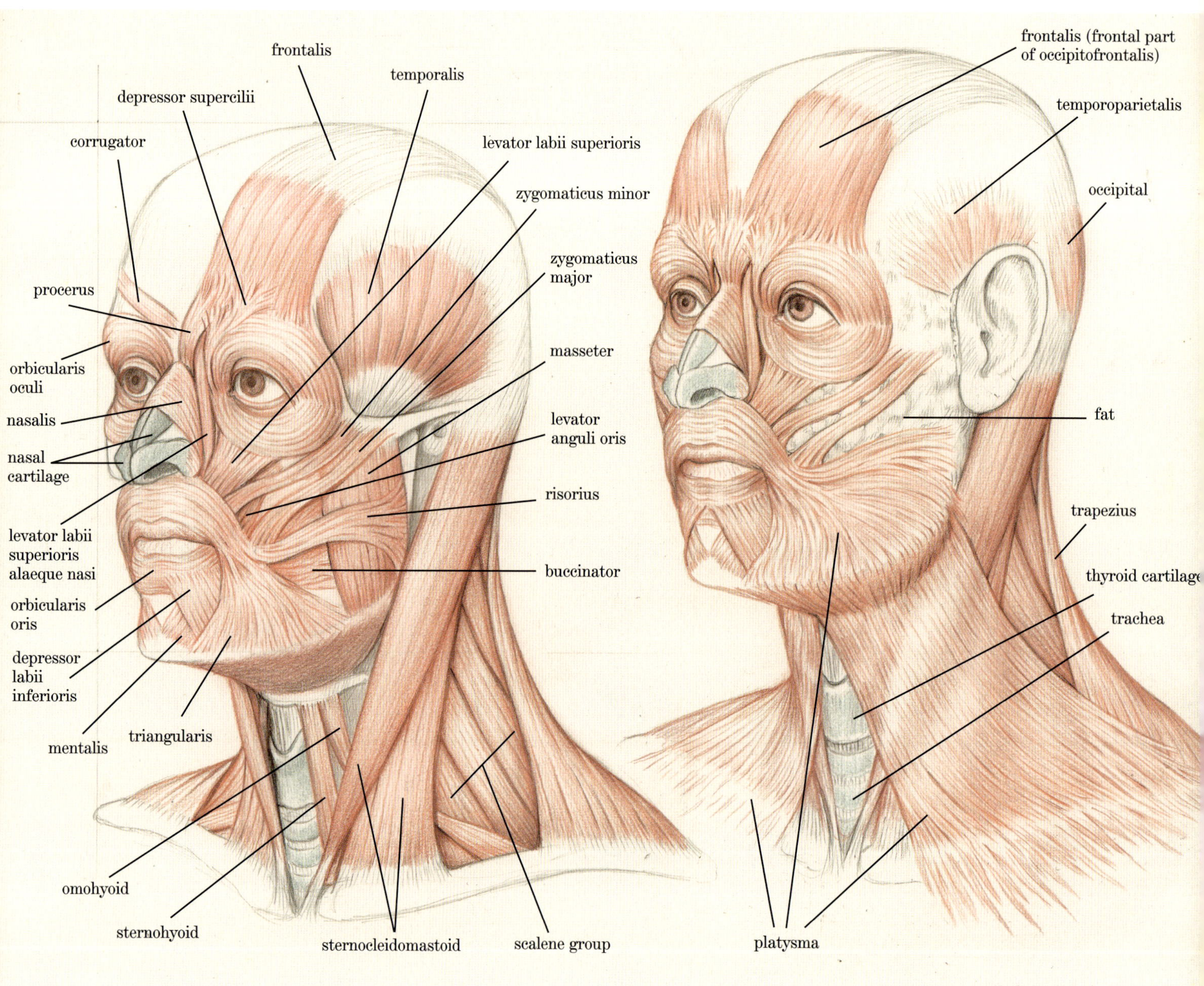

COLOR-CODING FACIAL MUSCLES

The colored-coded diagrams I prepare for my class demonstrations get a very positive response from my students, because they permit you to immediately isolate and identify the specific muscles. At the same time, this kind of conceptualization (as shown in the figure opposite) shows you the overall interconnections, patterns, rhythms, and harmonies between the muscles.

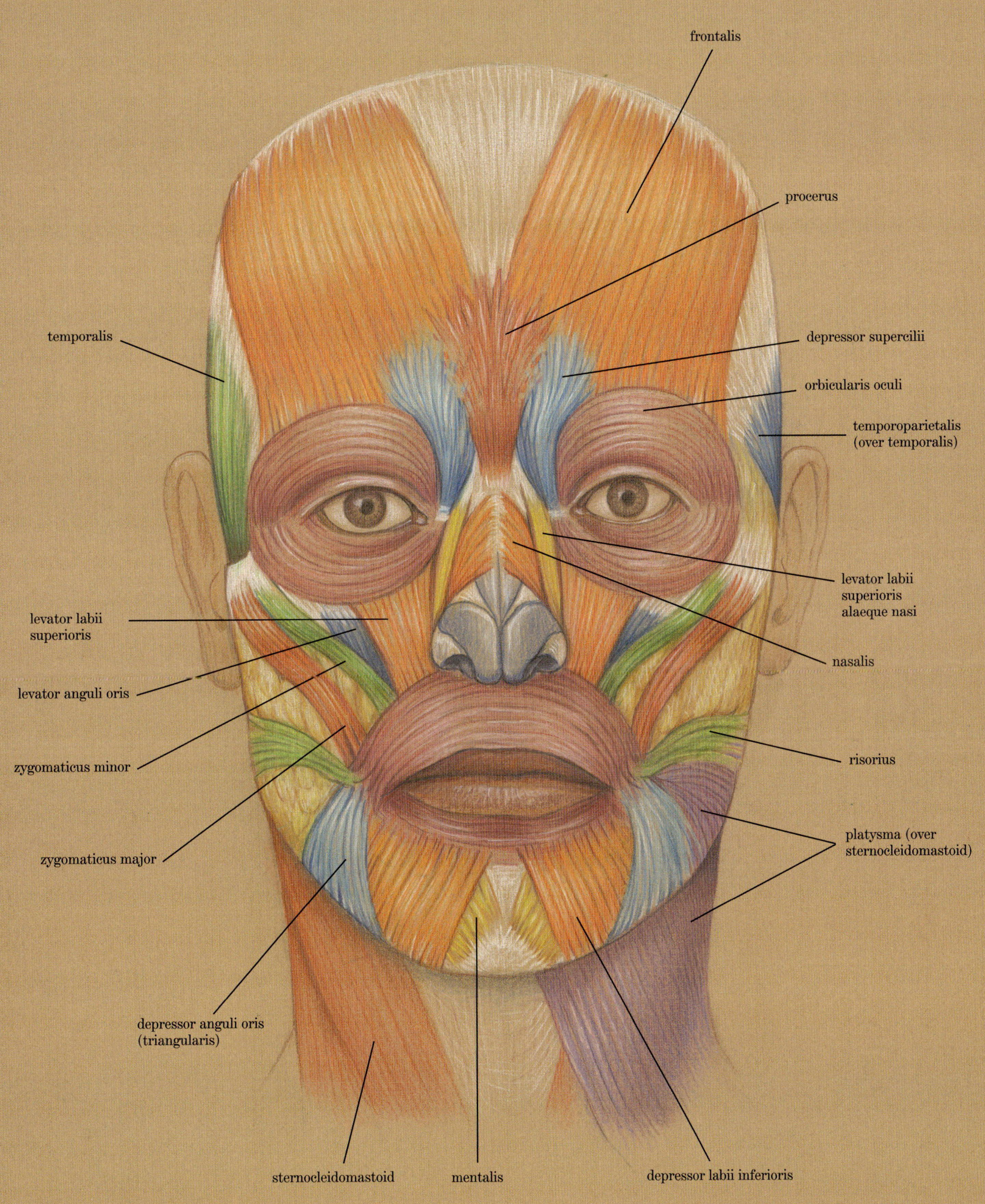

frontalis
procerus
depressor supercilii
orbicularis oculi
temporoparietalis
(over temporalis)
temporalis
levator labii
superioris
alaeque nasi
nasalis
levator labii
superioris
levator anguli oris
zygomaticus minor
risorius
platysma (over
sternocleidomastoid)
zygomaticus major
depressor anguli oris
(triangularis)
sternocleidomastoid
mentalis
depressor labii inferioris

THE NECK

This section provides a comprehensive view of both the deep and the superficial muscles of the neck (together with the head) and of the muscles' volumes and patterns. Although you are already familiar with the muscles of the head, it makes sense to include them in these images to show the continuity between the structures of the head and the neck.

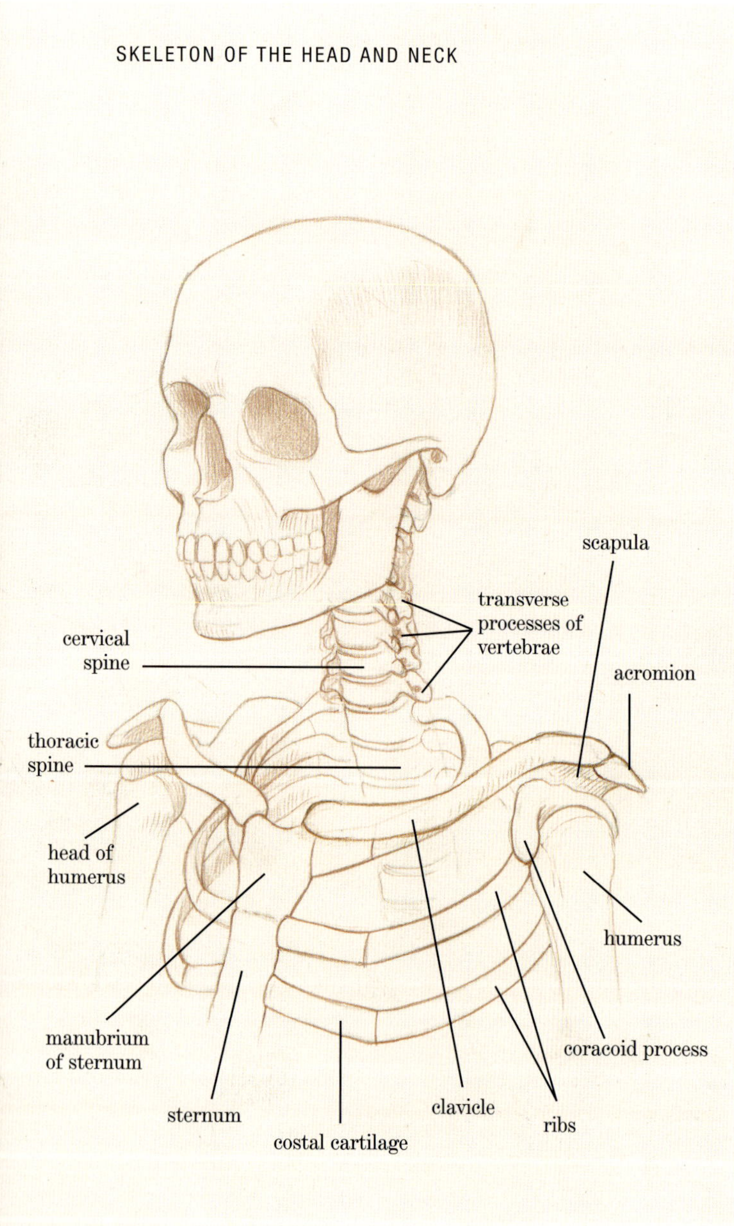

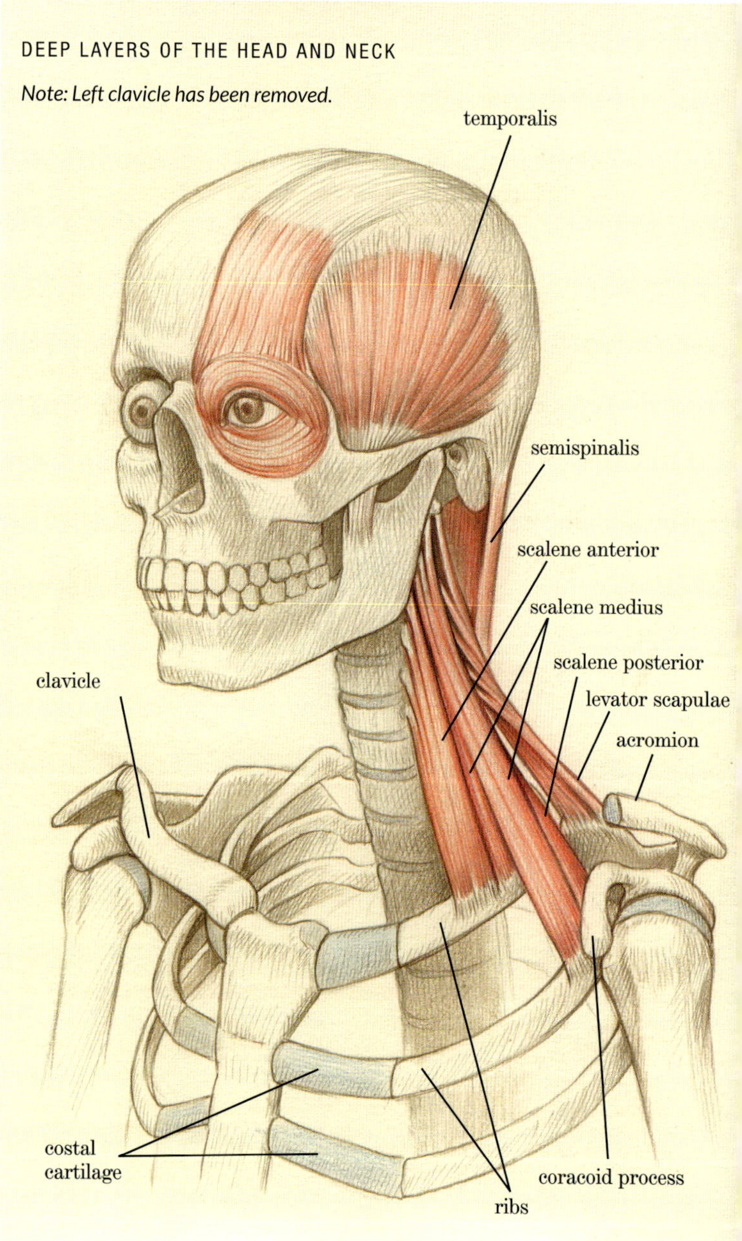

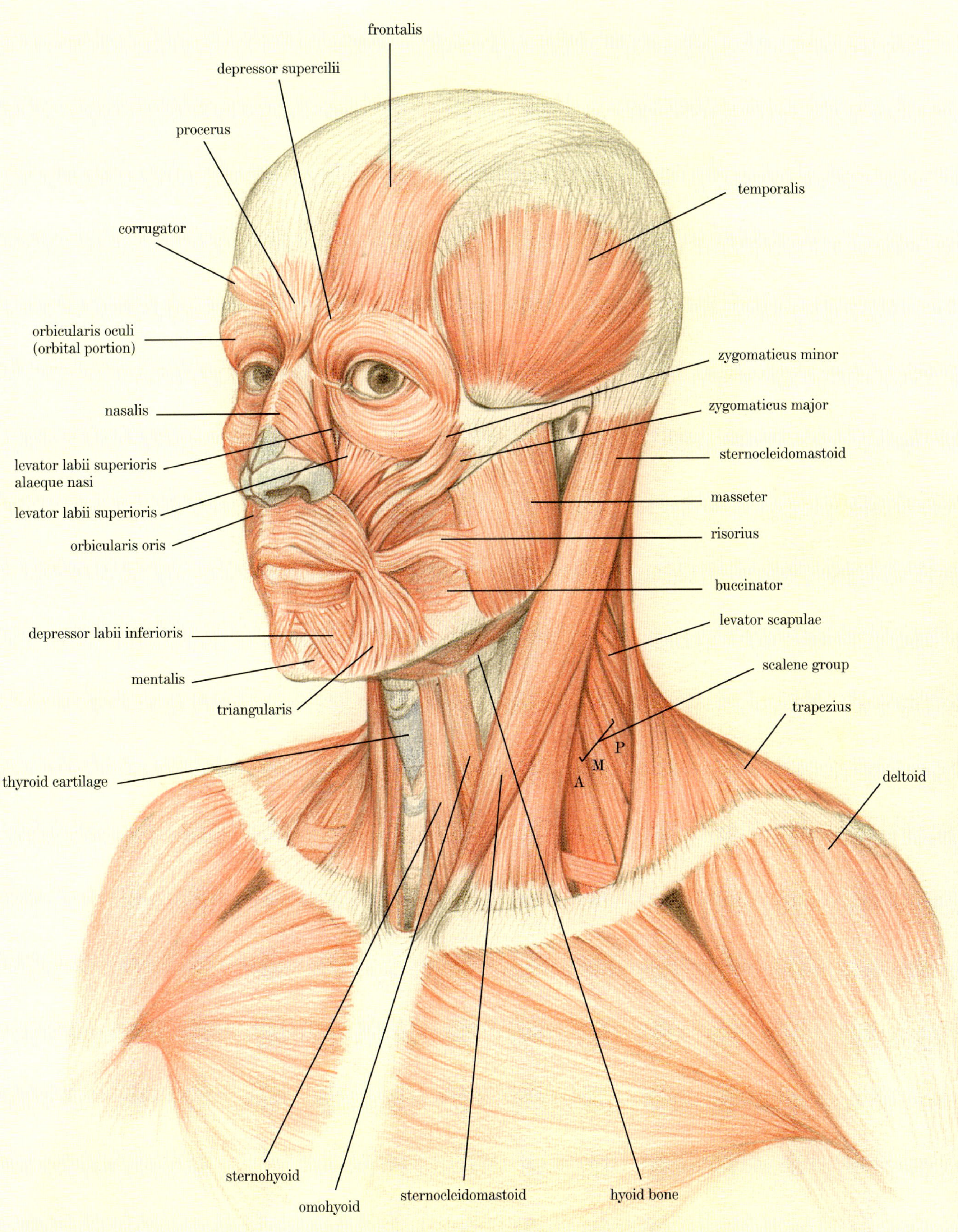

frontalis
depressor supercilii
procerus
corrugator
temporalis
orbicularis oculi
(orbital portion)
zygomaticus minor
zygomaticus major
nasalis
sternocleidomastoid
levator labii superioris
alaeque nasi
masseter
levator labii superioris
risorius
orbicularis oris
buccinator
levator scapulae
depressor labii inferioris
scalene group
mentalis
trapezius
triangularis
P
M
A
thyroid cartilage
deltoid
sternohyoid
omohyoid
sternocleidomastoid
hyoid bone
SUPERFICIAL LAYERS OF THE HEAD AND NECK

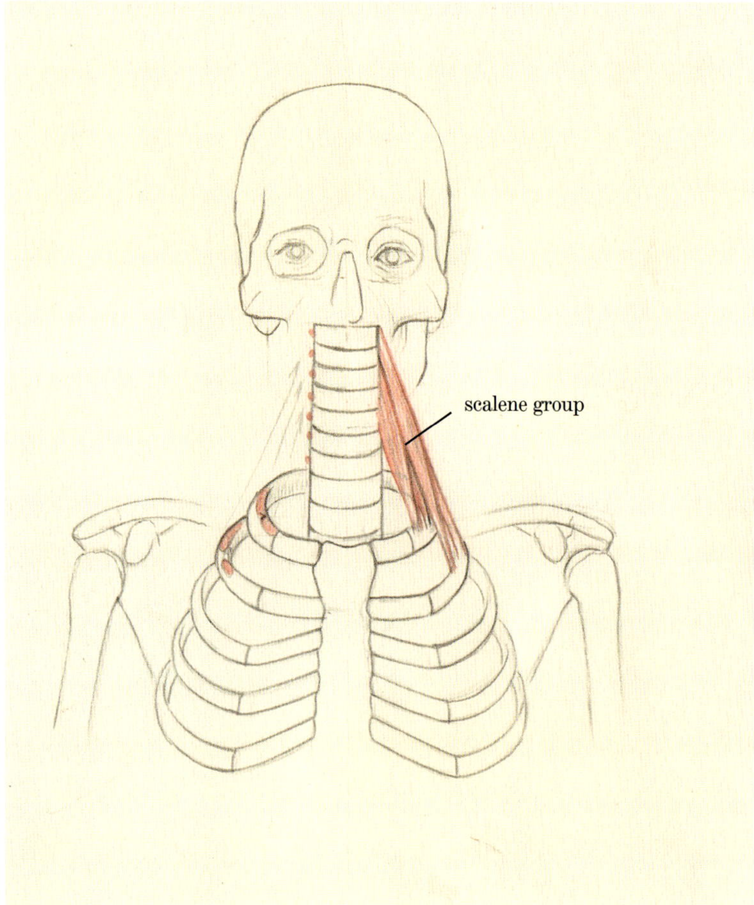

scalene group

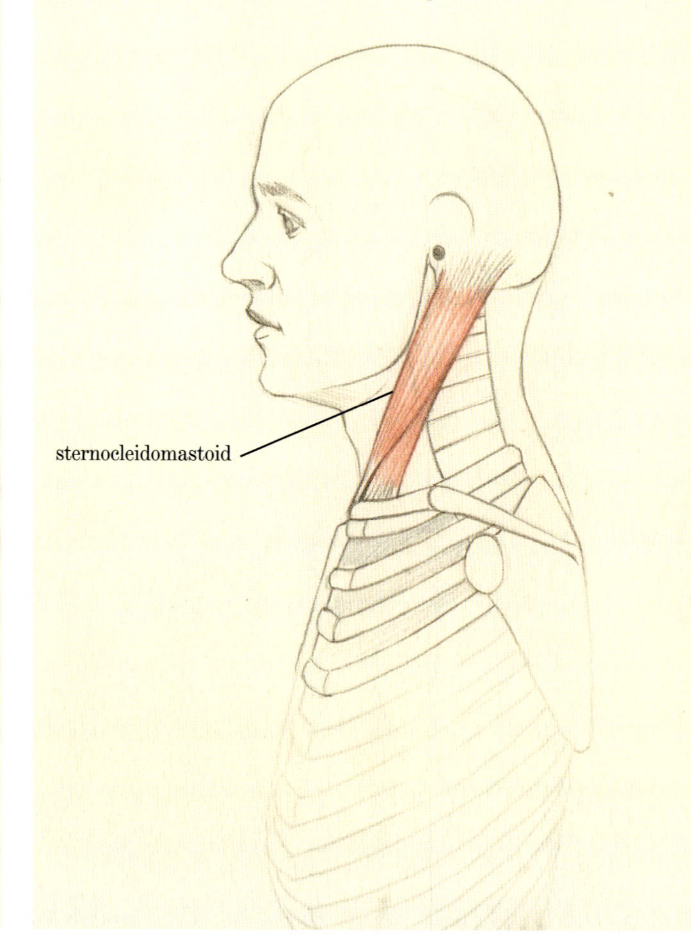

sternocleidomastoid

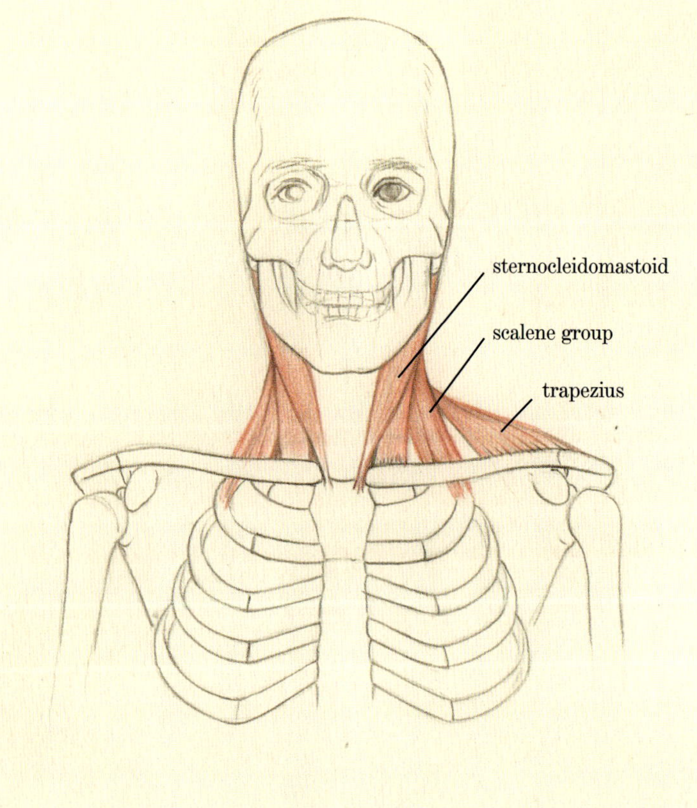

sternocleidomastoid
scalene group
trapezius

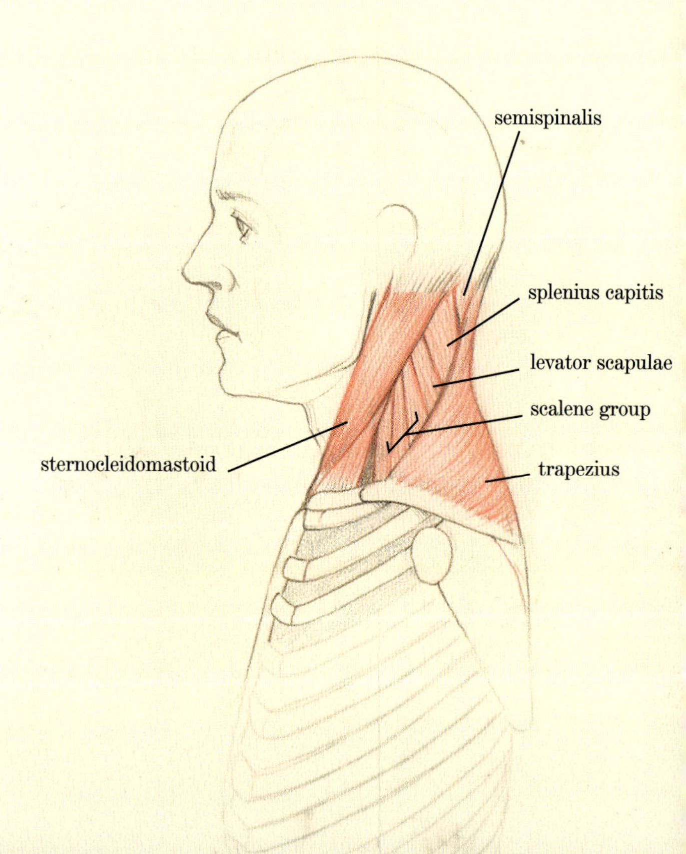

semispinalis
splenius capitis
levator scapulae
scalene group
trapezius
sternocleidomastoid

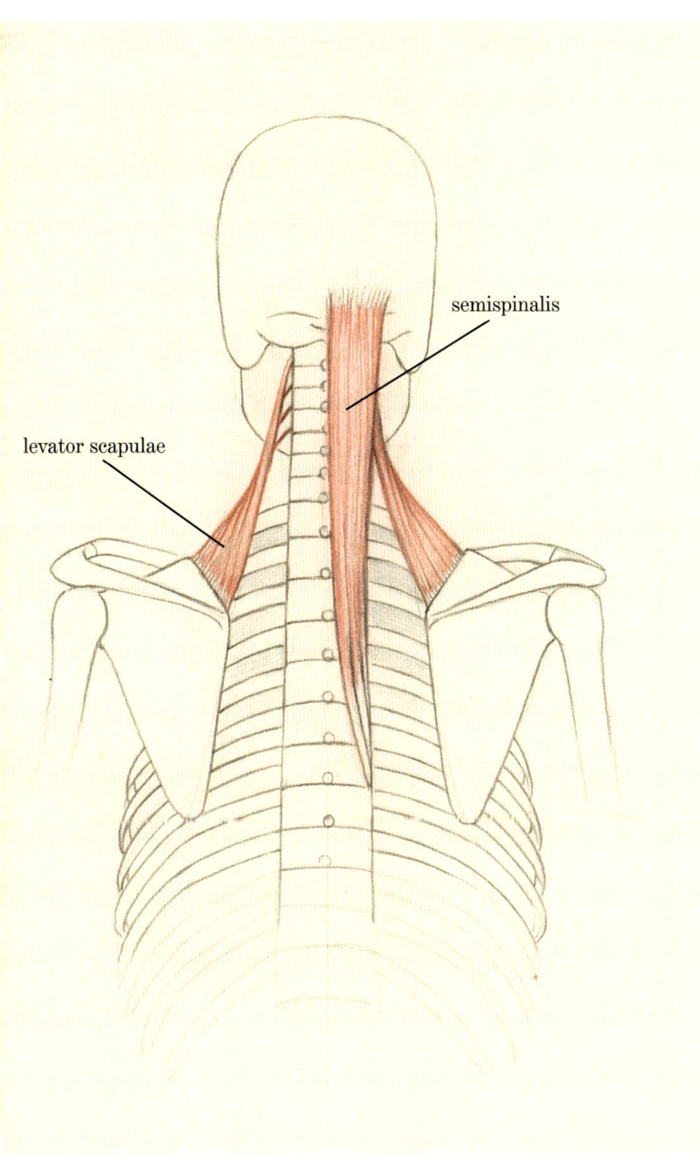

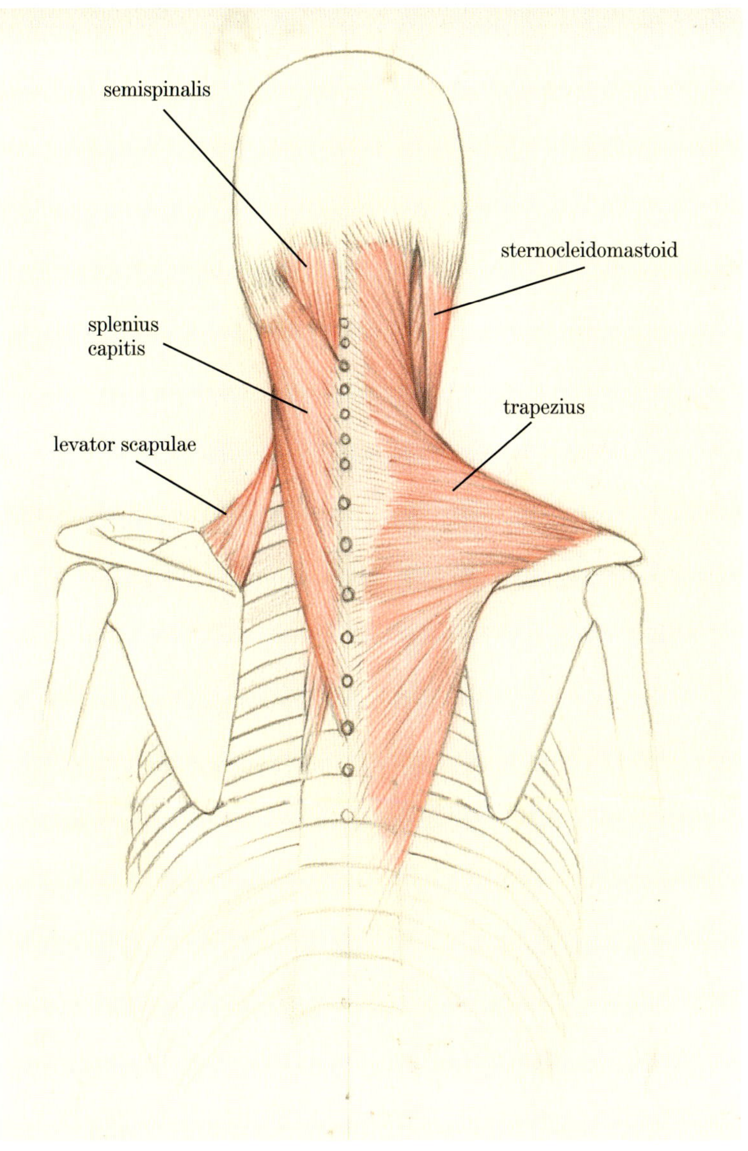

opposite, clockwise from top left
DETAIL OF SCALENE GROUP

DETAIL OF STERNOCLEIDOMASTOID, LATERAL VIEW

SUPERFICIAL MUSCLES OF THE NECK, LATERAL VIEW

SCALENE GROUP, STERNOCLEIDOMASTOID, AND TRAPEZIUS

above left to right
DEEP MUSCLES OF THE NECK, POSTERIOR VIEW

SUPERFICIAL MUSCLES OF THE NECK, POSTERIOR VIEW

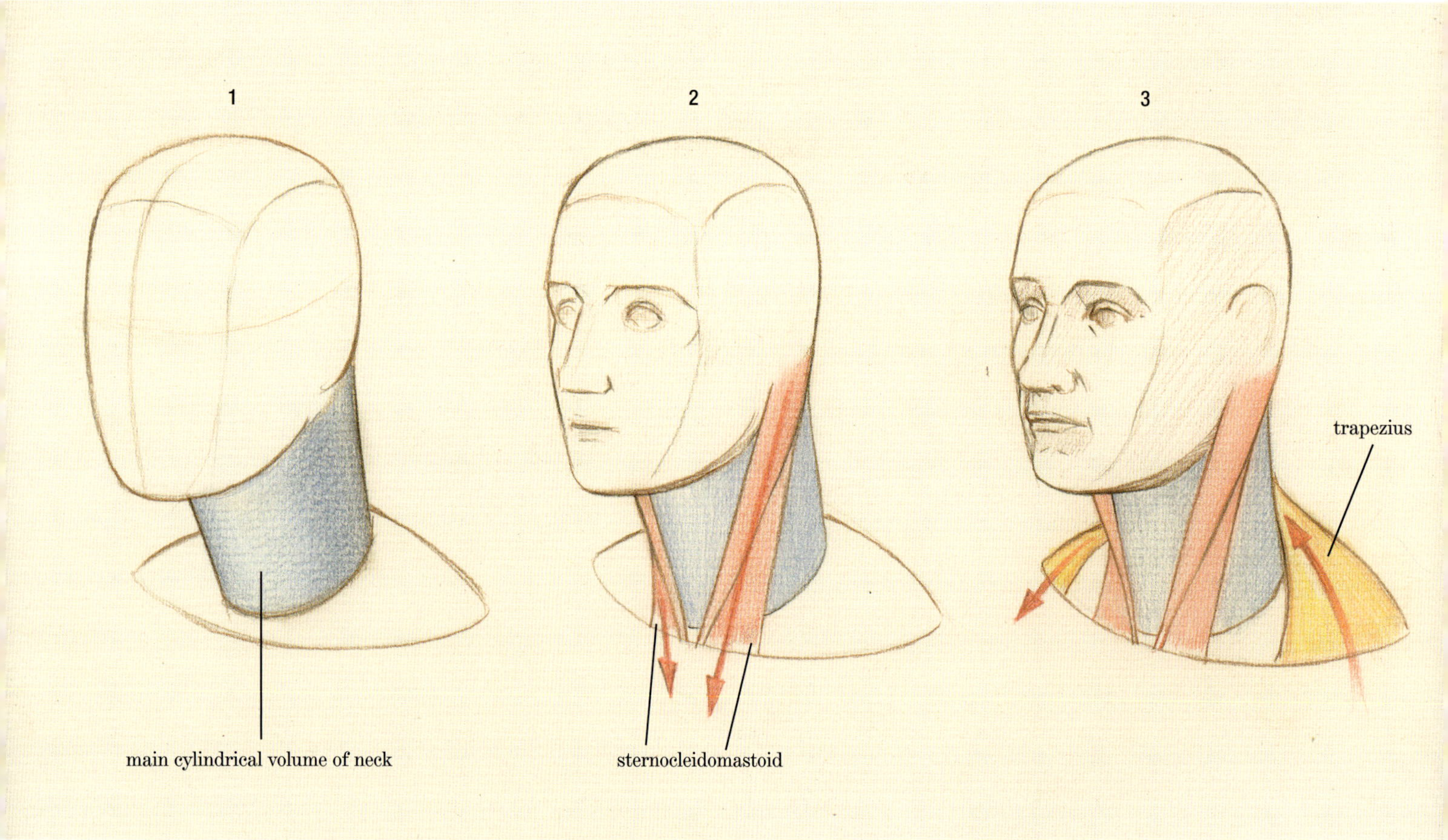

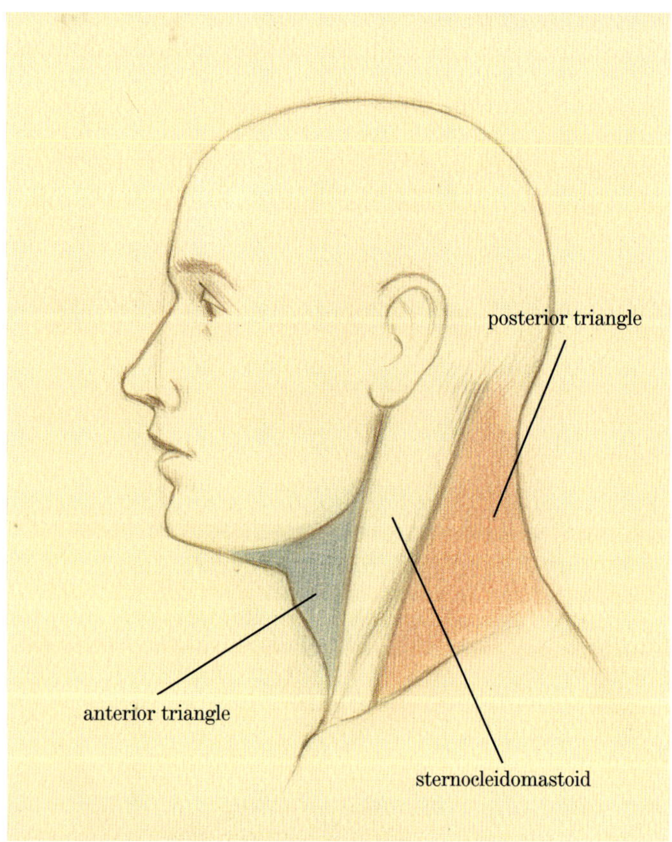

above

COLOR-CODED SEQUENCE SHOWING FORMS
OF THE NECK

The neck can be conceptualized as a cylindrical volume (1)
that is crossed diagonally by the strip-shaped sternocleidomastoid (2) and finally wrapped posteriorly by the form of the
trapezius (3).

left

TRIANGLES OF THE NECK

Moving from the top of the sternum diagonally upward and
backward to the mastoid process, the sternocleidomastoid
muscle divides the neck into two triangular sections, identified as the anterior triangle (blue) and the posterior triangle
(red).

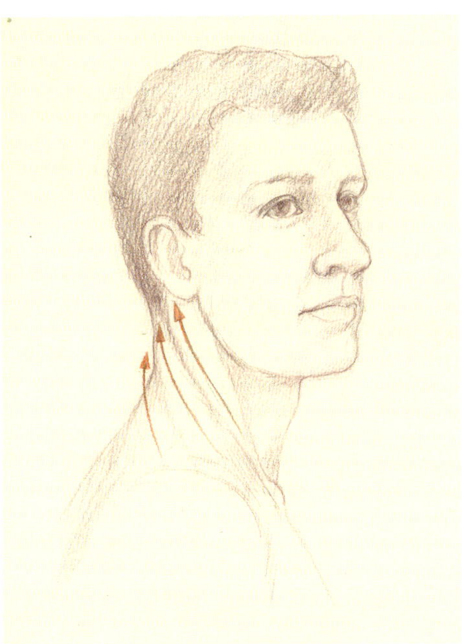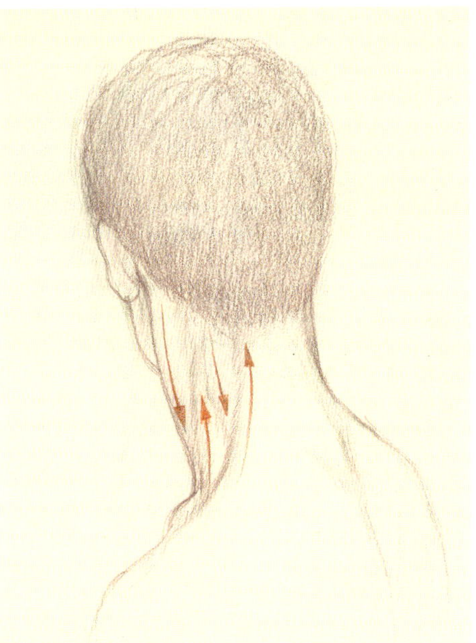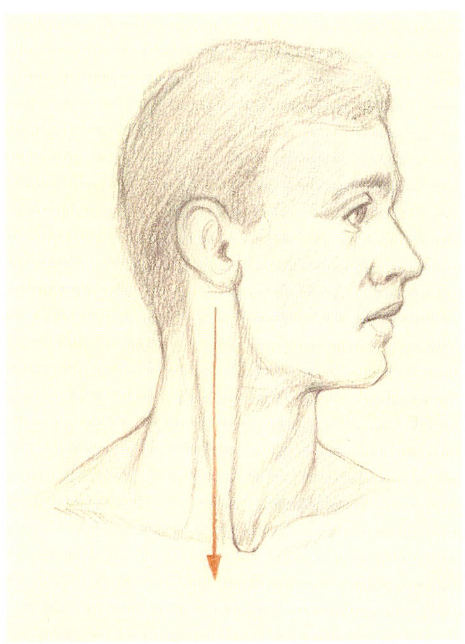

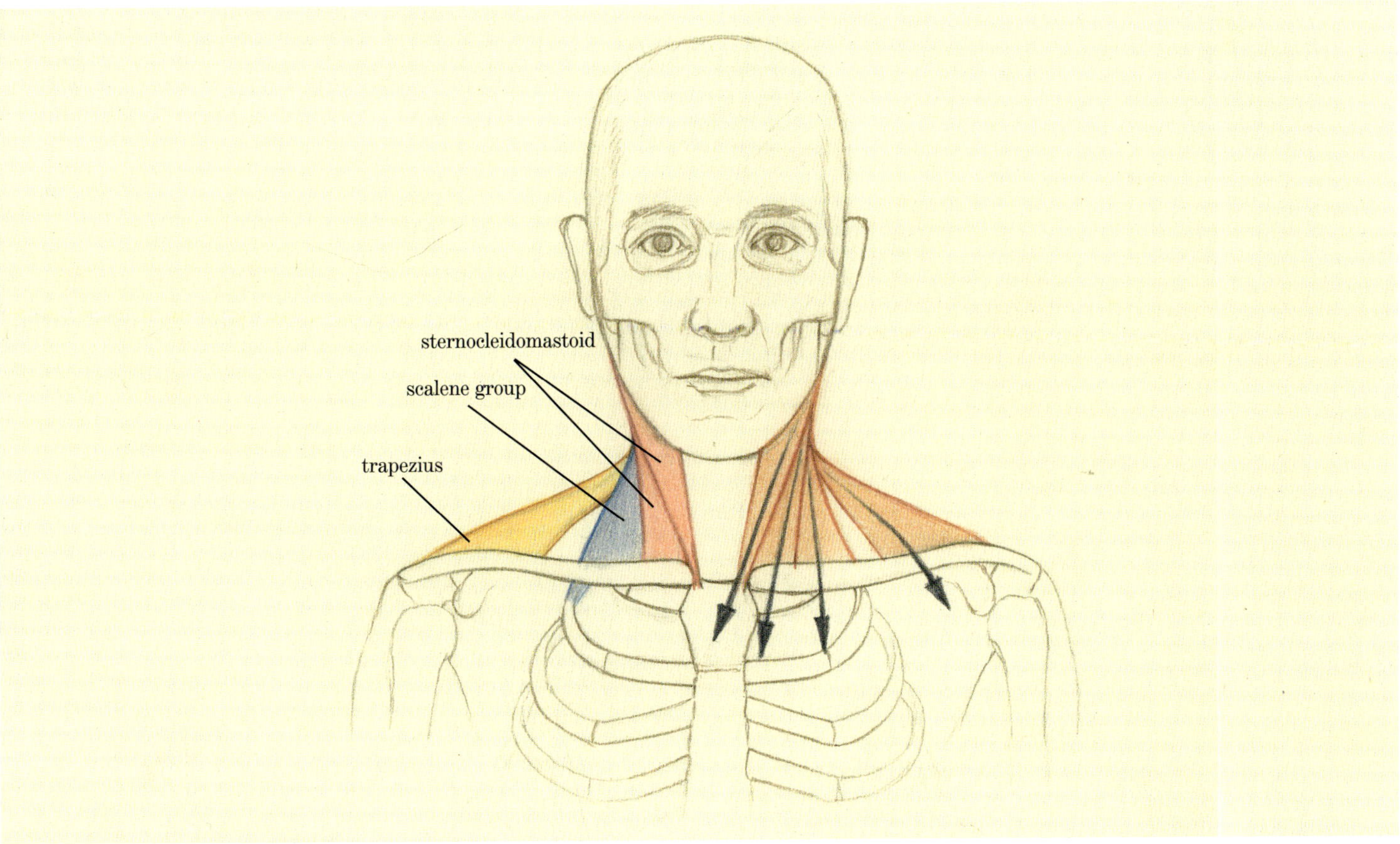

RADIATING MUSCULAR FORMS OF THE NECK

In these views of the muscles surrounding the neck, notice how they work together to create a beautiful radiating spiral. Being aware of this spiraling pattern—looking like ribbons wrapping around a pole—helps you draw the muscles in a more dynamic, harmonious, and lifelike manner.

IDENTIFYING FACIAL CHARACTERISTICS AND CAPTURING A LIKENESS

Now let's talk about identifying the specific proportions and characteristics of an individual face and head. First, we'll look at positions of facial features that represent the statistical majority of the population. Once you have learned these, you can adapt the facial characteristics to the specific characteristics of the individual being portrayed.

WIDTH-TO-HEIGHT RATIO

The figure at the center, below, shows common width-to-height ratios for the human head. The width of the head on the left is three-quarters of the height; for the head on the right, the width is two-thirds of the height. When drawing a portrait, you can quickly evaluate whether your subject's head is rounder (and therefore closer to the 3:4 ratio) or longer (closer to the 2:3 ratio).

Now look at the pair of drawings to the far left and right, below, which are tracings of photos of two of my students. As you see, the head of the person on the left has a width-to-height ratio of 3:4, while the head of the person on the right closely corresponds to the 2:3 ratio.

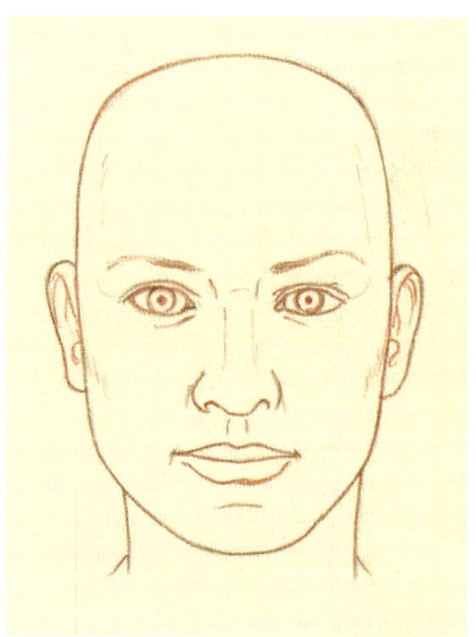

3:4 WIDTH-TO-HEIGHT RATIO

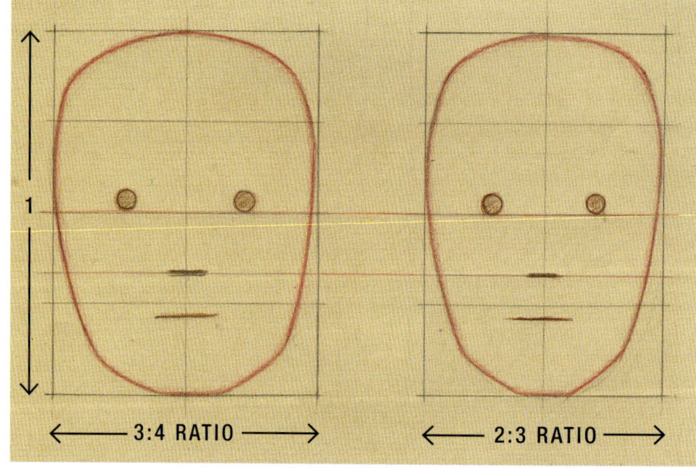

COMMON WIDTH-TO-HEIGHT RATIOS

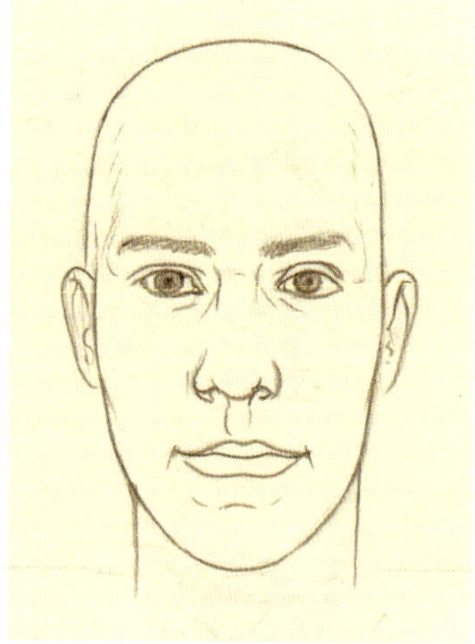

2:3 WIDTH-TO-HEIGHT RATIO

SKULL SHAPE—ROUND VERSUS OVIFORM

The cranial volume is never perfectly round (or, rather, spherical), but drawing the cranium as a circle is a good approach for capturing the narrower depth of some people's heads in a profile view. A horizontal oviform cranial mass is better for depicting a head with a deeper profile.

Now compare the two basic skull shapes shown in the figure at right, below, with the tracings of profile shots of the heads of two of my students, at left. The head at the top has an overall rounder appearance, while the head at the bottom is more ovoid. For fun, you might take some "mug shots" of friends' profiles, print the photos, and then draw cranial shapes on them to see whether the shapes are rounder or more oviform.

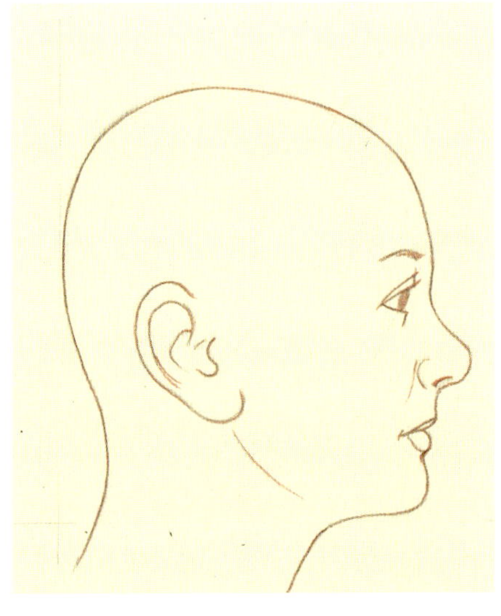

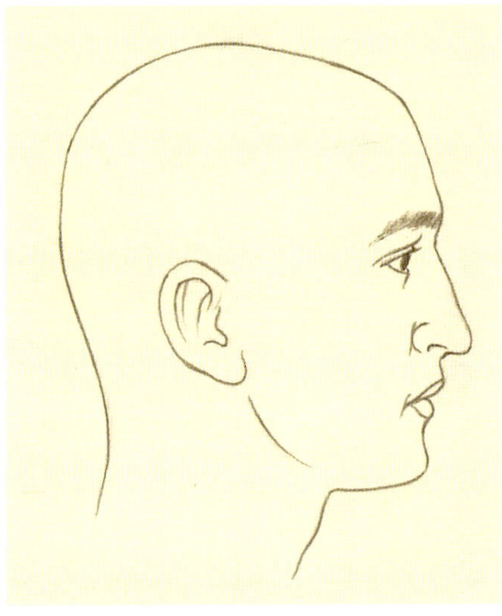

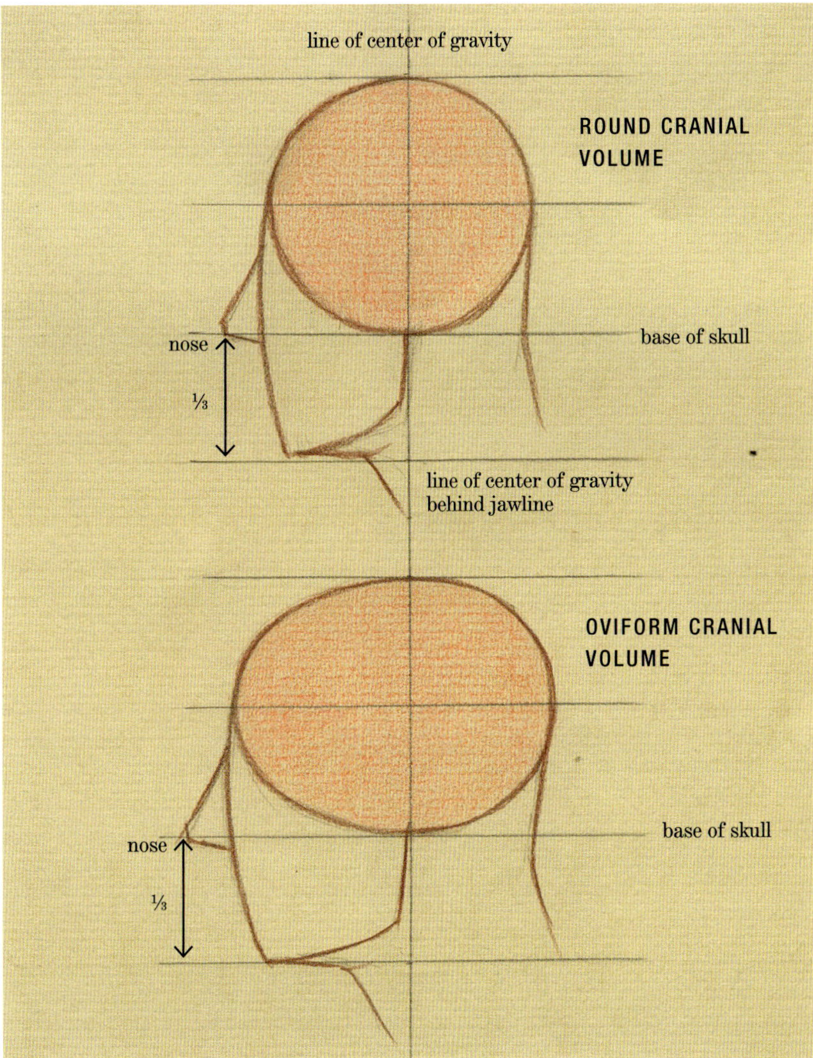

top to bottom
ROUNDER SKULL SHAPE
MORE OVIFORM SKULL SHAPE

ROUND AND OVIFORM SKULL SHAPES, PROFILE VIEW

POSITIONING FACIAL FEATURES

Now that you're familiar with the basic volumes of the head, its planes, and its general proportions, let's move on to positioning the features: the brow ridge, eyes, nasion, tip of the nose, and mouth. The figure below shows how to position the basic features on a front view of the face using a grid.

STEP 1: Establish the height of the head (line A–B) and subdivide it in halves, quarters, and thirds.

STEP 2: Establish the width and create the notional space of the box. In this case, the width of the head (at its widest point) is two-thirds of the height. Draw the cranial volume as a circle whose diameter is the same as the width of the head, and draw the facial volume in the shape of a mask below the cranial volume.

STEP 3: Establish the angles of the temporal ridge more or less at the upper sixth of the head. The temporal ridge marks the border between the top plane and the side plane of the head. Then mark the widest point of the head at the upper third; also at this level, but on the frontal plane (the face), describe the brow ridge. Mark the angles of the jaw and the chin. The irises are positioned above the horizontal midline and on the medial sides of the vertical lines that divide each side of the face in two. The base of the nose is at the lower third, and the mouth about halfway between the bottom of the nose and the chin, but a little closer to the nose. (So far, these steps are the same as those for the construction of the skull.)

STEP 4: Establish the front, top, and side planes of the head, and define the eyes, nose, mouth, and ears, giving them three-dimensionality by adding shading, as on the right half of step 4.

The figure opposite presents a four-step sequence for drawing a head in three-quarters view, which enhances the form's three-dimensionality.

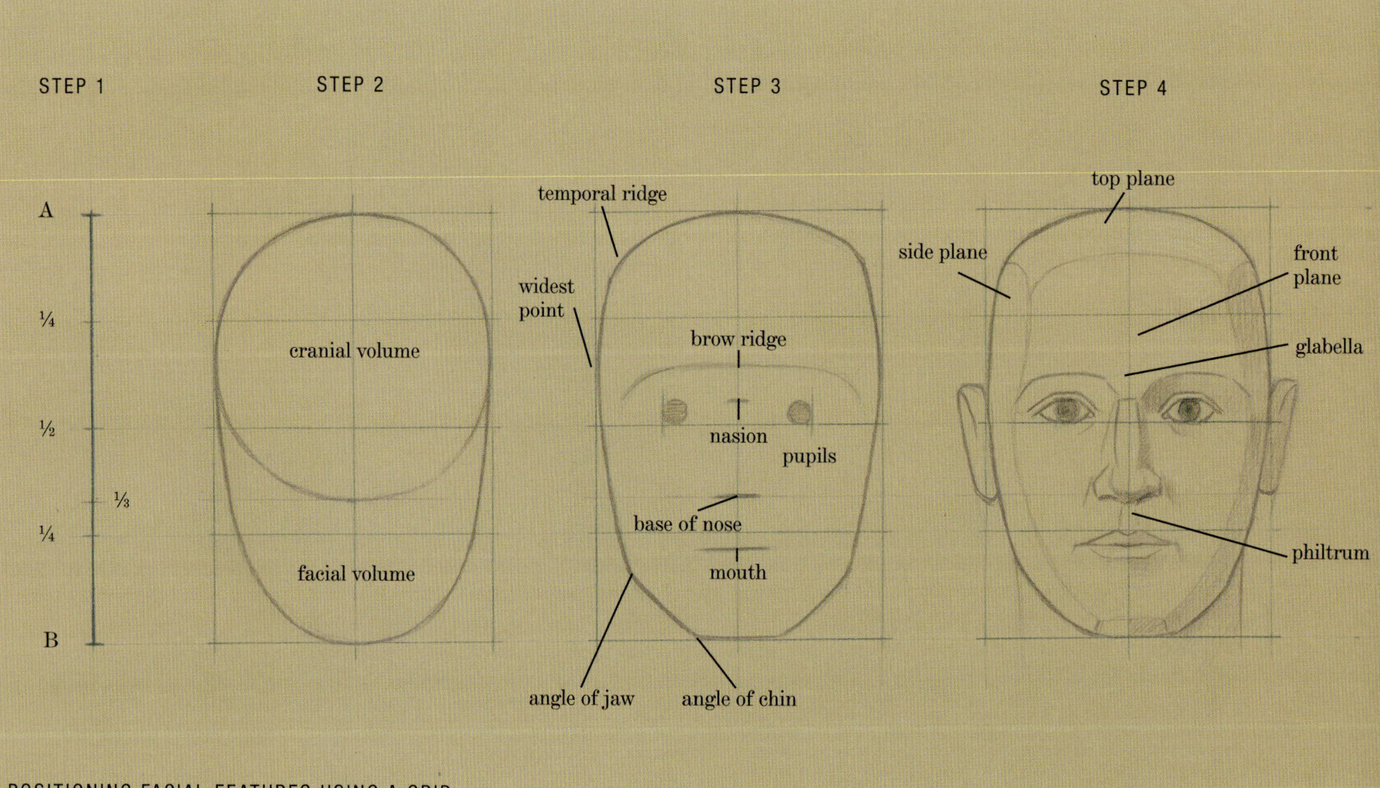

POSITIONING FACIAL FEATURES USING A GRID

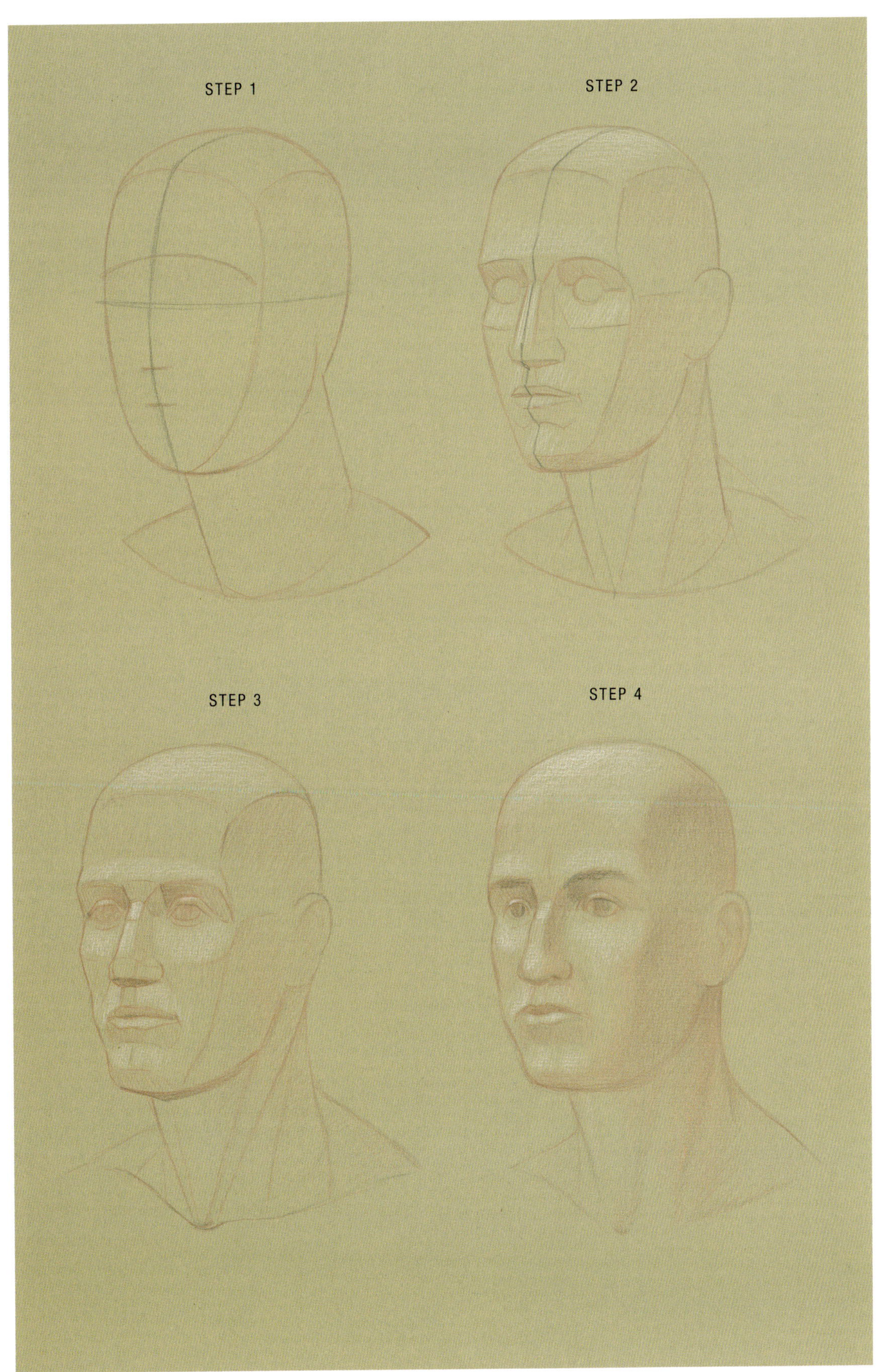

DRAWING A HEAD IN THREE-QUARTERS VIEW

Here, you see a gradual passage from the very basic forms of the head (step 1), to the definition of the head's basic planes (step 2), to the addition of smaller planes that hint of the facial features (step 3), to the rendering of the features of a specific person (step 4).

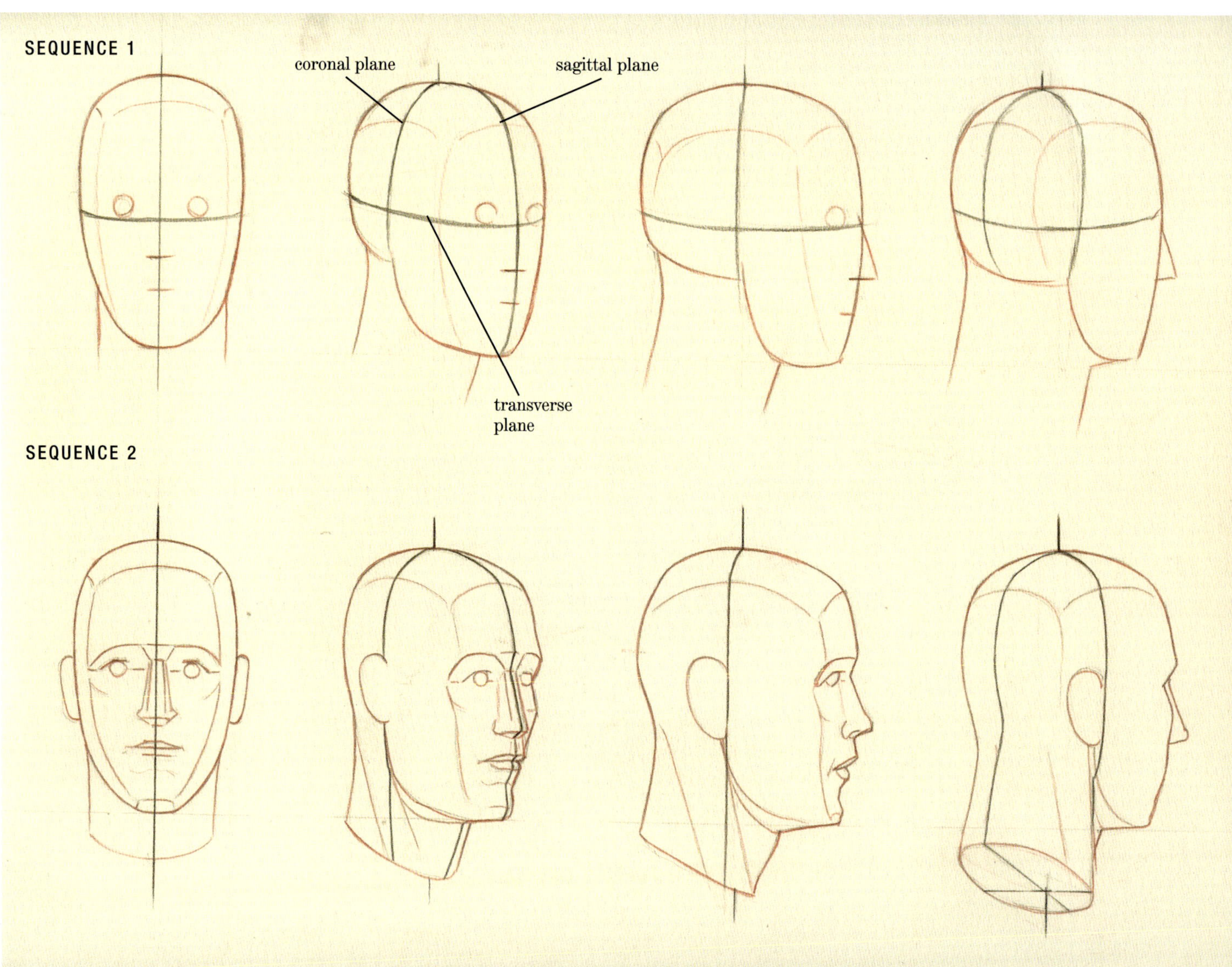

ROTATING THE HEAD

The figure above shows two levels of schematization of the head and how to rotate the head on its axis. The sagittal plane divides the head into right and left halves; the coronal plane into anterior and posterior; and the tranverse plane into superior and inferior.

Sequence 1, at top, shows how to position the basic features correctly, starting from a front view and gradually rotating the head to three-quarters, profile, and posterior three-quarters views. The section lines indicating the coronal, sagittal, and transverse planes will help you maintain consistent positions for the eye, nose, and mouth and will also help you visualize the variations in shape of the right and left halves of the head as it rotates. In sequence 2, at bottom, more details of the face are added.

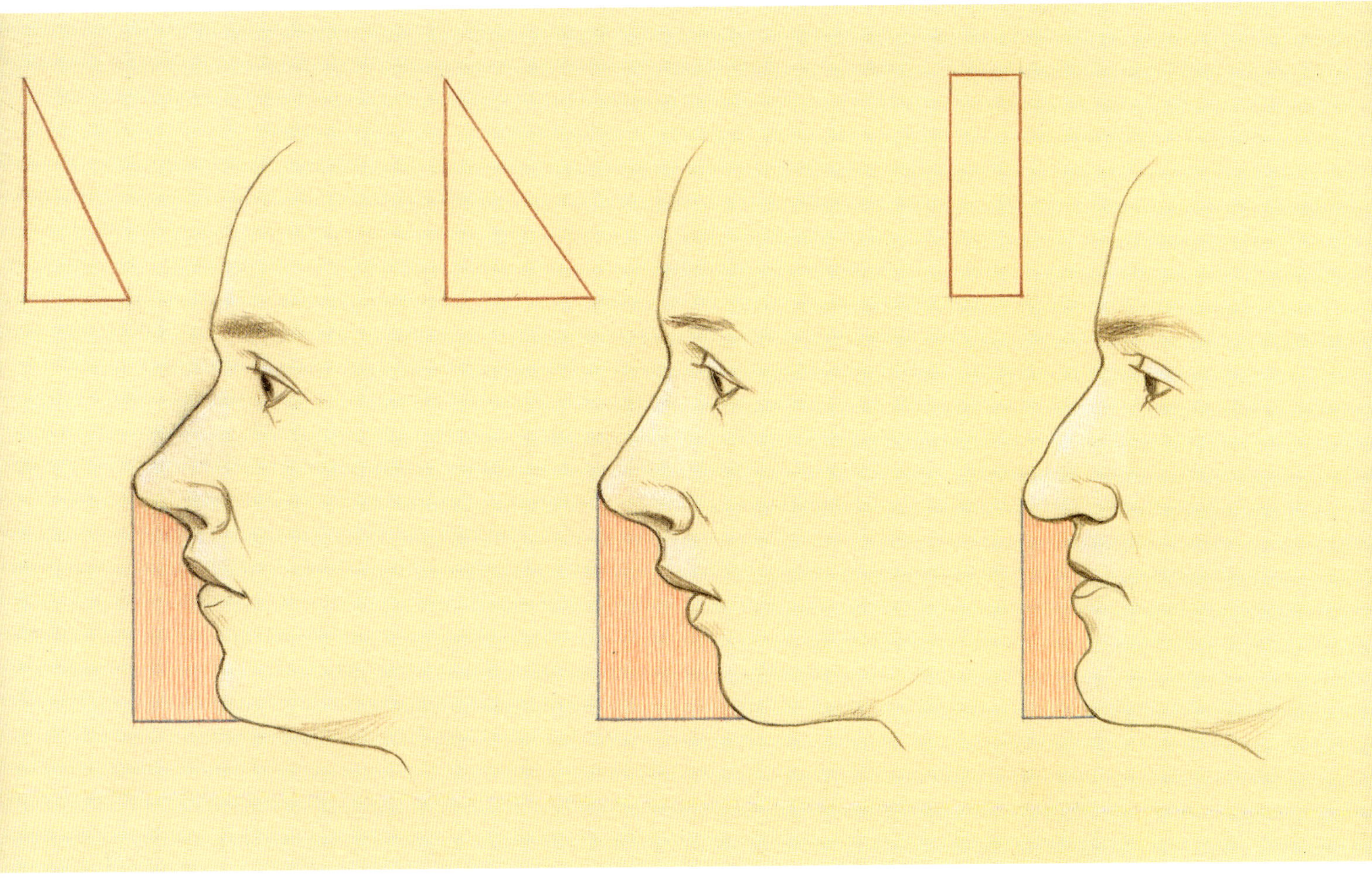

THREE TYPICAL PROFILES

When drawing a profile, I find it useful to isolate the negative space between a vertical line that starts from the tip of the nose and a horizontal line starting from the chin. Reducing this negative space to simple geometric shapes helps you accurately visualize specific characteristics of your subject's face.

Following Leonardo da Vinci's method of cataloguing the facial features, we can identify the main types of profiles. The figure above describes three typical profiles, but you can come up with your own classification and identify many more by creating a catalogue of the profiles of friends and relatives.

By now you have a good understanding of the volumes of the head, the planes of the head and face, and the positions of the facial features. This knowledge will make it much easier for you to create a variety of drawings of the head and face from different angles and in movement and to draw more accurate portraits from life. Illustrating the great diversity of real people's facial features, the final image of this chapter, on the next page, shows tracings of photos of the faces of some of my students. This is a fun exercise you can perform with the collaboration of your friends.

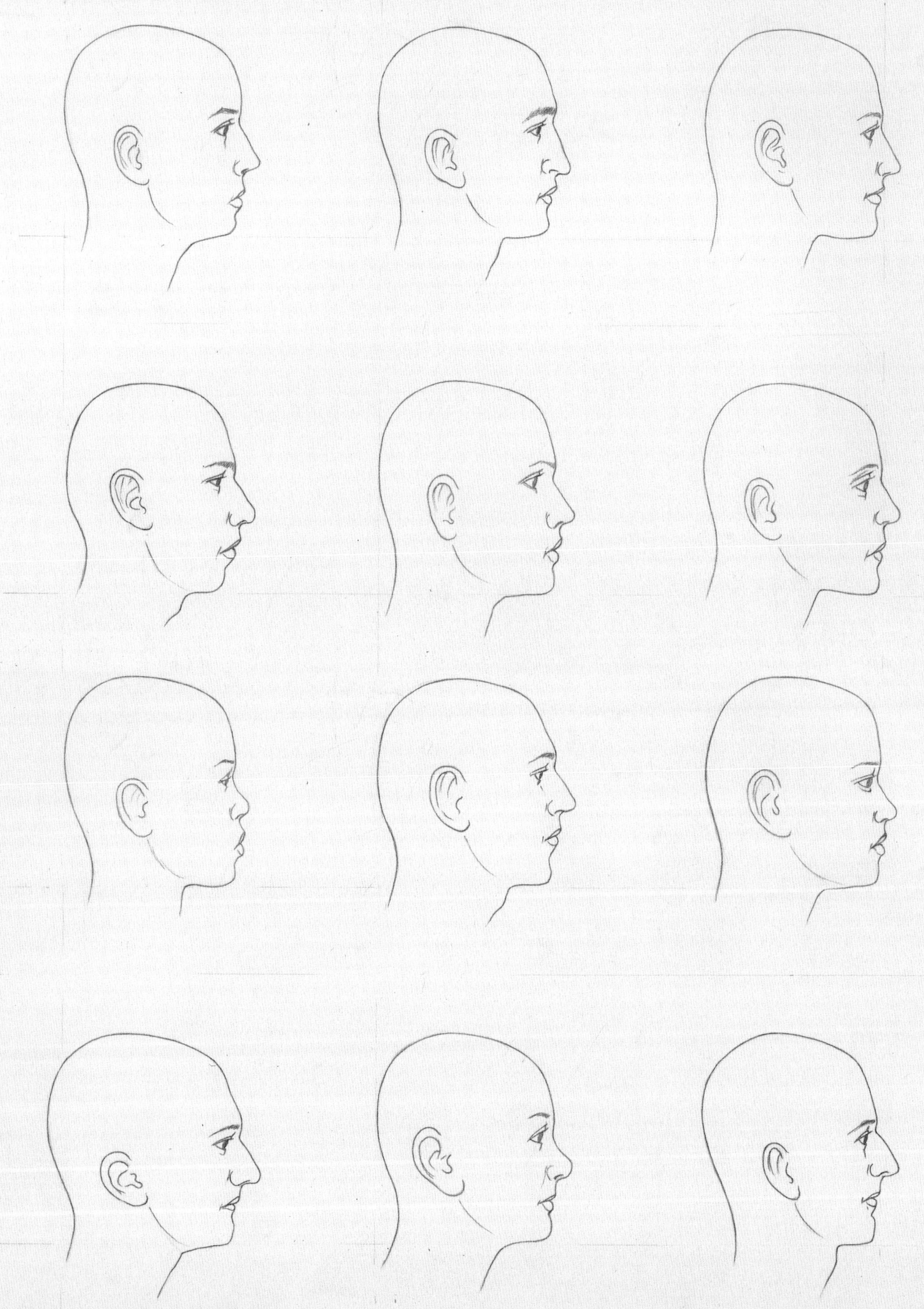

A DIVERSITY OF FACIAL FEATURES

EXERCISES

Drawing the figure is notoriously difficult, but drawing a person's facial features is even harder. These exercises will help you master the typical proportions of the human face, recognize the many possible variations in facial features, become proficient in capturing the likeness of a person, and, finally, understand the expressive qualities that emerge when light is shone on a face.

EXERCISE 1: DRAW HEAD SHAPES FROM IMAGINATION

From imagination, draw very simple head shapes seen from different angles. First draw the cranial and facial volumes and then the vertical center line, the median horizontal line, and the front, side, and top planes. Last, add the eyes, nose, mouth, and ears. Keep these drawings very simple. The more of these you draw, the better.

EXERCISE 2: DRAW FACES FROM PHOTOGRAPHS

Take photos of the faces of some friends and relatives. Using Photoshop, arrange them in groups of twelve or so, and print them on 8 ½ × 11 sheets of paper. Then copy the faces on separate pieces of drawing paper, making each head about one and a half or two inches tall. Start with basic shapes and feature positions, and then start adding more specific facial features and expressions. Keep it simple, and try to position the features as precisely as you can. Again, the more of these you draw, the better.

EXERCISE 3: DRAW THE EFFECTS OF A LIGHT SOURCE ON THE PLANES OF THE HEAD

Photocopy the drawing of the planes of the head, far left, making several copies. Now, imagine a directional light source and fill in the shadow masses, developing it tonally, as in the figure at left. Repeat the exercise, each time imagining a light source coming from a different direction.

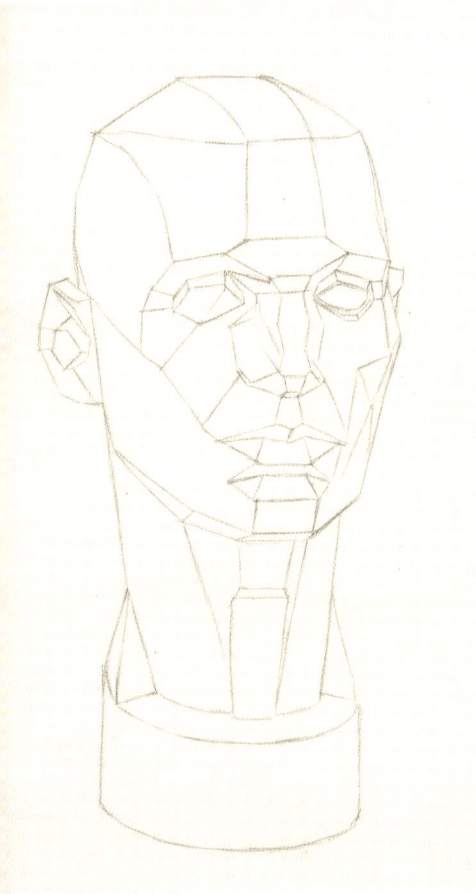

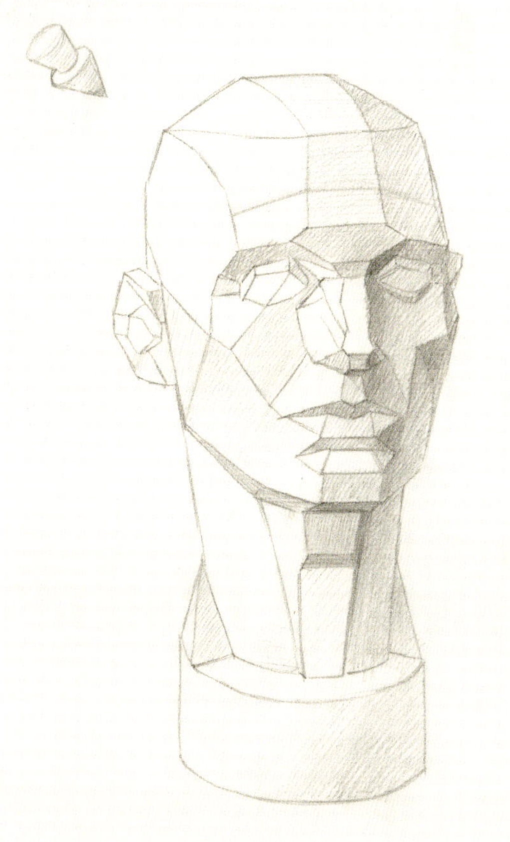

DRAW FORE-SHORTENED AND UNUSUAL POSES

Drawing foreshortened poses and unusual poses (like yoga poses) is a fantastic way of improving your skill and gaining a more complete understanding of the figure. Try many different poses from many different points of view.

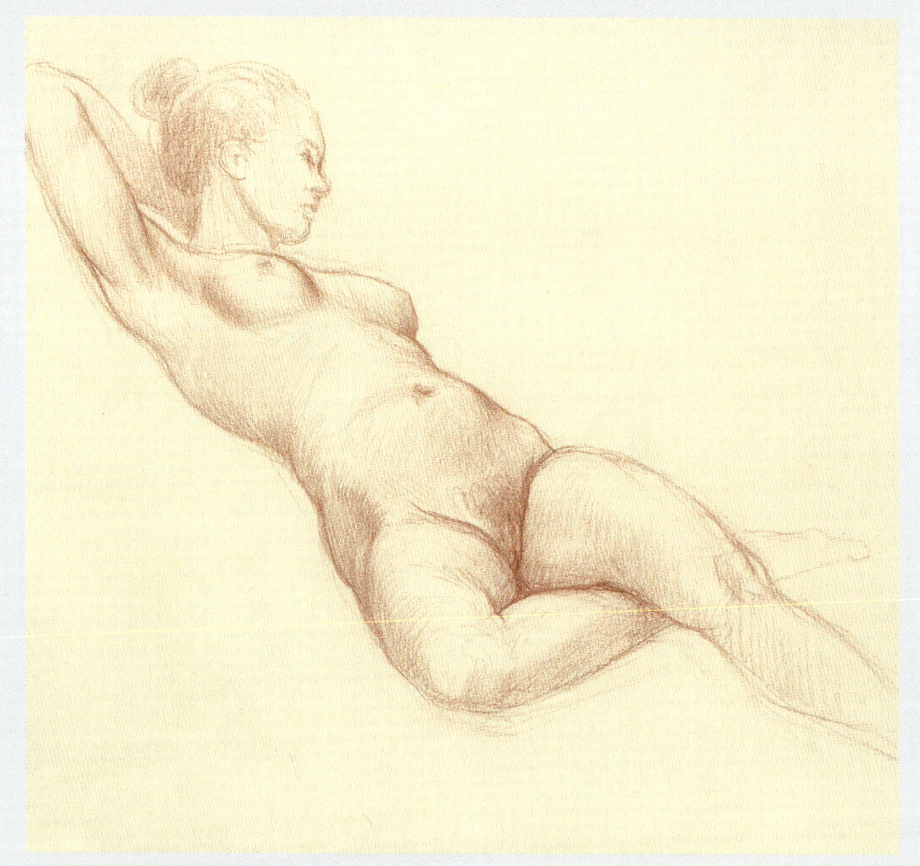

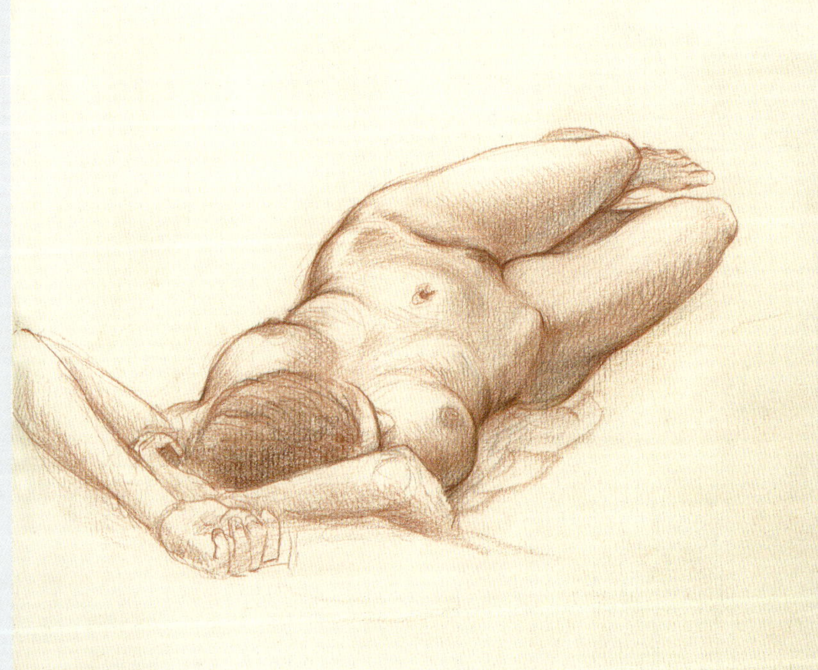

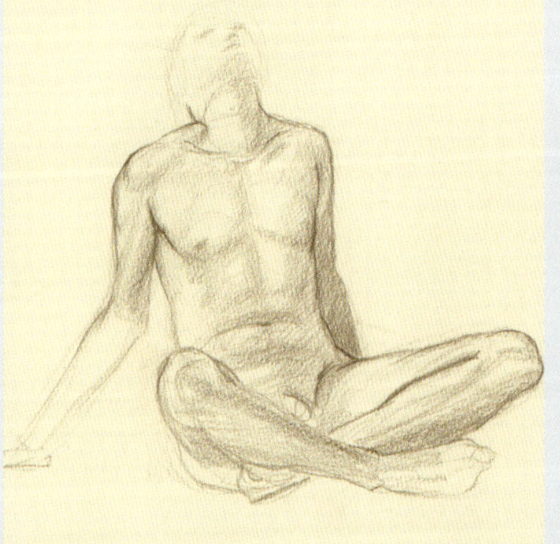

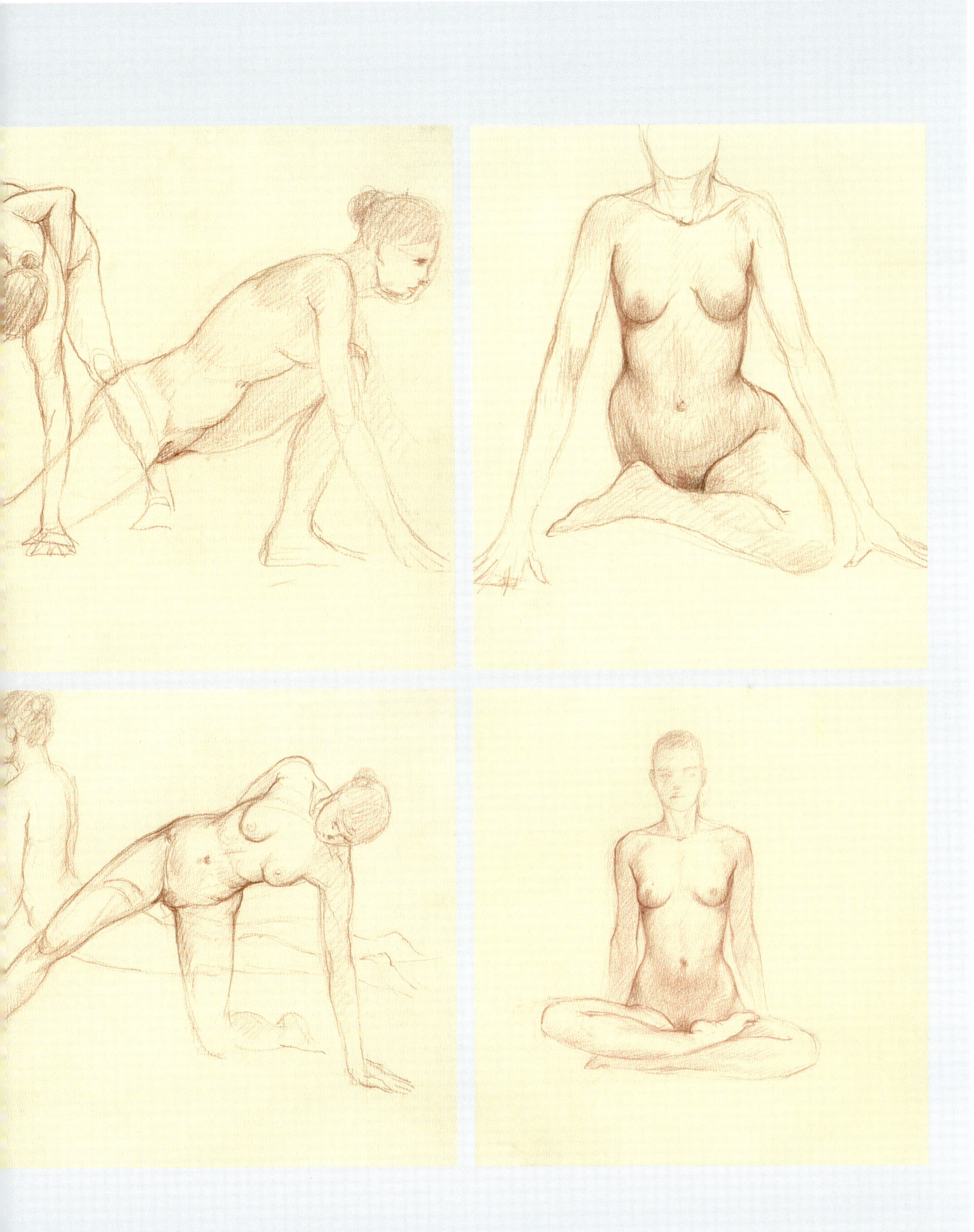

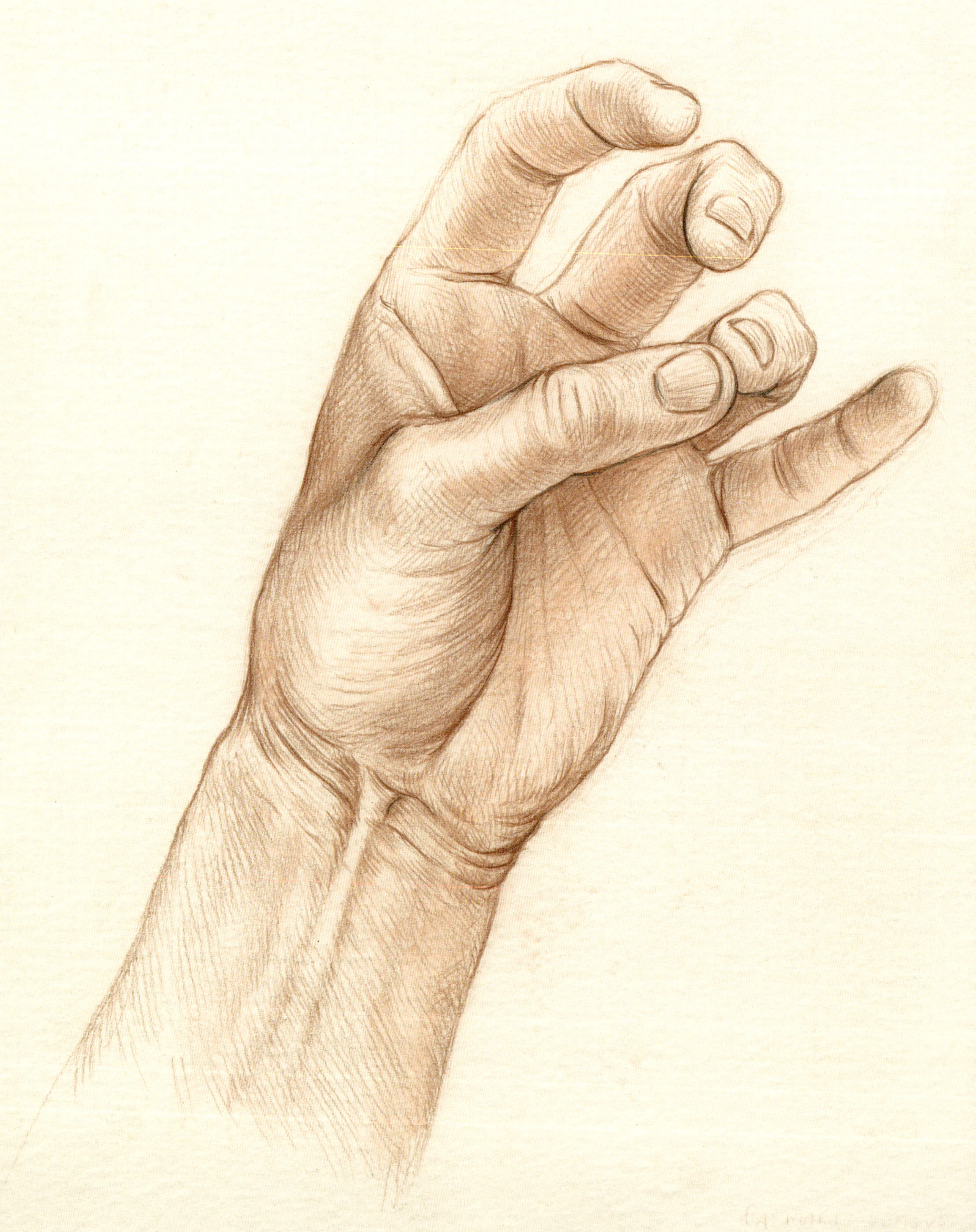

Chapter 6

THE HANDS AND FEET

long with the face, the hands and feet are the most difficult parts of the human figure to draw. In figure drawing classes, many students leave the hands and feet for last—or just leave empty spaces for them. The hand's structure is inherently complex, but it's made even more complicated by the great variety of shapes it can assume when it is flexed, extended, made into a fist, holds something, and so on. The feet are not quite as complicated, but when they are not properly proportioned, the figure will look unstable, awkward, or simply ridiculous.

PROPORTIONS AND SHAPES OF THE HANDS

Understanding the hands' essential structural characteristics is crucial if you want to overcome your reluctance to draw them. Many artists have conquered that fear, eventually deriving pleasure from creating correct, expressive, and elegant hands that look and feel right, solid, and functional. The illustrations in this section describe the proportions and shapes of the hands, helping you master their inherent complexity.

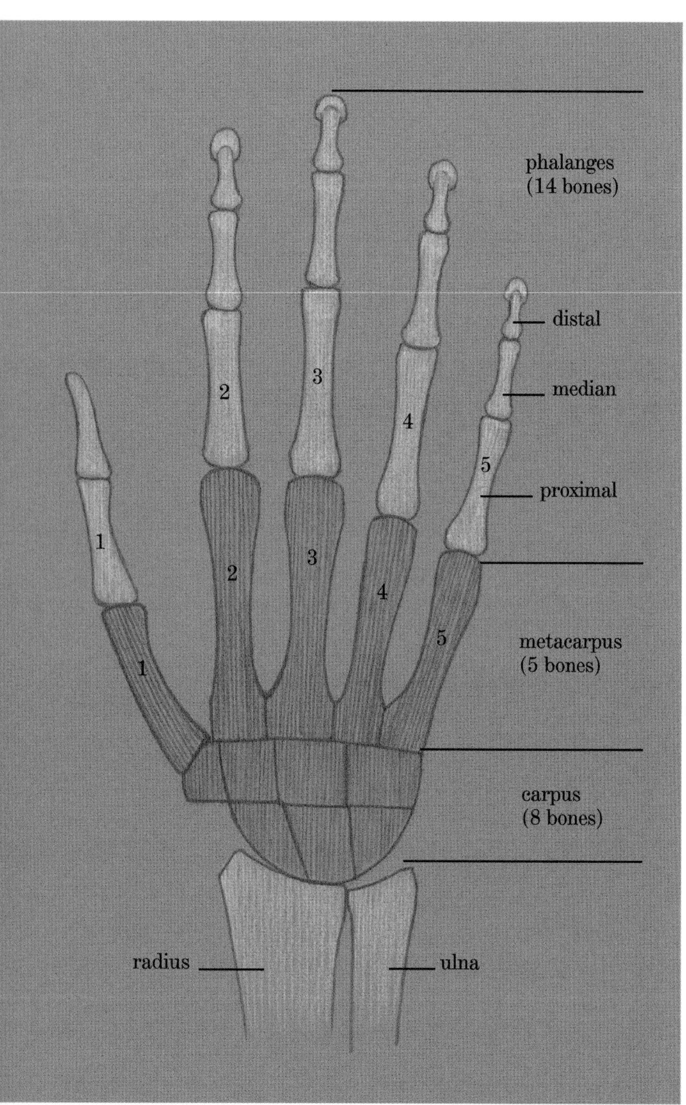

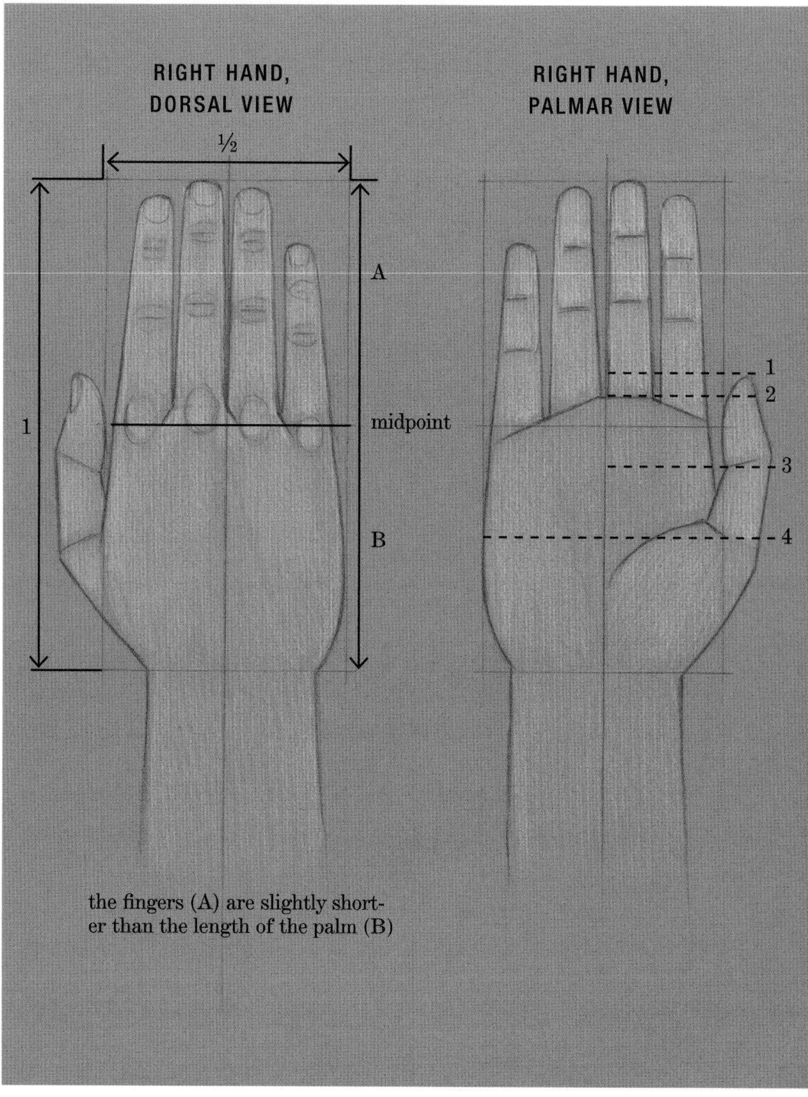

the fingers (A) are slightly short-
er than the length of the palm (B)

SCHEMATIC SKELETON OF THE HAND, DORSAL VIEW

The hand has 27 bones, as shown in this drawing. The progressive shortening typical of the bones of the limbs is clearly noticeable in the fingers. Take, for example, the middle finger: The metacarpal bone is the longest and the phalanges gradually decrease in length.

BASIC PROPORTIONS OF THE HAND

The width of the hand (excluding the thumb) is about half its length. The length of the fingers (segment *A* in the drawing at left) is slightly less than the length of the palm (segment *B*). As shown in the drawing at right, the distal phalanx of the thumb (1) reaches slightly above the base of the fingers at the palm of the hand (2). The proximal phalanx (3) reaches halfway up the upper half of the palm. The joint between the first metacarpal and the proximal phalanx of the thumb (4) is about halfway up the length of the palm.

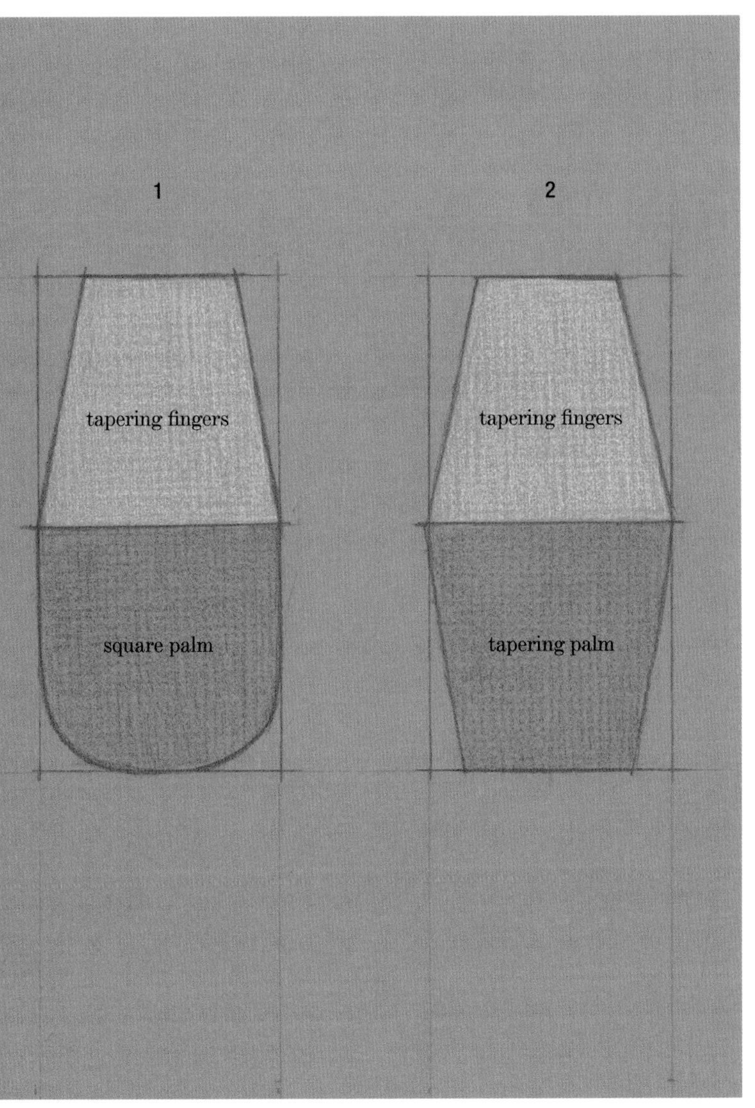

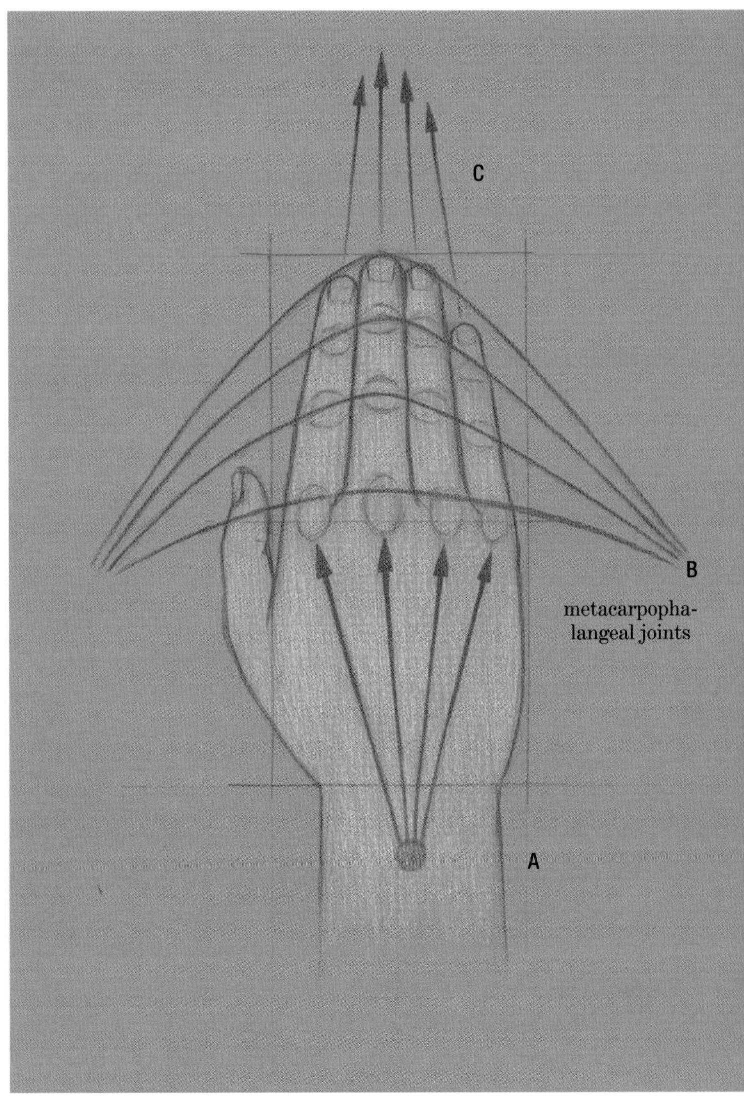

TWO COMMON HAND SHAPES

In hand 1, the palm is square and the volume of the fingers tapers; this shape describes a wider, stout hand. In hand 2, both volumes—palm and fingers—taper; this type of hand tends to be more elongated and narrow.

DIVERGENCE AND CONVERGENCE IN THE HAND

The tendons of the extensors of the fingers (black arrows) start diverging at a point, marked A, about an inch below the wrist joint. Then, from the metacarpophalangeal joints on, the fingers begin to converge. The lines of the knuckles are curved (B), with the curve growing sharper as you move toward the fingertips. The blue arrows (C) show the lines of the fingers' convergence.

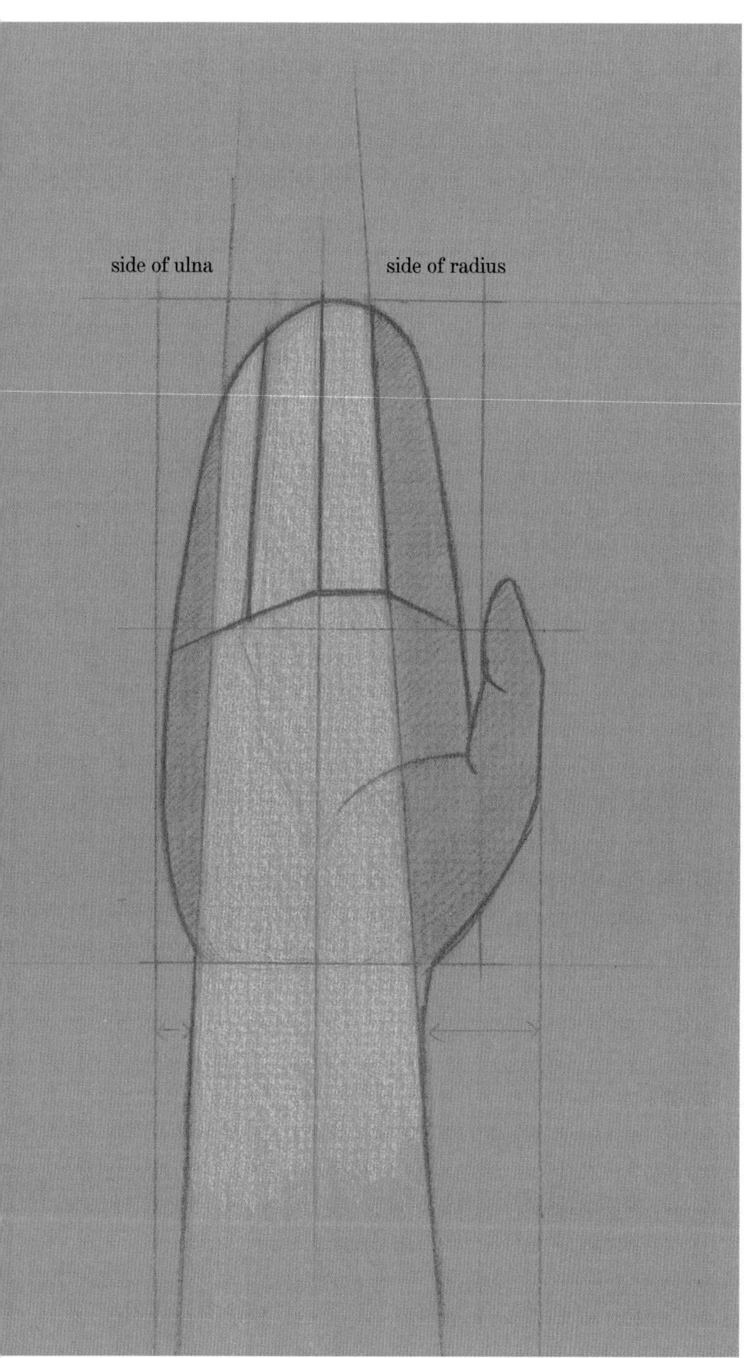

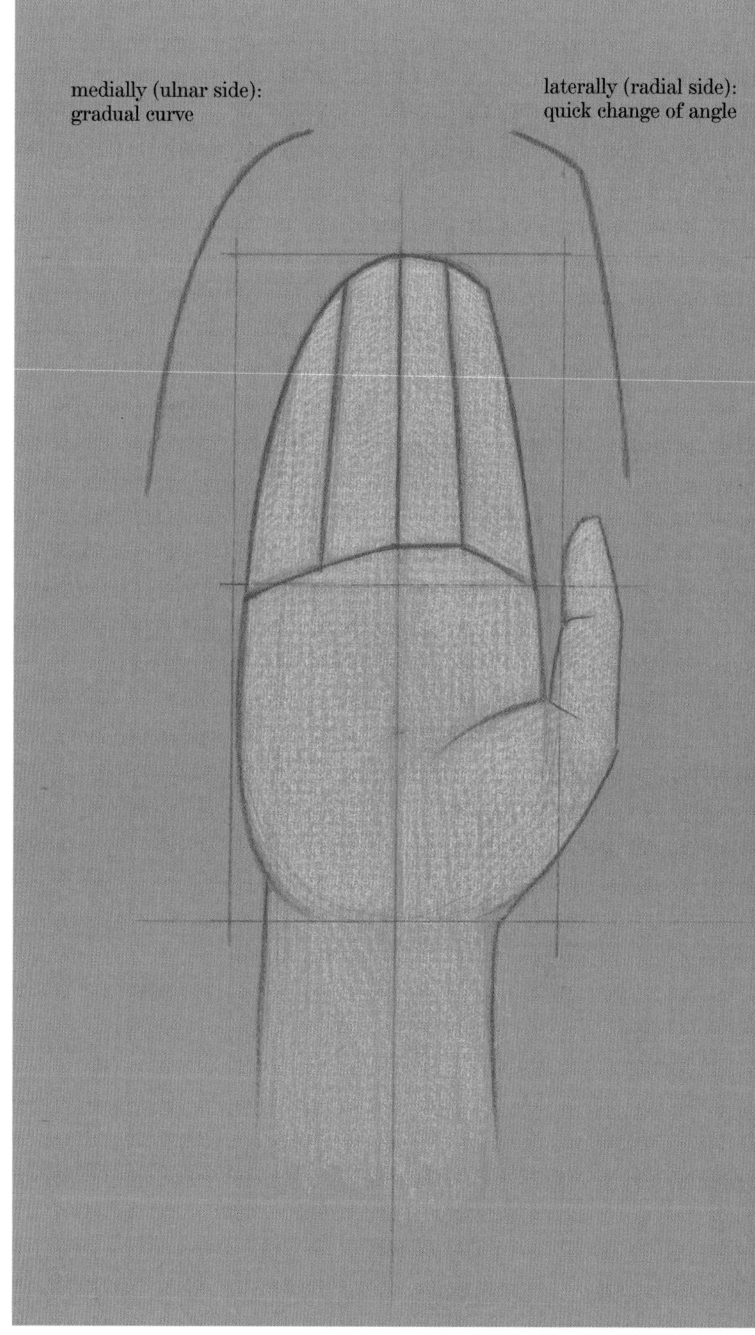

HAND SHIFTS TOWARD RADIUS

An imaginary line extending from the side of the ulna toward the fingertips cuts halfway through the width of the little finger. But an imaginary line extended from the radial side of the wrist excludes the whole width of the index finger and thumb. The hand is therefore slightly shifted toward the radius.

CURVES OF THE FINGERTIPS

Specific profiles are created by the alignments of the fingertips. Note how the thumb side of the hand has a steeper profile while the profile on the little-finger side is more gradual.

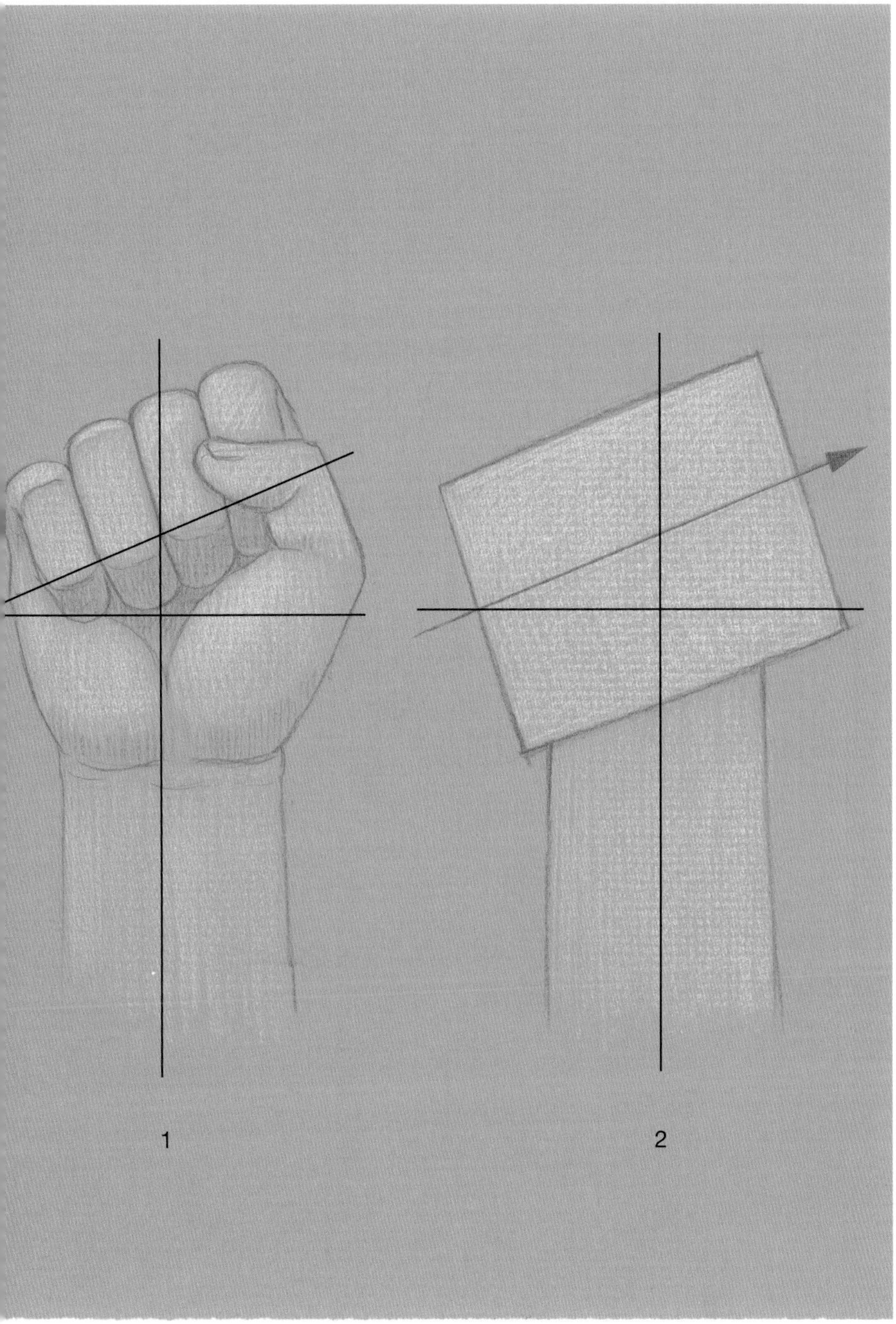

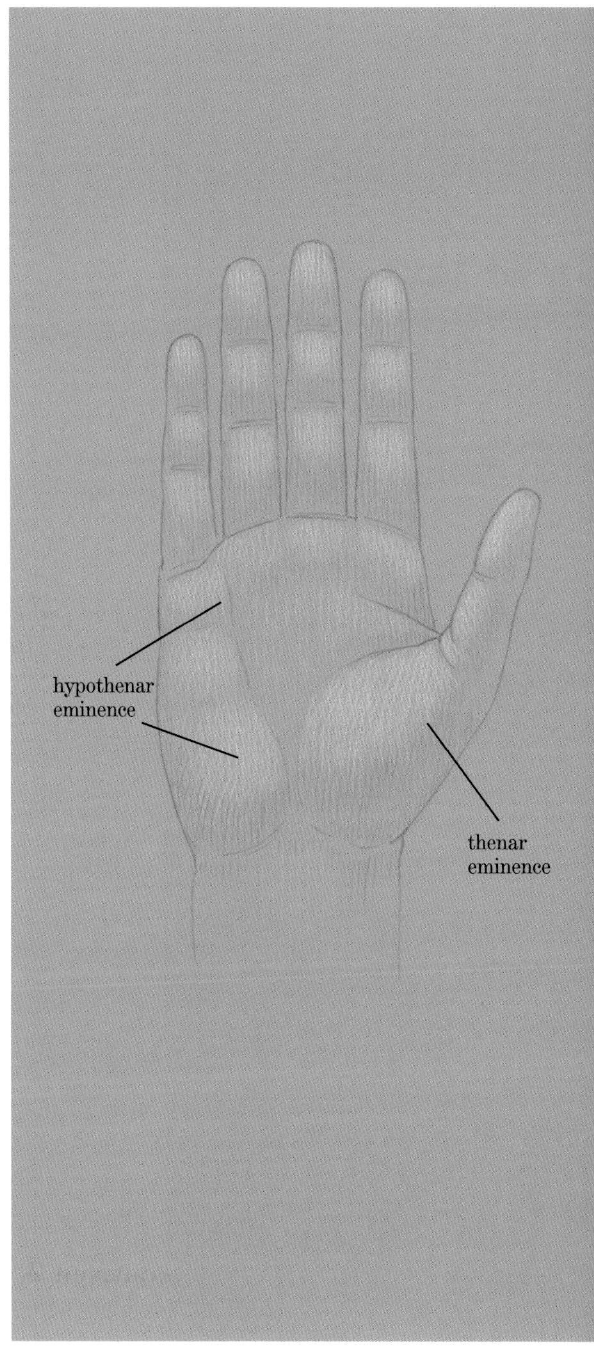

THE FIST

Starting with your hand extended with the palm facing you, and keeping the hand and forearm in a straight line, make a fist. You will immediately see that the volume created by the fingers (excluding the thumb) is not perpendicular to the wrist. If you reduce the fist to a rectangular shape as in the drawing at right, you can better appreciate how the fist is *not* perpendicular to the axes of the forearm but instead shifts laterally toward the radius side.

EMINENCES OF THE HAND (RIGHT HAND, PALMAR VIEW)

This image shows the main eminences of the palmar side of the hand. (An eminence is a small mound that stands above the general form.)

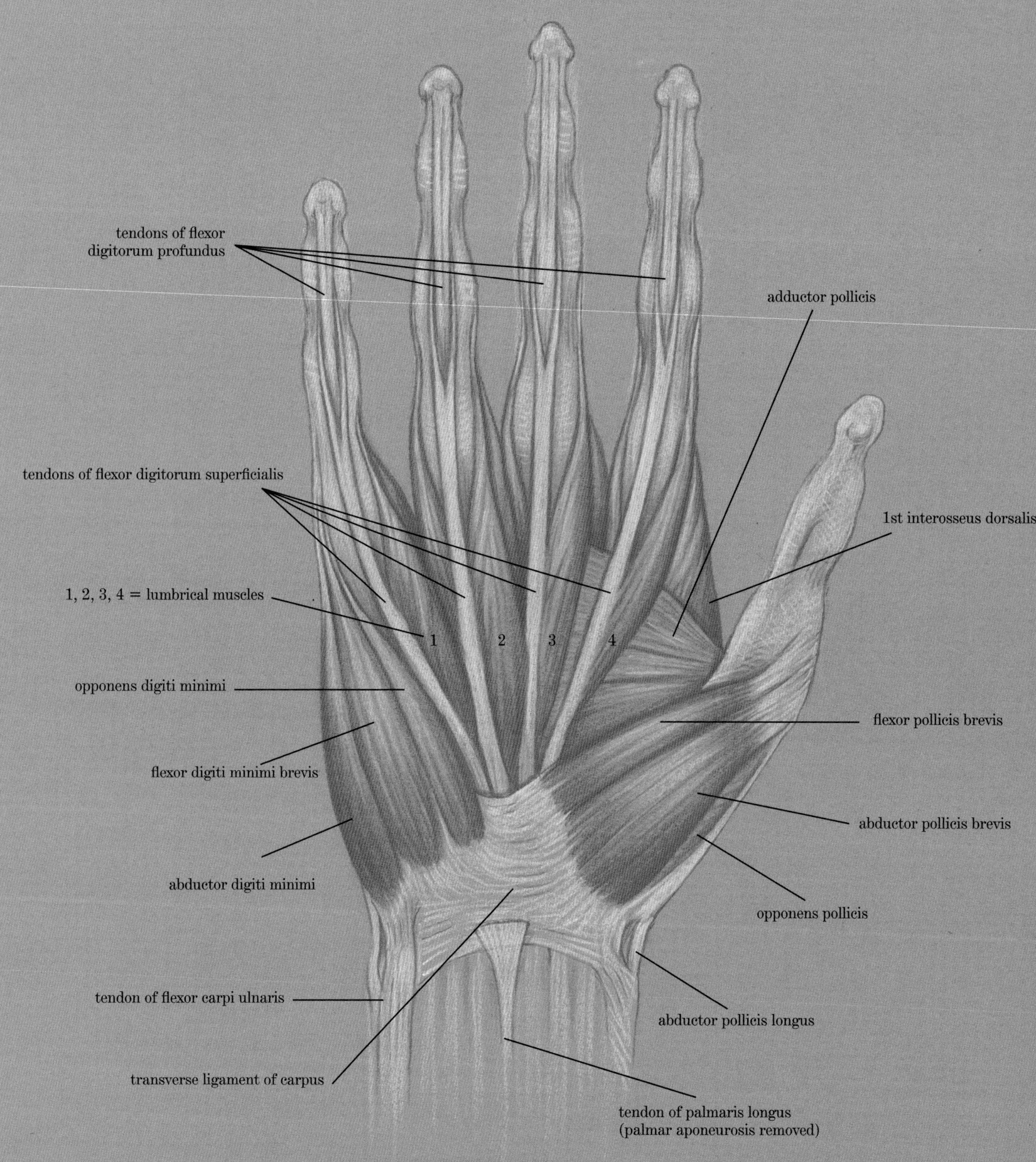

MUSCLES AND TENDONS OF THE HAND
(RIGHT HAND, PALMAR VIEW)

The image shows the superficial muscles of the palmar side of the hand with the palmar aponeurosis removed to better show the tendons of the flexors of the fingers.

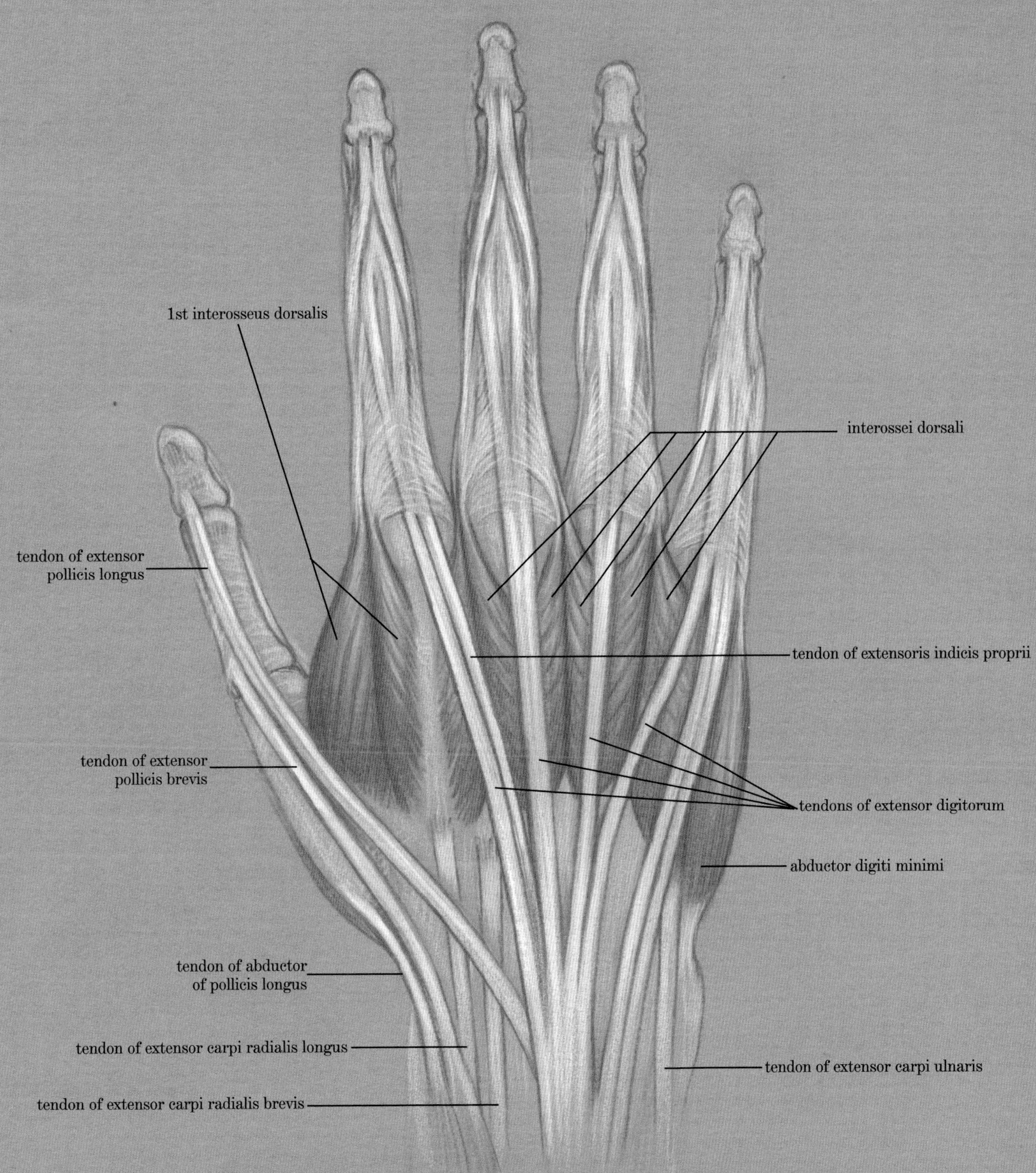

**MUSCLES AND TENDONS OF THE HAND
(RIGHT HAND, DORSAL VIEW)**

This image shows the amazing network of tendons connecting the muscles of the forearm with the wrist and fingers.

The drawings here show you how to recognize specific tendons of the hand. Connecting the tendons with specif- ic movements can help you to appreciate the complexity and beauty of the hand and to retain the information.

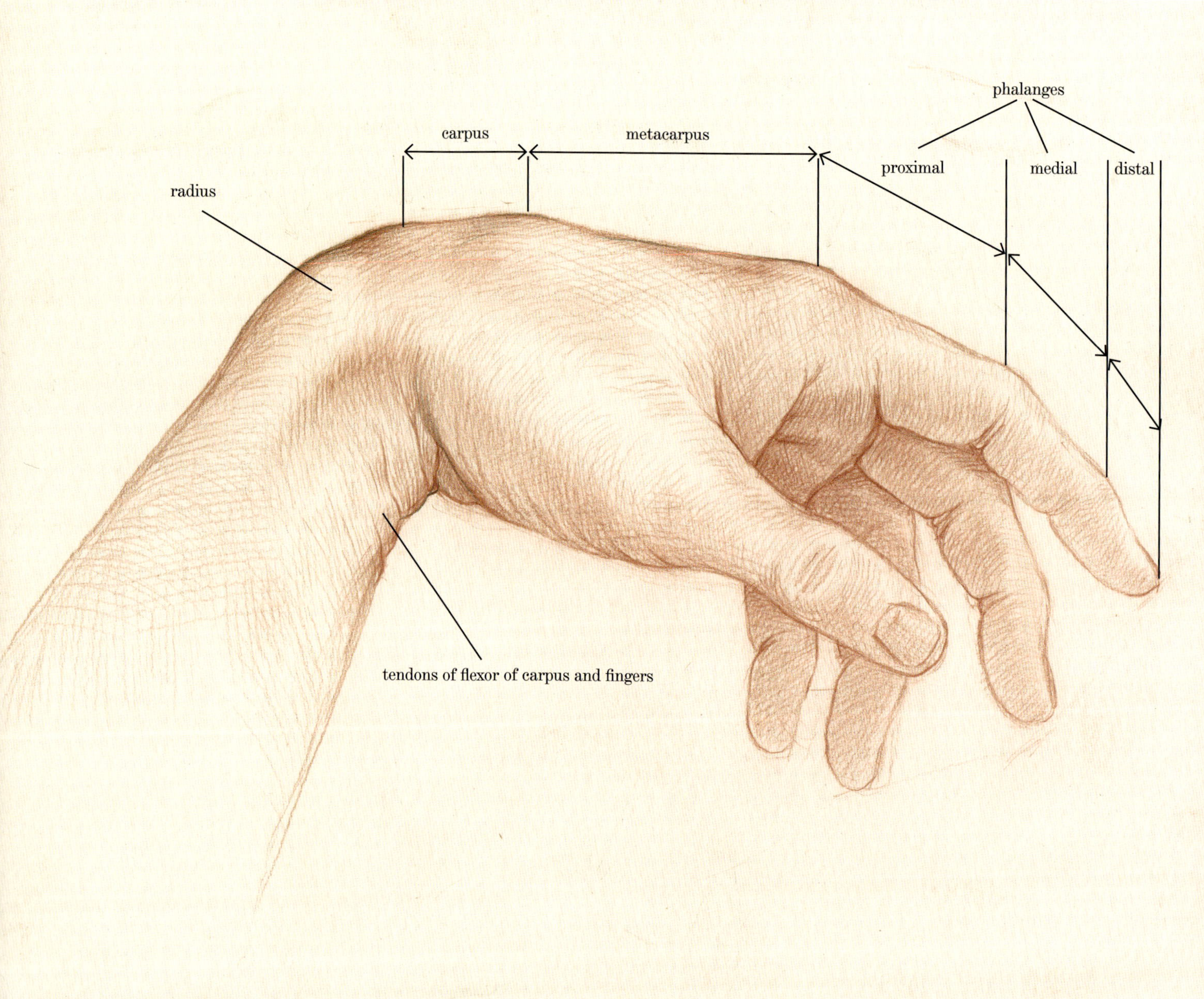

**SKELETAL FORMS AND
TENDONS ON THE HAND AND WRIST**

This image shows skeletal segments of the hand and their corre- sponding external forms.

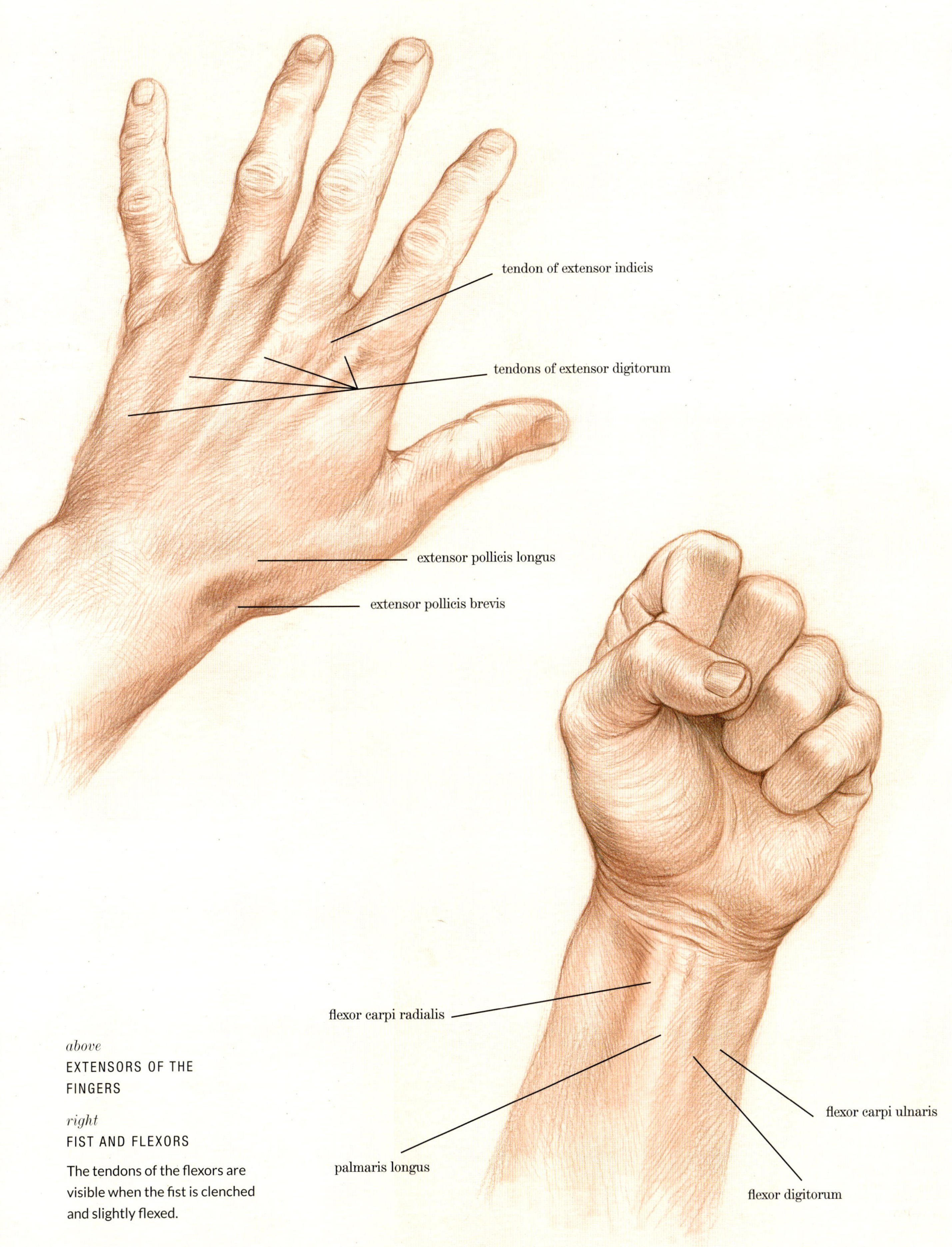

above

EXTENSORS OF THE FINGERS

right

FIST AND FLEXORS

The tendons of the flexors are visible when the fist is clenched and slightly flexed.

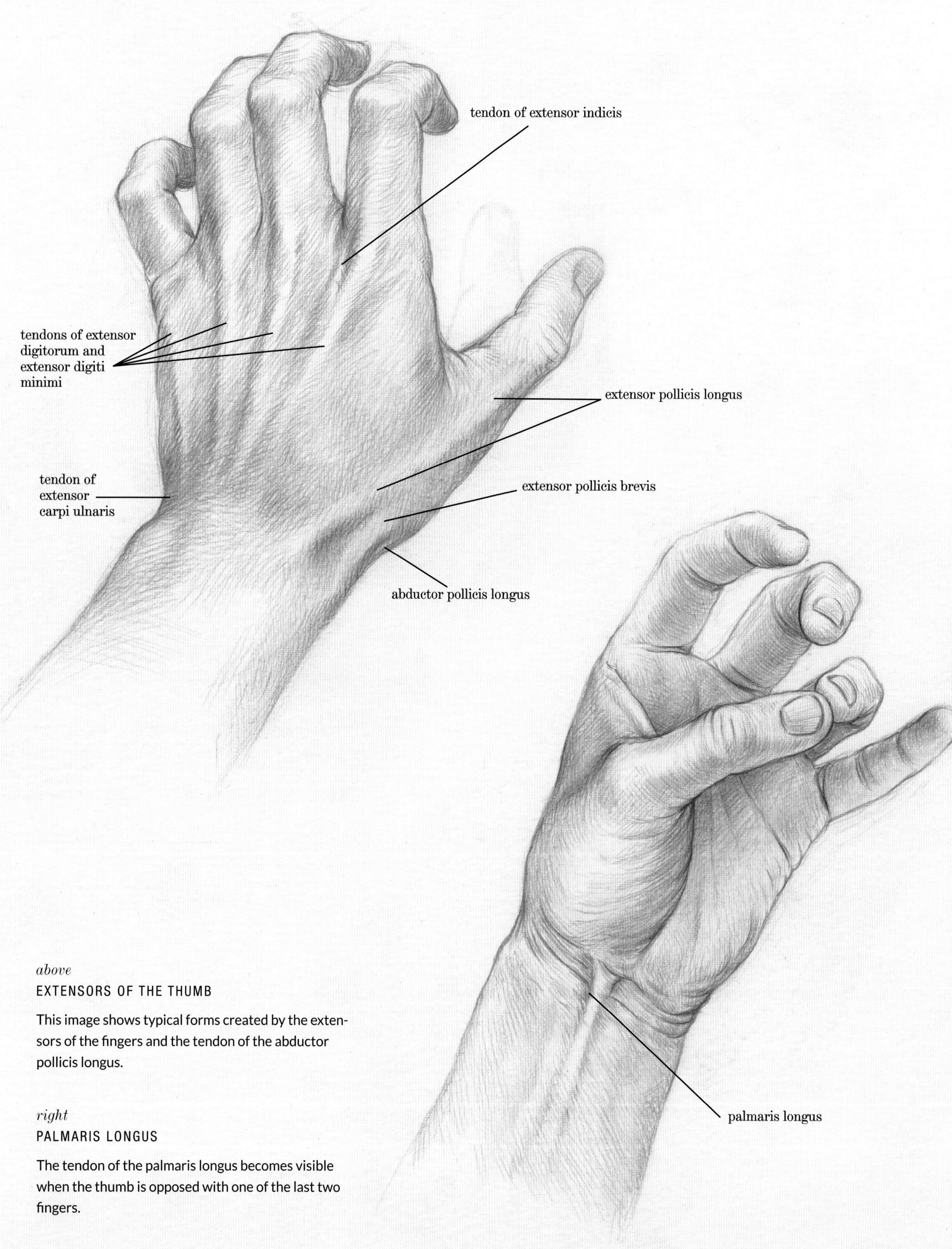

above

EXTENSORS OF THE THUMB

This image shows typical forms created by the extensors of the fingers and the tendon of the abductor pollicis longus.

right

PALMARIS LONGUS

The tendon of the palmaris longus becomes visible when the thumb is opposed with one of the last two fingers.

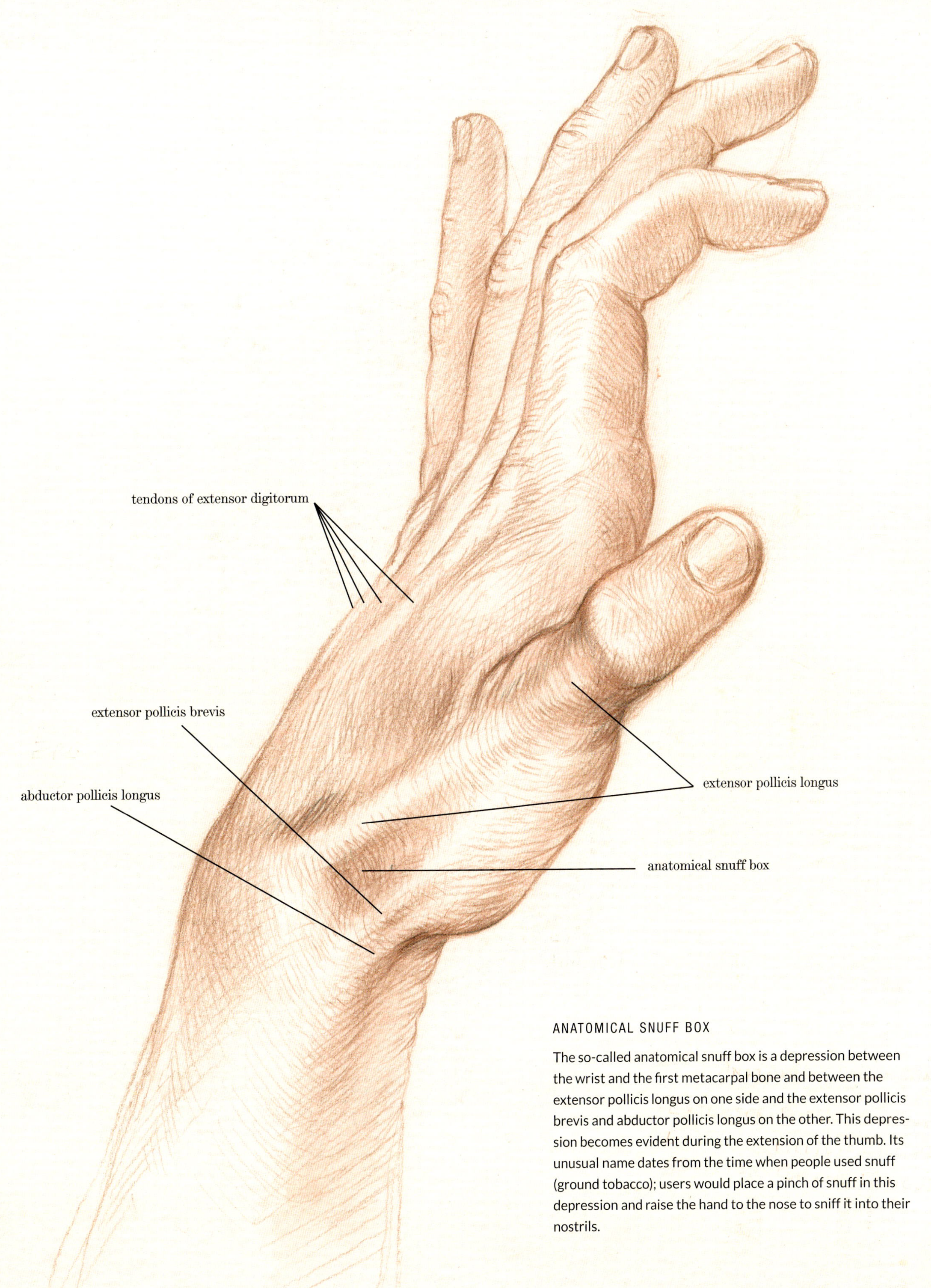

ANATOMICAL SNUFF BOX

The so-called anatomical snuff box is a depression between the wrist and the first metacarpal bone and between the extensor pollicis longus on one side and the extensor pollicis brevis and abductor pollicis longus on the other. This depression becomes evident during the extension of the thumb. Its unusual name dates from the time when people used snuff (ground tobacco); users would place a pinch of snuff in this depression and raise the hand to the nose to sniff it into their nostrils.

SCHEMATIC PROGRESSIONS FOR THE HAND

Drawing the complex forms of the hand in various poses is made easier by reducing the hand's various parts to basic volumes, as you have done for the rest of the body. The images here provide a few examples of how to conceptualize the hand.

PROGRESSION FOR DRAWING THE FINGERS

These steps will help you understand and draw the characteristic forms of the fingers.

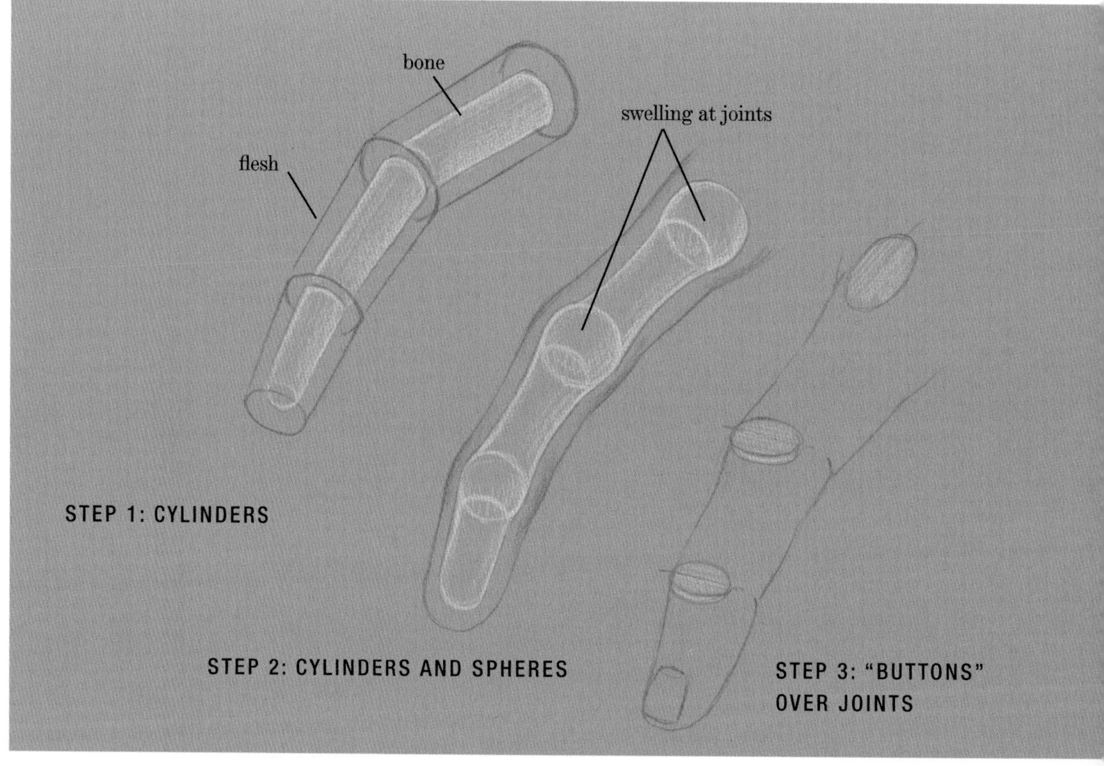

ESTABLISHING THE DIRECTIONS OF THE FINGERS

After establishing the main volume of the hand and the base of the fingers, you can mark their direction with simple lines and then develop the whole hand by adding volumes and details.

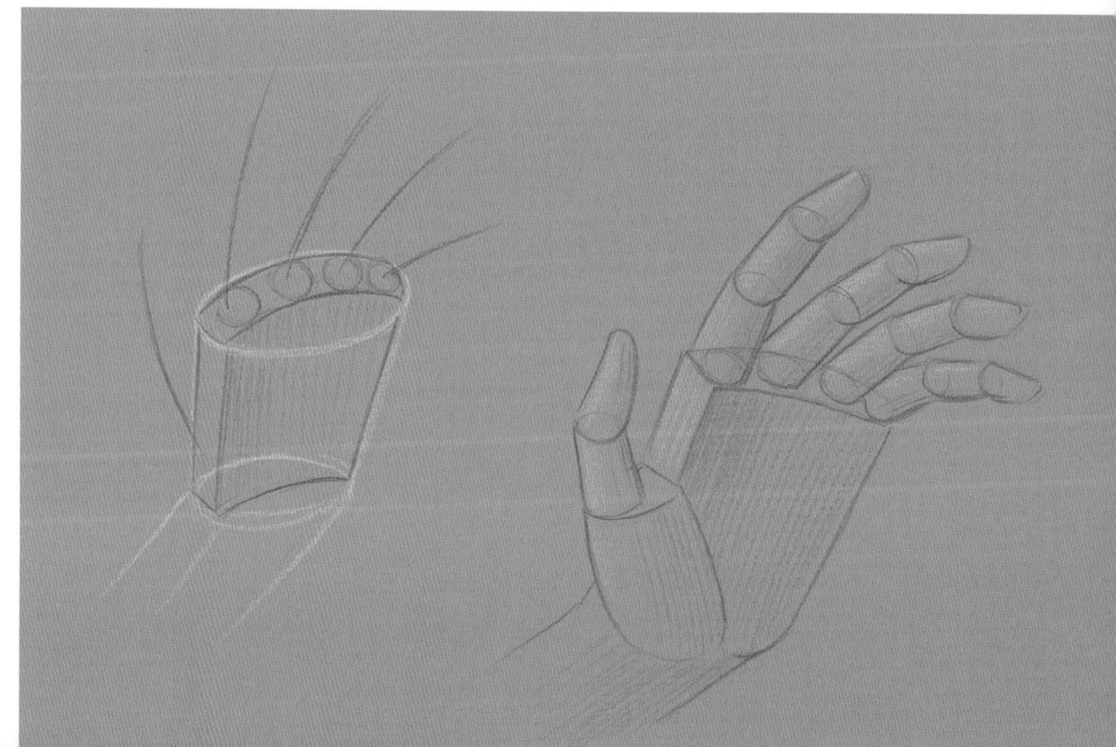

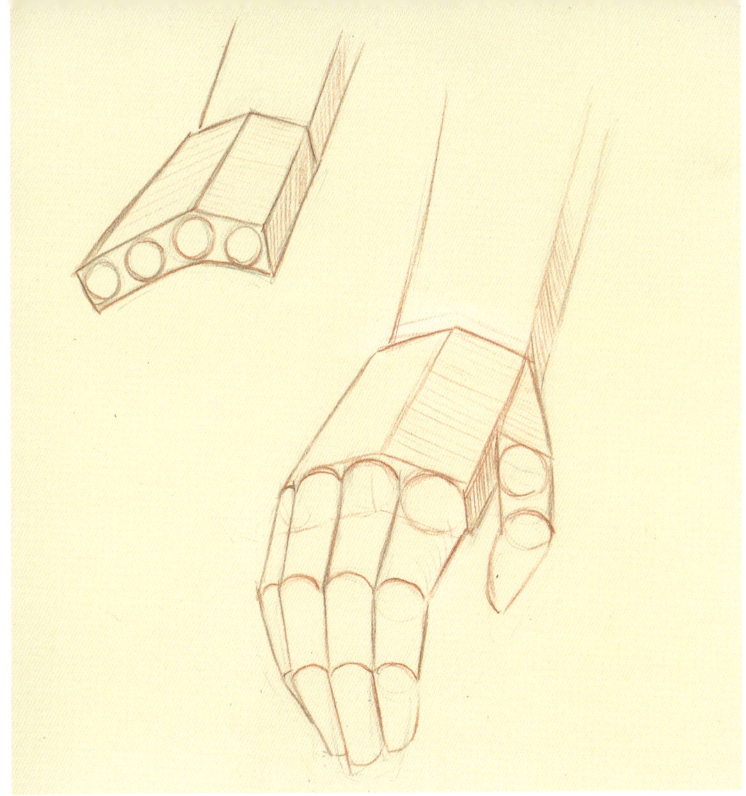

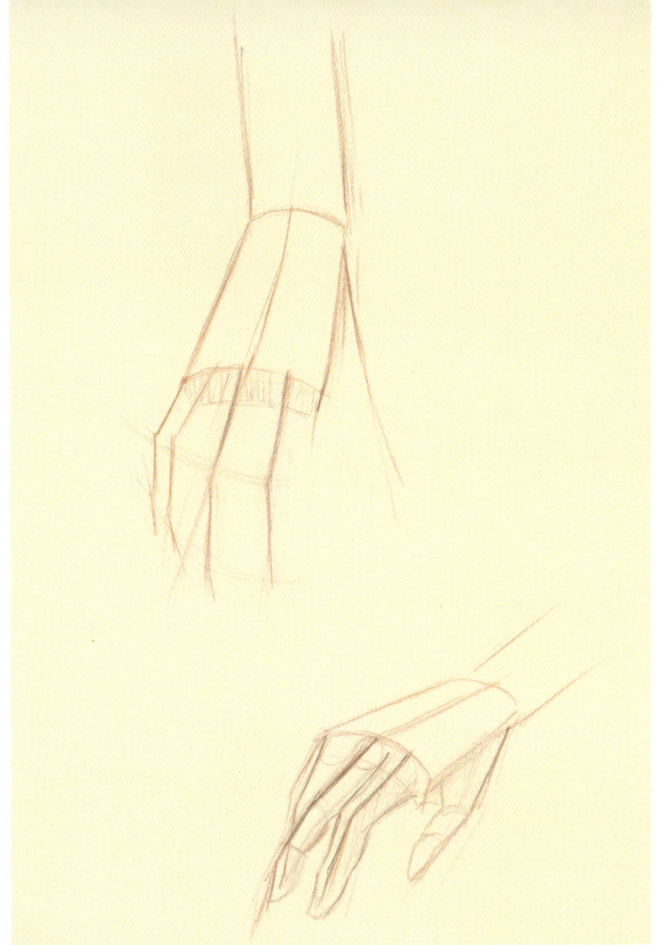

PEAK OF THE HAND ALIGNED WITH THE MIDDLE FINGER

In these images you can see how the peak of the back of the hand is aligned with the center of the middle finger.

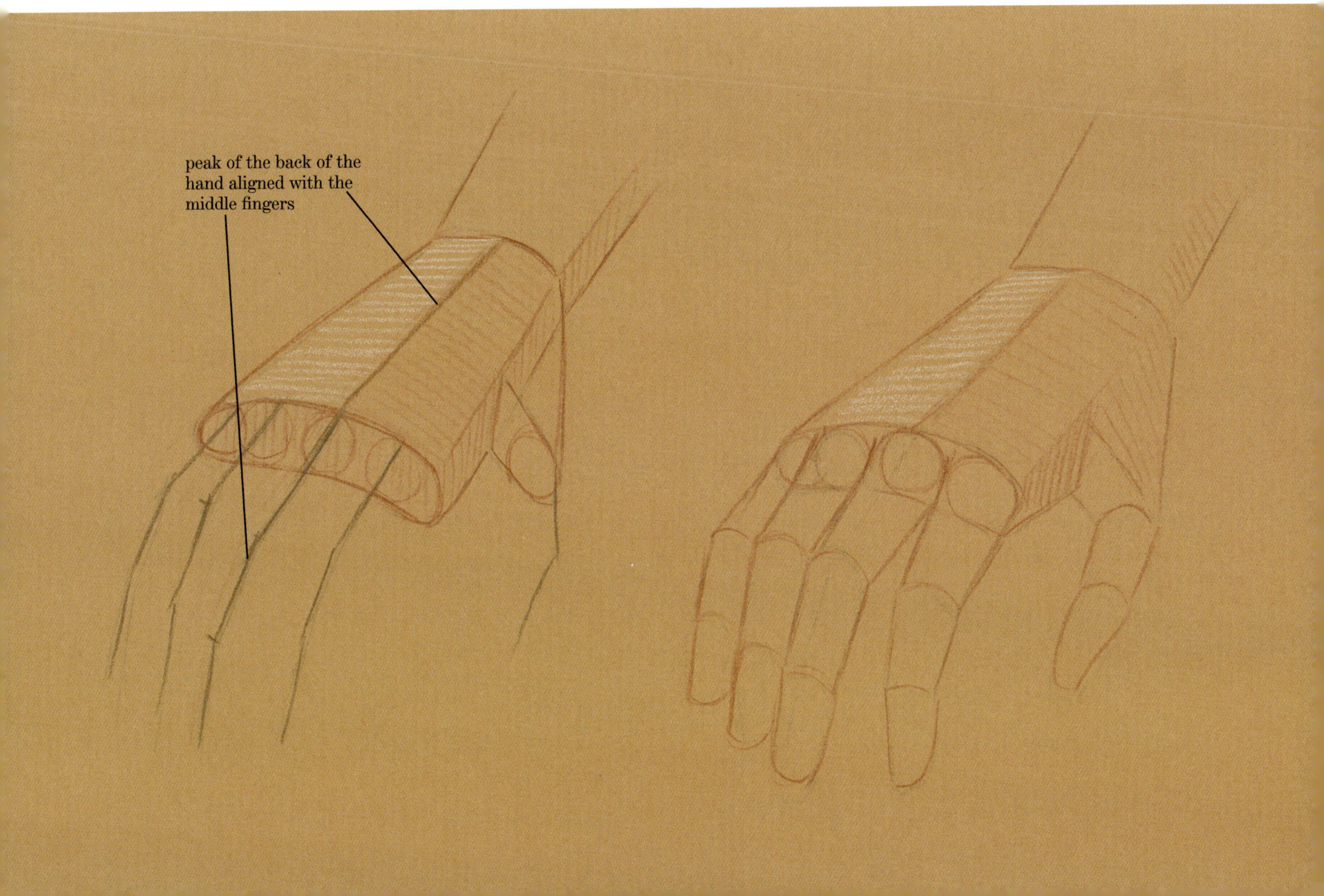

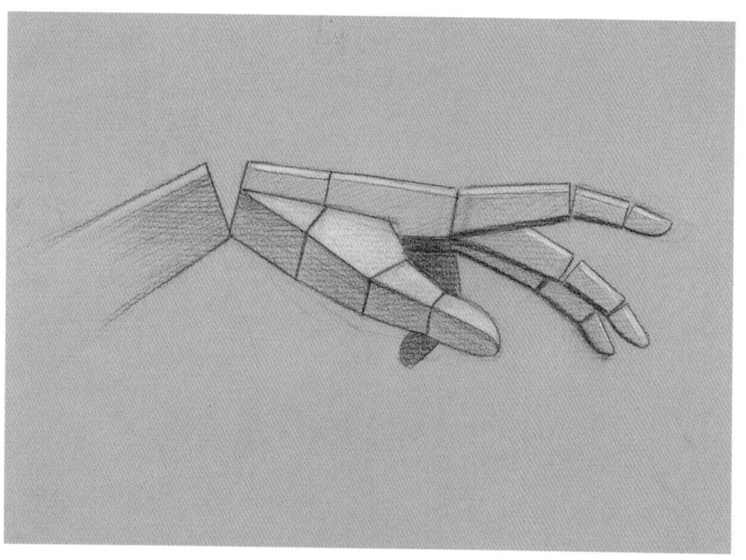
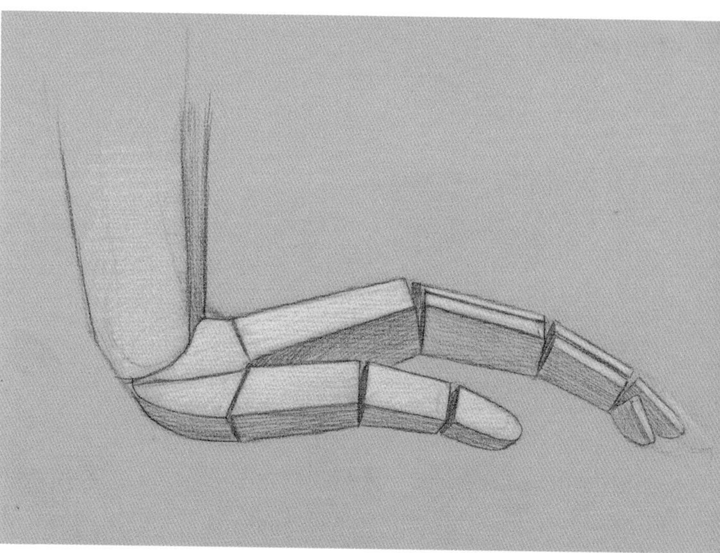
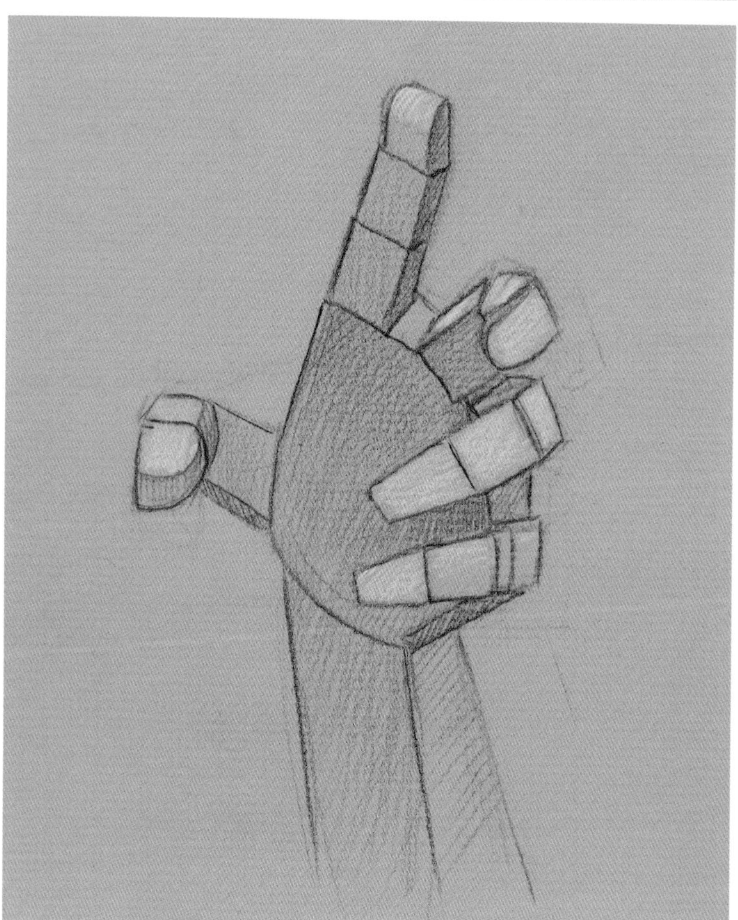
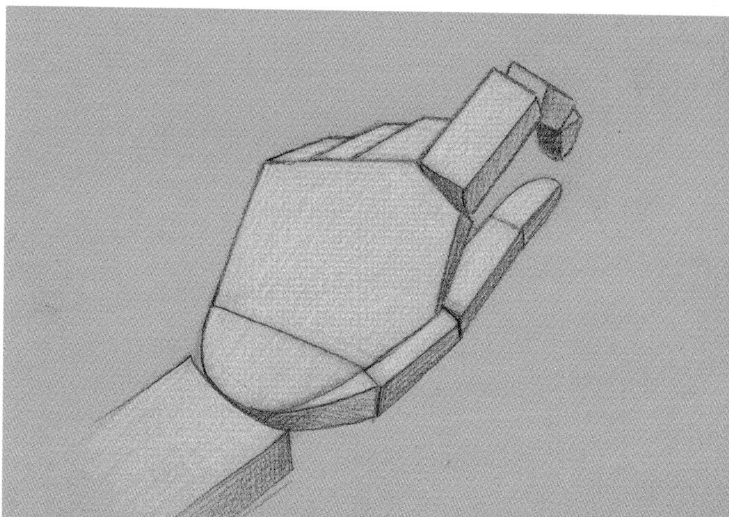
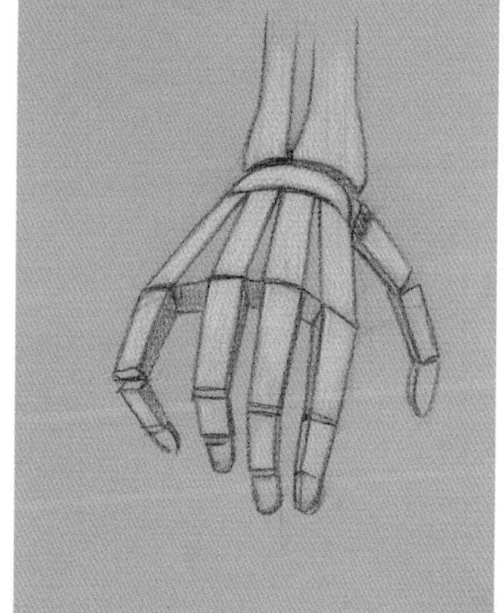
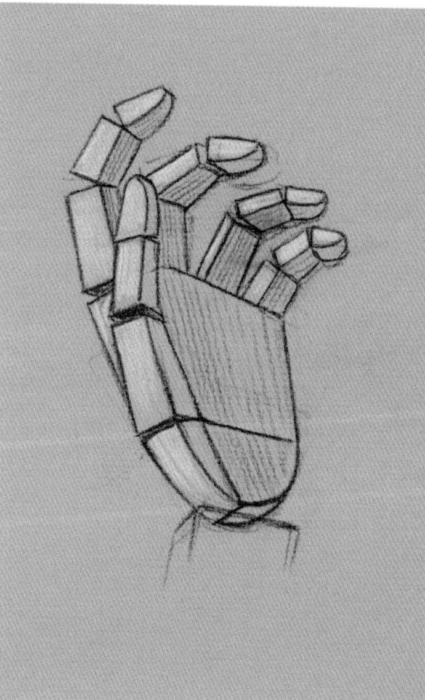

STEREOMETRIC INTERPRETATIONS OF THE HAND

These images show how stereometric renderings can be helpful when drawing the hand from life or imagination. The stereometric volumes make it easy to imagine complex hand positions and to place light and shadows on a drawing of the hand.

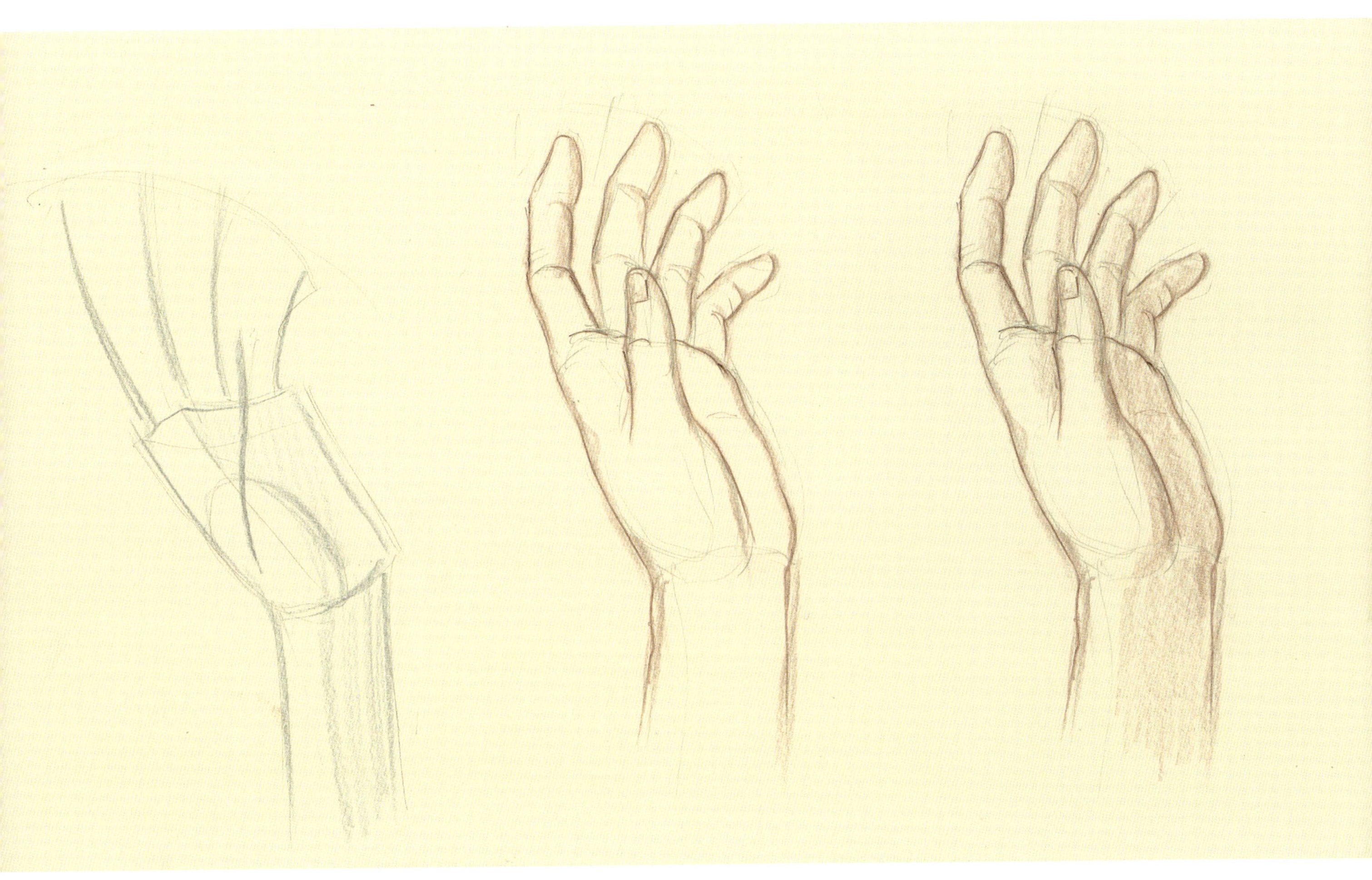

FROM STEREOMETRIC TO REALISTIC

Stereometric renderings can be helpful when drawing the hand from
life or imagination. Here, the drawing on the left shows a quick, almost
intuitive stereometric rendering of the hand. The drawing at center is
more realistic, and the hand on the right has been further enhanced
with a quick application of shadow to obtain a more volumetric effect.

PROPORTIONS AND SHAPES OF THE FEET

The form of the foot is not as complex as that of the hand, but subtleties in the form of the foot makes it equally difficult to draw. Creating simplified, schematic forms, as in the figures below, can be very helpful.

The small schematic rendering (1) is puppet-like, showing only the most basic of the foot's planes; the larger rendering (2) defines more specific planes, including those created by the angles of the toes.

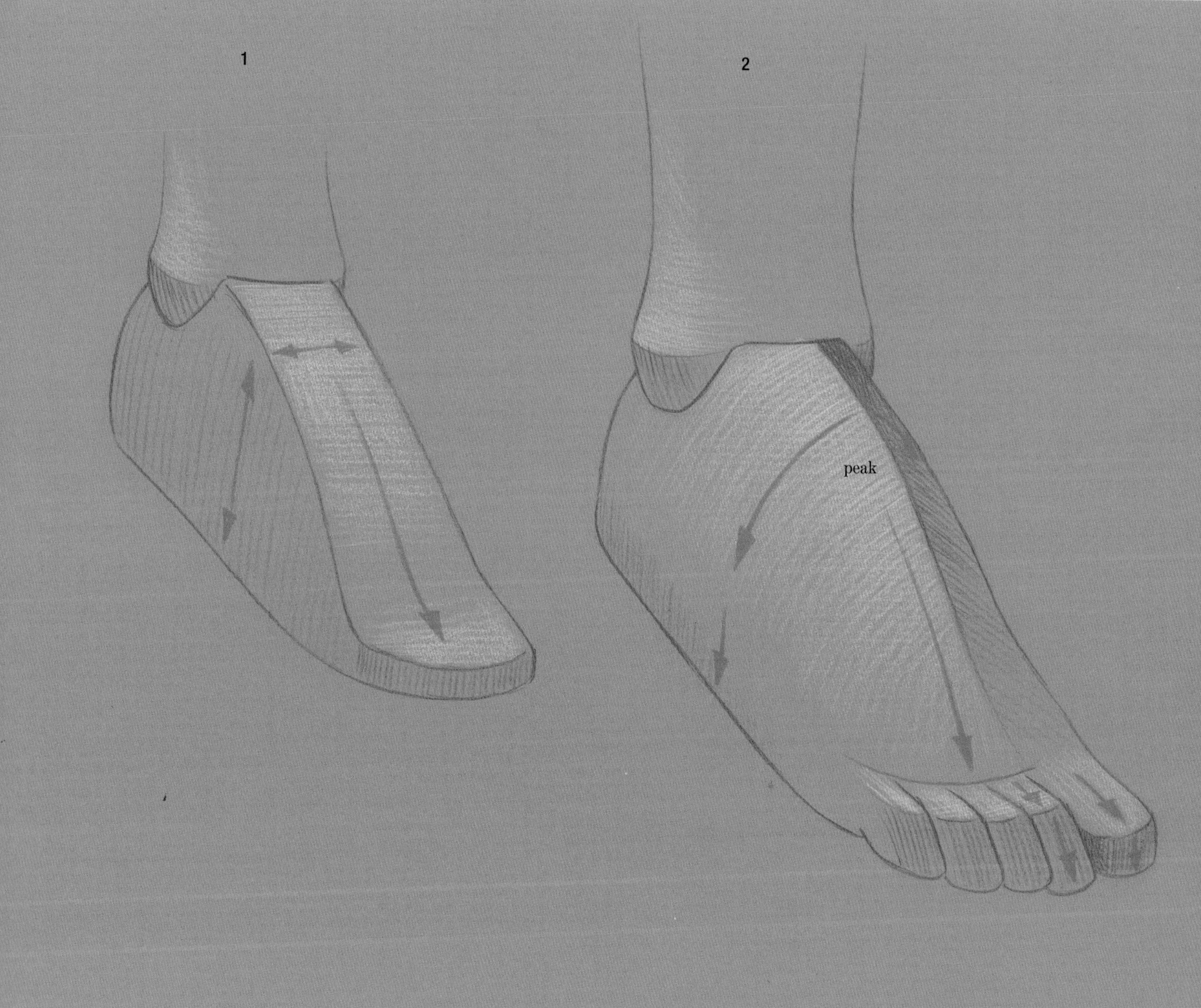

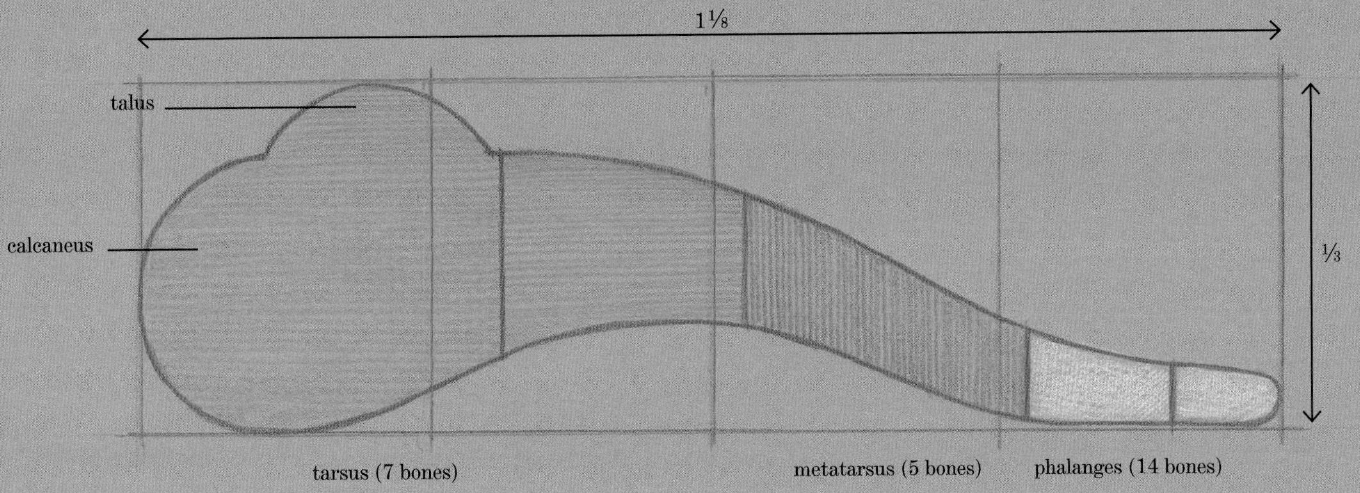

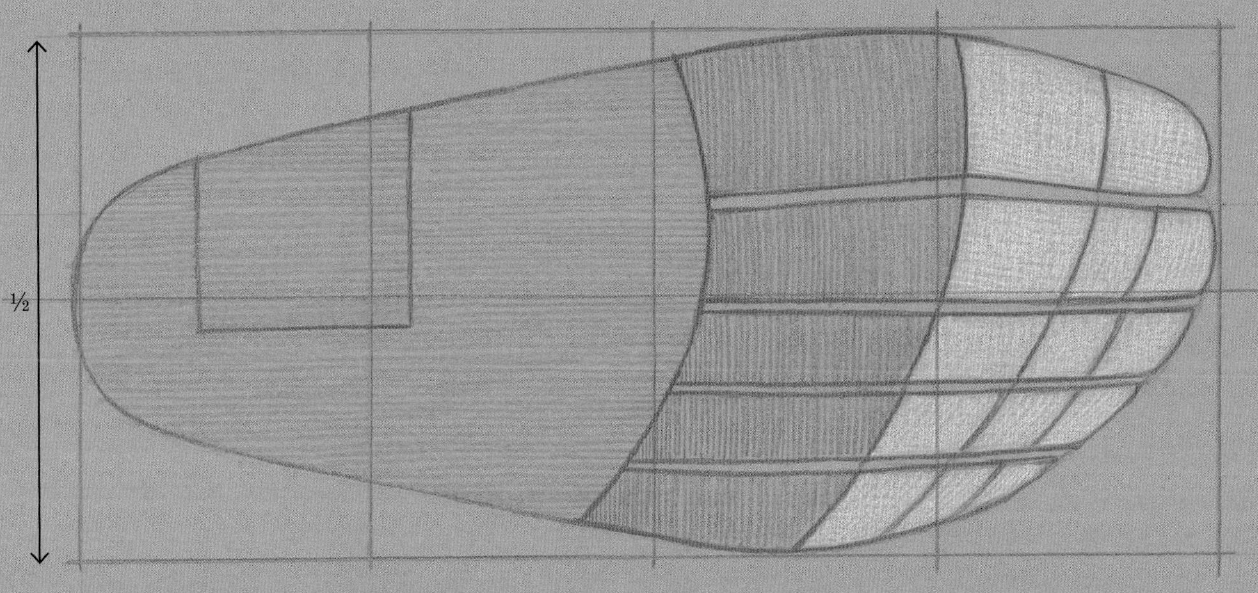

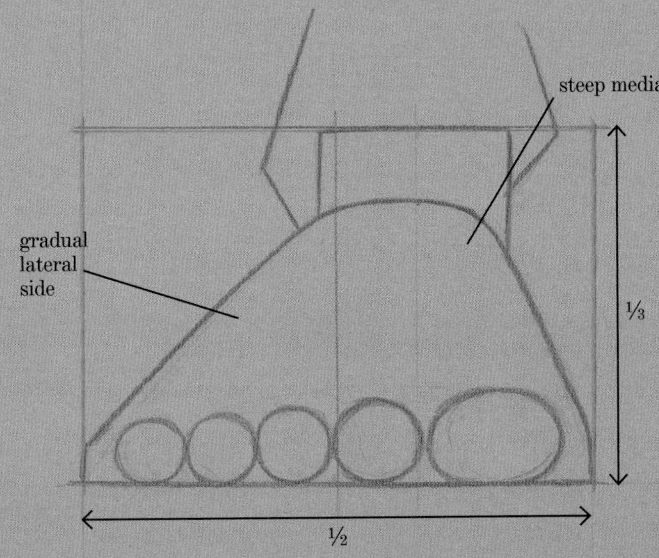

SCHEMATIC VIEWS OF THE MEDIAL SIDE, TOP, AND FRONT OF THE FOOT

The length of the foot is typically a little longer than the length of the head. Its height is about one-third of one head. The posterior half of the foot is occupied by the tarsus, the anterior half by the metatarsus and phalanges.

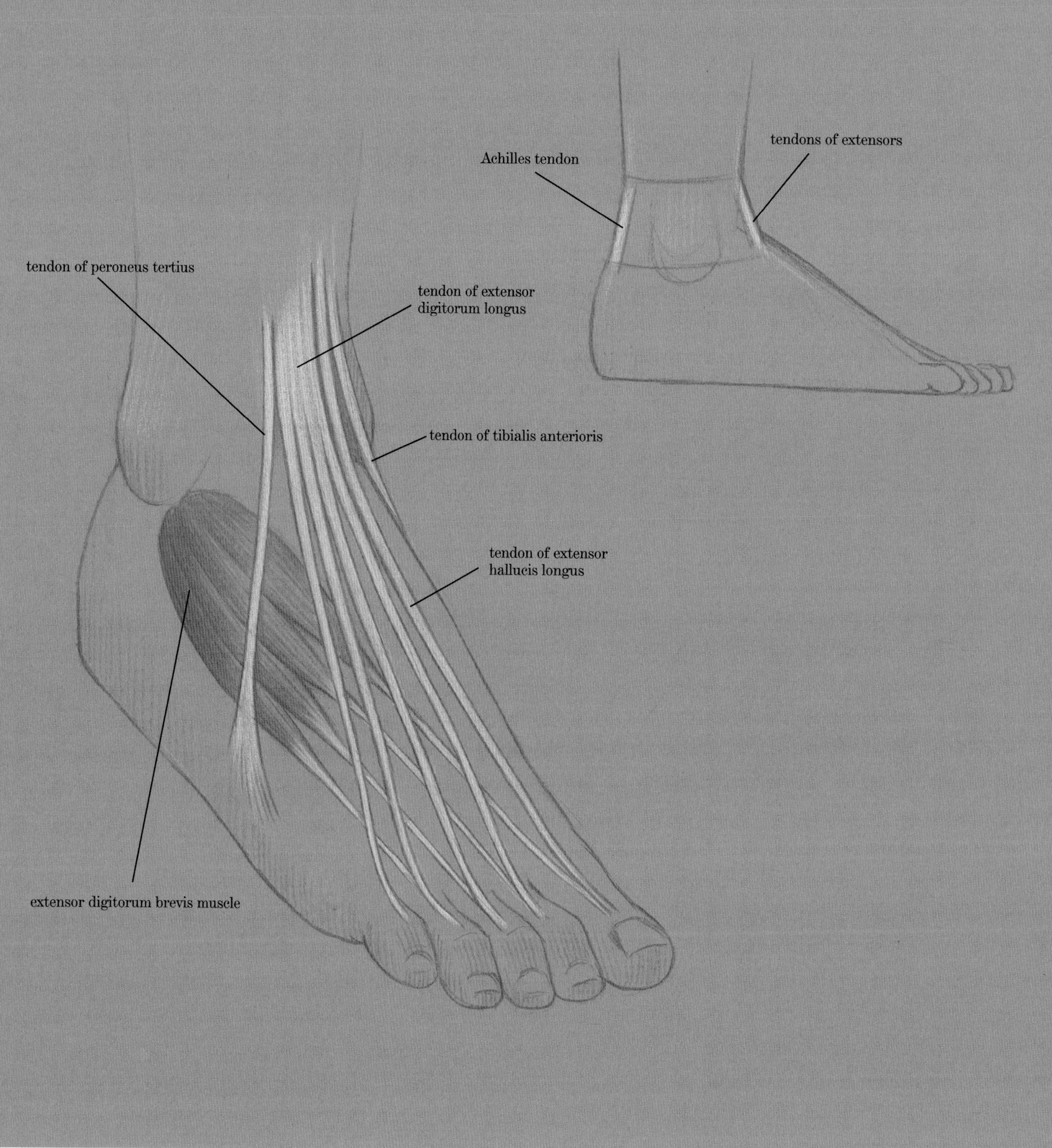

TENDONS OF THE FOOT

The larger, three-quarters view of the foot shows the complex pattern of the tendons of the foot. The smaller, the side view of the foot, shows how its widening profile at the ankles is created by the Achilles tendon posteriorly and the extensors of the toes anteriorly.

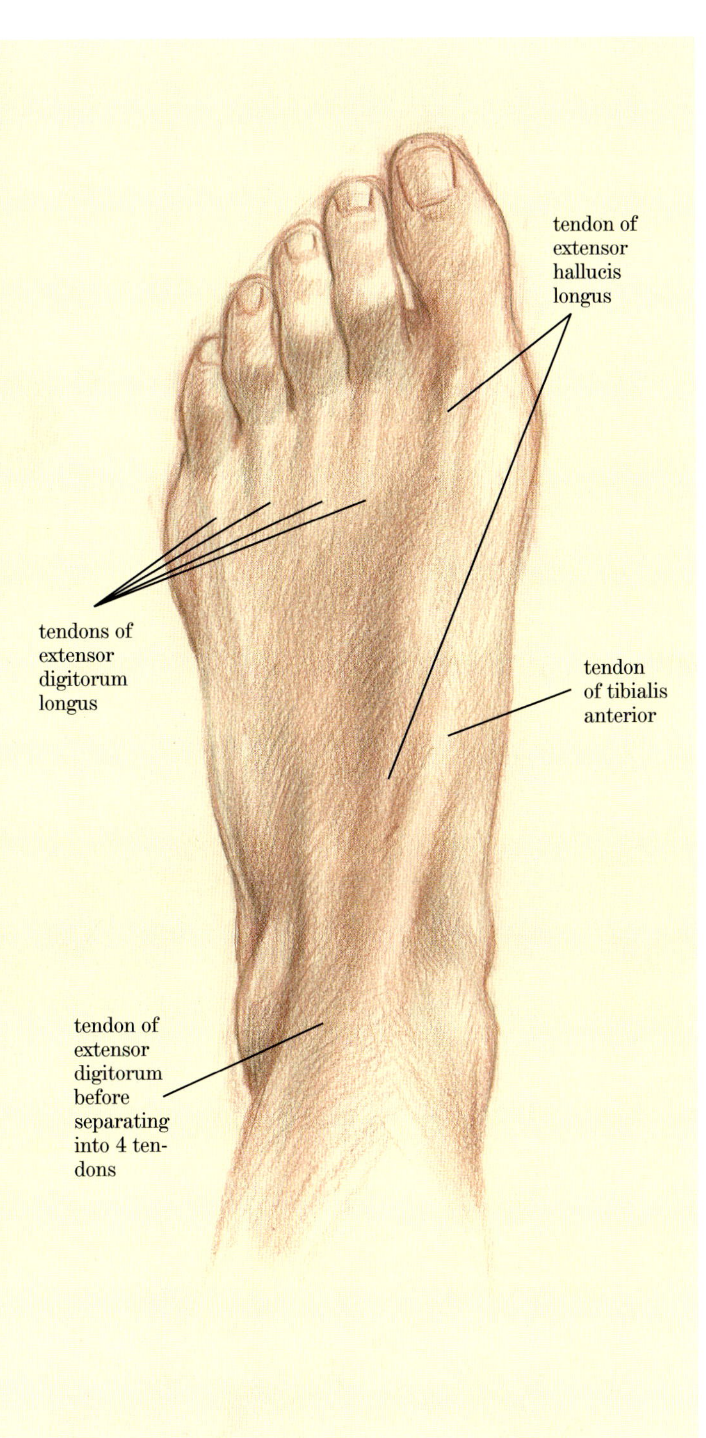

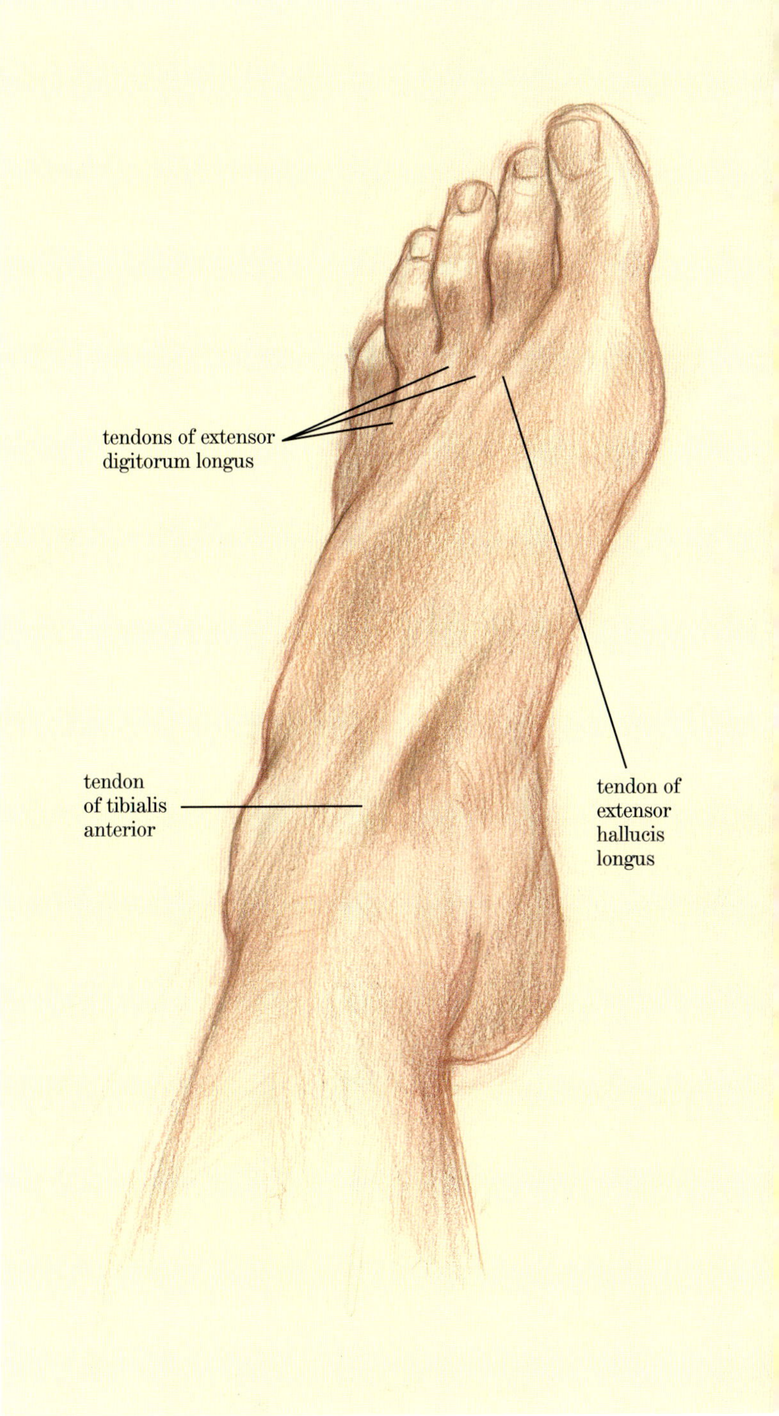

TENDONS OF THE DORSAL SIDE OF THE FOOT

These images of fully rendered feet show how several important
tendons are visible on the foot's surface.

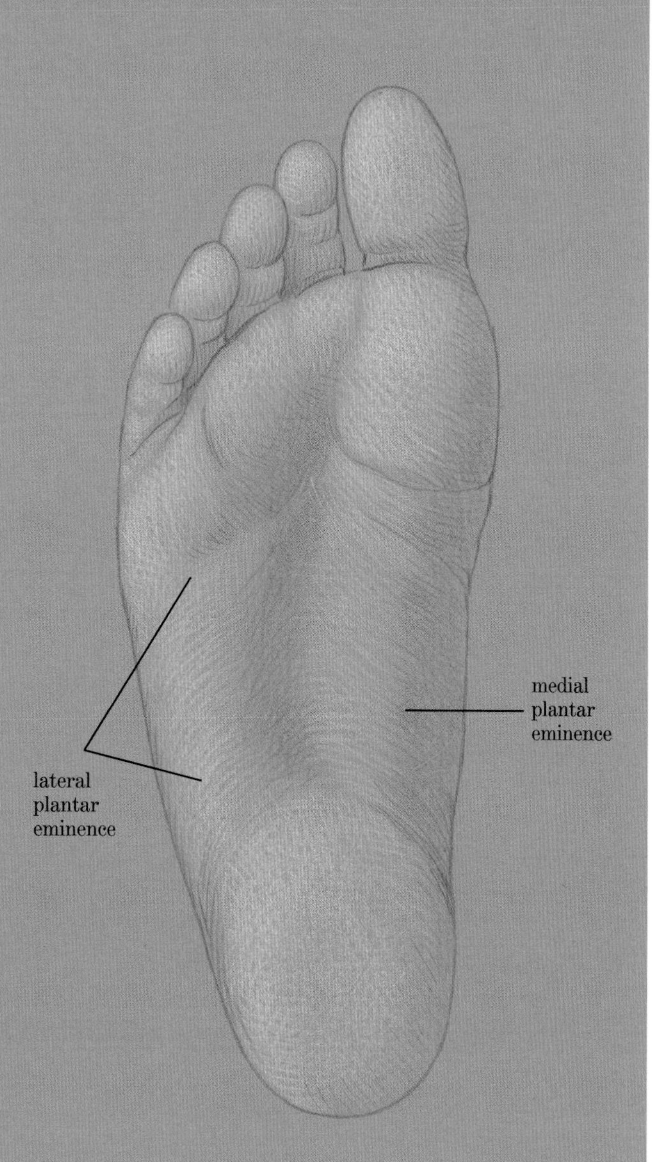

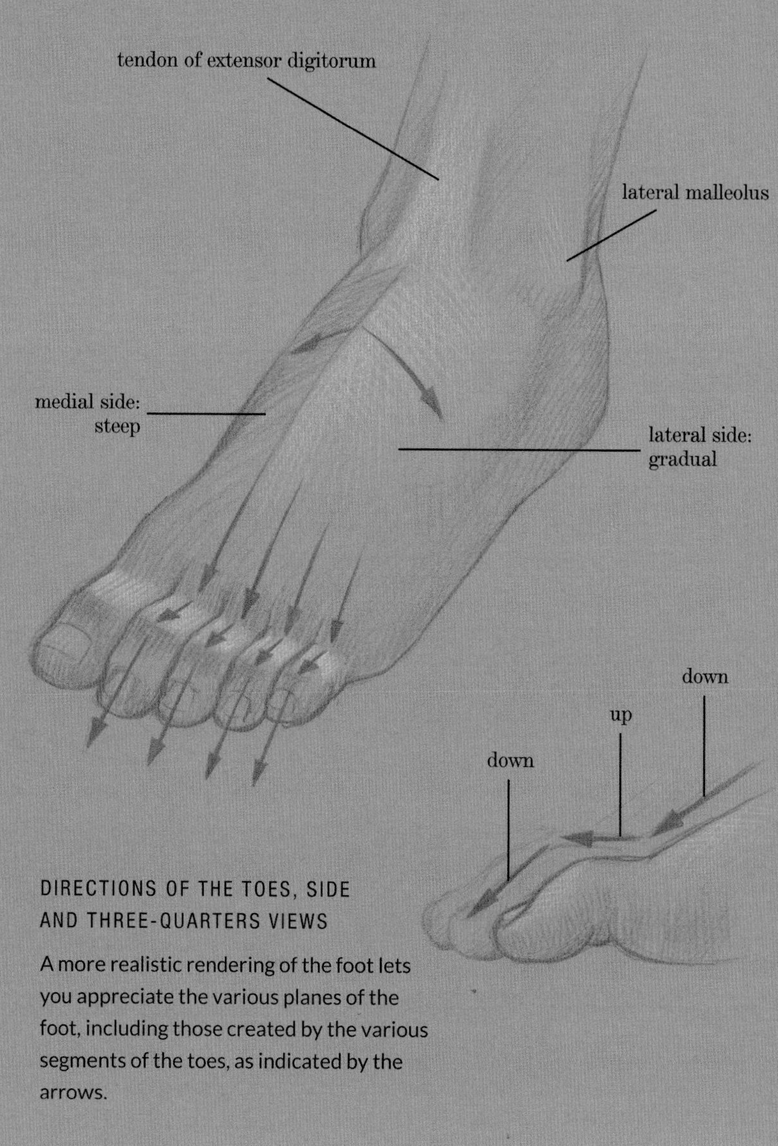

DIRECTIONS OF THE TOES, SIDE AND THREE-QUARTERS VIEWS

A more realistic rendering of the foot lets you appreciate the various planes of the foot, including those created by the various segments of the toes, as indicated by the arrows.

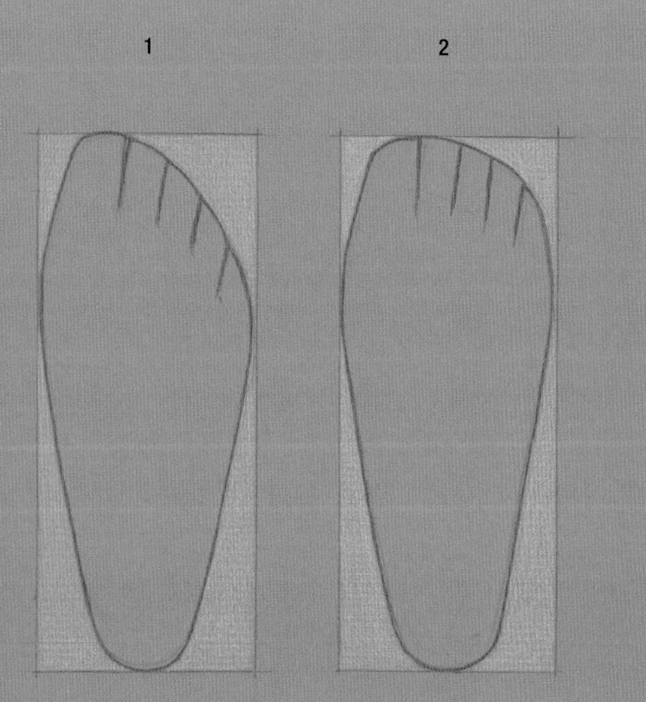

above left

EMINENCES OF THE FOOT, PLANTAR VIEW

This image shows the main eminences of the foot on its plantar side.

left

TWO BASIC FOOT SHAPES

The next time you take a walk on the beach, pay attention to the various footprints in the sand, and you will see a variety of foot types. Here are two of the most common. In footprint 1, the great toe (hallucis) protrudes beyond the other toes, which align to create a sharply declining curve. In footprint 2, the great toe and the second toe have a similar length, and the other toes are arranged along a much less pronounced curve. Sometimes the second toe is longer than the great toe (not shown). The contour of the foot also changes depending on whether it is being stood on or lifted off the ground.

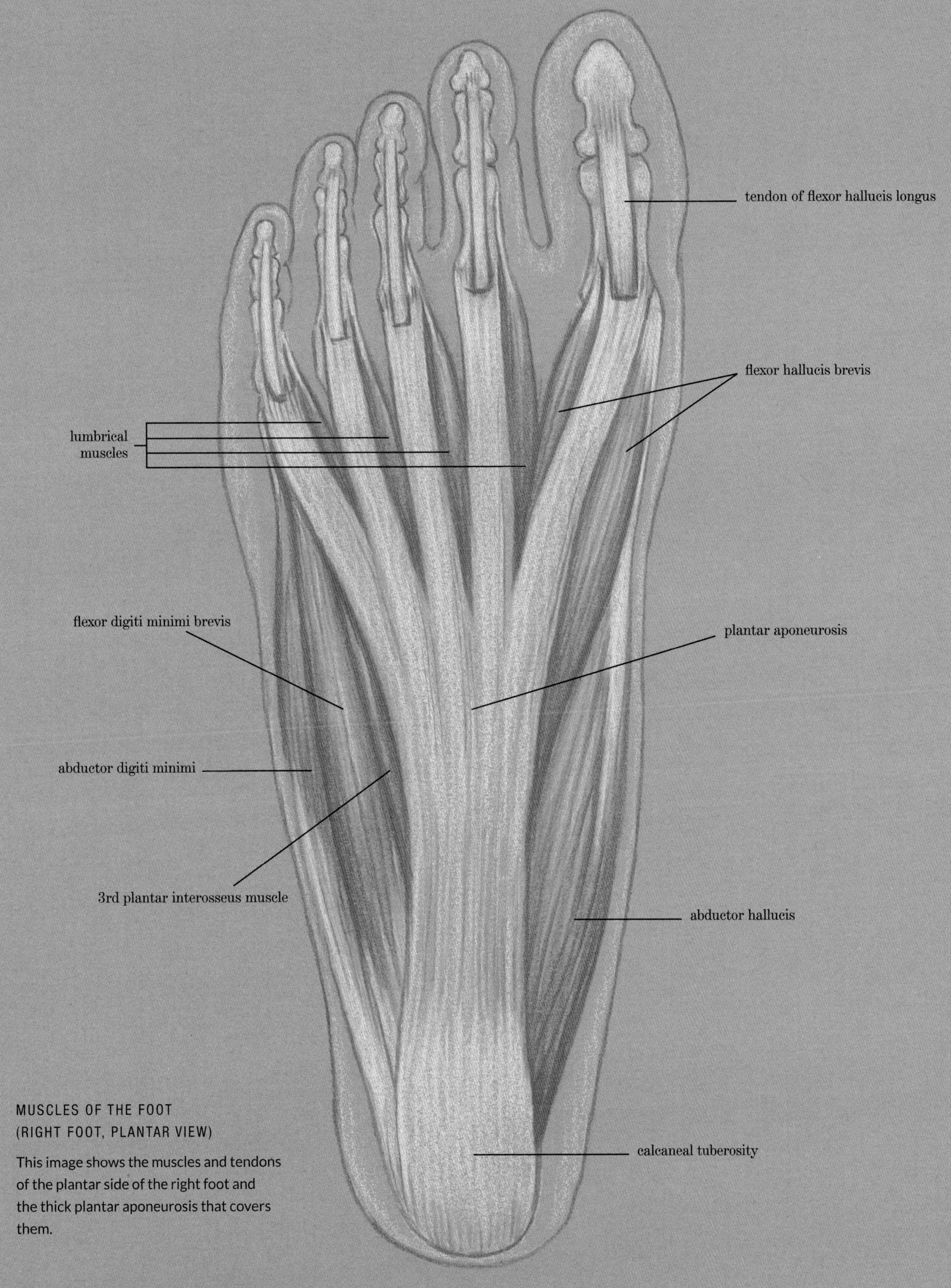

MUSCLES OF THE FOOT
(RIGHT FOOT, PLANTAR VIEW)

This image shows the muscles and tendons of the plantar side of the right foot and the thick plantar aponeurosis that covers them.

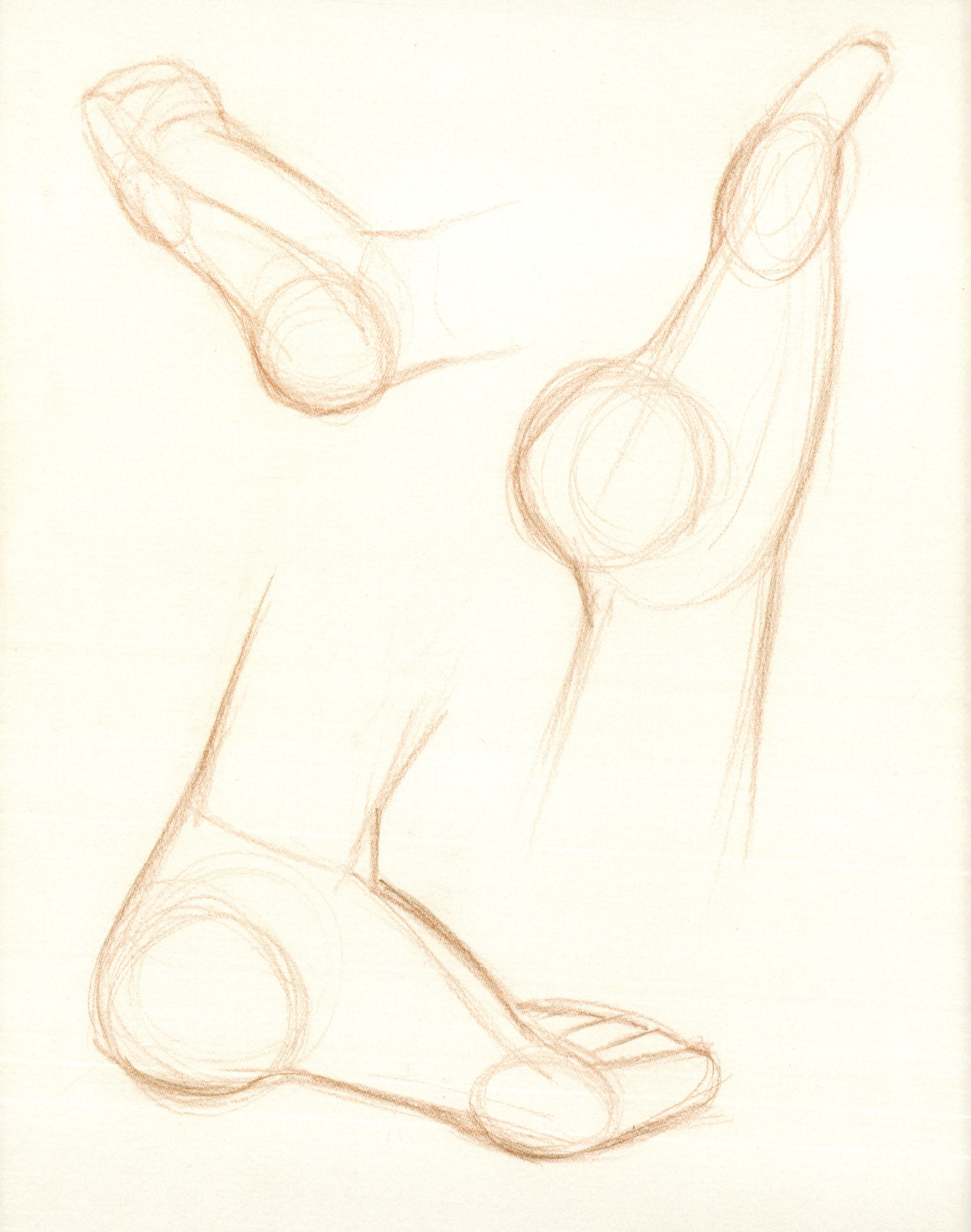

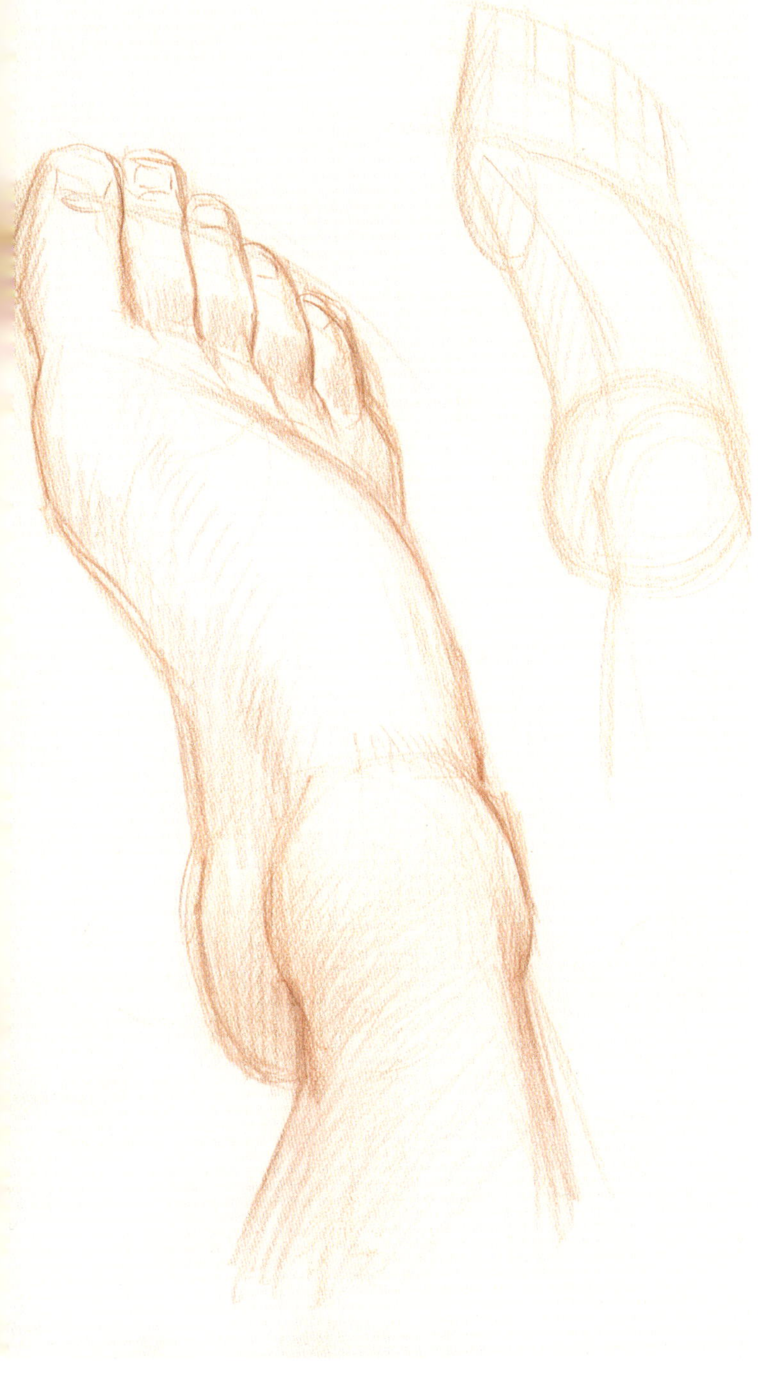

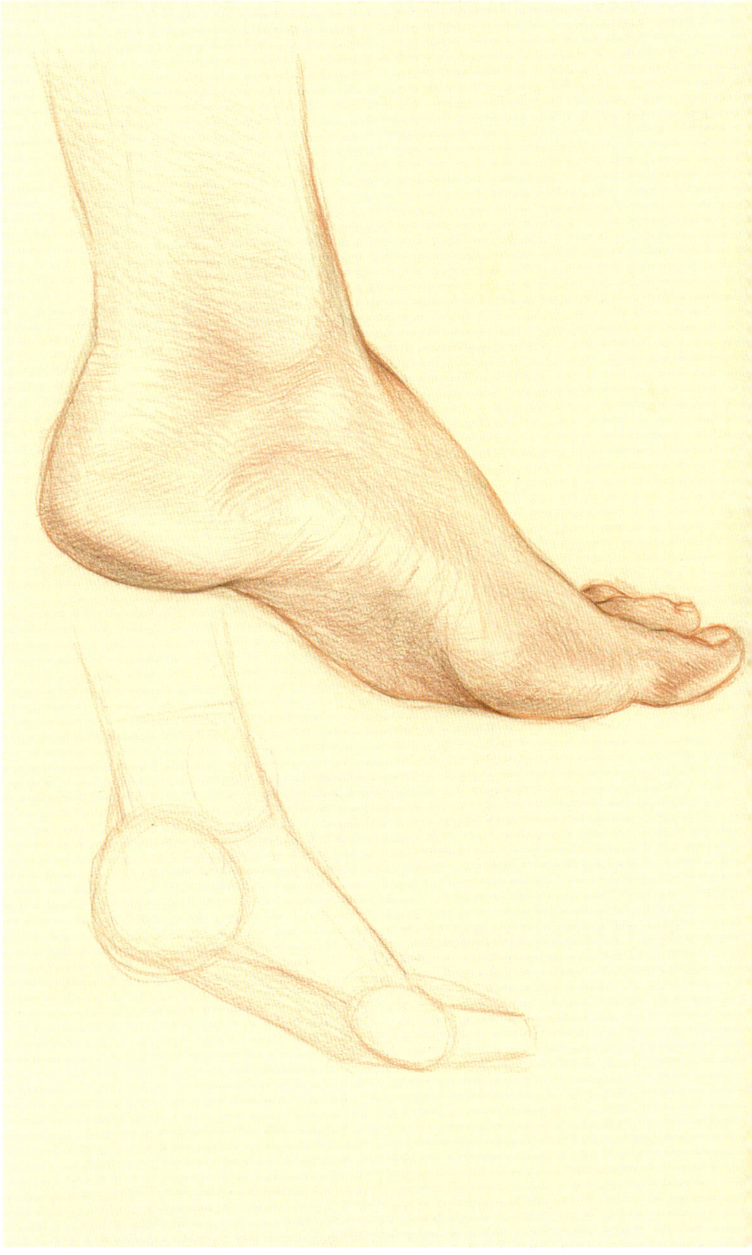

DRAWING THE FOOT—FROM SIMPLIFIED TO REALISTIC FORM

These images show a progression you can follow when drawing the foot. Start by reducing the foot to very simple forms, then gradually add more detail until the foot is fully rendered.

EXERCISES

The hands have a beautiful complexity that is notoriously difficult to draw, but if you draw them as often as you can you will soon gain the necessary skill. Try drawing your hand during idle moments on the bus or train or at home, using a small sketchbook for this purpose. You can, of course, also use your own bare feet as models for practice.

EXERCISE 1: DRAW YOUR HAND

Draw your hand—the one you don't use for drawing!—from life, but reduce it to its basic geometric forms. Concentrate only on the basic volumes, starting with very simple poses and gradually moving to more complex ones. Define the light and shadow masses to better understand the volumetric qualities of the hand.

EXERCISE 2: RENDER YOUR HAND MORE REALISTICALLY

Now move on to drawing more realistic renderings of your hand. Start by sketching the geometric shapes, but draw them very lightly, making the lines barely visible. The sketch is just to help you loosely visualize the pose and to guide you as you draw the hand more accurately and realistically.

EXERCISE 3: DRAW YOUR HAND IN MORE COMPLEX POSES

When you've mastered the basic proportions of the hand, move on to more complex poses. If the poses are too straining to hold for very long, take photos of them and work from the photos. It is always best to work from life, but it is also important to learn to use photographic references.

EXERCISE 4: DRAW YOUR HAND HOLDING OBJECTS

Now draw your hand holding a variety of objects of different sizes and shapes: a marble, a golf ball, a baseball, a pencil, a cup or glass, handles of several types, and so on. The objects you hold will hide part of the hand, but draw the whole hand, even the part that you don't see. Think of the hand as a transparent form so that you can gain a better idea of its three-dimensionality, and also draw the object as if it were transparent. Keep the lines very light until you have the structure correct, then use the sketch as a guide when rendering the hand more realistically and tonally.

EXERCISE 5: DRAW YOUR FEET

In the evening—maybe when you're watching TV—take off your socks and sketch your feet in various positions. Follow the same approaches used for the hand, above, to create different levels of conceptualization.

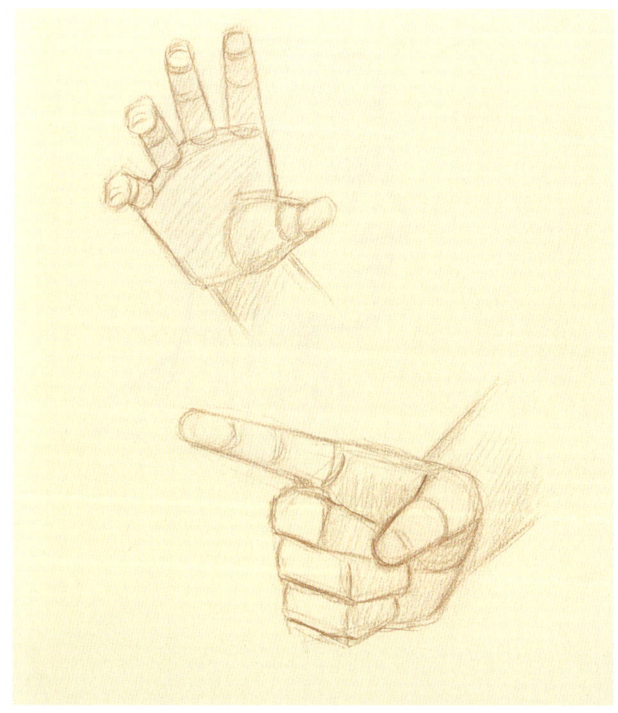

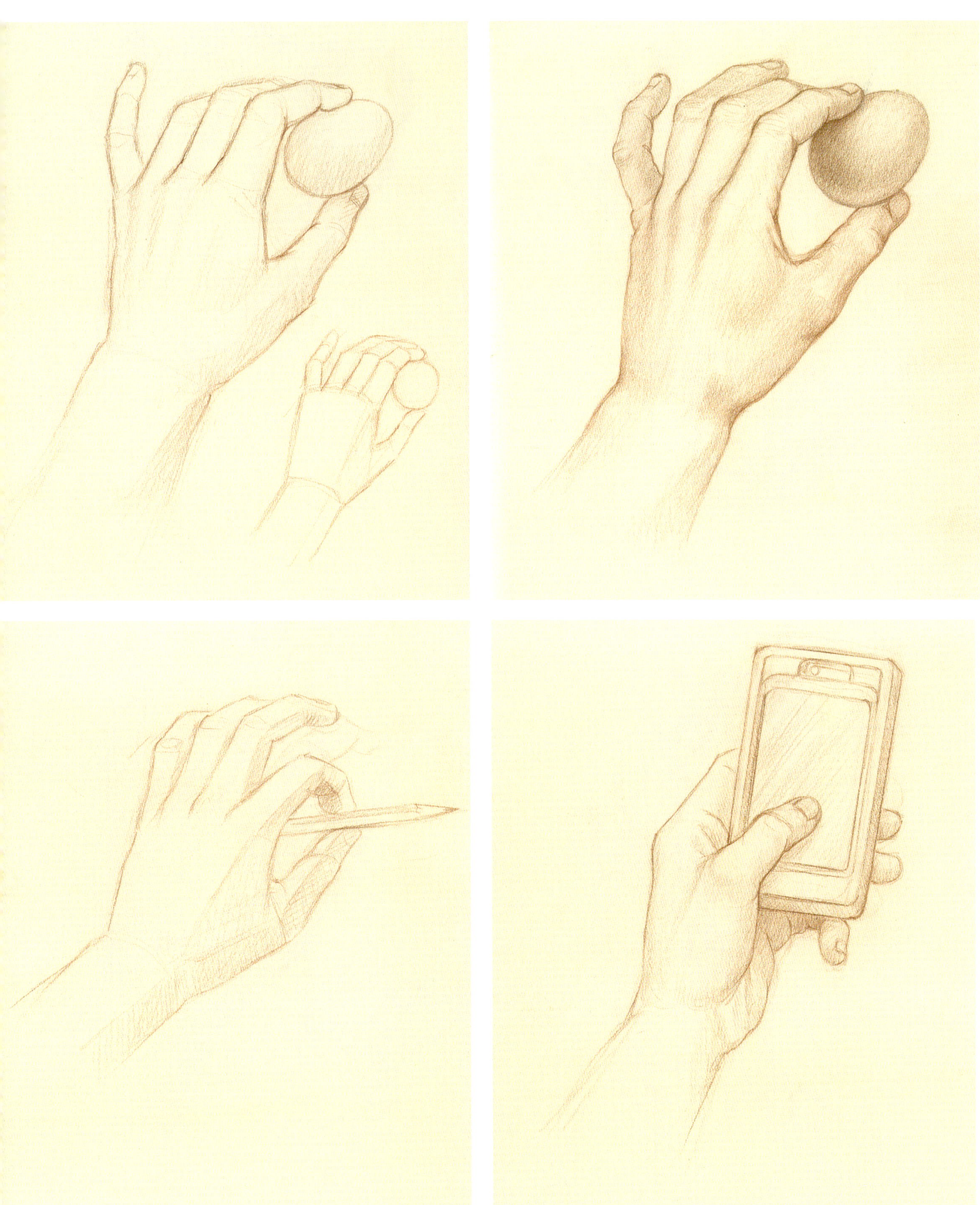

DRAW WITHOUT MEASURING

Eventually, you will get to the point where you can draw the figure without first sketching any volumes or landmarks or using any other measuring techniques. This will happen when you have internalized the measurements, proportions, and forms of the figure and your hand can create lines informed by this knowledge. You should try this exercise periodically. The figures here show the approach.

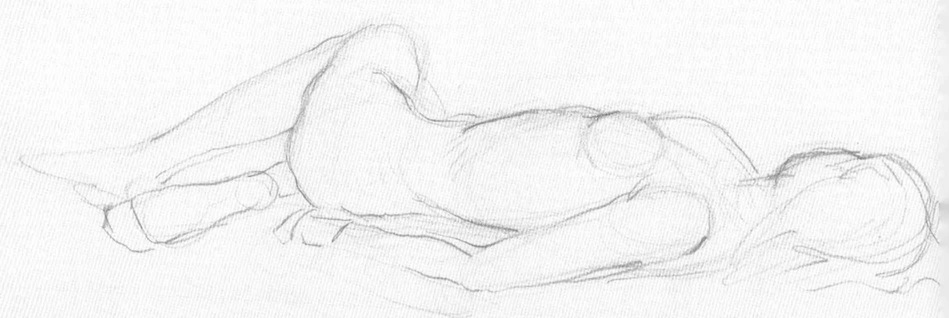

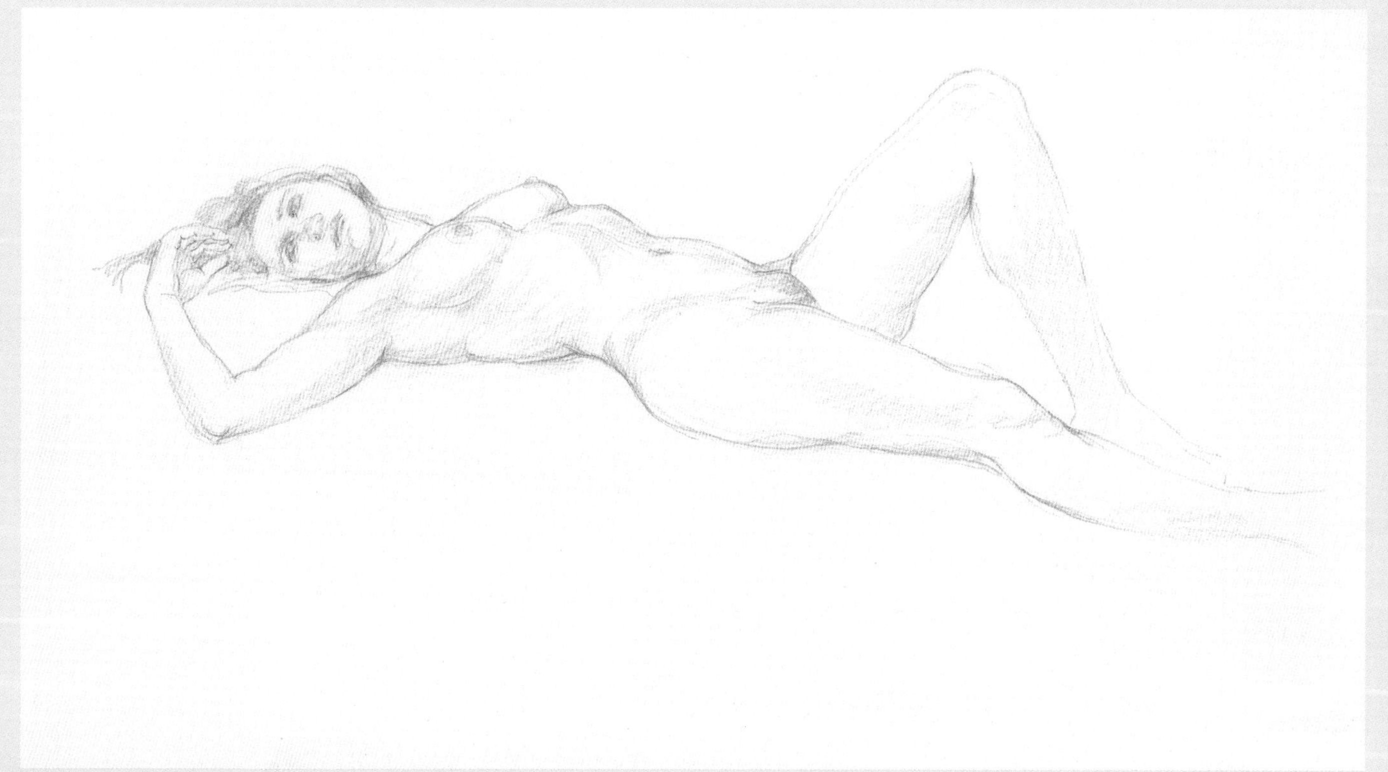

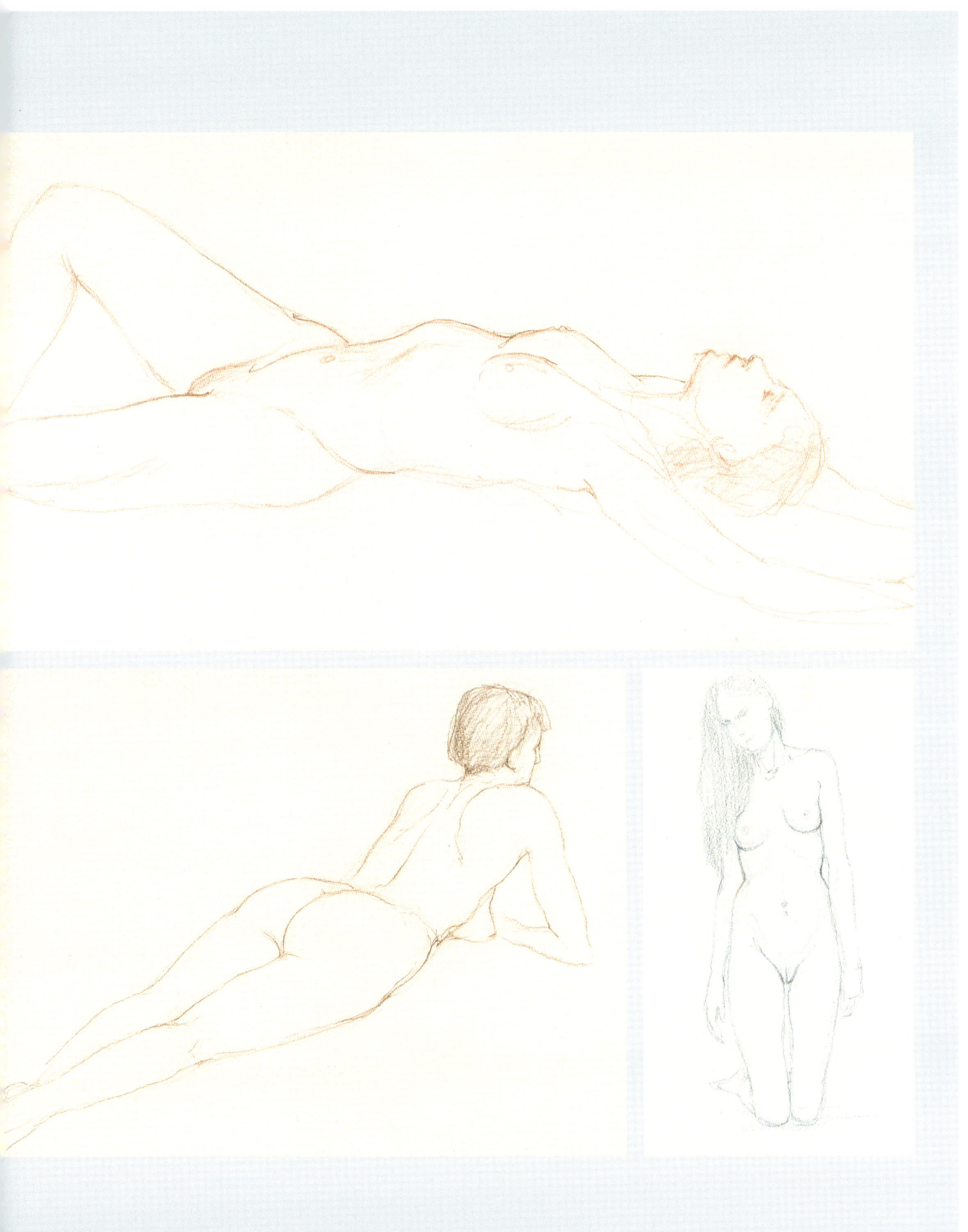

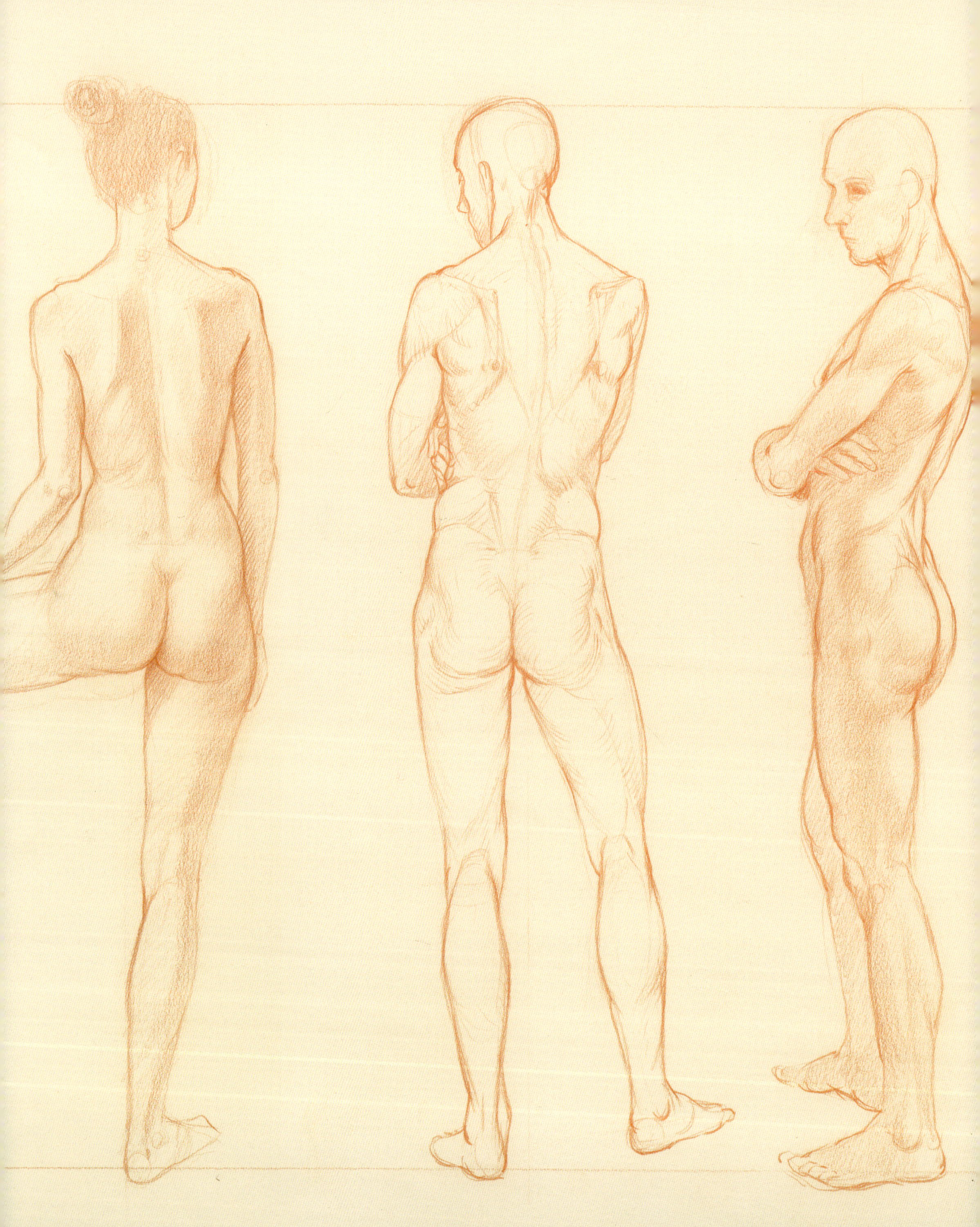

Chapter 7

DRAWING TECHNIQUES

A good understanding of human anatomy makes you see the figure differently. As you learn the anatomical structures, you start seeing the figure's forms more clearly and are able to draw them in a more complex, accurate, and realistic way. The more you know the more you see, and the more you see the better you draw. But to translate all the information you can extrapolate from a model into a drawing, you also need to know a few fundamentals about drawing itself—including the effect of light on forms, the technique of tonal drawing, and the essentials of measuring and foreshortening. For a realist artist, the techniques discussed in this chapter are just as important as grammar and vocabulary are to a writer. They're the basics you need in order to convey your visual message.

LIGHT ON THE FORM

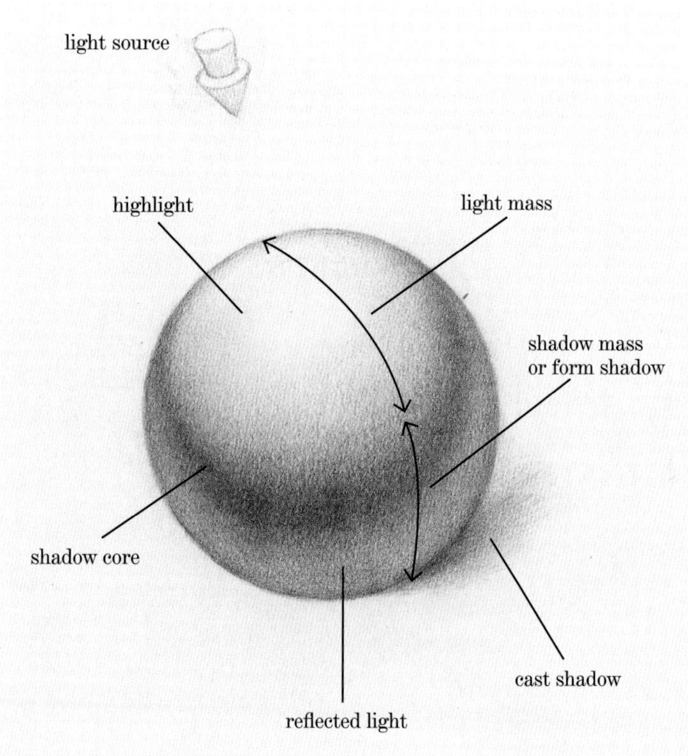

LIGHT CAST ON A SPHERE

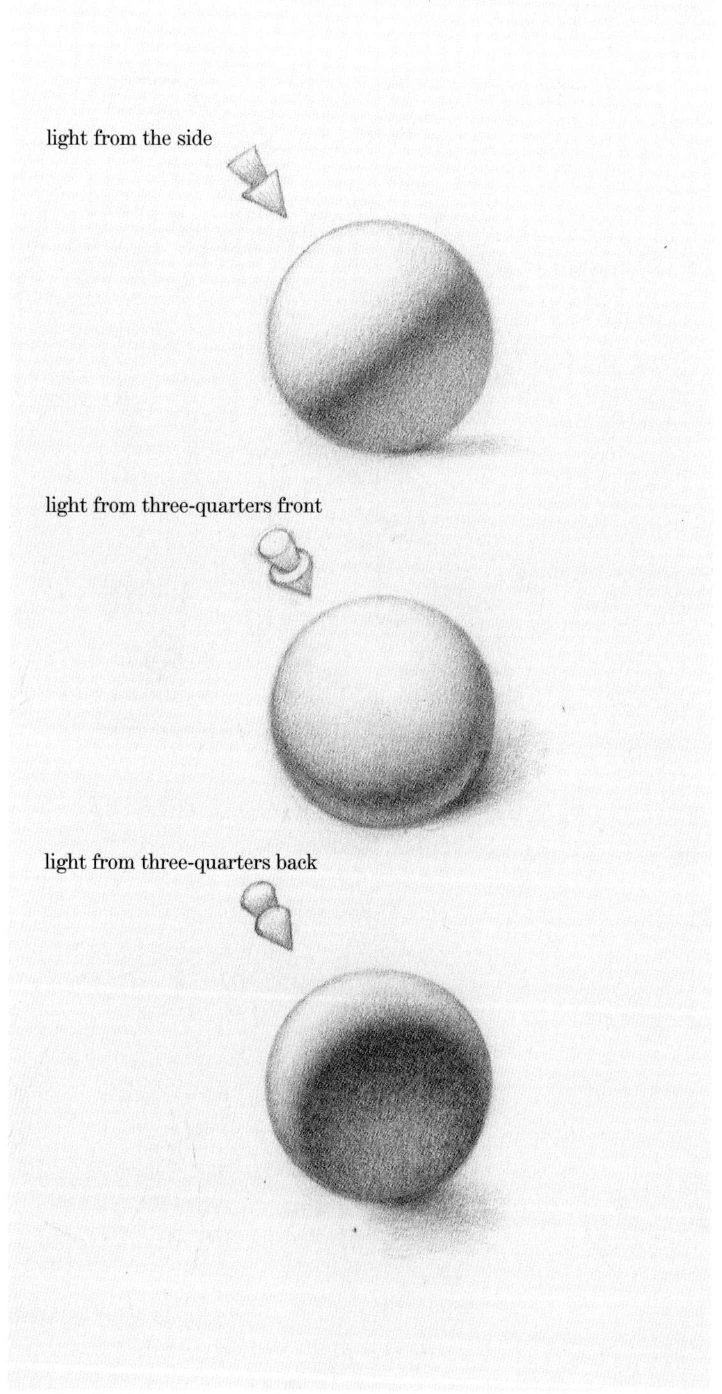

When light is cast on a sphere, as in the figure above, two areas are determined: the area that receives the light, called the light mass, and the area that does not receive the light, called the shadow mass or form shadow. Between the shadow mass and the light mass is a darker band of value called the shadow core. (The shadow core is also sometimes called the shadow accent, the tangency zone, or the form shadow core.) Past the shadow core but within the shadow mass, you can usually identify a lighter area of shadow caused by reflected light.

A careful examination of the light mass reveals different areas of value produced by the angle at which the

EFFECTS ON A SPHERE OF LIGHT CAST FROM DIFFERENT DIRECTIONS

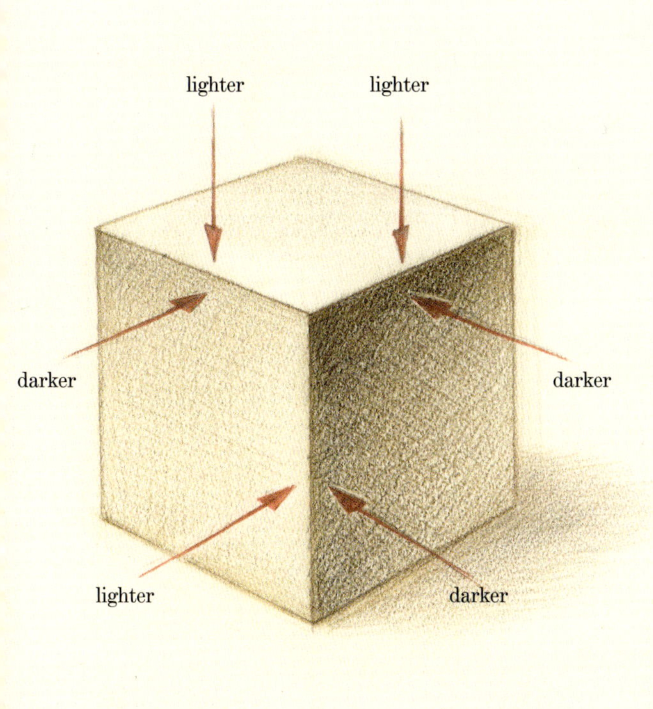

LIGHT CAST ON A CUBE

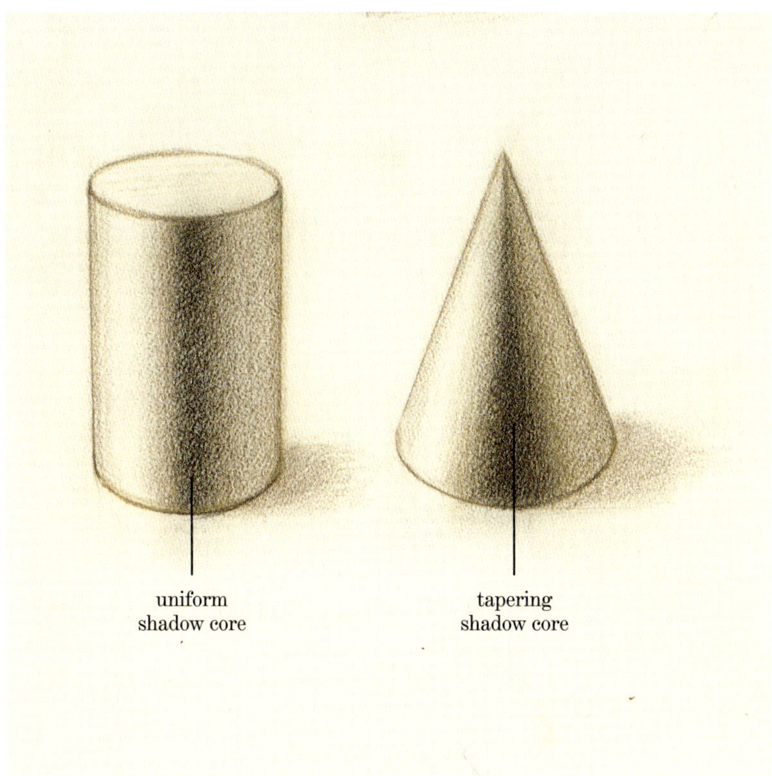

THE SHADOW CORES OF A CYLINDER AND CONE

light is hitting the form. The brightest highlight occurs where the light hits the form perpendicularly; as the angle of the light hitting the form grows narrower, the values seen on the form grow increasingly darker.

The next figure, at right, opposite, shows the basic light and shadow shapes produced by light coming from three different directions: the side, three-quarters front, and three-quarters back. Notice how the curvature of the shadow core changes from straight to concave to convex as the light source changes direction, and, from this, all the intermediate shapes the shadow core will take when light is shone on the sphere from intermediate directions.

Now look at the figure showing the effects of light cast on a cube, above. Notice the peculiar effect the light has on the contiguous areas where the planes of the cube touch (indicated by the arrows). Through a trick of the eye, these areas will appear slightly darker or lighter than the adjacent areas because of contrast.

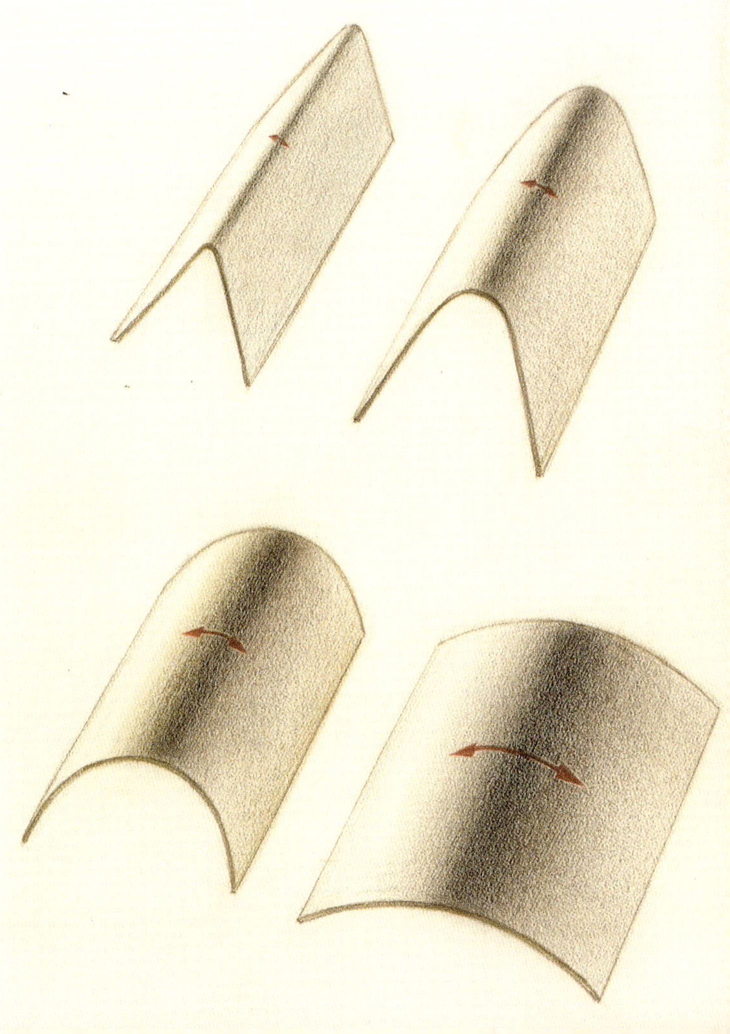

THE DIFFERENT CURVATURES OF THE SURFACE OF FORMS WILL CREATE WIDER OR NARROWER SHADOW CORES

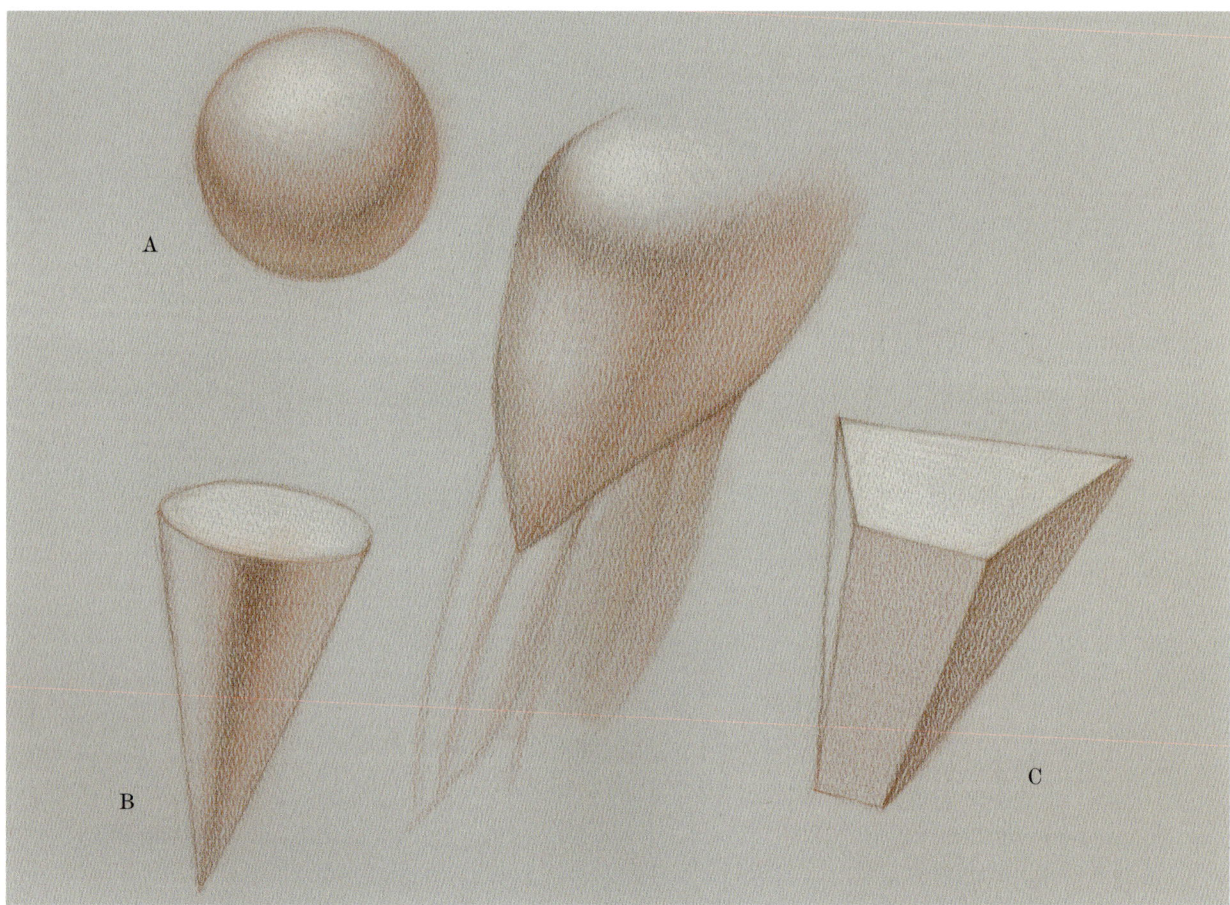

Examining the shadow core in detail can give you a great deal of information on volumetric characteristics of the form you are examining. The figure at top right on the previous page shows light cast on a cylinder and a cone. The shadow core on a cylindrical form will be wider or narrower depending on the cylinder's circumference. On a conical shape, the shadow core tapers from wide at the base to very narrow at the tip. The figure at bottom right on the previous page elaborates on the width of the shadow core, showing four examples of bent or curved planes. Notice how the sharper or more gradual changes of angle affect the width of the shadow core.

How is all this information of use for figure drawing? The image above shows how the complex organic forms of the body can be synthesized from basic geometric volumes: a sphere *(A)*, a cone *(B)*, and a trapezoidal solid *(C)*. Above, we see how a specific form, in this case the deltoid muscle, can be analyzed by further subdivision into geometric volumes. The page from a sketchbook, opposite, shows a few examples of basic volumes that can be visualized in the body overall. Notice how the shadow core is wider and softer in a big, tapering form such as the thigh but thinner and sharper where the passage from one plane to another is sudden or the form is narrower, such as the shin. This approach helps you better understand the organic forms and the effects of light shining on them, allowing you to draw tonally with greater accuracy.

above

THE DELTOID MUSCLE ANALYZED AS A SET OF GEOMETRIC VOLUMES

opposite

PAGE FROM A SKETCHBOOK SHOWING PURE GEOMETRIC FORMS AND A MODEL

The effect of light on pure geometric forms is replicated, to a greater or lesser degree, on similar forms appearing on the body.

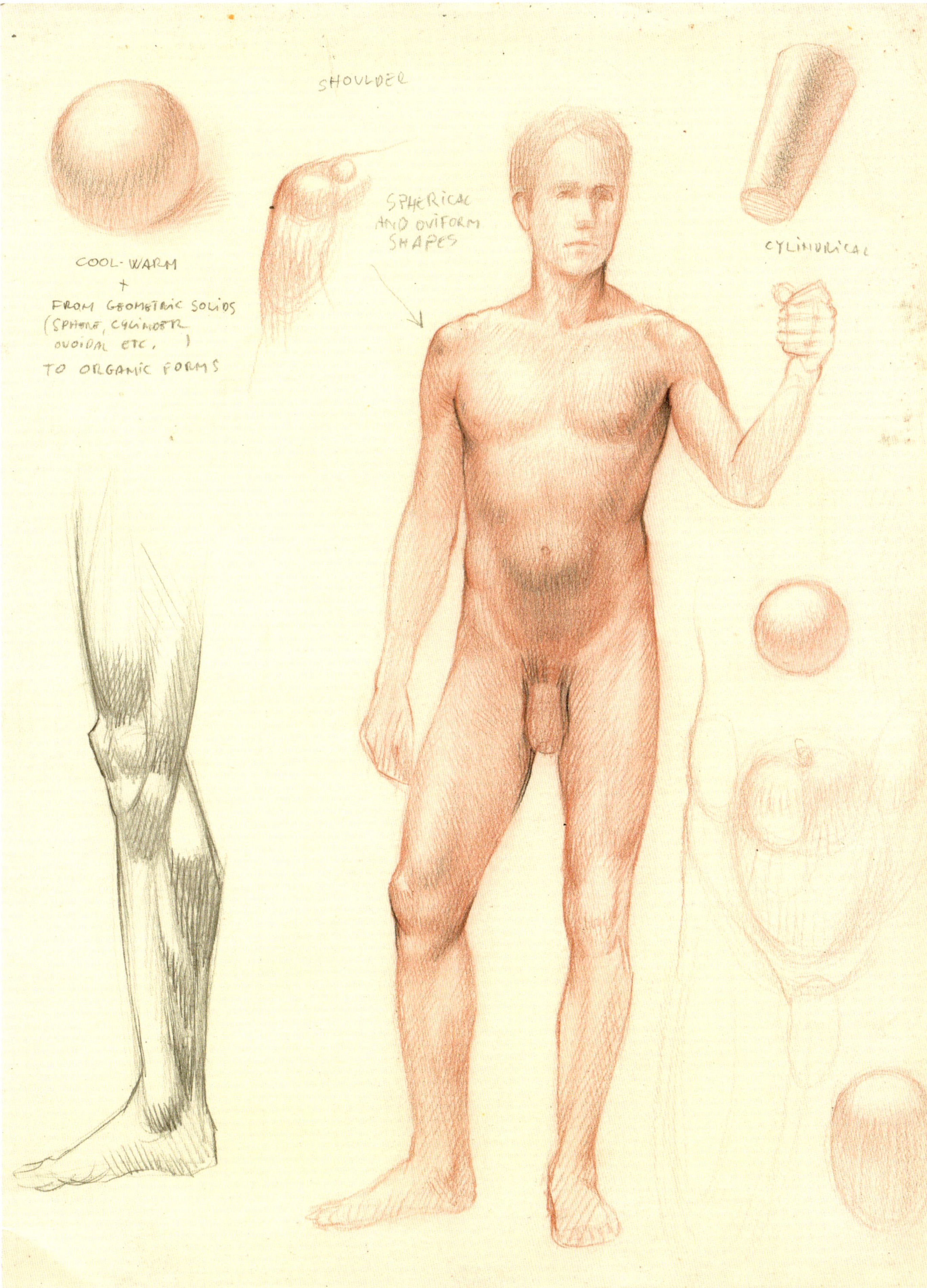

SHOULDER
SPHERICAL AND OVIFORM SHAPES
CYLINDRICAL
COOL - WARM
+
FROM GEOMETRIC SOLIDS
(SPHERE, CYLINDER
OVOIDAL ETC.)
TO ORGANIC FORMS

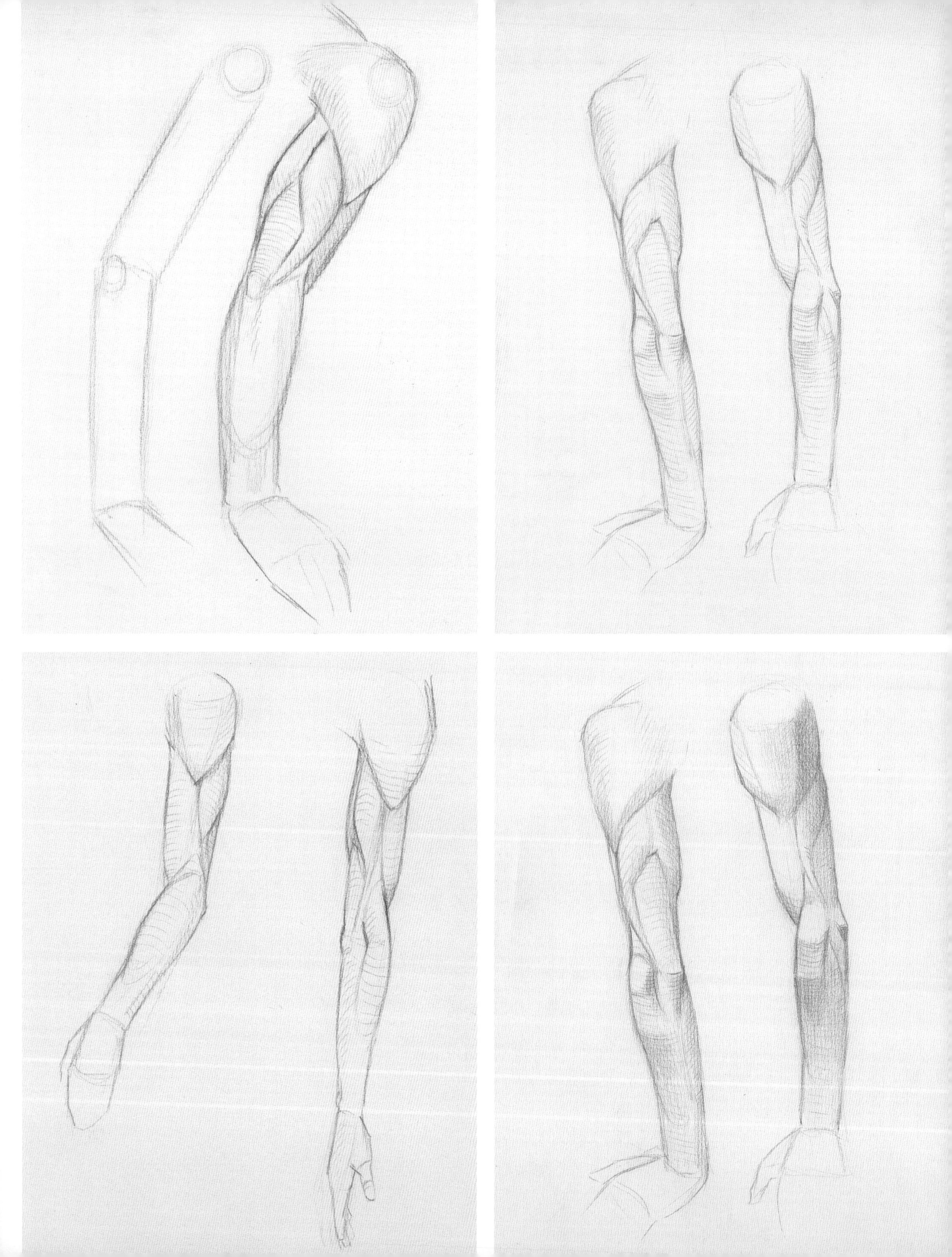

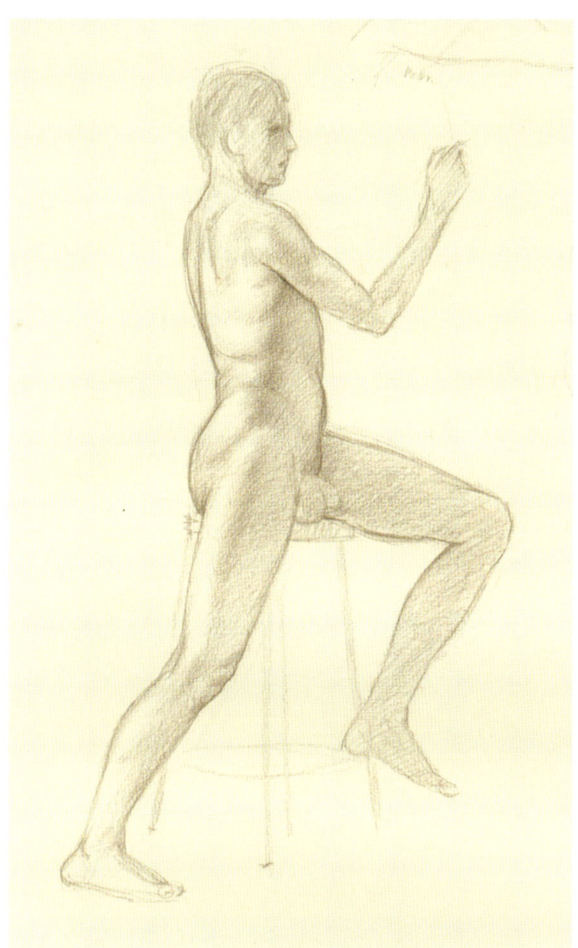

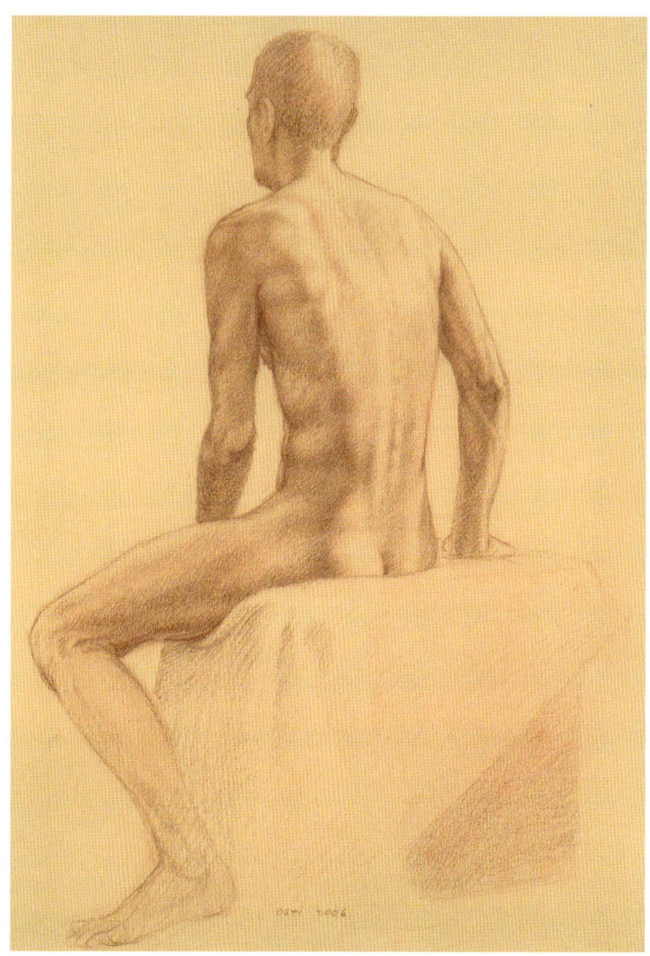

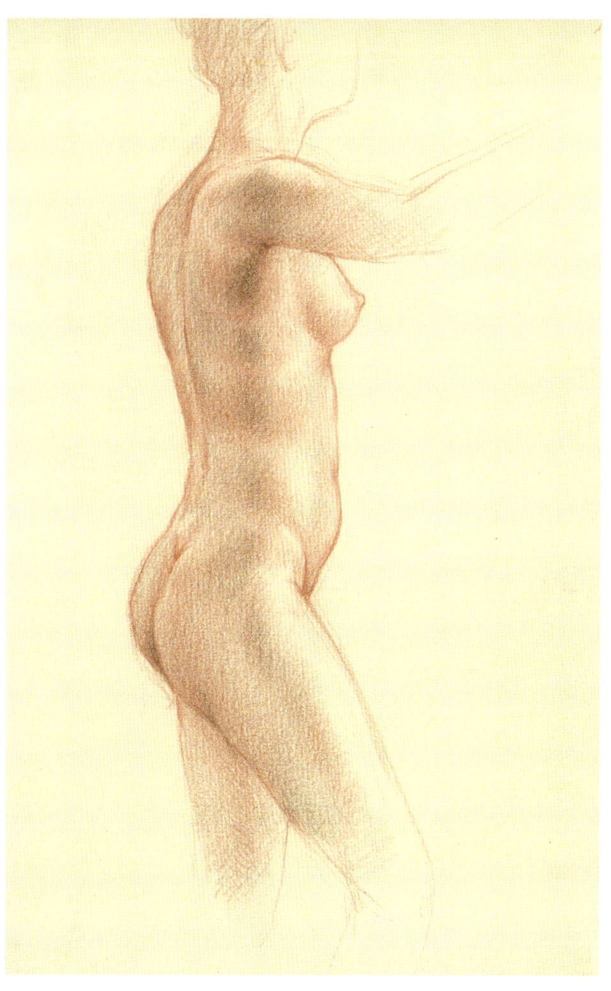

opposite
STUDIES OF ARMS REDUCED TO ESSENTIAL FORMS

These studies of arms show how you can better understand the body by reducing its parts to essential forms. You can also see how doing so makes it easier to understand the behavior of the light on these forms.

this page
FIGURE STUDIES SHOWING LIGHT AND SHADOW ON THE BODY

To extend this analysis of the effect of light on the form, look at the shadow cores produced by the various muscles of the torso and legs in these three figure studies. Following the direction of the shadow cores, you can see the directions of the muscles and also how the various muscles of the torso and legs interconnect. When the angle of a shadow core changes, it usually indicates a transition from one muscle to another. The width of the shadow core gives you an idea of the muscle's circumference. Finally, the division between light mass and shadow mass shows changes in temperature—that is, perceived warmth or coolness—in the various areas of light mass, shadow mass, and shadow core.

MATERIALS FOR TONAL DRAWING

When you first start drawing tonally, use graphite pencil on white paper. This time-honored technique is very versatile; you can obtain a great range of effects with it, from very sketchy and quick to incredibly precise and elaborate. You can also obtain a very extended tonal scale. I use mostly H, HB, and F pencils; with these gradations you can achieve a very extended tonal scale. If I want to extend it further, I add 2H and 2B pencils.

You can use colored pencils instead of graphite, but, if you do, I suggest that you work monochromatically at first, using red or brown earth colors such as Indian red, English red, sanguine, Venetian red, or sepia. My favorite brands of colored pencils are Caran d'Ache and Faber-Castell; both are lightfast—an important factor to consider. Faber-Castell pencils are a little bit harder than Caran d'Ache, which may make them better for really fine lines. Both brands offer a wide range of colors. These brands work for me, but you should feel free to experiment with a variety of brands to find what works for you. But do not compromise on quality; always buy the best materials you can.

For paper, I like to use Strathmore 400 Series or Strathmore 500 Series Bristol, either vellum or plate, though vellum has a slight texture and I like it better. I also love the paper in Moleskine sketchbooks; some have paper that looks slightly yellowish, and you can actually erase some of the paper's color to create very faint highlights. Canson papers are also very good. Experiment with various types of paper and then stick with those you like best. Knowing your material and what you can do with it lets you achieve the best results.

Whether you work with graphite or with colored pencils, build your values gradually. Never push down hard on your pencil, especially when using colored pencils. If you do, the waxy medium will create a burnished effect that will make your drawings look like schoolchildren's work. So build up your colors or tonal scale by gently layering the colors.

TONAL DRAWING—
THE *TROIS CRAYONS* TECHNIQUE

Next, let's look at some of the basics of one of the two fundamental approaches to drawing—tonal drawing. The other fundamental approach, structural drawing, has a direct link with Italian Renaissance methods and is based mainly on the use of line. The tonal drawing approach—based, as its name implies, on the tonal rendering of the subject—developed to its highest level in European art academies of the eighteenth and nineteenth centuries.

A drawing executed tonally starts with lines, but eventually all the lines will disappear and be replaced by a tonal scale. (The figure below shows a progression in tonal development.) The best examples of this technique are incredibly beautiful and realistic. When the academies developed the method, the aim was to "standardize" the quality of students' work. The drawback of such standardization is that it stifles creativity, leading a great many

TONAL DEVELOPMENT

These three steps quickly summarize how to approach tonal development on a sphere. The principle can be used to develop tones on any other surface.

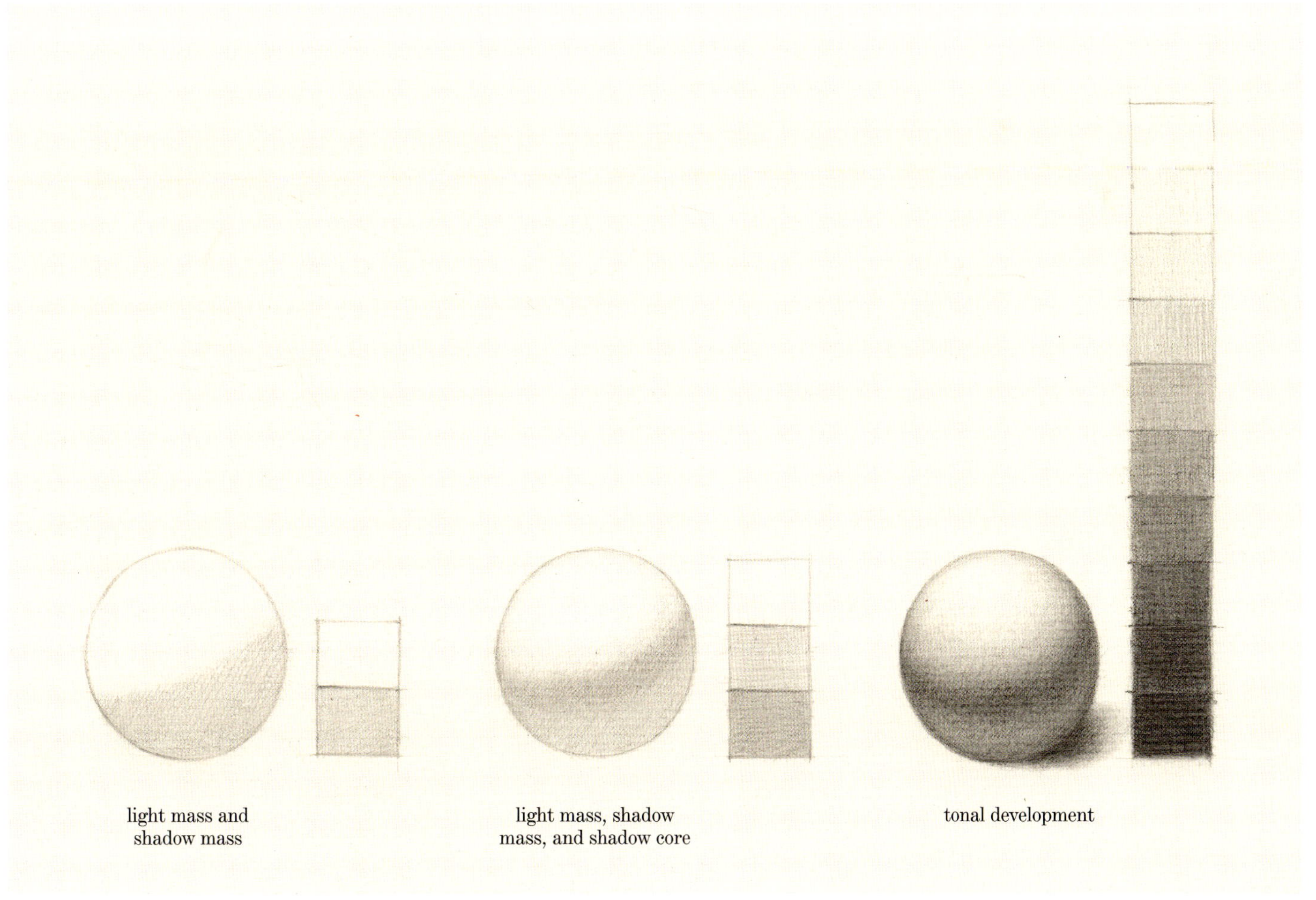

light mass and
shadow mass

light mass, shadow
mass, and shadow core

tonal development

artists to produce nearly identical work. That said, however, it is important to practice and master this approach if you want to improve your technical skill.

In my anatomy and figure drawing classes, I often teach what's called *trois crayons* ("three crayons") tonal technique, because it allows me to introduce the concepts of chroma and temperature manipulation. (The chroma of a color is its intensity; temperature has to do with the color's perceived warmth or coolness.) The three colors used in *trois crayons* are red, black, and white. You can use Conte crayons or similar crayons from other makers (e.g., Cretacolor, Faber-Castell PITT pastels), or you can use colored pencils. For the red, choose a red earth color, such as Indian red, English red, Venetian red, Pompeii red, or sanguine. Do not use a more highly chromatic red such as cadmium red, alizarin crimson, or magenta, which are not suited for this technique.

Work in this technique is typically done on toned paper. But, to begin with, use a red earth crayon or colored pencil on white paper, as in the three drawings here. Tonally develop your drawing as much as possible using only the red color.

below left
LIGHT ON A SPHERE, DONE IN RED EARTH COLORED PENCIL

below right
FIGURE DRAWING IN RED EARTH COLORED PENCIL

opposite
FIGURE DRAWING IN RED EARTH COLORED PENCIL

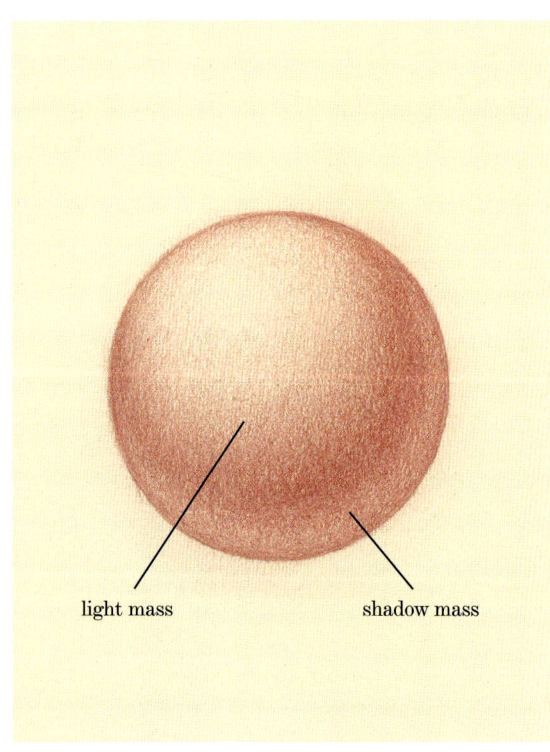

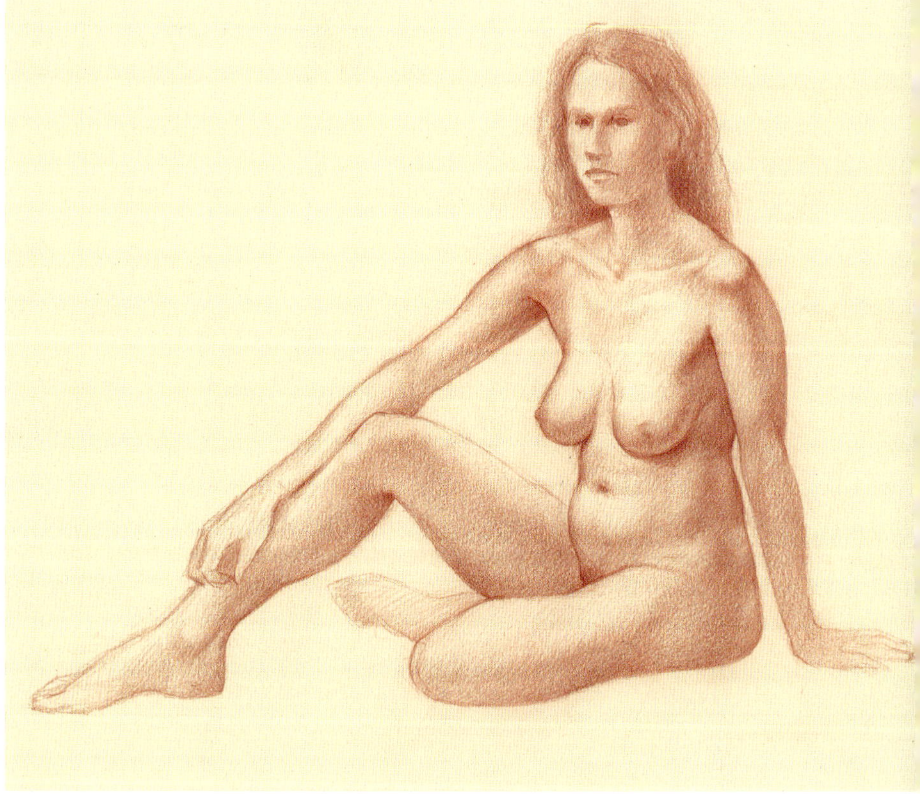

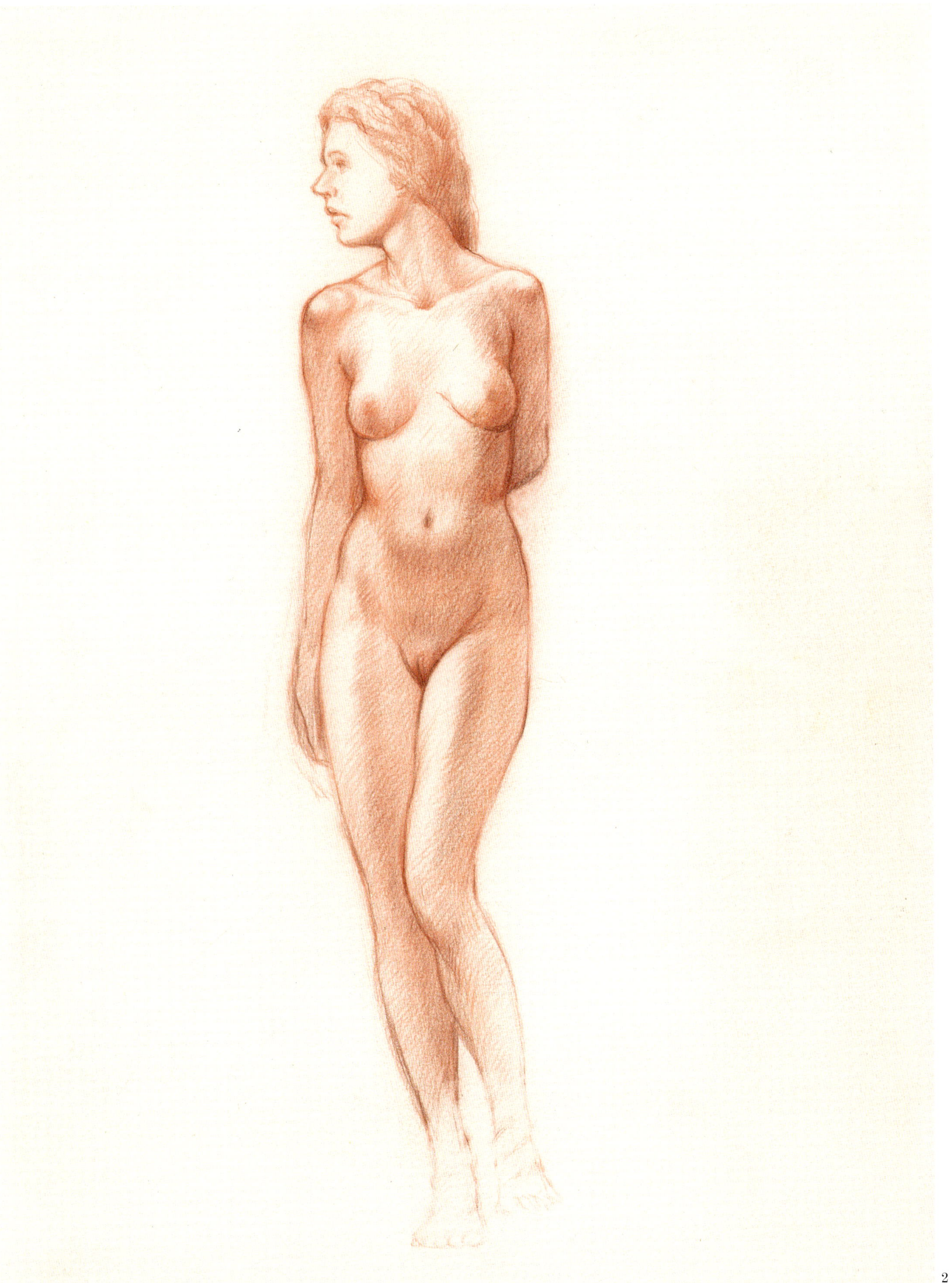

When the drawing is fully tonally developed, introduce the black to manipulate the chroma and temperature of the red, making it less chromatic and cooler, as in the drawings on this page.

So far you've used two of the three crayons. But to use the third—the white crayon—you'll have to switch to toned paper. Try cool, warm, and neutral papers to see the various effects you can obtain. Use white in the light mass only, *not* in the shadow mass. As you gradually develop the highlights with the white, you will obtain three specific effects: You will gradually cool down the color of the light mass (in this case red), lessen the chroma, and enhance the three-dimensional effect. Because the white crayon is opaque, it introduces another variable: opacity versus transparency. As you add white to the red in the light mass or to the toned paper, you make that area more and more opaque, enhancing the effect of volume. The areas where white is absent (as in the shadows) are relatively transparent, creating a sense of depth.

The drawing at top, opposite, shows a sphere done using the *trois crayons* technique on warm toned paper. In the drawing below it, the same technique is employed on cool toned paper; the four steps show the progres-

SPHERE IN RED AND BLACK COLORED PENCIL

FIGURE DRAWING IN RED COLORED PENCIL WITH BLACK ADDED TO MANIPULATE THE CHROMA

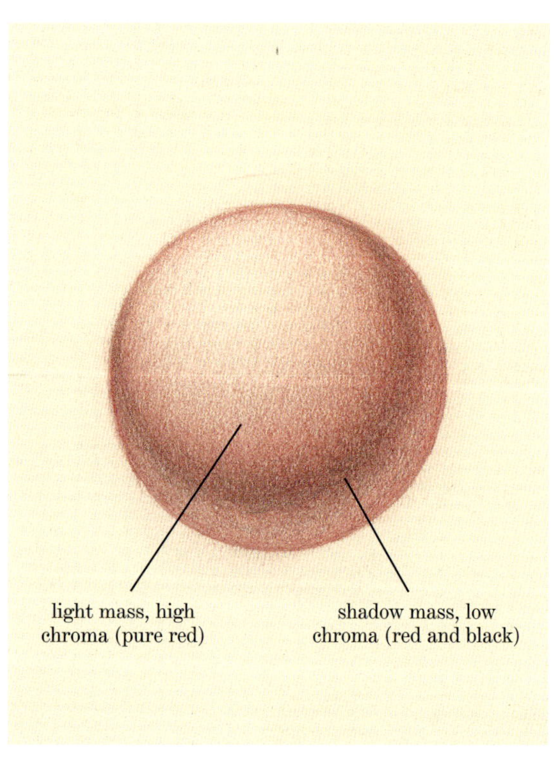

light mass, high
chroma (pure red)

shadow mass, low
chroma (red and black)

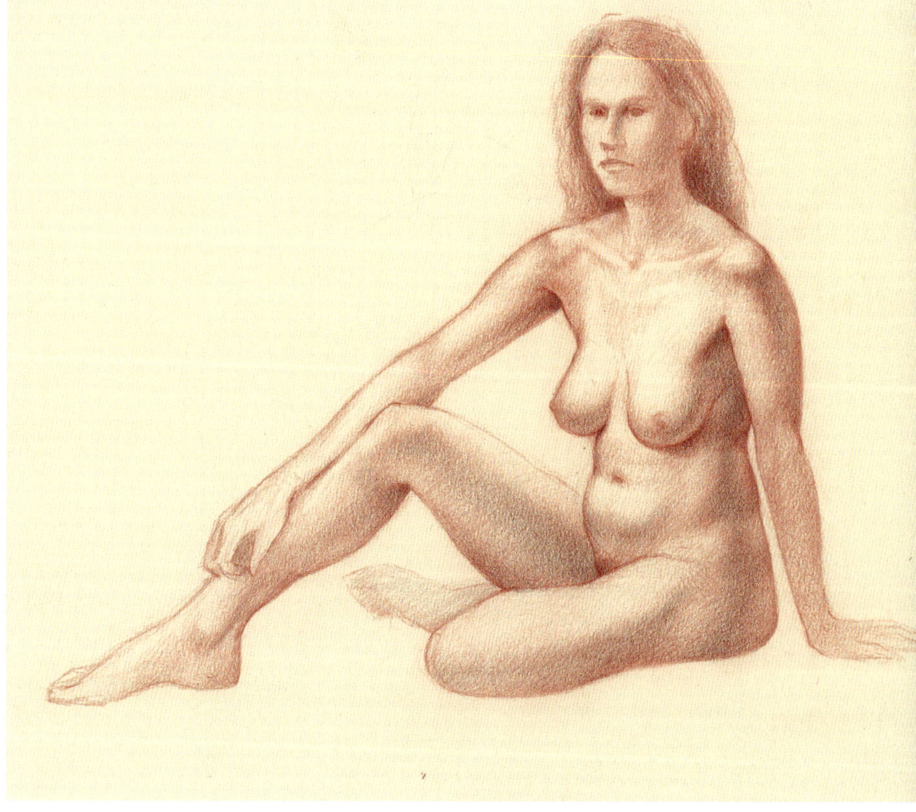

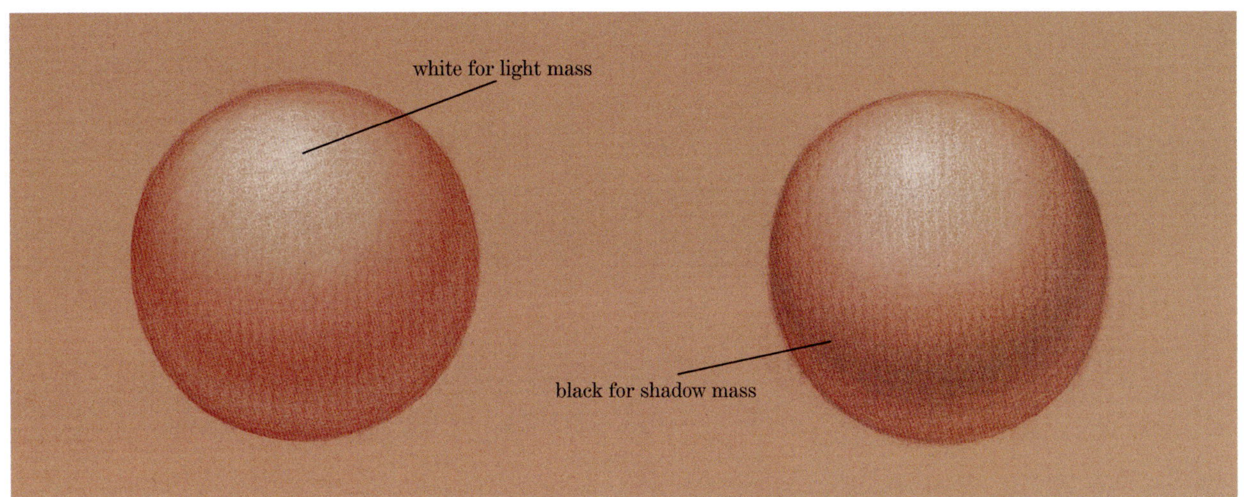

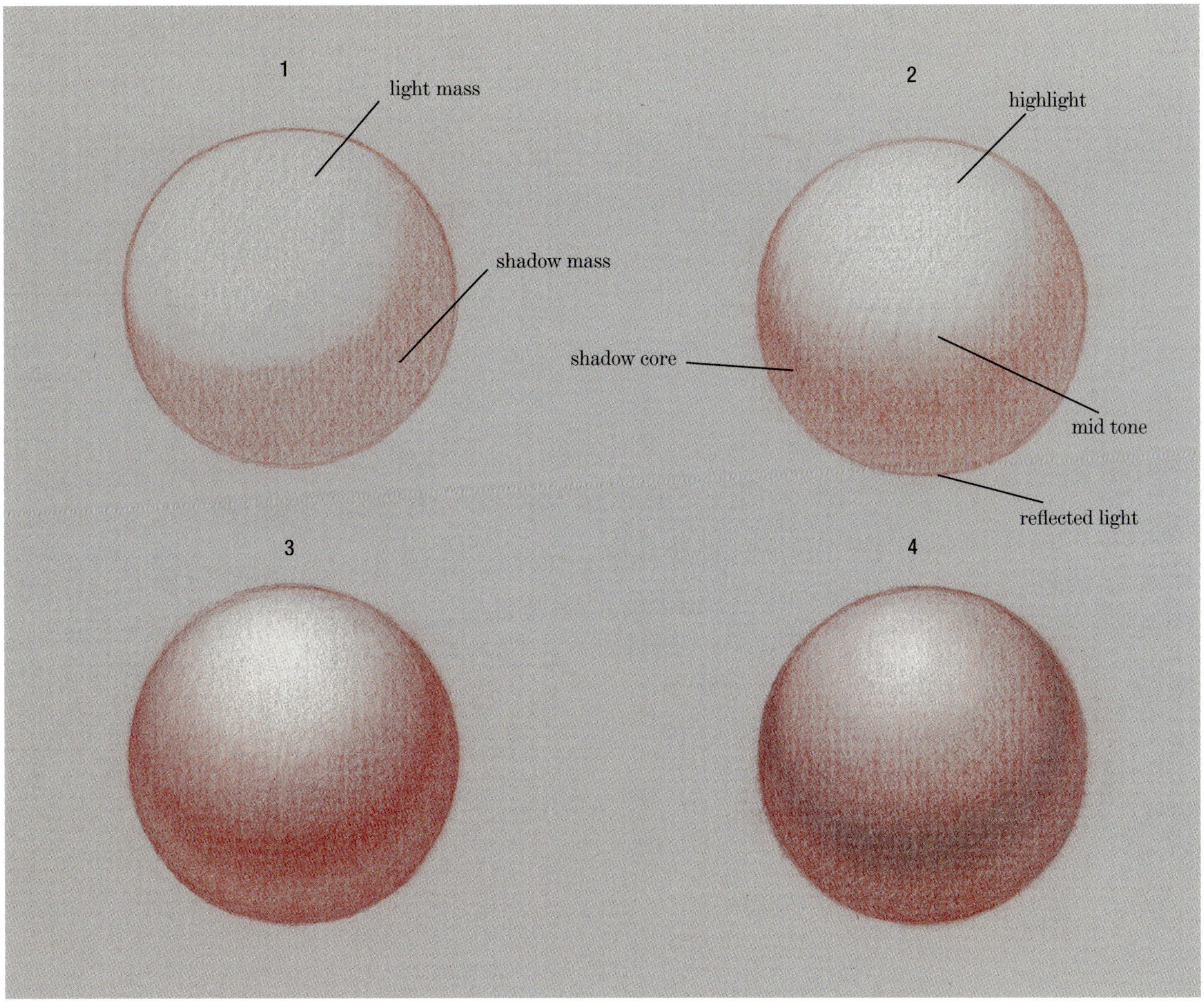

sive development of the sphere using color, temperature (cool and warm), opacity, and manipulation of chroma. Try copying these steps using various types of red earth crayons and various types of toned paper—warm, cool, neutral, light, medium, dark.

top
TROIS CRAYONS SPHERE ON WARM TONED PAPER

above
TROIS CRAYONS SPHERE ON COOL TONED PAPER

A GALLERY OF FIGURE STUDIES

The figure studies gathered here were executed using the techniques discussed in this chapter. Together, they give you an overview of possible technical approaches and the practical application of these techniques.

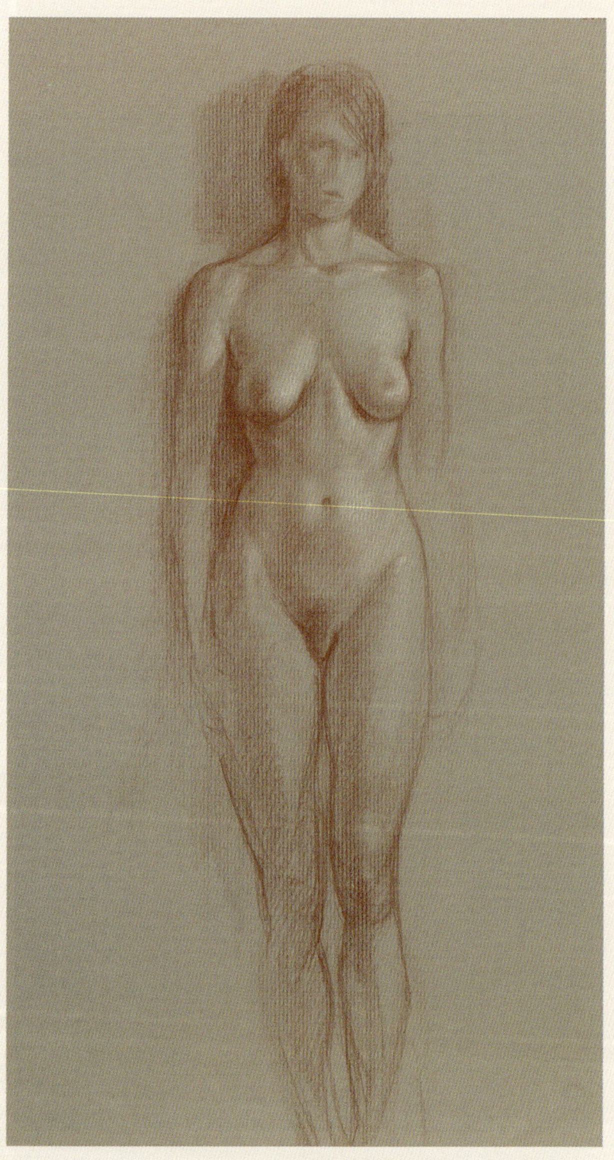

FIGURE STUDY IN BROWN AND WHITE COLORED PENCILS ON COOL TONED PAPER

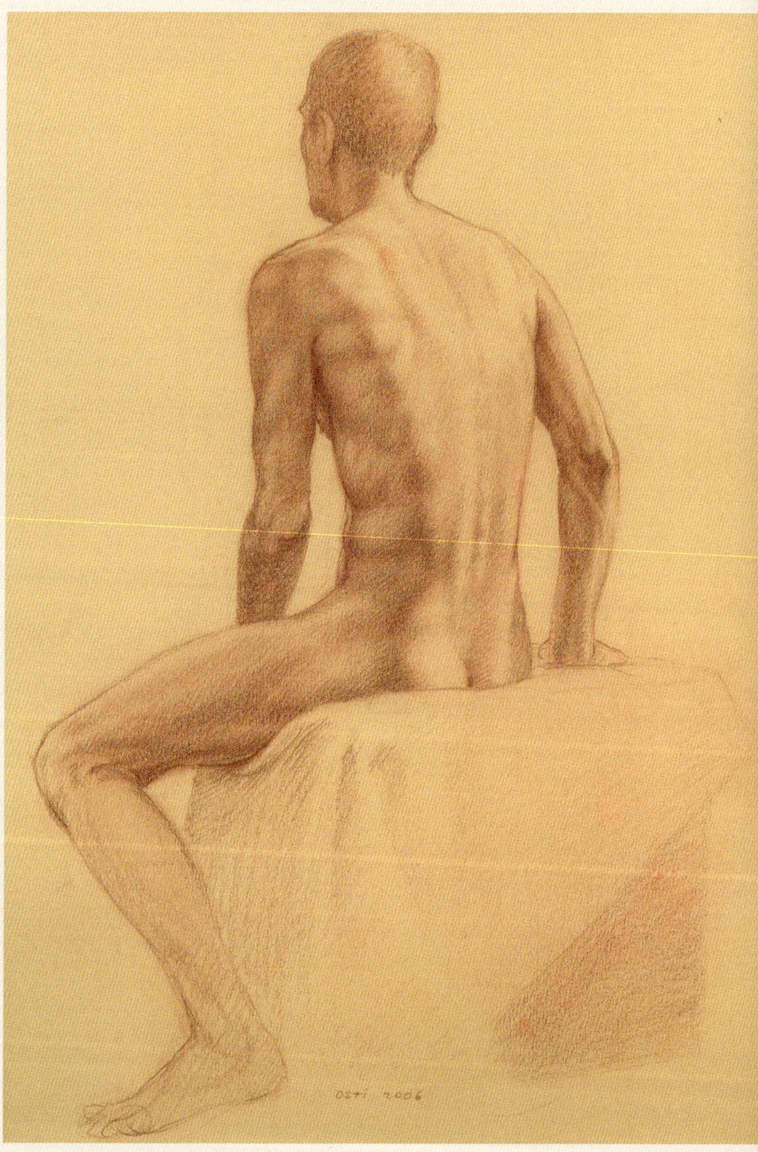

FIGURE STUDY IN SEPIA COLORED PENCIL ON WARM TONED PAPER

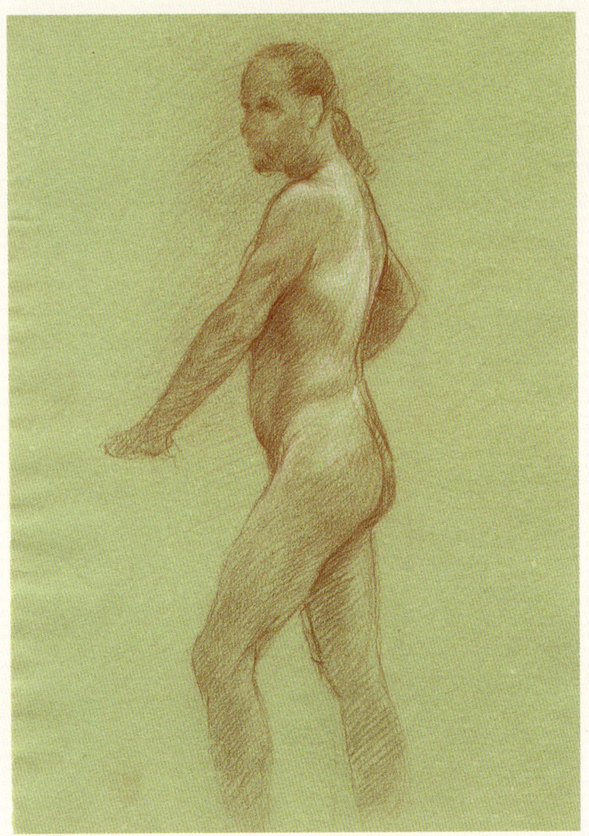

FIGURE STUDY IN BROWNISH RED AND WHITE PENCIL ON GREEN PAPER

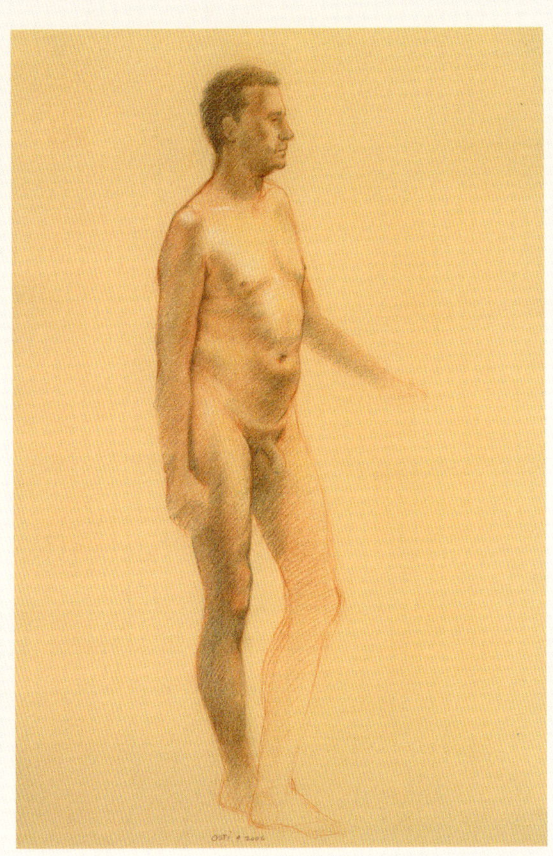

FIGURE STUDY USING *TROIS CRAYONS* TECHNIQUE ON WARM TONED PAPER

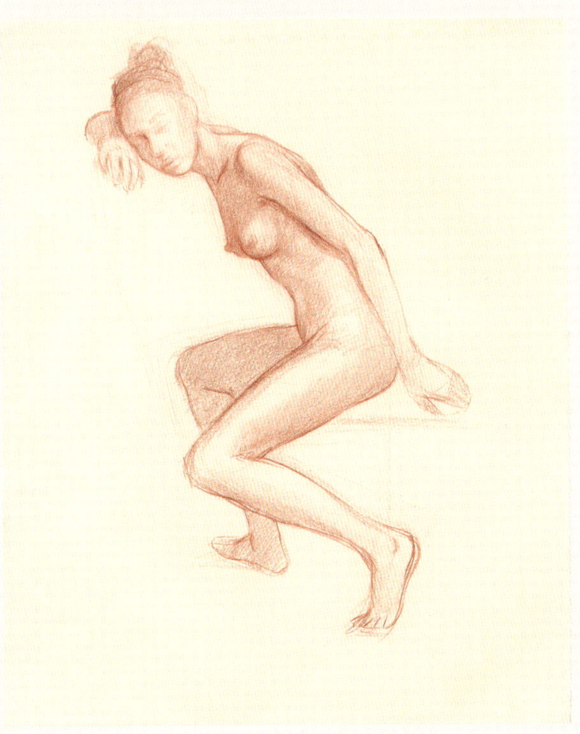

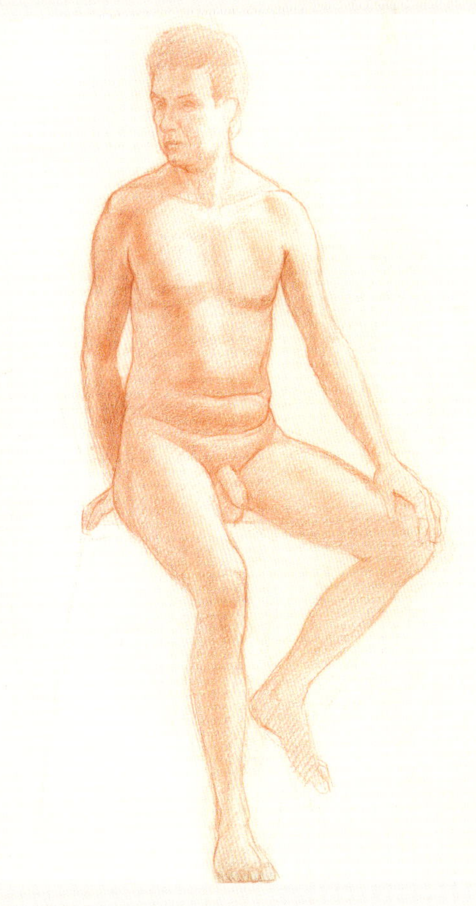

above and right
FIGURE STUDIES IN RED COLORED PENCIL ON WHITE PAPER

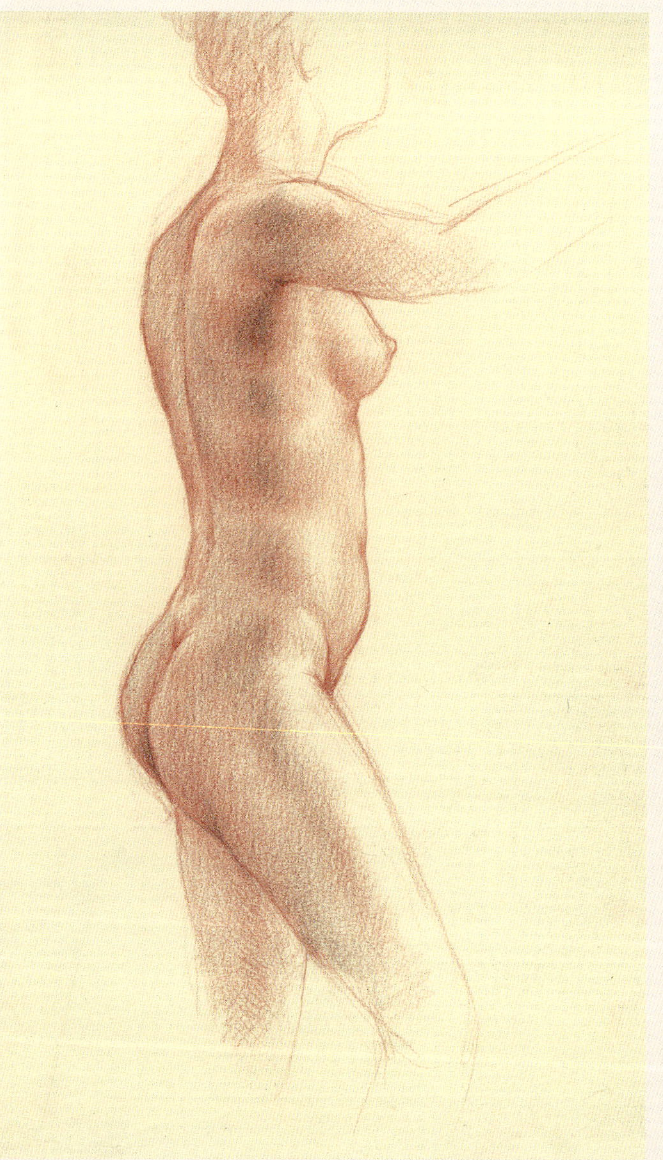

FIGURE STUDY IN RED AND BLACK COLORED
PENCILS ON WHITE PAPER

In this image you can see how the shadow core
describes the peaks of the muscle forms, adding to
the three-dimensional effect.

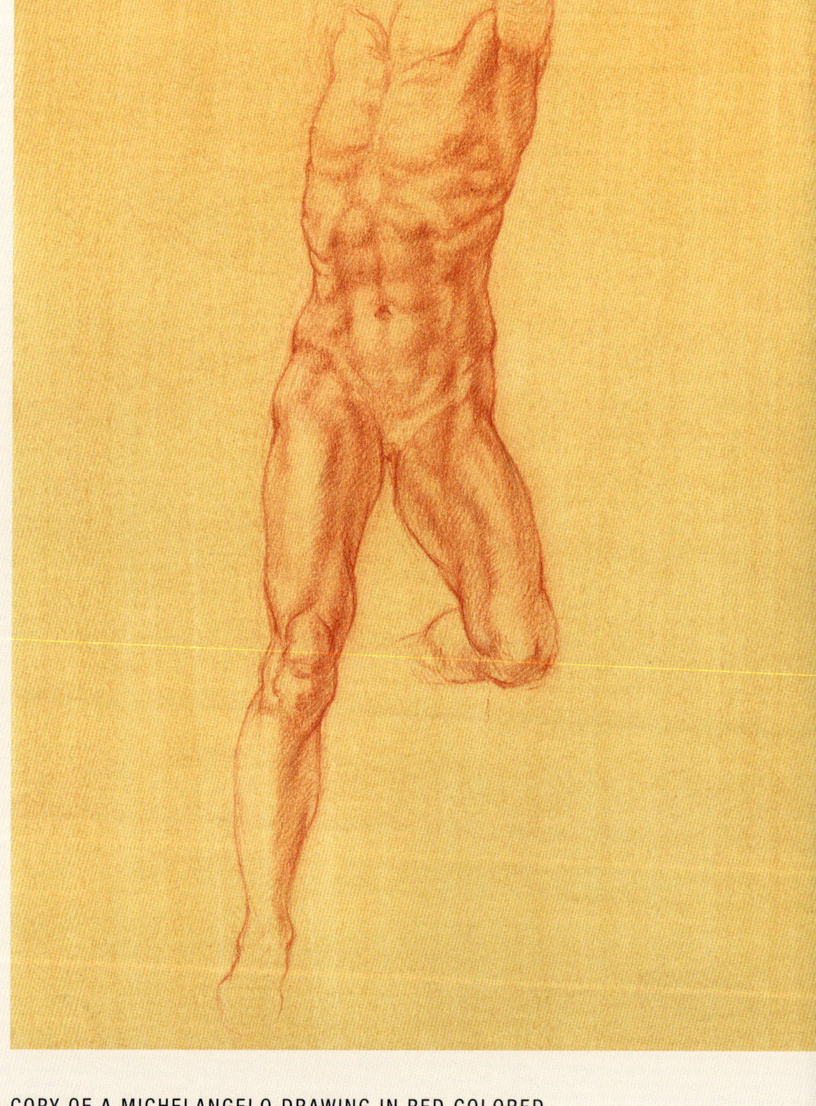

COPY OF A MICHELANGELO DRAWING IN RED COLORED
PENCIL ON PAPER PREPARED WITH A WATERCOLOR WASH

Copying the masters is always a great exercise. They still have a
lot to teach us.

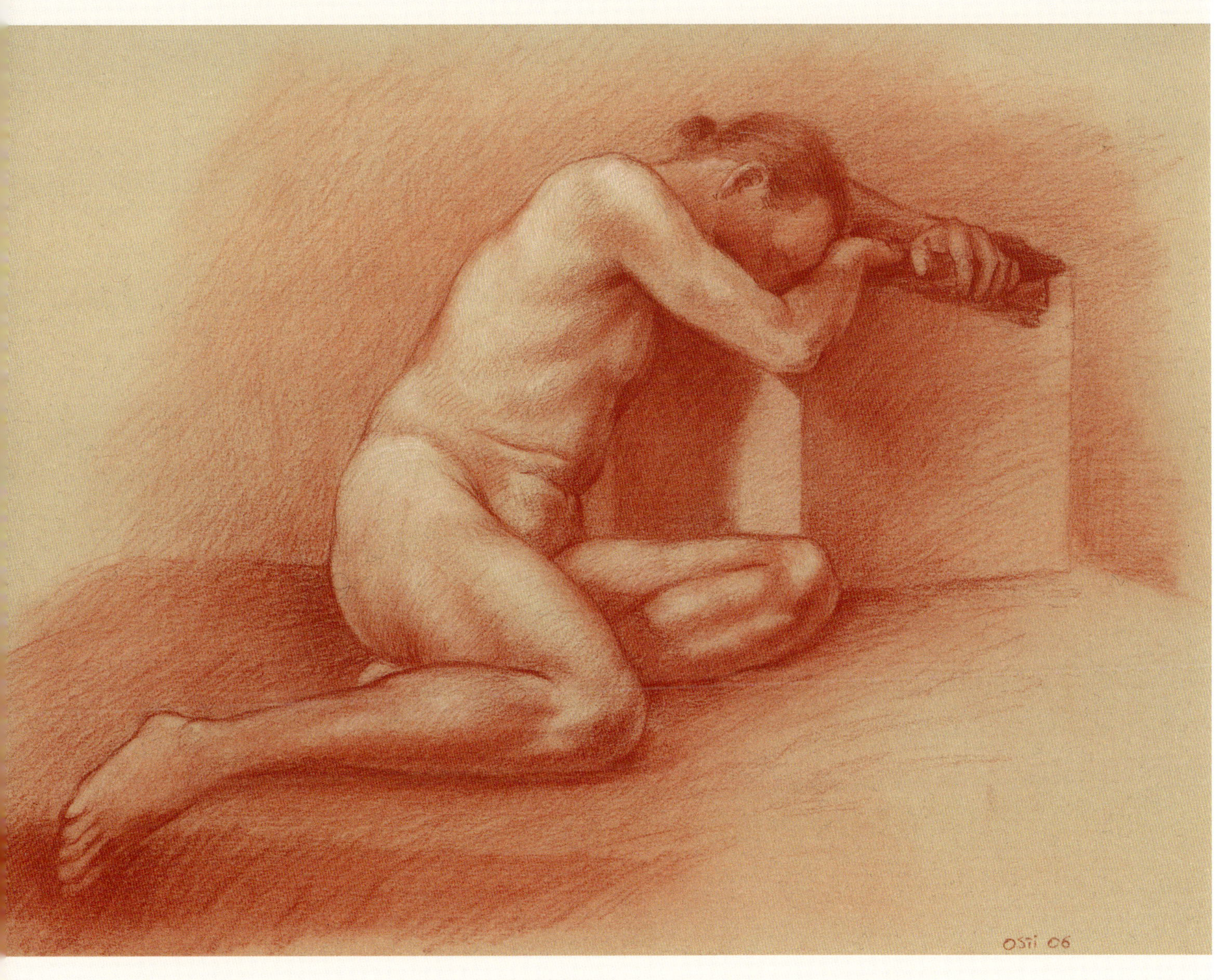

FIGURE STUDY IN RED AND WHITE CONTE CRAYONS ON TONED PAPER

The grainy quality of Conte crayons makes drawing details slightly more difficult, so when using them, draw a little bigger than you would in colored pencils.

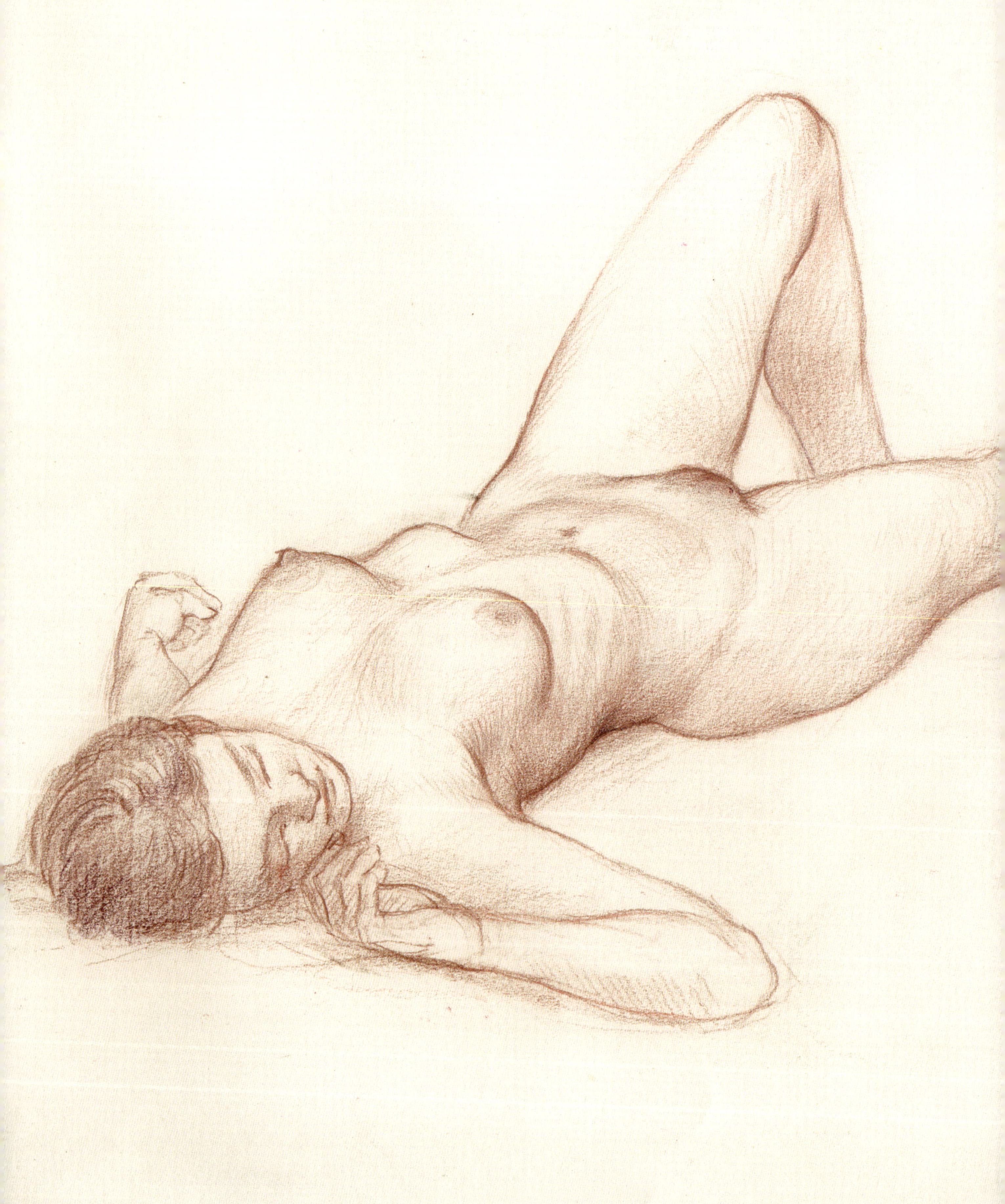

MEASURING AND FORESHORTENING

Have you ever wondered why some artists, when drawing, will stick their pencils up in the air while squinting and moving the pencil up and down? Well, this is probably the commonest measuring technique used by artists, and it can be fairly precise when performed correctly.

The figure at left, below, shows how to line up the top of the pencil with the top of the subject's head. If you position your thumb at the level of the bottom of the head, the segment of the pencil between the thumb and the pencil's tip gives you the measurement for the head. You can then use this measure to determine the measurements for the rest of the figure—marking off the corresponding landmarks, no matter whether you are using the 1:7 ½ or 1:8 proportions discussed in chapter 1 (see page 22). Of course, the measure of the head will change depending on your distance from your subject; the farther away you are, the smaller the measure will become. Note, too, that the measurements you obtain by using either the 1:7 ½ or 1:8 ratio are ideal proportions. Your model's proportions will differ, and you'll have to make adjustments to respect the model's specific proportions. (Also, this technique only works perfectly if your model is standing straight.)

The figure at right, below, shows how to continue measuring so as not to alter the proportions of the various segments of the figure as you move your pencil up and down. Each time you take a measurement comparing the height of the head with another segment of the body, make sure that your arm remains completely extended to maintain a constant distance between your eye and the pencil. Also, do not shift your position forward or backward. That way, the pencil will stay at the same distance from the model, and your measurements will remain true.

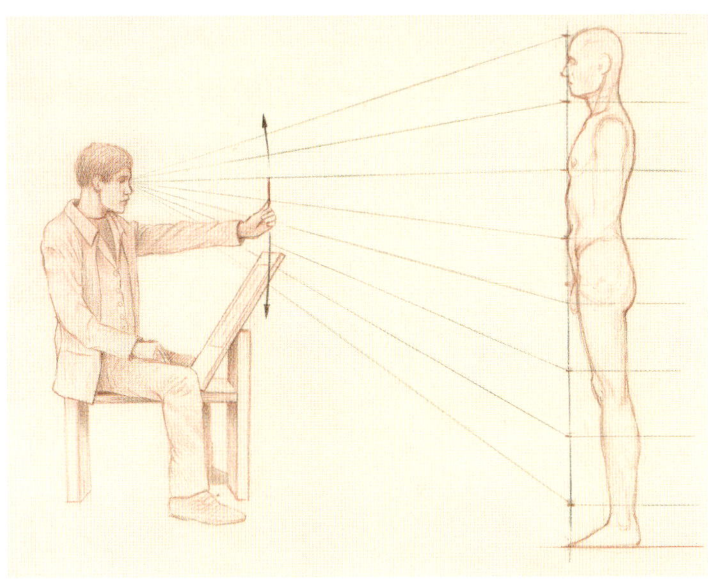

LINING UP THE PENCIL

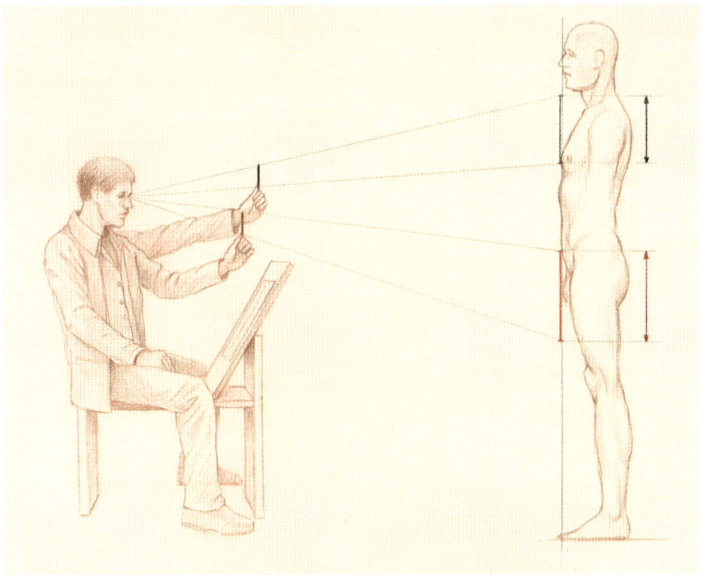

MOVING THE PENCIL TOWARD OR AWAY FROM YOUR SUBJECT WILL ALTER THE MEASUREMENT

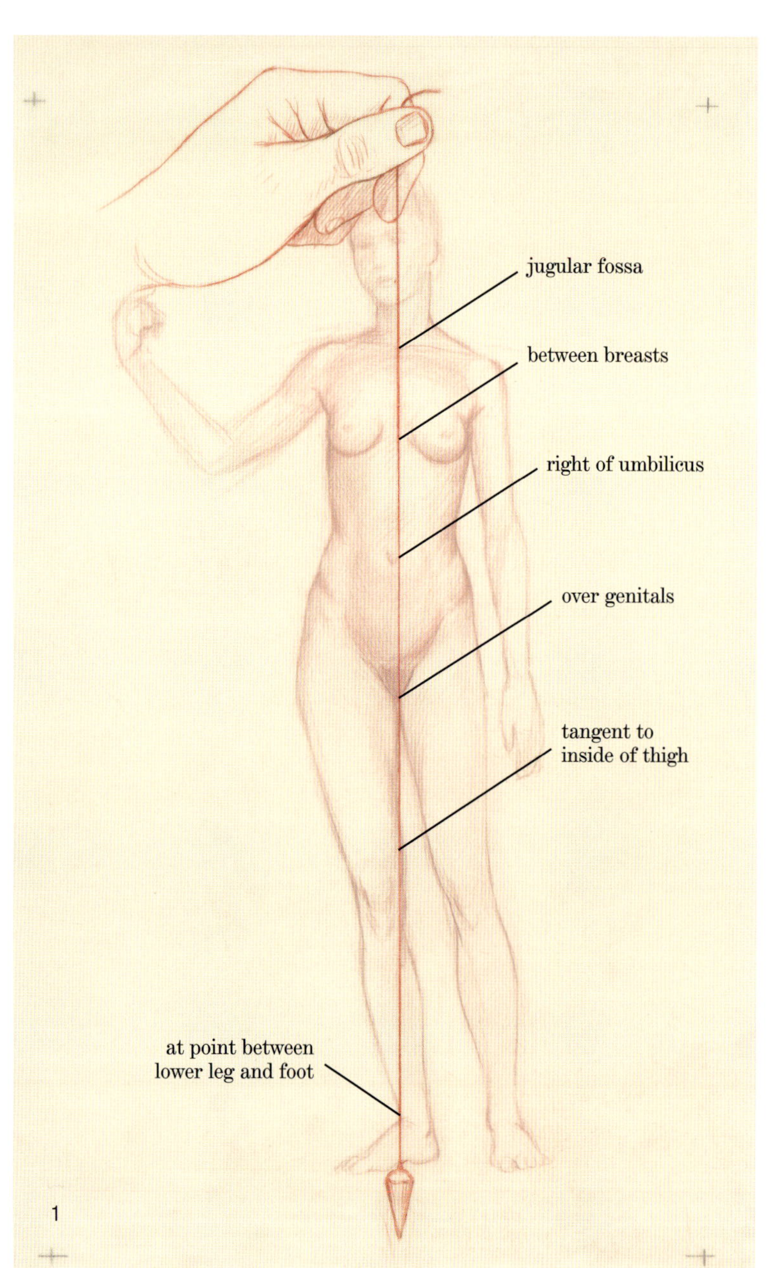

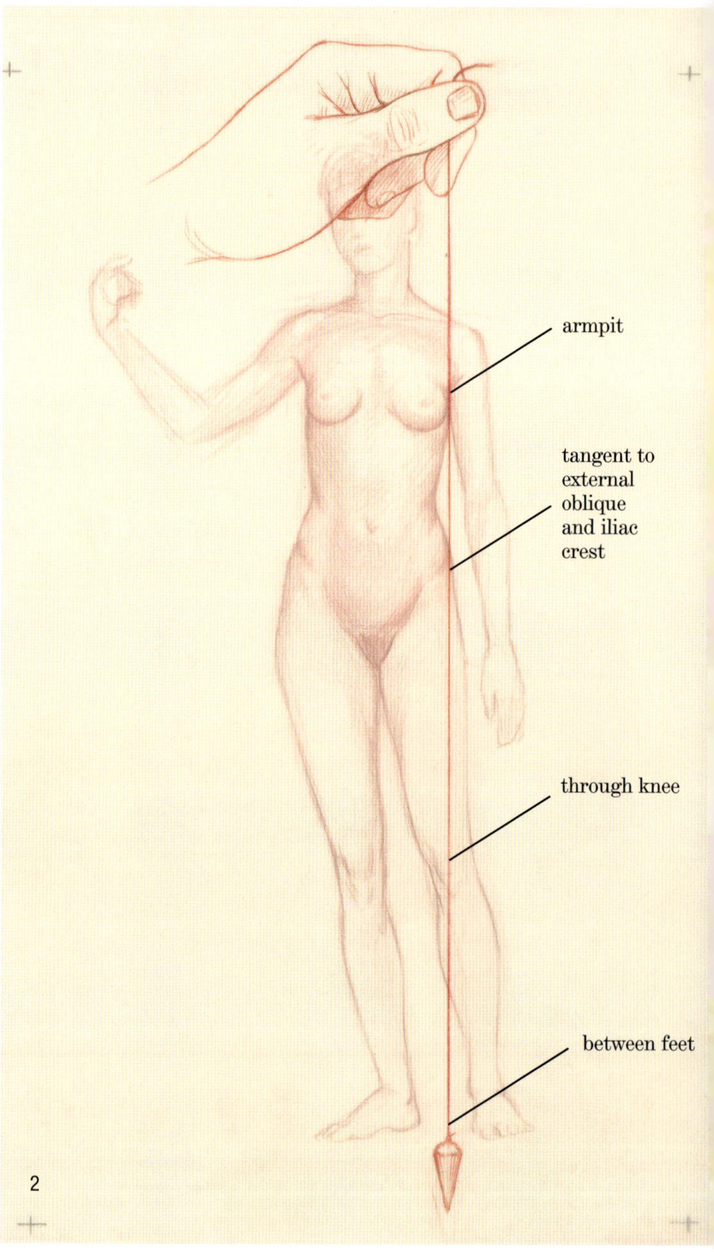

USING A PLUMB LINE

The American painter John Singer Sargent is said to have surrounded his models with plumb lines hanging from the ceiling so that he could immediately see the alignments between various parts of their bodies. The plumb line, a tool that is normally used in construction, consists of a weight suspended from a cord; the weight straightens the line vertically so that you can use it for reference when drawing. Holding the line in front of your subject will permit you to correctly relate distant parts of the body to each other by means of a virtual grid that lets you instantly visualize how, for example, the jugular fossa (figure 1) and the armpit (figure 2) relate to the rest of the body.

A PLUMB LINE HELD IN FRONT OF A STANDING FIGURE

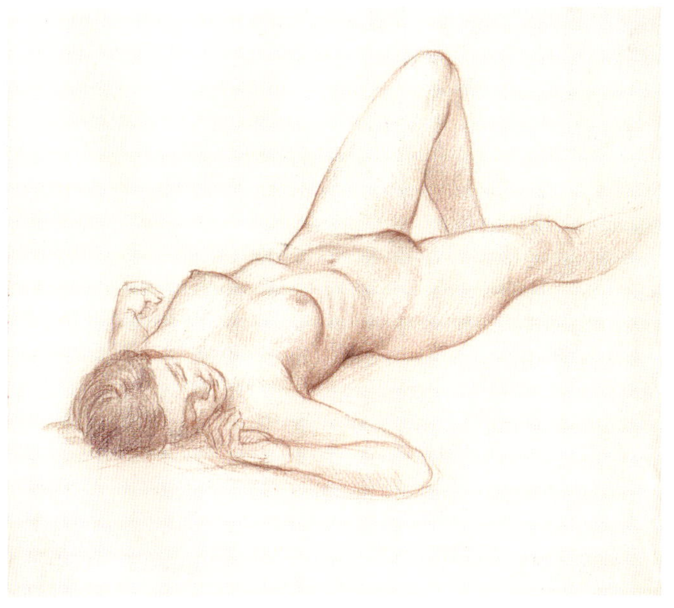

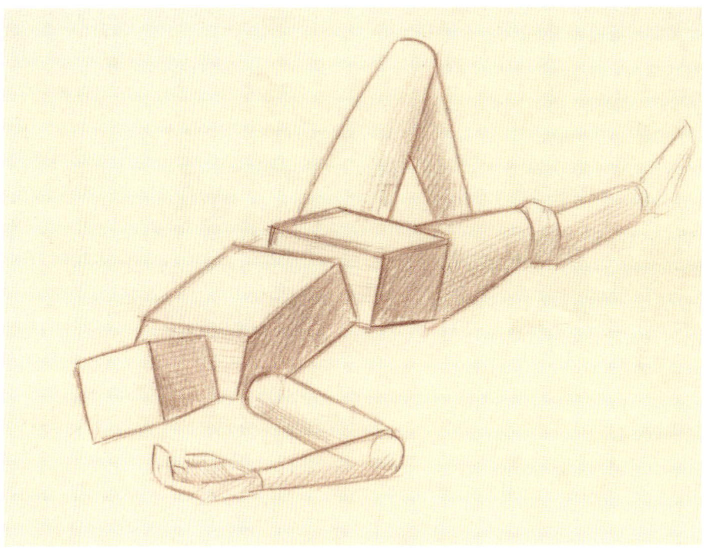

Plumb lines by themselves provide you with the vertical lines of the grid; the horizontal lines can be obtained holding the string of the plumb lines between the thumbs or by using a knitting needle or any other thin, straight object. The three figures at left show such a virtual grid, which you can use to compare horizontal and vertical landmarks of the body.

The use of stereometric volumes can likewise be helpful in "decoding" a foreshortened pose, as shown in the drawing above, because it makes it easier to appreciate the overlapping of volumes. It is easier to first focus only on the main volumes of the body, without paying attention to the smaller details such as the nose, ears, or breasts. You can place those after you have correctly positioned the larger volumes of the head and torso.

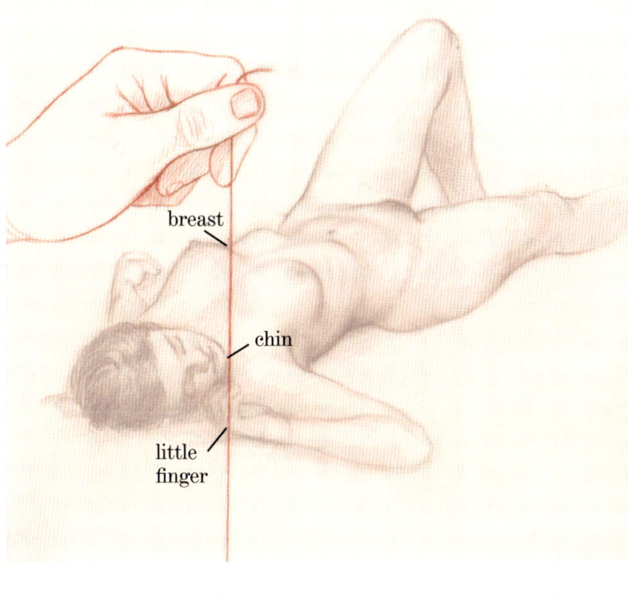

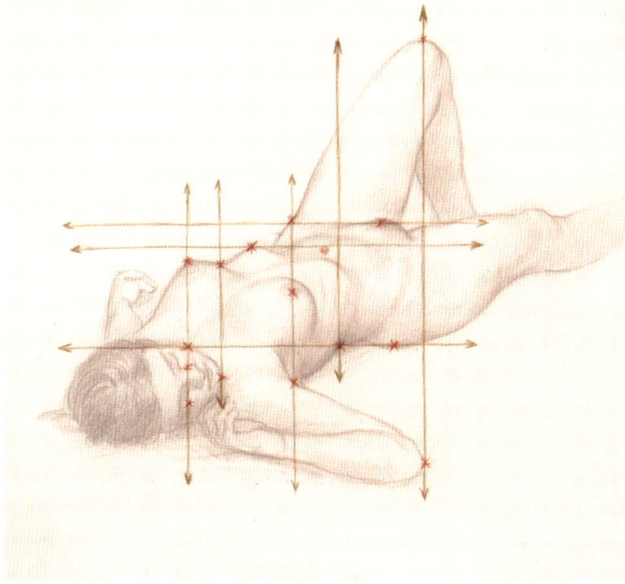

left column, top to bottom

RECLINING FIGURE

ESTABLISHING THE VERTICAL OF THE GRID

RECLINING FIGURE WITH SUPERIMPOSED GRID

The *x*'s on the grid's lines highlight the alignments between various parts of the body—especially those that are distant from each other, such as the left knee and right elbow in this pose. These alignments will help you capture a foreshortened pose with great accuracy.

top right

FORESHORTENED POSE DEPICTED AS STEREOMETRIC VOLUMES

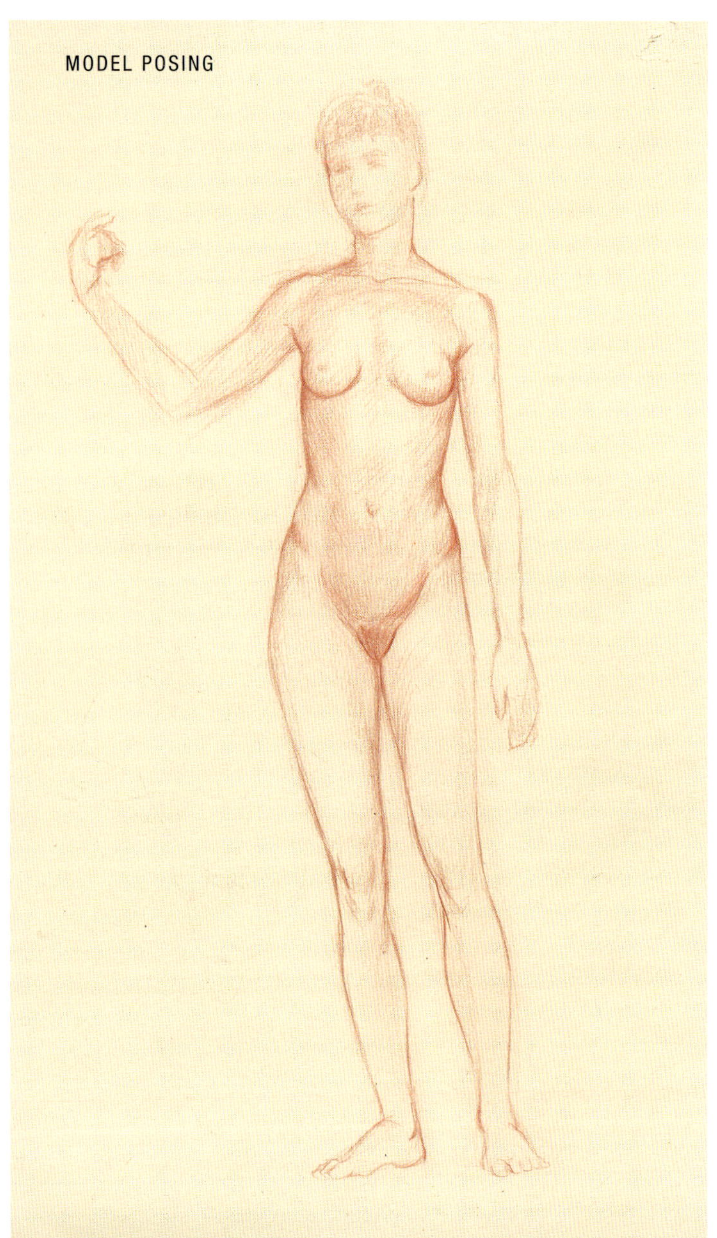

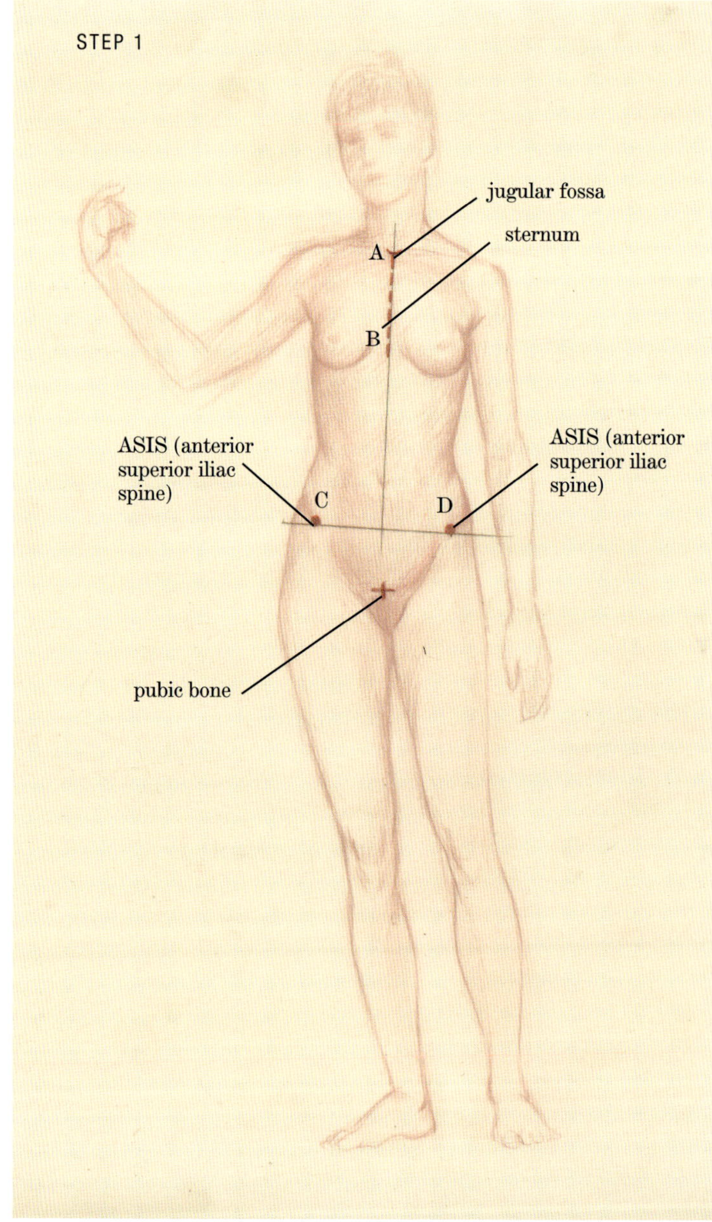

USING LANDMARKS

The body's landmarks give us access to the invisible internal structure of the body—the skeleton. As we have seen earlier, having a good understanding of the skeleton permits you to produce figure drawings that convey a sense of visual harmony and three-dimensionality. The drawings here show you how, in a step-by-step way, to read and use the landmarks when drawing the figure.

above left
THE MODEL POSING

This drawing represents the model posing for you.

STEP 1: Find the Axis of the Ribcage and the Tilt of the Pelvis

Identify the sternum, which starts just below the jugular fossa. The sternum gives you the axis of the ribcage (line *A-B*). Now align the anterior superior iliac spines (each labeled *ASIS* in the drawing) to find the tilt of the pelvis (line *C-D*). Locate the pubic bone.

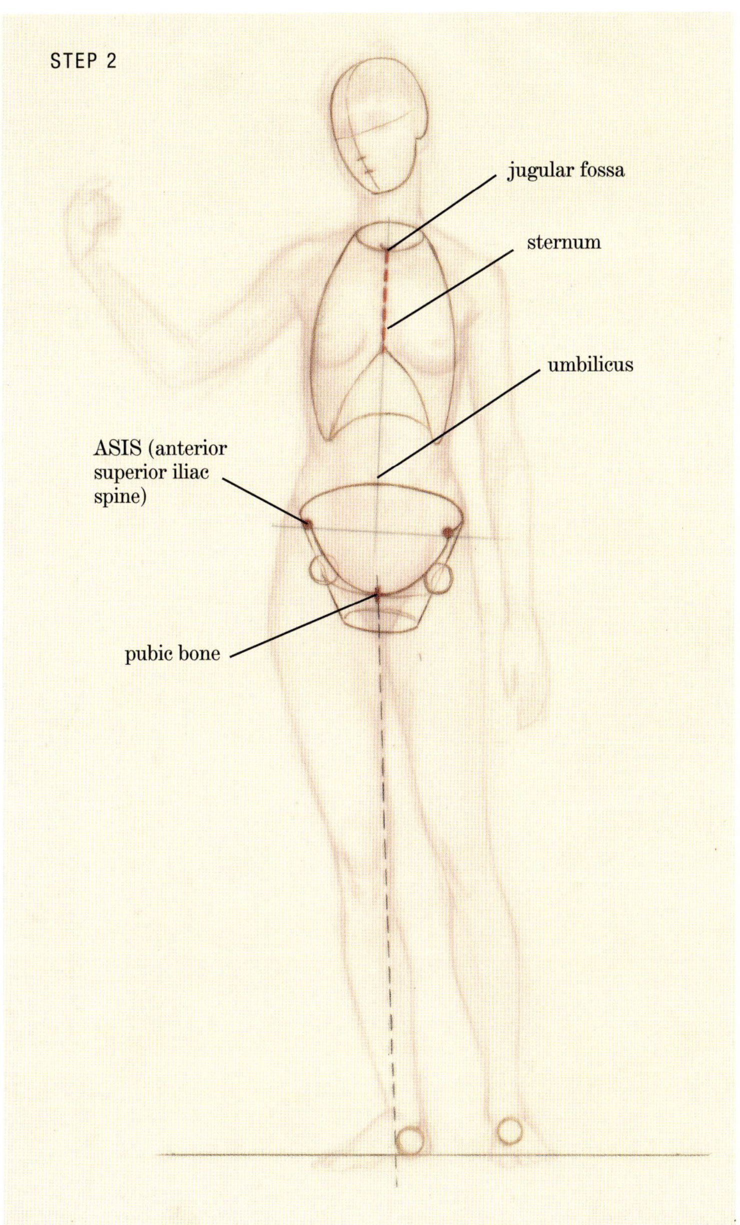

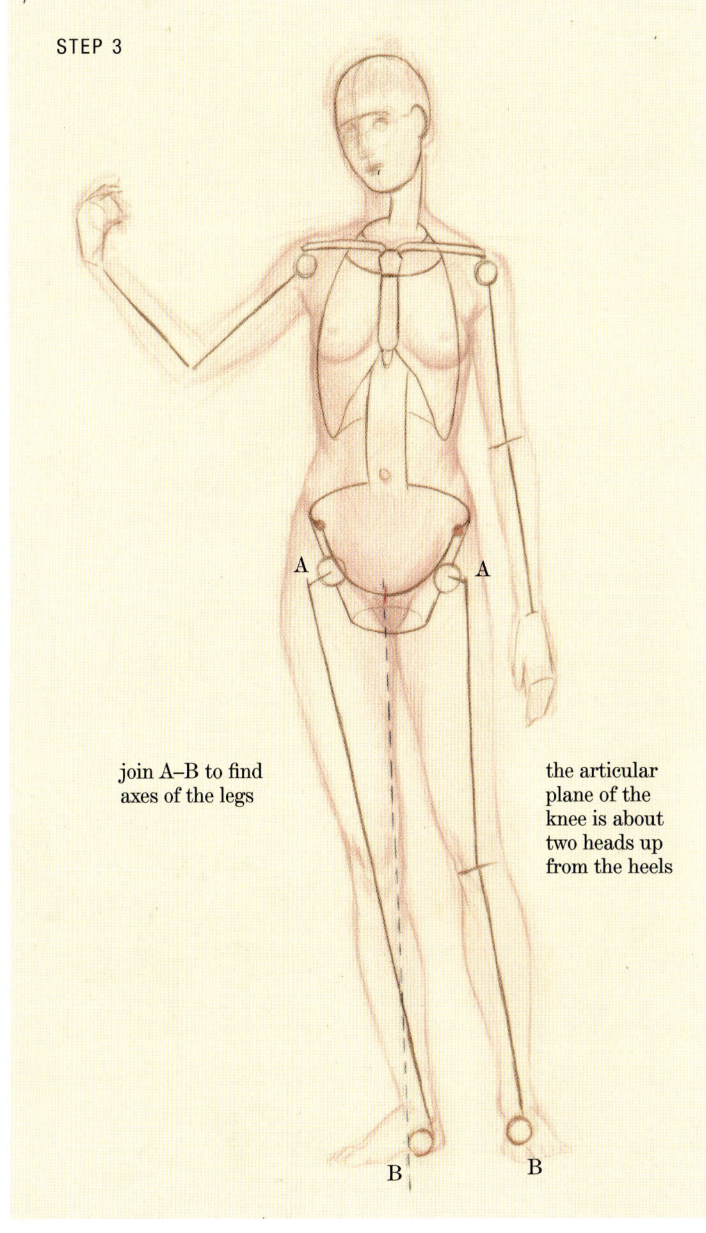

STEP 2: Draw the Basic Volumes

Draw the basic volume of the head, marking the transverse and sagittal sections and the eyes, nose, and mouth. Using the sternum, the jugular fossa, and the width of the ribcage, extrapolate the form of the ribcage. Then extrapolate the form of the pelvis, using the anterior superior iliac spines and the pubic bone. (The top of the pelvis is one-quarter of a head above the ASIS, or more or less at the level of the umbilicus. The bottom of the pelvis is one-quarter of a head below the pubic bone, or, in women, at the bottom of the genitals.) Now, drop a vertical line going from the pubic bone to the ground and see how this line relates to the heels. In the case

shown here, the heel on the left (the model's right heel) is tangent, or contiguous, to the vertical line. Establish the position of the right heel by eyeballing it or by measuring the head with your pencil and comparing that measure to the space between the heels.

STEP 3: Complete the Structural Skeleton

Draw the rest of structural skeleton, as shown in the image.

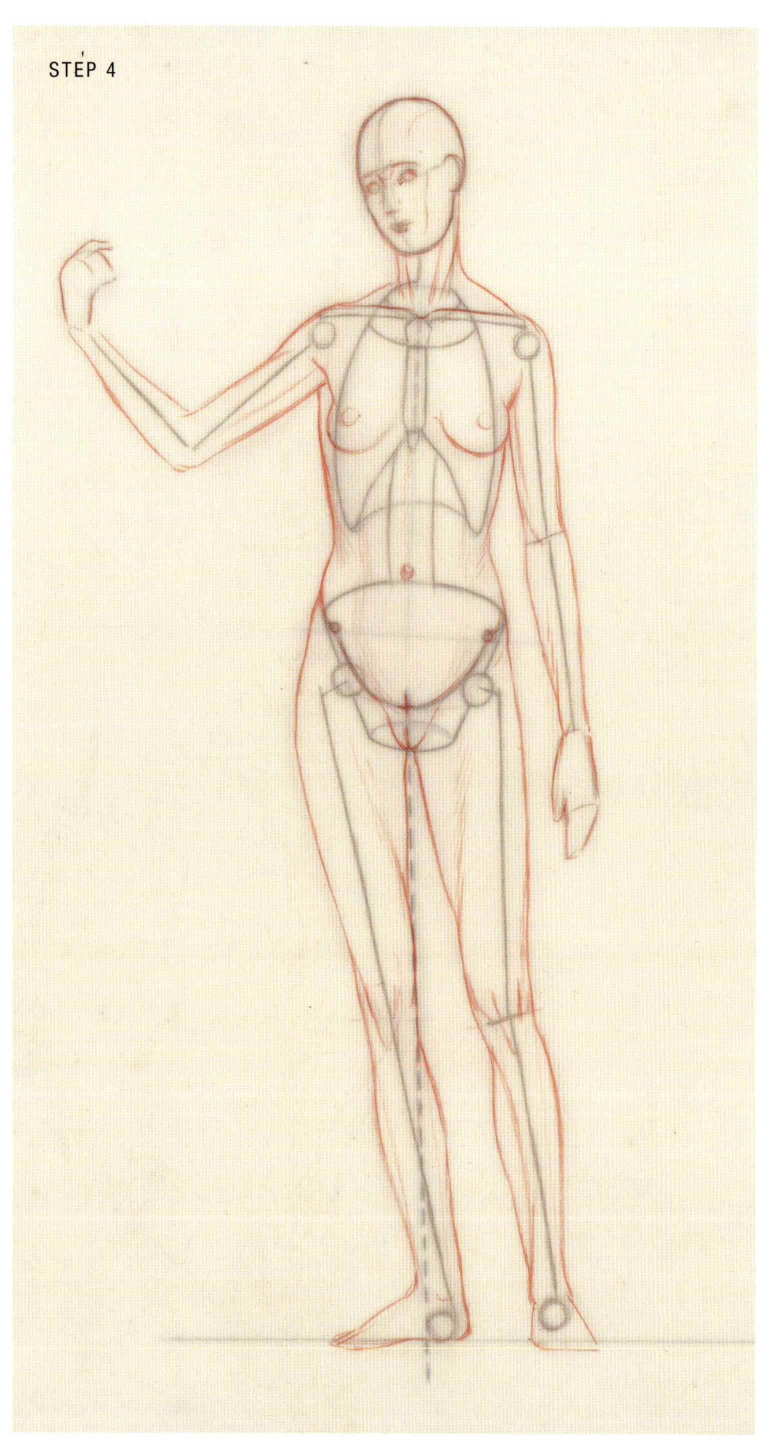

STEP 4: Define the Organic Forms with Line

Start defining the organic forms by creating a line drawing.

STEP 5: Define the Organic Forms with Tone

Once you've defined the organic forms with line, move toward a tonal rendering.

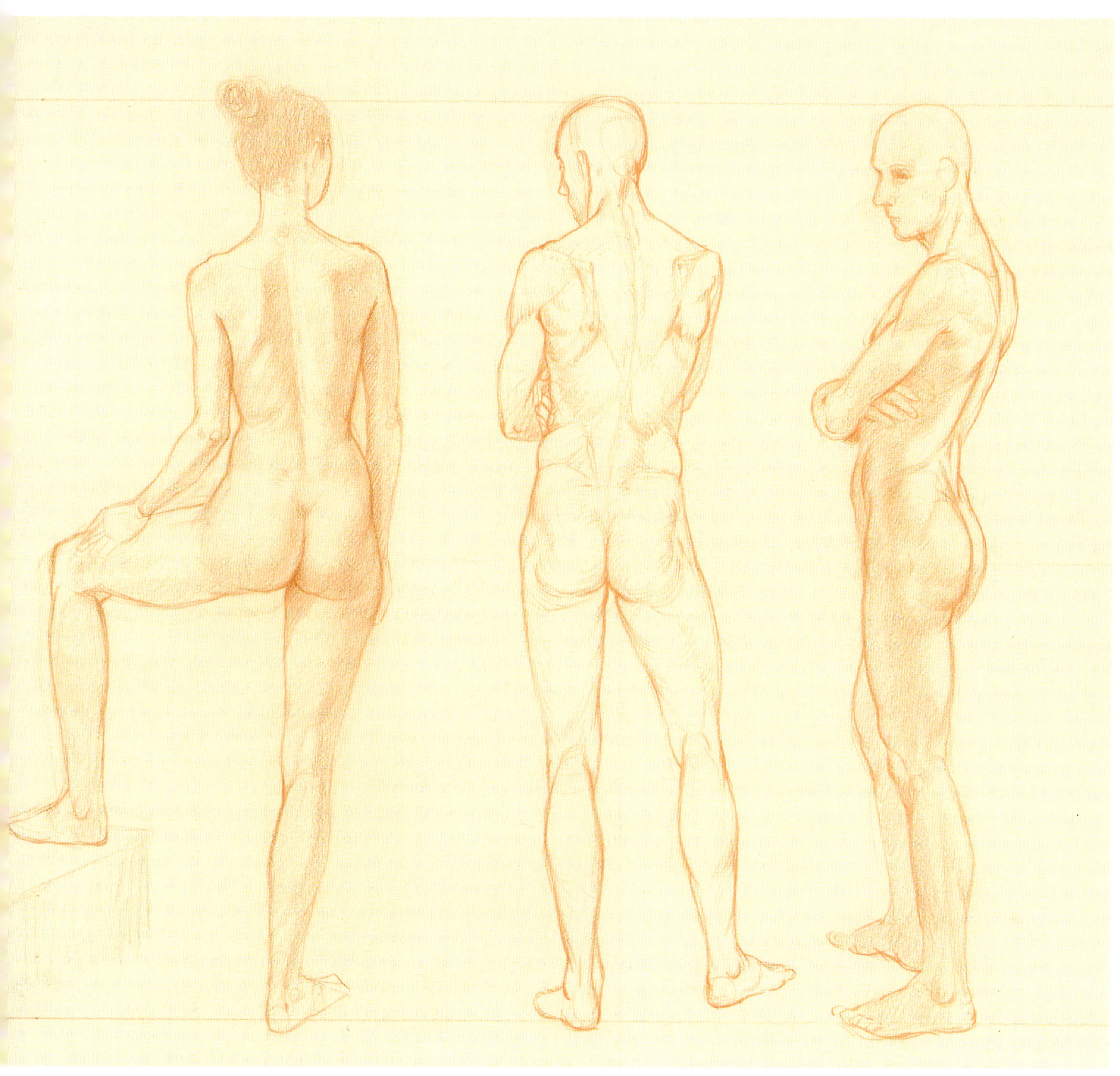

The drawings above provide further examples of the
progression from line drawing to tonal drawing.

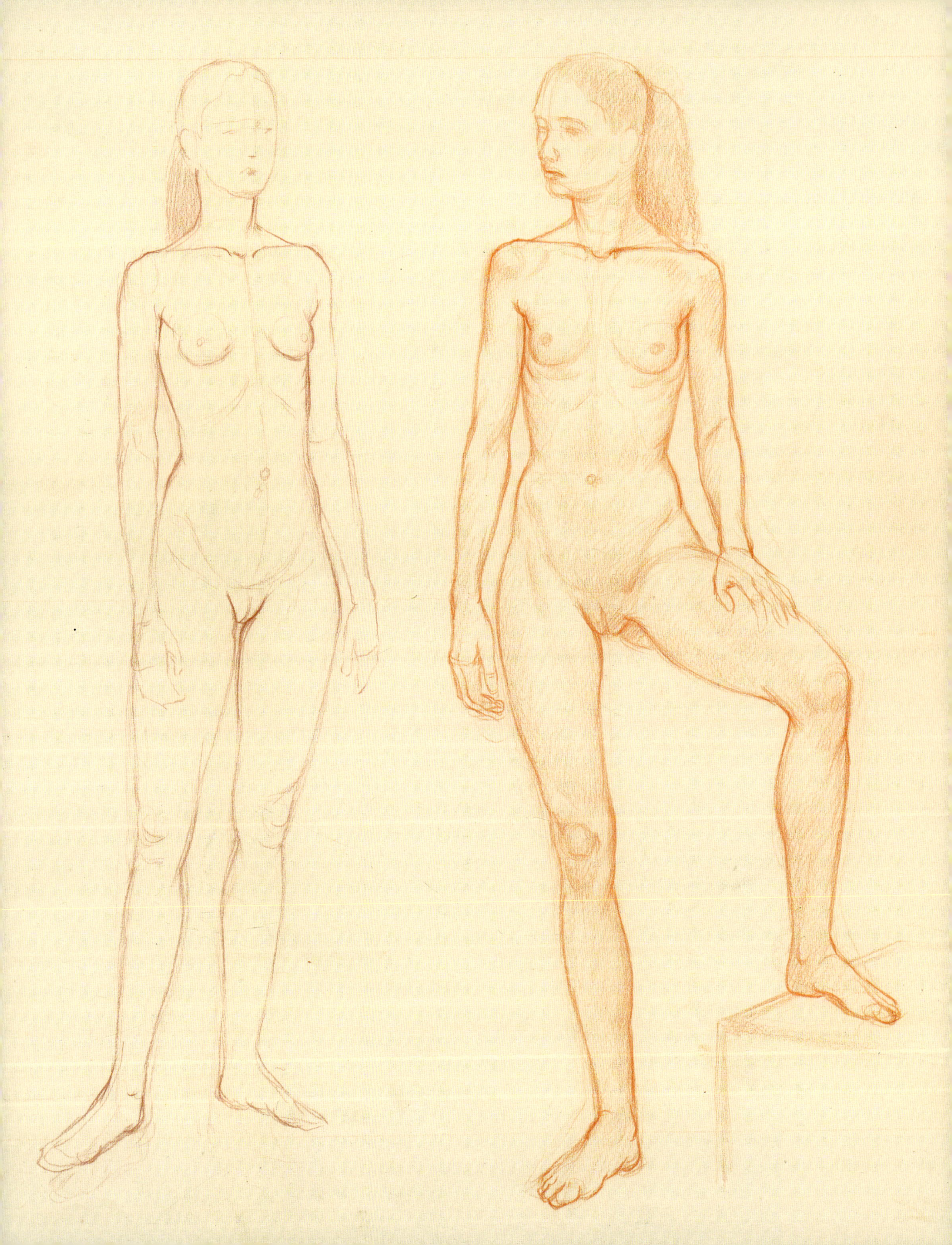

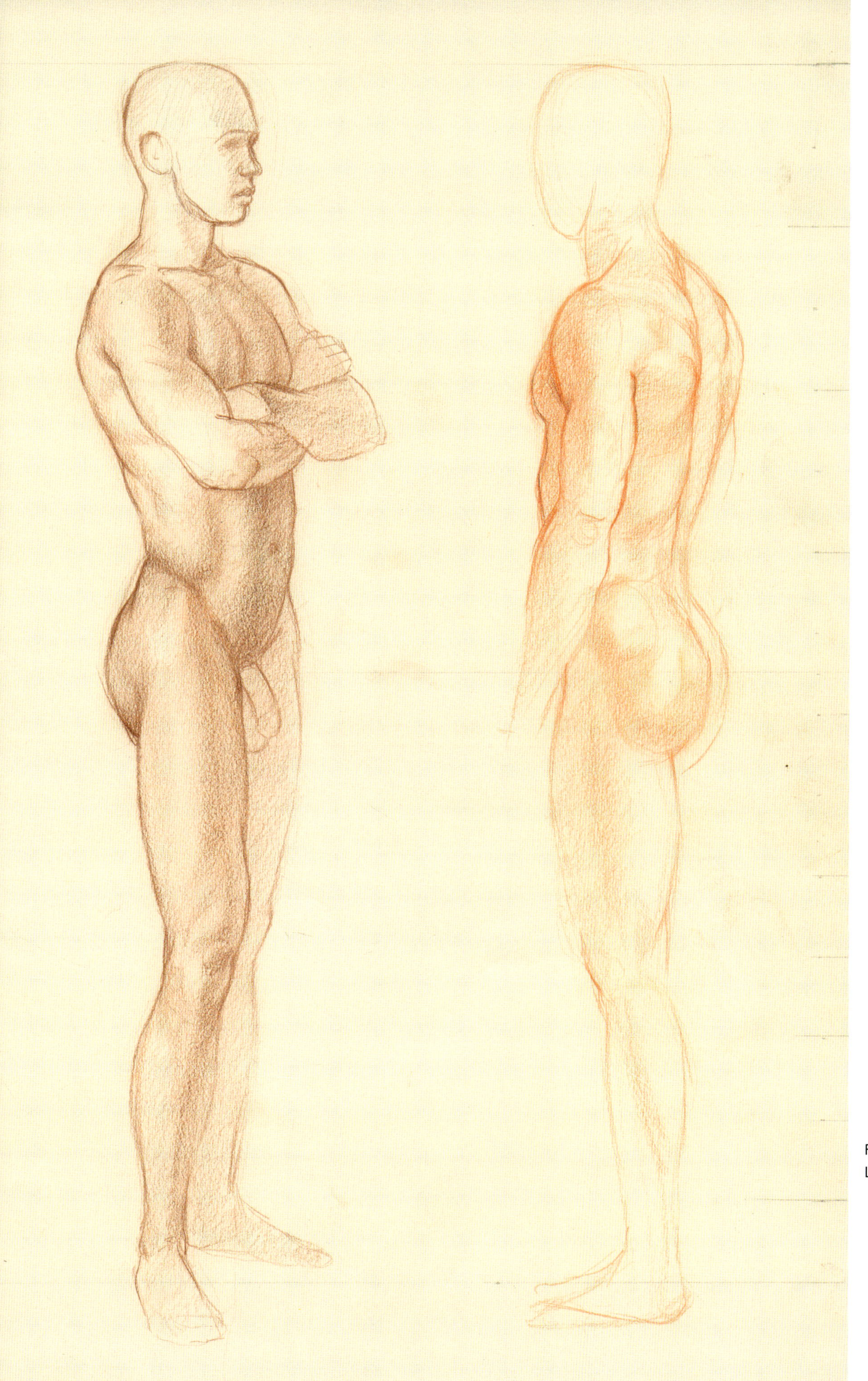

FIGURE STUDIES—
LINE AND TONE

USING GEOMETRIC SHAPES

Another method of measuring is to visualize
the posing model as a set of basic geometric
shapes. The drawings here show a sequence in
which the pose is measured through the use of
geometric shapes.

top right
REFERENCE POSE

This drawing represents the model in a foreshortened
pose.

right
THE POSE INSIDE THE ENVELOPE

First, create an "envelope," or frame, around the figure.
The sides of the envelope are determined by the maximum height and width of the figure. You can use any
measurement extrapolated from the figure to find the
dimensions of the box. For example, in this case, the
size of the head (line *A–B*) fits into the space between
the model's elbow (the highest point of the figure) and
her left heel (the lowest point) three and a half times.
The length of the lower leg (line *C-D*) fits two times
into the space between the side of the arm and the tip
of the little toe.

bottom right
VERTICALS AND HORIZONTALS, ANGLES AND
TRIANGLES

To better appreciate the various angles created by the
forms of the body, you can visualize vertical and horizontal lines (V1, V2, V3, H1) superimposed on it. You
can obtain these lines with a plumb line or by lining up
a knitting needle or your pencil horizontally over the
pose. The vertical and horizontal lines will show you—
immediately and with a good deal of accuracy—the
angles formed by the various segments of the body. It's
easy, for example, to tell whether a given angle is 90
degrees, or 45 degrees, or about 20 degrees.

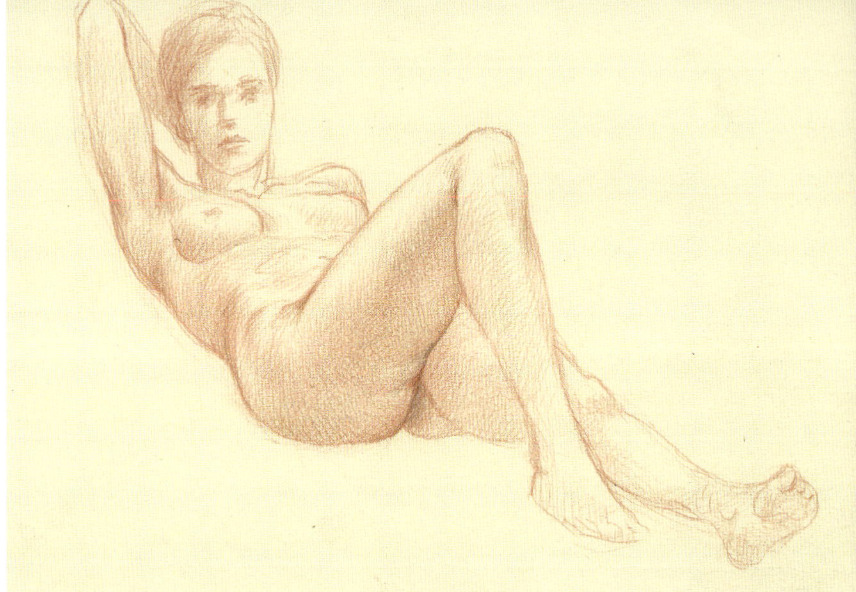

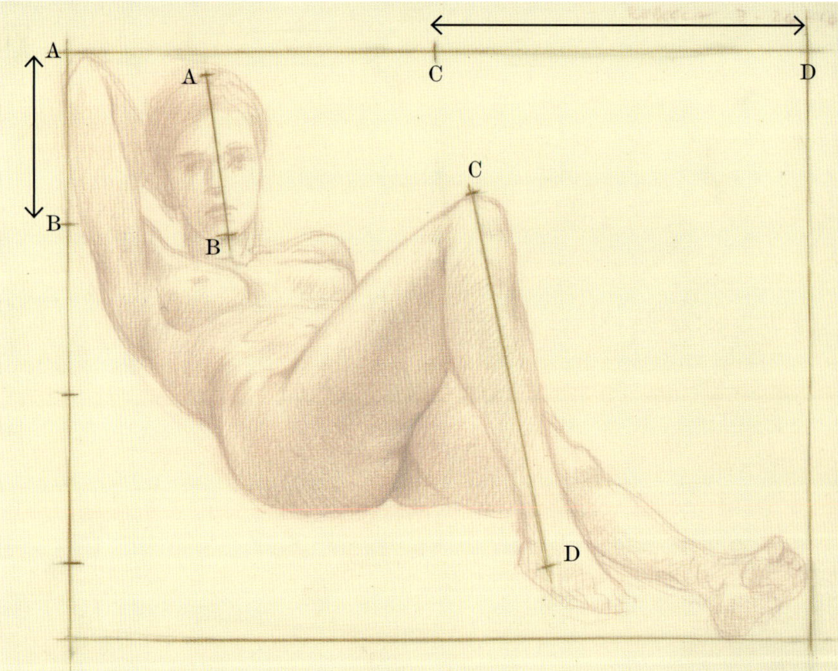

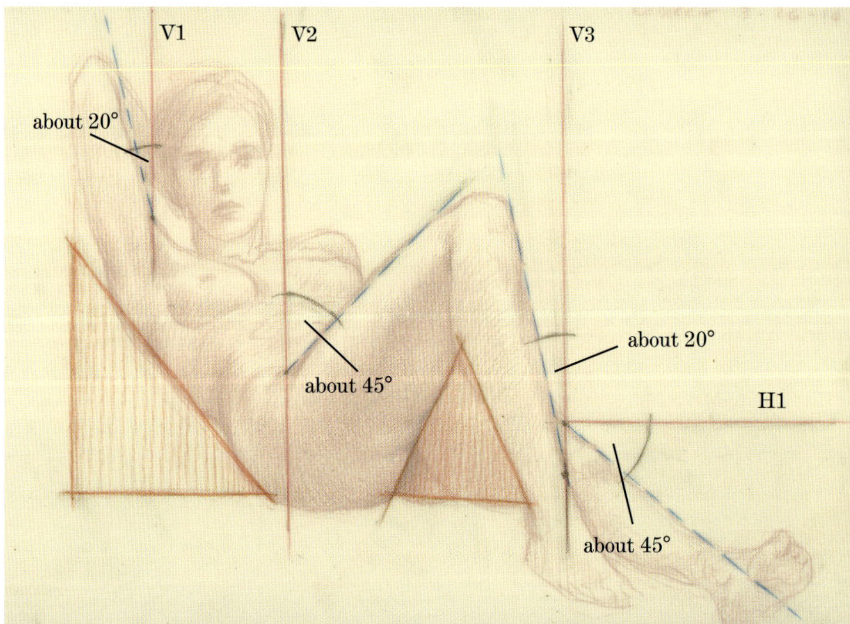

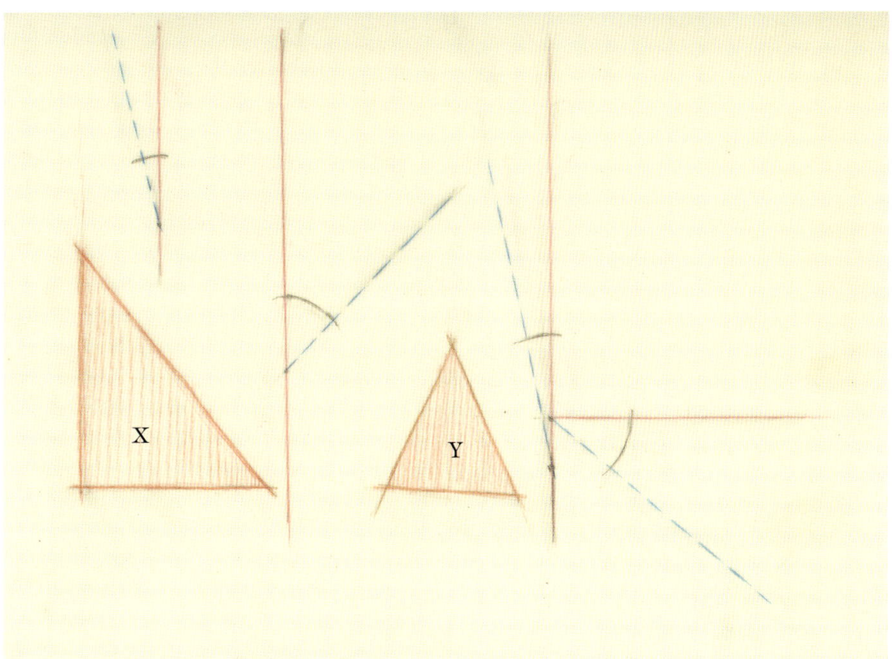

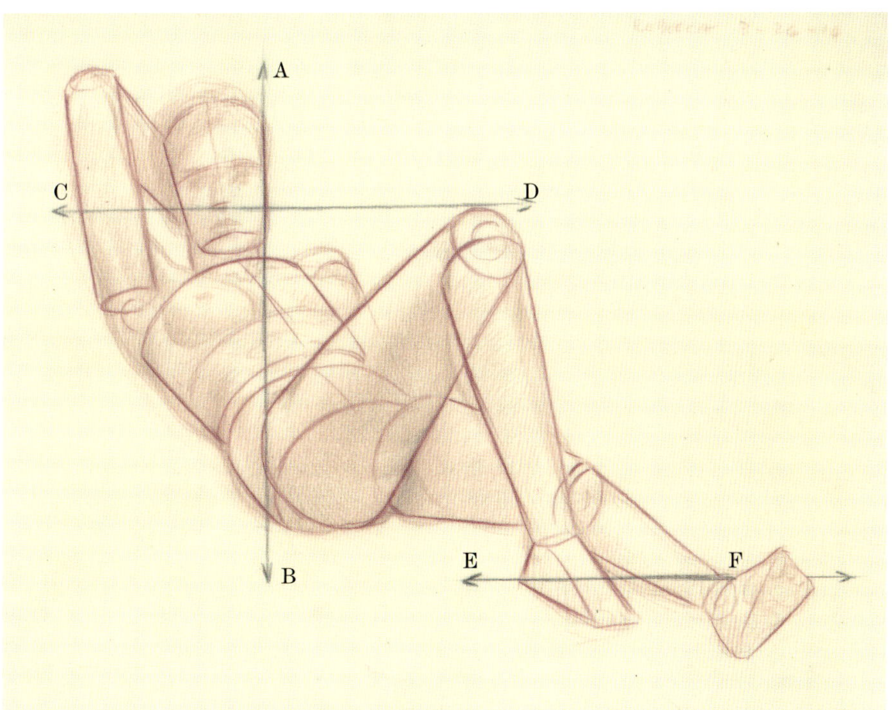

top

THE NEGATIVE SPACE OF THE POSE

You can also visualize the geometric shapes created by the negative space of the pose. The negative space is the empty space between parts of the body and/or objects and background in contact
with the figure. Here, I identify two triangles (*X* and *Y*) as examples
of simplified negative space, but there are also many irregular
negative spaces all around this figure. Seeing the types of triangles
(scalene, equilateral, isosceles) that are created by the negative
space and how they are oriented in relation to the figure can help
you refine the measures of the various body segments of the body.

above

THE POSE REDUCED TO GEOMETRIC SOLIDS

Reducing the segments of the body to basic geometric solids can
help you focus on the structural and three-dimensional aspects of
the figure. It also makes it easier to relate the various parts of the
body to each other. Line *A–B* shows how the side of the face aligns
with the side of the thigh at the hips; line *C–D* shows the alignment
of the nose and the knee; and line *E–F* shows the alignment of the
heel and the joint of the ankle.

EXERCISES

By now you have acquired a deep understanding of
human anatomy: You can draw the figure using a variety
of methods. You can use each method independently—
focusing, for example, on the structural, anatomical, or
aesthetic aspects of the figure—or combine them. This
knowledge enables you to see the figure completely,
giving complexity to your work. To help you completely
assimilate all this material, I propose a few more drawing
exercises that I think are very efficacious. They are noth-
ing new, but they work!

EXERCISE 1: DRAW A SPHERE

For this exercise, you need a spherical object of a neutral
gray color. (You can buy a plastic ball from a crafts store
and paint it gray with acrylic paint.) Place it on a piece
of paper or cardboard of the same neutral gray color and
cast a light on it from different directions, as in the figure
at right. Make drawings showing the various effects of the
light on the sphere.

   Alternatively, take a white sphere (you can paint a
plastic ball with white acrylic paint) and position it over a
colored piece of paper and cast a light on it. You will see
the effect of the reflected light in the shadow mass, with
the color of the reflected light influenced by the color of
the paper. Draw what you see. Then try the exercise using
different colors of paper—high chroma, low chroma,
primary colors, secondary colors, and so on. Or do the exercise using a cube, a cylinder, or other geometric solid.

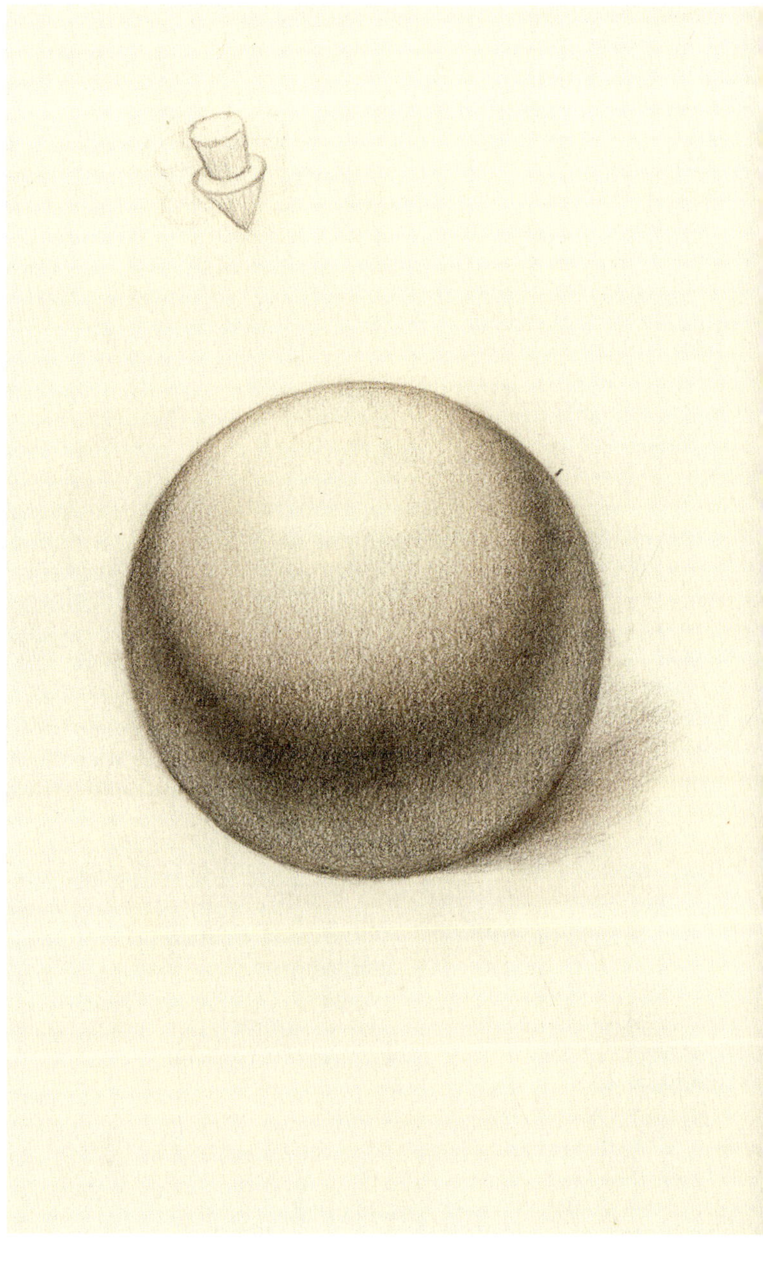

LIGHT CAST ON A SPHERE

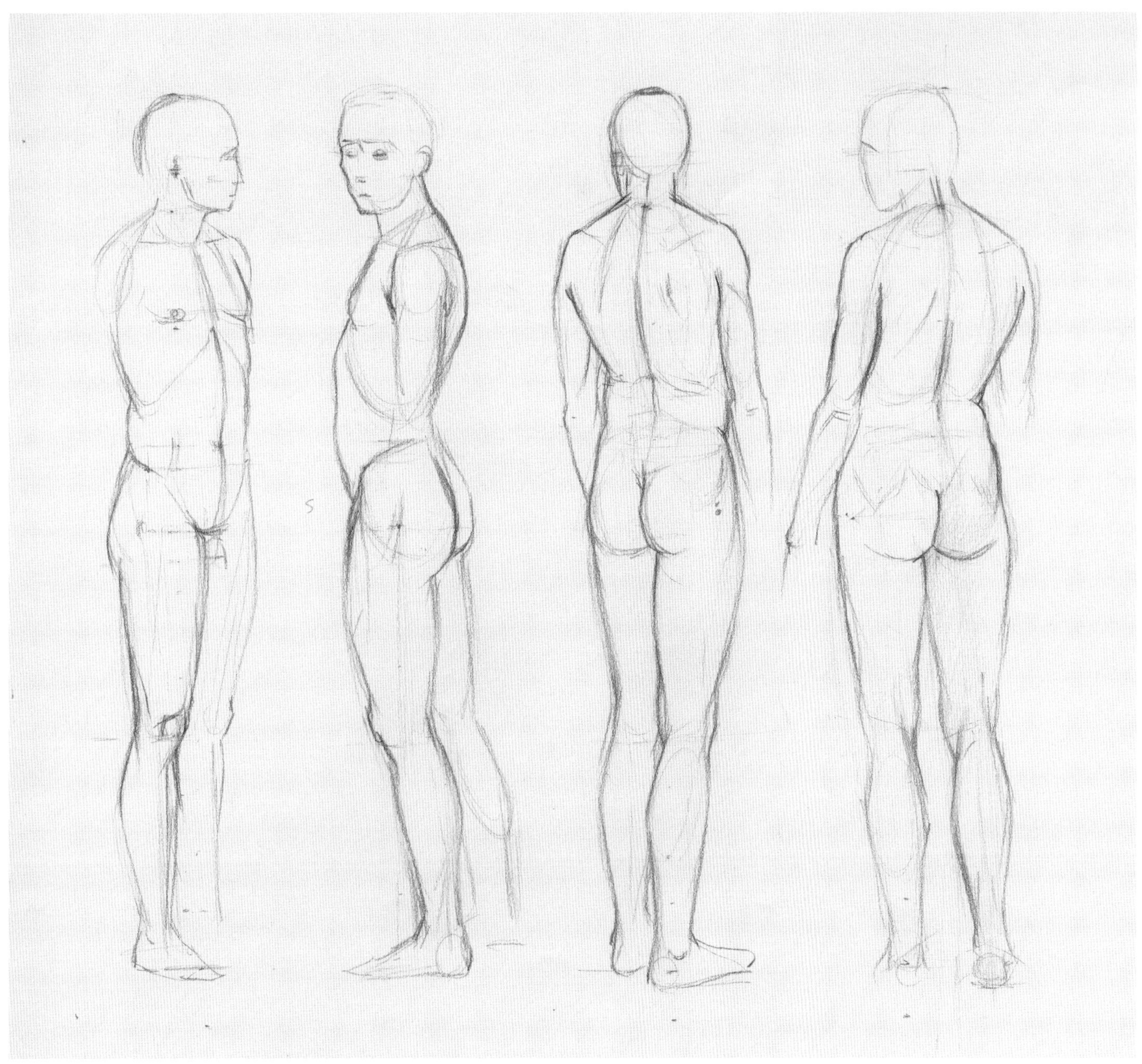

EXERCISE 2: "SCAN" THE FIGURE FROM DIFFERENT POINTS OF VIEW

This exercise, for which you'll need a live model, is
particularly useful for acquiring awareness of the figure's
three-dimensionality. Have the model take a pose that's
easy for him or her to hold, and move around the model,
drawing the pose from three, four, or more points of
view. This exercise is a little bit like a 3-D scanning: As
you move around the model, examining and drawing the
figure from different vantages, you'll learn how to "see"
parts of the figure that are not visible, increasing the im-
pression of depth in your drawings. The drawings here and
at the top of the following page provide examples of such
studies. You can also do this with quicker poses (of, say,
five minutes), since the point of this exercise is to study
the figure rather than to render it in great detail. In any
case, start with simpler poses and then move on to more
complicated ones.

SINGLE POSE DRAWN FROM MULTIPLE VIEWPOINTS

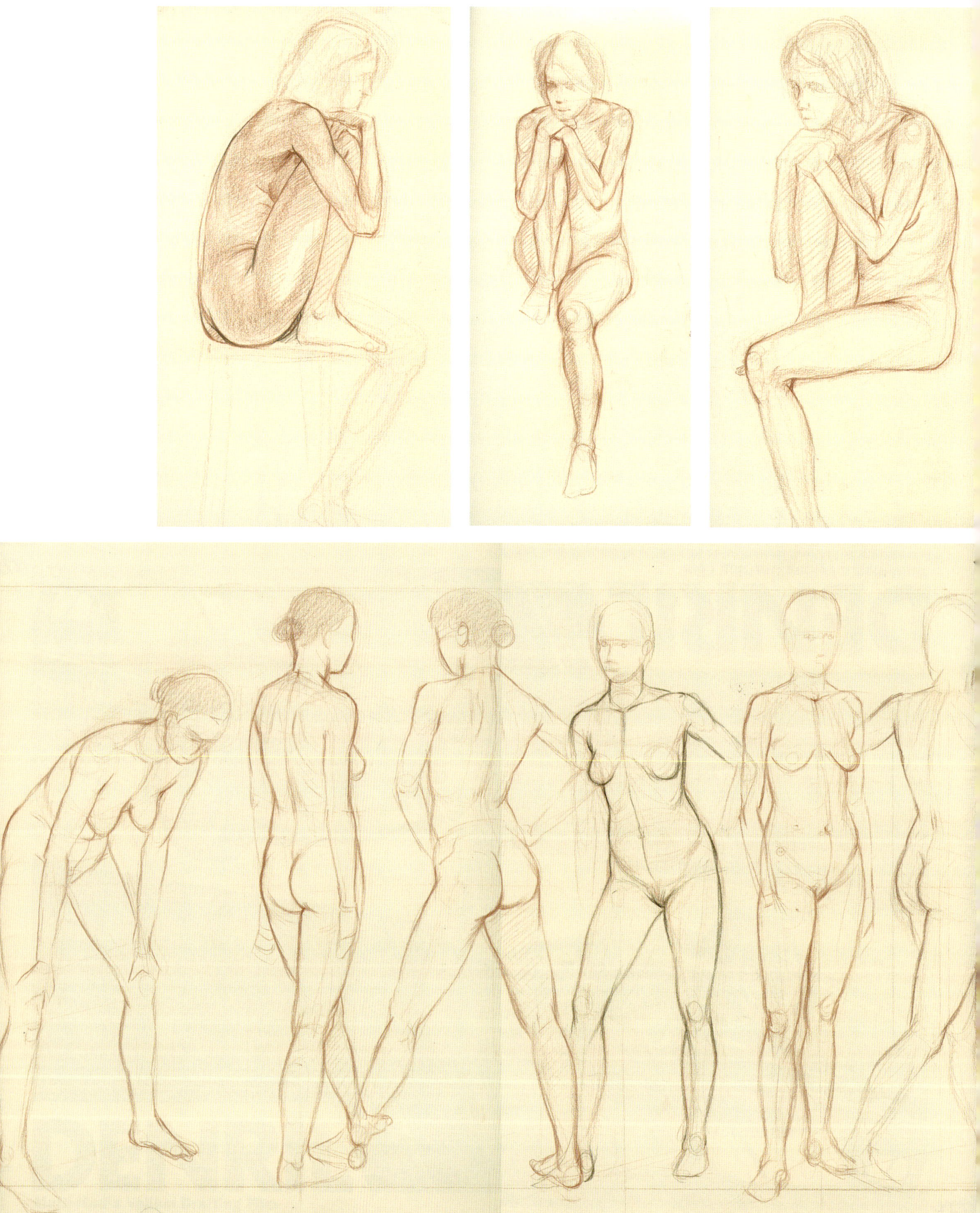

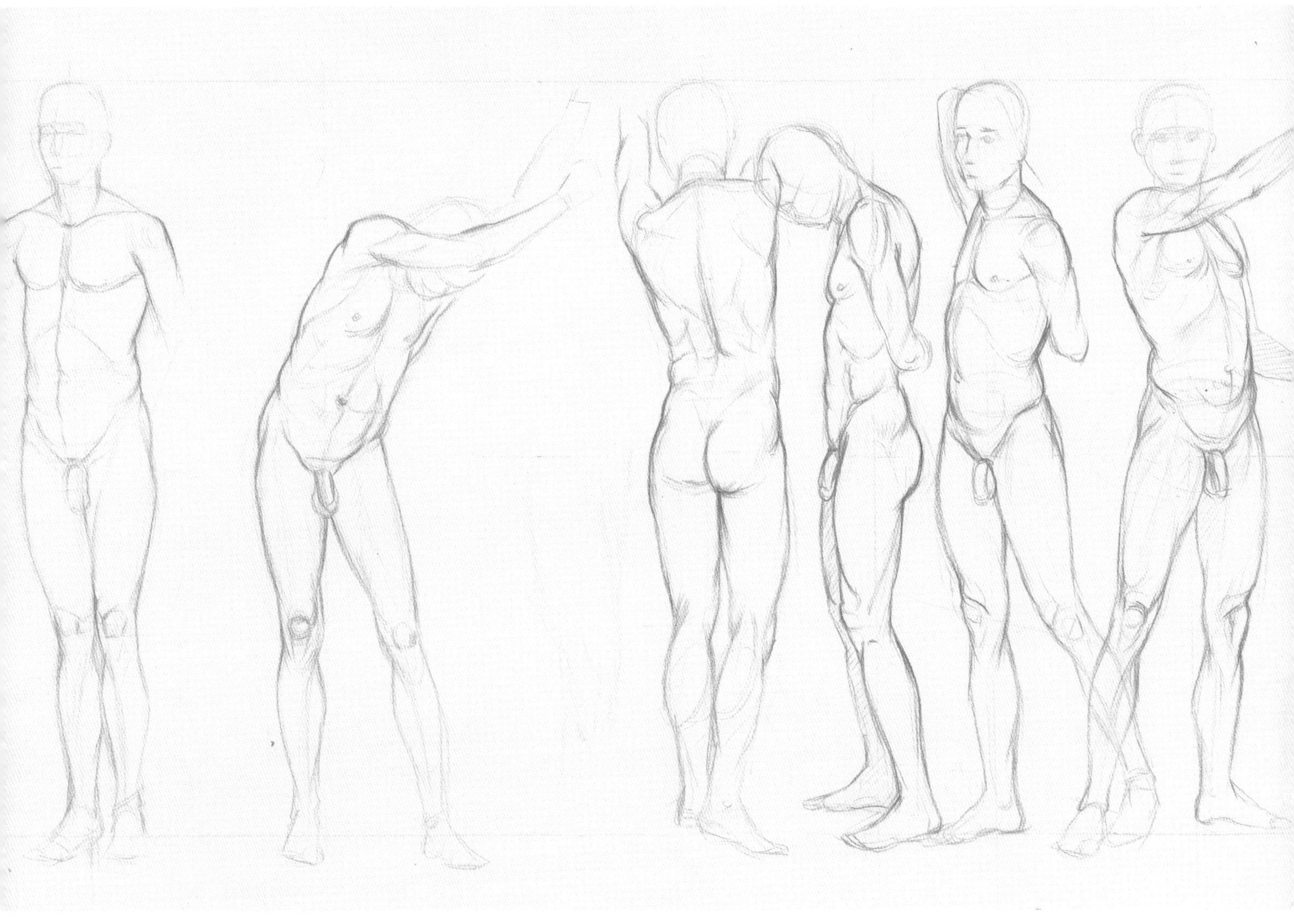

EXERCISE 3: DRAW THE FIGURE IN SEQUENTIAL DYNAMIC POSES

This exercise is similar to the previous one, but now you're drawing the model as he or she sequentially adopts different poses, as in the examples at bottom, opposite, and above. This exercise is very good for studying the expressive qualities of the body in movement and the variety of forms and postures it can assume.

opposite, top
SINGLE POSE DRAWN FROM MULTIPLE VIEWPOINTS

opposite, bottom, and above
STUDIES OF SEQUENTIAL POSES

EXERCISE 4: SIMPLIFY THE FIGURE TO BASIC PLANES

When you study a pose, it is always a good idea to conceptualize it using one or more of the conceptualizations described in this book. In the drawings below and opposite, bottom left, the small preliminary sketches have been simplified to basic planes to study the behavior of light on the figure. Try making such preliminary sketches yourself, before proceeding to a more fully rendered figure.

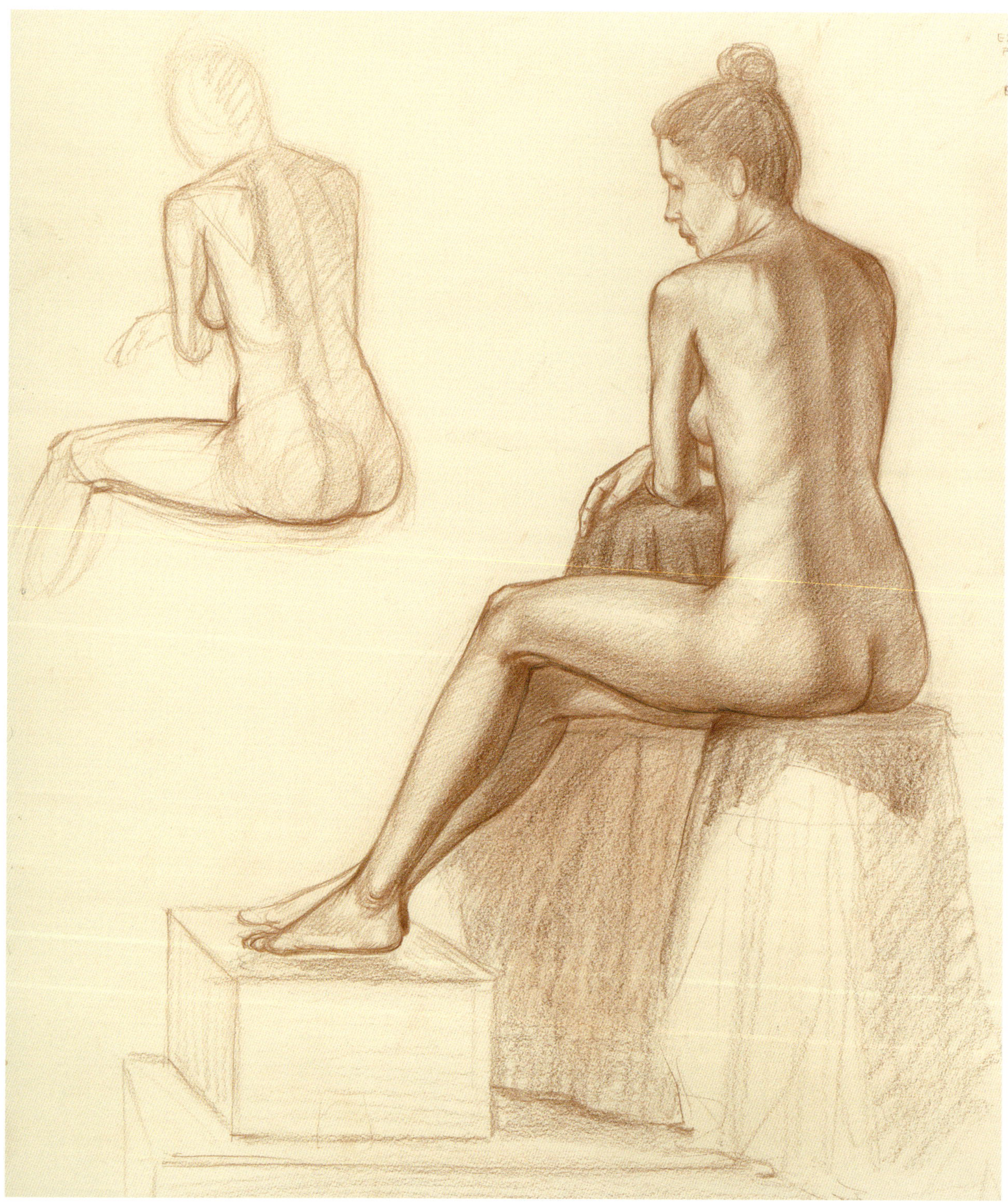

EXERCISE 5: RENDER THE FIGURE THREE-DIMENSIONALLY USING ONLY LINE

Rendering a figure only with line is a challenging but useful exercise. The lines have to describe the three-dimensional qualities of the figure without the use of tonal rendering, as shown in this study of a classical sculpture, right.

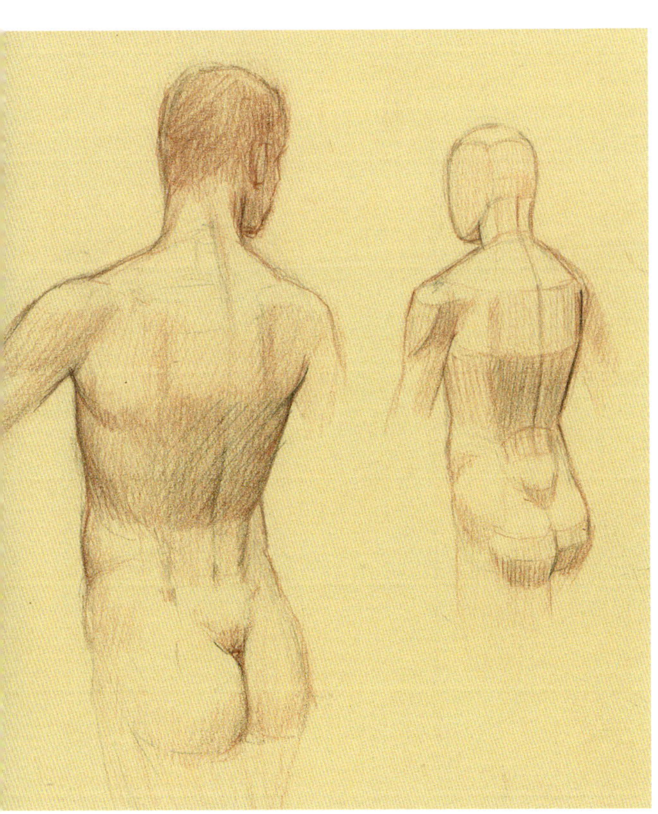

above
LIFE STUDY WITH A PRELIMINARY SKETCH

right
LINE-ONLY STUDY OF A SCULPTURE

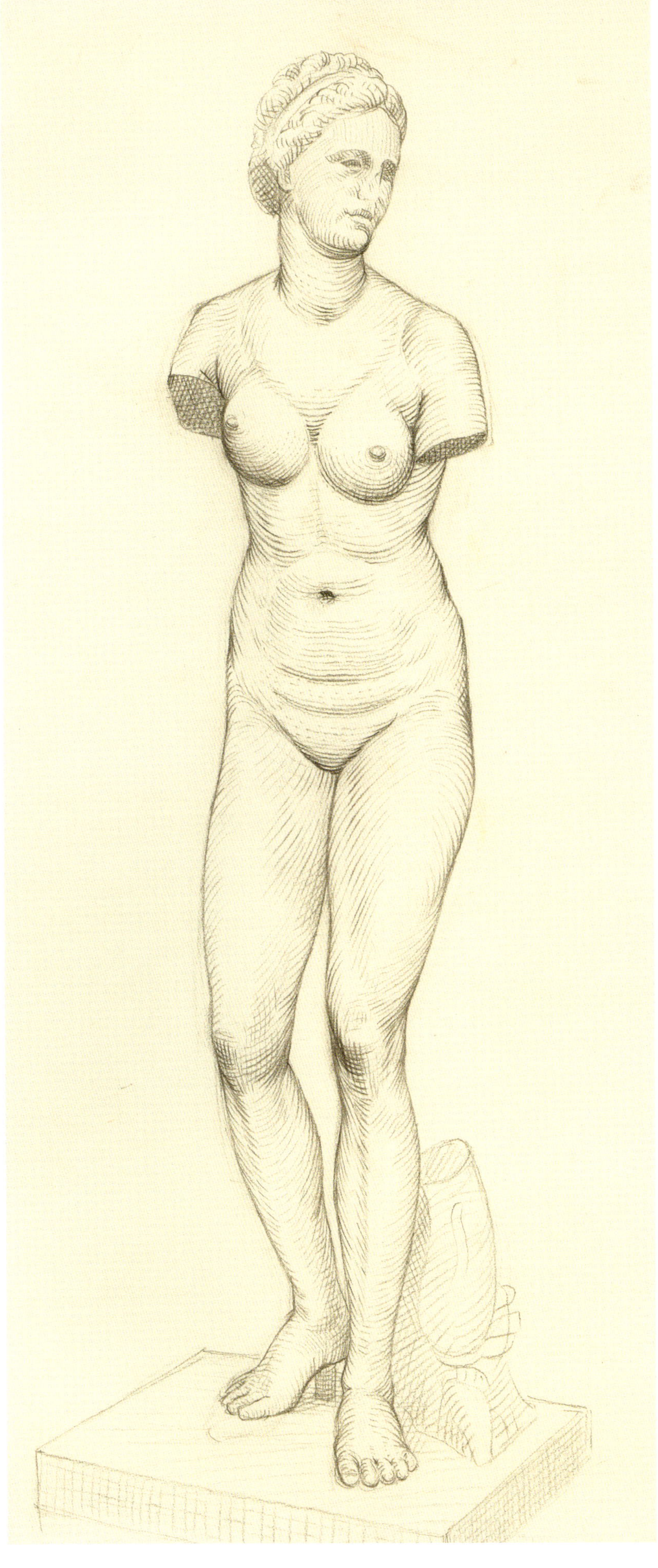

DRAW DIFFERENT BODY TYPES

Try drawing various body types and people of different ages. This will help you become more aware of the incredible number of variations of the human body based on individuals' gender, race, age, weight, and specific proportions.

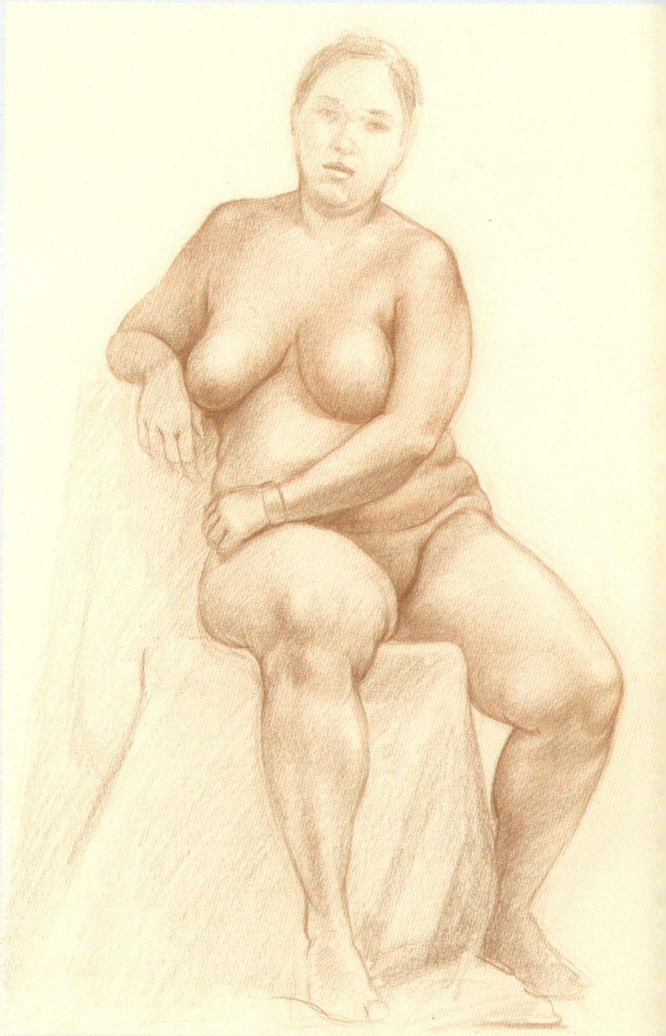

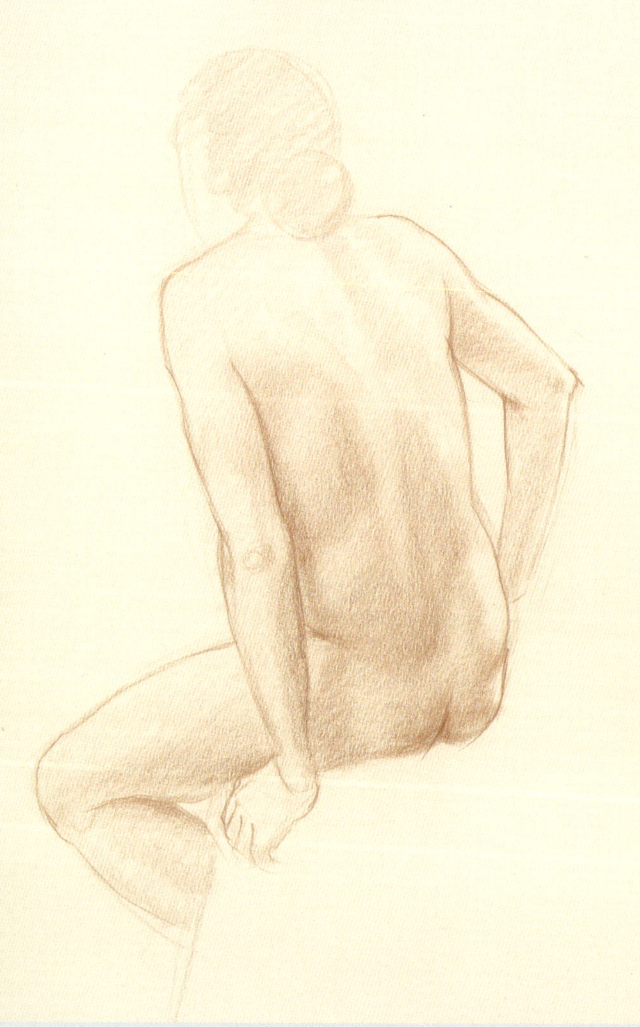

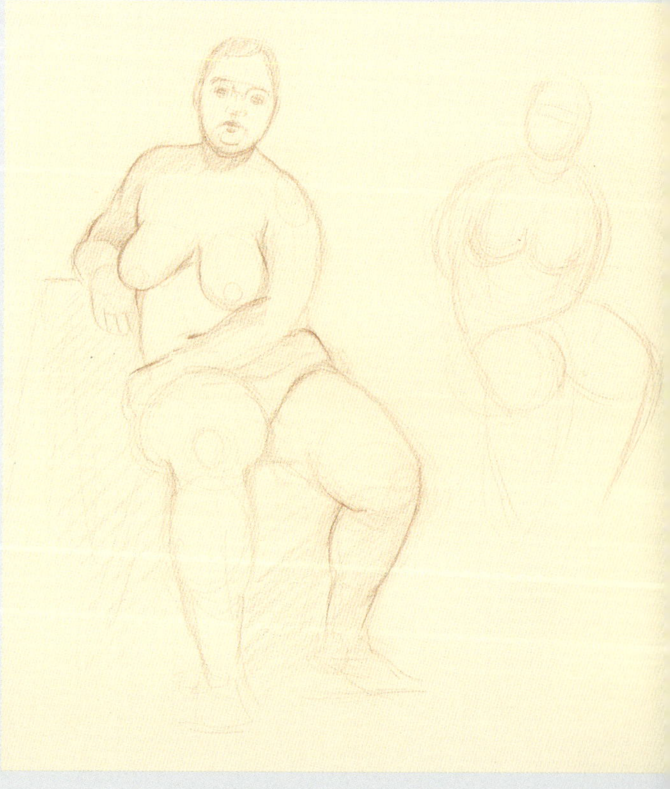

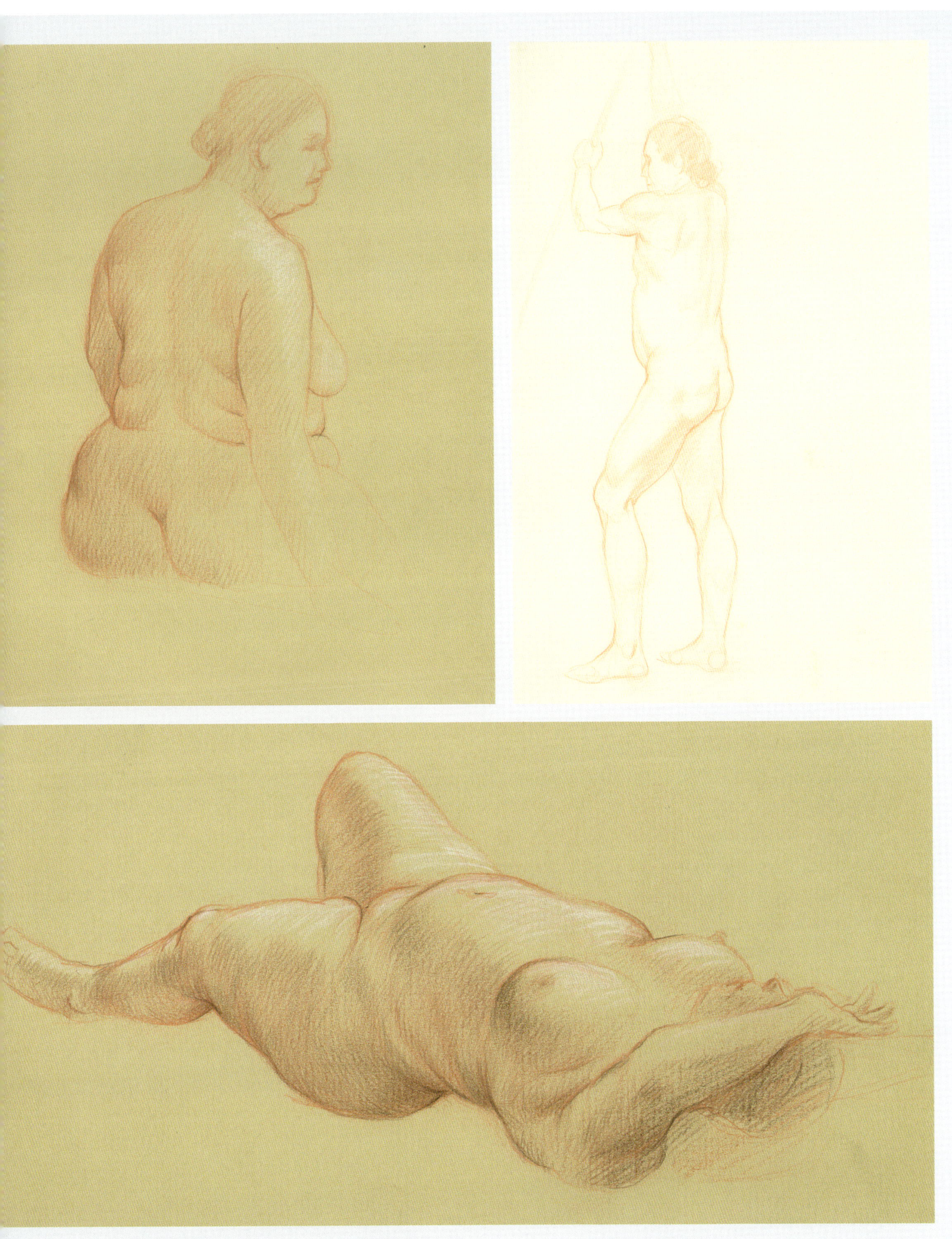

SELECTED BIBLIOGRAPHY

ANATOMY AND ART

Bammes, Gottfried. *Die Gestalt des Menschen.* Stuttgart: Urania, 2002.

———. *Complete Guide to Life Drawing.* Kent, United Kingdom: Search Press, 2011.

Goldfinger, Eliot. *Human Anatomy for Artists: The Elements of Form.* New York: Oxford University Press, 1991.

Lolli, Alberto, Mauro Zocchetta, and Renzo Peretti. *Struttura Uomo: Manuale di Anatomia Artistica.* Vicenza, Italy: Neri Pozza, 2000.

Richer, Paul. *Artistic Anatomy.* New York: Watson-Guptill, 1986.

ANATOMY AND SCIENCE

Clemente, Carmine D. *Anatomy: a Regional Atlas of the Human Body.* Philadelphia: Lippincott, Williams & Wilkins, 2011.

Netter, Frank H. *Atlas of Human Anatomy.* Philadelphia: Saunders/Elsevier, 2014.

Sobotta, Johannes et al. *Atlante di Anatomia dell'uomo.* Florence: USES, 1996.

Spalteholz, Werner et al. *Atlante di Anatomia Umana,* 6 edit. Milan: Vallardi, 1977.

Testut, L. and A. Latarjet. *Anatomia Umana.* Turin: Unione Tipografico Editrice Torinese, 1971.

ANATOMY AND THE HISTORY OF ART

Caroli, Flavio. *Leonardo: Studi di Fisiognomica.* Milan: Electa, 2015.

Cazort, Mimi, Monique Kornell, and K. B. Roberts. *The Ingenious Machine of Nature: Four Centuries of Art and Anatomy.* Ottowa: National Gallery of Canada, 1996.

Hall, James. *Michelangelo and the Reinvention of the Human Body.* New York: Farrar, Straus and Giroux, 2005.

Kwakkelstein, Michael. *Leonardo da Vinci as a Physiognomist.* Leiden, Netherlands: Primavera Pers, 1994.

Premuda, Loris. *Storia dell'Iconografia Anatomica.* Milan: Ciba Edizioni, 1993.

Rifkin, Benjamin. *Human Anatomy from the Renaissance to the Digital* Age. New York: Abrams, 2006.

ABOUT THE AUTHOR

Roberto Osti studied at the State Institute of Art and the School of Anatomical and Surgical Drawing, University of Bologna, Italy, and earned an MFA from the New York Academy of Art in 2007. As a scientific illustrator, he has collaborated with many publications and publishers including *Scientific American,* the *New York Times,* Rizzoli, Mondadori, and Scholastic. His illustrations have been exhibited at the Museum of Modern Art and the Aldrovandi Museum in Bologna, the Museum of Natural History in Milan, and the Oceanographic Museum in Monte Carlo, Monaco. His fine art paintings and drawings have been exhibited in galleries in New York, New Jersey, and Philadelphia and other locations in the United States and abroad and have been included in publications such as *Creative Quarterly, American Artist,* and the Drawing Center's *Drawing Papers.* Osti has taught anatomy to artists since 2005, and currently teaches courses on anatomy and figure drawing at the University of the Arts in Philadelphia, the Pennsylvania Academy of the Fine Arts, and the New York Academy of Art. He also teaches a popular course on anatomy for the online site Craftsy. He lives in New Jersey with his wife and two children.